American Business Regulation

Note on Electronic Materials

American Business Regulation: Understand, Survive, and Thrive is available on the Sharpe eTc electronic textbook center, at www.sharpe-etext.com

Online resources for adopting instructors are available at www.sharpe-instructor.com.

American Business Regulation

Understand, Survive, and Thrive

W. Lesser

M.E.Sharpe
Armonk, New York
London, England

Library of Congress Cataloging-in-Publication Data

Lesser, William, author.
American business regulation : understand, survive, and thrive / by William H. Lesser, Susan Eckert Lynch Professor in Science and Business, Dyson School of Applied Economics and Management, Cornell University.
pages cm
ISBN 978-0-7656-4378-0 (cloth : alk. paper)
1. Trade regulation—United States. 2. Administrative law—Economic aspects—United States. 3. Trade regulation—Economic aspects—United States. I. Title.

KF1600.L47 2014
658.1′20973—dc23 2014018402

Printed in the United States of America

The paper used in this publication meets the minimum requirements of American National Standard for Information Sciences Permanence of Paper for Printed Library Materials, ANSI Z 39.48-1984.

∞

EBM (c) 10 9 8 7 6 5 4 3 2 1

Dedicated to my wife Susan who is an ongoing,
enthusiastic supporter of this undertaking

Contents

Preface

This book is directed toward students who wish to understand multiple aspects of business regulation. These students may be either conventional college students or, unconventionally, employees or those interested in running a new business as well as those broadly interested in how to manage regulation (business), how to develop and interpret regulation (policy), or those who implement regulation (bureaucrats, politicians, lawyers). Because of the notable size and diversity of interest in the regulatory system, the base requirements (prerequisites) for utilizing this book are intentionally minimized. The single mandatory one is a basic understanding of microeconomic theory. This allows for the largest possible readership. But limiting the prerequisites should not be interpreted as an indication that the content is dumbed down. Rather, it begins at a base level, allowing those with a more limited background to enter at a comfortable level and progress to one needed to understand the concepts. For example, the righting, or offsetting, of "market failures" is an important justification for regulation, so an appreciation of the what and why of those failures is key to understanding why and how societies regulate. The text can be taught at a higher level, but it need not be. The subject is accessible at multiple levels.

This text differs from the usual economics text on the subject of regulation in two important ways. First, rather than starting with the economics rationale of why to regulate, each chapter frequently begins with the historical background of events that led to the development of a particular regulation. The economic rationale is then taken up to place the chapter in a wider setting. And second, the goal of the text is not to master a body of ongoing regulations and their rationale, but rather to understand and act aggressively on business "survival strategies" within a regulatory environment. That approach is accomplished by using a series of Harvard Business School cases and my own "quasi cases" to push students into hands-on activities and projects, including group projects.

The book is organized around three broad components: (a) why societies regulate; (b) how societies regulate and what is known of the consequences of different kinds of regulation; and (c) managing regulation. The *why* component incorporates the economic concepts of market failures and natural monopolies, but as well highlights the catastrophes that often led to regulation. We are talking here about the Stock Market Crash of 1929 as well as the near meltdown of 2007–2008. Events like the Triangle Shirtwaist Fire resulted in new workplace safety regulations, as did the sinking of the *Titanic*, which led to the regulation of wireless signals which became the basis of communications regulation. Also there are hugely influential books, such as *The Jungle, Silent Spring,* and *Unsafe at Any Speed,* each of which spawned various business regulations. I have found it a useful class exercise to have student groups report on each of these books and the results have been illuminating and instructive. The *how* and *to what end* section treats the various policy levers and the methodologies available to assess the consequences of regulation, which is largely to say cost-benefit analysis. That section examines among others the value of a statistical life, and willingness-to-pay approaches to value nonmarket goods. The regulatory system scope is then expanded to incorporate intellectual property rights and antitrust.

A significant contribution of the book, and the largest component in terms of pages, concerns the subject of managing under regulation. This is done through case studies in four sectors: consumer products, communication, environment, and the financial sector. Those sectors were selected on the basis of currency and relevance to the world of students. To keep the scope manageable, the text focuses on U.S. federal regulation. Localized state, county, and town regulations like zoning and building codes can be staggering in detail and so are largely excluded. But when state regulations in areas like insurance and trade secret law have a broader regulatory context, they are examined in some detail.

Some of the case studies (7) evaluated in the text are from the Harvard Business School (HBS). These are the full-scope cases including financial data and other background information. I typically have my students order selected cases directly online or have the bookstore assemble them in a course pack. As an instructor I can register for access to the teaching notes, which are useful guides for the classroom. In general, though, I seek breadth rather than depth with the case study analysis and rarely spend more than 20–25 class minutes on a case. After going over several cases in class, assigning presentations to small student groups works well to initiate discussion.

Most of the case studies (12), however, are unique to this book, what I call "quasi cases." These quasi cases lack the financial and other firm-specific detail of the HBS cases, but they do address very current issues. An example is, how should KFC executives respond to the voluntary decision of McDonald's to post menu item calories in all their restaurants when the timing and details of the pending (but delayed) FDA regulation are unknown? Or, how might the Federal Trade Commission under its merger guidelines program evaluate a merger of Comcast and Time Warner? Indeed, just such a merger was proposed in early 2014. The topics are selected to have some relevancy to the lives of students, such as the evaluation of the Facebook IPO in association with the JOBS (Jumpstart Our Business Startups) Act.

On a lighter note is applying analysis of the pending LEED bird-proofing credits (to reduce bird-strike deaths) to a classroom or other nearby glass buildings. A principal objective of these case studies is to imprint on students the added complexity of identifying a response strategy when the full dimensions of a regulation—or even whether a regulation will eventually be established—are unknown. As with the HBS cases, students respond well to being assigned to present these cases for class discussion. The subject matter is sufficiently current that students can readily find additional information online. Students also respond well in class to panel debate–like discussions, such as one on whether the Dodd-

Frank Act has gone too far, or not far enough. The competitive spirit of students is brought out and they will look at the topic in more depth than if given a written assignment.

The final term project I use is to have student groups select any regulatory issue for discussion. Most groups in my experience have selected controversial current issues—gun control, mortgage regulation—which simultaneously engage the class as relating to their world while identifying the complexities of regulation from the perspectives of both the regulated and the regulators.

In my own semester-long course it has been possible to cover the bulk of the material presented herein. My approach is largely linear, in the sense of front to back, with some meandering among chapters to balance the class period material. Alternative structures are of course possible—one for example might move from a discussion of *Silent Spring* to the environmental case studies and from there to the cost-benefit analytical approaches particular to those regulations. An abbreviated path like that would be suited to say a quarter system, half semester class, or shorter summer school offering. There is also no reason why instructors could not develop their own quasi cases dealing with a local or very contemporary topic. I begin each class with a segment on "regulation in the news" to which students respond well as they realize regulatory matters are arising and changing on literally a daily basis.

Instructors of courses with more of an economics of regulation focus may wish to approach the chapters in a different sequence. I still suggest motivating the analysis by examining why a particular set of regulations was adopted. In a few cases the motivation might have been economic efficiency, but more typically it was a response to some event; Glass-Steagall following the Great Depression and Dodd-Frank following the Great Recession are examples. From there methodologies are evaluated, first theoretically (effects of taxation), then empirically (willingness-to-pay). Other examples are the primers on antitrust and intellectual property rights, which have applicable case studies in several chapters in the text. The study questions at the end of each chapter can also be utilized to extend the level of economic analysis in the book.

A work like this, although it is single-authored, reflects more than my own efforts. The efforts and insights of my teaching assistants during the initial "working out the details" years should be recognized. For years one and two they were Adam Karmali and Fay Long, and Kyle Ezzedine and James Solomon. I remain in their debt. Ms. Susan Eckert Lynch, who has shown enough trust in my work to place her name on my chair title, should be recognized and thanked for her support. An anonymous reviewer who clearly spent considerable time on the process provided many helpful comments and suggestions. The book as presented benefited greatly from these insights.

And I would also like to recognize my editor at M.E. Sharpe, George Lobell, for taking on the publication of this book. It is a departure for books on regulation, those preceding it being primarily applied economics texts, important for sure but not my concept of the only way to instruct in the area of regulation. George recognized that a market needed to be created for this book and undertook the task regardless. For myself, I cannot claim to have been so prescient when first sitting down to put fingers to keyboard. And finally, my friend and colleague Bob Smith should be thanked formally for directing me to George.

American Business Regulation

Note on Electronic Materials

American Business Regulation: Understand, Survive, and Thrive is available on the Sharpe eTc electronic textbook center, at www.sharpe-etext.com

Online resources for adopting instructors are available at www.sharpe-instructor.com.

1 Introduction

Chapter Objectives

This chapter introduces and justifies the subject matter of this text: The emphasis is on management within the confines of regulation. The focus is on case studies to provide insight into the kinds of compliance decisions made by business. In addition, the author notes the significant level of detail involved with regulation and the need to appreciate it to comprehend regulatory compliance issues.

Business regulation is defined, and the term is explored as a guide to the subject matter and to explain the reasons for limiting the scope of this book, which is focused on U.S. federal regulation of business in four key areas: consumer products, environment, communications with emphasis on cable, and finance. Managing *regulatory risk* is mentioned as a key business management function.

Key Terms: *Consumer surplus, Producer surplus, Extraterritoriality*

To the saying that there are only two certainties in life, death and taxes, can be added a third surety: regulation. In its many forms regulation has existed throughout recorded human history. The first Olympic Games in 776 BCE required a detailed series of rules, laying out the nature of competitions and delineating the processes for scoring and identifying the winners. The beginnings of agriculture roughly 10,000 years ago enhanced the need for regulation, defining ownership and uses of land, including the activities of hunter-gatherers and herders.[1] In early Christian times Jesus drove traders from the temple, deemed an improper location for business, saying "Take these things away; you shall not make my Father's house a house of trade."[2]

But what exactly are business regulations? If they are to be studied, analyzed, and critiqued, it is essential that we understand just what they are. The term *regulation* must be defined and the scope and objectives of this book clarified. We begin with this book's objectives.

1.1 Objectives and Structure of the Book

a. Objectives

The objectives of this volume are (a) to guide interested students in understanding and recognizing the multiple motivations of society to control certain business activities,

(b) to set out the several general approaches to regulation and what is understood of their outcomes, and (c) to provide an appreciation through case studies of how different sectors manage in a regulated environment, including how they manage regulatory risk, the uncertainty underlying regulatory compliance.

To focus on the subject area, we limit the discussions to (a) U.S. regulations and (b) federal (in contrast to state and local) regulations. With the globalization of trade, however, it is becoming increasingly necessary to standardize international regulations (bank reserve requirements/Basel III; intellectual property rights). When relevant those agreements are described and analyzed, as well. Further discussion of the book's aims is included in this chapter, Section 1.3.

b. Book Structure

Chapter 2

In order to achieve these objectives it is necessary first to consider *why* societies regulate. In Chapter 2 the motivations are described as threefold: (1) responses to dramatic events (for example, the events of 9/11 leading to heightened airport security), (2) the quest for economic efficiency (for example, the formation of so-called public utilities), and (3) to support societal values (for example, antidiscrimination policies).

Chapter 3

Each motivation for regulation dictates a particular regulatory approach (see Chapter 3, Sections 3.1–3.4). For example, the pursuit of economic efficiency leads to the identification of the underlying problem and hence the appropriate regulatory response. Are consumers trying to cut down on fat in their diets or avoid gluten? Food products need to be labeled to allow informed choices.

The "invisible hand" of the free market is supposed to determine which products prevail, but consumers are often unable to apply sufficient pressure on manufacturers to produce the kinds of products they need. In such cases the government can step in and apply great persuasive force—minimum mileage standards for cars are an example.

Governments take on other oversight functions necessary for efficiency, and keeping the economy competitive is critical (Chapter 3, Section 3.5, discusses antitrust laws). In the long term what is most essential is that the economy continues to be innovative, for which incentives are needed. That is the role of intellectual property rights (see Chapter 3, Section 3.6, on patents, copyright, trademark). On what authority, however, rests the great regulatory power of the government? The Commerce Clause of the Constitution is discussed in Chapter 3, Section 3.7.

Chapter 4

Following our discussions of *why* and *how* we regulate, we move on to an understanding of what we know of the outcomes of regulation. Economists model these as if they were taxes (see Chapter 4, Section 4.1). The limitation, however, is that while the taxation approach can capture the *costs* of regulation (not easy in practice but generally possible), the *benefits* of regulation often involve human life and other nonmarket goods and values. That is where alternative approaches to valuation come into use. Most regulations require a showing that the benefits exceed the costs (cost/benefit analysis). However, evaluating the benefits of major legislation like the Clean Air Act (EPA) is not for the faint of heart—significant attention to detail is essential (see Chapter 4, Section 4.2).

Chapter 5

Of course, regulation is but one means to an end; other methods exist either as substitutes or complements to meet the needs of society, as shown in Chapter 5. For example, lawsuits or the threat thereof affect the behavior of manufacturers, and higher prices affect consumers (for example, taxes on alcohol and tobacco). Self-regulation within companies or professional associations (accountants, lawyers, doctors) is also important, and to that end there are codes of conduct and corporate compliance divisions.

Chapters 6 through 9

With this background we proceed to the core of the book, with four chapters on regulation within specific sectors:

- Consumer products (Chapter 6)
- Environment (Chapter 7)
- Communications, with emphasis on cable (Chapter 8)
- Finance (Chapter 9)

These sectors were selected in part based on their importance to society and relevancy to students, and in part on the availability of case studies.

Each chapter includes considerable background material on the history of sector regulations, specific issues that led to those regulations, and case studies, followed at the end by conclusions and study questions. Detailed source notes are included so the interested reader may search for additional information. Every effort is made to be factually correct and timely, but regulations can be opaque—it can be difficult to determine what laws actually have or have not been enacted—so the reader is cautioned that the purpose of the text is to promote understanding of the functions of regulations. This is not a legal text, nor is it an encyclopedia. Rather, this volume attempts to provide a general factual and conceptual background of regulation that, hopefully, will allow students to comprehend, evaluate, and respond to regulations in new and changing areas throughout their careers.

Individuals may or may not agree with a few or most regulations. But the fact remains that regulations form a large part of the business environment and must be managed. Management, however, necessitates understanding just what regulations mandate, and this requires delving into the details. Hence in this volume it is necessary to provide sufficient detail for the reader to appreciate the environment that businesses operate in when considering regulatory compliance decisions.

The reader will soon note that there are two forms of case studies presented herein, one being the familiar third-party (Harvard Business School) model and including financial statements and so forth. These are great but are surprisingly few in number, considering the importance of regulation to business. The HBS-type case studies do have one other limitation: they are written after the fact, often well after the fact, at which point the answer can appear obvious. In practice, a regulatory response decision is often needed before the regulations are fully set out, or even before it is completely clear there will even be regulations.

To supplement the third-party regulatory case studies, I created a number of my own, referred to here as "quasi-cases." These are current and often forward-looking. What they are not is detailed, in the sense of including financial statements and the like.

Intentionally, detailed guides/assessments of the cases are not included. Doing so would defeat their purpose, which is to prompt readers to puzzle out the appropriate responses for themselves. Indeed, there is often more than one "appropriate" response. The real value is in the consideration and the discussion of options, not in the final conclusion per se.

1.2 Definition of Business Regulation

Several synonyms exist for the concept of a regulation. These include "laws" and "rules" and "orders." Distinguishing among them is not critical for our purposes. Indeed, orders and laws can be substitutes for regulations. Unable to get a law approved by Congress, presidents sometimes invoke their rule-making authority, as with the Obama administration's decision to up the auto fleet mileage standards to 54.5 by 2025.[3] Nor is this use of executive authority particularly recent. The American Antiquities Act of 1906 authorizes the president "in his discretion, to declare by public proclamation historic landmarks, historic and prehistoric structures, and other objects of historic or scientific interest that are situated upon the lands owned or controlled by the Government of the United States to be national monuments . . ."[4] Presidents Theodore and Franklin Roosevelt, among others, used this authority to establish many national monuments that subsequently became national parks, including Olympic, Isle Royale, and spectacularly the Grand Canyon National Parks. One hundred and five national monuments have been established by the authority of several presidents (Figure 1.1).[5]

And regulations and laws can be complementary; regulations often consist of the operational details required to implement a law. What is critical is that an authority must exist to provide an incentive for businesses to follow the prescribed order. For purposes here then a regulation is *an order in the sense of a detailed mandate from an authoritative body.* In practice, a regulation often derives authority from the underlying law. Here our focus is limited to government regulations: *an order in the sense of a detailed mandate from a government body.*

Figure 1.1 **The Grand Canyon, One of the 105 National Monuments and Parks Established by Presidential Rule Making**

Source: National Park Service, www.nps.gov.

What regulations do is attempt to change behavior. If a regulation involves power-plant emissions, it will likely succeed in making businesses adhere to that change—penalties can be substantial. If the behavior to be changed, though, is reducing the consumption of high-calorie foods, posting the calorie count can but does not necessarily help. And so our definition now becomes: *an order in the sense of a detailed mandate from a government body intended to control behavior.* Since we are talking about business in particular, the scope of behavioral change sought can be expanded to product design and technologies: *an order in the sense of a detailed mandate from a government body intended to control behavior, including product design and technologies.* A major form of regulation is auto safety, which involves both product design and technologies (air bags). Since business is the focus of our regulatory analysis it should be noted specifically: *an order in the sense of a detailed mandate from a government body intended to control the behavior, including product design and technologies, employed by business.* This definition then excludes from our purview general regulations like zoning, which certainly affects businesses but affects the rest of society, as well.

Behavior can be controlled both directly and indirectly, such as through the price mechanism. Governmental efforts to reduce smoking extend to taxation, which is intended to make tobacco less accessible, particularly for young, beginning smokers. While indirect behavioral control mechanisms are part of the mix, here we limit ourselves to direct controls only: *an order in the sense of a detailed mandate from a government body intended to control directly the behavior, including product design and technologies, employed by business.* Direct regulatory control approaches to reducing smoking include outlawing sales to those below eighteen.

Finally, it is important to consider the motivation for a regulation. While many may consider regulations in general as misguided efforts that curtail freedoms, most recognize the underlying motivation as the enhancement of public benefit, as it is perceived by regulators: *an order in the sense of a detailed mandate from a government body for a perceived public benefit intended to control directly the behavior, including product design and technologies, employed by business.*

Of course "public benefit" is not easily measured. In this book we use the economists' measure of public benefit, that is, an increase in the consumer and producer surpluses (Example 1.1). One might legitimately ask "If the benefits are intended for consumers, why is the producer surplus included, as well?" Both surpluses are mentioned because economists strive to be value-neutral: No distinction is made regarding which group, consumers or producers, receives an increase in the surplus. By that standard, public benefit has improved if the total surplus expands, even if that represents a gain by producers over consumers or vice versa.

EXAMPLE 1.1 MEASUREMENT OF PUBLIC BENEFIT

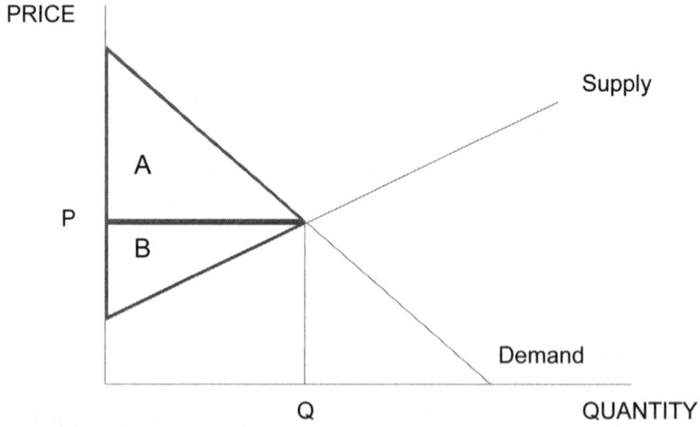

In this figure, the consumer surplus is represented by the area A, which is consumers' willingness to pay (as represented by the demand curve) minus what they must pay. Area B is the producers' surplus, the excess of revenue over costs, the supply, or marginal cost curve. The total surplus is then simply A + B.

Source: W. Lesser.

This discussion brings us to a working definition of "business regulation": *an order in the sense of a detailed mandate from a government body for a perceived public benefit intended to control directly the behavior, including product design and technologies, employed by business.*

1.3 Scope of Analysis

a. Further Scope Considerations

The definition above is one attempt to limit the breadth of this book; for example, it excludes general forms of regulation like zoning from consideration. Yet it still leaves too much for the purposes of our overview. A second way to limit scope is to emphasize U.S. regulations. Other countries have quite different systems operating in different legal/political/cultural environments: Attempting to address all of them at a useful level of detail is infeasible. The influence of cultural norms on regulation and business practice became very apparent to the author when studying fish marketing in the public markets of Guatemala.

An accounting of costs and returns for those miniscule businesses, each operating a stall in the market, soon revealed that the major fixed cost was the time of the proprietor/proprietress, then about a dollar a day, or the standard pay level (opportunity cost) in alternative occupations. Yet multiple vendors worked side-by-side selling the same kinds of fish from the same sources at near-identical prices. The obvious question was why some sellers did not lower prices so as to attract more customers, reducing their unit overhead. A consequence, of course, would be that some of the sellers would be displaced while survivors would benefit. When asked why they did not act that way, the sellers were shocked. They perfectly well understood the potential, as well as the inevitable consequences. Their bottom line: they felt they did not have the "right" to take away another's livelihood. In the United States, competition is considered not only acceptable but beneficial, which indeed it is for society, if not for all individuals within it. But in the Guatemalan fish markets, societal standards prevail, and regulations reflect those standards.

A second example of cultural differences in approaches to regulation was relayed to the author regarding taxis in Turkey. In the United States, if you are in a cab and the driver gets into a wreck, it is his or her fault, which makes perfect sense since the passenger was not in control. However, the Turks consider that the passenger is partially responsible because without the customer's directive, the driver would never have been in the locale of the accident in the first place. It is important to remember when addressing regulations that concepts of logic and responsibility differ across cultures.

More specifically related to regulation are differences in national levels of trust in government and regulators in particular. Every other consideration aside, successful regulation depends in no small part on the trust of the citizenry, and trust varies widely across countries. U.S. citizens are not great fans of regulations, but comparatively they trust the regulators more than do many other societies.

Furthermore there are multiple cases where regulation must be transnational to be effective. Examples are controls on sulfur dioxide (acid rain), which affects communities downwind of the discharge, and carbon dioxide emissions contributing to climate change, which has global ramifications. The latter in particular has been the subject of a major international agreement, the Kyoto Protocol[6] (1997) with several follow-up conventions. Pollution control is not the sole example; banking regulations are also involved, as with the Basel Accords. Because banking has such a large international dimension, a shaky national system can quickly contaminate other national systems, as has become all too obvious with the recent home mortgage and eurozone debt debacles. Hence, there is some logic to harmonizing reserve requirements across borders (see Chapter 9, Section 9.4d). When relevant to our subject, international agreements that have potential consequences for trade with the United States will be noted herein, although as previously stated this is not the focus of this volume.

Another method of limiting the scope of this work is by focusing on federal regulation. Certainly the national government is the dominant actor regarding regulation, but states also play a role, and at a local level even towns and communities have their own rules. States dominate insurance regulation, including health insurance, and typically have their own pollution regulations. New York State at this time, for example, is in the process of establishing regulations for fracking of natural gas, a process involving deep wells with horizontal extensions into which pressurized water and chemicals are injected to fracture the shale formations and release natural gas from myriad small pockets.[7] At the same time, towns are using land-use zoning ordinances effectively to ban fracking from their communities.[8] In other areas such as antitrust, state regulations are largely duplicative of national ones, with the redundancy significant during times of shifting attitudes on enforcement. While these more localized efforts are important in the overall scope of regulation, and will be identified when particularly relevant, maintaining focus and clarity requires that they be largely bypassed.

These justifications are intended to explain why the subject matter of this book is focused heavily on U.S. federal regulations, and on four business sectors within that. But some further justification for what has been excluded is called for, regarding two areas in particular: transportation and extraterritoriality.

b. Exclusions

Transportation Regulation

The exclusion of transportation regulation for a text on the topic of regulations is a seemingly odd choice. Transport issues, steam ships in particular, led to the Commerce Clause interpretation, the legal base for federal regulation (see Chapter 3, Section 3.7a). Subsequently ground transportation was regulated, and later deregulated through a number of laws in ways that foreshadowed regulatory treatment of other sectors:

- **Interstate Commerce Act (1887):** Required the publishing of rail rate charges and prohibited differential short- and long-haul freight rates; created the Interstate Commerce Commission (ICC), which eventually controlled freight services for rail, trucking, barges and the like, buses, pipelines, and telephone, telegraph, and cable companies.

- **Transportation Act (Esch–Cummins Act) (1920):** Returned railroads to private ownership following nationalization in World War I; authorized ICC to set minimum shipping rates, oversee financial operations of railroads, and regulate acquisitions and merger so as to allow a "fair return."
- **Motor Carriers Act (1935):** Added to the ICC's authority rate and entry control over trucks and buses.
- **Railroad Revitalization and Regulatory Reform Act (1976):** Allowed for more competition and cost-based rate setting; created the public Amtrak following the bankruptcy of Penn Central.
- **Motor Carrier Act (1980):** Removed most rate-making from the rate bureaus; eliminated most restrictions on commodities transported; deregulated routes used and geographic regions served; greatly facilitated entry.
- **Staggers Act (1980):** Removed most rail rate setting from ICC review; dismantled collective rate setting system.

Even at this early point it should be increasingly clear that understanding why regulations were imposed and how they functioned during regulation and following deregulation is not a straightforward matter. But to this list should be added the regulatory regimes for airlines, which are more familiar to most of us than those for shipping. Major airline regulatory acts include:

- **Air Commerce Act (1926):** Established Aeronautic Branch within Department of Commerce with a focus on safety. Renamed Bureau of Air Commerce 1934; began air traffic control 1936.
- **Civil Aeronautics Act (1938):** Established Civil Aeronautics Authority, later divided into Civil Aeronautics Administration (CAA) and Civil Aeronautics Board (CAB) with responsibilities respectively of traffic control and safety development, and accident investigation and economic regulation.
- **Federal Aviation Act (1958):** Created Federal Aviation Agency (FAA), transferring safety rule making from CAB. Accident investigations by the CAB transferred to a new National Transportation Safety Board in 1967.
- **Airline Deregulation Act (1978):** Phased out regulatory controls; CAB discontinued in 1984.

Then, there is the matter of assessing what effect all of this had on airlines and consumers. Many economists do agree that the regulatory era did indeed keep airfares inflated by the emphasis on avoiding "destructive competition." In practice that meant entry was limited and lines had to apply for permission to serve routes. As a result, airlines competed on the basis of quality of service (think meals). There was also an implicit cross-subsidization which meant that high-volume routes were paired with low-volume ones, with the former paying more than the true cost, and the latter, less. Following deregulation, fares certainly fell. In my personal experience, forty-five years ago when I traveled roundtrip from Seattle to New York for the holiday break, tickets cost about $300, the equivalent of $2,200 today. Needless to say, visits back East were rare. Yet figuring the net consequences of airline regulation is not so easy as comparing rates over time.

The reason for the complexity is simple: Multiple other changes occurred simultaneously, some as strategic responses to deregulation and some purely exogenous. Strategic responses included mergers among the established major lines, which tends to raise prices due to reduced competition. But despite that, formerly major airlines like Pan Am disappeared while others have been in and out of bankruptcy for decades. When American Airlines was in bankruptcy in 2012–13, were they negotiating to purchase U.S. Airways, or was it the other way around?[9] The merger was subsequently approved by a federal judge, with the agreement that certain gate-access privileges be relinquished to competitor lines.[10] Union employees were also hurt, with wages falling through rounds of "give backs," negotiations for reduced wages and benefits in exchange for continued employment.

The degree of successful new firm entry never materialized beyond a few low-cost lines like Jet Blue and Southwest Airlines. Economists at the time of deregulation called competition in the industry "contested," meaning firms could target high-price routes until fares fell more into line, at which point another target route would be identified. But it is not as easy as simply identifying the most profitable routes: One limiting factor is access to landing times and gates at popular airports.

Other concurrent changes included movements in the hub system, which channels flights through the originating line's hub airport and hence reduces competition. And then there are the recent efforts at reducing costs and generating new revenues that led to the cessation of most free meals while charging fees for checked luggage and choice seats. As for exogenous events, how about the tragedy of 9/11 and increased security measures? Where one comes out on the benefits of regulation and deregulation depends in part on one's vantage point and cost/quality of life trade-offs. Certainly the matter is complex and, given the time lapse, one where it is difficult to consider what appropriate corporate strategies might have been at the time.[11] What is clear, at least from the consumers' perspective, is that ongoing regulations/legislation is needed to curb some practices. Notable among these is "tarmac delays," currently limited for domestic lines to three hours before passengers are allowed to disembark and given access to water and lavatory facilities. The rule came in the aftermath of passengers being held for up to ten hours on a plane stranded due to a blizzard. This and a series of other regulations are referred to as the Air Passenger Bill of Rights (76 Federal Regulation 23110, April 25, 2011).

However, for the purposes of this text, transportation regulation was rejected as a topic both because of its relative antiquity and the difficulty of evaluating its consequences. It is simply too complex an issue for the confines of this book.

Extraterritoriality

Extraterritoriality in this context is simply an elaborate way of referring to legal and regulatory activities imposed outside national borders. The United States imposes regulations transnationally in many ways, as do other countries. One such area of regulatory/legal activity is anticorruption stipulations. The Foreign Corrupt Practices Act is a federal law making it a crime for American corporations or their subsidiaries to bribe foreign officials. Walmart de Mexico is under investigation for doing just that, not only for paying bribes (allegedly over $200,000) to alter zoning maps and allow the construction of a store within a mile of the ancient pyramids of Teotihuacán, Mexico's great archeological treasure and tourist attraction, and at eighteen other locations around Mexico, as well. Bribes for building at two other locations in the Mexico City area totaled over $1 million.[12] Nor is Walmart the only U.S. firm currently under a bribery investigation: Sheldon Adelson's firm, Las Vegas Sands Corp., is under scrutiny for the possible payment of tens of millions in bribes for operating a casino in Macau,[13] from which most of Adelson's personal fortune (and political largesse) stems. Yet this is but one dimension of international regulation, and one involving but a small number of firms, one hopes. In addition, federal authorities are examining allegations that JPMorgan Chase is hiring the children of China's elite with the expectation of receiving business from government-run companies.[14]

Another dimension is international agreements like Basel III, which establishes agreed-upon minimal reserve requirements for international banks (see above and Chapter 9, Section 9.4d). That situation is a little different though, as the agreement's recommendations are adopted and implemented under national financial regulations. There are countries U.S. citizens are told not to visit (Cuba) and to trade with (Iran, presently under extensive sanctions). More broadly, and the particular focus of this subsection, are stipulations over exports. Let us take as an example military arms exports.[15] Military arms are not necessarily on everyone's mind but the United States is the leading arms exporter ($66.3 billion in 2011).[16] Such exports make domestic needs more affordable and they allow countries to strengthen allies while restrictions hopefully limit access by foes. And of course arms are big business, involving some very large firms like Lockheed Martin and General Dynamics.

Arms exports are controlled by the Department of State Directorship of Defense Trade Control under the auspices of the Arms Export Control Act and the International Traffic in Arms Regulations. Regulated items are placed in twenty-one categories.[17] Export generally requires a license, which necessitates the firm be registered. License requirements were not significantly altered in the wake of 9/11 but processing times, even for priority shipments such as for Operation Iraqi Freedom, have increased from the target two-to-four days to seven-to-twenty-two days. Concerns expressed by Congress have delayed or prevented allies like the UK and Australia from being removed from the list of recipient countries requiring licenses.[18]

The purpose here is not to second-guess any specific governmental decision, particularly in the critical area of arms exports. It is rather to show by example the wide sweep of regulatory activities while emphasizing that regulatory management is central to the operation of business.

1.4 CONCLUSIONS

This chapter sets out the objectives of the book as well as delineating its scope. Objectives are:

- To help and guide interested students in understanding and recognizing the multiple motivations of society to control certain business activities.
- To set out the several general approaches to regulation and what is understood of the outcomes.
- To provide an appreciation through case studies of how different sectors manage in a regulated environment.

The scope of the book is U.S. federal business regulations focused in four areas and accompanied by case studies:

- Consumer products
- Environment
- Communications, with emphasis on cable
- Finance

The book makes the point that regulations are typically detailed, and complex. Understanding them and appreciating how the regulated might best respond therefore requires an exploration of details on our part, as well. At the same time, not all the factors are known or knowable, making regulation compliance (regulatory risk) a major risk for many firms.

1.5 STUDY QUESTIONS

1. Why do economists not differentiate between the consequences of changes in the producer or consumer surplus?
2. In what ways does the definition of business regulation used here differ from a standard dictionary definition?
3. What is "regulatory risk" and how does it enter into the subject matter of the book?
4. Please give your own examples of (a) when a calamity led to a regulation and (b) a substitute for a regulation (and no looking ahead in the text!).
5. Why in the annals of regulation is transport regulation so significant?
6. Identify a current issue potentially involved with regulation that might be suitable for use as a case study.

NOTES

1. See Jared M. Diamond, *Guns, Germs and Steel: The Fates of Human Societies*. New York: Norton & Co., 1997.
2. John 2:16.
3. Brit Liggett, "President Obama Announces 54.5 MPG Average Fleet Goal for All U.S. Automakers." *Inhabitat,* July 29, 2011.
4. American Antiquities Act of 1906 (16 USC 431–433), Sec. 2.

5. "The National Parks: America's Best Idea," Episode 5: 1933–45, Great Nature. Available at www.pbs.org/nationalparks/history/ep5/2/. "Theodore Roosevelt and the National Park System." Available at www.nps.gov/history/history/hisnps/npshistory/teddy.htm. Last visited 8/7/11.

6. United Nations Framework Convention on Climate Change. Available at http://unfccc.int/kyoto_protocol/items/2830.php. Last visited 8/8/11.

7. See New York State Department of Environmental Conservation, "Revised Draft SGEIS on the Oil, Gas, and Solution Mining Regulatory Program (July 2011)." Available at www.dec.ny.gov/energy/75370.html. Last visited 8/8/11.

8. Ithaca.com, "Dryden Accepts Measure to Ban Fracking." Available at www.ithaca.com/news/east/article_0d24a71c-9cf5–11e0-b712–001cc4c002e0.html. Last visited 8/8/11.

9. Ted Reed, "Analyst: Could AMR Acquire U.S. Airways in Bankruptcy?" *Forbes,* December 17, 2012.

10. David McLaughlin and Andrew Zajac, "American Airlines-US Airways Merger Settlement Approved," *Bloomberg.com,* April 26, 2014. Available at www.bloomberg.com/news/2014-04-25/american-airlines-settlement-over-us-airways-merger-approved.html.

11. For treatments of the subject, see S. Borenstein and N.L. Rose, "Chapter 2: How Airline Markets Work . . . Or Do They? Regulatory Reform in the Airline Industry." October 2008. Available at www.nber.org/chapters/c12570.pdf. Last visited 12/20/12.W.K. Viscusi, J.E. Harrington, Jr., and J.M. Vernon, *Economics of Regulation and Antitrust,* 4th ed. Cambridge, MA: MIT Press, 2005, Chapter 17.

12. David Barstow and Alejandra Xanic von Bertrab, "The Bribery Aisle: How Wal-Mart Got Its Way in Mexico." *New York Times,* December 17, 2012.

13. Michael Luo, Neil Gough, and Edward Wong, "Scrutiny for Casino Mogul's Frontman in China." *New York Times,* August 13, 2012.

14. Ben Protess and Jessica Silver-Greenberg, "JPMorgan Tracked Business Linked to China Hiring." *New York Times*, December 7, 2013.

15. I would like to recognize and thank my teaching assistant Kyle Ezzedine for bringing this example to my attention.

16. Thom Shanker, "U.S. Arms Sales Make Up Most of Global Market." *New York Times*, August 26, 2012.

17. See the United States Munitions List. Available at http://pmddtc.state.gov/regulations_laws/documents/official_itar/ITAR_Part_121.pdf. Last visited 12/21/12.

18. General Accounting Office, "Arms Export Control System in the Post-9/11 Environment." GAO-05–234, February 2005. Available at www.gao.gov/assets/250/245338.html. Last visited 12/21/12.

■ Part I ■

The Whys, Hows, Whos, and What Happened of Regulation

2 Why Regulate?

Chapter Objectives

Since there are so many regulations, there must also be clear and solid explanations for *why* societies regulate, correct? Not so—this chapter illustrates that there are multiple explanations for regulations—no single explanation suffices nor are all explanations taken together complete.

Justifications include economic, rational, and social metrics—such as catastrophes (real and literary) from which society demands protection. Economic justifications involve enhancements to efficiency (such as managing natural monopolies for which size economies are, for all practical purposes, infinite) and placing a value on nonmarket goods and externalities like pollution. Efficiency is measured in terms of producer and consumer surpluses and deadweight loss as determined by the supply and demand curves. Elasticities (three forms are predominant: own price, cross price, and income) can be used to help determine the effect of regulation-induced price increases on demand and hence the effect of many regulations. The Coase Theorem applied to externalities distinguishes between actual changes in efficiency and mere income transfers between parties.

Economic theories include the capture theory (not a true theory but instead an observation), which posits that over time regulators morph from protecting the public (known as the consumer protection model) to protecting the regulated. Capture theory predicts that small groups with strong preferences benefit most, and since producer groups are smaller they tend to be favored, but clearly not always. Political scientists take a more nuanced view of the distribution of regulatory benefits based on the distribution of costs and benefits among different-sized groups. Similarly the motivations of regulators are more varied than is often described, and the group is larger than assumed, including politicians, public employees, and judges.

None of this is static, as society's concept of what is a right versus what is an economic good available to those with the financial resources evolves as well.

Key Terms: *Natural monopoly, Deadweight loss, Capture theory, Elasticities, Economic good, Coase Theorem, Economies of scale, Static efficiency, Dynamic efficiency, Market failure*

The ubiquity of regulation is easily verified through observation. Much more elusive is the explanation of *why* societies regulate. Understanding the "why" is not central to this volume, which is focused on helping students work within regulations. Business, is noted for taking the position of "Tell us whatever the rules are and we will work within them." Nonetheless it is helpful to have some understanding of the origins of regulation as that helps generate acceptance, at least to the degree of appreciating that regulations serve understandable purposes.

Producers moreover are consumers as well as producers of goods and services and can appreciate regulations from that perspective. Nor can producers be considered to be purely passive responders to regulation. Business expends considerable effort and funds attempting to influence the type and implementation of regulations, whether through lobbying groups like the U.S. Chamber of Commerce,[1] trade associations,[2] media funding to influence opinions, or broadcasts supporting or critiquing a political candidate. The final area was recently effectively deregulated by the Supreme Court in *Citizens United vs. Federal Election Commission* (2010),[3] which ruled corporate funding of independent political broadcasts in candidate elections cannot be limited, either in amount or time frame (e.g., within sixty days) prior to primaries and elections.[4]

As a consequence of these factors, some exploration of sources, targets, and effects of regulation is called for. Herein, three bases for regulation are considered: (1) dramatic events (often tragedies) or accounts that capture the attention of the public, (2) economic explanations, and (3) basic societal standards, like concepts of what is "fair." Each of these is particular, ad hoc one could say, in explaining certain forms or reasons for regulation. Multiple attempts have been made over the years to formulate an encompassing theory of regulation; these are reviewed in subsection 2.2e. The theoretical treatment describes well the origins of regulation in several categories such as public safety, but less well in other areas that are also regulated. "It appears that we have a considerable journey ahead of us in understanding why regulation occurs when it does and why it takes the form that it does."[5] This absence of an encompassing explanation represents a gap in our understanding and likely contributes to the suspicions surrounding regulation held by many in the public arena and business alike. It is well beyond the scope of this book to fill that gap, but an attempt to provide at least a broad explanation is relevant and indeed needed.

2.1 Responses to Dramatic Events and Compelling Accounts

During the past several decades it has become common to personalize laws by naming them after a high-profile victim. One such law is New York's "Jenna's Law,"[6] named for Jenna Grieshaber, who was murdered by a parolee who had been released early despite his conviction for a violent stabbing. Jenna's Law ends parole for first-time violent felons while mandating that felons serve six-sevenths of their terms and imposes supervision on the felons postrelease.[7] Consider also Megan's Law, which requires the registration of sex offenders and involves both federal and state statutes.[8] And these are but two of numerous examples. In another context altogether, recent presidents have been inviting individuals to their State of the Union addresses who achieved national attention as heroes or doers, or who personify a group such as active-duty soldiers.

a. Dramatic Events

The purpose in recounting this personalization here is to note the approach is not particularly new and indeed has frequently played a major role in establishing regulations. It is far easier for the public to respond to specific human tragedies than to abstractions like appeals to economic efficiency. And the public does respond, with government not far behind, as in the following cases.

Sinking of the Titanic

The demise of the "unsinkable" *Titanic* on April 10, 1912, following a collision with an iceberg and the resulting loss of some 1,500 lives is well known. Less appreciated is how that tragedy led to the passage of the first U.S. regulation of the airwaves. Lives of many of the 705 survivors were saved when the *Carpathia* received a distress message, first via the distress call signal CQD (calling all stations) and only later using the recently agreed-upon SOS signal, and sped to the wreck site. But the trip took four hours, too long for those who died of hypothermia. There was a vessel far closer, within sight, but she could not be raised by wireless, likely because the operator had gone to bed for the night. That vessel was believed to be the *Californian,* which carried one telegraph operator; the *Titanic* had but two. A subsequent investigation revealed that amateur operators at that time often clogged the airwaves, masking or jumbling the messages, including the *Titanic*'s critical distress message. Indeed out of the confusion arose the belief that the *Titanic* was moving safely toward Halifax. The messages of distress were believed to be either a misunderstanding or a possible hoax. If only that had been true.

The direct aftermath of the tragedy was the passage of the Radio Act of 1912, which mandated for passenger vessels:[9]

- Licensing of radio operators
- 24/7 staffing of the wireless room
- Adherence to certain bandwidths
- A separate frequency for distress calls
- Absolute priority for emergency calls
- Reserving a large portion of the bandwidth spectrum for the navy
- Amateurs allowed to listen to any transmissions but not permitted to broadcast over them, and limited to transmitting on the shortest waves (considered useless)

Such measures are self-evident, but not self-enacting. An authoritative regulatory body is needed to establish and enforce them.

Triangle Shirtwaist Fire of 1911

At 4:45 P.M. on Saturday, March 25, 1911, 275 immigrant textile workers in New York City, mostly women aged thirteen to twenty-three, were ending their shift at the Triangle

Shirtwaist Company and preparing to go home. Within twenty minutes, 146 of them were dead as a fire spread rapidly through the ninth floor. Most appallingly, sixty-two leapt to their deaths to escape the flames (see Figure 2.1). "Thud—dead; thud—dead; thud—dead; thud—dead; thud—dead. Sixty-two thud—deads. I call them that, because the sound and the thought of death came to me each time, at the same instant," is the way United Press reporter William Shephard described the scene. Other charred bodies were found near the exit doors, which were either locked (allegedly to prevent theft) or opened inward. Still others were trapped when the fire escape collapsed. It took a century to identify the names of all the victims.[10]

Other factors contributing to the horrific loss of life included low water pressure: fire hoses could not reach the seventh floor, with the worst of the fire on the ninth. Cloth scraps stored in flammable baskets around the room accelerated the fire, and further impeded exit.[11]

Figure 2.1 **Bodies of Seamstresses Who Jumped from the Factory Floors of the Triangle Shirtwaist Company to Avoid Being Burned Alive**

Source: "Famous Trials" by Douglas Linder, University of Missouri-Kansas City School of Law.

Two years later one of the building owners—acquitted of manslaughter for the 1911 fire—was fined for locking an exit door during working hours. The fine? $20 (about $500 in current dollars).

The tragedy proved a turning point for worker safety regulations. Within one week the Committee on Safety was established in New York City. On June 30, 1911, the New York State Factory Investigating Commission was formed to report on factory conditions. Frances Perkins, who witnessed the fire from the ground, eventually became the U.S. Secretary of Labor under Franklin Roosevelt and helped bring in many new labor laws during her time in office.[12] Over time, legislation was enacted that required certain workplaces to have sprinklers, open doorways, fireproof stairwells, and functioning fire escapes. Labor legislation also followed, limiting women's workweeks to fifty-four hours and banning children under eighteen years old from certain hazardous jobs. Objections ensued; a spokesman for the Associated Industries of New York stated the changes in the fire codes would lead to "the wiping out of industry in the state." The regulations would force expenditures on precautions that were "absolutely needless and useless," according to George Olvany, special council to the Real Estate Board of New York City.[13]

Tragically, a century later very similar conditions of flammable material improperly stored, barred windows, and inadequate escape routes led to the deaths of 112 young female textile workers. What changed was the location; this time the tragedy occurred in Bangladesh, not the United States.[14] Then in 2014, again in Bangladesh, an illegally constructed textile factory collapsed. "Endemic corruption means owners and constructors can routinely ignore health and safety regulations." . . . "Authorities say the building owner added floors to the structure illegally and allowed the factories to install heavy equipment such as generators that the building was not designed to support." In this instance, though, the death toll was not in the hundreds but greater than 1,000.[15]

Great Baltimore Fire of 1904

On February 7, 1904, a small fire in the business district was wind-whipped into an uncontrollable conflagration that engulfed a large portion of the city by evening. When the blaze finally burned down after thirty-one hours, an eighty-block area of the downtown area, stretching from the waterfront to Mount Vernon on Charles Street, had been destroyed. More than 1,500 buildings across seventy city blocks were completely leveled, and some 1,000 severely damaged, bringing property loss from the disaster to an estimated $100 million (Figure 2.2). Miraculously, no lives were lost.[16]

Essentially the entire Baltimore fire department was involved, with assistance brought in from Washington and other communities as far away as New York City. Once there it was soon discovered that the other companies' hose couplings would not fit Baltimore's fire hydrants, so they were wrapped with canvas to connect them to the hydrants. This reduced their effectiveness and continued to cause problems with the subsequent arrival of other mutual aid companies.[17] "Until then, cities saw little reason to adopt a standard

Figure 2.2 **The Baltimore Fire of 1904**

Source: Wikimedia Commons. Original author Fred Pridha.

sized coupling, and local equipment manufacturers did not want competition."[18] Reform followed thereafter.

Stock Market Crash of 1929

On "Black Thursday" (October 24, 1929) the Dow Jones Industrial Average lost 9 percent of its value, and dropped an additional 11 percent the following "Black Tuesday" (October 29, 1929).[19] These are big numbers, but they merely demarcate what is generally considered to be the beginning of the crash. The crisis did not end until 1932, by which point stocks had lost 89 percent of their value compared to the market high of early September 1929.

The specific causes of the crash are complex, and contemporary scholars are not in full agreement even eighty years after the fact. At the time, however, speculation, also known as a "bubble," abetted by margin requirements (a partial payment) as low as 25 percent in mid-1929, was thought to be the cause. Also suspect were utility stocks, which sold at two or three times their book value, a particularly clear indicator of expected high returns despite utilities being a sector in which prices were regulated on a fair return to investment basis (see Chapter 3, Section 3.4).

Overvaluation, speculation, and low margin requirements are all linked: A decline in stock prices leads to margin calls which can necessitate further sales into a falling market, exacerbating the price declines. Many of these market problems remain with us today. For example, there have been calls for limits or outright bans on short selling (see Chapter 9, Section 9.4). In a short sale, a trader sells a stock he or she does not own (it may have been borrowed) with the expectation of a price fall and the stock can be bought back at a lower price. Clearly, though, if the price rises, then the trader/speculator will be in a losing position.

What was different in 1929 was that margin levels were not regulated but rather set by brokers. Perhaps more significant, there were few accounting standards, so investors knew little about the sales, assets, and liabilities underlying the firms they invested in. Moreover, with nonpublic interconnected boards of directors it was often not even clear who ran the firms. And then there was no demarcation between commercial and investment banking.[20]

Understandably the public, traumatized by the stock market declines during the Great Depression, wanted to avoid a reoccurrence, so many U.S. financial regulations date to the period, including the Glass-Steagall Act, which separated commercial banking from investment banking (partially repealed in 1999, see Chapter 9, Section 9.3). The trauma was even greater for at the time there was no unemployment insurance or Social Security to assist those in great need. Soup kitchens, including one supported by Al Capone, sustained many unemployed workers (see Figure 2.3).

Figure 2.3 **Chicago, November 1930: Notorious Gangster Al Capone Attempts to Help Unemployed Men with His Soup Kitchen, Big Al's Kitchen for the Needy**

Source: Wikimedia Commons. Original author unknown. Current source U.S. National Archives and Records Administration.

It was not only the Democrats who were involved in creating regulations. Conservative President Herbert Hoover was a foe of speculation, saying in a speech criticizing the mistakes of the Federal Reserve Board, "One of these clouds was an American wave of optimism, born of continued progress over the decade, which the Federal Reserve Board transformed into the stock-exchange Mississippi Bubble."[21]

But the banking system failures occurred closer to home, with multiple bank failures following "bank runs." Commercial banks, which make money by lending funds held on deposit, can keep only some of the deposits on hand at any time. That makes them vulnerable to running out of funds if an unexpectedly large number of depositors demand their money at any one time. Yet that is exactly what happened as depositors became nervous about the solvency of banks, 7,700 of which went under from 1929 to 1933.[22] And they had good reason to be nervous, for in those pre-FDIC days if the bank had no funds depositors/creditors were out of luck. The FDIC, an independent agency established by Congress in 1933 as part of the Glass-Steagall Act, now provides guarantees of deposits up to $250,000 per depositor per institution (see Chapter 9, Section 9.2). A famous scene in the holiday movie classic *It's a Wonderful Life* shows George Bailey (played by Jimmy Stewart) of Bedford Falls, New York, using his personal funds to pay off depositors and end a run on his family's imperiled savings and loan.

Accounting Scandals of the Early 2000s

The Stock Market Crash of 1929 happened long ago, and we have all learned since then. But further lessons are needed to stabilize our equity markets, as indicated by the dot-com bubble of 1995–2001 and the credit crunch of 2008. During the former, the NASDAQ peaked in spring 2000 at 5,132.52. At 4,045 in late 2013, it is only two-thirds restored. Clearly, serious losses were incurred. Prior to the credit crunch, the Dow Jones Industrial Average index exceeded 14,000 points; it was not until 2013 that level was reached again, rising from a 2009 low of 6,600. Again, serious losses were incurred overall and especially by particular firms. Lehman Brothers went under while Citigroup's stock price as it teetered near bankruptcy fell as low as $1 per share in the spring of 2009.

These financial traumas and the still-evolving regulatory responses are reviewed in detail in Chapter 9. Here the focus is on the accounting scandals of the early 2000s leading to the spectacular bankruptcies of Enron, in which investors lost more than $60 billion, and Adelphia, AOL, Global Crossing, and Halliburton, among other firms.[23] The regulatory response was the passage of the 2002 Sarbanes-Oxley Act.

Enron's rise and fall was indeed spectacular.[24] Founded in 1985 by Kenneth Lay, its stock price peaked at $90 before dropping to less than one dollar prior to the 2001 bankruptcy filing. Enron earned its keep by providing services such as wholesale trading and risk management in addition to building and maintaining electric power plants, natural gas pipelines, storage, and processing facilities. Financial irregularities ensued when Enron booked its brokered trading profits as the selling minus buying price, the so-called merchant model, rather than the more conventional brokerage fee earned, the agent model. The result was vastly overstated profits during good times, and a limited earning cushion to absorb other losses when incurred. Enron also booked the costs of discontinued projects as assets, a process known as "snowballing," along with other financial irregularities.

The legal outcome was messy.[25] Kenneth Lay was convicted on multiple counts of fraud and conspiracy but his conviction was commuted on a technicality as he died prior to sentencing. Jeffrey Skilling, the president, in a joint trial with Lay was convicted of securities and wire fraud, while Andrew Fastow, the chief financial officer, pleaded guilty to conspiracy in a plea bargaining deal. Of more relevance to the study of regulation was the fate of Arthur Andersen, Enron's auditor, and then one of the "Big Five" national accounting firms. Andersen was charged and convicted of obstruction of justice with evidence presented the firm had shredded tons of Enron documents before they could be examined as evidence, and the alteration of an internal memo critical of the way a loss was reported. The conviction was subsequently overturned by the Supreme Court, but Andersen disappeared as an accounting firm.

The regulatory outcome was the passage of the Sarbanes-Oxley Act, which expanded repercussions for destroying, altering, or fabricating records in federal investigations or for attempting to defraud shareholders. The act also increased the accountability of auditing firms to remain unbiased and independent of their clients (see Chapter 9, Section 9.3b).[26]

b. Compelling Accounts

Literature, fiction as well as nonfiction, can have major impacts on public opinion. That certainly was the case for Harriet Beecher Stowe's *Uncle Tom's Cabin*, which was written in response to the Fugitive Slave Act of 1850 and is credited with advancing the abolitionist movement.[27]

And so it has been with regulation; three examples will be highlighted here. *The Jungle* by Upton Sinclair (1906), which by exposing the unhealthy conditions of the meatpacking industry, led to strengthened food safety regulation. *Silent Spring* by Rachel Carson (1962) was one of the first of the popular environmental books that identified the effects of DDT, a then-common pesticide, on wild bird populations. DDT was subsequently banned in the United States. And finally, *Unsafe at Any Speed* by Ralph Nader (1965), which ushered in auto safety regulations, will be discussed.

The Jungle

Those with even a passing acquaintance with the Western genre will be familiar with cattle drives from Texas to rail heads in Dodge City, Kansas, and elsewhere whence live cattle

Figure 2.4 **Union Stockyards, Chicago**

Source: Photo by Jack Delano, 1943 (Library of Congress).

were shipped to the great stockyards in Chicago (see Figure 2.4). In Chicago's slaughterhouses cattle and hogs were preserved by drying, smoking, or salting (refrigeration other than with ice was not widely available at that time).

Upton Sinclair wrote about conditions in meatpacking plants where he had spent weeks as an undercover worker to acquaint himself with practices. The protagonist of his novelized report is Jurgis Rudkus, a young Lithuanian immigrant. In addition to serving as an exposé of working conditions—the book is dedicated "To the Workingmen of America"—Sinclair revealed much about the unsafe conditions of the food prepared there.

> It was only when the whole ham was spoiled that it came into the department of Elizabeth. Cut up by the two-thousand-revolutions-a-minute flyers, and mixed with half a ton of other meat, no odor that ever was in a ham could make any difference. There was never the least attention paid to what was cut up for sausage; there would come all the way back from Europe old sausage that had been rejected, and was moldy and white—it would be doused with boric and glycerin, and dumped into the hoppers, and made over again for home consumption. There would be meat that had tumbled out on the floor, in the dirt and sawdust, where the workers had tramped and spit uncounted billions of consumption germs. (Chapter 14)

Any man who knows anything about butchering knows the flesh of a cow that is about to calve, or who has just calved, is not fit for food. A good many of these came every day to the packinghouses—and, of course, if they had chosen, it would have been an easy matter for the packers to keep them till they were fit for food. But for the saving of time and fodder [] whoever noticed it would tell the boss, and the boss would start up a conversation with the government inspector, and the two would stroll away. [I]t was Jurgis's task to slide them into the trap, calves and all, and on the floor below they took out the "slunk" calves, and butchered them for meat, and used even the skins of them. (Chapter 5)

The people of Chicago saw the government inspectors in Packingtown, and they all took that to mean that they were protected from diseased meat; they did not understand that these hundred and sixty-three inspectors had been appointed by the United States government to certify that all the diseased meat was kept in the state. They had no authority beyond that []. And shortly afterward one of these, a physician, made the discovery that the carcasses of steers which had been condemned as tubercular by the government inspectors, and which therefore contained ptomaines, which were deadly poisons, were left upon an open platform and carted away to be sold in the city. (Chapter 9)[28]

Before the [pig] carcass was admitted to the [chilling room], however, it had to pass a government inspector, who sat in the doorway and felt of the glands in the neck for tuberculosis. This government inspector did not have the manner of a man who was worked to death; he was apparently not hunted by a fear that the hog might get by him before he had finished his testing. If you were a sociable person, he was quite willing to enter into conversation with you, and to explain to you the deadly nature of the ptomaines which were found in tubercular pork; and while he was talking with you you could hardly be so ungrateful as to notice that a dozen carcasses were passing him untouched. (Chapter 3)

It is easy to understand a visceral response from the public, first to stop consuming food they now believed was unsafe and second to demand steps to assure its safety.

Silent Spring[29]

Here in our village the elm trees have been sprayed for several years [to control the emerald beetles, spreader of the Dutch elm disease]. When we moved here six years ago, there was a wealth of bird life. . . . After several years of DDT spray, the town is almost devoid of robins and starlings . . . It is hard to explain to the children that the birds have been killed off . . ."

Our place has been a veritable bird sanctuary for over half a century. . . . Then suddenly in the second week of August, they all disappeared. . . . There was not the sound of a song of a bird. . . . Again, the spraying of DDT was identified as the cause.

[I]n spite of the assurances of the insecticide people that their sprays were "harmless to birds" the robins were really dying of insecticide poising. . . . The DDT it seems was being accumulated in earthworms which ate the sprayed leaves as they accumulated as leaf litter. . . . As few as 11 large earthworms can transfer a lethal dose of DDT to a robin.

And not only robins were affected. "Like the robin, another American bird seems to be on the verge of extinction. This is the national symbol, the eagle. . . . The insecticide being fat soluble it seems concentrated in egg yolks and so poisoned hatchlings within a few days of emergence."[30]

> DDT sprayed to control the spruce budworm was also found to be deadly to fish. . . . Soon after spraying had ended there were unmistakable signs that all was not well. Within two days dead and dying fish, including many young salmon, were found along the banks of the stream. . . . "A whole year's spawn had come to nothing."[31]

We too were, and are, affected.

> For the first time in the history of the world, every human being is now subjected to contact with dangerous chemicals, from the moment of conception until death. In less than two decades [following WWII] of their use, the synthetic pesticides have been so thoroughly distributed through the animate and inanimate world that they occur virtually everywhere.

And nasty stuff it is too. "They have immense power not merely to poison but to enter into the most vital processes of the body and change them in sinister and often deadly ways." The organic phosphates (e.g., parathion), for example, destroy the protective enzyme on nerve endings. That means once a nerve signal has been sent it continues leading to the spasms and convulsions associated with pesticide poising.[32]

Rachel Carson's message though was not a hopeless one, for she gave us two concepts of immense importance:

1. The imperative of studying ecology
2. The "right to know"

"We have subjected enormous numbers of people to contact with these poisons, without their consent and often without their knowledge." And, quoting Jean Rostard, "The obligation to endure gives us the right to know."[33]

Unsafe at Any Speed[34]

In 1965 Ralph Nader wrote *Unsafe at Any Speed* about the built-in safety limitations of automobiles. The particular target was the novel (for the United States) rear-engine air-cooled Corvair, which Nader charged was inherently unstable on turns. But the real culprit was the entire industry.

> For over half a century the automobile has brought death, injury, and the most inestimable sorrow and deprivation to millions of people. With Medea-like intensity, this mass trauma began rising sharply four years ago, reflecting new and unexpected ravages by the motor vehicle. A 1959 Department of Commerce report projected that 51,000 persons would be killed by automobiles in 1975. That figure will probably be reached in 1965, a decade ahead of schedule.

> Highway accidents were estimated to have cost this country in 1964, $8.3 billion in property damage, medical expenses, lost wages, and insurance overhead expenses. . . . But these are not the kind of costs which fall on the builders of motor vehicles (excepting a few successful law suits for negligent construction of the vehicle) and thus do not pinch the proper foot. Instead, the costs fall to users of vehicles, who are in no position to dictate safer automobile designs.
>
> A great problem of contemporary life is how to control the power of economic interests which ignore the harmful effects of their applied science and technology. The automobile tragedy is one of the most serious of these man-made assaults on the human body.

2.2 ECONOMIC EFFICIENCY

If you are a "right brain" kind of person swayed strongly by emotions, then the preceding explanations for regulations will be compelling. Problems of well-being have been identified dramatically and call out for government action to protect future victims, or something to that effect. For analytical left brainers, however, something is clearly lacking, some kind of documentation that regulation can indeed improve the situation. Moreover it would be helpful to understand more systematically when and how regulation is likely to be beneficial, and when not so clearly so. Acting purely responsively means attention may be given to the wrong areas, and at best only *ex post.* Regulation can perhaps avert future problems of the same kind, but without some anticipatory system for what to consider there will always be victims before the system can act. Is it possible to do better by identifying regulatory needs before major problems emerge? Can we determine *ex ante* which forms of regulation will give the greatest bang for the buck?

Here is where economic theory can be of assistance. It identifies, conceptually, when and what kinds of regulation are required. Theory even provides a conceptual basis for understanding the net benefits, while economists have attempted to quantify those benefits. Certainly theory has its critics. It, for example, can be based on assumptions some find unrealistic, raising questions about the real world applicability of the conclusions. And the measures of benefits, consumer surpluses, are abstractions which many cannot relate well to real people and events. Yet even with its limitations economic theory does provide an important, systematic pillar on which to understand and assess regulatory approaches, at least in some areas. At a very practical level, some laws specify that the estimated benefits of a regulation must exceed its costs, certainly a pragmatic approach to enhancing welfare to which economics is major contributor.

Take for example the "value of a life," not a subject many of us like to consider in such stark terms, but something nonetheless done regularly. Victims of the 9/11 tragedy were compensated differentially in part according to measures of their lifetime earning potential, a common way to place a value on a life. And regulatory agencies are frequently required to estimate the value of a life saved when calculating the benefits of a regulation.[35] Clearly even a rich country like the United States cannot afford to eliminate all notable risks, so it makes sense to invest where the payoff is highest. And so economics, and economists, are major players in the regulatory environment. We begin in this section though at the more conceptual level: how economists determine when regulation is needed, and how the potential benefits can be assessed. In a broad sense, those areas for which regulation can be justified are fourfold:

1. Incomplete, asymmetrical information between sellers and buyers
2. Externalities/pollution
3. Natural monopolies
4. Maintaining competitiveness in the economy

Each will be discussed in turn, but we begin with a basic overview of how economics evaluates efficiency, a key requirement for benefits. The intent here is to keep the explanation simple and intuitive; more advanced explanations will be identified in endnotes as appropriate. Yet even relying on the simplest of economic models, those for perfect competition and simple monopoly, is sufficient to give intuitive insights into much of what economic theory can explain about regulation. This is true even though it is immediately evident that the conditions for these models are so exacting as never to apply fully in any real-world situation. Here we are more interested in the insights gained than the practical limitations of the models. Indeed much of the field of resource and environmental economics is directed to understanding the effects of these variations from simple economic models. More on that later; here we begin with the basic perfect competition model.

a. Perfect Competition Model

Economists are enamored with the *perfect competition model* because it shows that when the conditions hold (a) production is at the lowest possible cost (known to economists as *production [or technical] efficiency*), and (b) products are priced at their lowest possible sustainable level (meaning profits are not so low that firms go out of business). This is known as *static allocative efficiency*. So-called *dynamic allocative efficiency* (innovativeness) is also considered in this volume.

A more precise definition of (static) allocative efficiency is an output level where price equals the Marginal Cost (*MC*) of production. This is because the Price (*P*) that consumers are willing to pay is equivalent to the marginal utility, the benefit, they get. Productive efficiency means a firm is producing at the minimum possible cost, the low point on the Average Cost (*AC*) curve. The nadir of the *AC* curve is the point where *AC* is equal to Marginal Cost (*MC*), the cost of producing one more unit. The *AC* curve also describes the Scale Economies (*SE*) of a sector, the proportion of units required to reach (nearly) the low point on the *AC* curve. And so we have a "holy trinity" for economists, $P = AC = MC$. Consumers are well-off because they pay the minimum possible (sustainable) price for what they desire while the entire economy benefits because it is operating at maximum efficiency. This is illustrated in Figure 2.5.

Figure 2.5 **Simple Perfect Competition Model**

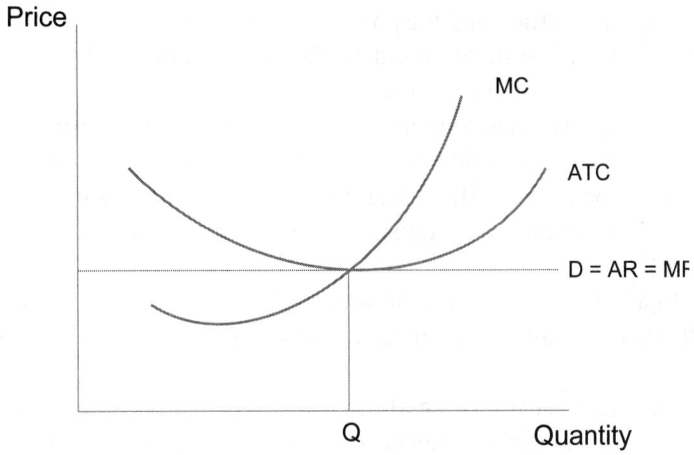

Source: W. Lesser.

This model applies to the firm level; output is adjusted by the entry and exit of firms.

This is obviously a great outcome for consumers and economy-wide efficiency overall, but does not come easily. The specific requirements of the model are as follows, but we will emphasize those which are relevant for understanding regulation:

a. Perfect information: Prices and quality of products are assumed to be known equally to all consumers and producers. This is a critical assumption for regulation if, for example, consumers unknowingly buy unsafe products (as described, for example, in *The Jungle* quotes in this chapter, Section 2.1b).
b. Infinite buyers and sellers: Buyers must at least be in sufficient numbers so that no consumer or producer is able to influence the market price.
c. Limited economies of scale: This is actually a subset of (b) as sectors with very large economies of scale cannot support many firms giving potential control over price. It is said for example that the cost of developing a new car "platform," the underpinnings including the engine system, is about $1 billion. Clearly recovering that investment alone requires large-scale sales, excluding many interested entrants.
d. Homogenous goods: Another subset of (b) as differentiated products means there are not infinite producers (or consumers) of each variant, which gives producers some potential control over price—think of the iPhone and iPad. Differentiated goods also make perfect information (see "a" above) more complex and problematic. Indeed it is difficult to think of true homogenous goods—bulk agricultural products like wheat are among a few which come to mind.
e. All inputs and outputs are priced at their true value/cost: This assumption really

rules out externalities like pollution. If, for example, a firm pollutes when there are no imposed costs, it is operating efficiently in a technical sense, but is not truly efficient if the pollution creates true, if unpriced, costs for the economic system. The situation is actually more complicated than this—see Coase's Theorem below—but is mentioned here to emphasize that the perfect competition model applies in a system where everything is efficiently priced.

f. Zero transaction costs: Buyers and sellers incur no costs in making an exchange (perfect mobility). It should be noted that reducing transaction costs, particularly regarding the acquisition of information, is a major justification for regulation.

In addition to these requirements of direct relevance for regulation, there are several others of less direct significance, but still needed for the model to apply:

g. **Zero entry and exit barriers:** It is relatively easy for a business to enter or exit in a perfectly competitive market. Without this when more or less of a product is required there would be considerable lags, periods of inefficiency, as the economy adjusts.

h. **Perfect factor mobility:** In the long run, factors of production (labor, capital) are perfectly mobile, allowing free long-term adjustments to changing market conditions. Factor mobility is a requirement for free entry and exit (see "g" above).

i. **Profit maximization:** Firms aim to sell where marginal costs meet marginal revenue, where it can be shown they generate the most profit.[36] This final assumption is not a difficult one to accept, although other incentives/goals for firms than profit maximization have been hypothesized.[37]

So, where are we in explaining why/where regulation is justified? Based on this simple overview there are several areas where regulation can be applied, or at least considered, on economic efficiency grounds. These are:

- **Natural monopoly:** The extreme relaxing of assumption (c) so that there can be but a single efficient firm in an industry.
- **Incomplete information:** Particularly asymmetrical information between sellers and buyers when (as frequently applies) collecting information is expensive.
- **Nonpriced inputs and outputs:** In short where there is pollution.
- **Maintaining a dynamic economy in the long run:** It is to everyone's benefit that an economy not only be but remains dynamic in terms of product innovation, enhanced efficiency, job creation, and so forth. Sometimes government intervention is needed to maintain the proper conditions.

Before proceeding to consider each of these in more depth it is necessary to describe how economists measure, conceptually, benefits—something they call *consumer* and *producer surplus.*

b. Conceptualizing Consumer and Producer Surplus

The demand curve measures what consumers as a group are willing and able to pay for a good or service. It is the familiar downward-sloping line or curve shown in introductory economics classes, downward sloping because usually less is bought of a product when the price is higher. The supply curve for its part shows how much firms are willing and able to produce at different prices. Supply curves slope upward as more firms are willing and able to supply at higher prices: For example, the cost of components and inputs like skilled labor or rare earth minerals for cell phone batteries could rise with greater demand. Where supply and demand intersects is the equilibrium point, setting the total quantity and its price. This equilibrium point is shown at 500 units at a price of $30 each in Figure 2.6.

Figure 2.6 **Supply/Demand Equilibrium**

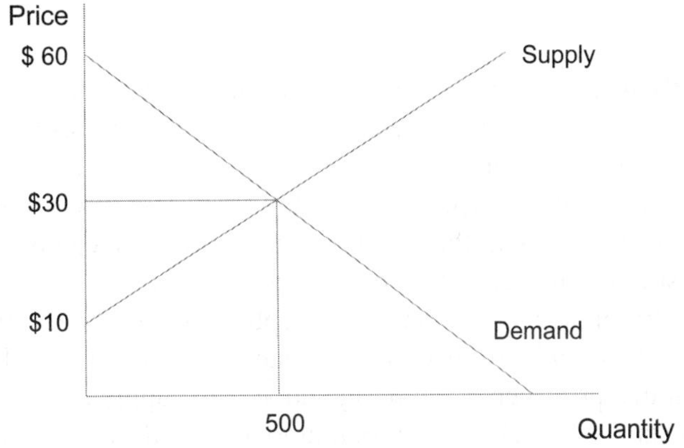

Source: W. Lesser.

This is all pretty basic, but nonetheless important to understanding consumer and producer surplus. Note that while 500 items are demanded at $30 each, there are a number of individuals who would be willing to pay more than $30. Indeed a few are willing to pay up to $60. For them the $30 market price is a relative bargain as they can keep money in their pockets. These retained funds, in aggregate, are termed *consumer surplus*, as shown in Figure 2.7. More formally, consumer surplus is the difference between the total amount that consumers are willing and able to pay for a good or service (indicated by the demand curve) and the total amount that they actually do pay, the market price. In short, the consumer surplus is the area bounded by the demand curve and price line. For this particular example the consumer surplus is $7,500, or ½ x ($60 – 30) x 500 as the simple figure is constructed as a Pythagorean (right) triangle.

Note now that the angle of the demand curve affects greatly the potential for consumer surplus. If the "curve" is flat—technically a perfectly elastic demand[38] (see subsection d below) meaning if the price is raised by any amount demand falls to nothing—there can be no consumer surplus. Conversely, if the demand curve is vertical the system is

Figure 2.7 **Consumer Surplus**

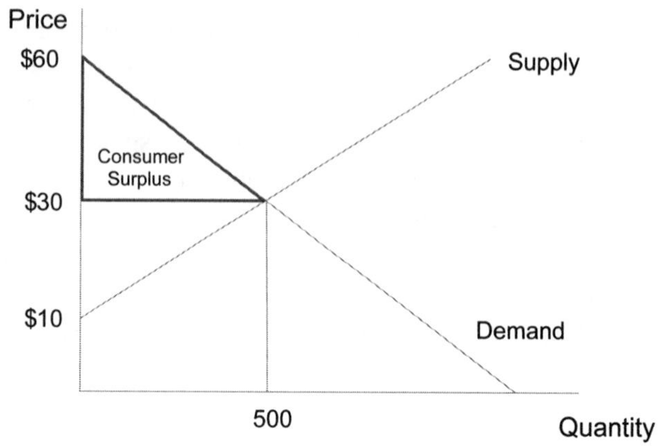

Source: W. Lesser.

perfectly inelastic—price changes have no effect on demand and the consumer surplus is infinite. At points in between—where the vast majority of demand curves would be found—one can generalize by saying the less elastic the demand the more potential for increased consumer surplus. As demand for necessities is typically less elastic, and electricity is a necessity in the contemporary world, one can begin to understand one of the populist forces for regulation of electric utilities.

A mirror image to the consumer surplus is the producer surplus. Using a similar conceptualization, the producer surplus can be defined as the difference between the total amount that producers are willing and able to supply a good or service for (as indicated by the supply curve) and the total amount that they actually sell for, the market price. This is shown in Figure 2.8.

Figure 2.8 **Producer Surplus**

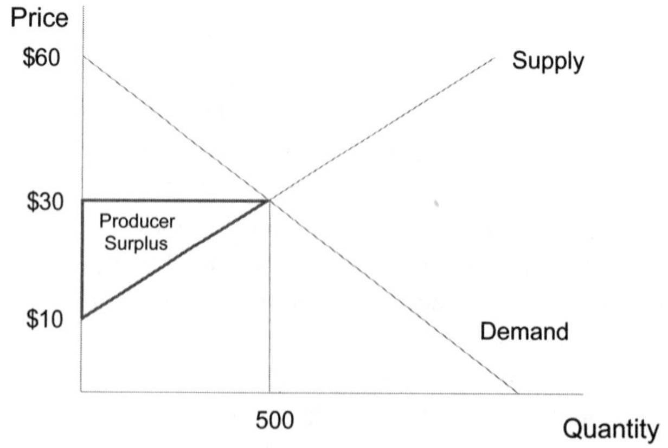

Source: W. Lesser.

One interesting point to note is that while most of us would see a sharp distinction between the consumer and producer surplus, depending on whether we were a consumer or a producer, a buyer or a seller, economists do not make those kinds of judgments. For economists producers and consumers are of equal importance, and the economy is better off if, say, the producer surplus created by a regulation is greater than the loss of the consumer surplus, as consumers can be compensated with some money left on the table. What occurs is "merely" a transfer of wealth from consumers to producers. This judgment applies even if no compensation is actually paid, it only potentially can be. This economic perspective is known as *positive economics* ("what is") as distinct from *normative economics* ("what ought to be" in economic matters). Positive economics is important for understanding some areas of regulation theory such as Coase's Theorem (see below).

c. Market Failures

The perfect completion model describes the market economic system at its best: efficiency, lowest possible prices, maximum satisfaction, and so forth. When any of the conditions required for the desired outcome are violated and all those goals are not achieved, a *market failure* exists. In the following subsections we examine four closely related to regulation, beginning with natural monopoly.

Natural Monopoly

A so-called natural monopoly violates perfect competition assumption c (which is part of b), limited economies of scale (see above). Economies of scale are represented by the average cost (*AC*) curve. Specifically, the *AC* curve is often drawn as u-shaped, or nearly so, for convenience of explanation as this gives a definitive, single minimum cost point (Figure 2.5). In reality, *AC* curves look more like the one shown in Figure 2.9, which has a long declining section; a slight uptick in costs at very large sizes may occur as inefficiencies (like logistics, management complexity) creep in, but they are difficult to observe in practice.

Figure 2.9 **Shape of a Typical Average Cost Curve**

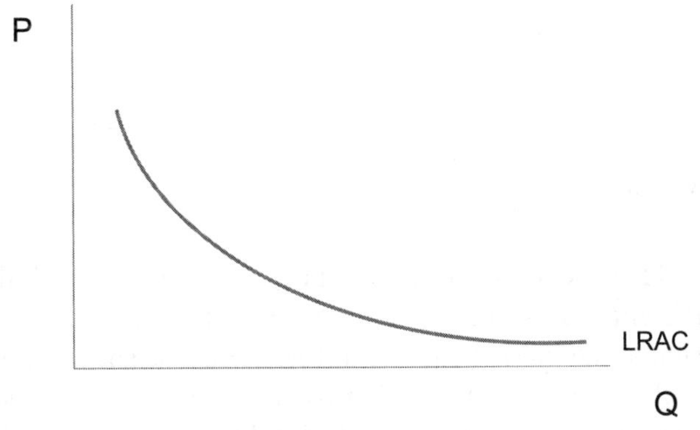

Source: W. Lesser.

What is shown is a simple curve, while for a fuller understanding of size economies we would like to know if the curve represents a single plant or a multiple plant firm. There are also considerable complexities in how one actually measures these economies. Here though our goal is a simpler one, some insight into motivations for regulation, and for that purpose a simple *AC* curve serves.

The problem for the economy is if total demand is 100 units, as shown in Figure 2.10. At that level of output, *MC* is still below *AC*, meaning *AC* could decline further if demand increased, which is inefficient. Producing 100 units with demand as shown in the figure would, however, mean losses to the producer of the amount between *MC* and *LRAC* x 100. This figure is consistent with an industry with high fixed costs and constant variable costs, indicating that average costs decline with increased output. Large electricity generation plants are an approximation of such an industry, which is why they are intended to operate continuously at full capacity. Producing eighty units as shown in Figure 2.11 would solve the loss problem, since where $P = AC$ there are no losses, nor are there any excess profits. This outcome is not efficient (as $P = AC > MC$), but at least it is sustainable. However there is a small deadweight loss created—see the shaded area in the figure, which illustrates a measure of the inefficiency of producing where $AC > MC$.

Figure 2.10 **Loss Resulting from Large-Scale Economies**

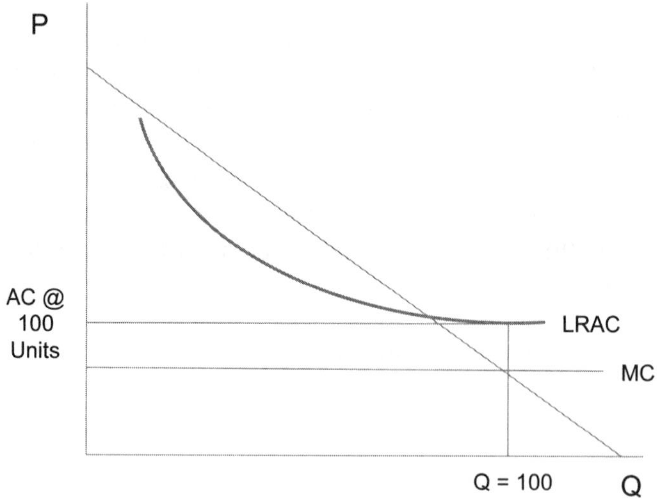

Source: W. Lesser.

Figure 2.11 depicts a natural monopoly, a sector in which the size economies allow but one efficient-size firm to operate. Note what would happen if a second firm entered and both shared the market equally at forty units, as shown in Figure 2.12. Under those conditions, the price would rise sharply to $P^* = LRAC$ to be sustainable, with firms at least covering their costs. So from a societal perspective there is reason to limit entry to the single firm to maximize production efficiency.

Figure 2.11 **Deadweight Loss Resulting from Large-Scale Economies**

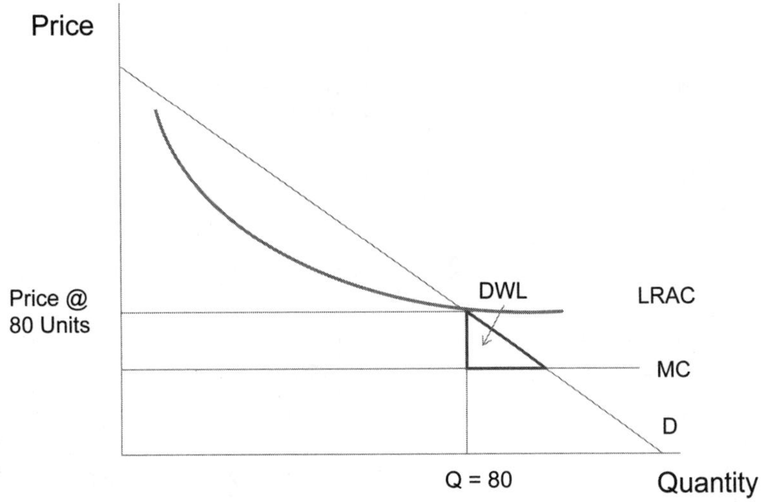

Source: W. Lesser.

Figure 2.12 **Price and Costs Effects of Multi-Firm Operations in a Natural Monopoly**

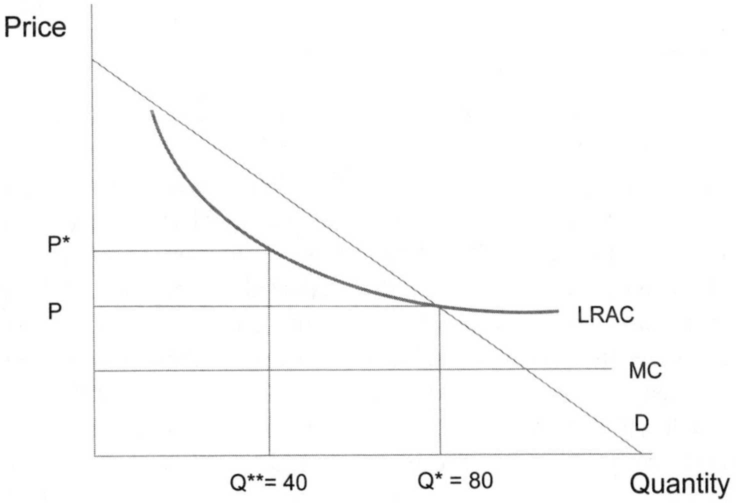

Source: W. Lesser.

All well and good, but a single firm (a monopolist) would not choose to produce forty units, but rather forty-two (see Figure 2.13). That is the profit maximizing level where $MR = MC$ and price is still higher at P^{**}. As a consequence the consumer surplus is reduced and the deadweight loss increased. What is the regulator to do? Often this natural monopoly situation occurs in so-called utilities like electricity transmission or cable

Figure 2.13 **Monopoly Equilibrium in a Natural Monopoly**

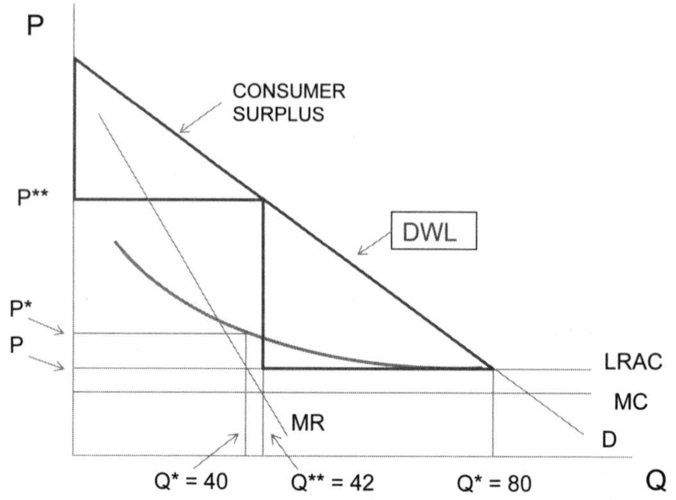

Source: W. Lesser.

networks, where it makes no sense to string up multiple service lines. The regulatory answer, though, is not easy and is explored in Chapter 3, Section 3.4.

Incomplete Information

If I sell you a car I know to be a lemon, and which indeed blows up within a month of the sale, you would rightfully consider yourself to have been cheated. Economists agree, but refer to the lopsided exchange as one where you, the buyer, has incomplete information, otherwise known as *asymmetric information*. Markets simply cannot function efficiently if buyers and sellers do not have full information. Often this is a problem for consumers: Is the milk fresh? Do a firm's reported profits and losses represent its true financial situation? Is this new brand of TV reliable or does the lower price merely reflect higher future repair costs? Sellers, though, are also sometimes imperiled, as if consumers bought life insurance only when they knew they were seriously ill.

Clearly there are multiple regulatory approaches to closing some of this information asymmetry. They are represented by grade standards (prime meat), labeling (fat content), quality standards (SAE grades of motor oils), all the way up to detailed accounting standards for public corporations. Information needs are many and while regulation cannot resolve all of them, there are nonetheless many such efforts (see Chapter 3, Sections 3.1 and 3.2).

Nonpriced Inputs and Outputs

This category of market failure refers to externalities, best known as pollution. Consider, for example, the iron ore (taconite) mines of northern Minnesota (in the city of Hibbing,

Figure 2.14 **The *Edmund Fitzgerald* Was Carrying Taconite from the Minnesota Mines When She Sank on November 10, 1975, with All Hands Lost**

Source: Wikimedia Commons. Original author Greenmars.

where Bob Dylan grew up). The *Edmund Fitzgerald* (Figure 2.14) was carrying taconite from these mines when she famously foundered, with all hands lost, in 1975. In the past, the tailings from the mines were simply dumped into Lake Superior,[39] with permits given from 1955 to 1980 allowing the dumping of up to 67,000 tons a day. This damaged fishing, recreation, and tourism, not to mention imposing ongoing health problems caused by the asbestos in the tailings entering water supplies, along with other health effects.[40] And because the cost of dumping was less than that of land processing, in economic terms, iron ore was overproduced and fishing and recreation, which bore the costs, underproduced. This situation leads to economic inefficiencies because the *AC* and *MC* of the polluter are below their true value if the environmental and health costs of pollution were included, while the costs of, for example, fishermen (recreational as well as commercial) are raised, reducing consumer surplus.

Because of the externalities caused by pollution, this is a major subject area for regulation (see Chapter 7). In the Lake Superior example there are clear polluters/evildoers and innocent victims, and certainly there was some shifting of wealth as a result. But the effects on overall societal welfare are not usually measured in such a straightforward manner, as is effectively described in what has become known as "Coase's Theorem."[41]

Coase Theorem

Coase begins by observing, "The question [of regulation] is commonly thought of as one in which A inflicts harm on B and what has to be decided is: how shall we restrain A? But this is wrong. We are dealing with a problem of a reciprocal nature. To avoid the harm to B would inflict harm on A. The real question that has to be decided is: should A be allowed to harm B or should B be allowed to harm A? The problem is to avoid the more serious harm."

His major expository example is that of crop and livestock farmers living side by side, with cattle sometimes crossing over and damaging the other's crops, the degree of the damage hypothesized to be related to the number of cattle. A standard regulatory response could require the rancher to erect a fence between the two, which of course damages him/her but leaves the crop farmer harmless. Coase's insights are threefold, one being that the simple solution assumes the property rights reside with the crop farmer, but that is not necessarily so. Indeed, a recent tussle emerged between transgenic (genetically modified or GM) and organic alfalfa growers. Alfalfa cross-pollinated over a distance, creating a problem for organic growers if the pollinated crop is no longer eligible for the organic classification. Under the "polluter pays" principle, the GM crop grower would be restrained, possibly by being limited in how close the GM crop could be planted to organic fields. But that was not the decision made by Agriculture Secretary Vilsack, who has allowed GM alfalfa growers to plant where they choose.[42]

But back to Coase. If the property right—the right to exclude unauthorized use—resides with the livestock rancher, then a number of possible resolutions arise beyond say who pays for the fence. The two farmers can negotiate multiple mutually agreeable outcomes. The rancher may compensate the farmer for crop damage (if that costs less than the annualized fence cost), or pay the farmer not to grow crops (or at least crops of interest to cattle) near the boundary. Conversely, the farmer may pay the rancher not to keep cattle near the crops, or pay to keep the numbers of cattle lower if damage is a function of stocking levels. The possibilities are multiple, but it is Coase's second insight to note that these agreements "would not affect the allocation of resources but would merely alter the distribution of income and wealth between the cattle-raiser and the farmer." The eventual outcome would be of great importance to the two participants, but society as a whole is unaffected as market forces see that resources are allocated most efficiently. Indeed regulation impedes this process as described for it prescribes a single outcome, which might not be the least costly overall.

Now comes Coase's third insight, that the preceding analysis is based on an assumption of zero transaction costs, meaning the negotiations are costless. One can perhaps imagine neighboring farmers negotiating efficiently, but when the numbers are large on both sides—Coase uses the example of smokers and nonsmokers—costs for deciding what areas are and are not to be smoke-free obviously rise. Under these conditions, "an alternative solution is direct government regulation" that states what people must or must not do.

This theorem was developed by Coase when considering the regulation of radio frequencies when multiple users of the same frequency interfered with each other so as to destroy the value of any transmission. He pointed out that regulating frequencies was not required because stations with the most to gain by broadcasting on a particular frequency—the most valuable user—would have an incentive to pay other broadcasters not to interfere.[43] What Coase seems to have missed here is if entry of broadcasters is easy—recall the problems wrought by amateur broadcasters on the *Titanic*'s distress signals (see this chapter, Section 2.1a)—then the number of entities to negotiate (and police) becomes very large indeed. Some may interfere for no other purpose than to extract a settlement.

What we learn is that pollution is a market failure, and regulation is one, but only one, possible resolution. Efficiency (as well as income redistribution) depends on both the allocation of property rights and the costs of negotiations.

Maintaining a Dynamic Economy in the Long Run

Current economic data on the United States—high unemployment, high debt, low growth—are indeed disturbing, but the economy retains its great strength: innovation. Known to economists as *dynamic allocative efficiency*, innovation can be measured in many dimensions: One particularly relevant measure is the ease of starting a business—which certainly supports business innovation. Here the United States ranks quite well—fourth in ease of doing business in the World Bank's "Doing Business: Economy Rankings" (2013 data).[44] The first ranked country was Singapore. However, the intrusiveness of regulations is far more significant; the United States ranks 80th of 148 on the "burden of government regulations" survey of corporate executives.[45]

There are nonetheless constant threats to maintaining a competitive edge. One of these is monopolies, which by restricting competition and suppressing the need for competitive advantage tend to limit innovativeness. But even in these cases, care in regulation is needed so as not to limit monopolies or near monopolies that achieve their status by being the best, possibly by holding key patents. Xerox is a good example of a monopoly in the early days of the copier, but of course no more. What is considered beneficial is to prevent monopoly firms from using their might to squelch competition. John D. Rockefeller, when setting up Standard Oil, was said to have used his influence as a major rail customer (trucking was less common in those days) to demand lower rates, which were used to subsidize low prices in competitive markets until the competitor gave up and Rockefeller could raise the price—and move on to another market. Whether this scenario is in fact true is not entirely clear but it does illustrate the concept (see Chapter 3, Section 3.5). More recently the U.S. government twice sued Microsoft, not for its high market share in the PC operating system, but rather for allegedly using that share to give away its Internet Explorer browser, so as to weaken Netscape and other browser companies. Again the details and competitive considerations are complex, as was the agreed remedy.

Dealing with a monopoly that is already established is problematic, so it is best to prevent it in the development stage. One approach is to prevent or restrict mergers believed to contribute to the development of a monopoly. The United States, for example, would be highly unlikely to approve a merger of BP and Exxon/Mobil.[46] The regulation of mergers is taken up in Chapter 3, Section 3.5d. Restricting monopolies and approving mergers is just one aspect of a field of economics known as *industrial organization* (IO). This is a complex subject that interacts with a number of laws known as antitrust. IO and antitrust also focus on price fixing, various other joint business actions like exclusive dealing, and, at one time, minimum markup laws. For an excellent intermediate text, see Carlton and Perloff.[47]

Maintaining competition, while critical, is in itself insufficient. The other requisite dimension is innovation. Ongoing innovation is particularly important in an advanced, relatively high-cost economy like that of the United States where competing internationally on the basis of low cost is not possible. What is needed is innovation in the production of new products and methods. The principal regulatory approach for stimulating inventive/creative activities is intellectual property rights (IPR). IPRs are discussed in Chapter 3, Section 3.6.

d. Elasticities

Most people, even those lacking Economics 101, recognize that when prices are higher they buy less. That is, the demand curve is downward sloping. This aspect is even called the "Law of Economics" even though there is no such law nor is there a complete absence of exceptions. However the question quickly expands from *how* will demand be affected by a price change to *how much* will the demand change? That is where *elasticities* come in, a measure of the effect of a price change on quantity demanded (technically this definition applies to *own-price elasticities*). There are also elasticities measuring the effect of a price change on a related product (*cross price elasticities*), and income on demand (*income elasticities*). *Supply elasticities* can also be computed.

At the extremes elasticities are easy to calculate and understand. If the demand curve is vertical—perfectly inelastic (elasticity = 0)—price affects demand not at all. Conversely a horizontal demand curve is perfectly elastic (elasticity infinite), and if the price changes at all, nothing is purchased. Clearly the slope of the demand curve is involved in measuring the elasticity: the steeper the slope, the less elastic is the demand. And since the demand curve is downward sloping, the slope is negative, although by convention the negative sign is often omitted—take note. The equation for the slope of a line is slope = dQ/dP: the d depicts a very small change in the price or quantity, Q stands for quantity (vertical axis), and P for price.

The limitation of using only the slope of the demand curve is that the demand curve for chewing gum and Jaguar cars could look the same. But a fifty-cent change in the price of chewing gum would have a whole lot more effect on demand than for a Jaguar. Hence elasticities are *scaled* by dividing by a point or range on the demand curve, Q/P, so that the formula for elasticity is $dQ/dP/Q/P = dQ/dP*P/Q$ (again ignoring the negative sign). The Q and P may be a point, a range, or the midpoint, that is, the average, which is the most common practice.

An elasticity estimate can be interpreted as the percent change in quantity demanded for a 1 percent change in price. Thinking in terms of percentages presents another way to visualize the elasticity formula. It is the percentage change in quantity demanded divided by the percentage change in price, or $dQ/Q/dP/P = dQ/dP*P/Q$, as above. Because P and Q change as one moves up and down the demand curve, the elasticity varies, as well.

When the elasticity is one, then quantity demanded changes proportionally with the change in price, which means total revenue ($P*Q$) remains unchanged. When demand is inelastic (< 1 absolute value—ignoring the sign), total revenue increases because the quantity demanded declines less rapidly than price rises, and vice versa. Typically essential products like food, medical care, and electricity have inelastic demand. Conversely, an elasticity greater than one (> 1 absolute value) is called elastic and means total revenue declines as prices rise. Products with more substitutes have more elastic demand simply because there are more options over which to spread the purchase.

Inverting the formula ($dP/dQ*Q/P$) gives the *price flexibility,* the effect of a quantity change on the product price. The effect of a regulation which limits the supply of a product on its price could be calculated through this formula. Elasticities and flexibilities are typically calculated from statistical models of demand curves. The approaches used exceed the scope of this book, but suffice it to say they are complex and allow for differences in methods and data. This means there can be multiple estimates for the same products with no clear preferred answer, but hopefully estimates do not vary greatly.

A way to measure the degree of substitution between products is with the cross elasticity of demand between two products, A and B. It is defined as $dQ_A/dP_B*P_B/Q_A$, where Q_A refers to the quantity of A purchased as the price of B changes. If the sign is negative, A and B are complements (hot dogs and mustard—price and quantity changes move in opposite directions), and if positive they are substitutes (coffee and tea). A positive sign means a price increase is driving consumers from one product to the other—as coffee gets more expensive, some consumers choose to drink more tea—so the two move in the same direction. Finally, if the elasticity is near zero the two products are independent, as with our Jaguars and chewing gum.

The income elasticity identifies how consumers spend the next dollar of their incomes. It is defined as (using Y as the economists' shorthand for income): $dQ/dY*Y/Q$. Typically the value is positive and the good is referred to as a normal one. On occasion, though, the value is negative—with higher incomes less of a product is purchased. The standard example used to be recapped tires but they have all but ceased to exist for passenger cars, so perhaps one can think of canned spinach. Popeye aside, its raison d'être is that this is the best spinach that one can afford.

Supply elasticities are defined in an analogous manner except, since supply curves are upward sloping, the sign is positive. They quantify the degree to which a price rise increases output.

When visualizing the different forms of elasticities, it is helpful to remember that the demand curve as presented in a simple diagram is strictly two-dimensional; the only components are P and Q. Changes in either causes movement *along* the curve. Changes in the price of substitutes or in incomes are not depicted on a demand-curve graph and hence represent a *shift* or *rotation* in the curve. This isn't something one needs to do anything about, but it does help in visualizing how multidimensional factors (P, Q, P of substitutes, and Y) are depicted on a two-dimensional graph.

Demand elasticities are useful for understanding the effect a regulation-based price rise will have on the quantity of a product demanded. If, for example, the FDA tightens up drug trials, that may save lives by keeping unsafe drugs off the market. But at the same time, any resulting higher price of approved drugs can keep them out of reach of the less well-off, which negatively affects public health. A price-elasticity estimate for the product would help determine the severity of the demand effect. Of course, prescription drug insurance which establishes a fixed price well below the market price for drugs greatly distorts the demand elasticity for the simple reason that users do not pay the true price. Indeed, the same applies to medical insurance in general.

e. Theoretical Explanations for Regulations

The purpose of this subsection is to give names and greater depth to the motivations for regulation treated in an ad hoc manner above. Those explanations for the font of regulations included safety and monopoly, particularly natural monopolies, as well as pollution. The mechanism in these instances would presumably be public pressure through the political system.

But even a casual observer of regulatory policy will note that more is involved. How else to explain (past) regulation of, say, trucking, which is neither a monopoly nor in itself particularly hazardous? Economists have tried their hand, more or less successfully, at additional explanations to capture these other factors. Not surprisingly, this is a broad and complex subject area with far-from-satisfactory outcomes.

Consumer Protection/Public Interest Model

The examples above (Sections 2.1a and 2.2c) of responding to public health threats like toxic medicines and controlling natural monopoly represent the earliest consumer protection model of regulation, more formally known as *positive analysis*. Normative analysis explains why regulation should occur (curbing monopoly pricing motivations in a natural monopoly) while positive analysis evaluates why regulation does occur.[48]

This consumer protection theory—actually more of an hypothesis than a theory, for there are no testable hypotheses generated—has been criticized for the absence of justification for regulations when the need for consumer protection is not evident (again, think truck-rate regulation). Perhaps more significant, there is no explanation of the mechanism for initiating regulations. One can easily imagine concerned voters pressuring elected officials after the *Titanic* distress-message debacle (Section 2.1a), but natural monopolies? Voters might well have complained about high electricity prices (as they do now about gas prices), but understanding the concept of natural monopoly and how best to manage? Less likely.

Capture Theory

The recognition of the limitations of the consumer protection model for explaining regulation led to the development of the *capture theory*. As described in Lowi's book *The End of Liberalism,* Congress has abdicated its responsibility for managing public policy, effectively leaving the responsibility to appointed bureaucrats, marking the move from the "First Republic" to the "Second Republic."[49] The central concept of capture theory is that regulatory agencies, following perhaps an initial public interest focus, move to protecting the sector they oversee rather than consumers, their public constituents. More formally, it can be defined as the process through which regulated industries end up manipulating the agencies that are supposed to control them.

As a theory, the capture theory has no actual theoretical base, only observations like the so-called revolving door, through which government regulators as well as elected officials move from public service to the employ of those whom they previously regulated, although such moves now typically require at least a one-year "cooling-off" period.[50] Sometimes the revolving door rotates the other way, as in the case of former Vice President Richard (Dick) Cheney, who immediately previously was chairman and CEO of Halliburton, which specializes in oil field and other services. As vice president, Cheney established energy policy under the George W. Bush administration. Another possible example is high-ranking military officials taking postretirement positions with military contractors. Another example is studies showing that government regulation did not necessarily lead to lower prices, notably in the electricity market.[51]

Possible examples of capture include the 2010 Deepwater Horizon oil spill. The Minerals Management Service (MMS) (since renamed the Bureau of Ocean Energy Management, Regulation, and Enforcement), which had had regulatory responsibility for offshore oil-drilling, was widely cited as an example of regulatory abuse[52] MMS had allowed British Petroleum BP and dozens of other companies to drill in the Gulf of Mexico without first attaining permits to assess threats to endangered species, as required by law. BP and other companies were also given a blanket exemption from having to provide environmental impact statements.[53]

Of course, the motivations and outcomes for capture need not be nefarious. Regulators over time may become sympathetic with the situation of the regulated, a group they spend considerable time with compared with the far more numerous and diverse consumers. And there can be distinct benefits for government officials being familiar with how industry really functions, as in the case of Vice President Cheney. We do wish our regulators, elected or appointed, to be completely impartial, but that is a high standard. In another sphere altogether, are referees and umpires, a group of "regulators" of sports behavior, strictly impartial to the home team?[54]

Certainly the capture theory helps in understanding some regulatory behavior, but only some, for the regulated are not always triumphant. Auto manufacturers for example struggled against mileage mandates, but unsuccessfully so. Moreover, as has been noted, it is possible to support any observation by applying observations selectively. As an example, James Q. Wilson, a political scientist, cites the days when the airline industry was heavily regulated by the Civil Aeronautics Board. The board was widely noted for supporting existing carriers by strictly limiting entry, thus protecting the entire sector. But difficult decisions over rates and service areas were imposed on some individual airlines so the story is by no means one-sided. The sheer workload for agencies can also be an issue distorting public perceptions of performance. Wilson reports that OSHA (which regulates workplace safety) assigned 80 percent of its staff to workspace inspections, but nonetheless could visit only 2 percent of establishments annually. Even Stigler and Friedland's results regarding the price effect of electricity regulation can be questioned, as their study period encompassed a time when scale economies and new technologies meant that prices were generally falling anyway, followed by the oil embargo with its inflated fuel prices—a challenging period for regulators charged with lowering prices. For Wilson, government agencies are more risk-averse than imperialistic.[55]

Economic Theory

The economic theoretical treatment of regulation, initiated by George Stigler (who won the Nobel Memorial Prize in Economic Sciences in 1982) in his "Theory of Economic Regulation" article,[56] adds little explanatory power beyond the capture theory.[57] It predicts that producers are better organized than consumers/the public, who therefore always lose out. Nonetheless, Stigler made significant contributions to the understanding of regulation by casting regulation as a market with buyers and sellers. He begins with the observation that the power of government is to coerce legally. Firms in particular can benefit from the correct kind of coercion, particularly direct subsidies or limiting entry. But subsidies are dissipated with more entrants so that entry limits are preferable for established firms. In particular, he predicts:

- Regulation tends to favor small groups with strong preferences (more per capita to gain) over larger ones with weak preferences (less individually to gain). This is one explanation for why producer groups often trump weakly allied consumers.
- Even when producers prevail, policies (and prices in particular) are typically set below profit-maximizing levels due to the influence of consumer groups.
- Regulation is more common in sectors leaning to either competition (think taxies—hacks benefit from the limitation of competition) or monopoly (utilities—consumers benefit from the restriction of monopoly pricing), because it is at these extremes where regulation will have the strongest effects on one group or another. This focuses attention on the regulatory process.
- Regulation is more likely when market failure is present (natural monopoly, pollution) than when not.

While this theory applies to regulation, and hence is of interest here, it is really a theory about the distribution of income between producers and consumers, and about the dynamics of group size. Regulation is treated as a tax paid by the losing party, a reduction in consumer surplus (see Chapter 4, Section 4.1).

One key limitation of Stigler's work is the near-exclusion of the supply side of regulation. That gap was subsequently addressed by Sam Peltzman,[58] who models the supply (legislator) side of regulation as well. He treats politicians as rational players with a preference for re-election who must choose between the competing demands of producers and consumers. Since producers benefit more individually, they can provide greater benefits and hence win. But the victory is not complete, not as great a benefit as a party under complete control of industry would provide, because politicians do not wish to aggrieve consumers. There is, though, another benefit to regulated industries—the reduction in diversifiable as well as systematic risk.

Peltzman's inclusion of the supply side of regulation does substantially generalize Stigler's theory. Limitations nonetheless remain, not the least of which is the ability to explain how industries sometimes lose a regulatory contest to consumers when consumers are not necessarily well-organized or motivated to support legislators. An example is minimum car gas mileage standards (Corporate Average Fuel Economy, or CAFE standards). Other limitations apply to the scope of the model. He considers only legislators as supplying regulation, when in fact agency bureaucrats and judges are significant contributors as well with markedly different preference functions. A significant limitation of the theory is the treatment of regulation as a zero-sum game; the loss by one party is the gain of the other. But this approach, necessary for the focus on income distribution, completely ignores how regulation can overcome market failures. Consider for example common property resources which belong to no one but are accessible to all. They are invariably overexploited with a reduction in benefits to all without some controlling force (regulation) to restrict the limited perspective of individual gain. This situation is referred to as the *Tragedy of the Commons*. One needs only consider the tragic collapse of one after another of the great wild fish stocks due to uncontrolled exploitation: whales, Atlantic halibut, bluefin (giant) tuna, cod, king crab, and more.

Peltzman's applications of his expanded theory are all to price regulation. This is likely because placing a value on the regulation of safety or environmental benefits is a complex matter in itself (but it is done nonetheless—see Chapter 4, Section 4.2). The ability to measure properly all the benefits of regulation does not diminish the value of a theory, but it definitely influences the perceptions. Consider, for example, the tendency for regulation to cross-subsidize, that is, use income from one activity to underwrite another. That was done frequently in the days of airline regulation when it was common to charge a rate based on distance. Since many costs are fixed, that approach had the attribute of having customers on longer flights subsidize those on shorter hops. And since short flights are disproportionally from small airports, these typically rural airports were subsidized. Cross-subsidization is not efficient in economic terms, but it did constitute a real, if difficult to measure, benefit for small airports and their customers. Today, in a different context, we are going through the same debate over the importance of subsidizing post offices in small towns where they may be all the town there is.

In a related effort at explaining where regulations are applied, Becker took a somewhat different approach by focusing on competition between interest groups. His theory is driven by the relative pressure applied by the competing parties, and not by the absolute amounts.[59]

Of course, the real test of an economic theory is (or should be) its predictive power, so it is important to consider the empirical support for the capture theory even if a review article concludes that evidence is "well short of abundant."[60] On the matter of the effects of the revolving door, there are several available studies. Regarding moves from industry to regulation, that group tended to vote slightly more in favor of the industry than those without an industry background. However, political-party affiliation mattered as much, and sometimes more, than background. Republicans tend to vote consistently in favor of industry interests. However, and somewhat surprisingly, regulators who subsequently move to industry are typically less supportive of industry.

Political Science Perspective

As Wilson argues, regulation is far too complex and dynamic to be explained by any single theory. Rather than using Stigler and Peltzman's narrow concept of the distribution of benefits based on individual benefits and optimal group size, he classified four forms for distribution, describing how each form affects the resultant regulations. The groups and outcomes are as follows:

- **Costs and benefits widely distributed:** Most of society will both benefit and pay, so there is little incentive for interest groups to form. Social Security is an example.
- **Costs and benefits narrowly concentrated:** Affected groups have an incentive to organize, but the broader population is unaffected.
- **Benefits concentrated but costs widely distributed:** This is the case assumed in the capture theory of regulation and its derivatives, but it constitutes only one alignment of interest groups.
- **General (if small) benefits with costs narrowly distributed:** The capture and economic theories would have it that these forms of regulation are rare. But in practice they are not so rare. The additional factor is what Wilson identifies as the entrepreneurial regulator, one with the skills and motivation to direct latent public sentiment while placing the opposition on the defensive. Examples are Ralph Nader, who parlayed early safety problems with the Corvair into a major program for auto safety. The use of the elixir sulfanilamide poisoning tragedy to gain passage of FDA approval for drug-efficacy testing is another example (see Sections 2.1b and 6.1b).

Wilson similarly considers the diversity in the motivations of the regulators, dividing them into three groups: careerists, politicians, and professionals. Careerists, to pick a large group of regulators, typically have civil-service protection and hence are not personally threatened, but neither are they rewarded by an expansion of regulation, which is to say they with their classifications and corresponding "pay bands" are not greatly benefited by agency growth. Rather Wilson argues they act in a risk-averse manner, which does not imply they are timid—doing nothing in the face of a real or imagined problem is not a scandal-minimizing position. At the same time their actions are controlled by avoiding ridicule—such as for requiring stoves to display "Caution—Hot when in use." Professional staffers, like doctors who work for the Food and Drug Administration, are also motivated by their professional stature within the broader community and act to protect their reputations. By considering the motivations of those who form regulation, Wilson provides a far more nuanced insight into the regulatory process. He also solicits some sympathy for the regulator's task of appeasing broad spectrums of interest.

Of course none of this says that the governmental role in regulation is always benign. Regulatory authority can be abused for political or financial gain, as Robert Cato laid out in detail in his extensive biographies of President Lyndon Johnson. In this example, President Johnson sought to silence a Dallas reporter who was asking questions about the operation of Johnson's Texas Broadcasting Company. "All his life, Lyndon Johnson had made use of any political weapon on which he could lay his hand, or which he could invent, any power that he could find or devise, as a means to attain his ends. . . ." "A President had a lot of weapons. . . ." "If a newspaper is investigated by the federal government, a particularly vulnerable area would be its profitable radio and television stations, since all broadcasting stations are under the authority of the Federal Communications Commission, and in few businesses was the role of government as critical as in broadcasting, for not only were the very licenses which allowed the uses of the airways granted and periodically reviewed solely at the FCC's sufferance, but the agency possessed virtually unchangeable authority over every aspect of a station's operations. Johnson brought the Dallas stations' operations into the conversation [with the reporter's editor]."[61]

Another potent regulatory force is the courts. Judges frequently are called upon to interpret laws, in effect making policy decisions in areas in which they often have no technical competence. The result is all too often unrealistic expectations—as with air pollution control (see Chapter 7, Section 7.1).

Finally, Wilson emphasizes the dynamic aspects of regulation, a component missing in the more formal theories. One aspect is the evolution of concepts of what constitutes a problem. Consider foods made from genetically modified crops, in particular corn and soybeans. Even though those nearly ubiquitous foods have been on the market in the United States since 1996 and to date (to my knowledge) there is not a single food-based problem documented, a large portion (93 percent) of U.S. consumers, when asked, still favor mandatory product labeling, even if no specific information beyond the likely inclusion of GM components is provided.[62] A second dynamic area is the most potent of all. It is *ideas*.

For decades, the utility sector consisting of electric generation and distribution was jointly regulated as a natural monopoly. Then economists realized it is the distribution component that is the monopoly—not generation. The consequence has been the separation of generation from distribution and the establishment of markets for electric power, while distribution remains quasi-regulated as a monopoly (see Chapter 3, Section 3.4). In a similar way, it was recognized that pollution reduction was cheaper for some entities than others, and so overall pollution reduction could be achieved more economically if permits could be bought and sold (see Chapter 7, Section 7.3c).

Perhaps no further examples are needed to document that our conceptual understanding of the why and who of regulation is indeed very limited and that no simple approach is or will be adequate.

2.3 Social/Religious/Moral Concepts of Equity

The intent of this subsection is not to be entirely systematic in exposition but rather simply to establish that the standards of a society can influence greatly its actions, whether they be "rational" in some broader context or economically efficient or not. In the U.S. context, it is easy to see how some basic societal standards, however formed, translate into particular regulations, as in:

a. Age Discrimination

Given the long and troubled history of U.S. racial discrimination, combined with a founding national principle of freedom from religious discrimination, it is easy to understand a movement to prohibit age discrimination. However, age-related policies are not completely consistent, for discounts for seniors and children are common, and a ninety-day lower minimum wage for youths is permitted.[63]

b. Polluter Pays

This principle, referring here to domestic pollution and not the formalities called for under international trade, says simply that he who causes the pollution should pay for its cleanup or compensate those whose interests or health are injured. However, as pointed out by Coase (see Section 2.2c), this can be a very inefficient approach, and thus can be seen in part as an expectation of taking personal responsibility for one's own actions in a society where personal responsibility is highly prized. In a parallel sense, a conversion of automobile insurance to "no fault" was long impeded by those who believed the guilty should pay, no matter how cumbersome and costly it was to determine who indeed was guilty.

c. Rights versus Economic Goods

To a large degree, the "polluter pays" principle is an embodiment of the concept of absolute rights in contrast to a perspective on the use of a resource as economic goods that can be negotiated à la Coase's Theorem. Yet in a society which places such emphasis on property rights, it is easy to understand why positions become so absolute, with regulations reflecting those positions. The significance of this distinction in societal attitudes should not be underestimated.

One key area this distinction can be observed in is access to medical care. In 1941 President Roosevelt declared "freedom from want" to be one of four essential liberties, and "the right to adequate medical care and the right to achieve and enjoy good health" one of those freedoms.[64] The right to medical care is enshrined in the United Nations "Universal Declaration of Human Rights," along with the right to free education.[65] Of course, such declarations mean nothing unless or until established in national laws and regulations. The United States indeed has advanced only little regarding universal medical care since Roosevelt's time, but the Affordable Care Act of 2010 does begin making access more available and affordable.[66] The purpose of mentioning these aspects of health care here is to highlight the difference in perspective between those who see health care as a right in contrast to those who view it as an economic good, available to those who can afford it.

d. Extension to Other "Rights"

It is easy for a society to identify some good or service as a "right" and subsequently to see it is provided through law or regulation. The right to a trial is established in the Sixth Amendment to the Constitution (part of the Bill of Rights): "the accused shall enjoy the right to a speedy and public trial, by an impartial jury." That amendment also provides the right to legal counsel—and subsequently was extended to state trials by several Supreme Court decisions. But of course the right to counsel means little for the indigent so that Legal Aid has been established as a welfare provision by states to people who could otherwise not afford access to the legal system. Why this society recognizes the right to affordable council as more important than the right to affordable health care is not very clear, although providing subsidized council is clearly far less costly than health care, plus far more legislators are lawyers than are doctors. And in the case of free primary and secondary education, it can be justified as an economic benefit to society at large as well as a personal right.

What is a "right" versus a privilege evolves over time. After all, for many centuries, including in the United States until 150 years ago, the right to personal freedom was not accepted. Pets and livestock are presently given legal rights for protection from maltreatment and suffering, but possibly at some future date pets may no longer be considered as property. Already fringe groups call for the ending of the use of animals for medical experiments,[67] and the Humane Society of the United States considers keeping laying hens in cages to be inhumane ("battery cages present inherent animal welfare problems, most notably by their small size and barren conditions"),[68] and they are no longer permitted in Switzerland, among other places.[69] There are even suggestions that the physically ugly, who have a documented loss in lifetime earnings "in a typical case" of $230,000, be given some legal/regulatory protection from the more comely.[70]

The purpose of mentioning these examples, including those presently outside the mainstream, is not to advocate for or against any or all. Rather they are used as illustrations of how social consciousness influences laws and regulations, and how consciousness is mutable over time, generally toward recognizing more rather than fewer "rights." However in these as in many other areas, social norms are not necessarily consistent.

2.4 Conclusions

The question of "why do we regulate" is a straightforward and obvious one. It is a question all of us wish to answer, but nothing clear-cut is forthcoming. In some cases—personal safety—justifications are evident. In others, such as natural monopoly, the answer is also relatively apparent—for economic reasons. Theories of political and influence applications suggest that regulation will occur where it has the greatest effect on particular parties; that is, in either competitive or monopolistic sectors. Yet there are many forms, perspectives, and players, all in a dynamic mix. This means there is not, nor is there ever likely to be, a single explanation for why and how we regulate. There is no unified theory. Societies don't work that way. While this is not a completely satisfactory outcome, if we cannot provide an encompassing answer to the why, perhaps we can do better at approaching how best to regulate and operate under these regulations.

Assisting with the effort for enhancing the efficiency of regulation is the measurement of elasticities. Calculated elasticities can help in projecting, for example, how regulation-induced price increases will affect demand and possibly diminish the benefits intended from regulation. For example, costly pollution-reducing devices on autos will cause consumers to hold on to older (more polluting) cars for longer, but to what degree and for how long? Estimates are possible.

But costs and efficiencies are not the only motivating factors for societies. Societies also have core values that motivate actions—economic rationale be damned. For example, "we" often believe the polluter should be held accountable, even when, as Coase points out, that is often not effective or efficient nor is it always clear who the violator is. We just know what should be done, what is right and proper. Business leaders need to appreciate that an emotional response underlies much of what societies do, and respond accordingly.

2.5 Study Questions

1. What is a common form of nonpriced inputs and outputs and how do they figure into regulation?
2. What are the insights that the Coase Theorem provides for considering the roles and types of regulation?
3. According to George Stigler in "The Theory of Economic Regulation," what are three economic conditions that often lead to the implementation of regulations?
4. Can you identify a recent book, article, or event that had the effect of a *Silent Spring*–like book in leading to new regulations at the federal or state level?
5. Wilson identified four categories of the distribution of regulatory costs and benefits. Can you give an example of the classes of "costs and benefits narrowly concentrated" and "benefits concentrated but costs widely distributed"?
6. Explain how the deadweight loss is a measure of economic inefficiency.
7. Is there a logical connection between the Tragedy of the Commons and the "polluter pays" principles?
8. What sectors other than electrical power have the attributes of a natural monopoly?

9. Search the Web for some estimates of the cost of auto safety and/or efficiency regulations along with own-price demand elasticities and calculate the effect of the regulations on domestic automobile demand.
10. Regulations which promote the fuel efficiency of cars may add costs initially but can lead to long-term savings at the gas pump, as the saying goes. Consumers sometimes though have a difficult time comprehending the net effect over the initial cost consideration. Is there a theory of regulation that explains that lack of understanding?

NOTES

1. See, for example, U.S. Chamber of Commerce, "Regulations: Restoring Balance." Available at www.uschamber.com/regulations. Last visited 8/22/11.

2. See, for example, American Seed Trade Association, Government Affairs, "ASTA Statement on Field and Greenhouse Planted Seed and Human Pathogens." Available at www.amseed.org/pdfs/issues/phytosanitary/planted-seeds-human-pathogens.pdf. Last visited 5/20/14.

3. 558 U.S. 08-205.

4. See, for example, Dan Eggen, "The Influence Industry: 'Candidate Super PACs' Surge Ahead in the 2012 Money Race." *Washington Post,* August 24, 2011.

5. W.K. Viscusi, J.E. Harrington, Jr., and J.M. Vernon, *Economics of Regulation and Antitrust*, 4th ed. Cambridge, MA: MIT Press, 2005, p. 393.

6. See the Sentencing Reform Act of 1998. Available at www.parole.state.ny.us/legislation-jl.html. Last visited 8/8/11.

7. Evelyn Nieves, "Our Towns; Lost Crusader Inspires 'Jenna's Law.' " *New York Times*, May 3, 1998.

8. See overview and list of state laws at Klass Kids Foundation. Available at www.klaaskids.org/pg-legmeg.htm. Last visited 8/9/11.

9. D.W. Johnson, "The Radio Legacy of the R.M.S. *Titanic*." Available at www.avsia.com/djohnson/titanic.html. See also Encyclopedia.com, "The *Titanic* and the Radio Act of 1912." Available at www.encyclopedia.com/doc/1G2–3468300546.html. Last visited 8/15/11.

10. Joseph Berger, "A Century Later, the Roll of the Dead in a Factory Fire Now Has All 146 Names." *New York Times,* February 21, 2011.

11. "Leap for Life, Leap of Death." Yaz Page. Available at www.csun.edu/~ghy7463/mw2.html. Cornell University, ILR School Kheel Center, "The Triangle Factory Fire." Available at www.ilr.cornell.edu/trianglefire/story/introduction.html. Detailed history available in David von Drehle, *Triangle: The Fire That Changed America.* New York: Atlantic Monthly Press, 2004.

12. EHS Wire, "The Triangle Shirtwaist Fire (1911)—A Turning Point for Workplace Safety." March 23, 2011. Available at http://ehswire.com/2011/03/the-triangle-shirtwaist-fire-1911-a-turning-point-for-workplace-safety/. Last visited 8/15/11.

13. Harold Myerson, "The Mindset That Survived the Triangle Shirtwaist Fire." *Washington Post,* March 22, 2011.

14. Jim Yardeley, "Recalling Fire's Horror and Exposing Global Brands' Safety Gap." *New York Times,* December 7, 2012.

15. Jason Burke, "Bangladesh Eases Trade Union Laws after Factory Building Collapse." *The Guardian,* May 13, 2013.

16. History.com, "The Great Baltimore Fire Begins." Available at www.history.com/this-day-in-history/the-great-baltimore-fire-begins.

17. See Maryland Digital Cultural Project, "Great Baltimore Fire of 1904." Available at www.mdch.org/fire/. Last visited 8/15/11.

18. Steve Lohr, "Seeing Promise and Peril in Digital Records." *New York Times,* July 17, 2011, p. 3.

19. Kimberly Amadeo, "Black Tuesday." About.com. Available at http://useconomy.about.com/od/glossary/g/Black_Tuesday.htm. Last visited 11/19/11.

20. See any number of accounts of the 1929 stock market crash, including Harold Bierman, Jr., *The Causes of the 1929 Stock Market Crash: A Speculative Orgy or a New Era?* Westport, CT: Greenwood Press, 1998.

21. Quoted in Harold Bierman, Jr., "The 1929 Stock Market Crash." EH.net. Available at http://eh.net/encyclopedia/article/Bierman.crash. Last visited 11/29/11.

22. John R. Walter, "Depression-Era Bank Failures: The Great Contagion or the Great Shakeout?" *Economic Quarterly* 91, 1 (Winter 2005): 39–54.

23. List of recent scandals available at http://en.wikipedia.org/wiki/Accounting_scandals.

24. Wikipedia, "Enron Scandal." Available at http://en.wikipedia.org/wiki/Enron_scandal#Revenue_recognition. Last visited 8/17/11.

25. Cathy Booth Thomas, "Called to Account." *Time,* June 18, 2002. Available at www.time.com/time/business/article/0,8599,263006,00.html. Last visited 8/17/11.

26. See the executive summary of P.L. 107-204, the Sarbanes-Oxley Act of 2002. Available at www.csbs.org/legislative/leg-updates/Documents/ExecSummary-SarbanesOxley-2002.pdf. Last visited 8/17/11.

27. Brandi McCandless, "Slavery's Destruction of Domestic Life in Stowe's *Uncle Tom's Cabin.*" *Ampersand* 2, 1 (Fall 1998).

28. A footnote contains the text of U.S. Dept. of Agriculture Order No. 215, which makes explicit reference to interstate or foreign commerce.

29. Rachel Carson, *Silent Spring.* Boston: Houghton Mifflin, 1962.

30. Ibid., Chapter 8.

31. Ibid., Chapter 9.

32. Ibid., Chapter 3.

33. Ibid., Chapter 2.

34. Ralph Nader, *Unsafe at Any Speed.* New York: Grossman, 1965. Quotes presented are from the Preface.

35. Binyamin Appelbaum, "As U.S. Agencies Put More Value on a Life, Businesses Fret." *New York Times,* February 16, 2011.

36. For a simple proof, see Inflate Your Mind, "Section 4: Profit Maximization Using a Purely Competitive Firm's Cost and Revenue Curves." Available at http://inflateyourmind.com/index.php?option=com_content&view=article&id=122&Itemid=153. Last visited 1/2/13.

37. For example, sales volume maximization, revenue maximization, sales growth.

38. Demand elasticity is defined as $dQ/dP \times P^*/Q^*$, or the slope of the curve defined at point P^*/Q^*. Often rather than using a point elasticity the average over the demand curve is utilized.

39. Minnesota Historical Society, "Taconite." Available at www.mnhs.org/library/tips/history_topics/24taconite.html. Last visited 8/25/11.

40. "Pollution, the Classic Case." *Time,* May 6, 1974.

41. Ronald H. Coase, "The Problem of Social Cost." *Journal of Law and Economics* 3 (October 1960): 1–44. The "theorem" is not one which Coase actually developed as such, but rather a name given to the ideas in this and related papers.

42. Andrew Pollack, "U.S. Approves Genetically Modified Alfalfa." *New York Times,* January 27, 2011.

43. Investopedia, "Coase Theorem." Available at www.investopedia.com/terms/c/coase-theorem.asp#axzz1W3b1LuZ3.

44. The World Bank Group, International Finance Corp., "Doing Business." June 2013. Available at www.doingbusiness.org/rankings. Last visited 7/18/13.

45. World Economic Forum, "The Global Competitiveness Report 2013–2014," Section 2.1, Indicator 1.09. Available at http://reports.weforum.org/the-global-competitiveness-report-2013–2014/. Last visited 11/18/13.

46. Interestingly, Exxon is an outgrowth of Rockefeller's Standard Oil.

47. Dennis W. Carlton and Jeffrey M. Perloff, *Modern Industrial Organization*, 4th ed. Boston: Addison-Wesley, 2005.

48. W.K. Viscusi, J.E. Harrington, Jr., and J.M. Vernon, *Economics of Regulation and Antitrust*, 4th ed. Cambridge, MA: MIT Press, 2005, p. 377.

49. T.J. Lowi, *The End of Liberalism*. New York: W.W. Norton, 1979. See also W.A. Niskanen, "Bureaucrats and Politicians." *Journal of Law and Economics* 18 (1975): 617–643.

50. Details at Sourcewatch, "Revolving Door Regulations." Available at www.sourcewatch.org/index.php?title=Revolving_door_regulations. Last visited 8/26/11.

51. See, for example, G.J. Stigler and C. Friedlander, "What Can Regulators Regulate? The Case of Electricity." *Journal of Law and Economics* 15 (April 1962): 1–16.

52. See, for example, Thomas Frank, "Obama and 'Regulatory Capture.' " *Wall Street Journal,* June 24, 2010.

53. Ian Urbina, "U.S. Said to Allow Drilling without Needed Permits." *New York Times*, May 13, 2010.

54. See, for example, Tobias J. Moskowitz and L. Jon Wertheim, *Scorecasting: The Hidden Influences behind How Sports Are Played and Games Are Won*. New York: Crown Publishing, 2011.

55. See Chapter 10, "The Politics of Regulation," in J.Q. Wilson, ed., *The Politics of Regulation.* New York: Basic Books, 1980.

56. George Stigler, "The Theory of Economic Regulation." *Bell Journal of Economics and Management Science* 3 (1971): 3–18.

57. For a more detailed overview of the Stiglarian model and subsequent embellishments see Ernesto Dal Bó, "Regulatory Capture: A Review." *Oxford Review of Economic Policy* 22, 2 (2006): 203–25.

58. Sam Peltzman, "Toward a More General Theory of Regulation." *Journal of Law and Economics* 19 (1976): 211–40.

59. Gary Becker, "A Theory of Competition among Pressure Groups for Political Influence." *Quarterly Journal of Economics* 98, 3 (1983): 371–400.

60. Dal Bó, "Regulatory Capture," references suppressed.

61. Robert A. Cato, *The Years of Lyndon Johnson: The Passage of Power.* New York: Alfred A. Knopf, 2012, Chapter 21.

62. Thomson Reuters/NPR, "National Survey of Healthcare Consumers: Genetically Engineered Food." October 2010. Available at www.factsforhealthcare.com/pressroom/NPR_report_Genetic-EngineeredFood.pdf. Last visited 1/2/13.

63. U.S. Department of Labor, "Youth Minimum Wage-Fair Labor Standards Act." Available at www.dol.gov/whd/regs/compliance/whdfs32.pdf. Last visited 8/26/11.

64. Quoted in Center for Economic and Social Rights, "The Right to Health in the United States of America: What Does It Mean?" Available at www.nhchc.org/Advocacy/RighttoHealthinAmerica.pdf. Last visited 8/29/11.

65. See United Nations Universal Declaration of Human Rights, Articles 25 and 26. Available at www.un.org/en/documents/udhr/. Last visited 8/29/11.

66. The Affordable Care Act of 2010. Overview available at www.whitehouse.gov/healthreform/healthcare-overview#works. Last visited 8/29/11.

67. For various articles regarding the ban of animal testing, see the Web site for People for the Ethical Treatment of Animals. Available at www.peta.org/. Last visited 8/29/11.

68. See Humane Society of the United States, "Cage-Free vs. Battery-Cage Eggs." Available at www.humanesociety.org/issues/confinement_farm/facts/cage-free_vs_battery-cage.html. Last visited 8/29/11.

69. Heinzpeter Studel, "How Switzerland Got Rid of Battery Cages." Zurich: United Poultry Concern, 2001. Available at www.upc-online.org/battery_hens/SwissHens.pdf. Last visited 8/29/11.

70. Daniel S. Hamermesh, "Ugly? You May Have a Case." *New York Times, Sunday Review,* August 8, 2011.

3 Approaches to Regulation

Chapter Objectives

Chapter 2 focuses on why societies regulate. The objective of this chapter is to explore how regulations are implemented. Chapter 4 subsequently describes what we know about the effects of those regulations (including costs and benefits), and how those assessments are made. None of this is easy.

This chapter introduces the concept of market failures and the roles of regulation in overcoming them. Here the reader is exposed to four specific mechanisms for offsetting market failures:

- Provision of information/ratings
- Grade standards
- Mandates, known as *performance* and *process standards* (the latter less formally known as *command and control*—thou shall or thou shall not!)
- *Rate of return* regulation for natural monopolies, which must balance too-low and too-high returns on investments

The types of regulation in the list above apply mainly to existing products, services, and so forth currently available. Societies are concerned as well about the long-term outlook, particularly the competitiveness of a society and its innovativeness. Two major forms of legislation/regulation address these longer-term concerns: *antitrust*, focused on maintaining competitiveness, and *intellectual property rights*, which encourage investments.

Antitrust, a form of industrial policy, strives to prevent uncompetitive activities by prohibiting certain forms of corporate behavior such as price fixing and mergers that would reduce competition. Antitrust is an enormously significant aspect of regulatory policy but is ensconced in only a few major laws, the Sherman and Clayton Acts, as well as a part of the Federal Trade Commission Act.

Intellectual property rights grant limited temporary monopolies for inventions (patents), creations (copyright), or product names (trademark) as protection from direct copying. Generally protection is national, placing a premium on evolving agreements to standardize systems internationally.

Federal regulation, it must be recognized, is restricted based on interpretations (led by *Gibbons vs. Ogden*) of the authority granted in the Commerce Clause of the Constitution. In the simplest terms, federal regulation applies when commerce is interstate, and state regulation applies when commerce is intrastate; however, distinguishing the boundary is not always straightforward.

Key Terms: *Averch-Johnson Effect, Horizontal merger, LEED, NAICS, Nonobviousness, Nonrivalrous, Novelty, Standard of identity, Trade secret, TRIPS, Utility*

For a regulation to be functional, it must have (a) an objective/purpose/intent, (b) an operational approach (how that objective is to be achieved), (c) a mechanism (which can be a positive or negative incentive) to foster compliance, and (d) some means of measuring whether the goal has been achieved or compliance assured. Given the ubiquity of regulation, it is unsurprising that there are many variants under a, b, and c, and once the permutations among them are counted the number is indeed quite large. Some organizational principal is therefore required for categorizing the several general approaches and summarizing their success, or lack thereof, in achieving such goals.

In this chapter, the organizational format is structured around the kinds of regulatory mechanisms applied. This organizational system, in contrast to organizing around a sector (utilities) or objective (pollution reduction), is in itself not all inclusive but does encompass the major forms of regulation. The intent here is to provide a broad overview of regulatory approaches and their general characteristics/effects. Details of selected sector regulation with case studies are provided in Chapters 6–9. Four such mechanisms are evaluated:

- Enhance information availability
- Specify performance standards
- Establish outcomes, whether rigid or flexible
- Maintain a dynamic, competitive market system

The final point has two dimensions, the short run involving antitrust and the long term having a reliance on intellectual property rights. These are very important forms of business regulation but are not often spoken of in the same category as, say, pollution control, and indeed their mode or operation is quite different. In recognition of those differences the first three bulleted items, corresponding to this chapter's Sections 3.1–3.5, are treated as a group, while the fourth bullet point, corresponding to this chapter's Sections 3.6 and 3.7, is a second group.

Alternatively, the material presented in the first five sections of this chapter can be viewed as a means of categorizing regulations. Basically, there are but three main ways to regulate behavior: regulate inputs, regulate outputs, or regulate functionality/behavior and preconditions. In highly simplified terms consider a family attempting to get a teenage son to focus more on his high school studies. They can ask him to study two hours a night (input) or to achieve an A–average (output). Alternatively they can remove distractions such as video games while seeing that his laptop is up to date (preconditions). The lever for extracting the first two outcomes is access to the car on weekends.

In the regulatory environment, the principal policy levers available are:

- Enhance information availability
- Mandate a particular performance/behavior or outcome
- Establish standards
- Specify a particular allowable return

The first and fourth points above are direct curatives to specific market failures, respectively inadequate information and natural monopoly (see Chapter 2, Section 2.2c). The second and third are more the "command and control" approach—do this or else. The two differ as the "particular performance/behavior or outcome" (as worded here) relates to more generalized requirements such as the Food and Drug Administration's (FDA's) mandate that pharmaceuticals must be shown to be "safe and effective." Just what constitutes safety and efficacy is established on a case-by-case basis. Standards are intended to be very detailed and particular, for example, the requirements for the crash strength of seat belts (see Section 3.3a).

3.1 MANDATED INFORMATION/RATINGS

a. Warnings

If the justification for a regulation is incomplete or asymmetric information then the appropriate response is enhancing information. This takes several forms, the simplest of which is the *warning*, such as the notices printed on cigarette packs and liquor bottles. Actually, most users of these products are aware of the basic health messages, and so the warnings serve more to emphasize a point than to educate. In that sense, these warnings attempt to change behavior, but then so does the provision of any information. Cigarette warning labels were supposed to have changed by September 2012 from the simple "SURGEON GENERAL'S WARNING: Quitting Smoking Now Greatly Reduces Serious Risks to Your Health" and "WARNING: SMOKING IS ADDICTIVE" to nine much more graphic warnings under the Family Smoking Prevention and Tobacco Control Act.[1] Needless to say, this change was controversial. Other warnings include those of side effects on prescription and over-the-counter drugs.

The antismoking graphic images indeed proved to be highly controversial—and illegal, according to an August 2012 ruling by the U.S. Court of Appeals for the District of Columbia Circuit in response to a lawsuit against the Food and Drug Administration by several major tobacco companies.[2] The case was one of First Amendment free speech, but as advertising is commercial speech the standards for limitations are looser than for personal and political speech. The plaintiffs charged that the graphic images were "not warnings, but admonitions," the message "ideological and not informational."[3] Much of the case hinged on determining the applicable standards, with the majority (two judges) opting for the more rigorous standard under which the government must show that its interest in the issue of reducing smoking is "substantial" and "whether the regulation directly advances the governmental interest asserted, and whether it is not more extensive than is necessary to serve the interest."[4]

The government's interest in reducing smoking rates is evident—just consider the ongoing debates over funding Medicare and Medicaid at a time when 400,000 Americans are dying prematurely due to smoking-related illnesses. But that interest does not in itself substantiate the efficacy of the program, according to Judge Brown, writing for the majority. "[The] FDA has not provided a shred of evidence . . . showing that the graphic warnings will 'directly advance' its interest in reducing the number of Americans who smoke." Judge Brown continued by critiquing the evidence presented from other countries, and Canada in particular, using similar graphical warnings. While Canadian smoking rates fell from 24 to 21 percent, the direct effect of the graphics could not be deduced because several other smoking control initiatives, including higher prices, were initiated at the same time.[5] The FDA did undertake an Internet-based 18,000-consumer survey in which the participants after viewing the graphics answered questions regarding the effects of the images on their intentions to quit or refrain from smoking. The study was, however, criticized for measuring only intentions, and not the absolute, long-term effects.[6]

Of course, it is not possible to measure long-term effects unless the program is in effect, at least locally, and then there are likely to be other changes over the long term, making the test impure. That is, the strict standard of proof the court suggested as required is not feasible. Economists do, however, have statistical techniques (econometrics) capable of separating the relative effects of concurrent changes, which could go a long way to meeting the evidence requirement.

Perhaps, though, the legal standard is too high as well, as Judge Rogers wrote in dissent. He states the applicable law is *Zauderer vs. Office of Disciplinary Council*,[7] which follows a more relaxed standard of proof that the disclosure requirements are "reasonably related" to the State's interest.[8] Because another appeals court[9] found differently from the District of Columbia Circuit it was possible for the FDA to appeal the case to the Supreme Court. However, in 2013, the agency decided against that approach and instead will be creating new warning labels.[10]

b. Grade Standards

A second form of information is *grade standards*. On food products these are familiar to shoppers as "Grade A" eggs and milk, or prime and choice beef. The Grade A references typically apply to food safety standards—Grade B milk (about 10 percent of U.S. milk supply), for example, is produced under conditions that make it acceptable only for use in manufacturing products such as certain cheeses, where it undergoes further processing. Indicating prime and choice meat standards, based largely on intramuscular fat content and done on a voluntary basis at the cost of meat-packers, provides consumers with indications of quality. Many other food standards, however, serve the needs of the industry more than consumer needs directly. Prices for fruits, for example, are often quoted on a grade basis, which facilitates arm's-length transfers.

Still other standards define what may be called by specific names. For instance, whole milk must contain a minimum of 3.25 percent milk fat.[11] Commercial mayonnaise must contain (by U.S. law) at least 65 percent oil by weight (except reduced-fat and fat-free mayonnaises). The *standard of identity* law[12] also requires that all commercial "real mayonnaise" use only egg as an emulsifier. Those mayonnaise-like products not meeting these standards are called "dressing." Other composition requirements apply to ice cream (versus ice milk or other dairy or nondairy frozen dessert products). These standards, about

Figure 3.1 **The Department of Agriculture's Food Choice Recommendations Are Presented in the Form of a "Plate" of the Major Food Groups**

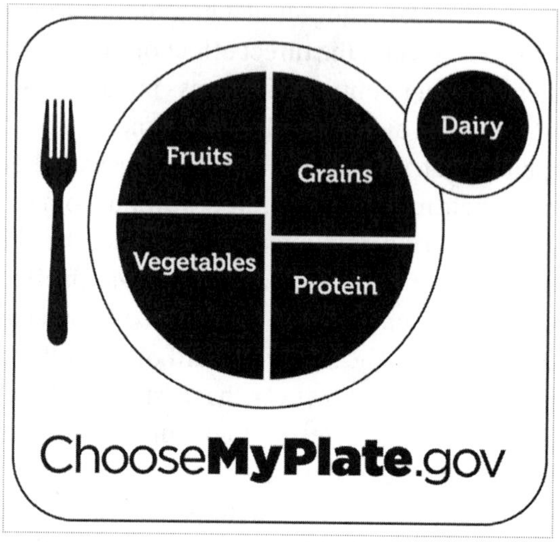

Source: USDA, ChooseMyPlate.gov.

which few consumers are cognizant, nonetheless make the marketplace more efficient by establishing a minimum truth-in-naming for many processed food products.

More familiar to average consumers is the Department of Agriculture's dietary guidelines, presently illustrated as "MyPlate," and showing the recommended daily proportions of the major food groups (Figure 3.1).[13] To comply for processed foods it is then necessary to know the nutritional composition of foods, which is mandated by the Federal Food, Drug, and Cosmetic Act (FD&C) and its amendments.

Nutritional labeling is required by the Nutrition Labeling and Education Act (NLEA) of 1990 for most prepared foods, such as breads, cereals, canned and frozen foods, snacks, desserts, drinks, and so on (Figure 3.2).[14] According to a 2005–2006 survey, a majority of food consumers (52 percent) use food label information sometimes or often/always versus 27 percent who never do. These figures represent a decline from a decade earlier when nearly two thirds of consumers were sometimes or frequent users of label information. Of the data provided, information on fat content is most frequently used, followed closely by calories. The decline in use has been most pronounced for young adults, ages twenty to twenty-nine.[15]

For further information on the use and competitive effects of product ratings, see Chapter 6.

c. Financial Disclosure

A completely different category for mandated information applies to financial disclosure for publicly held firms. As was noted in Chapter 2, Section 2.1, inadequate and misleading

Figure 3.2 **Sample FDA-Mandated Label for Processed Foods**

Nutrition Facts
Serving Size 1 cup (228g)
Servings Per Container about 2

Amount Per Serving	
Calories 250	Calories from Fat 110
	% Daily Value*
Total Fat 12g	**18%**
Saturated Fat 3g	**15%**
Trans Fat 3g	
Cholesterol 30mg	**10%**
Sodium 470mg	**20%**
Total Carbohydrate 31g	**10%**
Dietary Fiber 0g	**0%**
Sugars 5g	
Proteins 5g	
Vitamin A	4%
Vitamin C	2%
Calcium	20%
Iron	4%

* Percent Daily Values are based on a 2,000 calorie diet. Your Daily Values may be higher or lower depending on your calorie needs:

	Calories:	2,000	2,500
Total Fat	Less than	65g	80g
Saturated Fat	Less than	20g	25g
Cholesterol	Less than	300mg	300mg
Sodium	Less than	2,400mg	2,400mg
Total Carbohydrate		300g	375g
Dietary Fiber		25g	30g

For educational purposes only. This label does not meet the labeling requirements described in 21 CFR 101.9.

Source: Wikimedia Commons. Original author Trounce. April 12, 2008.

financial reporting was considered to be a contributor to the stock market crash of 1929. How, after all, can a firm be valued if its finances are essentially unknown? Legislation establishing mandatory financial reporting regulation followed.

That 1930 legislation, though, was found wanting during the Enron, WorldCom, and other accounting scandals of the early 2000s (see Chapter 9), leading to the passage of the Sarbanes-Oxley Act of 2002.[16] The act, which specifies both civil and criminal penalties, has numerous sections, the most relevant to information reporting being 302 and 401.

Section 302 of the act mandates a set of internal procedures designed to ensure accurate financial disclosure. The signing officers must certify that they are "responsible for establishing and maintaining internal controls" and "have designed such internal controls to ensure that material information . . . is made known to such officers by others within those entities, particularly during the period in which the periodic reports are being prepared." The act in Section 401 requires the disclosure of all material off-balance-sheet items, such as were fraudulently used by Enron to overstate profits. The financial crisis of 2008 has led to further corporate disclosure requirements, but at the time of this writing new regulatory procedures are just being introduced (see Chapter 9).

The kinds of information required to offset an informational market failure clearly must be customized for the specific market needs. Many of these informational needs can be met by labels, whether the label functions as a reminder, such as this product is not really good for you (cigarettes); provides complete information, such as describing potential side effects (prescription drugs); or deconstructs the contents (listing food nutrition information). Another category of information provision reveals otherwise unknown factors (financial disclosure for investors). While the role and general form of the informational provisions is evident, the specifics of just what information to provide, when to provide it in the purchase decision, and what form to use is surprisingly complex (see generally Chapter 5).

3.2 PERFORMANCE STANDARDS

Sometimes regulations are keyed to a particular performance (outcome) standard. Well known among these are the corporate vehicle mileage requirements (CAFE). First established in 1975,[17] they have been raised several times with the most current minimum, an average of 35.5 miles per gallon (Figure 3.3), to be implemented beginning in 2012 and culminating in 2016. This change will harmonize national standards at levels proposed in California, which has long had more stringent standards made possible by a series of exemptions over forty years (but not for these most recent standards).[18] Target mileage standards rose from 18 miles per gallon (passenger cars) in 1978, leading in 2002, according to a National Academy of Sciences report, to actual mileage being 14 percent above that projected without the mandate.[19] Post-2016 standards call for increasing fuel economy to the equivalent of 54.5 miles per gallon for cars and light-duty trucks by model year 2025.[20]

Figure 3.3 **CAFE Effects on Vehicle Mileage, 1978–2011**

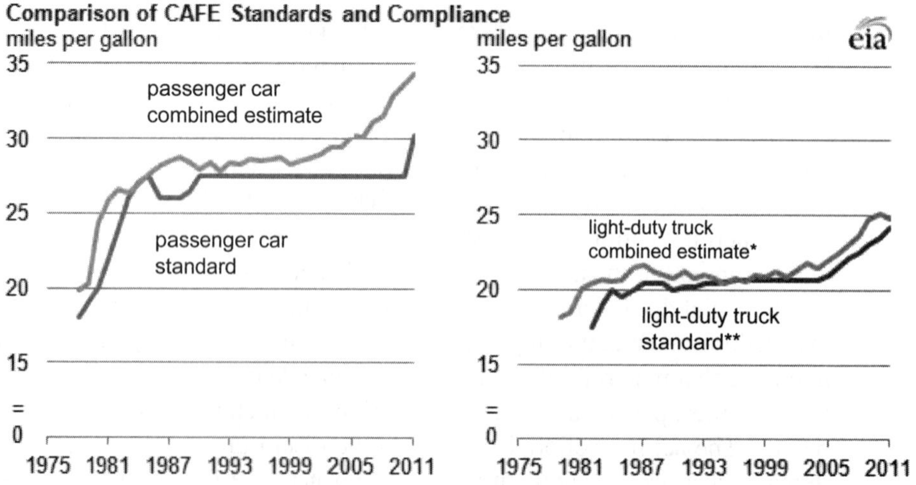

Source: U.S. Energy Information Administration, "Fuel economy standards have affected vehicle efficiency," August 3, 2012. www.eia.gov/todayinenergy/detail.cfm?id=7390.

Note that the standards apply to the corporate average so that firms have the option of manufacturing a range of vehicle size and engine types so long as the average mileage meets the requirement (buyers have to pay a "gas-guzzler tax" for individual vehicles whose mileage falls below a specified minimum). A financial penalty applies for each .1 mile-per-gallon the average falls below the target, times the number of vehicles sold. The National Highway Traffic Safety Administration regulates CAFE standards and the Environmental Protection Agency measures vehicle fuel efficiency.

In another example of regulating performance standards, the major securities and futures exchanges have procedures for coordinated marketwide trading halts if a severe market price decline reaches levels that may exhaust market liquidity. These procedures, known as circuit breakers, may halt trading temporarily or, under extreme circumstances, close the markets before the normal end of the trading session.

The circuit breakers provide for marketwide trading halts during a severe market decline as measured by a single-day decrease in the Dow Jones Industrial Average (DJIA). There are three circuit-breaker thresholds—10 percent, 20 percent, and 30 percent —set by the markets as point levels that are calculated at the beginning of each quarter.[21] Regulations also exist for circuit-breaker trading suspensions in individual equities as well as derivative contracts. Indeed on May 6, 2010, the first detected of the so-called flash crashes occurred, during which the Dow Jones Industrial Average sunk about 900 points—about 9 percent (7 percent in only 15 minutes)—only to recover the losses within minutes. Major individual stocks sunk to pennies while others soared to $100,000 a share. This dramatic market event led to a trial of the effect of imposing circuit breakers.[22]

A major form of performance regulation is that for pharmaceutical products (including medical devices) where, to be given market approvals, the FDA requires new drugs to demonstrate both safety and efficacy.[23] Safety testing is commonplace and the results are easy to understand; this kind of testing also is performed on insecticides and chemical products. Regarding efficacy though, generally in a marketplace like the United States the prevailing approach is more in line with "buyer beware." That concept though is inappropriate when individuals' health and well-being are at risk, if only by taking a less effective medicine, and where individuals and their doctors are hard put to assess the relative merits of one medication over another. Double-blind clinical trials (meaning neither the patients nor the attending clinicians know who is taking the experimental drug or a placebo) required for approval can take years and cost an average of $800 million (in 2000 dollars) per approved drug, including the cost of failures, which approximately doubles the total cost.[24]

Premarket approval, as with medicines, requires judgment that, among other considerations, must balance the potential benefits with the documented side effects. Known side effects (some very serious, if rare) must be included with the product description and compiled in the annual *Physicians' Desk Reference*; disclosures of side effects are familiar to anyone who has seen print or TV ads.[25]

Also to be taken into consideration are the risks versus the benefits of accelerated access, and the sickness of the patients for whom distant, low-probability side effects are

Table 3.1

Comparison of Approval Times for Priority and Standard Review Drugs, 1993–2003

Calendar Year	Priority Number Approved	Priority Median FDA Review Time (months)	Standard Number Approved	Standard Median FDA Review Time (months)
1993	13	13.9	12	27.2
1994	13	15.0	9	22.2
1995	9	6.0	19	15.9
1996	18	7.7	35	14.6
1997	9	6.4	30	14.4
1998	16	6.2	14	12.3
1999	19	6.3	16	14.0
2000	9	6.0	18	15.4
2001	7	6.0	17	15.7
2002	7	13.8	10	12.5
2003	9	6.7	12	13.8

Source: Original source FDA, Fast Track, Accelerated Approval and Priority Review. http://archive.is/9UBmx.

less of a concern than immediate survival. As a consequence, the process is fraught with errors of Type I (erroneously rejecting a safe and effective drug) and Type II (approving one that is not safe and/or effective). In 1987 an accelerated approval process for life-threatening diseases such as AIDS was adopted.[26] The reduction in approval time is shown in Table 3.1.

There are of course potential problems with preapproval systems as actual experiences with patients may differ from those observed in trials, no matter how well conducted. There also have been cases where, contrary to initial research, new studies have indicated that the benefits do not outweigh the risks. An example is Avastin for treating late-stage breast cancer. It costs $8,000 a month and, as an FDA advisory panel concluded, does not provide benefits exceeding its risks.[27] In June 2011, the FDA stopped endorsing it as a breast cancer treatment, although it retains approval for use in treating other cancers.[28] The decision has been controversial, if only because the removal of the recommendation means insurance companies no longer pay for it. Those wishing to continue its use must rely on private funds.

Among the several forms of regulation, performance standards are relatively rare despite having the conceptual advantage of adjusting dynamically as conditions evolve. Some of the reasons for this rarity presumably include the difficulty of implementation/enforcement when requirements do evolve. Monitoring can also be complex and costly, as in the case of pharmaceuticals. Perhaps most complex though are decisions about degree and coverage of regulations—let's consider again the pharmacological industry. Detailed tests are costly and delay access to new treatments; however, they can and have averted domestic tragedies such as the one caused by Thalidomide (see Chapter 6, Section 6.1c). How is the proper balance between cost and benefit, between caution and accelerated access, to be identified?

3.3 MINIMUM/MAXIMUM AND PROCESS STANDARDS

Among the common forms of regulation is the specification of a standard that must be achieved, with penalties for noncompliance. This form of regulation is known as command and control and often involves very particular and exacting standards. Examples of such regulations that do allow flexibility are given in Section 3.4 of this chapter.

a. Product Standards

An example of product standards familiar to most of us is the ubiquitous seat belt. Seat belts are regulated by the Department of Transportation, Federal Motor Carrier Safety Administration as Standard No. 209, "Seat belt assemblies" to include such aspects as web width and breaking strength, complete with descriptions/drawings of approved testing methods.[29] Despite data showing seat belts are the most effective safety devices in vehicles today, estimated to save over 12,000 lives each year,[30] only 87 percent of motor vehicle occupants were buckled in 2013.[31] In 2011 (the last year for which data are available), 44 percent of the occupants killed in fatal crashes were not wearing seat belts.[32]

The overall safety effect of seat belts is, however, not so readily calculated (even for those who use them) for the added safety they promise may cause drivers to take other risks, principal among them driving faster. Driving faster is of course more dangerous, leading to more accidents and more serious accidents, which at least partly offsets the benefits of the belts. There are other auto safety devices that evolved concurrently—air bags, side beams in doors, antilock brakes, and so forth, some driven by regulation and some not—and therefore determining the net effect of a single device is no simple matter (see also Chapter 4, Section 4.2).[33]

A straightforward example of consumption-related quantitative regulations is that for arsenic in drinking water. Arsenic, as any murder mystery fan would know, is an acute poison, but its nonlethal effects can include thickening and discoloration of the skin, stomach pain, nausea, vomiting; diarrhea; numbness in hands and feet; partial paralysis; and blindness. Arsenic has been linked to cancer of the bladder, lungs, skin, kidney, nasal passages, liver, and prostate. The EPA has set the arsenic standard for drinking water at .010 parts per million; water systems must have complied with this standard by January 23, 2006. Arsenic may come from natural or farm and industrial sources.[34]

A somewhat more complex standard, in that it has a three-hour, day, and annual value, is that for sulfur dioxide (SO_2), familiar as a major contributor to acid rain. More formally, sulfur dioxide is one of a group of highly reactive gases known as "oxides of sulfur." The largest sources of SO_2 emissions are from fossil-fuel combustion at power plants (73 percent) and other industrial facilities (20 percent). Smaller sources of SO_2 emissions include industrial processes such as extracting metal from ore, and the burning of high-sulfur-containing fuels by locomotives, large ships, and nonroad equipment.

The EPA first set standards for SO_2 in 1971. It set a 24-hour primary standard at 140 ppb (parts per billion) and an annual average standard at 30 ppb to protect health. The EPA also set a 3-hour average secondary standard at 500 ppb to protect the public welfare.[35]

Sulfur dioxide has both human health and ecological effects. Current scientific evidence links short-term exposures to SO_2 (5 minutes to 24 hours) with an array of adverse respiratory effects including broncho-constriction and increased asthma symptoms. Studies also show a connection between short-term exposure and increased visits to emergency departments and hospital admissions for respiratory illnesses, particularly in at-risk populations, including children, the elderly, and asthmatics.[36]

The ecological effects of acid rain are most clearly seen in aquatic, or water, environments, such as streams, lakes, and marshes. Lakes and streams become acidic (i.e., the pH value, that is the measure of acidity or alkalinity, goes down from the average of 6–8) when the water itself and its surrounding soil cannot buffer the acid rain enough to neutralize it. Many lakes and streams examined in a National Surface Water Survey (NSWS) of over 1,000 lakes larger than 10 acres and in thousands of miles of streams believed to be sensitive to acidification suffer from chronic acidity. Of the lakes and streams surveyed, acid rain caused acidity in 75 percent of the acidic lakes and about 50 percent of the acidic streams.

As acid rain flows through soils in a watershed, aluminum is released from soils into the lakes and streams located in that watershed. So, as pH in a lake or stream decreases, aluminum levels increase. Both low pH and increased aluminum levels are directly toxic to fish and amphibians, but plants and animals have differing tolerance to acidity. At a pH of 5, most fish eggs cannot hatch, although frogs are more acid-tolerant than trout (Figure 3.4), and adult trout are more tolerant than their young. Acid rain also damages buildings and monuments (Figure 4.10).

Figure 3.4 **Tolerance of Aquatic Species to Water Acidity Levels**

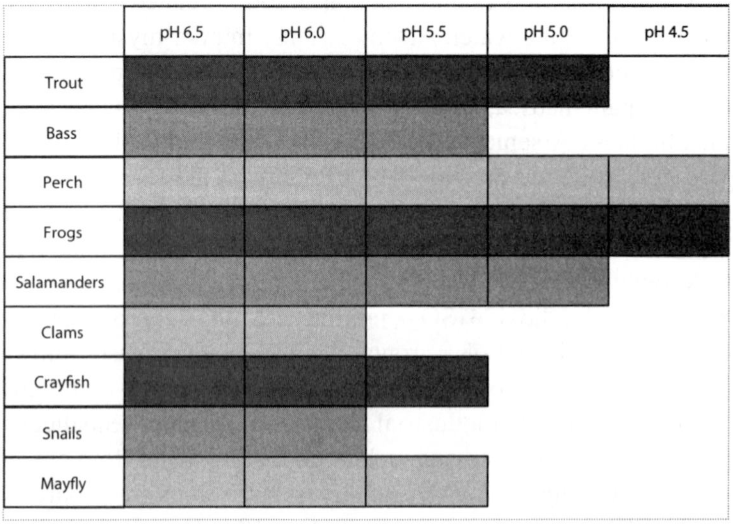

pH 6.5
pH 6.0
pH 5.5
pH 5.0
pH 4.5
Trout
Bass
Perch
Frogs
Salamanders
Clams
Crayfish
Snails
Mayfly

Source: United States Environmental Protection Agency, "EPA Effects of Acid Rain—Surface Waters and Aquatic Animals," December 4, 2012. www.epa.gov/acidrain/effects/surface_water.html.

In the case of sulfur dioxide pollution, a national program is critical because acid rain falls hundreds of miles east of where the source air pollution is emitted (given the prevailing west–east wind direction in North America). For that reason in the United States, a significant amount of the ecological problem has befallen the Adirondack region of New York State.[37]

Indeed the problem was so significant for the Northeast region that the northeastern states joined with the EPA in a four-year lawsuit of FirstEnergy Corp. over four power plants in Ohio, the first of many suits planned. The settlement against FirstEnergy Corp. for violating the Clean Air Act was valued at $1.1 billion in fines and cleanup costs, and would lead to an annual reduction of 212,000 tons of sulfur dioxide and nitrogen oxide, another contributor to acid rain.[38]

b. Process Standards

When it is not possible or reasonable to regulate the outcome, the focus is shifted to the process of how to accomplish the outcome. So while it is conceivable to monitor, or at least sample, the emissions of the approximately 600 coal-fired power plants in the United States,[39] doing so for all 250 million cars[40] is clearly not feasible. Hence the EPA requires firms seeking emission certification to demonstrate that new motor vehicles will comply with EPA emission standards throughout their useful lives (defined as the first 100,000 miles or ten years). The proposed Compliance Assurance Program (CAP) 2000 rules specify the sampling process for selecting vehicles for testing and the test procedures.[41]

Residences are responsible for an estimated 70 percent of electricity consumption in the United States and for 40 percent of the emission of greenhouse gases.[42] Yet once finished and approved for use (typically through the issuance of a Certificate of Occupancy), the government has little control over efficiency during the life of the structure, unless and until there is a major renovation. Hence energy efficiency standards are included in building codes.[43]

The system in the United States, though, is quite a hodgepodge with most (but not all) states having statewide energy efficiency standards to be enforced on the local or county level, with some communities like Austin, Texas, adopting stricter standards. This approach, however, means that seasonal structures—think a summer home or hunting camp—must be built to comply with the same standards as year-round buildings. Alternative approaches include voluntary standards like LEED and EnergyStar. These are described in Chapter 5, Section 5.1e.

c. Inspection

The final type of regulatory approach to be considered in this subsection is that of the use of inspection, whether for an entire population or a sampling. Sampling is a systematic approach to identifying a subset of the whole, the population. Sampling is familiar through opinion surveys and can be highly accurate, sometimes more accurate than a population survey once the inevitable errors which creep in when surveying large numbers is considered.

Regarding the inspection of food products, regulatory policy is somewhat inconsistent. For livestock, all animals must be inspected prior to slaughter for the identification of diseased specimens.[44] However, with food processing, companies in the juice, seafood, meat, and poultry sectors must develop and, when approved, implement a Hazard Analysis and Critical Control Point (HACCP) system. The seven principles of the system include hazard analysis, critical control point (CCP) identification, establishing critical limits, monitoring procedures, corrective actions, verification procedures, and record-keeping and documentation. In short, firms are expected to use science to establish their own monitoring system. Why, though, is this different from preslaughter safety review regulation?

There are of course a number of differences between live animals and flow processes for foodborne pathogens. A major distinction, though, is the recognition that "the use of microbiological testing is seldom an effective means of monitoring CCPs because of the time required to obtain results."[45] That is, if there has been a breakdown in sanitation control, it is essential to identify and remedy it as soon as possible, before contaminated food is produced and possibly distributed. And the best way to accomplish that goal is to know what to look for, and where in the process it is most likely to be detected. Live animals for their part are not part of a flow process and indeed are assembled from multiple sources. Thus there is less of a basis for selecting individual animals to examine; rather, all animals must be.

Of course, no system is perfect, and in the case of the HACCP system there is the recurring problem of salmonella outbreaks. The Centers for Disease Control and Prevention list eight notable outbreaks for 2013, down from twelve in 2012. Those involving poultry were the most significant, responsible for over 700 reported illnesses.[46] In aggregate over time, nearly 48 million U.S. residents (one in six) get some form of foodborne illness annually, leading to 128,000 hospitalizations and 3,000 deaths.[47]

The ongoing health problem with eggs led the FDA to develop a new "Egg Safety Rule" for large operations, effective in 2010. Among the required steps is the microbial testing of at least 1,000 eggs every two weeks.[48]

Then, in January 2011, the Food Safety Modernization Act was signed into law, signaling a shift from inspection and outbreak response to prevention and risk-based management practices. Specifically, the requirement for implementing a HACCP system is extended to virtually all food processors, manufacturers, and packers. It gives the FDA added recall authority when outbreaks occur, as well as enhanced traceability systems for food products so that the source of a problem can be more readily identified.[49]

3.4 RATE-OF-RETURN REGULATION: U.S. ELECTRICAL POWER INDUSTRY

Recall that the public management problem with natural monopolies is that of a trade-off between productive and allocative efficiency (see Chapter 2, Section 2.2c). That is, if a natural monopoly is allowed to operate as a monopoly, then it charges monopoly prices, but if reduced in size so there is competition, then efficiency in production is sacrificed, and prices are higher.

A standard regulatory approach has been to permit natural monopolies, but effectively to regulate prices. In this chapter, the focus is on the U.S. electrical power industry. Certainly other sectors include natural monopolies and are regulated as such (see, for example, Chapter 8 for a treatment of communications), but electrical power is an early and significant subject of natural monopoly regulation.

a. Who Regulates What?

Based on the natural monopoly model concept, it is easy to imagine that the entirety of electricity production and distribution, from generation to use, is regulated as a natural monopoly. And until 1994 you would have been largely correct. At that time and beginning in California the sector was deregulated, also called restructured, to separate generation from distribution.[50]

The deregulation created three stages of the system: generation, transmission (high voltage), and retail distribution (low voltage). The concept was that while transmission and retail distribution were natural monopolies, generation was not. Restructuring then separated out the generation portion that, in theory at least, sells power to a competitive marketplace, while transmission and distribution remained regulated. Separating the generation component meant that in many states utilities were required to sell off their generation plants while retaining distribution networks.

Under the new system, the federal role is limited to interstate commerce (see Section 3.7a), or transmission and overseeing interstate electricity sales, along with most hydroelectric power (which typically is also interstate). There are exceptions—New York, Texas, Alaska, and Hawaii, where interstate connectedness is limited or nonexistent—along with some federal programs like the Tennessee Valley Authority.[51] Here the focus is on the transmission and distribution functions, which are typically managed using rate-of-return regulation.

b. Regulatory Mandates

To explain the processes involved, I use the example of the New York State Public Service Commission (PSC), which has the following mission statement:

> The primary mission of the New York State Department of Public Service is to ensure safe, secure, and reliable access to electric, gas, steam, telecommunications, and water services for New York State's residential and business consumers, at just and reasonable rates.[52]

Many other state power authorities have similar multidimensional responsibilities. Those multiple goals typically include some mandates for encouraging energy efficiency and providing a minimum supply from renewable sources, as well as environmental regulations that recognize that electricity production is a—if not *the*—single most concentrated source of air pollution (see Chapter 6). At the same time, regulators are cognizant of the need for a regulated utility to be prudent in its investments: otherwise the cost of borrowed capital rises and along with it the rates for electricity consumers. Serving all these goals simultaneously while attending to the underlying charge of safe, secure, and reliable power at reasonable rates greatly complicates the regulatory process.

c. The Rate-Setting Process

The rate-setting process is described in brief as follows, again using an example from the New York State Public Service Commission:[53]

Rate-Setting Process: To begin, the utility company submits a filing to demonstrate the need for a rate increase. Items to be included in the rate filing are estimates of expenses, including operating expenses (labor, pension costs, materials, fuel); depreciation costs; taxes; a return on investor-provided capital; and recognition of utility plant additions and capital expenditures.

Rate-Setting Timeline:

- Months 1–4: Analyze the utility rate filing and represent the public interest.
- Months 5–7: The testimony filed by staff and other interested groups are received; rebuttal testimony by utility company is allowed; hearings with cross-examination of all expert witnesses are conducted.
- Months 7–9: Initial and reply briefs are filed with the Administrative Law Judge.
- Months 9–11: Additional briefs are filed with the PSC. Commission deliberations are held in open and public meetings and a written order resolving all outstanding issues and matters necessary to determine the utility company's revenue requirements and the amounts to charge customers.

A 2011 rate decision for Orange and Rockland Utilities, Inc. (O&R) gives an indication of the way the PSC operates:[54]

- Original increase requested, $61.7 million
- Increase granted, $26.6 million (12.1 percent revenues or 4 percent electric bill, which includes charge for power)
- Due to elimination of temporary surcharges, net consumer increase is 6.7 percent
- Major portion of the reduction is linked to the established return on equity of 9.2 percent instead of the requested 11 percent
- Plan continues system reliability and customer performance targets; if not met, up to $3.1 million in revenues could be forgone
- Plan effective for one year

d. Issues and Incentives

This quick overview indicates several aspects of the rate-setting process. Clearly it is a lengthy one; a rate request decided today will at best be in effect for two years, including the review period. This delay requires utilities to plan well in advance. At best, it encourages utilities to be frugal during the set rate period; at worst, it encourages padding requests. Additionally—and this is based on personal observations and not documented evidence—typically the approved rates are lower than the request by some amount. Whether that difference reflects protection of consumers by the PSC or requests to the PSC being initially overstated is unclear. Penalties and incentives reflect another problem with regulating utilities: the need to encourage good service, since fixed-price monopolists have little incentive to maintain quality.

Most significant here is the reduction in the allowed return on invested capital, known as the rate base. Essentially rate regulation operates by allowing a return on invested capital above its cost. Variable costs—labor, other inputs—are typically allowed at cost. Setting the appropriate return is clearly a complex and critical decision. Set too low and the system is starved of capital; set too high and consumers are overcharged, as well as providing an incentive for firms to overinvest in capital equipment—the Averch-Johnson Effect.

In practice, the regulators must use a weighted return to invested capital. Imagine that a utility has three sources/types of capital: investor capital, long-term loans for facility construction, and short-term loans for working capital, for example, for meeting a twice-monthly payroll when customers pay monthly. Now imagine investors are satisfied with a 5 percent return, long-term loans are at 4 percent (because they use the facility as collateral and so have lower risk of default), while the working capital is valued at 5.5 percent—short term but unsecured. The following table shows the percentages of capital.

Source of Capital	Percent Capital	Rate %	Weighted Cost Capital
Investor Capital	40	5	2
LT Loans	50	4	2
ST Loans	10	5.5	0.55
Average Cost Capital			4.55%

Regulators must determine the appropriate cost for each of these sources of capital. The "appropriate" one may be above or below the actual, depending on whether the regulators believe management is accepting higher rates than required or, alternatively, not paying enough to assure access to needed future capital needs. They must also determine the appropriate depreciation rate for the equipment and buildings—which may be different from the allowed income tax rate—which is often set for achieving policy objectives such as accelerated depreciation as an inducement for business to increase investment. The process is quite detailed overall and utilizes a number of rates for which there is a discretionary range.

In the example above, the rate request period coincided with the beginning of the Great Recession, during which interest rates fell notably and general corporate profitability fell as well (for a time anyway). In addition to the reduction in the return, the PSC also reduced the requested amount for operation and maintenance expenses.[55]

Another complexity associated with rate regulation is the encouragement of technical change. If firms are rewarded on a return on invested capital basis with a direct pass-through of variable costs, then there is little incentive to improve long-term efficiency (that is, beyond the single year when rates are fixed). The PSC deals with that important inconsistency with its mission in several ways. It has a program to award grants for technical improvements. Other incentives are negative: as part of the rate decision, O&R is required to make an additional $478,000 in savings to meet its established goal of $875,000 in austerity savings[56] under the PSC Great Recession requirement.[57]

Other approaches to encouraging technical advances under regulation include setting performance standards, price caps, and yardstick regulation. Each has its own attributes and limitations, but describing them exceeds the appropriate level of detail for our purposes. What has been presented should be sufficient to indicate the complexities involved, and that is just for a single product! With multiple products—selling electricity to commercial customers is essentially a separate product from residential consumers—the complexities magnify. And this treatment applies only to electricity.

Over time, domestic oil and natural gas prices and pipeline pricing have been regulated, as are radio and television, and also quasi-natural monopolies. Cable, too, was once regulated (see Chapter 8), and there are presently discussions of the need to regulate Internet access. Natural monopolies are perhaps more ubiquitous than they might initially appear to be, yet no one has as yet devised a more efficient regulatory means than that described above.

3.5 ANTITRUST

The very lifeblood of capitalism, a market economy, is competition. Competition is why new products and methods are introduced, why firms invest in R&D, why efficient firms enter a market, and why inefficient ones go out of business. Without competition, market systems stagnate, and therefore society has a huge stake in a competitive economy.

At the same time, firms prefer monopoly with its stable high profits. In the words of the eminent economist J. R. Hicks, "The best of all monopoly profits is a quiet life," free from the stresses and complexities of competition. If not for the benefits of monopoly, why would firms attempt to fix prices, buy out competitors, or lobby Congress for ways of making it more difficult for new firms to enter a sector, among other self-beneficial acts?

Clearly there is a tension here between business pushing its own benefits versus the public good, a situation not conceptually different from conditions underlying other regulations. What is distinct are the stakes involved. An auto-safety recall may affect the health of hundreds of individuals, but the competitiveness of an economy affects almost everyone in terms of the prices they pay and the available job opportunities. Into this complex terrain steps a system of law known as antitrust, the legal base for regulating a competitive business environment.

One of the early scholars of this branch of economics, Joe Bain, identified in the simplest terms a system where the structure of a sector (the number and size distribution of firms) affects how the firms act (behavior, such as ad expenditures or the degree of deference to other sector firms), which leads to the outcome or performance. Performance is defined in terms of innovativeness, price levels, growth, and so forth. Further, Professor Bain recognized that the entry point for public policy is through behavior. If firms want to lessen competition by purchasing a competitor, don't let them. And in the case of the proposed merger of Staples and Office Max, the merger was indeed denied. More simply, if firms fix prices, they should not be permitted to do so.

Needless to say, antitrust economics and policy is not a simple topic. But its functionality is central to any regulatory system. Here I provide an introduction to the subject through an overview of the major legislation, as amended. Chapter 8, Section 8.6, contains a case applying a part of those regulations to the communication industry. For those interested in studying this issue in more depth, an excellent overview is available in Dennis W. Carlton and Jeffrey M. Perloff's *Modern Industrial Organization*.[58]

When introducing a topic, newspapers often exemplify an issue by citing a human-interest story. To illustrate our topic, we can begin by referring to the Rockefellers, and the clan founder John D. Rockefeller (1839–1937) in particular.[59] The Rockefeller name lives on as the personification of wealth long after other dynasties have outstripped the family. For example, we do not say to a big spender "Who do you think you are, Bill Gates?" even though David Rockefeller is ranked 159th in wealth by *Forbes* while Bill Gates is first.

In his day John D. Rockefeller, who established the Standard Oil Company, the first U.S. trust, was indeed fabulously wealthy. He established Standard Oil in 1870 and by 1882 had a near monopoly over oil refining and distribution in the United States. The company grew largely by acquisition, but it was the highly aggressive way the purchases were handled that led Rockefeller afoul of the law. Standard Oil became a major customer of the railroads—oil at the time was shipped primarily by rail—which facilitated negotiating lower rates. Standard Oil could then charge lower prices in competitive markets because of its lower costs, or if necessary it could cross-subsidize from other markets, until the competitor went bust. At that point the formed competitor would become a cheap acquisition. As a further step to reduce potential competition, Standard Oil owned the components needed to make the barrels that the oil was shipped in, preventing competitors from shipping to markets. Reputedly Standard Oil would then focus on other markets, continuing this process, and ultimately raise prices in markets where competition had just been diminished.

Whether Standard Oil actually behaved in that way is in some doubt, but the anecdotal account serves two roles. It describes what came to be regarded as unfair business behavior, because a company could grow larger at the expense of others simply because of the benefits of size and not its business acumen. It is also just the kind of account that incensed public opinion and led to the first, and in some ways the greatest, of the antitrust laws, the Sherman Act of 1890.

If the Standard Oil account is potentially factitious, or even partially so, there are many documented examples of how monopolies have exploited many groups. One such group was farmers who, because of their small individual scale and lack of group organization, were easily exploited by, among other sectors, the railroads. "The railroads charged more for a short haul under monopoly conditions than a long haul under stiff competition. The railroads also gave rebates to certain favored shippers. These abuses were heavy on the farmer because he had no other reasonable way to carry his products to market . . ." In response the farmers organized the Patrons of Husbandry, later renamed the Grange, for social, economic, and political improvement.[60] The Grange proved to be highly effective in supporting the Sherman Act. "The Sherman Act would not have been passed if it had not been for the pressure of the Grange against the growing monopoly power in the United States. Big business wanted high tariffs. Agriculture adopted the slogan that tariffs were the mother of monopoly."[61]

Attentive readers will recognize that the antitrust laws come close to establishing an "industrial policy," the concept of which is so reviled in the United States. It does this by operating on the principal that competition is the foundation for an efficient capitalist system. Therefore when a market operates in a noncompetitive manner it is necessary to restore competition, whether by stopping anticompetitive behaviors such as price fixing or, in extreme cases, by breaking a monopoly into several components. As always, the devil is in the details, and there are lots of nuances to consider under antitrust law.

a. Antitrust Legislation: The Sherman Act of 1890[62]

A trust is defined as a combination of firms or corporations formed by a legal agreement, *especially* one that reduces or threatens to reduce competition. Standard Oil was a trust, as Rockefeller put it under the control of nine directors, with himself as the head. In 1892 the Ohio Supreme Court held that the Standard Oil Trust was a monopoly in violation of an Ohio law prohibiting monopolies. Rockefeller evaded the decision by dissolving the trust and transferring its properties to companies in other states, with interlocking directorates so that the same nine men controlled the operations of the affiliated companies. In 1899 these companies were brought back together in a holding company, Standard Oil Company (New Jersey), which existed until 1911.[63]

At that point, Standard Oil was found in violation of the Sherman Act and split into thirty-four unrelated companies, including Jersey Standard, Socony, and Vacuum Oil. In 1926, combining the "s"s and "o" from Jersey Standard, a new trade name of Esso was launched. Then in 1972 the name was officially changed to Exxon (Figure 3.5). The 1999 merger of Exxon with Mobil Oil completes the link from the 1911 antitrust decision to the present.

Sherman Antitrust Act of 1890

The Sherman Antitrust Act, for all its regulatory might, is very broadly stated in two dominant sections (abbreviated to remove mention of the level of penalties allowed):

> Section 1—Trusts, etc., in restraint of trade illegal; penalty: Every contract, combination in the form of trust or otherwise, or conspiracy, in restraint of trade or commerce among the several States, or with foreign nations, is declared to be illegal. Every person who shall make any contract or engage in any combination or conspiracy hereby declared to be illegal shall be deemed guilty of a felony. . . .

Figure 3.5 **Exxon, Now ExxonMobil, Is the Direct Descendent of the Original Standard Oil Company**

Source: W. Lesser.

Section 1 of the Sherman Antitrust Act is a bar on price fixing, the agreement among independent enterprises to charge set prices. Prior legal defenses against set prices focused on the "reasonableness" of the prices—that is, no harm was done to consumers. The legal decision, however, was that the infraction itself was the violation, not any particular set of prices. That is, price fixing is *per se* illegal—if there is evidence of a conspiracy to set prices, an active meeting of the minds, then Section 1 has been violated.

The lead case is *U.S. vs. Trenton Potteries Co.* (SC 1927). The Sanitary Potters Association fixed prices for 80 percent of pottery products for bathrooms and lavatories, arguing that the prices were reasonable and so did not harm the public. Justice (later Chief Justice) Stone wrote memorably, "[I]t does not follow that agreements to fix or maintain prices are reasonable restraints and therefore permitted by the state, merely because the prices themselves are reasonable. . . ." Indeed, it is possible for firms to conspire to fix prices even if they prove unsuccessful in actually influencing those prices.

However, there must be evidence of the conspiracy—merely demonstrating that prices are similar is insufficient. Perfectly competitive prices, for example, should be identical for identical goods. As the *Trenton Potteries* case suggests, trade associations were frequently involved with Sherman Section 1 cases. Trade associations frequently publish valuable sales and price data, and so it is easy to step over the legal line in an attempt to control those prices. Typically today at trade association meetings there will be a disclaimer announcement that none of the proceedings are intended to restrain trade, or words to that effect.

Sometimes the conspirators are clever at hiding their activities. A classic case was revealed in 1961 when GE and several other large electrical suppliers were convicted for price fixing in bids for generators and transformers and the like. The group met secretly to agree on prices and market shares, but to hide the plan they established a system under which the phase of the moon identified the successful bidder; for example, full moon for GE, first quarter for Westinghouse, and so forth. The scheme unraveled when a buyer noticed that the losing bids, submitted in secrecy, were all identical. Often, though, it requires inside information of the fix for a conviction.

Conversely, price leadership under which one firm raises prices in the expectation competitors will independently choose to follow suit is normally legal. Price leadership was common in the airline and other industries for many years. That being said, some sectors are exempt. Farmers, for example, are exempt for the purpose of running cooperatives, where the intent is to market jointly.

> Section 2—Monopolizing trade a felony; penalty: Every person who shall monopolize, or attempt to monopolize, or combine or conspire with any other person or persons, to monopolize any part of the trade or commerce among the several States, or with foreign nations, shall be deemed guilty of a felony. . . .

Section 2, under which Standard Oil along with several railroads, American Tobacco (the tobacco trust), and the DuPont explosives business were convicted, is more complex. Note particularly that the act outlaws "monopolization," not the mere presence of monopoly. Monopolization refers to the conscious drive for monopoly power, and not the monopoly market share that occurs from supplying, for example, clearly superior products. Stated differently, Sherman Section 2 does not prohibit mere size nor the existence of market power if unexploited. What is illegal is the utilization of market power to extend or enhance a monopoly.

Far more recently than the Standard Oil case, the government charged Microsoft with an attempt at monopolization of, among other charges, the market for Internet browsers because such browsers would create competition for operating systems. One of the alleged methods for monopolizing the browser market was Microsoft's bundling its browser (Internet Explorer) free with Windows, making it more difficult for competitors to sell their browsers. That case spread over four years, from 1998 to 2002, with a lower court initially ordering the breakup of Microsoft; however, on appeal, the Department of Justice (which administers the Sherman Act) eventually essentially dropped the case in 2002.[64]

The duration of that case suggests the complexity of Sherman Section 2 cases. They are adjudicated on the basis of the so-called *rule of reason*, which in the simplest terms means each case is decided on its own factual evidence, the circumstances of the case. For example, while Microsoft in the 1990s was potentially liable for bundling its Internet Explorer, Apple, which at the time had something like a 10 percent market share, would be unlikely to be similarly charged. Apple simply lacked the market power to monopolize Internet access whatever its preferences might have been.

And if the cases are difficult, remedies are as well. For very entrenched monopolies—such as the trusts of the early 1900s—the only cure was breaking them up. But that is a disruptive and in some cases not very effective remedy. Sometimes the government will seek a consent decree, the antitrust version of a plea bargain where there will be a "voluntary" agreement to divest or to end certain practices. Section 2 has its exemptions as well. Often regulated sectors will be exempt, and since 1911 Major League Baseball

(MLB) has had an exemption based on the court's treatment of it as a game, and not a business.[65] In another example, the government-directed breakup of AT&T in 1984 went through a different legal process due to the regulated nature of the Bell telephone system (see Example 8.1). Patented products also receive specific antitrust exemptions, but not a carte blanche.

Even with this limited introduction, it should be clear that this section of the Sherman Act, while very powerful, is hampered by the complexity of the monopolization cases, as well as the need to wait until significant market power has accrued, at which point damage to competition has already occurred. Would not it be preferable to target certain actions in their incipiency to prevent the development of market power—simply defined as the power to set prices—rather than addressing market power once it exists? That is the basic justification for the Clayton Act of 1914.

b. Clayton Act of 1914[66]

The Clayton Act prohibited exclusive sales contracts, local price cutting to freeze out competitors, rebates, interlocking directorates in corporations capitalized at $1 million or more in the same field of business, and intercorporate stock holdings.

Specifically, the Clayton Act consists of eight sections of relevance here as they directly or indirectly affect business activities. Due to the ambiguous nature of many of the sections—such that underlying activities may under different circumstances help or hinder competition—Clayton cases generally illustrate rule of reason decisions.

Section 2—Price Discrimination:

> It shall be unlawful . . . to discriminate in price between different purchasers of commodities . . . where the effect of such discrimination may be to substantially lessen competition or tend to create a monopoly. . . . Provided . . . nothing herein contained shall prevent differentials that make only due allowance for differences in the cost of manufacture, sale, or delivery resulting from the differing methods or quantities in which such commodities are to such purchasers sold or delivered. . . . That nothing herein contained shall prevent persons engaged in selling goods, wares, or merchandise in commerce from selecting their own customers in bona fide transactions and not in restraint of trade. . . .

The clause regarding due allowance for differences in cost or quality rendered Section 2 essentially unenforceable, so that in 1936 the Robinson-Patman Act was passed essentially as an amendment. That Act reads:

> It shall be unlawful . . . either directly or indirectly, to discriminate in price between different purchasers of commodities of like grade and quality . . . where the effect of such discrimination may be substantially to lessen competition or tend to create a monopoly in any line of commerce, or to injure, destroy, or prevent competition. . . . Provided, That nothing herein contained shall prevent differentials which make only due allowance for differences in the cost of manufacture, sale, or delivery resulting from the differing methods or quantities in which such commodities are to such purchasers sold or delivered: . . . Provided, however,

> That nothing herein contained shall prevent a seller rebutting the prima-facie case thus made by showing that his lower price . . . was made in good faith to meet an equally low price of a competitor, or the services or facilities furnished by a competitor. . . . It shall be unlawful . . . knowingly to induce or receive a discrimination in price which is prohibited by this section.

While far more specific and detailed than Section 2 of the Clayton Act, the Robinson-Patman Act nonetheless contains a number of legal defenses which made it equally difficult to enforce. These include "due allowance for differences in the cost of manufacture, sale, or delivery resulting from the differing methods or quantities in which such commodities are to such purchasers sold or delivered; showing that his lower price . . . was made in good faith to meet an equally low price of a competitor; knowingly to induce or receive a discrimination in price."

In practice, rebutting the "good faith" defense or showing an illegal discount was offered or received "knowingly" proved difficult to substantiate in court. At the same time, there were real concerns that strict adherence would lead to fewer legitimate discounts being offered, resulting in higher and not lower prices. In any event, in *Brooke Group Ltd. vs. Brown & Williamson Tobacco Co.* (1993), the Supreme Court developed strict standards for proving that price discrimination did in fact "substantially lessen competition." Those standards have effectively rendered moot further price discrimination cases.

Section 3—Tying and Exclusive Dealing:

> It shall be unlawful . . . to make a sale . . . of goods . . . on the condition . . . that the . . . purchaser . . . shall not use or deal in the goods . . . of a competitor . . . where the effect . . . may be to substantially lessen competition or tend to create a monopoly. . . .

Section 3 makes illegal so-called tying arrangements (sometimes known as full line forcing) under which sellers use a scarce or sought after product as leverage for requiring purchases of related products. In one major case, the American Can Company rented and would not sell the preferred equipment for sealing cans, and rented on condition that the renter bought all the metal for fabricating the cans ("tin plate") from American Can. That is, strength in one market is utilized to enhance market power in other product markets. Microsoft's bundling of its Internet Explorer with its operating system is a form of tying. However, tying can be beneficial if the required ancillary product purchases allow the underlying product to function better. In 1984 in *Jefferson Parish Hospital vs. Hyde,* the Supreme Court made tying a more difficult case to prove.

Exclusive dealing/supply (also known as requirements contracts) applies when a firm insists that retailers handle its brand exclusively, as would apply if, for example, Samsung required retailers like Best Buy to sell only its brand of televisions. The antitrust concept is that exclusive dealing requirements can be exploited by major firms to restrict market access by smaller rivals. However, the courts have recognized exclusive dealing may be beneficial if it prevents consumers from being defrauded. The courts have also been more tolerant of small market share firms requiring exclusive dealing arrangements based on a concern that they will not be well represented when mixed with larger rivals.

Section 4—Private Lawsuits:

> Any person who shall be injured in his business or property by reason of anything forbidden in the antitrust laws may sue therefore in any district court of the United States . . . and shall recover threefold the damages by him sustained, and the cost of suit, including a reasonable attorney's fee.

This provision creates a major inducement for private suits because it means that a private plaintiff can obtain a damage award three times as large as the actual loss. Further, if the plaintiff wins, the defendant will have to pay the plaintiff's attorneys' fees. Largely as a consequence, 90 percent of antitrust lawsuits (including Sherman cases) are brought by private parties such as consumers or business firms.

(Section 5 is intended to reduce the difficulty and expense of proving a violation and calculating the resultant damages and so is not of direct relevance here).

Section 6—Labor Exemption: The labor of a human being is not a commodity or article of commerce.

This section put an end to the use of the antitrust laws against labor unions under previous interpretations that did not distinguish between the price of goods and the price of labor.

Section 7—Mergers:

> No person engaged in commerce . . . shall acquire . . . the whole or any part of the stock or other share capital . . . another person engaged also in commerce . . . where in any line of commerce or in . . . any section of the country, the effect of such acquisition may be substantially to lessen competition, or to tend to create a monopoly.
>
> No person shall acquire, directly or indirectly, the whole or any part of the stock or other share capital . . . where in any line of commerce . . . the effect of such acquisition, of such stocks or assets, or of the use of such stock by the voting or granting of proxies or otherwise, may be substantially to lessen competition, or to tend to create a monopoly.

This is the most significant of the sections of the Clayton Act, and the one of particular relevance to the case in Chapter 8. However, while the Clayton Act prohibited stock purchase mergers that resulted in reduced competition, it was possible to bypass those provisions by simply buying up a competitor's assets. The Celler-Kefauver Act (1950) prohibited that practice by applying to assets as well as stock acquisitions. The Act also gave the government the ability to prevent vertical mergers and conglomerate mergers that could limit competition. The second clause of this section effectively prohibits the formation of trusts, if their effect is substantially to lessen competition. Applications of Section 7 to mergers is developed below and further in Chapter 8, Section 8.6c.

Section 8—Interlocking Directorships: prohibits one person serving as director of two or more corporations if the certain threshold values are met, pursuant to the Hart–Scott–Rodino Antitrust Improvements Act of 1976.

c. Federal Trade Commission Act of 1914

Before completing this quick overview of federal antitrust law it is necessary to make some notice of the Federal Trade Commission (FTC). The commission was established by the 1914 Federal Trade Commission Act, which also defines a number of its functions. Recall, for example, that the FTC is responsible for verifying advertising claims.

In the antitrust context, though, it is Section 5 (amended by the Wheeler-Lea Act of 1938) which is relevant. It reads simply, "Unfair methods of competition in commerce and unfair or deceptive acts or practices in commerce are hereby declared illegal." The courts have interpreted "unfair methods of competition" to cover acts that would also violate the Sherman Act. Therefore, while the Federal Trade Commission Act contributed a second public administrative body, it adds no significant new antitrust authority. In addition, the Clayton Act gives the FTC certain legal and administrative roles.

d. Managing Mergers under Section 7 of the Clayton Act, as Amended

Concept of Restricting Mergers

For explaining the concept behind Section 7, an example would perhaps be helpful. A good one is *Federal Trade Commission vs. Heinz, Inc.* (2001), which prohibited a merger between two manufacturers of baby food. Gerber, Heinz, and Beech-Nut were the three major producers of baby food in the United States. Then Heinz offered to purchase Beech-Nut. Under the law, large mergers have to be reported to the Department of Justice or the Federal Trade Commission (see below). In this instance the FTC challenged the merger.

The court accepted the FTC's analysis that with three firms in the market there was a significant amount of competition in the baby food market, and this tended to keep prices low. If the merger were permitted, the market would have only two major firms, and these would not compete as fiercely as firms in a three-firm market. As a result of the court's decision, Heinz abandoned the merger plans, and the market continued to have three major baby food producers.[67]

Amendments to Section 7: The Premerger Notification Program

From the preceding example it is immediately evident that to function as it does the responsible antitrust authorities must have prior notification of proposed significant (to be defined below) mergers. Otherwise, the government could act only after the fact of a completed merger, limiting responses to more complex and costly remedies.

It is the Hart–Scott–Rodino Antitrust Improvements Act of 1976 (HSR) that establishes the federal premerger notification program to provide the FTC and the Department of Justice (DOJ) with information about large mergers and acquisitions *before* they occur. The parties to certain proposed transactions must submit premerger notification to the FTC and DOJ.

Premerger notification involves completing an HSR Form, also called a "Notification and Report Form for Certain Mergers and Acquisitions," with information about each party's business.[68] The parties may not close their deal until the waiting period outlined in the HSR Act (typically thirty days, but extendable under certain circumstances) has passed, or the government has granted early termination of the waiting period. The premerger notification program is administered by the FTC.[69]

Notification Requirements and Resolutions[70]

The rules generally require both the acquiring and acquired persons (persons in a legal sense of corporations, not individuals) to report if all the following conditions are met:

1. Postmerger, the acquirer will hold assets of the acquired in excess of $200 million (adjusted for size of the GDP), regardless of the sales or assets of the acquiring acquired persons, or
2. Postmerger, the acquirer will hold assets of the acquired between $50 and $200 million (adjusted), and
3. One party has sales or assets of at least $100 million (adjusted), and
4. The other party has sales or assets of at least $10 million (adjusted)

In addition to providing balance sheet data, the reporting entities must disclose whether they derive revenue from businesses that fall within the same industry and product category of the North American Industry Classification System (NAICS), and if so in which geographic areas they operate. A second, more detailed information request may follow if considered necessary by the reviewing agency (either DOJ or FTC). This information will assist the antitrust agencies in determining if the parties engage in similar lines of business so that a merger could possibly reduce competition in the business (as with the baby food example above). Typically, if the acquired firm is failing, the review conditions are less stringent. After all, a bankrupt firm will be a less effective competitor, to say the least.

There are three possible outcomes from the prenotification process:

1. No action—the merger may proceed as proposed
2. Conditional, negotiated approval
3. Recommend injunction actions to halt the merger

Of these, only the conditional approval is not self-explanatory. The no-action option, according to the FTC, applies to 95 percent of premerger notifications. What is sought in the conditional approval case is some mitigating actions that would make the merger, in the assessment of the evaluating agency, less damaging to competition. Often those steps will involve a sale or other distancing from some of the components of the postmerger firm. We will see one example of such an arrangement in Comcast's pre–NBC Universal merger agreement not to manage Hulu (Chapter 8, Section 8.6).

As a second example we can consider a supermarket merger in upstate New York between Tops Markets and P&C Foods (Penn Traffic). The FTC approved the merger provided Tops sold seven stores acquired in the portfolio of seventy-nine across the upstate region.[71] Three of those stores were in Ithaca, where Tops with two pre-existing stores was first or second in market share, and a takeover of the P&C stores would have moved it decidedly into top place in a more concentrated market.

Understanding how these kinds of decisions are made brings us to the Merger Guidelines, which are explored below. Understanding those guidelines, however, necessitates some background in the terminology and measurements used.

Horizontal, Vertical, and Potential Competitor Mergers[72]

Making the understanding of mergers more complex is the fact that there are actually three categories of mergers, although an individual merger could combine more than one of them:

1. Horizontal mergers, which involve two competitors
2. Vertical mergers, which involve firms in a buyer-seller relationship
3. Potential competition mergers, in which the buyer absent the merger is likely to enter the market and become a potential competitor of the seller

In this subsection, attention is focused on the first two types of mergers.

As regards the competitive effects of *horizontal mergers,* there are two ways that a merger between competitors can lessen competition and harm consumers: (1) by creating or enhancing the ability of the remaining firms to act in a coordinated way on some competitive dimension (coordinated interaction), or (2) by permitting the merged firm to raise prices profitably on its own (unilateral effect). The idea of coordinated interaction is that fewer larger firms are more conscious of the effects on each other of a price change by one of them, while finding it easier to coordinate their pricing actions without the need for direct (and illegal) agreements.

Vertical mergers for their part involve firms in a buyer-seller relationship—for example, a manufacturer merging with a supplier of an input product, or a manufacturer merging with a distributor of its finished products. Vertical mergers can generate significant cost savings and improve coordination of manufacturing or distribution. Indeed, early on, car manufacturing was split between those who built the engine and chassis, and the constructors of bodies. Bringing these activities together on the Model T assembly line as Ford did (luxury cars held onto custom bodies far longer) made for great efficiencies. Anyone who noticed the "Body by Fisher" seal on the door sills of pre-1984 General

Figure 3.6 **The Fisher Body/GM Merger in 1919 Is an Example of an Efficiency-Enhancing Vertical Merger**

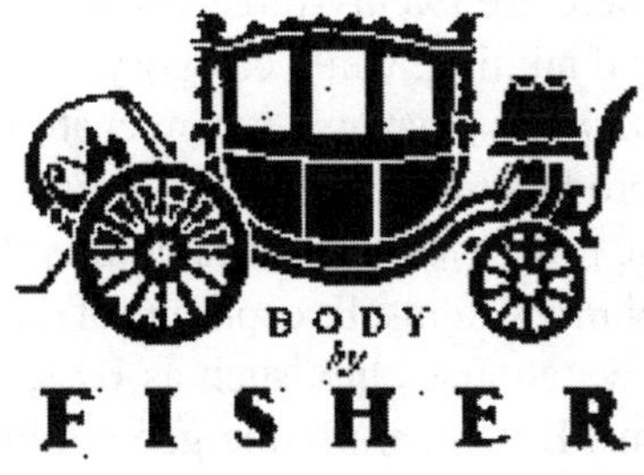

Source: United States Patent and Trademark Office. http://tmsearch.uspto.gov/.

Motors (GM) cars (the separate division was eliminated that year) will be interested to know that Fisher Bros. (there were six brothers) provided bodies for several companies before being purchased by GM in 1919. It remained a separate GM division until 1984, explaining the door sill seal (Figure 3.6).[73]

But some vertical mergers present competition problems. For instance, a vertical merger can make it difficult for competitors to gain access to an important component product (think of a steel mill acquiring iron ore) or to an important channel of distribution. This problem occurs when the merged firm gains the ability and incentive to limit its rivals' access to key inputs or outlets.

e. Defining Horizontal and Vertical Markets[74]

For *horizontal markets,* it is one thing to refer to a "competitor" and another formally to define what a competitor is. The law bars mergers that have potential harmful effects in a "line of commerce" in a "section of the country." In practical terms, this means the FTC will examine the businesses of the merging parties both in terms of *what* they sell (a product dimension) and *where* they sell it (a geographic dimension).

In the most general terms, a product market in an antitrust investigation consists of all goods or services that buyers view as close substitutes. That means if the price of one product goes up, and in response consumers switch to buying a different product so that the price increase is not profitable, those two products are in the same product market because consumers will substitute those products based on changes in relative prices (i.e., the cross elasticity of demand). When it is not possible to examine directly consumers' price responses, investigators will often look at firms in the same product market as identified under the North American Industry Classification System (NAICS) starting in 1997 (previously known as the Standard Industrial Classification system or SIC).

The NAICS[75] works on a two- to seven-digit system, where the increasing number of digits identifies narrower and narrower product categories (industries). For example, category 31 is all manufacturing while category 311 is food manufacturing and category 3111 is animal-food manufacturing. Finally, category 311111 identifies dog- and cat-food manufacturing. There are twenty-three two-digit industries: category 11 is agriculture, forestry, fishing and hunting, while category 61 is educational services.

A *geographic market* is that area where customers would likely turn to buy the goods or services in the product market. With supermarkets, for example, the geographic market is largely local due to the obvious time and travel costs of frequent trips, not to mention the perishability of many items. Exceptions, of course, occur as some shoppers will travel to a more distant warehouse club, such as BJ's, Sam's Club, or Costco, to stock up on a selection of items. But generally the geographic market is contained so that the FTC will use the Metropolitan Statistical Areas (MSA) as the geographic market for all but the largest cities (Figure 3.7).

Measuring the Degree of Concentration of Markets[76]

To this point in the discussion of markets and competition we have noted the definition of those markets, yet lack a direct means of quantifying and describing them. In the antitrust area that is done using the Herfindahl-Hirschman Index (HHI). It is calculated by squaring the market share of each firm competing in the market and then summing the resulting numbers. For example, for a market consisting of four firms with shares of 30, 30, 20, and 20 percent, the HHI is 2600 ($30^2 + 30^2 + 20^2 + 20^2 = 2{,}600$).

Previously, the Concentration Ratio was used, which is simply the combined share of the largest four (CR_4) (the government will not release figures on fewer than four combined firms as it is possible for one of them to estimate the share of the other[s]), eight (CR_8), and so forth. The HHI, however, takes into account the relative size and distribution of the firms in a market and approaches zero when a market consists of a large number of firms of similar size.

For a monopoly (single firm) the HHI is 10,000. The HHI increases both as the number of firms in the market decreases and as the disparity in size between those firms increases. Markets in which the HHI is between 1,000 and 1,800 points are considered to be moderately concentrated, and those in which the HHI is in excess of 1,800 points are considered to be concentrated.

Decision Process under the Merger Notification Program[77]

While the analysis is applicable to both horizontal and vertical mergers, guidelines for filing the premerger notification are provided only for horizontal mergers. As an assist to businesses, there is an attempt to indicate which proposed mergers are likely to be questioned as potentially harmful, as distinct from those that are beneficial or neutral. The guidelines describe the principal analytical techniques used and the main types of evidence used.

As a hypothetical test, the agencies attempt to determine if a completed merger would lead to a small but significant and nontransitory price increase, including at least one

Figure 3.7 **The North American Industry Classification System Is Sometimes Used to Outline Geographical Markets, Such as for Supermarkets**

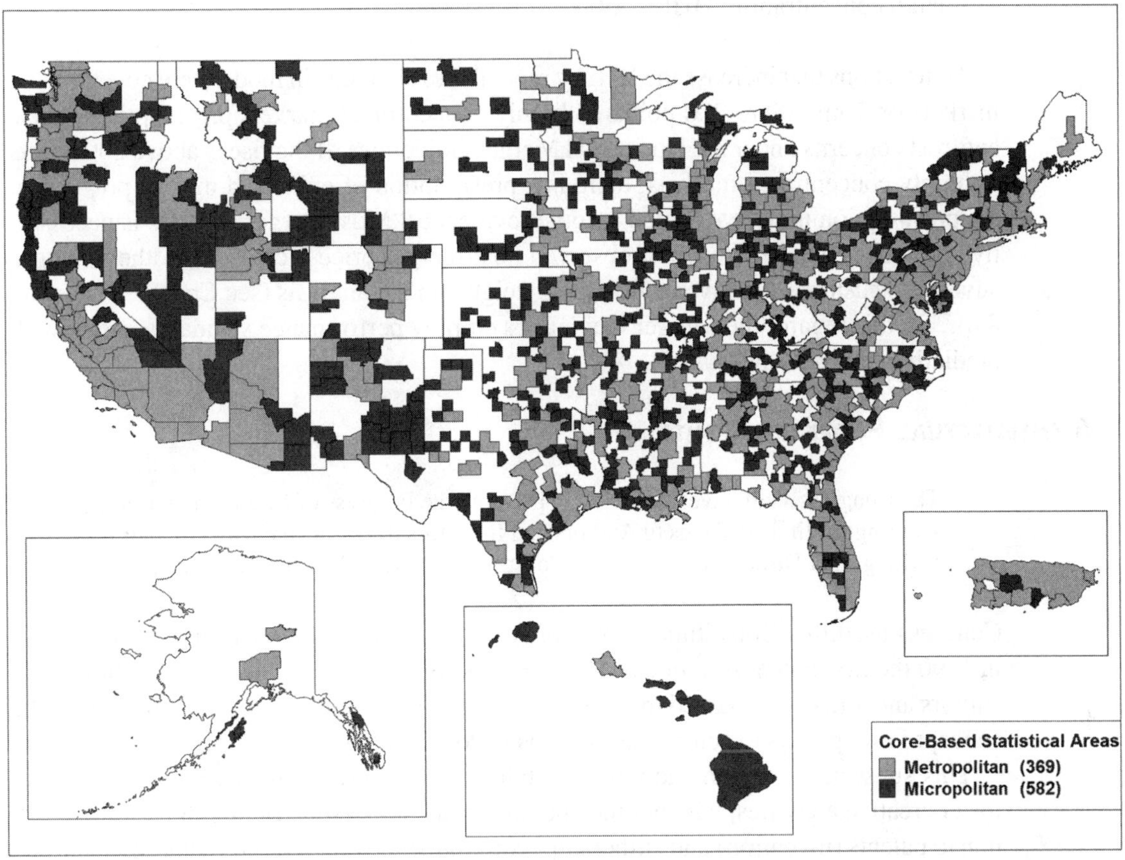

Source: Wikimedia Commons. Map of the Core-Based Statistical Areas of the United States, based on 2005 U.S. Census data. Created by Rarelibra. October 25, 2006.

product sold by one of the merging firms. This test, known as SSNIP, is not a tolerance test for a proposed merger, but rather a methodological tool for, among other uses, ensuring the market is not defined too narrowly. A narrowly defined market will typically lead to a higher HHI than one defined more broadly.

Market shares may be determined based on observing the responses of consumers to price changes. Do they buy less if prices rise, suggesting the market is centered on that product, or do they shift to substitute products, which indicates the product market should be defined to incorporate those substitutes as well?

Alternatively the FTC may rely on the North American Industry Classification System (see above). Regarding market concentration, for the purposes of analyzing the competitive effect of a merger, product markets are defined as follows:

- Low concentration: HHI < 1500
- Moderate concentration: HHI 1500–2500
- High concentration: HHI > 2500

Transactions that increase the HHI by more than 100 points in moderately concentrated markets or from 100 to 200 points in highly concentrated markets presumptively raise antitrust concerns under the Horizontal Merger Guidelines. If the rise is above 200 points in highly concentrated markets, there is a presumption of enhanced market power, but the presumption may be rebutted by other evidence. "Most merger analysis is necessarily predictive, [but] evidence of observed post-merger price increases or other changes adverse to customers is given substantial weight" in the analysis (see Chapter 8, Section 8.6).[78] In this regard, the Merger Guidelines employ performance standards, along with predictive (*ex ante*) measures.

3.6 Intellectual Property Rights

> The Congress shall have Power to . . . promote the Progress of Science and useful Arts, by securing for limited Times to Authors and Inventors the exclusive Right to their respective Writings and Discoveries. . . . (U.S. Constitution Article 1, Section 8, Clause 8)

Congress used this Constitutional power from this so-called Copyright Clause to pass in 1790 the first Patent Act, one of the first laws for the new nation. A copyright law for authors and artists was passed that same year although several state laws predated it. The concept is simple, its execution intricate as is documented below.

This subsection explains how these intellectual property rights (IPR) are applied to foster creative activities, whether they be invention, authorship, or branding, for in addition to patents (invention) and authorship (copyright), IPR includes trademarks and trade secrets. Other more specialized forms exist but are less common and are not reported on here. Since patents are the earliest form of intellectual property rights internationally (traced by scholars to fifteenth-century Venice), as well as domestically, it is treated first. But initially an overview of the concept of IPR is needed.

a. Concepts of Intellectual Property

Intellectual property is inherently different from other forms of property for it can be copied without excluding others from its use. That is, only one person at a time can drive a car. If I am that person, you are excluded; our use is competing (rivalrous). Not so with an idea—an idea can be shared infinitely without reducing access to anyone: just think of images going viral on Facebook. That is why economists refer to ideas as nonrivalrous and nonexclusionary. And inventions are nothing but applied ideas. Zuckerberg's concept for Facebook is said to be based on a program to rank the attractiveness of photos, which itself likely evolved from a practice of private schools. He applied and extended those early efforts.

This all sounds fine, but the infinite usability of ideas creates its own problem. Whereas use does not diminish the utility of an idea, it does diminish its commercial value. The initial insight, the inspiration, may or may not have been costly to develop. The glue for Post-it® notes is said to have evolved from a failed effort at making a more secure glue; it took insight to realize a whole new market for a weak glue existed. The insight may not have been costly in itself, but what is costly is taking a basic idea and transforming it to a commercial one. *Reduction to practice* is the term used in the patent world, but it is best known as R&D (research and development) funding.

An example of the role of patents in R&D funding is penicillin, one of the greatest lifesaving inventions of all time. Its inventor, Sir Alexander Fleming, chose for humanitarian reasons—increasing availability—not to patent it following his discovery in 1928. The problem was that much additional development—among others, a way to retain penicillin in the body long enough to be effective—was required before it became a really functional product. But with no patent no private firm had the incentive to invest. So it was not until the mid-1940s when the U.S. Army badly needed an antibiotic to prevent infection from war injuries that the U.S. government invested in the R&D required to refine the product we still rely on today. Many who might have been saved by the drug suffered and died in the interim.

Then there was Edison with his 1,000+ patents who is credited with saying "invention is 1 percent inspiration, 99 percent perspiration." Well, R&D is the perspiration, but it does not flow as cheaply. What happens, then, is if the commercialized idea can be copied freely, the investor in the R&D loses out as his or her costs are higher than those of imitators.

In the terms of economists, the inventor's long-run average cost are raised compared to noninvesting competitors and sales are lost (see Chapter 2, Section 2.2a). It does not take an economist to recognize that such a system is a loser because there is no incentive to invest in new inventions, and by extension in writing, composing, and similar creative activities. Governments of course can invest but not as much or as broadly and possibly not as effectively, meaning that innovation stagnates.

The solution to this unhappy situation is to prevent copying the developed ideas, essentially making the products/ideas private property. The regulation of that transformation to private property involves intricate definitions as well as judgment calls. But the basic concept is a simple one: provide an incentive for investing in new products of whatever type by making them private property, which is to say excludable.

While the basic concept may seem reasonable enough, there are reasons to reject it. For one, IPR creates a monopoly. The monopoly is limited in many ways, but it is a monopoly nonetheless, which leads to higher prices and reduced market supply (see Chapter 2, Section 2.2a). The higher prices mean some consumers will be priced out of a market (think of some pharmaceuticals costing $500,000 annually), as well as delaying dissemination. Both are counter to efficiency and detrimental to societal well-being, but the real issue is how society comes out ahead overall, with or without IPR. That is far too large a question to be resolved or even explored here, so instead let us just address the basics of how IPR actually functions and is utilized strategically by business. Here the particular areas of application focus on international markets and how the forms and operation of IPR in other countries affect investment decisions by U.S.-based companies. In practice, IPR is national law so that protection of each form must be secured in each country of interest (although there are some multiple country agreements available—see below).

b. Patents

Patents are not only the earliest form of IPR protection, they are the most expansive in terms of protectable subject matter. In a 1980 decision *Diamond vs. Chakrabarty* the Supreme Court interpreted the Constitution as allowing patents for "anything under the sun that is made by man." This definition should not be taken to mean literally *anything*. The words "made by man" limit the scope by excluding abstractions like formula ($E = MC^2$ is out) (judicial interpretation). Patents are intended to be applied knowledge of possible practical value. That said, the scope of patentable subject matter in the United States is vast, generally products and processes (specific ways of making things) as well as combinations of the two (products made by a particular process).

The "made by man" definition also recently ruled out so-called "products of nature" (isolated genes, as determined in a recent decision) and "rules of nature." More specifically, engineered living organisms (from the *Chakrabarty* decision) including seeds can be patented, as can some forms of computer programs and business methods (a policy interpretation that is especially controversial). There are also special forms of patents known as design patents (35 USC 171–73) which are intended to protect aesthetic, not functional, designs, but they will not receive much attention here.

Once the subject matter has been identified, the system must choose what is protectable and what is not. From a policy perspective it makes no sense to grant patents to what already exists—a patent on fire or the wheel would simply allow monopoly pricing with no new product to benefit the public. Nor is it sensible to grant a patent for really trivial inventions—say a new flavor of gum. These considerations underlie the three basic requirements for being awarded a patent, as follows, using patent law terminology:

1. Novelty
2. Utility
3. Nonobviousness (elsewhere called Inventive Step).

Novelty requires an invention be new, not previously known (35 USC 102). In the United States the invention can be publicly exposed (by publication, presentation, or public use) for a year prior to the initial patent application. Otherwise the invention is not considered new and cannot be patented (there go patents for fire and the wheel). Many other countries prohibit *any* public exposure prior to filing an application, so the U.S. law in that regard is quite accommodating.

The utility requirement (35 USC 101) states that the invention must function as described, not that it is somehow better in a practical sense (the Patent Office disallows being able to make those judgments). The item must work, even if it is silly (Figure 3.8).

Figure 3.8 **This Is an Example of a Silly (Obvious) Patent: Exercising a Cat Using a Laser**

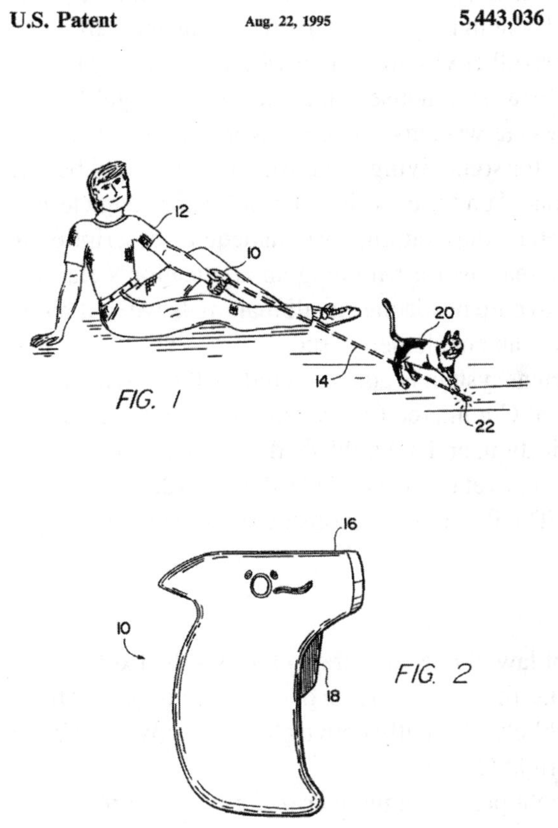

Source: U.S. Patent # 5,443,036, United States Patent and Trademark Office.

The nonobviousness determination (35 USC 103) is inherently subjective and made by Patent Office employees known as examiners. The examiners weigh the claimed invention (as set out in a part of the application known as the patent claims) against the known state of the technology. If the invention gets over the bar, a patent is awarded; if not, it is denied (although in practice there is often some back and forth between the inventor and the examiner which may result in some reduction in the patent claims).

The claims combined with the novelty search determine the scope of the patent. This will generally be larger for pioneering patents than for important but modest extensions of older technologies, like pipe connections. Under the U.S. system a patent will get some "'halo'" of protection around the exact description of the invention.

Because of the involvement of examiners the patent review process takes time, and frequently backs up. Often there is a two-year backlog, more for some technologies. Securing a patent in the United States typically costs between $10,000 and $30,000, the great bulk of which goes to patent attorneys who must be experts on the technologies as well as on patent practice, not to the Patent Office.

There is one additional patent requirement, referred to variously as the description or the enablement requirement (35 USC 112). It says that the patent must be described completely enough so that a person of ordinary skill in the art can recreate it once the patent expires (otherwise the patent would effectively be everlasting). The requirement also provides for a "storehouse of technical knowledge" to aid subsequent inventiveness. Most disclosures are written—the great working models from the nineteenth century are long gone. But for some living organisms which would be difficult to recreate from a written description—"undue experimentation" is the patent term—a deposit of a sample may also be required by the examiner. An inadequate description for all the forms claimed may be one of the reasons for trimming an application's claims as noted above. An application claiming to cure headaches in all mammals when it has only been demonstrated in mice would have an enablement issue.

The patent system is administered by the Patent and Trademark Office within the Department of Commerce (www.uspto.gov). Patents have a twenty-year life from date of first application, and are published eighteen months after the first application even if the patent has not yet been awarded (35 USC 122), excepting inventions limited to domestic use only. The first to file is considered to be the true inventor (35 USC 135).

c. Copyright

Copyright law allows authors and artists the exclusive right to make and sell copies of their works, the right to create derivative works, and the right to perform or display their works publicly. Presently copyright law is governed by the Copyright Act of 1976 under the Copyright Office.

Copyright protects a number of forms of expression, including:

- Literary
- Musical
- Dramatic
- Pantomimes and choreographic works
- Pictorial, graphic, and sculptural works
- Audiovisual works
- Sound recordings (nationally since 1972)
- Derivative works (works containing major components of a copyrighted work)
- Compilations (including databases)
- Architectural works
- Some forms of software

What copyright protects is the form of expression, not the ideas contained therein. "In no case does copyright protection for an original work of authorship extend to any idea, procedure, process, system, method of operation, concept, principle, or discovery, regardless of the form in which it is described, explained, illustrated, or embodied in such work" (17 USC 102(b)).

Thus the basic plot of *Romeo and Juliet* of young love thwarted by tribal conflict with tragic consequences is free for all to use, although the exact approach used by Shakespeare (if it were copyrighted, which it is not) or in *West Side Story* would not be. Compilations such as data sets and encyclopedias are protectable to the degree there is originality in structure or presentation. Any public data contained therein is not protected, nor can a standard alphabetical presentation, as used in a telephone book, be copyrighted (*Feist vs. Rural,* Supreme Court 1991). That is, a copyrightable act must have a component of creativity and not simply reflect effort.

The protected expression must be in tangible form, meaning that a dance can be protected if filmed or depicted as a diagram of foot movements. In 1980 the Copyright Act was amended to allow protection of computer software to the degree it represented an original creation (17 USC 101 and 117). IPR including copyright have a "first sale" limitation (17 USC 109), meaning all rights are surrendered on first sale—that is how libraries and Netflix can lend out their purchased copies. For software that would be a problem, as users could copy the originals and then pass them on to others to do the same. Hence, software firms "license" rather than sell copies—the basis for the annoying, lengthy agreement statement before a program can be used. Generally a work is the property of its creator (and can be bought and sold as such) unless produced as part of an employment arrangement—a "work for hire" (17 USC 101), in which case it is the property of the employer.[79]

The copyright system differs from patents in several significant ways. First, since 1988, copyright is automatic. If you prepare an original work, even an unpublished paper like a class paper, it is automatically copyrighted. No formal act is required, not even the posting of the copyright symbol "©" (the symbol ℗ is used for recordings). Registration, which involves sending a copy of the work to the Copyright Office and paying a small fee, is nonetheless encouraged, because it simplifies any legal proceedings as well as allowing for the recovery of legal costs if successful. The Copyright Office does not examine a submission as does the Patent Office, but gives only a cursory evaluation and determines if the subject matter is copyrightable.

Second, a work published in one of the Berne Convention member countries or by a national or resident of one of those countries automatically receives protection in the other member nations. The extent of protection depends on national law (see Section f below).[80] There are at present 167 contracting states adhering to the convention.[81]

A third difference is the limited allowed use of copyrighted material known as "fair use" (17 USC 107). Fair use permits quoting from protected works for scholarly or critique purposes. While the act identifies four standards for determining the extent of allowances under fair use, the decision in individual case is difficult, and certainly creates a headache for class materials. Individuals are generally permitted to make a single copy of a copyrighted work for personal use.

These exclusive rights are subject to a time limit, and generally since 1998 copyright expires seventy years after the author's death. If the work is corporate owned, however, the term is 102 years from creation or 95 years from first publication, whichever is shorter (17 USC 301). Reregistration is no longer required. These periods have been extended periodically (the duration in the first Patent Act of 1790 was only twenty-eight years) and are sometimes referred to as the "Disney" terms. Clearly there is little public benefit from extending the protection period for a work already in existence.

d. Trademark

A trademark is a word, phrase, symbol, and/or design that identifies and distinguishes the source of the goods of one party from those of others. A trademark is indicated by a registration mark, or "®" symbol, when federally registered, and a trademark, or "TM" symbol, when not. A service mark (SM) is a word, phrase, symbol, and/or design that identifies and distinguishes the source of a service rather than goods.

The term *trademark* is often used to refer to both trademarks and service marks.[82] That is, a trademark is a brand name. It allows the owner to invest in a product or service without worrying that the value of the investment will be undermined by inferior copies. Some trademarks are hugely valuable and frequently copied, as is evident in the number of Rolex watches at the "night markets" in Bangkok or New York City. Trademarks are regulated by the Lanham Trademark Act of 1946, as amended (37 CFR Part 2). National in form, trademarks must be acquired in each country of use, although a simplified system for doing that is available (see this chapter, Section 3.6f).

A U.S. trademark can be acquired either through use in the marketplace or through federal registration with the Trademark Office (part of the Patent and Trademark Office), or both. The assigned examiner evaluates an application for procedural matters as well as determining if a trademark would be overly general or confusing with a pre-existing mark. For example, the office might reject an application for Ferrari clothing, particularly sport clothing, because of the concern that the clothes could be confused with the legendary sports car. There are, however, Ferrari Chocolates, a name that is presumably nonconfusing, and Ferrari is of course a family name, although the chocolates are made in China. To make matters yet more confusing, there also are the well-known Ferraro chocolates. The "prancing horse" logo of Ferrari cars could not be used by either chocolate company without permission. Slight variations of a trademark that could be confusing to consumers also would be disallowed.

Following tentative approval there is a thirty-day comment period known as an Opposition Proceeding that allows for public objections. Following five years of unchallenged registration, a federally registered trademark reaches "incontestable" status and is no longer subject to challenge by third parties.

Unlike other forms of IPR protection, trademarks can conceptually be indefinite, so long as the product is in commerce. Nonuse for three years in the United States can lead to deactivation, at which point it can be reactivated by anyone with a suitable product or service. Another way to lose—have revoked—a trademark is for a name to be judged as generic for a product. Examples are linoleum, zipper, aspirin, escalator, and yo-yo. It is due to concerns over the generalization of a trademarked name that companies such as Kleenex® are careful to use the "registered trademark" symbol and phrases like "Kleenex® brand of tissues."

An evolving area is that of the protection of nontraditional trademarks such as shape, color, and smell. Owens-Corning succeeded in trademarking the traditional pink color of its insulation (*In re Owens-Corning Fiberglas Corp.*, Federal Circuit 1985). These novel kinds of trademarks can however be difficult to register.

e. Trade Secrets

A trade secret is anything of value for which an effort has been made to keep secret. The prime example is the formula for Coca-Cola, said to be held in a vault in the Atlanta headquarters, opened only by using multiple keys held by several top officials. More common are corporate secrets such as customer lists and efficient processing steps.

In the United States trade secrets are controlled by the Uniform Trade Secrets Act (UTSA; 1979, amended 1985), which codified and standardized a disparate set of state laws. The concept is simple: a firm is due damages if a trade secret is improperly acquired, which is to say by theft, bribery, misrepresentation, or breach of trust (UTSA 1.1). Breach of trust applies to such acts as a former employee passing on information to a new employer.

Trade secrets remain only as long as the secret is maintained. Inventors sometimes must decide whether to seek a patent or protect the idea with a trade secret. The trade secret route has the benefit of lower cost and potential permanency versus the twenty years for patents. However, if another company independently develops the same idea, there is no protection. Furthermore, if investor funding is sought it would be necessary to reveal the idea, in which case a confidentiality clause may provide less protection than a patent. Inventors may combine the two; for example, patenting the basic ideas while holding some aspects of the invention as trade secrets.

f. International Harmonization

Viewed from a national perspective, two factors tug at the writers of intellectual property legislation. There is a temptation in international relations to protect your own rights while sticking it to foreigners. In the IP world, that takes the form of protecting your own inventors while discriminating against foreigners. The controlling factor is that if all countries play the same game, then no one has anything. Conversely, from the perspective of the rights holders in an increasingly internationalized world, the more it is possible to obtain multicountry protection, the better. Failing that, the more standardized is protection, the easier it is to manage across countries.

The prejudicial position against foreigners was a principal aspect of the first of the international IP agreements, the Paris Convention of 1883. Article 2, the so-called equal treatment clause, requires that the same protection granted to a country's own nationals must be granted to the nationals of the other contracting states. Another dimension (Article 4) grants an applicant in any of the contracting states a priority of up to one year to apply in any of the others (six months for trademarks). This allows an additional year to consider the economic realities before committing to multinational applications. This and many of the treaties identified below are administered by the World Intellectual Property Organization (WIPO), a specialized agency of the United Nations charged with supporting IPR worldwide. There are presently 175 signatory countries to the Paris Convention.[83]

WIPO does have a major program under the name of the Patent Cooperation Treaty (PCT) that aids multiple country patent applications. Under the system applicants can select up to all of the 148 member countries for an application while receiving a preliminary search report (on novelty) from a major patent office. At the end of the year the applicant can select which of the countries to continue an application with, at which point the process reverts to the individual national routes. While there are efficiencies to be gained by using this system, the principal reason it is utilized is to delay for up to eighteen months the decision (and substantial costs) over which countries to apply to.[84]

The Berne Convention followed shortly thereafter in 1886 but applies specifically to copyright (see also this chapter, Section 3.6c). It too is administered by WIPO. Article 5(1) is nondiscrimination and parallels Article 2 of the Paris Convention (also see above) while Article 5(2) mandates an absence of any formalities in securing protection (i.e., allows for automatic copyright protection). Article 2(6) allows protection across the member states. There are presently 167 of those member states.[85] The Berne Convention is limited to literary and artistic works; the Rome Convention (1961) extends similar protection to performers and recordings as well as broadcast organizations.

International trademark protection can be sought through the Madrid Protocol (1996). (There is an earlier Madrid Agreement [1891] to which the United States does not belong.) Under the Protocol, applicants file a separate international application identifying the member states in which protection is sought. After a technical review by WIPO, which administers the agreement, the international application is forwarded to the designated countries where it is treated as a national application.[86] There are presently ninety-one member states adhering to the Protocol.[87]

While these several international agreements facilitate protection among the willing states, they do nothing for securing protection in other countries, some of which often show skepticism, even prejudice, against strong IPR systems. The United States addressed that critical matter in the Uruguay Round of the General Agreement on Tariffs and Trade (GATT; 1994). The GATT began post-World War II to reduce trade protection measures such as tariffs and quotas. In the Uruguay Round (named for the location of major discussions) the United States extended the argument by declaring inadequate IPR to be trade barriers, hence falling under the auspices of GATT.

The argument was that for economies such as the United States where major exports are technology and entertainment (movies, recordings, and the like), both of which are easily copied, the absence of IPR systems in a country limits trade. From that came the TRIPS (Trade-Related Aspects of Intellectually Property Rights) Annex 1C to the World Trade Organization (WTO), as GATT has been renamed. Countries seeking the member benefits of most-favored-nation trading status under WTO concurrently agreed to TRIPS mandates.

Not surprisingly, TRIPS is a lengthy and complex document, but in its essence it requires certain minimal forms/levels of protection for patents, copyright, trademarks, and trade secrets (other less common forms of protection are covered as well, but are not discussed here):

- **Copyright:** To be protected under the terms of the Berne Convention, including computer programs (Article 9–10)
- **Trademark:** Any sign capable of distinguishing goods or services shall be protectable as a trademark (Article 15)
- **Patents:** Shall be available for all inventions whether products or processes with the exception of diagnostic, therapeutic or surgical methods, and plants and animals other than micro-organisms. However if plants are excluded there must be made available a specialized system of protection (Article 27). Revocations and the like must have the opportunity for judicial review (Article 32), and the term of protection is standardized at 20 years from first application (Article 33).
- **Trade secrets:** Referred to as undisclosed information shall be protected in accordance with the Paris Convention (Article 3).

Member states (159 to date)[88] were given various periods to update their laws based on the level of development. At present all but a few of the least-developed countries are compliant. TRIPS is administered by the WTO under an agreement with WIPO.

g. Enforcement

IP is treated like personal property as it can be exchanged, but unlike the theft of real property, the theft of intellectual property—known as infringement—is a private enforcement matter. That is, if you believe someone is infringing your IP, it is your responsibility to remedy the matter. If a negotiated settlement is not possible, court cases are notoriously complex and costly ($1 million is not unusual) due to the often arcane subject matter involved. Further complicating matters, a patent infringement case of company A charging company B often results in a countersuit by B that A's patent isn't valid and so there can be no infringement. The court then must consider the validity of the underlying patent, which raises some risks for the patent holder.

In practice, process patents can be very difficult to enforce for the simple reason the process being used is not known. For that reason, some businesses (and universities) do not seek process patents. If the process is applied overseas, even though an infringing product can be turned back at the point of importation, proof is doubly difficult to come by.

In 1982 the United States created the United States Court of Appeals for the Federal Circuit, giving it exclusive jurisdiction to hear appeals in patent cases. The intent was for a specialized court to become more conversant on technical matters and hence speed the resolution of complex cases. Results though have been mixed, with the Appeals Court taking a more expansionary position than the Supreme Court, which repeatedly strikes down decisions. In any case, domestic IPR issues are difficult to adjudicate.

Internationally the complexities magnify in part because the courts are often even less equipped to consider complex technical and business matters, and in part because courts can be corrupt and slow—India is said to have a backlog of some 5 million civil cases. Foreigners sometimes also find themselves disadvantaged in some national courts, especially if a multinational is seen as going after a small national firm. And even if a favorable ruling is handed down, actually getting the settlement is a task in itself. In part for these reasons, WIPO along with other entities has established an alternative dispute resolution system comprising mediation and arbitration.[89] While helpful, these steps have been only partly successful, as they are optional and clearly will not be followed by those who anticipate a more favorable outcome under the national courts.

The drafters of the TRIPS Annex were of course well aware of these enforcement issues, but obviously hesitated to place too many demands on national court systems. Even without any further stipulations, the TRIPS agreement has received considerable push back for favoring developed countries, for being too complex and costly, and for being counter to the more communal property orientation of many societies. As a result, TRIPS mandates only that IP issues be open to judicial review, but does not specify anything about the form or operation of the legal system (Part III). Those mandates were left to be addressed by future negotiations, now seemingly a long way into the future.

3.7 Overview of Major Federal Regulatory Legislation

a. Federal Authority to Regulate: The Commerce Clause

The underlying issue of federal regulation is its authority to impose requirements at the state level. Authority is found in the "Commerce Clause"—Article 1, Section 8, Clause 3—of the Constitution. That clause empowers Congress "to regulate Commerce with foreign Nations, and among several States, and with the Indian Tribes." This article, which uses similar language found in the Articles of Confederation, limits the powers otherwise granted to the states under the Tenth Amendment, the so-called Reserve Clause. That amendment reads as follows:

> The powers not delegated to the United States by the Constitution, nor prohibited by it to the States, are reserved to the States respectively, or to the people.

Gibbons vs. Ogden (1824) was the landmark Supreme Court decision which held that the power to regulate interstate commerce was granted to Congress by the Commerce Clause of the Constitution. The case applied to the rights to control navigation between the states. Specifically, New York State had granted Ogden a monopoly to operate steamships between New York and New Jersey. Gibbons, who had a federal coasting license, challenged the requirement he pay substantial fees to New York State for the right to operate between New York and New Jersey. The Court found that New York's licensing requirement for out-of-state operators was inconsistent with a congressional act regulating coastal trade. In his opinion, Chief Justice Marshall developed a clear definition of the word *commerce*, which included navigation on interstate waterways. He also gave meaning to the phrase "among the several states" in the Commerce Clause.[90]

For nearly a century after *Gibbons*, the Court's Commerce Clause decisions dealt but rarely with the extent of Congress' power, and almost entirely with the Commerce Clause as a limit on state legislation that discriminated against interstate commerce. Indeed, the Civil Rights Act (1964) draws its authority from the Commerce Clause as two key challenges were decided on the grounds of the Commerce Clause.

In *Heart of Atlanta Motel Inc. vs. United States* (1964) the Supreme Court held that Congress could use the Commerce Clause to compel private businesses to abide by the Civil Rights Act of 1964. In that case, the owner of a large motel in Atlanta, Georgia, refused to rent rooms to black patrons, in direct violation of the terms of the Civil Rights Act. The owner of the motel filed suit in federal court, arguing that the requirements of the Act exceeded the authority granted to Congress over interstate commerce. The Supreme Court (unanimously in this instance) for its part ruled that the restrictions in adequate accommodation for black Americans severely interfered with interstate travel, giving Congress the authority under the Commerce Clause to prohibit discrimination.[91]

A second pivotal case regarded a local restaurant which refused to serve African Americans. *Katzenbach vs. McClung* (1964) regarded Ollie's Barbecue, a small, family-owned restaurant operating in Birmingham, Alabama, that provided sit-down service for white customers but only take-away service for African Americans. Sued under the Civil Rights Act, the owner and Ollie McClung argued that the Civil Rights Act was unconstitutional, at least as applied to a small, private business such as Ollie's. In response to the interstate-derived food served there, McClung argued that the amount of food purchased by Ollie's that actually crossed state lines (about half the total) was so minuscule that Ollie's effectively had no effect on interstate commerce. Justice Clark writing in the unanimous decision held that racial discrimination in restaurants had a significant impact on interstate commerce, and therefore Congress has the power to regulate this conduct under the Commerce Clause. His conclusion was based on prior testimony that African Americans spent significantly less in areas with racially segregated restaurants, and that segregation imposed an artificial restriction on the flow of merchandise by discouraging African Americans from making purchases in segregated establishments. The Court gave great weight to evidence that segregation in restaurants had a "direct and highly restrictive effect upon interstate travel by Negroes."[92]

At that stage, interpretations of the Commerce Clause seemed both broad and stable. Then came *United States vs. Lopez* (1995), which dealt with a twelve-year-old bringing a loaded gun to school. He was charged under a federal act and appealed, arguing that schools were not involved in interstate commerce, and hence Congress had no authority to pass the Act under which he was charged and convicted. The Supreme Court ultimately decided 5–4 in his favor, and while doing so laid out the three broad categories of activity that Congress could regulate under the Commerce Clause:

1. The *channels* of interstate commerce
2. The *instrumentalities* of, or *persons or things* in, interstate commerce
3. Activities that *substantially affect* or *substantially relate to* interstate commerce

Subsequently in *United States vs. Morrison* (2000), the Supreme Court again struck down (and again by 5–4) an incitement under a federal act, this one the Violence Against Women Act of 1994, for lack of authority under the Commerce Clause. In this instance Brzonkala, a student at Virginia Polytechnic Institute and State University, was allegedly raped by a Morrison and Crawford, and, following a university judicial process she found inadequate, sued her alleged attackers as well as Virginia Tech. The suit in Federal District Court alleged that Morrison and Crawford's attack violated 42 USC Section 13981, part of the Violence Against Women Act of 1994, which provides a federal civil remedy for the victims of gender-motivated violence. The District Court found, and the Court of Appeals ultimately affirmed, that Congress lacked authority to enact Section 13981 under either the Commerce Clause or the Fourteenth Amendment, which Congress had explicitly identified as the sources of federal authority for it. Subsequently, Chief Justice William Rehnquist held that Congress lacked the authority to enact a statute under the Commerce Clause or the Fourteenth Amendment since the statute did not regulate an activity that substantially affected interstate commerce, nor did it redress harm caused by the state. The remedy rather was the responsibility of the Commonwealth of Virginia. In a dissent, though, Justice Souter noted that the Violence Against Women Act contained a "mountain of data assembled by Congress . . . showing the effects of violence against women on interstate commerce."[93]

Much of the difference in interpretation seen first in *Lopez* relates to the interpretation of the term *commerce.* As used in the Constitution, it means business or commercial exchanges in any and all forms between citizens of different states, including purely social communications between citizens of different states by telegraph, telephone, or radio, and the mere passage of persons from one state to another for either business or pleasure. Or, more formally, the dictionary definition of "commerce" is two-fold:[94]

1. The buying and selling of goods, especially on a large scale
2. Intellectual exchange or social intercourse.

Hence, *Gibbons* in part evokes the broader, social interpretation of "commerce" while *Lopez* and *Morrison* apply to the narrower "buying and selling" context.

A similar disagreement appeared early in the United States over the taxation authority of Congress. Madison and Jefferson applied the "strict construction" argument that the only rights were those specifically identified in the Constitution. Hamilton for his part argued for the broader "general welfare" interpretation, now known as "implied powers." To his mind, a narrow interpretation of Congressional powers would soon stultify the new nation, freezing it in the world of the eighteenth century.[95]

Such matters of interpretation may seem arcane, but can have great practical effect. Indeed, the key 2012 Supreme Court decision on the constitutionality of the Patient Protection and Affordable Care Act of 2010, often referred to as "Obamacare," relates in part to how commerce is defined. *National Federation of Independent Businesses vs. Sebelius* (132 S. Ct. 2566, June 2012) had both taxation and Commerce Clause aspects of the key provision if the government could somehow penalize individuals under the "individual mandate" for *not* purchasing health insurance. In short, can the government penalize individuals for not doing something, or only for specified prohibited acts? Chief Justice Roberts provided the pivotal (and surprise) support for the interpretation that the penalty was indeed a "tax" and hence allowable under the broad federal taxation authority. More significant for regulatory authority was what was not upheld—that the federal government had authority under the Commerce Clause to mandate participation.

> The power to regulate commerce presupposes the existence of commercial activity to be regulated. If the power to "regulate" something included the power to create it, many of the provisions in the Constitution would be superfluous. . . .
>
> The individual mandate, however, does not regulate existing commercial activity. It instead compels individuals to become active in commerce by purchasing a product, on the ground that their failure to do so affects interstate commerce. Construing the Commerce Clause to permit Congress to regulate individuals precisely because they are doing nothing would open a new and potentially vast domain to congressional authority. . . . The Framers knew the difference between doing something and doing nothing. They gave Congress the power to regulate commerce, not to compel it.

The effect of this decision on federal authority is debatable. "The rejection of the Commerce Clause," wrote Lyle Denniston, "should be understood as a major blow to Congress's authority to pass social welfare laws." Other legal scholars, however, are not so sure that this curtails Congress's power. Douglas Laycock, a constitutional law professor at the University of Virginia, says it was unexpected that the Supreme Court would make a distinction between activity and inactivity. But, he continues, it is difficult to think of a situation where this will matter much. What could prove more significant, as Jonathan Adler, a law professor at Case Western Reserve University notes, is that the Supreme Court placed limits on Congress's ability to withhold Medicaid funds from states that refuse to expand the program.[96]

That component of the decision by the Supreme Court was based on 42 USCS 1303, which reads, "If any provision of this Act, or the application thereof to any person or circumstance, is held invalid, the remainder of the Act, and the application of such provision to other persons or circumstances shall not be affected thereby." For the Affordable Care Act this says that, while the government can withhold additional Medicaid funding from states not in compliance with the requirements, it cannot withhold *all* Medicaid funding. Yet the withholding of funding to prod state compliance with federal law is frequently done. An example is the National Minimum Drinking Age Act of 1984, which says that states not limiting the purchase and public possession of alcoholic beverages to those twenty-one and older were subject to a 10 percent reduction in federal highway funding. In that regard it is worth noting that while both *Gibbons* and *Lopez* limit the extent of the Commerce Clause, neither abrogated past decisions. Nor does the more recent decision on the Patient Protection and Affordable Care Act.

Table 3.2

Major Federal Regulatory Acts by Departmental Jurisdiction

	Agency	Year	Authority
Interstate Commerce Act	ICC	1887	Regulates railroad industry; established ICC
Pure Food & Drug Act	FDA	1906	Specifies drugs labeled with contents and dosage; created FDA (1930)
Federal Meat Inspection Act	FSIS	1906	Prevents sale of adulterated/misbranded meat; ensures sanitary slaughter and processing practices
Federal Trade Commission Act	FTC	1914	Prevents unfair competition, deceptive acts; created FTC
Radio Act	FRC	1927	Regulates frequencies; created FRC
Communications Act	FCC	1934	Created FCC to parallel ICC
Food, Drug, and Cosmetic Act	FDA	1938	Authorizes FDA to oversee the safety of food, pharmaceuticals, cosmetics, and tobacco
Clean Air Act	EPA	1963	As amended; to improve air quality
Telecommunications Act	FCC	1966	Deregulated access to sector, incorporated cable service, allows cross-ownership
Consumer Products Safety Act	CPSC	1972	Protects public from unreasonable risks of injury or death from thousands of consumer products; created CPSC
Energy Policy Conservation Act	DOT	1975	Establishes car manufacturers' mileage standards
Nutrition Labeling and Education Act	FDA	1990	Requires FDA-approved health claims on food labels
Small Business Regulatory Enforcement Fairness Act	SBA	1996	Allows court review of agency compliance
Telecommunications Act	FCC	1996	Emphasis is on telephone industry; allows media cross-ownership; access to be given by incumbents; oversees spectrum allotments to Internet
Sarbanes-Oxley Act	SEC	2002	Accounting standards
Dodd-Frank Wall Street Reform and Consumer Protection Act	Multiple	2010	Financial reform
Food Safety Modernization Act	FDA	2011	Expands safety precautions; enhances recall authority

Abbreviations:

CPSC Consumer Product Safety Commission
DOT Department of Transportation, National Highway Traffic Safety Administration
EPA Environmental Protection Agency
FCC Federal Communications Commission
FDA Food and Drug Administration
FRC Federal Radio Commission
FTC Federal Trade Commission
FSIS Food Safety and Inspection Service of U.S. Department of Agriculture
ICC Interstate Commerce Commission
SBA Small Business Administration
SEC Securities and Exchange Commission

Source: Compiled by W. Lesser.

b. Major Acts

Table 3.2 lists the major federal regulatory acts by departmental jurisdiction. Further details of these major laws are included in the corresponding chapters.

3.8 CONCLUSIONS

There are many reasons *why* a society may wish to regulate, as is discussed in the preceding chapters. But once a decision is made to regulate, there are a limited number of options regarding *how* to regulate and what steps/approaches can be taken to rectify the issue of concern. The problem may have been identified in any number of ways (tragedy, theory, public sentiment, etc.), but the resolution typically involves one of a very few approaches, right out of economics textbooks.

Paramount among these is providing missing information in response to market failure due to inadequate information. Whether the object is to facilitate better product selection (low salt foods) by labeling, or improving the ability of investors to select a promising stock by providing reliable corporate financial information, the key is providing enhanced information. Theory tells us that markets cannot operate efficiently without complete information. So if the information is lacking, the public steps in to see that needed information is provided universally. Information provision in its many forms is a major policy lever.

As a remedy, however, information works only to the degree individuals are able and willing to use it. Surveys inform us that only some one half of shoppers use food nutrition labels. Yet short of banning some products (a limited option, as seen with the proposed ban on large soft-drink containers) or telling individuals what they should not buy (which will not happen), it is one of the best regulatory options available. Another approach is identifying a more user-friendly information system. The Department of Agriculture has been tweaking its required formats for years while private systems such as the good-better-best Guiding Stars® approach of the Hannaford Brothers supermarket chain is proving effective.

Another economic failing is monopoly, where economic theory prescribes remedies. One is to stop a monopoly from forming, or if it has formed, to end it. The policy lever in these cases is antitrust law. Prohibition of price fixing (monopoly in the sense that supposedly independent companies are in fact operating in concert) is effective. Breaking up major monopolies is far more fraught. The major tool, then, is prevention by limiting mergers and acquisitions, a major path to monopoly. Antimerger legislation is effective, when there is the political will.

One subcategory of monopoly, the natural monopoly (very large economies-of-scale market failure), is not readily manageable except through rate or return means, effective but complex and costly. Franchise bidding (see Chapter 5, Section 5.1i) can work also, but not for electrical power distribution and similar sectors where there are too few franchises to create competition among them.

If the regulatory problem cannot be codified as informational or monopoly then the old standby of force comes into play—do this, do it right, and do it right now. That works too, but its rigidity causes inefficiencies. Flexibility has been injected to good effect in some cases, primarily with tradable emission permits (see Chapter 7). Tradable permits reintroduce a partial market mechanism into rate-of-return regulation. As a society, however, we seem too suspicious, too litigious, or perhaps just too big to extend that approach. Or is it just a lack of imagination?

These approaches are directed to preventing something from happening. Hence most of the incentives for compliance are negative—fines and the like. When a society wants to have something positive happen, it makes sense to offer positive incentives. That is the role of Intellectual Property Rights protection: incentives to invest whether it be in a product (patents), creative activities (copyright), or brand names (trademark). The mechanism is the awarding of a (temporary and limited) monopoly of use rights. IPRs work in the sense of incentivizing investment at no public (government) expense as any benefits come from the market.

Yet it is difficult to determine if such systems grant too much or too little return. The instruments are blunt and do not distinguish by varying protection according to subclasses. So we use what we know works, even if we don't know exactly how well it works. Ultimately, federal regulation has a narrow, and seemingly narrowing, base, the Commerce Clause.

3.9 STUDY QUESTIONS

1. The introductory portion of this chapter lists three organizational categorizations of types of regulations. What are the general concepts of those lists? The conceptual similarities?
2. Trusts have been outlawed in the United States since 1890 (under what legislation?), but that does not mean they do not exist elsewhere. Can you name a prominent trust presently operating?
3. The Patient Protection and Affordable Care Act (also known as Obamacare) represents a major new form of regulation of access to and payment for health insurance. The act, among other things, prohibits insurance companies from denying coverage for pre-existing conditions while requiring that everyone be covered by insurance, public or private. How are the interpretations of the "Commerce Clause" fundamental to its legality?
4. There is no optimal means for regulating natural monopolies, but rate of return regulation is frequently used as one of the better alternatives. Please describe *briefly* the regulatory problem created by natural monopolies and the functioning of rate of return regulation, and then go into more detail on the problems/limitations of rate of return regulation.
5. Electric Slide, Inc., an energy distributor like NYSEG, purchases electricity from power plants and transports energy to customers. The company is subject to rate of return regulation, as applied by the New York State Public Service Commis-

sion, in order to encourage fair pricing in what is a natural and legal monopoly. Assume no taxes when answering the following questions:

i. Last year the rate of return on invested capital was set at 9 percent. Owner's equity (capital) was $50 million at the beginning of the year. What is the maximum return in dollars Electric Slide can expect? Baring other regulations, are there any incentives under rate-of-return regulation for Electric Slide, Inc., to control the pass through of electricity and other costs to consumers given a generally inelastic demand?

ii. Now imagine that the New York State Public Service Commission raises the rate-of-return limit to 10 percent while imposing a price ceiling of $50 per unit of energy. Given inelastic demand, for 2 million energy units, what is the maximum average cost Electric Slide can pay suppliers and still maximize the allowed profit on its $50 million of equity?

6. The evolving definition of "commerce" has affected the judicial interpretation of the Commerce Clause. Can you identify another situation where the changing definition of a word or phrase has affected the law?
7. Identify two additional food products not described in this text where the composition is specified by regulation.
8. Nutritional food labeling requirements would seem to be generally applicable, but many dairy products such as some brands of milk and ice cream nonetheless lack them. Can you explain why that is so?
9. One line of thought argues that safety devices such as seat belts lead to greater risk taking, largely or possibly wholly offsetting the benefits. Please identify and summarize an example of counter evidence.
10. Please report on a (any) study of the effects of the Food Safety Modernization Act of 2011 on reducing food contamination.
11. One dimension of regulation that firms must contend with is regulatory risk, the uncertainty of a regulatory decision. Certainly this is a major factor for pharmaceutical companies. But what of regulated utilities, the electricity system in particular? What sources of regulatory risk do those sectors face?
12. Identify three key articles in the Constitution/Bill of Rights that are central to our regulatory system.
13. Do the Sherman and Clayton Acts generally function as complements or substitutes for each other? What about the Clayton Act and the FTC Act Section 5?
14. For heavy products like steel, the delivery charge is an important part of the total cost for users. For many years the U.S. steel industry used a system known as "base point pricing" in which prices were quoted on a delivered basis with just a few base or source points across the United States. Would such arrangements violate Section 1 of the Sherman Act? Why in any case would the industry get involved in such complex arrangements?
15. If the DOJ were to develop some form of vertical merger guideline, what components would need to be included?

16. Widgets Corp is considering a merger with either Trinkits, Inc., a competitor in their industry, or with Supply Co., one of their suppliers. What options does the government have in response to each proposal? What necessary information does the government need to make a decision, and what are some potential outcomes of regulatory intervention?
17. What is it about intellectual property that makes it so different from real property?
18. Critics of the patent system charge it with allowing protection for trivial, nonsensical inventions. If true, what aspects of the system would have to be changed to remedy that problem?
19. What prevents the government from using Sherman Section 2 to go after patent-based monopolies?
20. Draw a simple economic diagram showing the competition problem that IPR protection is intended to resolve.
21. What is it about copyright law/practice that facilitates the granting of multicountry protection not available for patents and trademarks?
22. A subform of IPR not discussed here is *appellations of origin*, which protect the names of producing regions for wines and spirits (such as Champagne). Which basic form of IPR—patents, copyright, and trademarks—are appellations of origin most like?

NOTES

1. CNN Health, "FDA Reveals Bigger, Graphic Warning Labels for Cigarette Packages," June 21, 2011. Available at www.cnn.com/2011/HEALTH/06/21/cigarette.labels/index.html. Last visited 8/29/11.
2. *R.J. Reynolds Tobacco Co. vs. FDA,* U.S. Court of Appeals for the District of Columbia Circuit No. 11-5332, August 24, 2012.
3. Ibid., p. 10.
4. Ibid., quoting *Central Hudson Gas & Electric Corporation vs. Public Service Commission,* 447 U.S. 557, 566 (1980), p. 22.
5. Ibid., pp. 25–26.
6. Ibid., pp. 6–8.
7. 471 U.S. 626 (1985).
8. 471 U.S. 626 (1985) Rogers dissent pp. 1–2.
9. U.S. Appeals Court for the 6th Circuit, March 2012.
10. Steve Almasy, "FDA Changes Course on Graphic Warning Labels for Cigarettes," CNN, March 20, 2013. Available at www.cnn.com/2013/03/19/health/fda-graphic-tobacco-warnings. Last visited 6/14/13.
11. How Products Are Made, Vol. 4, "Milk." Available at www.madehow.com/Volume-4/Milk.html. Last visited 8/29/11.
12. Food, Drug, and Cosmetic Act (FDCA) (21 U.S.C. §341) directs the FDA to establish definitions and standards for food. See TLC, "What Is Mayonnaise?" Available at http://recipes.howstuffworks.com/food-facts/question617.htm. Last visited 8/29/11.
13. See the United States Department of Agriculture Web site "ChooseMyPlate.gov."
14. See U.S. Food and Drug Administration, "Food and Nutrition Labeling." Available at www.fda.gov/Food/IngredientsPackagingLabeling/LabelingNutrition/ucm114155.htm. Last visited 6/14/13.

15. Jessica Todd and Jayachandran Variyam, "The Decline in Consumer Use of Food Nutrition Labels, 1995–2006." United States Department of Agriculture, Economic Research Report No. 63, August 2008, Tables 1, 3, and 4.

16. Public Law 107-204, 116 Stat. 745.

17. National Highway Safety Traffic Administration, "CAFE Overview—Frequently Asked Questions." Available at www.nhtsa.gov/cars/rules/cafe/overview.htm. Last visited 8/30/11.

18. John M. Broder, "Obama to Toughen Rules on Emissions and Mileage." *New York Times,* May 18, 2009.

19. National Research Council, *Effectiveness and Impact of Corporate Average Fuel Economy (CAFE) Standards*. Washington, DC: The National Academies Press, 2002. Available at www.nap.edu/openbook.php?record_id=10172&page=R1. Last visited 6/14/13.

20. National Highway Traffic Safety Administration press release, "Obama Administration Finalizes Historic 54.5 mpg Fuel Efficiency Standards," August 28, 2012. Available at www.nhtsa.gov/About+NHTSA/Press+Releases/2012/Obama+Administration+Finalizes+Historic+54.5+mpg+Fuel+Efficiency+Standards. Last visited 6/14/13.

21. See NYSE Euronext "Circuit Breakers." Available at http://usequities.nyx.com/markets/nyse-equities/circuit-breakers. Last visited 8/30/11. Formulas are set forth in the New York Stock Exchange Rule 80B.

22. See "Findings Regarding the Market Events of May 6, 2010." Report of the Staffs of the Commodities Futures Trading Commission and Securities and Exchange Commission to the Joint Advisory Committee on Emerging Regulatory Issue, September 30, 2010. Available at www.sec.gov/news/studies/2010/marketevents-report.pdf. Last visited 8/30/11.

23. See U.S. Food and Drug Administration, "Federal Food, Drug, and Cosmetic Act, Chapter 5: Drugs and Devices." Available at www.fda.gov/RegulatoryInformation/Legislation/FederalFoodDrugandCosmeticActFDCAct/FDCActChapterVDrugsandDevices/default.htm. Last visited 8/31/11.

24. J.D. DiMasi, R.W. Hansen, and H.G. Grabowski, "The Price of Innovation: New Estimates of Drug Development Costs." *Journal of Health Economics* 22 (2003): 151–85.

25. See, for example, "Lipitor side effects" (a popular cholesterol-lowering drug). Available at http://www.lipitor.com/aboutLipitor/sideEffects.aspx?source=google&HBX_PK=s_lipitor+side-effects&HBX_OU=50&o=23127370|166376222|0&skwid=43000000210101631. Last visited 8/31/11.

26. U.S. Food and Drug Administration, "Fast Track, Accelerated Approval and Priority Review: Expediting Availability of New Drugs for Patients with Serious Conditions." Available at www.fda.gov/forconsumers/byaudience/forpatientadvocates/speedingaccesstoimportantnewtherapies/ucm128291.htm. Last visited 8/31/11.

27. Rob Stein, "FDA Considers Revoking Approval of Avastin for Advanced Breast Cancer." *Washington Post,* August 16, 2010.

28. Newsy, "Sci/Health News: FDA Revokes Avastin—FDA Panel Doesn't Back Popular Cancer Drug," June 30, 2011. Available at www.newsy.com/videos/fda-panel-doesn-t-back-popular-cancer-drug/. Last visited 8/31/11.

29. U.S. Department of Transportation, Federal Motor Carrier Safety Administration, Standard No. 209, "Seat Belt Assemblies." Available at www.fmcsa.dot.gov/rules-regulations/administration/fmcsr/fmcsrruletext.aspx?reg=571.209. A complete list of safety standard requirements can be found on the National Highway Traffic Safety Administration Web site, www.nhtsa.gov. Last visited 8/31/11.

30. National Highway Traffic Safety Administration, "Lives Saved in 2010 by Restraint Use and Minimum Drinking Age Laws." Traffic Safety Facts, DOT HS 811 580, February 2012. Available at www-nrd.nhtsa.dot.gov/Pubs/811580.pdf. Last visited 10/9/12.

31. National Highway Safety Administration, "Seat Belt Use in 2013—Overall Results." Traffic Safety Facts, DOT HS 811 875, January 2014. Available at www.nrd.nhtsa.dot.gov/Pubs/811875.pdf. Last visited 5/21/14.

32. National Highway Traffic Safety Administration, "Seat Belt Use in 2011—Overall Results." DOT HS 811 544, December 2011, Figure 1. Available at www-nrd.nhtsa.dot.gov/Pubs/811544.pdf. Last visited 8/30/12.

33. National Highway Traffic Safety Administration, "Lives Saved Calculations for Seat Belts and Frontal Air Bags." DOT HS 811 206, December 2009. Available at www-nrd.nhtsa.dot.gov/Pubs/811206.pdf. Last visited 10/9/12.

34. U.S. Environmental Protection Agency, "Arsenic in Drinking Water." Available at http://water.epa.gov/lawsregs/rulesregs/sdwa/arsenic/index.cfm. Last visited 8/31/11.

35. U.S. Environmental Protection Agency, "Sulfur Dioxide." Available at www.epa.gov/air/sulfurdioxide/. Last visited 9/8/11.

36. U.S. Environmental Protection Agency, "Sulfur Dioxide: Health." Available at www.epa.gov/air/sulfurdioxide/health.html. Last visited 9/8/11.

37. New York State Department of Environmental Conservation, "Acid Rain: Sources and Environmental Impacts of Acid Rain and Acid Deposition in New York State." Available at www.dec.ny.gov/chemical/283.html. Last visited 5/21/14.

38. Environmental News Network, "EPA, Northeast States Settle Pollution Lawsuit with Ohio Utility," March 20, 2005. Available at www.enn.com/top_stories/article/1197. Last visited 9/8/11.

39. Union of Concerned Scientists, "Coal vs. Wind: You Be the Judge." Available at www.ucsusa.orgclean_energy/coalvswind/c01.html. Last visited 9/9/11.

40. Sebastian Blanco, "Report: Number of Cars in the U.S. Dropped by Four Million in 2009—Is America's Love Affair Ending?" Autoblog.com, January 4, 2010. Available at http://green.autoblog.com/2010/01/04/report-number-of-cars-in-the-u-s-dropped-by-four-million-in-20/. Last visited 9/9/11.

41. U.S. Environmental Protection Agency, "Emission Durability Procedures for New Light-Duty Vehicles, Light-Duty Trucks and Heavy-Duty Vehicles." Available at www.epa.gov/oms/regs/ld-hwy/cap2000/dura_preamble_regs.pdf. Last visited 9/9/11. There are additional ways of monitoring the operation of the emission control systems during mandatory annual vehicle safety tests, either by directly sampling the tail pipe emissions, or by not passing cars with the check engine light illuminated. The check engine signal often indicates a malfunction of some part of the emission system.

42. Linda Baker, "Reconstructing Building Codes for Greater Energy Efficiency." *Governing,* May 2011. Available at www.governing.com/topics/energy-env/reconstructing-building-codes-greater-energy-efficiency.html. Last visited 9/9/11.

43. For example, see New York Department of State, Office of Planning and Development, Building Standards and Codes, "2010 Energy Conservation Construction Code of New York State." Available at www.dos.state.ny.us/DCEA/energycode_code.html/. Current code status by state, available at www.energycodes.gov/states/. Last visited 9/9/11.

44. Cornell University Law School, Legal Information Institute, "21 U.S. Code §603. Examination of Animals Prior to Slaughter; Use of Humane Methods" ("an examination and inspection of all amenable species before they shall be allowed to enter into any slaughtering, packing, meat-canning, rendering, or similar establishment, in which they are to be slaughtered"). Available at www.law.cornell.edu/uscode/21/usc_sec_21_00000603—000-.html. Last visited 9/9/11.

45. U.S. Food and Drug Administration, "Hazard Analysis and Critical Control Point: Principles and Application Guidelines," Executive Summary. Available at www.fda.gov/Food/FoodSafety/HazardAnalysisCriticalControlPointsHACCP/HACCPPrinciplesApplicationGuidelines/default.htm#execsum. Last visited 9/9/11.

46. Centers for Disease Control and Prevention, "Salmonella." Available at www.cdc.gov/salmonella/outbreaks.html. Last visited 5/21/14.

47. Data reported in Sandra Hoffman, "U.S. Food Safety Policy Enters a New Era." *Amber Waves* 9, 4 (December 2011): 24–29 (online publication of U.S. Department of Agriculture, Economic Research Service).

48. Details at U.S. Food and Drug Administration, "Egg Safety Final Rule." Available at www.fda.gov/Food/FoodSafety/Product-SpecificInformation/EggSafety/EggSafetyActionPlan/ucm170615. Last visited 9/10/11.

49. Hoffman, "U.S. Food Safety Policy Enters a New Era."

50. W.M. Warwick, *A Primer on Electric Utilities, Deregulation, and Restructuring of the U.S. Electricity Markets,* Version 2.0, Chap. 6. U.S. Department of Energy, Office of Energy Efficiency and Renewable Energy, May 2002. Available at www1.eere.energy.gov/femp/pdfs/primer.pdf. Last visited 2/28/12.

51. Regulatory Assistance Project, *Electricity Regulation in the U.S.: A Guide.* Montpelier, VT: Author, 2011, Chapter 6.

52. New York State Public Service Commission, "Mission Statement." Available at www3.dps.state.ny.us/W/PSCWeb.nsf/ArticlesByTitle/39108B0E4BEBAB3785257687006F3A6F?OpenDocument. Last visited 9/10/11.

53. New York State Public Service Commission, "Major Rate Case Process Overview." Available at www3.dps.ny.gov/W/PSCWeb.nsf/0/364D0704BEEC5B7D85257856006C56B3?OpenDocument. Last visited 5/21/14.

54. New York State Public Service Commission, "PSC Adopts 1-Year Electric Rate Plan for O&R." Available at www3.dps.ny.gov/pscweb/WebFileRoom.nsf/Web/E11E97293546C75C852578B1005CB453/$File/pr11056.pdf?OpenElement. Last visited 5/21/14.

55. The Averch-Johnson Effect argues that rate-setting systems that are based on an allowed rate of return essentially encourage too much capital compared to variable inputs. See Harvey Averch and Leland L. Johnson, "Behavior of the Firm under Regulatory Constraint." *American Economic Review* 52 (1962): 1052–69.

56. New York State Public Service Commission, "PSC Adopts 1-Year Electric Rate Plan for O&R."

57. "PSC Orders Gas, Electric Utilities to File Austerity Plans." *North Country Gazette,* May 16, 2009. Available at www.northcountrygazette.org/2009/05/16/austerity_utilities/. Last visited 9/10/11.

58. For an excellent intermediate text on the subject, see D.W. Carlton and J.M. Perloff, *Modern Industrial Organization,* 4th ed. Boston, MA: Addison Wesley, 2005.

59. For those living in upstate New York, it is worth noting that he was born in Richford. The story goes that his family home was dismantled and then stored by a speculator hoping to sell it back to him at a profit. Rockefeller's response is said to have been "Why do you think I worked so hard all my life but to get out of Richford?" Richford was, and remains, a hardscrabble farming community.

60. The National Grange, *Legal and Economic Influence of the Grange 1867–1967.* Washington, D.C: Author, 1967, p. 85.

61. The National Grange, *Legal and Economic Influence of the Grange 1867–1967,* p. 1.

62. See Federal Trade Commission, "Guide to Antitrust Laws." Available at www.ftc.gov/bc/antitrust/index.shtm. Last visited 11/10/11

63. See Biography.com, "John D. Rockefeller." Available at www.biography.com/people/john-d-rockefeller-9461341. Also, U.S. History.com, "John D. Rockefeller: The Ultimate Oil Man." Available at www.u-s-history.com/pages/h957.html. Company history of ExxonMobil, "Our History." Available at www.exxonmobil.com/Corporate/history/about_who_history_alt.aspx. All last visited 11/8/11.

64. "U.S. vs. Microsoft: Timeline." *Wired,* November 2, 2002. Available at www.wired.com/techbiz/it/news/2002/11/35212. Department of Justice documents available at www.justice.gov/atr/cases/ms_index.htm. Both last visited 11/8/11.

65. David Greenberg, "Baseball's Con Game." *Slate,* July 19, 2002. Available at www.slate.com/articles/news_and_politics/history_lesson/2002/07/baseballs_con_game.html. Last visited 11/8/11.

66. See, for example, Herbert Hovenkamp, "Clayton Act (1914)." Major Acts of Congress. 2004. Encyclopedia.com, March 7, 2014.

67. Ibid.

68. The "Notification and Report Form for Certain Mergers and Acquisitions" is available at www.ftc.gov/sites/default/files/attachments/form-and-instructions/hsrform-instructions1_0_0.pdf. Last visited 11/9/11.

69. Federal Trade Commission, Bureau of Competition, "The Hart–Scott–Rodino Antitrust Improvements Act of 1976." Available at www.ftc.gov/bc/hsr/. Last visited 11/9/11.

70. Federal Trade Commission Premerger Notification Office, "What Is the Premerger Notification Program? An Overview," March 2009. Available at www.ftc.gov/bc/hsr/introguides/guide1.pdf. Last visited 11/9/11.

71. Federal Trade Commission, "FTC Order Requires Tops Markets to Sell Seven Penn Traffic Supermarkets," August 4, 2010. Available at www.ftc.gov/news-events/press-releases/2010/08/ftc-order-requires-tops-markets-sell-seven-penn-traffic. Last visited 5/21/14.

72. Federal Trade Commission, Guide to Antitrust Laws, "Mergers: Competitive Effects." Available at www.ftc.gov/bc/antitrust/competitive_effects.shtm. Last visited 11/10/11.

73. See Cartype.com, "Body by Fisher." Available at www.cartype.com/pages/346/body_by_fisher. Last visited 11/10/11.

74. Federal Trade Commission, Guide to Antitrust Laws, "Mergers: Markets." Available at www.ftc.gov/bc/antitrust/markets.shtm. Last visited 11/10/11.

75. U.S. Census Bureau, "North American Industry Classification System." Available at www.census.gov/cgi-bin/sssd/naics/naicsrch?chart=2007. Last visited 11/10/11. The site allows for searching for numbers for individual industries.

76. U.S. Department of Justice, Antitrust Division, "The Herfindahl-Hirschman Index." Available at www.justice.gov/atr/public/testimony/hhi.htm. Last visited 11/10/11.

77. U.S. Department of Justice and Federal Trade Commission, "Horizontal Merger Guidelines," August 19, 2010. Available at http://ftc.gov/os/2010/08/100819hmg.pdf. Last visited 11/10/11.

78. Ibid.

79. Universities apparently for historical reasons generally allow faculty to retain the copyright to their books and other research papers, as is the case with this volume. Software, however, is considered the property of the university, as are patents through a special mandatory license agreement. Cornell University's patent policy ("Inventions and Related Property Rights") is available at www.dfa.cornell.edu/cms/treasurer/policyoffice/policies/volumes/academic/upload/vol1_5.pdf. Last visited 10/21/13.

80. See U.S. Copyright Office, "International Copyright." Available at www.copyright.gov/fls/fl100.html. Last visited 10/21/13.

81. A list of WIPO-administered treaties can be found at www.wipo.int/treaties/en/ShowResults.jsp?lang=en&treaty_id=15. Last visited 10/21/13.

82. U.S. Patent and Trademark Office, "Trademark, Patent, or Copyright?" Available at www.uspto.gov/trademarks/basics/definitions.jsp. Last visited 10/21/13.

83. Member list available at www.wipo.int/treaties/en/ShowResults.jsp?lang=en&treaty_id=2. Full text of the "Paris Convention for the Protection of Industrial Property" is available at www.wipo.int/treaties/en/text.jsp?file_id=288514. Both last visited 10/21/13.

84. Full text of the "Patent Cooperation Treaty." Available at www.wipo.int/pct/en/treaty/about.html. Last visited 10/23/13.

85. Member list available at www.wipo.int/treaties/en/ShowResults.jsp?lang=en&treaty_id=15. Full text of the "Berne Convention for the Protection of Literary and Artistic Works" is available at www.wipo.int/treaties/en/text.jsp?file_id=283698. Both last visited 10/21/13.

86. Nina Shreve, "International Trademark Registration: The Madrid Protocol Takes Effect in the United States," November 2, 2003. Available at http://corporate.findlaw.com/intellectual-property/international-trademark-registration-the-madrid-protocol-takes.html. Last visited 10/22/13.

87. List available at www.wipo.int/treaties/en/ShowResults.jsp?treaty_id=8; full text of the "Protocol Relating to the Madrid Agreement Concerning the International Registration of Marks" is available at www.wipo.int/treaties/en/text.jsp?file_id=283484. Both last visited 10/22/13.

88. Membership list available on WIPO Web site, www.wipo.int; full text of "Protocol Relating to the Madrid Agreement Concerning the International Registration of Marks" is available at www.wipo.int/treaties/en/agreement/trips.html. Last visited 10/22/13.

89. "WIPO Arbitration and Mediation Center." Available at www.wipo.int/amc/en/index.html. Last visited 10/22/13.

90. Oyez Project, *Gibbons vs. Ogden.* Available at www.oyez.org/cases/1792–1850/1824/1824_0. Last visited 2/12/12.

91. Oyez Project, *Heart of Atlanta Motel vs. U.S.* Available at www.oyez.org/cases/1960–1969/1964/1964_515. Last visited 2/12/12.

92. Oyez Project, *Katzenbach vs. McClung.* Available at www.oyez.org/cases/1960–1969/1964/1964_543. Last visited 2/12/12.

93. Oyez Project, *United States vs. Morrison.* Available at www.oyez.org/cases/1990–1999/1999/1999_99_5. Last visited 2/12/12.

94. From *The American Heritage Dictionary of the English Language.* Boston, MA: Houghton Mifflin, 1979.

95. See The Founders' Constitution, Volume 3, Article 1, Section 8, Clause 18, Document 11, "Alexander Hamilton, Opinion on the Constitutionality of the Bank" (1791). Available at The University of Chicago Press, http://press-pubs.uchicago.edu/founders/documents/a1_8_18s11.html. Last visited 2/12/12.

96. Quoted in Brad Plumer, "Supreme Court Puts New Limits on Commerce Clause. But Will It Matter?" Wonkblog, *The Washington Post,* June 28, 2012.

4 Results of Regulation

Chapter Objectives

Economic models of the effects of taxes are shown to project the consequences of regulation-imposed costs on prices and quantities. Effects differ if the industry is competitive or a monopoly, and based on the relative elasticities between consumers and producers. Most (but not all) federal regulations must document that benefits exceed costs (a positive ratio between them).

A major objective of this chapter is to describe the principal methods used to compute the benefits of regulation. Benefits are generally more complex to assess than costs because they frequently involve nonmarket goods like the absence of air pollution. This is typically done using *contingent valuation* procedures for determining *willingness to pay* or *willingness to accept.*

Among nonmarket goods is human life, which must be valued for many studies. This is done either by determining the *risk premium* required for risky jobs or calculating the *value of a statistical life (VSL).* Complicating the analysis is the tendency for reductions in risks or costs to be offset at least in part by riskier or less frugal behavior, known as the *Peltzman Effect.*

The subsequent subsections of this chapter include a discussion of who regulates (state or federal and principal federal agencies), a synopsis of studies of regulatory outcomes (including how cost-benefit analyses are conducted when required), an overview of alternatives to regulation (such as liability litigation), and, finally, corporate responses to regulation (such as utilizing compliance divisions).

Key Terms: *Travel cost method; Hedonic pricing; Risk premium; Lifetime earning method; Value statistical life; Contingent valuation; Willingness to pay; Willingness to accept; Peltzman Effect*

Comprehending why, and how, we regulate is essential. Understanding the outcomes—consequences, both positive and negative—of regulation also is important. Documenting those outcomes, though, is an enormous subject in itself, due both to the vast quantity of analyses available and the differences in approaches used. Differences in approach include the time periods covered, assumptions incorporated, methods used to incorporate nonpriced components (also known as nonmarket goods), ranging from the mere existence of wilderness to the value of a human life, discount rates (the degree to which current use is valued over future users), and so forth.

This is a very broad subject, and only an introduction can be provided here. Hopefully, this introduction will give students sufficient background to pursue subsequently specific issues of interest on their own. Business students are reminded that the principal requirement of business is to comply with regulations in the most expeditious and cost-effective manner possible, whatever the analysis shows or personal opinions may be. Understanding just what the regulations require and how best to comply are topics for the latter part of this text.

The second subsection here provides relevant background on understanding how regulations, as a group and individually, function. Of course, formal regulations, in the sense of legally binding ones, represent but one means of achieving a set of goals. Alternatives to formal regulations as well as corporate responses to regulations, though, are held off until Chapter 5.

However, before considering the specifics of how regulations function and can be assessed, it is useful to develop a concept, a model, of what we might expect to happen. Whether the predicted result actually comes to be is an empirical matter, but at least the models illustrate what to look for. Economic models are intended for just that purpose, so we begin there.

4.1 MODELING THE EFFECTS OF REGULATION

The government can intervene in the marketplace in numerous ways, including combinations of interventions, each of which can be modeled using a different economic graph. In the vocabulary of economists, many of these cases can be treated as a "tax" on prices and output. To an economist, a tax is more than a payment to a government entity and consists of any government/externally imposed cost. That broad definition applies to many cost-imposing regulations, such as those mandating the use of a scrubber to remove pollutants from power plant effluents.

The overview presented here is intended only as a refresher. Readers who seek more background are directed to one of many introductory microeconomic textbooks, or to a micro MOOC. Major forms of intervention with common examples include:

- Unit tax (fixed amount per unit)
- Lump sum tax (license fee)
- Ad valorem tax (sales tax)
- Minimum price (minimum wage rates)
- Maximum price (rent control)
- Prohibited goods (illegal goods)
- Price supports (milk)
- Production quotas (crops, taxi licenses)
- Import quotas
- Import tariffs

All of these cases can be modeled, but only the three "taxes" apply to the kinds of regulations examined here, so the models presented below are restricted to them. However, it is also necessary to examine the effects on (purely) competitive industries as well as (simple) monopolistic ones, considering as well as the deadweight social loss imposed (see Chapter 2, Section 2.2). The degree of elasticity of supply and demand also must be taken into consideration (see Chapter 2, Section 2.2d) so that our undertaking will not be a trivial one. We begin with the simplest model to demonstrate, a unit tax.

a. Unit Tax

A unit tax, say 50 cents per gallon of gas, shifts the supply curve up and to the left, as shown in Figure 4.1, which applies to a competitive industry. This happens because the supply curve in the long run is akin to an average cost curve, which increases by the amount of the tax. The diagram shows the expected effect: price rises while demand falls with the "distance" between S and S′ reflecting the amount of the tax.

By observing the figure, it is apparent that some but not all of the increase is passed onto consumers; a portion is also absorbed by the supplier. The apportionment of the division of the tax paid by the two parties depends on the relative elasticities. *In general, the party with the lowest elasticity (in absolute value) pays the largest share* simply because there are fewer alternatives.

The figure also notes the deadweight loss (DWL) created by the tax. A DWL (see Chapter 2, Section 2.2) is a loss of social value. Based on the resulting DWL, many people oppose taxes (read: regulations) as inefficient. However, it is important to recall that with regulations like smog reduction, beneficial results are generated as well as costs, but they are not reflected in the graph.

Figure 4.1 **Unit Tax in a Competitive Industry**

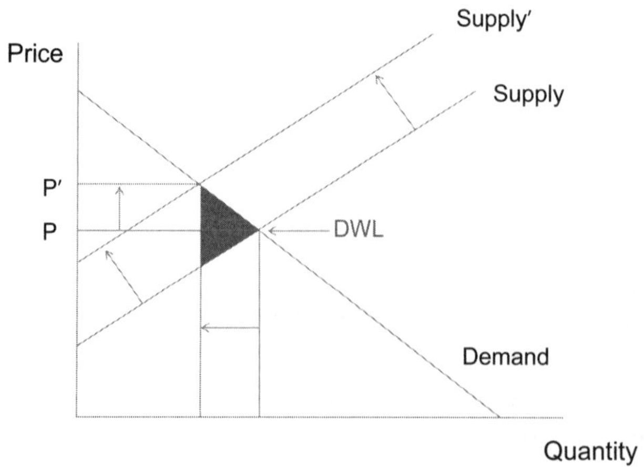

Source: W. Lesser.

Figure 4.2 **Unit Tax in a Monopolistic Industry**

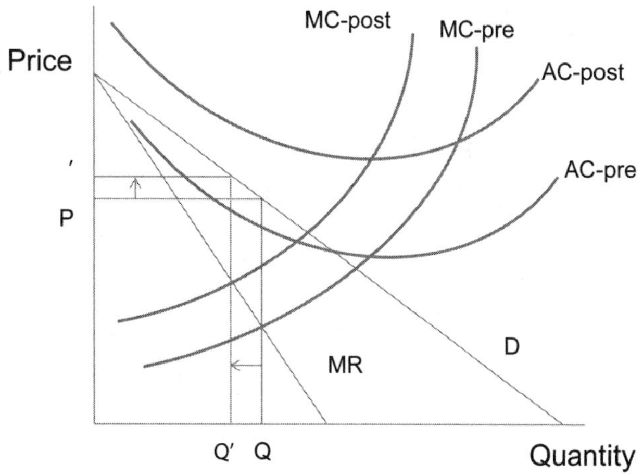

Source: W. Lesser.

Modeling a unit tax in a monopoly leads to a very different outcome, as shown in Figure 4.2. As can be seen in the diagram, the same general effect is achieved: quantity declines and price rises. However, quantity declines proportionally more than price rises (as is evident from the relative sizes of the rectangles), meaning the monopolist absorbs most of the tax, passing on some. Again, the amount passed on depends on the demand elasticity. The less elastic the demand (the more vertical the curve), the more tax is passed on.

b. Lump-Sum Tax

In a competitive industry we can view the supply curve as the average cost curve. A tax will shift the supply curve out (to the left). The distinction from the unit tax (see Section 4.1a of this chapter) is that the shift will not be parallel, but rather will depend on the output level as the fixed tax amount is averaged over more units. This is shown in Figure 4.3. The results are generally in line with the unit tax outcome as regards quantity decline and price rise, the division being dependent on the supply and demand elasticities. The only real distinction is that the greater the tax, the more pronounced the effect on the supply curve at lower outputs.

With a monopoly, the government can reduce or even eliminate the monopoly profit without affecting either the price or output level. It is taxing the profit away, as shown in Figure 4.4. There we begin with the typical monopolist's price and output of *P* and *Q*. The government then "merely" needs to determine what the typical monopolist's profit is at that *P* and *Q* (indicated in the figure by the distance from point a to b) and set the lump-sum tax at that level. Because the tax is the same for any level of output, it affects only the *AC*, not the *MC*. We know there is no residual profit because the demand curve is

Figure 4.3 **Lump-Sum Tax in a Competitive Industry**

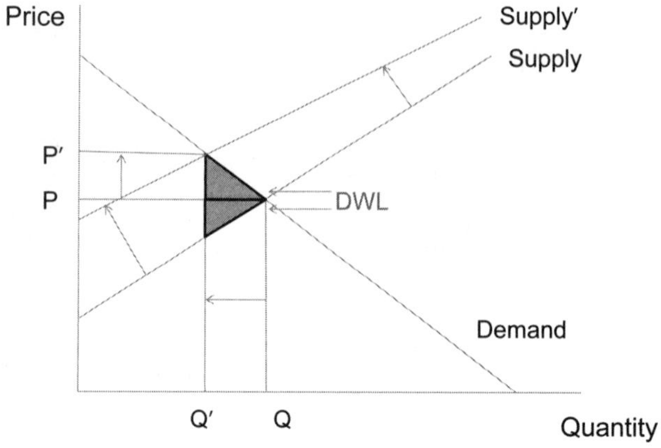

Source: W. Lesser.

Figure 4.4 **Lump-Sum Tax in a Monopoly**

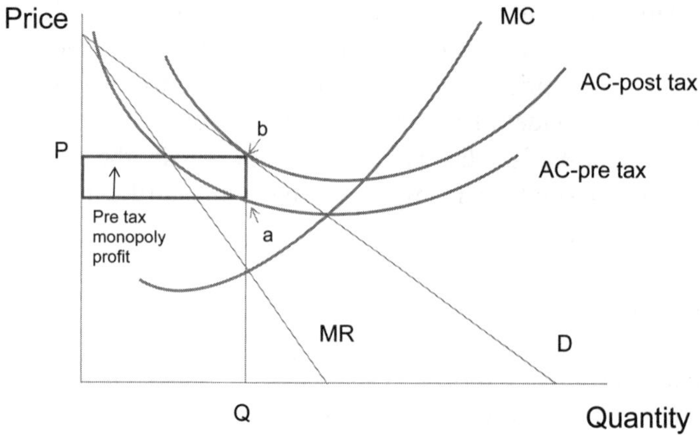

Source: W. Lesser.

tangent to the AC curve at the optimum output level. Of course it is difficult to achieve that precise tax level, but any level of lump-sum tax will shift monies from the pocket of the monopolist to government coffers.

c. Ad Valorem Tax

A sales-type tax (ad valorem) applies a fixed percentage of the purchase price and so can be viewed again as an upward shifting of the supply curve. At zero quantity there is of course no tax while the amount of tax rises with the quantity, shown as S′ in Figure 4.5. Comparing this figure with Figure 4.1, it is evident that for a particular tax level there is no

Figure 4.5 **Ad Valorem Tax in a Competitive Market**

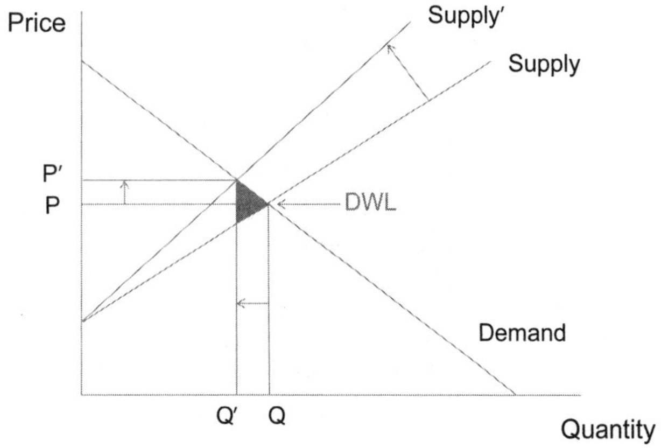

Source: W. Lesser.

difference in the revenue raised or in the social effect between the two forms of taxation in a competitive market. There may be practical political, management, or acceptance differences, but in terms of economics the effects are the same.

Note however from the figure that an ad valorem tax makes the supply curve less elastic (steeper sloped). Referring back to the observation that the party with the lowest elasticity in terms of supply and demand pays the greater portion of the tax (see Section 4.1a of this chapter), ad valorem taxes do shift more of the tax burden onto suppliers and away from consumers.

All of the examples here apply the tax to the seller, meaning a shift in the supply curve. However, we could as easily have modeled the effect on the demand curve. A tax shifts the supply curve out (the cost of the goods sold rises) or the demand curve in (a tax raises the cost of the good). Which one we choose to model is arbitrary: the outcomes on price, quantity, and tax income are identical. This result can be generalized into the observation that *it is immaterial if a tax in a competitive market is imposed on the consumer or the supplier—the outcome in terms of price and quantity, and tax revenue, is the same.*

The effect of a supply shift due to an ad valorem tax is shown in Figure 4.6, in this case applied to a monopoly. The tax causes the demand curve (as perceived by the monopolist) to pivot downward as the product becomes progressively more costly—the higher the price with the added tax. As quantity demanded falls, price rises (from P to P′) as shown in the figure.

Of interest here, the tax revenue for the government is the area depicted in the figure. It can readily be shown that a tax that leads to the same post-tax Q′ and P′ raises more tax revenue when applied as an ad valorem tax than as a unit tax. The demonstration is given as an exercise (see Section 4.5 of this chapter).

Figure 4.6 **Ad Valorem Tax under a Monopoly**

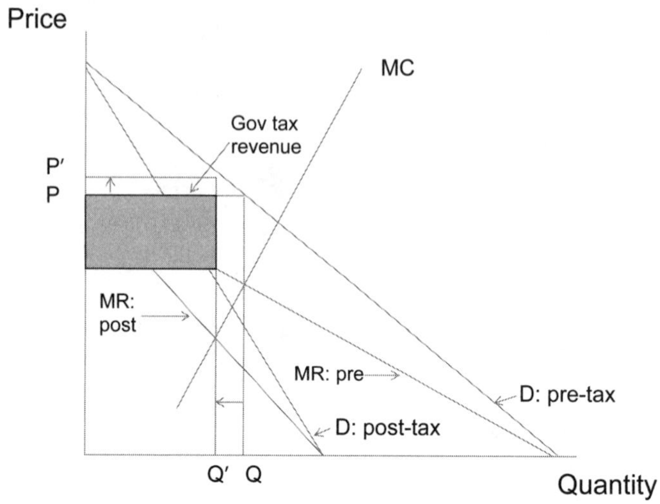

Source: W. Lesser.

d. Lessons

While there is considerable detail involved even at this initial level of analysis, the major insights from this modeling of the effects of taxes/regulatory costs can be summarized succinctly:

- Under competition taxes raise prices, reducing quantities sold, which creates a social cost.
- The social costs imposed lead many to oppose regulations, but it is important to remember the models consider costs but not necessarily the nonmarket benefits generated.
- Costs are shared between producers and consumers; the one with the lower elasticity in terms of supply and demand absorbs the greater proportion.
- Modeling can be done as affecting either supply or demand—the outcome is identical.
- Again in a competitive sector, the form of the tax (unit, lump sum, or ad valorem) at the same tax level makes little difference. Ad valorem (sales) taxes, though, do make the supply less elastic, which increases the proportion of tax paid by the supplier.
- Tax effects in a monopoly are very different. Under a monopoly the seller absorbs most of the tax. Indeed with a unit tax the level can be set to tax away all the excess profit while leaving the level of price and quantity unchanged. An ad valorem tax raises the taxed amount relative to a unit tax of the same level.

4.2 INTRODUCTION TO ANALYTICAL METHODS

Developing these theoretical models is one thing, but measuring what actually occurs is another. This subsection provides an overview of how the assessments of outcomes are actually done. I begin with a brief introduction to the major methodologies used to calculate the costs and benefits of regulation, including those for valuing nonmarket goods and for placing a value on a human life. We then examine aggregate government costs and benefit studies as reported by agencies to the Office of Management and Budget, followed by a more detailed look at a particular study. The subsection concludes with a brief overview of third party, principally academic, studies to provide a flavor of that literature.

Please note that no claim is made here to assess the "weight of the evidence" regarding the overall balance of costs and benefits of regulation. That is simply too broad and uncertain an undertaking to be attempted in this context. Readers interested in this aspect of regulation are directed to Viscusi, Harrington, and Vernon[1] for further information.

a. Introduction to Analytical Methods

In 2000, Congress passed the Regulatory Right-to-Know Act (31 USC 1105) as a part of the Treasury Department's Fiscal Year (FY) 2001 appropriations bill. The act makes permanent—similar reports had been requested annually from 1997 on—a requirement for the White House Office of Management and Budget (OMB) to submit to Congress annually a report on the costs and benefits of federal regulations for the previous year. OMB is to provide estimates of costs and benefits by major rule and by agency and agency program. OMB is also to tally the costs and benefits of all regulations adopted in a given year in order to provide aggregated figures to Congress.

The act depends in part on Executive Order 12866 (September 30, 1993), "Regulatory Planning and Review," which, among other mandates, requires agencies to adopt regulations only when "required by law, are necessary to interpret the law, or are made necessary by compelling public need, such as material failures of private markets to protect or improve the health and safety of the public, the environment, or the well-being of the American people." In the process, "agencies [are to consider] all costs and benefits of alternative regulatory approaches" (Section 1). To these mandates, Executive Order 13563 (January 18, 2011) adds a requirement when allowed by law to "adopt a regulation only upon a reasoned determination that its benefits justify its costs" (Section 1(b)1). Readers are reminded that law does not allow all agencies to consider costs and benefits when adhering to regulations—see this chapter, Section 4.2b. Additionally, agencies are required to consider how best to promote retrospective analysis of "rules that may be outmoded, ineffective, insufficient, or excessively burdensome" (see this chapter, Section 4.2b).

Agencies not required to report to the OMB under Executive Order 12866 must do so to the Government Accountability Office (GAO) under the Small Business Regulatory Enforcement Fairness Act of 1996 (PL 104–121, March 29, 1996, as amended). These so-called independent agencies have jurisdiction largely over financial matters and include the Federal Reserve System and the Securities and Exchange Commission, among others. They differ on requirements for cost and/or benefit reporting. Finally, the Unfunded Mandate Reform Act of 1995 (PL 104–4, March 22, 1995 Sec. 202) requires federal agencies to report prior to adoption on rules which will cost state, local, or tribal governments, or the private sector more than $100 million annually (adjusted for inflation). The OMB works with those agencies to assure compliance.

Two years following then President Clinton's signing of Executive Order 12866, the OMB's Office of Information and Regulatory Affairs released an overview of "'best practices' for preparing the economic analysis of a significant regulatory action called for by the Executive Order."[2] That overview provides a basis for this explanation of accepted analytical methods for calculating the costs and benefits of regulations. More detailed discussions of analytical methods are placed in boxes in the text.

Here only the means of calculating costs and benefits are considered—recognizing that the distinction between them is somewhat arbitrary, as a cost can be considered a negative benefit. So it is the maximization of *net* benefits to which regulators strive, as required by the Executive Order. Agencies are to adopt a regulation "only upon a reasoned determination that the benefits of the intended regulation justify its costs."[3] Just how that determination is reached is not considered here. The OMB does caution however that cost-benefit ratios, the common way that net benefits are presented, should be used with care. "Selecting the alternative with the highest cost-benefit ratio may not identify the best alternative, since an alternative with a lower cost-benefit ratio than another may have higher net benefits."[4]

The OMB-endorsed approach consists of the following key steps, which are explored in turn:

- Baseline
- Discounting
- Risk and uncertainty
- Distributional effects and equity
- Valuing benefits for directly traded products
- Valuing benefits for indirectly traded products
- Valuing nontraded goods
- Nonfatal illness and injury
- Fatal risks

Baseline

"The benefits and costs of each alternative must be measured against a baseline. The baseline should be the best assessment of the way the world would look absent the proposed regulation."[5] The baseline calculation must consider that other factors may as well change during the period of analysis; for example, other regulations may be adopted or the market may change. In some cases more than one baseline may be used.

The baseline will often depend on scientific calculations. In the air pollution cost-benefit example given below (Section 4.2c), for example, meteorological models are used to project the future levels of ozone with and without the proposed control regulations.

Discounting

The stream of costs and benefits associated with a regulation will occur at different points in time. Smokestack scrubbers, for example, must be installed prior to reducing particulate emissions. Simply adding up annual costs and benefits then gives an incorrect representation of their consequences given preferences for consumption today over tomorrow, as well as the impacts of inflation. Moreover, if costs or benefits continue indefinitely (at least for purposes of the analysis), then unadjusted values will become infinite, which is not very useful for policy-making decisions.

The OMB posts annual estimates of real interest rates (those from which the inflation premium has been removed) and utilizing economic assumptions from the current year federal budget. These real rates are to be used for discounting constant-dollar flows, as is often required in cost-effectiveness analysis such as cost-benefit analysis. For 2013, the ten-year discount rate is 2.0 percent.[6] The discounted value is an estimate of the *opportunity cost of capital*, the before-tax return to incremental private capital. A basic explanation of methods for discounting cash flows is available from any introductory finance book; it also can be found at online sources.[7]

Risk and Uncertainty

Future events frequently cannot be forecast with certainty, leading to a lack of precision in calculating the costs or benefits of those events. The unpredictable costs may be physical or scientific events (temperature; efficiency of scrubbers in removing soot) or values (future price of oil independent from inflation; future interest rates).

If the likelihood of an event occurring is known, then that is referred to as a risk. For example, if the lifetime likelihood of developing lung cancer for smokers is 20 percent higher than for nonsmokers, then the smoking-induced risk is 20 percent. Or, more simply, the risk of losing a bet on a coin toss is 50 percent, as the chance of a coin landing showing heads (or tails) is 50 percent. If the likelihood is not known, or not known with any precision, then the situation is known as uncertainty. For instance, the effect of global warming on sea levels fifty years from now is uncertain.

Estimating the benefits and costs of risk-reducing regulations includes two components: a risk assessment that, in part, characterizes the probabilities of occurrence of outcomes of interest, and a valuation of the levels and changes in risk experienced by affected populations as a result of the regulation. For example, if property values are reduced due to high levels of smog, smog-reducing regulations should raise those values. The amount of the increase will depend on the amount of smog reduction actually achieved (risk assessment), and the specific relationship of smog levels and property values (valuation), along, of course, with the general drivers of property values like interest rates, and so forth.

If either or both of those values are unknown, there are several approaches that can be followed. One is to use the best estimates available but be very explicit about the assumptions used. That will allow readers to understand how the estimates were derived and permit them to compute alternative values using substitute assumptions.

A second common approach is to employ sensitivity analysis. Say, for example, a regulation will reduce a cancer risk by an amount estimated to be between 10 and 20 percent. With sensitivity analysis the cost-benefit ratio can be calculated using the 10 and 20 percent values (and possibly 15 percent as well), which will indicate how sensitive the result is to the value picked. When there are more than a few uncertain values, then a more systematic, computer-based approach known as Monte Carlo analysis may be employed.

There is another matter to which risk applies: the computation and use of the risk premium. Imagine you are offered \$5 if you toss heads or \$10 if you toss heads twice in a row. To the statistician, the two are identical in value because coin tosses are independent with the chance of a head on each toss being 50 percent. Then: $\$5 \times \frac{1}{2} = \$2.50$ while $\$10 \times \frac{1}{2} \times \frac{1}{2} = \$2.50$.

Many players, however, will choose the single toss option believing (incorrectly) that the chance of tossing heads after having just produced one is somehow less than 50 percent. If players will select the second option only if the payoff is raised to \$12 from \$10, then the risk premium, the required compensation for taking on a higher perceived risk, is \$2. With this premium we can easily calculate the perceived probability of tossing the second head: $\$12 \times 1/x = \$2.50$, $1/x = 0.21$, so $x = 4.75$ rather than the correct value of 4 ($\frac{1}{2} \times \frac{1}{2} = \frac{1}{4}$). Now assuming all players believe the odds of tossing heads on the first try is 50 percent, then the perceived odds of the second head in a row is $0.5 \times y = 0.21$, $y = 0.42$, rather than the actual 0.5. The risk premium is used for, among other things, determining how much compensation is required for individuals to work in less safe occupations.

Distributional Effects and Equity

Often, those who pay the costs of regulation are different from the beneficiaries. When considering power-plant scrubbers, those living on the leeward side of the smokestacks will benefit most while all users of power produced by the plant, and possibly the shareholders, pay the costs. Thus the regulation has the effect of redistributing costs and benefits, which raises equity issues.

Distributional consequences can be very important—it is often said that dumps are located in poorer neighborhoods because the residents are less effective at petitioning the political process—but there is no generally accepted methodology for determining when one distribution is more or less equitable than another. As a result no decisions on equity are included in regulation cost-benefit analysis, although the redistributional effects can be described.

Valuing Benefits for Directly Traded Products

A product or service is worth what people are willing to pay for it. When products and services are sold on open markets, the true and best measure of people's willingness to pay is the market price. This applies unless the market is somehow distorted, as, for example, with solar collectors, which presently are subsidized by the government to encourage use. In that case, the opportunity cost to the homeowner is less than the true opportunity cost consisting of both the paid amount and the subsidy value. But in general, market prices are excellent measures of directly traded product values.

Valuing Benefits for Indirectly Traded Products

Sometimes products and services are traded, marketed, but as composite goods when the interest is in one of the component parts. A convenient example to use is the effect of air pollution obscuring a view on house prices. A smog-reducing regulation increases the value of those homes, which should be included in the benefit calculations. But how can this benefit be valued?

A second (though not regulation-related) example is valuing the stocking of a stream with trout. The costs are evident. But, unless there is an entrance fee for public access to the stream, how is the benefit to be measured?

In the trout stream example, the common approach to use is the *travel-cost method.* Under that method, the value is what fishermen in aggregate pay to reach the stream, ideally measured in years before and after the stocking took place.

For the pollution-house price example, the standard approach to use is known as *hedonic pricing.* Imagine there is a large data set for house sales in an area where some views are affected by smog and others are not. The data set includes the sale price, neighborhood, size, number of bedrooms, garage, pool, and so forth, while the researcher adds measures of pollution using a standard measure such as miles of visibility on a smoggy day. Applying a statistical technique known as regression analysis, it is possible to value each of the components of the house price separately, including the effect of pollution levels on visibility. That measure then becomes the benefit value for reducing pollution. There are, to be sure, assumptions made and limitations to the analysis, including the need for a large data set with variations in visibility, as well as the assumption that enhancing visibility will not so greatly expand the houses available in a particular category of the market that prices will crash. Even with these limitations, hedonic pricing analysis provides a useful pricing tool in multiple instances.

Finally, the *risk premium* described above can be used to place a value on, say, hazardous occupations and hence on the benefit from reducing those hazards. Consider times past when logs were transported by river and on occasion would form enormous jams. The loggers who freed the jams, often by climbing over the piles and placing dynamite charges, took enormous risks and were the best-paid members of the crews (Figure 4.7). The difference between their salaries and those of equally skilled but safer logging operators is the risk premium, a measure of the market rate for taking on greater risk.

At present one could evaluate pay levels for other dangerous occupations such as mining, fishing, and farming for measures of the risk premium and use that information to value the benefits of reducing risks through regulation. One simple example: a leading cause of death and injury for farmers was rollovers by tractors. When regulations

Figure 4.7 **What Would You Have to Be Paid to Work on a Log Jam?**

Source: Wikimedia Commons. Original author Benjamin Franklin Upton, "On the drive, Pineries of Minnesota."

required manufacturers to install roll bars, risks were reduced along with, presumably, wages for farm workers.

As with all the other approaches described here, there are limitations, assumptions, to the risk premium approach. For example, workers must have (and recognize that they have) alternative employment opportunities before one occupation could be considered more risky than another. Certainly the Welsh coal miners in the novel *How Green Was My Valley* knew a working life in the mines resulted in black lung, but they had few options other than to take those jobs.

With greater information and mobility in the twenty-first century, options are enhanced, but labor mobility is far from perfect, meaning many are caught in risky occupations through lack of choice. Some though do seek out risky work, and risky lives in general—risk seekers. Put another way, there is some self-selection in risky job holders, so that surveying only those holding those positions may not represent an average valuation.

Finally, the amount of the premium is very dependent on income. Consider a simple case where the premium demanded is 10 percent, but the dollar amount is $4,000 for those earning $40,000, and $20,000 for those in the $200,000 income bracket. And since better-paying jobs tend to be less risky (lawyers, stockbrokers, doctors, and so forth), the survey sample will greatly affect the measured risk premium. Despite these limitations, the risk premium approach does provide a method for valuing workplace safety regulations in particular.

Valuing Nontraded Goods

If a product or service truly has no market, direct or indirect, then the only real way to valuate it is to ask individuals about their preference values. Of course, the technique, known as *contingent valuation* (CV), is not so simple as that and indeed requires sophisticated approaches to drafting the questions. The "contingent" part of the name refers to values for a specific hypothetical situation.

A CV study done in California attempted to measure the value of different degrees of water salinity in Mono Lake. Mono Lake, an ancient lake (over 1 million years old) in California near Yosemite National Park, is particularly known for its spectacular "tufa towers," calcium-carbonate spires and knobs (Figure 4.8). It has no outlet (hence the salt buildup), but its freshwater inflow over the years has been diverted to Los Angeles residents.

As a prominent water body in a dry region, Mono Lake is a major bird habitat and rookery, and it has been designated as part of the Western Hemisphere Shorebird Reserve Network. Over 100 species use its waters and many islands. Waterfowl though are scarce, with the number of ducks falling from over 1 million to only 14,000 over a forty-year period to 1988.[8] The decline is attributed to the rising salinity due to the high water diversion; as salt levels continue to rise, other bird species will be unable to use its water as well. The catch is that reducing the water diversions will require more costly substitute sources, including conservation and recycling. This brings us to the application of contingent valuation: Does maintaining a bird habitat justify the costs in the eyes of residents?

The California State Water Resources Control Board was eventually mandated by court order in the 1990s to release more water to the lake to raise the level by 20 feet.[9] By 2011, it had risen by 13 feet. By 2014 an additional 13 feet rise was needed to reach the specified "stabilization" level of 6,392 feet.[10] But of interest here is the process of determining how area residents valued the nonmarketed use of the lake as a bird habitat.

Figure 4.8 **Mono Lake**

Source: Mono Lake in California, NASA Landsat 7 image. Available at http://americanliberalprogressiveidea.blogspot.com/2009/10/primordial-earth-most-likely-was.html.

The Control Board conducted two rounds of surveys, one by mail and one in-person survey of California residents, followed by a more systematic contingent valuation analysis by the firm that was completing the environmental impact statement (Example 4.1). The results for the initial survey indicated that benefits (willingness to pay) exceeded costs by an order of fifty (see Example below). The follow-up analysis supported the costs of an intermediate water level increase.[11] The results are believed to have contributed to the acceptance of the water restoration project, although many other factors were involved as well.

A second CV example considers the costs and benefits of banning a fungicide called SOPP (sodium ortho-phenlyphenate) Soap, which is used as a postharvest cleaner for grapefruits.[12] Banning the suspected carcinogen would increase spoilage by an estimated

EXAMPLE 4.1: CONTINGENT VALUATION ESTIMATES OF MONO LAKE WATER LEVELS

Mail Survey: A mail survey was conducted by the California State Water Resources Control Board. Five hundred and fifty-eight residents received a mail survey stating that biologists indicated a higher lake level was required to maintain a food supply for migratory and nesting birds, and were asked their willingness to pay extra for substitute water supplies so that less water could be diverted from the lake.

With follow-up there was a 44 percent response rate with an average annual valuation of $156, or, aggregated across all California households, fifty times the water diversion costs of $26 million annually.

Visitor Survey: Also conducted by the Control Board, every fifth visitor (152 in total) was asked the same questions, leading to an annual household valuation over twice as high as the valuation gathered from the mail survey. (That higher result is expected, as generally those who visit a site value it more than the general public).

Contingent Valuation: Mail and phone respondents were shown photo-simulations of three lake levels:

1. Current
2. Diversion reduced by 50 percent
3. Really substantial diversion reduction

The respondents were asked their willingness to pay for each level. Results indicated a positive cost-benefit result for the intermediate level of reduction.

10 percent, which constitutes the major cost to growers/packers (in terms of lost product) and consumers (due to higher prices for a smaller supply). For growers/packers the higher consumer prices offset some of the supply reduction value with a net estimated annual loss of $9 million. Consumers were estimated to sustain annual consumer surplus losses of $18.6 million. Given the limited number of substitute fungicides available, the variable costs were found to be negligible (86 percent were already using the best alternative option). In the longer term, though, heavier usage of the remaining fungicides would promote resistance and impose significant costs if new substitutes were not identified. That possible cost, however, was not quantified.

To calculate the benefits, a two-part survey was employed. The first stage involved a telephone survey to identify fresh-grapefruit consumers in all fifty states. The follow-up survey of 548 purchasers (response rate 78 percent) utilized a contingent valuation method for eliciting the willingness to pay (WTP) for safer grapefruits. Conveying the risk-reduction benefits of a ban on SOPP was a complex matter because most respondents were unfamiliar with the risks involved, which were relatively small. Specifically, the Environmental Protection Agency (EPA) estimated the cancer risk of eating SOPP-treated grapefruits at 10/100,000 while the risk from eating grapefruits treated with TBZ (thiabendazole), the alternative fungicide, were 10/10,000,000. The risk of a fatality was set at half of the cancer rate.

To convey this information in a comprehendible form, the "risk ladder" method was applied. Under that system, the risk of contracting cancer from various foods, including treated grapefruits, is presented in ascending order. Respondents were then asked to circle the additional price per fruit they were willing to pay to forgo treatment with SOPP.

The computed average WTP for the safer product was 38 percent, or 28 cents (19 cents if nonrespondents were added at a presumed WTP value of zero). Using the lower (conservative) figure and multiplying by the number of affected grapefruits yields a benefit estimate of over $80 million annually, a figure well in excess of the computed costs. In terms of the value of life imputed from these figures, the 19-cent WTP was multiplied by the average per capita grapefruit consumption by the average lifespan of 75.3 years to give a value of $204.22. That figure was then divided by the risk reduction of 4.995 per 100,000 grapefruit consumers, giving a value of statistical life (VSL) figure of $4.1 million (1995 dollars). While the $4.1 million figure is not high compared to the current median value of $7.4 million (see explanation below), the median increase in WTP of 38 percent does seem high. The researchers do note that had the WTP questions been based on a year's supply rather than individual fruits, the value would likely have been lower and the estimated benefits and VSL correspondingly reduced.

Contingent valuation studies in general have several limitations. Particular to these studies is the matter of framing the questions so as not to generate bias against a particular answer. In another context, I once saw a marketing study which reported that sophisticated people typically preferred darker colors—which color did the respondent prefer? Guess the answer.

Other problems are so-called whole-part bias: if a participant is asked to estimate the value of two halves and then also the whole, typically the valuation of the parts exceeds the whole. More perplexing, most respondents will place a higher value on their willingness to accept a payment to give up an object than they will offer for it. This anomaly can be explained (at least in part) by an inertia component of human nature, but it does highlight the importance of how questions are asked.

Those issues are in addition to the general concerns about survey results, which include:

- Sample size and representativeness—increased issues with cell-phone-only households, unwillingness to respond to questionnaires

- Self-reporting bias—imperfect recall and tendency to answer in ways intended to please the questioner
- Ordering of questions
- Gap between what people say they will do and their actual behavior
- Interpreting nonresponse and protest answers

There are statistical methods for overcoming some of these limitations, but they can be costly and are not always followed.

Nonfatal Illness and Injury

This category includes the valuation of regulations to reduce workplace injuries or injuries associated with auto accidents, home falls, and the like. The common approach for valuation is the direct one of calculating medical and other costs associated with an illness or injury, or costs for averting them (installing seat belts).

Excluded from those costs are valuations for pain and suffering, which incidentally are typically the largest component of many injury lawsuits. The value of leisure time lost is also not captured. Finally, the value of associated losses in production is included—say an assembly line is stopped for a time in the wake of an injury. The wage compensation for accepting riskier jobs approach described above can also be applied.

Fatal Risks

Many regulatory benefits are based on the value of lives saved, and although it may seem repugnant to place a value on a life, in fact that is done all the time. Two approaches to placing a value on human lives are considered here, one better suited for individual lives and the second appropriate for more aggregate analysis, although they can and are used interchangeably.

The first approach to consider is based on economic losses for a premature death—the lifetime earning approach. Example 4.2 describes how the lifetime earning approach was applied to calculating benefits for 9/11 victims. That compensation plan was based on a special law, the Air Transportation Safety and System Stabilization Act establishing the September 11th Victim Compensation Fund of 2001. The fund specified the methodology to be applied in calculating benefits and so it is not intended as an example directly applied to regulation benefits, but rather to document how such benefits were/are calculated, including the issues that arise. In that instance, the 2,880 claims averaged $2 million, but the figure is based on the earning potential of the particular population of individuals afflicted by the attacks.

The second more population-based approach to valuing a life is known as *value of a statistical life* (VSL) as there is no application to an identifiable individual. VSL applies to

EXAMPLE 4.2: CALCULATING COMPENSATION UNDER THE SEPTEMBER 11TH VICTIM COMPENSATION FUND PROVISIONS[13]

Compensation is to be based on the extent of harm to victims and their families, including any "economic . . . losses."

- Starting point is income from a base period (generally the average of 1999–2001); for those with no work history the average income of all U.S. wage earners was used.
- Incomes were specified to increase by an annual inflation amount (2 percent), an annual productivity adjustment (1 percent) and age-specific growth rates (higher in early career than later).
- Adjustments were made for the duration of the work life (i.e., age at the time of death).
- Deductions were made for any employer-provided benefits, for self-consumption using national data, and for tax liabilities.
- Annual figures were adjusted to present value using after-tax discount rates.
- The value of home-based services (cooking, cleaning, child care, etc.) was computed based on purchased service rates, and added; for those working full-time in the home, the value of these services served as their income value.

small changes in the risk of death and begins with a willingness-to-pay valuation for avoiding a particular risk. Say that risk is contracting asthma and the proposed regulation will reduce the risk of death by 0.1 percent.[14] The calculated willingness to pay for avoidance is $15,000. The VSL = willingness to pay/change risk = $15,000/.001 = $15 million.

At present, the calculated VSL used by the EPA (2006 dollars, adjusted for inflation) is $7.4 million, as derived from the mean (Weibull distribution) of twenty-six prior studies. The value has a standard deviation of $4.7 million, indicating it is not very precise.[15] By 2010 the value of $9.1 million was used by the EPA.

Different agencies use different VSLs in part based on the different emotional turmoil caused by deaths of various causes: for example, for cancer there is a proposed 50 percent "cancer premium." The Department of Homeland Security has suggested that the value of preventing deaths from terrorism might be 100 percent higher than that of preventing other deaths.[16] Clearly, the value placed on VSL is not very precise and is subject to multiple interpretations, but placing some sort of value on a human life is necessary and instrumental for placing a dollar figure on regulatory benefits.

b. Aggregate Government Cost and Benefit Estimates

For background on regulatory agency mandates to calculate the costs and benefits of regulations anticipated to cost more than $100 million across all sectors of the economy (federal, state, local and private), see Section 4.2a.

As a beginning point, some concept of the sheer size of the regulatory system in the United States will be helpful. According to testimony given at hearings for the Regulatory

Table 4.1

Federal Regulatory Spending Summary, Selected Fiscal Years, 1960–2013 ($ million current dollars)

	1960	1970	1980	1990	2000	2010	2011	2012	2013
Social Regulation									
Consumer H&S	102	222	1,252	1,830	3,650	7,389	7,699	8,634	8,976
Homeland Security	145	335	1,589	3,359	7,874	22,863	23,481	26,166	25,004
Transportation	42	177	550	810	1,493	3,062	3,002	3,338	3,094
Workplace	36	115	748	1,012	1,428	2,083	2,098	2,103	2,151
Environment & Energy	29	248	1,919	4,118	6,673	8,345	8,523	8,399	8,363
Economic Regulation									
Finance & Banking	40	98	392	1,309	1,968	3,167	3,584	4,128	4,193
Individual-Specific	91	276	486	513	744	1,258	1,290	1,416	1,443
General Business	48	113	357	727	1,674	3,754	4,102	4,960	5,510
TOTAL $	533	1,584	7,293	13,678	25,504	51,921	53,779	59,144	58,734
% Annual Change—Nominal		11.5	16.5	6.5	6.4	7.7	3.6	10.0	–0.7
% Annual Change—Real		8.5	8.9	2.2	4.3	5.4	-2.0	8.6	–2.1

Source: Susan Dudley and Melinda Warren, "Growth in Regulator's Budget Slowed by Fiscal Stalemate: An Analysis of the U.S. Budget for Fiscal Years 2012 and 2013." 2013 Annual Report, July 2012, Table 1. Regulatory Studies Center, George Washington University and Weidenbaum Center, Washington University (St. Louis). Available at http://wc.wustl.edu/files/wc/imce/2013regreport.pdf. Last visited 10/11/13.

Right-to-Know Act, regulation involves "more than fifty-five agencies, 125,000 rule-writers, and [a] $17 billion budget" producing more than 4,000 final rules every year.[17]

A snapshot like this, while effective at conveying the size of the U.S. regulatory machinery, says little about changes over time. Table 4.1 contains those data in percentage terms, in nominal and real values.

The very rapid increases of the earliest period, particularly to the EPA, seem a token of the past. More recent major increases have been focused on homeland security and financial regulation. The financial stimulus program was partly behind budget increases in FY2012 while banking regulatory costs jumped following the financial near-meltdown in 2008 and, previously, the savings and loan debacle (see Chapter 9, Section 9.4). The most recent budget declines are attributable to budget constraints in particular and the broad policy disagreements in Congress in general.

Clearly it is impossible to develop specific, precise cost and benefit estimates for such a vast undertaking. The OMB emphasizes that point in its 2012 report covering FY2011 by noting that the estimates "should not be taken to be either precise or complete."[18] Sources of possible error include erroneous assumptions, substantial uncertainty regarding likely consequences, and the lack of relevant information, as well as benefits and costs that cannot be quantified. Reductions based on disability discrimination are presented as an example of nonquantifiable benefits.

The OMB evaluated the aggregate costs and benefits for October 1, 2000, through September 30, 2010, for 105 major rules (benefits or costs exceeding $100 million annually), providing detailed cost and benefit estimates. Benefit estimates are available for between $132 billion and $655 billion in benefits and $44 billion and $66 billion in costs (in 2001 dollars).[19] These numbers reflect estimated budgetary impacts; it should be noted that in all but a few cases, estimated benefits far exceed costs.[20]

The distribution of benefits though is not uniform with the EPA's air pollution rules accounting for 62 percent to 84 percent of benefits and 46 percent to 53 percent of costs.[21] And most of that benefit is attributed to reductions in fine particulate matter.[22] On average, an estimated $5 billion have been added to private regulatory costs annually.[23]

Regarding major new rules established in FY2011, of the fifty-three reported, only twelve include detailed cost-and-benefit estimates. Of those (believed to represent the majority for FY2011), benefits are from $34.3 billion to $89.5 billion and costs are between $5 billion and $10.1 billion.[24] EPA rules again represent the largest share of benefits but not costs.

c. Specific Governmental Cost and Benefit Analysis

The intent here is to provide a detailed description of a federal agency's cost-benefit analysis of a rule or series of rules. In doing that, it makes sense to choose a major piece of legislation for which the analysis is likely to be more thorough. Hence the focus here is on air pollution rules, which constitute the majority of the calculated benefits and costs of federal regulation.

Specifically, the analysis reported was conducted by the EPA and applied to the Clean Air Act. The major benefits (and costs) are attributed to "fine particulate matter" reductions, which include acids (nitrates and sulfates), organic chemicals, metals, and soil or

Figure 4.9 **Smog in New York**

Source: Wikimedia Commons. Original author Dr. Edwin P. Ewing, Jr. 1988.

EXAMPLE 4.3: AIR QUALITY INDEX DEFINITIONS

What Is the Air Quality Index (AQI)?

The Air Quality Index (AQI) measures and reports daily on regional air quality. It tells you how clean or polluted your air is, and what associated health concerns you should be aware of. The AQI focuses on health effects that can happen within a few hours or days after breathing polluted air. EPA uses the AQI for five major air pollutants regulated by the Clean Air Act: ground-level ozone, particulate matter, carbon monoxide, sulfur dioxide, and nitrogen dioxide.

Air Quality Index (AQI)Scale

AQI Range	AQI Category	AQI Colors
0 - 50	Good	Green
51 - 100	Moderate	Yellow
101 - 150	Unhealthy for Sensitive Groups	Orange
151 - 200	Unhealthy	Red
201 - 300	Very Unhealthy	Purple

Source: Environmental Protection Agency, "Air Quality Index: A Guide to Air Quality and Your Health," EPA-456/F-09–002, August 2009.

dust particles (Figure 4.9). Fine particulate matter is the cause of smog, leading to "red alert" days as well as environmental, health, and quality of life effects, such as acid rain (see also Chapter 7, Section 7.3). Air-quality index definitions are shown Example 4.3 and Table 4.2 offers an overview of the health and environmental effects of the most common sources of air pollution.[25]

Over time there have been three such studies:[26]

1. Retrospective Study (1997) B/C 1970–1990, including 1997 amendments
2. First Prospective Study (1999) B/C 1990–2010, including the increments associated with the 1990 Clean Air Act amendments. Also considered were effects of reductions in stratospheric ozone depletion due to the phasing out of chlorofluorocarbons (CFCs).
3. Second Prospective Study (2011) 1990–2010, including the 1990 Clean Air Act amendments

The Clean Air Act as of 1990 is described in brief in Example 4.4 (p. 135). (For more detail see Chapter 7, Section 7.1.) Of the pollutants identified, the most widespread and persistent urban pollution problem is ozone. Over 100 million Americans live in cities that are not in compliance with the public health standards for ozone.[27] Note, however, that the Title V provisions which provide for pollution permits, and the trading of those permits, are the most significant administrative changes in the act.

Table 4.2 **Synopsis of Health, Environmental, and Climate Effects of Air Pollution**

Pollutant	Health Effects	Environmental and Climate Effects
Ozone (O_3)	Decreases lung function and causes respiratory symptoms, such as coughing and shortness of breath; aggravates asthma and other lung diseases leading to increased medication use, hospital admissions, emergency department (ED) visits, and premature mortality.	Damages vegetation by visibly injuring leaves, reducing photosynthesis, impairing reproduction and growth, and decreasing crop yields. Ozone damage to plants may alter ecosystem structure, reduce biodiversity, and decrease plant uptake of CO_2. Ozone is also a greenhouse gas that contributes to the warming of the atmosphere.
Particulate Matter (PM)	Short-term exposures can aggravate heart or lung diseases leading to symptoms, increased medication use, hospital admissions, ED visits, and premature mortality; long-term exposures can lead to the development of heart or lung disease and premature mortality.	Impairs visibility, adversely affects ecosystem processes, and damages and/or soils structures and property. Variable climate impacts depending on particle type. Most particles are reflective and lead to net cooling, while some (especially black carbon) absorb energy and lead to warming. Other impacts include changing the timing and location of traditional rainfall patterns.
Lead (Pb)	Damages the developing nervous system, resulting in IQ loss and impacts on learning, memory, and behavior in children. Cardiovascular and renal effects in adults and early effects related to anemia.	Harms plants and wildlife, accumulates in soils, and adversely impacts both terrestrial and aquatic systems.
Oxides of Sulfur (SO_x)	Aggravate asthma, leading to wheezing, chest tightness and shortness of breath, increased medication use, hospital admissions, and ED visits; very high levels can cause respiratory symptoms in people without lung disease.	Contributes to the acidification of soil and surface water and mercury methylation in wetland areas. Causes injury to vegetation and local species losses in aquatic and terrestrial systems. Contributes to particle formation with associated environmental effects. Sulfate particles contribute to the cooling of the atmosphere.
Oxides of Nitrogen (NO_x)	Aggravate lung diseases leading to respiratory symptoms, hospital admissions, and ED visits; increase susceptibility to respiratory infection.	Contributes to the acidification and nutrient enrichment (eutrophication, nitrogen saturation) of soil and surface water. Leads to biodiversity losses. Impacts levels of ozone, particles, and methane with associated environmental and climate effects.
Carbon Monoxide (CO)	Reduces the amount of oxygen reaching the body's organs and tissues; aggravates heart disease, resulting in chest pain and other symptoms leading to hospital admissions and ED visits.	Contributes to the formation of CO_2 and ozone, greenhouse gases that warm the atmosphere.
Ammonia (NH_3)	Contributes to particle formation with associated health effects.	Contributes to eutrophication of surface water and nitrate contamination of ground water. Contributes to the formation of nitrate and sulfate particles with associated environmental and climate effects.
Volatile Organic Compounds (VOCs)	Some are toxic air pollutants that cause cancer and other serious health problems. Contribute to ozone formation with associated health effects.	Contributes to ozone formation with associated environmental and climate effects. Contributes to the formation of CO_2 and ozone, greenhouse gases that warm the atmosphere.
Mercury (Hg)	Causes liver, kidney, and brain damage and neurological and developmental damage.	Deposits into rivers, lakes, and oceans where it accumulates in fish, resulting in exposure to humans and wildlife.
Other Toxic Air Pollutants	Cause cancer; immune system damage; and neurological, reproductive, developmental, respiratory, and other health problems. Some toxic air pollutants contribute to ozone and particle pollution with associated health effects.	Harmful to wildlife and livestock. Some toxic air pollutants accumulate in the food chain. Some toxic air pollutants contribute to ozone and particle pollution with associated environmental and climate effects.

Source: EPA, "Air Pollution," p. 4. Available at http://www.epa.gov/airtrends/2010/report/airpollution.pdf.

EXAMPLE 4.4: OVERVIEW OF THE CLEAN AIR ACT INCLUDING THE 1990 AMENDMENTS

Title I: The Clean Air Act requires states to make constant formidable progress in reducing emissions. It further requires the federal government to reduce emissions from cars, trucks, and buses; from consumer products such as hairspray and window-washing compounds; and from ships and barges during loading and unloading of petroleum products.

The federal government must also develop the technical guidance that states need to control stationary sources.

Title II: Tighter pollution standards for emissions from automobiles and trucks to reduce tailpipe emissions of hydrocarbons, carbon monoxide, and nitrogen oxides on a phased-in basis were established, beginning in model year 1994.

Automobile manufacturers are required to reduce vehicle emissions resulting from the evaporation of gasoline during refueling.

Fuel quality is controlled in part by requiring cleaner fuel (so-called reformulated gasoline), with stricter standards imposed on the nine cities with the most severe ozone problems. Scheduled reductions in gasoline volatility and sulfur content of diesel fuel are required.

Title III: Title III gives a list of 189 toxic air pollutants for which emissions must be reduced.

The EPA must issue "Maximum Achievable Control Technology" (MACT) standards for each listed source category. Unlisted categories of pollutants must be controlled within ten years.

Title IV: Title IV mandates a permanent 10-million-ton reduction in sulfur dioxide (SO_2) emissions from 1980 levels in two phases.

The first phase (effective 1995) requires 110 power plants to reduce emissions to 2.5 pounds of SO_2/mmBtu x an average of their 1985–1987 fuel use. Special five-year allowances are specified for plants in Illinois, Indiana, and Ohio.

The second phase (effective in year 2000) requires approximately 2,000 utilities to reduce emissions to a rate of 1.2 pounds of SO_2/mm Btu x the average of their 1985–1987 fuel use.

The law allows utilities to trade allowances within their systems and/or buy or sell allowances to and from other affected sources.

Title V: Title V introduces an operating/tradable permits program.

Title VI: Under the provisions of Title VI, the EPA was required to ensure that Class I stratospheric ozone-depleting chemicals (CFCs, halons, and carbon tetrachloride methyl chloroform) be phased out by 2000–2002. Class II chemicals (HCFCs) will be phased out by 2030.

Title VII: Title VII enhances enforcement provisions.

It is the Second Prospective Study,[28] the most recent and detailed, that is evaluated here. The report objectives include:[29]

- Estimate the direct costs and benefits of the Clean Air Act, with emphasis on the incremental effects of the 1990 amendments. Direct costs are defined as the first-order economic effects, like the costs of purchasing, installing, and operating pollution control equipment, while a direct benefit is the reduction of a pollution-related health effect.
- Gauge the economy-wide effects, including the effects on the overall growth of the U.S. economy and the economic well-being of American households. This objective adds to direct costs and benefits indirect ones, such as the higher costs of producing other goods due to, say, the cost-based increase in electricity; on the benefit side, an example of an indirect benefit is an improvement in worker productivity attributable to reduced pollution-related sick days.
- Be as comprehensive as possible within budget and data limitations by considering a wide range of human health and welfare issues, and ecological effects.
- Assess the limitations and uncertainties of the analysis.

The major benefits of the Clean Air Act, as well as the computed costs and benefits, are summarized in Example 4.5. Note that here we are particularly interested in the specifics of how these conclusions are reached.

EXAMPLE 4.5: OVERVIEW OF EPA SECOND PROSPECTIVE STUDY—MAJOR CONCLUSIONS BY 2020[30]

Costs of adhering to the Clean Air Act will reach $65 billion annually, the major components including:

- $28 billion for on-road vehicles, 40 percent of which is for fuel composition requirements
- $10 billion for electric utilities

Economic benefits are estimated to reach almost $2 trillion.

Health benefits of the Clean Air Act are as follows:

- Prevention of premature deaths of 23,000 Americans
- Prevention of over 1,700,000 incidences of asthma attacks and aggravation of chronic asthma
- Prevention of 67,000 incidences of chronic and acute bronchitis, 91,000 occurrences of shortness of breath, 4,100,000 lost work days, and 31,000,000 days in which Americans would have had to restrict activity due to air-pollution-related illness
- Prevention of 22,000 respiratory-related hospital admissions, as well as 42,000 cardiovascular (heart and blood) hospital admissions, and 4,800 emergency-room visits for asthma

(continued)

Air quality benefits include:

- Reduction of 14 million tons of volatile organic compounds (56 percent)
- Reduction of 23 million tons of nitrogen oxide (70 percent)
- Reduction of 20 million tons of sulfur dioxide (74 percent)
- Reflecting 75 percent reductions attributable to the 1990 amendments

Costs and benefits are not distributed uniformly, with:

- Larger urban areas receiving the greatest benefits, but also representing the largest population numbers
- Older industrialized areas (Northeast and upper Midwest) receiving the greatest benefits

Report Overview

An analysis of this magnitude—the report runs to 238 pages with additional technical appendices—is a complex undertaking, so it is appropriate first to lay out the study prior to considering the major components in detail. The basic approach is to develop two scenarios, one (actual) including the 1990 Clean Air Act amendments, and one (hypothetical) which assumes no change from 1990 levels except those due to a growing population and output.[31] Benefits are then associated with differences between the two trend lines.

Quantifying the costs and benefits requires an analysis on a sector-specific basis. Five were selected:

- Electricity generation
- Nonutility industrial (boilers, cement kilns)
- On-road vehicles and fuel
- Nonroad vehicles and fuel (aircraft, construction equipment)
- Area sources (wildfires, construction dust, dry cleaners)

Costs are computed for each of these sectors, plus local and "additional" costs are added. Additional costs are also local, but are less certain than the other local category. About half of total 2010 costs are attributable to the "On-road vehicles and fuel" sector, with electric utilities the second largest at $10 billion annually.[32]

Benefits are more difficult to compute, and hence are considered less specific, as is reflected in part by the large range in estimated values. Computations require several steps: the projection of the abatements on air quality and the subsequent quantification of those improvements in terms of lives saved, reduced work days lost, and so forth. Economics then become involved when valuing a human life—necessary if lives saved are to be quantified—and the value of work days saved. These are the direct, first-round effects.

Second-round effects consider that, for example, pollution reduction costs are passed on in part as higher electric rates, which raises the cost of most products. Higher fuel prices for the reformulated gas and lower particulate diesel have similar economy-wide consequences.

Computing these indirect costs requires a large-scale model of the U.S. economy. Quality-of-life factors such as increased visibility (smog reduction) involves additional economic approaches for valuing nonmarket goods (see Section 4.1a of this chapter).

Here, in terms of providing detail on the EPA's analytical approach, priority is given to the direct benefit estimates, including both human and ecological components. Cost calculations, while clearly important, are relatively less complex/more technical and are not covered here in detail. Additionally, no attempt is made to review the macroeconomic models for calculating the indirect benefits and costs. They are too complex for the technical backgrounds of the target audience for this book. Readers interested in other aspects of the report are directed to it.

Climate Modeling

The first step in the EPA analysis is climate modeling—projecting the concentration of pollutants from 1990 to 2020. This is done using an existing model—the Community Multiscale Model.[33] Inputs include hourly files of emission inventories, locations, and meteorological parameters like wind, precipitation, solar radiation, cloud cover, and so forth.[34] The model, which covers the lower forty-eight states, operates on a grid basis with three distinct grid systems. One applies to the entire forty-eight state region (36-kilometer grids), while two others at a higher level of detail (12-kilometer grids) cover the west and east with a slight overlap from North Dakota through Texas.[35]

The model is a "one-atmosphere" one, meaning it simulates "ozone, particulate matter, and other species in a single simulation which captures interaction effects among these pollutants."[36] There are differences in the composition across grid locations—Tucson, for example, ranks higher in dust due to the level of construction activity in this rapidly growing area.

Climate modeling is a complex task and is estimated to contribute "greater than 10 percent uncertainty, of indeterminate direction, to the overall uncertainty in benefit estimates."[37] Among the individual emissions, only secondary organic aerosol formation is believed to constitute a major source of uncertainty—but one that underestimates benefits.[38]

Human Health Benefit Calculation

The second step involves translating improved air quality into human health benefits (reduced premature deaths, heart disease, and respiratory illness), and monetizing those benefits. Specifically, three steps are followed using the EPA's Environmental Benefits Mapping and Analysis Program:

- Estimate individual exposure to outdoor air pollutants.
- Develop "concentration response functions" to map exposure levels to incidences of healthy effects.
- Value reduced health effects using third-party estimates.[39]

The exposure analysis draws directly on the climate modeling results (see immediately above), so we begin with the concentration response functions.

Epidemiological studies are used to relate the incidence of disease to exposure levels. The studies are both long and short term; the EPA uses only the long-term cohort studies (following individuals across time) as they are superior in associating differences in exposure levels as well as allowing for details on individual risk factors like smoking that otherwise would confound the statistical results. These studies are augmented by an EPA panel of experts who review and comment on the individual studies.[40] The studies include an estimate of the statistical error in the form of confidence intervals. However, the intervals relate only to the sampling errors, while another unquantified uncertainty exists: the relationship between health outcomes and exposure levels.[41]

The epidemiological studies are sufficiently detailed to allow the development of concentration response functions for only two health impacts: premature mortality and ozone. To the degree other possible health benefits are excluded due to a lack of information, the valuation results represent underestimates.[42]

The important—because it accounts for the great plurality of reported benefits—concentration response functions used by the EPA are used to measure premature deaths avoided. A Weibull distribution is used with a mean of 1.06 percent decrease in annual all-cause mortality per microgram per cubic meter of air (ug/m^3) reduction in particulate matter.[43] The Weibull is a versatile continuous distribution function frequently used in life-data analysis. The function treats all particulate matter as having equal potency, which is a simplification. A developing literature relates health effects to particular pollutants but at the time of this writing is insufficiently detailed to be incorporated in the analysis.

The report uses a "value of statistical life" approach, which is the value times the incidence times the population size. Calculation is of course not as simple as that, particularly as regards the method of calculating the value. There are several general approaches, each with its own benefits and limitations (see Section 4.2a of this chapter). The report applies a figure derived from twenty-six studies, five of which are contingent valuation studies, with the remainder of the wage-risk type. Since these kinds of studies solicit opinions on the reduction of specific life risks, each of which imposes a small risk, it is necessary to aggregate the individual risks until a life is represented—what is termed the "value of statistical life" approach.[44] For purposes of the report, the selected value is $7.4 million (2006 dollars) in 1990. Values for nonlethal benefits such as reduced hospital visits from asthma are also calculated.[45]

Two additional adjustments are required. One recognizes that a life-lengthening risk reduction today also enhances longevity in future years. Hence it is necessary to avoid the compounding of benefits to use a survival curve approach, which can be thought of as a continuous density distribution function. The survival curve approach, however, necessitates a national value of changes in air pollution exposure be used.[46] That is, important detail is lost. Moreover, an ideal system would consider individual differences in susceptibility— the very young and old for example are particularly vulnerable. Combined with that dimension, health status prior to exposure also affects susceptibility, as does the nature and context of the risk reduction.[47] None are possible to incorporate with the available levels of data and methodologies.

A second adjustment recognizes that an improvement in air quality today enhances health at some future date. That is, measuring benefits from the initiation of quality improvement activities would overstate the benefits. Note also that several of the components of the 1990 amendments are phased in over five or so years. To accommodate these factors, the benefits are counted with a lag:[48]

- 30 percent in year 1
- 50 percent in years 2–5
- 20 percent in years 6–20

The report includes a sensitivity analysis of the parameters used in the study, as well as a qualitative assessment of the component assumptions and methodologies. Most are considered to be "minor" while others lead to an underestimate of benefits. However, a few are judged to be potentially major and could overvalue the benefits.[49] No overestimate of the uncertainty of the analysis is provided.

Ecological Benefits

While presented last here and in the report, it was ecological benefits in the form of reduced acidification effects which led to the passage of the Clean Air Act. "[I]t was only after passage that it became clear that these provisions also provide very large human health benefits."[50]

The analysis is in two parts: qualitative (acid deposition, nitrogen deposition, tropospheric ozone, and hazardous air pollutants, notably mercury) and quantitative. The qualitative benefits make the uneven geographic distribution of benefits abundantly clear. Acidification is predominately a problem in Indiana, Ohio, and western Pennsylvania; nitrogen deposition affects the eastern half of the country, while ozone's notable effects are limited to the major East Coast megacities.[51]

Quantified benefits are provided for ozone depletion, visibility, and materials (structure) damage. Ozone reduces the growth of both annual and tree crops, and hence represents a loss to consumers. Producers, however, benefit because the inelasticity of demand for food in particular means that prices rise more than proportionally as production falls. The analysis is complicated by the option: farmers and timber growers have to switch to less sensitive crops. As a result, a partial equilibrium model, the Forest and Agriculture Sector Optimization Model, is used with elasticities inputted to account for induced changes in trade. While the model has been used and verified in multiple applications, this use is not one of them. The results show a projected 2010 increase in combined producer and consumer surplus of $10.7 billion (in 1996 dollars), or 32 percent. The agriculture sector receives all the benefits as production shifts to forestry while consumers bear all the costs.[52]

Reduced visibility affects individuals both in residential and recreational environments. As with health-benefit quantification, it is possible to quantify the value of visibility enhancements by using contingent valuation analysis. As before, estimates from academic studies are used.[53] Residential benefits are drawn primarily from the eastern half of the contiguous states, while recreational values relate to national parks. The results indicate total 2020 benefits of $67 billion (in 1996 dollars), with 72 percent attributable to residential benefits.[54]

The final quantified area is materials damage—for example, the corrosive effect of acid rain, and in particular sulfuric acid, on buildings and other structures. One affected monument is Cleopatra's Needle (which actually predates her lifetime by 1,000 years), moved from Egypt and erected in New York's Central Park in 1880 (Figure 4.10). "Within a matter of a few decades, the acid rain in New York had deformed it. It no longer had the sharp edges it used to have. Designs were faded. What appeared to be large dents in the stone figure were noticeable. This came from the acid rain."[55] Indeed recently a prominent Egyptian Egyptologist wrote to Mayor Bloomberg "describing how some of the hieroglyphs had all but disappeared and that if they couldn't take care of the obelisk, he'd 'take the necessary steps' to bring it back to Egypt."[56] And further, the Needle is made from granite, which is far more impervious to acid than limestone and marble.

Figure 4.10 **Cleopatra's Needle, Millennia Old, Has Over Merely a Century Been Severely Damaged by Acid Rain in New York City**

Source: Wikimedia Commons. Original author Captain-tucker. July 11, 2008.

The report quantified acid rain's effect through the Air Pollution Emissions Experiments and Policy analysis model, which quantified seasonal and average county by county (contiguous states only) concentrations for SO_2, along with other pollutants.[57] Translating SO_2 concentrations into a damage function requires a concentration/damage function. Four such functions were developed—one each for carbonate stone (sandstone and limestone), galvanized steel, carbon steel, and painted wood.[58] Only maintenance costs are considered, which misses the losses associated with monuments like Cleopatra's Needle, among others.

Costs were found to vary by region, due both to SO_2 concentration levels as well as density of structures, with the largest costs found in the Upper Midwest. Overall 2010 costs (in 1996 dollars) were calculated to be $110 million. This number obviously is relatively small compared to the other calculated damages, but it does increase across time.

Overall

The EPA concludes that benefits of the 1990 amendments significantly exceed their costs, and by such a large margin that the conclusion holds even when recognizing the significant uncertainties in the benefits estimations.[59] It should additionally be noted that in 2001 the Supreme Court decided unanimously that the EPA's authoring legislation allows it to establish standards solely on public health considerations without consideration of costs.[60]

4.3 THIRD PARTY/ACADEMIC STUDIES CRITICAL OF AGENCY VALUATION ANALYSIS

The intent of this subsection is to provide a flavor of the kinds of critiques directed to regulatory agency cost and benefit analyses. The literature is far too massive to provide a comprehensive overview here. (In the case of auto safety regulations alone, Google Scholar lists more than 18,000 articles.) Rather, the intent is to provide some exposure to the kinds of critiques which are being aired.

The treatment here goes beyond a mere reporting of those critiques by exploring the methods and assumptions used, and how they can affect the conclusions. Hopefully this approach will help students interpret the conclusions. Three categories of studies are considered: (1) methodological critiques, (2) the notion of unintended consequences and net-net benefits, and (3) public versus private benefits.

a. Critiques of the EPA Aggregate Cost-Benefit Study

Lutter and Belzer are very critical of the EPA report (see Section 4.2c of this chapter) on several counts.[61] They begin dramatically by noting "EPA's first report on rules issued from 1970 to 1990 gave a 'best estimate' of net benefits of $22 trillion—roughly the aggregate net worth of all U.S. households in 1990. We know of no professional economist independent of EPA who takes that estimate seriously."

As it happened, several prominent environmental economists in fact did take the estimate seriously and identified themselves—nine current and former members of the EPA's Advisory Council on Clean Air Compliance Analysis. They note that the comparison is "misleading in that it is comparing the discounted future value of a flow [of benefits from regulation] with a net asset value [household net worth]." When both benefits and income are calculated as streams of benefits, the EPA costs correspond to about 20 percent of the discounted stream of future personal income. "Many might feel that this is still too high. . . . But it is not wildly implausible."[62]

Lutter and Belzer continue with the following critiques of the report and the role of the Advisory Council:

- "Agency deliberately neglected the cost of complying with a well-known, and expensive requirement of the act and ignored its own scientific advisory board's advice to include indirect costs."
- "[EPA does] not analyze a range of reasonable policy alternatives."
- "EPA typically extrapolates [at the low end] the relationship between observable death and disease rates and high exposures." But "individuals often have thresholds of exposure below which they do not experience adverse health effects."
- "[The] scientific understanding of the health effects of [particulate matter] is notoriously weak."
- "Given that people spend a large majority of their time indoors, pollutants from indoor sources may be the true culprit," but the EPA uses outdoor values.
- "By failing to account for differences in wind speed, rain, or other determinants of intercity activity patterns," estimates of levels of pollutants may be overstated.
- "Premature mortality from PM [particulate matter] is associated with much older people" than the thirty-five to forty year olds who are the focus of the EPA analysis. This could bias upward the estimated value of a statistical life.
- "More puzzling is the ineffectiveness of the review performed by EPA's Science Advisory Board [SAB]. . . . SAB also lacked authority to determine that the report failed to meet minimum professional standards."

Recalibrating the costs with indirect costs included, Lutter and Belzer come up with an estimate of $104 billion, rather than the EPA's $27 billion estimate, which calls into question the balance of costs and benefits. Their overall conclusion? Studies of this kind done by in-house staff are "inherently self-serving. . . . Instead, Congress should direct policy-neutral institutions that are independent of regulatory agencies and protected from political interference to perform such evaluations."

The SAB members were not in agreement on many of these points. In particular, regarding their role, Brown et al. note, "But we could tell the [EPA] administrator that the results of the analysis were not valid or had no utility." That, though, was not their overall assessment: "[W]e believe that the study's conclusions are generally consistent with the weight of the available evidence."

At a more general level, the Committee on Risk Characterization and others in a 1996 report were highly critical of the use of cost-benefit analysis in the presence of uncertainty. "Unfortunately, the unrecognized sources of uncertainty—surprise and fundamental ignorance about the basis processes that drive risk—are often important sources of uncertainty, and formal analysis may not help if they are too large."[63] Among the suggested improvements are less analytical procedures and, significantly, more transparency in describing the processes used so that they can be better understood by readers.

b. Net, Net Benefits of Safety Regulation—Are They Negative?

As noted in the discussion of Executive Order 12866 (see Section 4.2a of this chapter), regulatory agencies are mandated to report annually the benefits and costs of their regulations with cost implications in excess of $100 million. This net is computed by subtracting the computed costs from the benefits, using the approach described above. But regulation is (frequently) expensive, with funds coming either directly (taxes) or indirectly (higher prices) from consumers, reducing available disposable income. (There is no room in this approach for considering efficiency enhancements from regulation which would increase disposable income economy-wide. Nor is there any mention of the job and other benefits generated from regulation-mandated expenditures). As health/preventative care is a purchased product like any other, reductions in available income reduce health care, which leads to increased mortality—or so goes one line of reasoning.

The general concept is certainly plausible, but measuring the degree to which this actually occurs is complex and requires a number of assumptions to calculate. Here, as representative of this approach, Hahn, Lutter, and Viscusi's analysis of twenty-four federal regulations from 1990 through mid-1998 is evaluated.[64] There is a clear statistical correlation between income and longevity, but for this analysis the relationship must be shown to be causal—higher incomes directly lead to greater longevity—and not a possible statistical anomaly as could happen, for example, as chronically sick people often have lower incomes. This causality is substantiated in large measure by showing that risky behaviors like drinking, smoking, and being obese are inversely related to income. Other possible explanations such as cumulative stress and depravations early in life are less coincident with the theory proposed.[65] A computed value of $15 million in increased national income is used to define one "saved" statistical life.[66]

This $15 million value is critical to the interpretation, so the source document was evaluated as well.[67] The authors use regression analysis to quantify the relationship between family income and three forms of risky behavior (or its absence): smoking, lack of regular exercise, and five or more drinks at an "episode." A survey was used to determine the beliefs regarding association between smoking and lung cancer, being overweight and heart disease, and drinking and cirrhosis, and so forth. The intent was to isolate the effects of beliefs regarding health risks from the income effects. The analysis shows that these three behaviors are indeed significantly associated with income, and by measuring in terms of the proportion of deaths (assuming they occur between thirty-five and seventy-nine) attributable to each, and a value of life leads to the reported estimate of $15 million increased national income being associated with a saved statistical life.

As a general matter, there are several ways theoretical/empirical studies like this can be critiqued. These include the data and statistical methods used, the structure/internal consistency of the analysis, and the theory/logic used in constructing the model. Here I focus on the "smoking" results because the basic parameters are quite clear: smoking is one of the major preventable health risks, and lower-income/education individuals smoke more in the United States. The empirical results are consistent here. The belief variables intended to separate income effects from understandings of health risks are also consistent—smokers are significantly less likely to believe smoking leads to lung cancer, heart disease, and so forth. One wonders if the survey captures a true understanding of smoking/health risks or rather reflects denial—one way to deal with a risk is to act as if it does not exist. In any case, there is one anomaly—a positive and significant association of heavy smoking with cirrhosis—that is not discussed. In general, though, the empirical results are straightforward.

A second line of inquiry is the way the analysis is structured and what that implies about underlying behavior, and cause and effect. For one thing, the proportion of deaths due to the three causes are fixed for the analysis, yet we know the smoking rate is and has been declining while the obesity rate increases. At minimum, this structural aspect means care must be used when projecting the results into the future. The model also implies that the distribution of income is fixed. This is important because the mechanism of the model says that rises in income (including but not limited to reduced regulatory costs) reduce risky behavior like smoking. For that to happen, income increases must reach lower income groups in some proportional way.

Yet recent data show that real national income increases since 1982 have largely benefited higher-income groups while lower-income quadrants have been flat or even declining; the share of national income captured by the bottom 80 percent of wage earners fell from 48.1 in 1982 to 38.6 in 2006.[68] Lower-wage earners were actually earning less in real terms, and the lower the base income the greater the decline in earnings. So a $15 million rise in national income would raise income for low-income workers—just those who smoke predominately—by a very small amount, raising questions about the theory of the model based as it is on rising incomes reducing risky behavior, given the reality of income distribution in the United States.

Conversely, Table 3.1 in the Hahn et al. study reports that regulations restricting the sale of tobacco products to minors cost $170 million (in 1995 dollars). As lower-income groups are disproportionally smokers, these regulations represent a wealth transfer not equally to all residents, but to lower-income groups in particular. The number is not large, but it does again raise the issue of including in the statistical analysis not only national family income, but measures of income distribution.

Finally, there is the issue of model development. Economic models based on theory reflect a particular kind of logic. The difficulty with logic is that it can be correct but still completely wrong in terms of reflecting the underlying cause and effect. The Lutter et al. study uses cross-sectional data to reflect time series decisions by individuals. That is, as national income rises by $15 million, one "statistical life" switches from risky to nonrisky behavior, reflected from the basis of a thirty-five-year-old to allow time for the risk to affect mortality. A limitation of this approach is that cigarettes are habit forming, highly so for many, while the habit is typically begun by teenagers (or else restricting access by minors would have limited effect). We also know that habits are affected by family and friends (otherwise known as peer pressure): if your parents smoke, you are more likely to smoke as well.

The authors include risk knowledge variable so as to "isolate the independent effect of income on risky behaviors as opposed to the role of health-risk information that may be correlated with one's income status."[69] However, as smoking is affected by one's environment, which is also correlated to income, then the study should have included a survey variable capturing whether smokers' parents smoked as well. Not doing so confounds the interpretation of the income variable as it reflects two distinct subgroups: those who have smoking parents and those who do not.

Returning to the Hahn et al. study and applying the $15 million income/mortality cutoff, the twenty-four examined regulations have an overall lifesaving effect. But that is because several are low cost with significant mortality-reducing effects, led by regulations limiting access by minors to tobacco products (noted above). Of the twenty-four, however, fewer than half have a net positive effect on saving lives, while thirteen are counterproductive. The most costly in terms of lives lost is an EPA regulation regarding land disposal of certain wastes.

In aggregate though, and accepting the studies analysis, the number of lives lost is but 600 annually ($9 billion/15 million),[70] not inconsequential but a limited basis for raising questions about the value of the entire regulatory system. And then the analysis applies to but 38 percent of causes of mortality.

Another sector to which the "counterproductive" charge of regulation—that users undercut the benefits by engaging in more risky behavior when other risks are reduced—has been applied is to auto-safety regulation. Peltzman, an economist, applied empirically the "Peltzman Effect" to the regulation of auto safety during the 1960s when it was being considerably enhanced. He concluded, based on both cross-section and time series analysis, that "The one result of this study that can be put forward most confidently is that auto safety regulation has not affected the highway death rate.". . . "On one interpretation, safety regulation has decreased the risk of death from an accident by more than an unregulated market would have, but drivers have offset this by taking greater accident risk."[71] What are among the risks identified? The growth of both drunken driving and driving by younger drivers.

However, one must be careful about applying statistical procedures to policy analysis, for reasonable changes in the empirical model can lead to major changes in the results, as was observed by Graham and Garber.[72] It is not the intent of this volume to parse the different conclusions of numerous academic studies, but as regards Peltzman's analysis, the interpretation of increased driving by the young as a risk factor associated with greater safety regulations can be questioned. Younger drivers statistically are more accident prone—insurance companies know this and charge accordingly. But in terms of numbers of young drivers, the period Peltzman evaluated, the 1960s, was the beginning of the baby boomer generation coming of age, when there simply were more young drivers. (This I know for certain because I was one of them.)

Hedlund reviewed a number of studies, including prior reviews, of what he calls "risk compensation" covering a number of consumer and workplace risk-reducing goods in the United States and internationally.[73] Most studies conclude that auto-safety regulations overall enhance the safety of occupants but not by as much as originally predicted. Nonoccupants (bicyclists, pedestrians) are either weakly benefited or have their safety reduced, but not by enough to offset all the benefits.

But perhaps the situation is indeed less complicated: while more than 90 percent of all motorists believe safety belts are good idea, only 87 percent actually use them routinely (2013 data). Of the approximately 33,000 passenger vehicle occupants who died in motor vehicle crashes in 2009, 44 percent were unrestrained. Over a fifteen-year period beginning in 1994, seatbelt use rose by 26 percentage points while deaths to restrained motorists fell by 7 percentage points,[74] aided by the introduction of other safety devices such as air bags (passive in this case, as they require no action by drivers). That is, the 16 percent of nonregular seat belt users accounted for 44 percent of daytime crash fatalities. These data do not support Peltzman's contention that safer cars lead to less safe driving. Rather, there seems to a small group of high-risk drivers who do not use seat belts and are involved in a disproportionally high percentage of serious accidents.

Peltzman also overlooked one other consumer response to an emphasis on auto safety—associating it with an inherently less safe car—which would deter any market response. One example was Ford's drop in sales in 1956, which has frequently been linked to its safety campaign—which may or may not be valid. Spurred by Cornell University's research efforts and the first year of its own safety crash program in 1955, Ford decided to go all out for safety in 1956 with its "Lifeguard design" advertising campaign. Standard equipment included stronger "double-grip" door latches, "deep-center" dished steering wheel, recessed instruments, and safety-designed door and window handles. For a few dollars extra, buyers could order a safety package consisting of padded dash and sun visors, as well as seat belts, first offered by Ford in 1955. Marketing studies soon showed that talk about safety actually turned off some buyers, but Ford continued to push such safety features right up until 1968, when the feds made it mandatory for all manufacturers.[75]

This same unintended consequences result is referred to as the "rebound" or "take-back" effect when applied, for example, to the tendency of drivers to use their cars more when fuel costs decline or for vehicles with better gas mileage. However the rebound *is* computed and explicitly included when calculating fuel expenditure savings from improved CAFE standards (see Chapter 3, Section 3.2). For the recent National Highway Traffic Safety Administration (NHTSA) cost-benefit study, the rebound effect was pegged at 10 percent, lower than prior studies due to recent evidence the effect is declining. Additional travel, of course, imposes further costs on society in the forms of noise, congestion, and more vehicle crashes. For the cost-benefit analysis the NHTSA calculated those costs as 7.8 cents per additional mile traveled (median value, 2007 dollars).[76]

c. Public versus Private Benefits

The EPA cost-benefit study presented above (see Section 4.2c of this chapter) is an example of a "public" benefit analysis as it applies to benefits (in that case from improved air quality) which accrue to all individuals within the project area without their needing to take any specific actions. Clean air enhances the lives of everyone, albeit not equally. Private benefits conversely accrue only to those who do something specific, such as purchase a product like gasoline.

The issue of public versus private benefits is important for the computation of benefits from the CAFE standards 2011—201516 (see Chapter 3, Section 3.2). As calculated by the NHTSA, the combined net benefits over the service life of the vehicles are $475,465–483,211 million (2010 dollars) (preferred alternative; 3 percent discount). Of the benefits, some three quarters come from (and accrue to) reduced gasoline purchases, while the remainder is attributable to a range of factors including reduced carbon dioxide emissions, lower world oil price, reduced military expenditures for patrolling oil production and shipping regions, as well as personal benefits from increased driving.[77]

Placing two-thirds of the benefits on personal savings from reduced gasoline use does, however, raise an ancillary question. Why if consumers desire higher-mileage cars is a regulation needed—can't the auto industry respond to demand through normal market mechanisms? That question does concern the NHTSA, which explains the seeming anomaly in terms of market failures. These can include consumers' misperceptions of the aggregate value of fuel savings, sharp discounting by consumers of future savings versus current costs, and purchase decisions made by short-term users like rental fleets, which do not pay fuel costs, or by corporate fleets, which quickly pass inefficient vehicles on to the used-car market. Similar explanations can be used for inefficient household appliances when purchased by landlords who do not pay electric charges.

4.4 CONCLUSIONS

Using economic models of taxes to provide insights into the consequences of imposed regulatory costs by no means answers all the questions one might have. But the models do make very clear that the effects are entirely different depending on whether the industry is competitive or a monopoly. For the former, some costs are borne by both consumers and suppliers, while with the latter most/all are paid by the monopoly. In competitive industries the share distribution is determined by the relative elasticities: the less elastic party pays more. Without even probing empirical estimates of elasticities we can surmise that demand for food and energy is relatively inelastic. The food system is overall reasonably competitive while energy is highly concentrated. That gives some insights into how regulatory costs in aggregate are shared in those key sectors.

One limitation of the economic modeling approach, practically if not conceptually, is that it is difficult to capture all the benefits generated. The overview of how the regulatory agencies go about that indicates why. Regulatory appraisal is detailed and complex. For air pollution control estimates, multiple steps are required across diverse scientific fields. First it is necessary to know the implications of pollutants on human health, ideally by degree of susceptibility, such as for the very young and very old. Then the distribution of the pollutants needs to be determined, at which point the economic valuation of the costs and benefits comes into play.

The economic calculations are themselves involved because many of the benefits are nonmarket benefits, such as the value of a human life. Several techniques have been developed to place a value on those components, many of which (known as contingent valuation) are based on asking a sample of individuals what their valuation would be. Asking individuals to place a value on an abstraction like the willingness to pay to avoid a low-probability illness raises some legitimate questions. It is well established that individuals overweigh low probability events (airplane crashes) while underweighing high-probability ones (lung cancer for heavy smokers). At the same time we value more highly what we have versus acquiring it (WTP versus WTA). Other valuation techniques have different but distinct flaws of their own.

This all suggests that many nonmarket value estimates likely are overstated, inflated. Are we all on average really willing to pay 38 percent more to avoid a small chance of illness from eating SOPP-tainted grapefruits? We may say yes with complete sincerity, but will our actions follow our rhetoric? At the same time the valuation techniques are the best available. Certainly all these limitations explain why the value of calculated benefits is spread across such a large range.

Approaching a consensus value then requires a comparison of a range of studies (meta-analysis). Those are available for specific assessments like VSL studies, but note the wide range of values generated. However, broad-based studies like assessments of pollutants are too complex and costly for multiple replications. That situation provides great opportunities for detractors, of whom there are many. While it is easy to identify limitations of the evaluation methods applied by the regulatory bodies, critics have been no more effective in identifying a superior methodology. More often their critiques are dismissive and picky; the different conclusions as likely to be attributable to variations in assumptions which are inherently no more and possibly less believable than those of the study they are critiquing.

Those who advise the net benefits of a regulation are less than what would result from universal compliance (the Peltzman Effect) have a legitimate point. We all have within ourselves the option to subvert any safeguard, and some of us do so whether knowingly or unknowingly. I am referring here to actions like driving faster because we believe accident survivability is improved. But to state the net benefit is less than the pre-regulation situation wildly overstates the situation.

Automobiles are indeed far safer as a result of regulation-imposed safety devices; one needs only look at declining auto accident death rates per mile traveled to verify that observation. Whether you believes the cost-benefit ratio of those safety improvements depends in a large part on how you views such valuations as VSL. The same can be said about removing pollutants. It is costly, but the benefits are real, even if difficult to quantify.

The Chinese are belatedly learning that lesson. A precise cost-benefit calculation, however, is something that will not be achievable for the foreseeable future.

4.5 STUDY QUESTIONS

1. Prepare a graph showing that in a monopoly an ad valorem tax raises more tax revenue than a unit tax of the same amount (see Figure 4.6).
2. The models of the effects of taxes on prices and quantities presented here apply to pure competition and simple monopoly. Yet few firms/industries precisely fit those extreme structural molds. How would you evaluate tax effects in industries that are neither purely competitive nor strict monopolies?
3. How would you respond to critics of regulation who point to economic models as showing that in competitive industries imposed regulatory costs always lead to socially inefficient deadweight losses?
4. As we have seen, in competitive markets the share of a tax burden paid by producers and consumers depends on their relative elasticities. Please locate some elasticity estimates in a sector or two (such as food or energy) and determine which group would pay the larger share.
5. The approach for valuing a life related to the victim of 9/11 is different from other approaches. What is the basis and justification for the differences?
6. What is the distinction between "risk" and "uncertainty"? How is it relevant for regulatory analysis?
7. Formally, cost-benefit analysis does not consider the redistribution effects of regulations as that would require a value judgment. However, many regulations recognize more vulnerable subpopulations like the very young and old, or the allergic, when setting standards. Does that approach indirectly involve a targeted redistribution of wealth?
8. The travel cost method measures (approximately) the value placed on a nonmarket good like a wilderness area by calculating the expenditures undertaken for utilizing it. Contingent valuation approaches, for their part, often elicit values placed on a resource by those who will never utilize it—something known as existence value. How comparable are the resultant values produced by the two approaches?
9. Identify a controversial environmental issue in your vicinity—say a plan for a new development—and prepare some willingness-to-pay questions which could be used to calculate a value for proceeding (or not proceeding).
10. The calculation of benefits from air pollution reduction as reported by the EPA is clearly a complex, multistep process. Which step do you believe is the most error-prone, and why?
11. Calculate for yourself the value of your life, based on your anticipated lifetime earnings. How does that figure differ from the VSL currently in use?
12. What are the roles of the EPA's Science Advisory Board?
13. Identify and critique a study attempting to measure the Peltzman Effect. Is the argument compelling, whether it be in support or critical of that theory?

14. Some professions use a self-licensing authority to establish high licensing barriers, restricting the supply and raising wages for those who are certified. Can you identify some professions where that approach may be in use?

NOTES

1. W.K. Viscusi, J.E. Harrington, Jr., and J.M. Vernon, *Economics of Regulation and Antitrust*, 4th ed. Cambridge, MA: MIT Press, 2005.

2. Office of Management and Budget, "Economic Analysis of Federal Regulations under Executive Order 12866." January 11, 1996. Available at www.whitehouse.gov/omb/inforeg_riaguide#iii. See also C. Dockins, K. Maguire, N. Simon, and M. Sullivan, "Value of Statistical Life Analysis and Environmental Policy: A White Paper." U.S. Environmental Protection Agency, National Center for Environmental Economics, April 21, 2004. Available at http://yosemite.epa.gov/ee/epa/eerm.nsf/vwAN/EE-0483–01.pdf/$file/EE-0483–01.pdf. Both last visited 8/30/12.

3. Executive Order 12866 Section 1(6).

4. OMB Executive Order III.A.2.

5. Ibid., at III.A.1.

6. OMB, "Discount Rates for Cost-Effectiveness, Lease Purchase, and Related Analyses," Circular A-94 Appendix C. Revised December 2012. Available at www.whitehouse.gov/sites/default/files/omb/memoranda/2013/m-13–04.pdf . Last visited 6/17/13.

7. The basic formula for discounting is:

$$\text{NPV} = \frac{C_1 \text{ or } B_1}{(1+d)^1} + \frac{C_2 \text{ or } B_2}{(1+d)^2} + \ldots + \frac{C_n \text{ or } B_n}{(1+d)^n}$$

Where C_1 is cost year I, B_1 is benefit year I, d is discount rate, n is years

More complex issues arise when capital is scarce and government borrowing "crowds out" private investment funds, distorting the price of capital. In the present depressed state of the world economy, however, capital is abundant and the "crowding out" issue much reduced.

8. "Birds of the Basin: The Migratory Millions of Mono." Available at www.monolake.org/about/ecobirds. Last visited 8/30/12.

9. "Summary of Mono Lake Litigation and Legislative Designations" Available at www.monobasinresearch.org/timelines/polchr.htm. Last visited 8/30/12.

10. Mono Lake Committee, "Mono Lake Level." Available at www.monolake.org/today/water. Last visited 5/22/14.

11. John B. Loomis, "Estimating the Public's Values for Instream Flow: Economic Techniques and Dollar Values." *Journal of the American Water Resources Association* 34, 5 (October 1998): 1007–1014.

12. J.C. Buzby, R.C. Ready, and J.S. Skees, "Contingent Valuation in Food Policy: A Case Study of a Pesticide-Residue Risk Reduction" *Journal of Agricultral and Applied Economics* 27, 2 (December 1995): 613–625.

13. U.S. Department of Justice, "Final Report of the Special Master for the September 11th Victim Compensation Fund of 2001," Volume 1, II.C.2.

14. There are 3,300 annual asthma deaths in the United States. See "Asthma Facts and Figures." Available at www.aafa.org/display.cfm?id=8&sub=42. Last visited 6/18/13.

15. U.S. Environmental Protection Agency, National Center for Environmental Economics, "Guidelines for Preparing Economic Analyses," p. B-1. Available at http://yosemite.epa.gov/ee/epa/eed.nsf/pages/guidelines.html#download. Last visited 8/30/12.

16. Binyamin Appelbaum, "As U.S. Agencies Put More Value on a Life, Businesses Fret." *New York Times*, February 16, 2011.

17. Angela Antonelli, "Regulatory Right to Know Act of 1999," March 24, 1999 (quoting Angela Antonelli, director of the Thomas A. Roe Institute for Economic Policy Studies at The Heritage Foundation). Available at www.heritage.org/research/testimony/regulatory-right-to-know-act-of-1999. Last visited 9/23/11.

18. OMB, Office Information and Regulatory Affairs, "2012 Report to Congress on the Benefits and Costs of Federal Regulations and Unfunded Mandates on State, Local, and Tribal Entities." Available at www.whitehouse.gov/sites/default/files/omb/inforeg/2012_cb/2012_cost_benefit_report.pdf. Last visited 5/23/14. (Hereafter OMB Report.)

19. OMB Report, Table 1–1.

20. Ibid., Table 1–5a.

21. Ibid., Table 1–2.

22. Ibid., p. 16.

23. Ibid., p. 19.

24. OMB, Office Information and Regulatory Affairs, "2011 Report to Congress on the Benefits and Costs of Federal Regulations and Unfunded Mandates on State, Local, and Tribal Entities," Table 1–4. Available at www.whitehouse.gov/sites/default/files/omb/inforeg/2012_cb/2012_cost_benefit_report.pdf. Last visited 5/23/14.

25. U.S. Environmental Protection Agency, "Air Pollution," p. 4. Available at www.epa.gov/airtrends/2010/report/airpollution.pdf. Last visited 9/24/11.

26. Mandating legislation is the Clean Air Act PL 91–604 Sec. 312, as amended.

27. U.S. Environmental Protection Agency,"OVERVIEW: The Clean Air Act Amendments of 1990." Available at www.epa.gov/air/caa/overview.txt. Last visited 9/25/11.

28. U.S. Environmental Protection Agency, Office of Air and Radiation, "Benefits and Costs of the Clean Air Act from 1990 to 2010," March 2011. Available at www.epa.gov/oar/sect812/feb11/fullreport.pdf. Last visited 9/27/11. (Hereafter EPA Report.)

29. EPA Report, pp. 1–5to6.

30. Ibid., Table 7–4.

31. Ibid., p. 7–8.

32. Ibid., p. 9–10.

33. Ibid., p. 4–3.

34. Ibid., p. 4–5.

35. Ibid., p. 4–6.

36. Ibid., p. 4–3.

37. Ibid., p. 4–24.

38. Ibid., p. 4–25.

39. Ibid., p. 5–2.

40. Ibid., p. 5–5.

41. Ibid., p. 5–7.

42. Ibid., pp. 5–5to6.

43. Ibid., p. 5–10.

44. Ibid., p. 5–22.

45. Ibid., Table 5–4.

46. Ibid., p. 5–21.

47. Ibid., p. 5–17.

48. Ibid., pp. 5–22to23.

49. Ibid., Table 5–11.

50. Ibid., pp. 6–1.

51. Ibid., pp. 6–11to17.

52. Ibid., pp. 6–17to25.

53. Ibid., pp. 6–28to29.

54. Ibid., Table 6–7.

55. Oracle ThinkQuest, "Acid Rain Drops Keep Falling on My Head." Available at http://library.thinkquest.org/11353/acidrain.htm. Last visited 9/28/11.

56. Sean McLachlan, "Zahi Hawass Tells New York City: Fix Cleopatra's Needle or Give It Back." *Gadling.* Available at www.gadling.com/2011/01/07/zahi-hawass-tells-new-york-city-fix-cleopatras-needle-or-give/. Last visited 9/28/11.

57. EPA Report, p. 6–33.

58. Ibid., p. 6–34.

59. Ibid., p. 7–1.

60. *Whitman vs. American Trucking Associations,* 99–1257, and *American Trucking Associations vs. Whitman,* 99–1426, February 2001.

61. R. Lutter and R.B. Belzer, "EPA Pats Itself on the Back." *Regulation* 23 (3): 23–29.

62. G. Brown et al., 2000. "Misrepresenting ACCACA." *Regulation* 23 (3): 4–5.

63. P.C. Stern and H.V. Fineberg (eds.), Board on Environmental Change and Society, Natural Resources Council, 1996. "Understanding Risk: Informing Decisions in a Democratic Society," p. 5. Available at www.nap.edu/openbook.php?record_id=5138&page=R1. Last visited 9/5/12.

64. R.W. Hahn, R.W. Lutter, and W.K. Viscusi, "Do Federal Regulations Reduce Mortality?" AEI-Brookings Center for Regulatory Studies, 2000.

65. Ibid., pp. 8–10.

66. Ibid., p. 7.

67. R. Lutter, J.F. Morrill III, and W.K. Viscusi, "The Cost-per-Life-Saved Cutoff for Safety-Enhancing Regulations." *Economic Inquiry* 37, 4 (October 1999): 599–60.

68. G. William Domhoff, "Wealth, Income, and Power." In *Who Rules America?,* Table 6. Updated July 2011. Available at http://sociology.ucsc.edu/whorulesamerica/power/wealth.html. Last visited 9/29/11.

69. Lutter, Morrill, and Viscusi, "The Cost-per-Life-Saved Cutoff for Safety-Enhancing Regulations," p. 604.

70. Hahn, Lutter, and Viscusi, "Do Federal Regulations Reduce Mortality?" Table 3–1.

71. Sam Peltzman, "The Effects of Automobile Safety Regulation." *Journal of Political Economy* 83 (1975): 677–725, 717.

72. J.D. Graham and S. Garber, "Evaluating the Effects of Automobile Safety Regulation." *Journal of Policy Analysis and Management* 3 (1984): 206–224.

73. J. Hedlund, "Risky Business: Safety Regulations, Risk Compensation, and Individual Behavior." *Injury Prevention* 6 (2000): 82–89.

74. Department of Transportation, National Highway Traffic Safety Administration, "Seat Belt Use in 2011—Overall Results." DOT HS 811 544, December 2011, Figure 1. Available at www-nrd.nhtsa.dot.gov/Pubs/811544.pdf. Last visited 8/30/12.

75. HowStuffWorks, "1955–1956 Ford Fairlane Crown Victoria." Available at http://auto.howstuffworks.com/1955-1956-ford-fairlane-crown-victoria4.htm. Last visited 9/8/11.

76. Department of Transportation, National Highway Traffic Safety Administration, "Corporate Average Fuel Economy for MY2012–MY2016 Passenger Cars and Light Trucks: Final Regulatory Impact Analysis." March 2010, pp. 369 and 400. Available at http://federalregister.gov/r/2127-AK79. Last visited 5/23/14.

77. Ibid., Tables 2 and X-7.

5 Alternatives to Regulation

Chapter Objectives

This chapter shows how alternatives to formal regulation exist in multiple forms, including self-regulation such as the international *Codex Alimentarius* (Latin for "Book of Food") and Hazard Analysis and Critical Control Points (HACCP) procedures for foods, private grades and certification, and franchise bidding. Corporate reputations serve to signal quality and reliability, a regulatory substitute, but that may be changing while concurrently firms are increasing their commitment to compliance divisions. Companies to varying degrees become involved in shaping regulations with some benefiting from high regulatory standards which thwart entry.

Key Terms: *Franchise bidding; LEED; Grade standards; HACCP;* Codex Alimentarius

Of course regulation is but one of many ways to achieve a particular outcome. Firms and individuals may choose voluntarily to act in particular ways—perhaps for moral/religious reasons or for social standing. Professional groups may recognize a mutual benefit from monitoring its members: the American Medical Association, for example, is involved in defining requirements for practicing medicine, as is the American Bar Association for lawyers. Firms also may adopt their own control mechanisms in hopes of warding off the imposition of regulations. (Though, in some cases, regulations are actually beneficial to a firm, as when they limit entry and competition.) In this chapter's first subsection we explore these and other alternatives to regulation, as well as supplementary steps that support the goals of regulatory legislation.

At the same time, firms and individuals have much at stake regarding regulation, and it is unrealistic to expect them to be purely passive observers. That is especially true in the United States, where "persons" (individual and corporate) have a right to petition the government. Persons act in their perceived best interest, both in terms of internal management of regulation and externally to influence the regulatory process. Approaches and responses to regulation by firms in particular are the subject of the second subsection in this chapter.

5.1 ALTERNATIVE/COMPLEMENTARY APPROACHES

This subsection identifies alternate approaches to regulations for changing behavior. These approaches may be—and are—applied as substitutes as well as complements to regulations. The intent is to convey that regulation is not the sole approach to achieving the stated goals. These alternate approaches are presented not to undermine the role or effectiveness of regulation—no comparative analysis is attempted here—but rather as a way of providing a deeper insight into how regulations function and, particularly, how the private sector can function in parallel ways without the inflexibility of regulatory rules.

Nine approaches are identified here and discussed in some detail. Given the regulatory focus of this volume, though, this treatment is not intended to be encyclopedic, but rather suggestive. The approaches, considered in turn, are:

- Litigation
- Insurance costs
- Nonmandatory government grade and standards information
- Private grade standards
- Independent assessments
- Competitive effects
- Taxing socially undesirable products
- Rating agencies
- Franchise bidding
- Self-regulation

a. Litigation

A common response to a schoolyard bully in my day was to say, "If you hit me, I'll sue you!" While never an effective deterrent in that context to a thug with green teeth, the threat of litigation is frequently used explicitly or implicitly in the United States as a means of controlling behavior. Consider, for example, class-action lawsuits (in which a few act on behalf of a large class of individuals with a common characteristic), which are frequently seen in TV ads. "Have you or a member of your family been injured by X!??@#??[? You may be eligible for compensation!" The best-known class action suit is the master agreement with the four largest tobacco companies (there have and continue to be numerous individual and small group suits, as well), followed closely by claims by mesothelioma victims against asbestos firms.

Here I will focus on the decision in which the attorneys general of forty-six states prevailed so that the four major U.S. tobacco firms (notably Philip Morris and R.J. Reynolds, being the largest) agreed to curtail or cease certain tobacco marketing practices, as well as to pay in perpetuity various annual payments to the states to compensate them for some of the medical costs of caring for persons with smoking-related illnesses. Under the settlement, established in November 1998, the defendants agreed to pay a minimum of $206 billion over the first twenty-five years of the agreement.

In the regulatory context of this volume, the particularly relevant matter is the voluntary restrictions on advertising. The participating manufacturers agree not to "take any action, directly or indirectly, to target Youth within any Settling State in the advertising, promotion or marketing of Tobacco Products, or take any action the primary purpose of which is to initiate, maintain or increase the incidence of Youth smoking within any Settling State." Of particular concern was the alleged targeting of youth for smokeless tobacco (moist snuff, often flavored to appeal to youth).[1] Similar restrictions had been sought through legal means but were only partially successful due to considerations of free speech and other rights. The lawsuit then achieved that goal in the absence of regulation.

Product damage lawsuits like this frequently include settlements for actual losses or costs incurred as well as (typically the larger component) payments for "pain and suffering," which act as a financial deterrent. Indeed, the U.S. antitrust acts (see Chapter 3, Section 3.5) make this role explicit by allowing for "treble damages": "Any person . . . may sue therefore . . . and shall recover three-fold the damages by him sustained."[2] In this way, the system encourages others to address antitrust and product liability matters outside the regulatory role of government.

Another area where litigation serves a constraining, regulatory-like role is with malpractice. More than 60 percent of doctors over the age of fifty-five have been sued at least once, according to a survey by the American Medical Association.[3] At their best, such lawsuits more quickly end faulty practices, devices, and medications. In *Wyeth vs. Levine* (Supreme Court 2009), for example, Diana Levine filed suit alleging that Wyeth failed to warn adequately of the risk of directly injecting its antinausea medication, Phenergan, into a patient's vein.[4]

Critics, however, charge that such suits raise the cost of medical care, as doctors use more tests, referrals to specialists, and other precautions to minimize their susceptibility to charges of inadequate or improper care; also impacting medical costs is the resulting increase in the malpractice insurance rates. The success of some suits also are said to encourage "frivolous" suits which have some possibility of a large award.

b. Insurance Costs

High insurance rates for some practices and activities have a chilling effect similar to the threat of litigation. Consider, for example, the aftermath of Hurricane Hugo, which struck Charlestown, South Carolina, in 1989, destroying many beachfront homes (Figure 5.1). Subsequently there was a legislative initiative to rezone properties not to allow building in particularly vulnerable areas, including many locations along the shoreline.

The zoning proposition led to accusations of the "taking" of property without adequate compensation, which was beyond the resources of the municipalities to cover. As a result, nothing was done legislatively. But much the same outcome was achieved through the marketplace, when insurance companies refused to provide homeowners insurance for vulnerable locations: no insurance meant no mortgages and little building followed.

Figure 5.1 **Hurricane Hugo Damage of Coastal Communities in South Carolina, 1989**

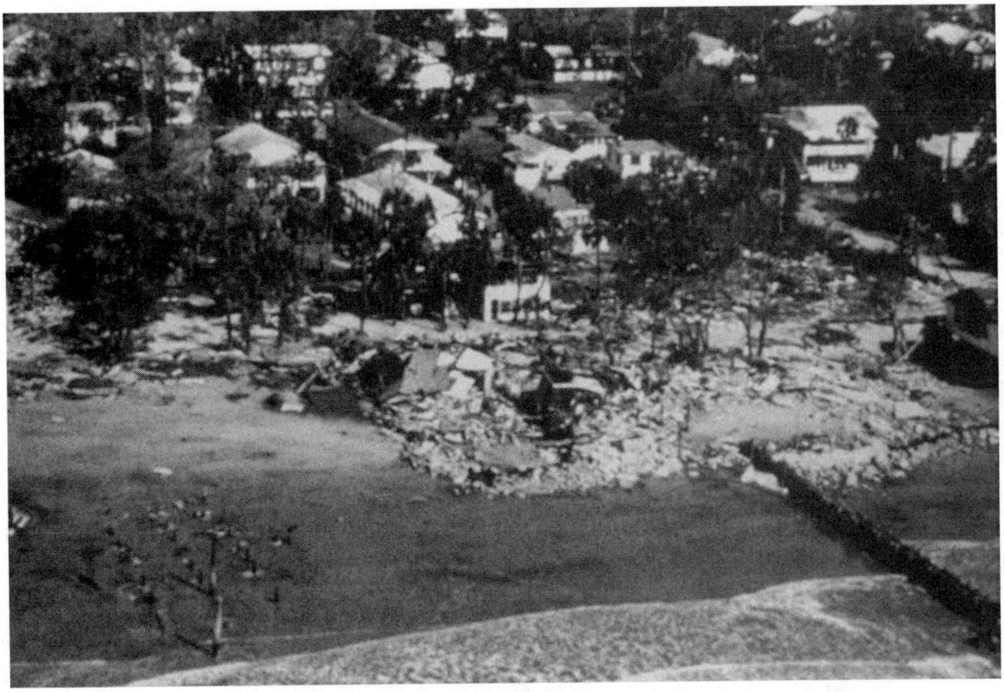

Source: Wikimedia Commons. Original author Storm05; original source www.photolib.noaa.gov.

For the same reason, super-high auto insurance fees may keep many nineteen-year-olds out of the 2014 580-horsepower Camaro ZL1 even if they are not deterred by the $55,000 to $60,000 base price.

c. Nonmandatory Government Grade and Standards Information

We are all familiar with at least the concept of mandatory government grades and standards information. Fluid milk, for example, must qualify as Grade A to be sold, and tires must carry wear, traction, and durability ratings (see Chapter 6, Section 6.4).

Less frequently recognized is that the federal government also provides various voluntary grading systems on a fee-for-use basis. Principal among these is meat quality standards: Prime, Choice, and so forth (see Figure 5.2). Venders, both supermarkets and restaurants, may or may not choose to use these grades as an added source of quality information for consumers. Since the quality standards apply only to sensory attributes and not to health- and safety-related matters—the rating of Grade A for milk by contrast is based on sanitation aspects—and are readily discernable on consumption, it makes sense that they are voluntary.

Certainly this is the kind of rating service the private sector could provide. But then, since government inspectors are already present in processing plants for food-safety

Figure 5.2 **Government Beef Grade Standard Seals, a Voluntary Program**

Source: U.S. Department of Agriculture (USDA), Agricultural Marketing Service.

inspection, it makes some sense for them to provide this information as well. Nor does the availability of the government grades exclude the possibility for private standards, although admittedly they would face obstacles in substituting for such well-recognized designations as "prime."

d. Private Grade Standards

Examples abound of private firms which rate or otherwise provide quality standards for products. Restaurant guides are a well-known example, with Zagat and Michelin guides (the latter in the United States only since 2005) prominent examples. Stars are a familiar and popular symbol of food quality, with ratings of one to four or five stars commonly used. Note these ratings are distinct from consumer reviews, for they follow standardized ranking practices.

Voluntary movie ratings represent a different category of standards, these generally are intended to help parents decide which movies are appropriate for young audiences. PG-13, for example, carries the notice that "Parents are urged to be cautious. Some material may be inappropriate for pre-teenagers," while an R-rating requires an accompanying guardian for viewers seventeen years old and younger.

e. Independent Assessments

Private grade standards are just one means by which the private sector provides quality and safety information. Perhaps best known in this category is *Consumer Reports* (*CR*), which publishes a magazine and booklets ranking the quality of products. While particularly known for their auto reviews, *CR* also reviews a range of appliances, computers, supermarkets, and even fast-food restaurants. On occasion, *CR* also flags safety problems, such as the tip-over risk of some SUVs. It makes scrupulous efforts to remain impartial by banning all advertising and purchasing all products tested, a practice not followed by auto enthusiast and other motorsports magazines. More narrowly focused, online sellers provide comparable quality information to assist their consumers. TireRack, for example, evaluates many tires as well as posting users' reviews. In fact, the practice of merchandisers providing users' reviews has become commonplace in Internet commerce.

On a broader product basis there are testing companies which provide a range of test and certification services. One of the best known of these is Underwriters Laboratory (UL),

EXAMPLE 5.1: A VISIT TO U.S. TESTING

Years ago I took a class on a field trip to U.S. Testing (now defunct), where we saw a number of machines which:

- Certified the strength of seat belt through a specified number of extensions and retractions
- Measured tar and nicotine content of cigarettes using a series of automatic smoking machines
- Checked the interior sound of a car (to verify a claim for being "quieter than a Rolls Royce")
- Tested product use in miniature washing machines to verify a claim that a detergent cleaned "whiter than white" (and, yes, the industry has agreed on a cloth swatch that is considered "white").

which offers expertise across five key strategic businesses: Product Safety, Environment, Life and Health, University, and Verification Services. There are presently over 20 billion UL marks on products worldwide. Readers may have noticed the UL mark on appliance cords, which certifies they have met a safety standard. Care must be taken, though, for the mark may apply to the cord only and not necessarily the entire electric appliance.[5]

Testing companies also may provide a range of other services. These might include certifying truth in advertising claims (required by the Federal Trade Commission) or confirming compliance with technical requirements (Example 5.1).

Some certification systems target other product attributes, such as energy efficiency under the Energy Star system. Energy Star is a hybrid, joint program of the U.S. Environmental Protection Agency and the U.S. Department of Energy which assists consumers and businesses in identifying energy-efficient appliances and homes/structures. Participating firms may voluntarily use the Energy Star logo to highlight their products, which must be 20 percent more energy efficient than government standards. Energy Star homes are at least 15 percent more energy efficient than homes built to the 2004 International Residential Code (IRC) and include additional energy-saving features that typically make them 20 percent to 30 percent more efficient than standard homes.[6]

An activity related to energy-efficient buildings i]Leadership in Energy and Environmental Design, an internationally recognized green building certification system. Developed by the U.S. Green Building Council in March 2000, LEED provides building owners and operators with a framework for identifying and implementing practical and measurable green building design, construction, operations, and maintenance solutions. LEED promotes sustainable building and development practices through a suite of rating systems that recognize projects that implement strategies for better environmental and health performance.[7] The LEED system applies throughout the process from new construction to the operation of existing buildings. For new construction, it operates on a 100-point system with four levels of certification, as follows:

Standard	Points
Certified	40–49
Silver	50–59
Gold	60–79
Platinum	80 +

Businesses and individuals use LEED systems to save money on energy use, and gain credibility by using third-party certification. But certification standards also highlight commitments to sustainability generally, including among public institutions. Cornell University, for example, uses LEED/30 standards as part of a university-wide sustainability initiative that requires new construction projects to be certified under the United States Green Building Council's LEED program and also achieve a minimum 30 percent reduction in building energy use as compared with the ASHRAE 90.1 standard (2007).[8] (See also Chapter 6, Section 6.8.)

Note should be made that LEED (and other) standards use a combination of standards and actual testing, or more formally, process and performance standards. Process standards apply to requirements for green building certification under which participants must meet construction guidelines but the buildings are not tested following completion. Testing to verify for example that an appliance meets certain standards involves the actual examination of products postproduction. Generally, post testing (performance) is more indicative of actual compliance than adherence to production standards, but the fixed standards remove much of the uncertainty of being awarded a particular designation.

f. Competitive Effects

This category is a subset of the immediately preceding but the emphasis here is on the use of standards for competitive purposes. Reference is to such third-party certifications as "dolphin-safe tuna," "sustainable forestry," "fair trade" goods, and the like. Consumers self-identify with an attribute or cause associated with a product, but ones which are not evident from examining the products. Economists call these "credence goods," which require third-party certification.

Consider the case of dolphin-safe tuna. Dolphin sightings are frequently used by large tuna boats for locating schools of tuna. That practice also puts dolphins at risk of being caught and drowned during netting operations. Sharks, sea turtles, and other species are also inadvertently caught as part of the "bycatch"; independent measures apply to saving them. The Earth Island Institute, which claims 7 million dolphins have been killed by non-dolphin-safe fishing practices, monitor tuna companies around the world to ensure tuna are caught by methods that do not harm dolphins or other species in the marine ecosystem.[9]

The Dolphin Safe logo (Figure 5.3) is appended to the products of participating firms to assist concerned consumers in identifying canned tuna with that attribute. The Earth Island Institute claims 90 percent of all firms worldwide participate. In many cases though it is difficult to identify/confirm the methods and credentials of agencies which do the certifying. Plus there are multiple seals in use in the United States and worldwide with different criteria and oversight.

Figure 5.3 **The Dolphin Safe Logo**

Source: Wikimedia Commons. Original source National Oceanic and Atmospheric Administration, United States Department of Commerce.

g. Taxing Socially Undesirable Products

For a long time governments have been taxing alcohol and tobacco—so-called sin taxes—as a source of revenue. According to the PBS series *Prohibition*, in the pre–World War I era, prior to the start of the income tax, up to 70 percent of federal revenues were derived from taxing beer. The more recent approach though targets reducing use, rather than revenue creation, following the old prescription that the higher the price, the lower the demand. This approach is also evident in taxing cigarettes.

"The general consensus is that every 10 percent increase in the real price of cigarettes reduces overall cigarette consumption by approximately 3 to 5 percent, reduces the number of young-adult smokers by 3.5 percent, and reduces the number of kids who smoke by 6 or 7 percent."[10] Hindering children from taking up smoking is considered particularly important, as they are then likely to remain nonsmokers for life.

More recently there have been calls for a "sugar" tax on soft drinks as a means of reducing obesity, particularly among children. Experts believe "based on experience with tobacco taxes, a soda tax would be 'highly effective' in reducing the $79 billion in annual health care costs associated with obesity and overweight across the country." They argue that an excise tax would be more effective than a traditional sales tax and provide an incentive to buy less soda. The article says that since the mid-1990s, children have been drinking more beverages containing sugar than they do milk."[11] Presently, one out of three children is now considered overweight or obese,[12] while the American Obesity Association places the rate of obesity for children (aged six to eleven years) at 15 percent.[13] To date, no state has adopted a sugar tax, something strongly opposed by the soda industry, but efforts continue.

h. Rating Agencies

Regarding the roles and responsibilities of third-party rating agencies, none are as prominent as those firms which rate the credit worthiness of bonds, securities, insurance companies, and the like. Notable among these are Moody's, Standard & Poor's (S&P), and Fitch Ratings, although there are ten such firms in all. "A credit rating is Standard & Poor's opinion on the general credit worthiness of an obligor, or the credit worthiness of an obligor with respect to a particular debt security or other financial obligation."[14] S&P uses a scale of AAA to C; other firms use slight variations of this system. Ratings have particular relevance for both lenders and borrowers because some institutional investors are prohibited from investing in "junk" corporate bonds, those graded BB and below.

A number of observers believe the Great Recession of 2008 began because these credit agencies grossly overstated the credit worthiness of "collateralized debt offerings," a repackaging of mortgages. Others see an inherent conflict of interest as the rating firms are paid by the companies whose securities they grade (see Chapter 9, Sections 9.3 and 9.4b).[15]

i. Franchise Bidding

Franchise bidding applies to natural monopolies as an alternative to regulation. Unregulated or unconstrained, natural monopolies lead to monopoly pricing to the detriment of consumers. Regulation by fixing a service price (electric rates) averts that problem, but at the cost of considerable complexity and inefficiency (see Chapter 3, Section 3.4). Franchise bidding averts both problems by auctioning the right to provide the service. Given enough competition in the auction, prices will be bid down to average cost, which while not as low or as efficient as variable cost pricing will still be preferable to monopoly prices. Government's sole role is to serve as the auctioneer; it is not necessary to be as knowledgeable about the costs of the sector as when regulating rates directly.

There are two forms the auction can take, with different outcomes for users. One is to auction the franchise right to the highest bidder, resulting in the government capturing the monopoly revenue. But the franchise cost is partially passed along to consumers as higher prices so the effect is to capture the monopoly benefits for the public and not the private sector. A second approach is to base the auction on the lowest service price; whoever bids lowest gets the franchise. This approach passes the benefits on to consumers in the form of lower prices.

Using either approach, an ongoing issue is assuring service quality maintenance; say uninterrupted power for electric service. True monopolies have little incentive to maintain quality so that government monitoring and some kind of penalty/reward system will be required. Further exploration at this level of detail exceeds our objectives here in identifying alternatives to regulation, but such issues do imply that no system is without its limitations.

j. Self-Regulation

Self-regulation at the extreme applies to any entity which is not otherwise regulated. More specifically it is used for entities which have taken on (or been sanctioned with) particular regulatory tasks. A closely related concept is self-policing organizations. Thus the American Medical Association accredits some 17,000 health care organizations and programs in the United States,[16] while the National Association of Realtors regulates the use of most (but not all) of the local Multiple Listing Services.

For lawyers, a degree from an American Bar Association–accredited school is a requirement to sit for a state bar examination. Their Model Rules of Professional Conduct are not legally binding in and of themselves. However, they have been adopted, in whole or in part, as the professional standards of conduct by the judiciaries or integrated bar associations of forty-nine U.S. states. The American Institute of CPAs is another of many professional associations which have a *Code of Professional Conduct* setting standards, for example, for maintaining the appearance of independence.[17]

More particular to the topics in this volume, the Financial Industry Regulatory Authority is a private organization operating under the supervision of the Securities and Exchange Commission (SEC) (see Chapter 9, Sections 9.3 and 9.4). Its mission is to protect investors by registering and educating all brokers, examining securities firms, writing the rules they must follow, and enforcing those rules and federal securities laws. It also monitors trading in the U.S. stock markets and administers the largest securities-related dispute resolution forum in the world. In particular it works to ensure that:[18]

- Anyone who sells a securities product has been officially tested, qualified, and licensed
- Every securities product advertisement used is truthful, and not misleading
- Any securities product promoted or sold to an investor is suitable for that investor's needs
- Investors receive complete disclosure about the investment product before purchase

In many ways, professional organizations in particular are best positioned to understand the needs of their field and hence to regulate members' activities in ways not readily achieved by third-party regulators like government. Self-regulation can be less adversarial, more flexible, and timelier than government regulation. Motivations include a sector establishing its own "rules" in the absence of action by governments. In other cases, self-regulation appears to be driven by a wish to prevent or forestall external regulation when perceived as a threat.

The latter motivation appears to apply to the American Beverage Association's 2006 adoption, in collaboration with the Alliance for a Healthier Generation, of School Beverage Guidelines (see also Section 5.2c of this chapter). The guidelines are staged by age so there are different standards for primary, middle, and high school children. By 2010, the most recent detailed study data available, the following successes are claimed:[19]

- An 88 percent reduction in total beverage calories shipped to schools from baseline 2004 to 2005 and 2009 to 2010

- Dramatic shift toward lower calorie and higher nutrient beverages such as juices and water
- Participation of 99 percent of school districts

The dominance of the beverage sector by three giant players certainly facilitates compliance with the guidelines. However a highly concentrated industry does not guarantee forthrightness with guidelines. "The tobacco industry's development of youth smoking prevention campaigns [in the 1980s] is arguably one of the most extreme examples of an industry abusing self-regulation to deflect legislative action."[20] Due to suspicions aroused by these kinds of cynical self-regulation approaches, a hybrid model of self-policing with government oversight has developed. An example is the Beer Institute's "Advertising and Marketing Code," which pledges:[21]

- Not to imply any laws regarding the sale and consumption of beer not be complied with
- To adhere to contemporary standards of good taste in advertising
- To reflect that brewers are responsible corporate citizens
- To strongly oppose the abuse or inappropriate consumption of their products

The alcoholic beverage sector's advertising activities are nonetheless carefully scrutinized by the Federal Trade Commission (FTC; see Chapter 3, Section 3.5c). In 2008 in its third report, the FTC documented, among other things, that the industry was in compliance with targeting advertising to media with 70 percent of viewers twenty-one years and older, up from the prior suggestion of 50 percent, with 70 percent being the proportion of the legal drinking-age population in the 2000 census.[22] The fourth report reflecting 2011 data documents that 93 percent of traditional ad placements met the 70 percent standard for drinking-age viewers. The standard has now been raised to 71.6 percent.[23]

5.2 CORPORATE RESPONSES TO REGULATORY RISK

Thus far in this chapter we have discussed various dimensions of how to regulate, which is to say that we have examined regulation as viewed by the governmental regulators. The regulated—businesses, principally—must by law comply with regulations, but they are not completely hapless agents. They, too, have their stratagems and methods for influencing the regulatory/deregulatory process. Indeed, the remainder of this book uses case studies to focus on mechanisms for managing regulations in a profit-maximizing way.

But we get ahead of ourselves. In this subsection we examine more general approaches firms use to manage and avert regulation. Considered from a firm's perspective, regulation constitutes one of many risks which must be managed—the risk that a product will not gain regulatory approval, or that new regulations will be imposed in the future. Such risks must be contained.

a. Compliance Divisions

For a 2011 report, PriceWaterhouseCoopers and Compliance Week surveyed over 100 firms with annual revenues of $1 billion plus regarding their compliance activities. Compliance activities extend to information technologies and financial reporting and audits. Of those surveyed, 48 percent anticipated a "compliance risk" as being high or very high over the next eighteen months, the highest of the anticipated risks. When lapses do occur, respondents anticipate the consequences to be severe; 68 percent expect the impact on the firm to be high or very high.

This appraisal suggests firms should take compliance very seriously, and indeed the surveyed firms do have a Chief Compliance Officer. But for most the position is recent; half created it within the past decade. The stature and influence of the compliance office, as always, depends heavily on the organizational structure, to whom the office reports. According to the survey, the office reports most frequently to the chief council or the chief executive officer, but only rarely to the board, as is recommended by the U.S. Sentencing Guidelines.[24] Compliance officers though do hold appropriate titles of vice president or senior/executive vice president to provide the requisite status and chain of reporting within firms.

"Ethics" is the sole activity wholly owned by the compliance office. Staffing for other functions is borrowed from audit, human resources, and other divisions. As this approach suggests, the compliance offices on average are small, with nearly a third having annual budgets of $1 million or less, and a fifth with ten or fewer employees.[25]

It is recommended that firms establish a corporate compliance policy. "The purpose of the *corporate compliance policy* is to provide collaborators with a point of reference in their daily activities to avoid potential compliance violations."[26] While attention here is focused on the private sector, it should be noted that public institutions like universities and hospitals frequently also have compliance offices. There is even a Society of Corporate Compliance and Ethics.[27]

While the survey may capture the trends in staffing and managing compliance office among larger firms, sectors such as pharmaceuticals and chemicals, for which regulatory approval is critical to the business, typically have well-established offices which work closely with regulators during product-review periods. For example, Merck & Co., a leading pharmaceutical research and manufacturing firm, has as a major division called Merck Research Laboratories. Reporting directly to the head of the division is the Office of Clinical and Regulatory Development.[28]

Sometimes these compliance divisions have a far broader task: preserving the corporate reputation. This was the case with Goldman Sachs in 2010 when the Business Standards Committee was established to conduct a thorough review of business standards and practices (Example 5.2). The committee receives additional guidance from a four-member subcommittee of the Goldman Sachs Board of Directors.

EXAMPLE 5.2: GOLDMAN SACHS ACTS TO PROTECT ITS REPUTATION AND CLIENT RELATIONSHIPS

The financial crisis of 2008 created great animosity toward the financial sector, which is widely seen as precipitating the crisis, while the subsequent regulation has led to ongoing adjustment and loss of profit opportunities (see Chapter 9, Section 9.4). This is particularly true of Goldman Sachs, which is often perceived as the flagship of the investment bank sector, the best managed, most profitable, and enviably politically connected, with two recent secretaries of the Treasury, Robert Rubin (Clinton administration) and Hank Paulson (G.W. Bush administration), as former chief executive officers (CEOs).[29] This stature, though, has had the downside of focusing special attention on the firm's actions before and after the crisis.

"For Goldman Sachs, this has been a challenging period. Our industry, and our firm in particular, have been subjected to considerable scrutiny. Our senior management and Board of Directors recognized this as an opportunity to engage in a thorough self-assessment and to consider how we can and should improve."[30] With this justification, the Goldman Sachs Business Standards Committee was established in 2010 with the objectives of strengthening client relationships and reputational excellence. In recent years, the company has experienced notable losses of both the trust of their clients and its reputation:

2010 and 2011: For 2010, Goldman Sachs set aside $15.38 billion for pay, mostly bonuses, for a ratio of compensation to revenue of 39 percent. That dollar amount was down 5 percent from the $16.19 billion allocated for compensation in 2009 when the ratio of compensation to revenue was at a record low of 35.8 percent. There are frequent complaints about the level of executive compensation in investment banks, particularly in cases like Goldman Sachs where bonuses were granted in 2010 even though reported earnings were down 37 percent from 2009. Goldman Sachs, though, was the first Wall Street bank to seek shareholder approval for its executive compensation plan ("say-on-pay"—see Chapter 9, Section 9.4).

The case did not raise issue with the product per se, but rather with the firm for not revealing that Paulson intended to bet against it, "in effect duping some investors into believing that their financial interests were aligned with those of the hedge fund. [Goldman Sachs] also failed to properly disclose that Paulson helped select those underlying securities," the SEC said. Goldman Sachs earned a $15 million fee for the transaction while Paulson's profits were $1 billion. Then in August 2013 a mid-level Goldman Sachs trader in charge of developing the product Fabrice Tourre was found guilty of fraud.[31]

April 2010: The Securities and Exchange Commission (SEC) sued Goldman Sachs for defrauding investors by misstating and omitting key facts about a financial product tied to subprime mortgages. Goldman Sachs, the lawsuit alleged, structured and marketed a synthetic collateralized debt obligation (CDO) based on the performance of subprime residential mortgage-backed securities. It was charged with failing to disclose to investors the role that a major hedge fund played in the portfolio selection process and the fact that the hedge fund had taken a short position against the CDO.

According to the SEC, "Goldman wrongly permitted a client that was betting against the mortgage market to heavily influence which mortgage securities to include in an investment portfolio, while telling other investors that the securities were selected by an independent, objective third party."[32] One of the four involved CDOs, known as ABACUS, soon collapsed, losing investors a reported $1 billion.

The case was settled with Goldman Sachs paying a $550 million penalty (including returning the fees for the ABACUS deal) but without admitting or denying liability. Rather, Goldman Sachs "admitting that it made a 'mistake' in not disclosing that 'that Paulson's [a client which shorted the CDO] economic interests were adverse to C.D.O. investors.' "[33] An additional but unrealized concern for Goldman Sachs was whether its statements about its ethical standards, like "Integrity and honesty are at the heart of our business," were indeed fraudulent. Judge Paul A. Crotty wrote, "Given Goldman's fraudulent acts, it could not have genuinely believed that its statements about complying with the letter and spirit of the law—and that its continued success depends upon it, valuing its reputation, and its ability to address 'potential' conflict of interests—were accurate and complete."[34]

January 2011: Goldman Sachs first opened a $1.5 billion private placement of Facebook stocks to its principal clients only to close it to United States–based customers, citing "intense media coverage."[35] The underlying issue though was a Securities and Exchange Commission rule requiring companies with more than 499 investors to file financial statements, as would a public company. Goldman Sachs, however, had proposed lumping investors in a mutual fund–like arrangement which would have been treated as a single investor.

April 2011: Senator Levin, chairman of the Senate Permanent Subcommittee on Investigations, publicly accused Goldman Sachs (among other banks, as well as critiquing the laxity of the federal regulatory process) of profiting at clients' expense as the mortgage market crashed in 2007. "In my judgment, Goldman clearly misled their clients and they misled Congress."[36]

May–September 2011: A merger/buyout between El Paso and Kinder Morgan, two gas exploration/transfer and storage firms, was proposed, with Goldman Sachs serving as a mergers and acquisitions (M&A) advisor for El Paso. The complicating factor was that Goldman Sachs held a $4 billion stake in Kinder Morgan. Among Goldman Sachs's activities was a reduction in the valuation of the gas exploration business, which was not being sought by Kinder, by $2 billion, "making the merger appear better than [the] alternative."[37]

March 2012: A long-term employee wrote embarrassingly for the opinion page of the *New York Times*:

> Today is my last day at Goldman Sachs. After almost 12 years at the firm—first as a summer intern while at Stanford, then in New York for 10 years, and now in London—I believe I have worked here long enough to understand the trajectory of its culture, its people and its identity. And I can honestly say that the environment now is as toxic and destructive as I have ever seen it. . . . To put the problem in the simplest terms, the interests of the client continue to be sidelined in the way the firm operates and thinks about making money."[38]

The article was expanded into a book released that October.

May 2012: Goldman Sachs, along with other underwriters, was sued by Facebook initial public offering (IPO) investors who lost big as prices dropped following the opening price of $38. Goldman Sachs was not the lead underwriting firm—that was assigned to Morgan Stanley—but was sued as an underwriter as prices fell by nearly half. The banks named in the lawsuit reduced their estimates for Facebook revenues for the second quarter and full year of 2012 as new users were primarily mobile and did not receive the ads, which are the predominant source of Facebook's income. The lawsuit charges the banks did not inform potential investors before the IPO (see also Chapter 9, Section 9.6f).[39] Goldman Sachs had a direct investment of about $450 million in Facebook, about half of which was off-loaded at the market peak on the day of the IPO.

July 1, 2013: The antitrust division of the European Commission reached a "preliminary conclusion" that thirteen major banks, including Goldman Sachs, had conspired to limit competition in the credit default swap market. Specifically they are being investigated for cooperating to prevent swaps from being traded on open exchanges between 2006 and 2009 by refusing to provide licenses for exchange trading. Over-the-counter trades have larger spreads than exchanges—75 percent higher, leading to $55 billion in additional profits for these banks, according to studies. "This was their cash cow, and they did not want to give it up," is the way one observer summarized the situation. A related U.S. Justice Department investigation is ongoing since 2009.[40]

July 21, 2013: An investigative report by the *New York Times* revealed that Goldman Sachs had inflated the price of aluminum by shifting product among its Detroit warehouses. The commodity price as set by the London Metal Exchange is not affected directly, but the price paid by users, and subsequently consumers, also adds an exchange-approved logistics premium, which includes the storage fee. The scheme, according to the article, works by offering traders a premium to store their metal in the Goldman Sachs warehouses, where the approved rate is 48 cents/day/ton. The metals, according to the exchange regulations, must be moved at a minimum level of 3,000 tons daily, but in Goldman Sachs's case, rather than the material being shipped out, it was simply being moved from one of their Detroit warehouses to another. Since Goldman Sachs entered the storage business three years previously, the quantity stored soared from 850,000 to 1.5 million tons, while the average period for aluminum to be received and shipped to users rose from six weeks to sixteen months. The aluminum premium doubled since 2010 at a total estimated cost to consumers of over $5 billion. In unit terms that is about $12 per car for the 200 pounds of aluminum used.

Goldman Sachs benefited directly from the storage fees and indirectly as the supply reductions involved drove up the price of aluminum. The London Metal Exchange had proposed changing the regulations in April 2014 to discourage the practice, but it earns 1 percent of the storage fees so such a change would cost the Hong Kong investors billions, a clear disincentive. Until late 2012 the exchange belonged to members, including Goldman Sachs, which set their own regulations on storage fees and so forth.

It should be noted there is nothing illegal about the alleged practices by the banks. However, until recent deregulation banks were prohibited from engaging in storage and transportation, but with deregulation the Federal Reserve was granted the authority to determine which activities were considered appropriate and which not. According to a Federal Reserve document quoted in the article, approval is granted when it can "reasonably be expected to produce benefits to the public, such as greater convenience, increased competition, or gains in efficiency, that outweigh possible adverse effects, such as undue concentration of resources, decreased or unfair competition, conflicts of interests, or unsound banking practices." Some of that is up for renewal, but indications are the Federal Reserve will be extending them.

Into the future Goldman Sachs along with other major banks are poised to extend their activities into copper and other commodities.[41] Indeed on July 30, 2013, JPMorgan Chase paid without admitting or denying wrongdoing a $410 million fine to settle a probe into allegations of fixing electricity prices in California and the Midwest.[42]

These public and client relations setbacks led to the creation of the Business Principles and Standards Committee. As Greg Smith continued in his *New York Times* op-ed,

> It astounds me how little senior management gets a basic truth: If clients don't trust you they will eventually stop doing business with you. It doesn't matter how smart you are.[43]

The creation of the committee was an indication that senior management was indeed getting it, and prepared to remedy the problems. But what did the committee do, and to what end?

The committee began by reaffirming the relevance of the thirty-year-old Fourteen Business Principles, the first two of which read:[44]

1. Our clients' interests always come first. "Our experience shows that if we serve our clients well, our own success will follow."
2. Our assets are our people, capital, and reputation. "If any of these is ever diminished, the last is the most difficult to restore."

The core client-service values are identified as "integrity, fair dealing, transparency, professional excellence, confidentiality, clarity, and respect."[45] In total, the committee made thirty-nine recommendations under five headings, as follows:[46]

1. Strengthening Client Relationships
2. Strengthening Reputational Excellence: "Goldman Sachs has one reputation. It can be affected by any number of decisions and activities across the firm."
3. Strengthening Committee Governance
4. Enhancing Transparency of Communication and Disclosure: Need to better explain our business activities and how these activities relate to our performance and to our mission to serve clients.
5. Strengthening Training and Professional Development

Under governance, five new committees were established to enhance accountability and the "client franchise at the center of our decision-making processes."

Several commentators have been highly critical of the committee report. *Bloomberg Businessweek* said it "rehashed the bank's mantras about putting its clients' interests before its own," adding "But Goldman's supposedly pristine reputation has always been more invented than earned."[47] Others were more pointed yet, calling the report banal:

> The business standards review produced a paper that is aimed at addressing the first gripe against Lloyd Blankfein, and the firm he has run for several years—that

> it is not client-oriented. It uses the word *client* some 372 times. It is meant to reassure Goldman's clients, to placate regulators, and to direct employee activity. Unfortunately, the paper ignores the second gripe. It lacks any attention at all to a higher understanding of the purposes of Goldman Sachs.[48]

Part of this "irrelevancy" is the issue of "too big to fail," which led to the Troubled Asset Relief Program (TARP) payments (see Chapter 9, Section 9.4) but is not mentioned in the report.

> What is most notable about the report, however, is what it does not say. No mention is made of any issues of first-order importance regarding how Goldman (and other banks of its size and with its leverage) can have big negative effects on the overall economy. The entire 67-page report reads like an exercise in misdirection.[49]

Goldman Sachs is known for its charity, both corporate and employee, support for small businesses, and opportunities for women, although giving declined by three-quarters in 2012 in response to falling profits.[50]

Issues:

- How serious has the damage to Goldman Sachs's reputation been, and what are the consequences?
- Are current steps sufficient to restore clients' trust?
- What else might be done?
- In 2012 Goldman Sachs donated almost $316 million to charity, 3.9 percent of its 2011 earnings compared to the top level of 2 percent for most firms, presumably in an effort to win favor with the public.[51] Was that money well and fairly spent?
- Is it the prerogative of a major firm like Goldman Sachs to define its role in society, and how might that be done?
- Goldman Sachs very recently has modified its internal rules for dealing with clients in several ways including (a) for most clients placing a limit on the kinds of transactions permitted and (b) informing clients of Goldman Sachs's earnings and roles in each transaction.[52] Are these modifications sufficient?

See also Study Question #5.

b. Competitive Effects of Compliance Divisions

While it is understandable why large firms in heavily regulated sectors would establish "regulatory development" offices, critics see more nefarious motivations.

> Contrary to conventional wisdom, Monsanto and other industry giants love EPA regulation. It adds another stamp of approval to their products, and it squeezes out smaller companies that can't afford the time and money the regulatory process demands. The big firms will spend whatever it takes to topple the competition, and Monsanto's lobbying is so masterful that once regulation is in place, manipulating the process is a breeze.[53]

Perhaps this quote from *Mother Jones* is a bit left of center, but others also reached this conclusion. For instance, Jennifer Ferrara writes in *The Ecologist*:

> From their position at the top, Monsanto and other corporations have actually favored some seemingly tight regulations, but, it turns out, only when the regulations serve corporate marketing purposes. Regulations that require corporations to submit a plethora of costly scientific data to regulatory agencies, for example, discourage competition from smaller biotechnology and seed companies while giving the public the illusion that new biotechnology products undergo rigorous safety evaluations and are therefore safe. . . .
>
> Furthermore, corporations could only get their *Bt* products [crops genetically engineered to contain *Bacillus thuringiensis* to resist insect damage] to market if they had extensive money and resources to jump through all the regulatory hoops. Big corporations alone can meet data requirements and, once in the system, manipulate and pass the EPA's safety evaluation process. With the competition out of the way, the market is theirs.[54]

As Brian Shaffer notes in a survey article,

> Thus firms may support legislation and regulation that benefits their positions vis-à-vis rivals, entrants, substitute products, buyers, and suppliers. This may be termed the strategic use of public policy for the purpose of gaining competitive advantage. In addition, regulation often has asymmetric effects on competing firms. As a result, firms with superior capabilities for adapting to regulatory dictates may also attain a position of competitive advantage over their rivals.[55]

Another more procompetitive use of regulations is as an indication or affirmation of quality or safety. For example, in the United Kingdom this would be like noting on the label of a jar of jam, "By Appointment to Her Royal Highness," suggesting the Queen is a good judge of the quality of preserves (which could well be true).

In the earliest days of biotech, the 1990s to be specific, Calgene, a California biotech firm, sought to have the Food and Drug Administration (FDA) declare its delayed-ripening tomato, the Flavr Savr®, as safe to eat. FDA approval could be viewed as a "competitive weapon."[56] Alas for Calgene, U.S. regulations do not work that way (as is true in most countries). The FDA can rule that a food product is unsafe to eat, but cannot declare one as "safe" on the logical basis that it is never possible to establish complete safety for a food, even conventionally developed ones.

More recently, the Supreme Court in *Mutual Pharmaceutical vs. Bartlett* (2013) ruled that drug design deficits of FDA-approved medications could not be litigated under state product liability laws. Previously in *PLIVA, Inc. vs. Mensing* (2011), the Court had ruled that manufacturers of federally approved drugs could not be sued under state failure-to-warn claims. Both cases primarily affect generic drug manufacturers, who under federal statutes are prevented from altering either the chemical composition or the labeling of their federally approved products without obtaining further approvals. As such, they fit under federal regulatory preemption over state law.[57]

Of course, regulatory approval connotes benefits only in societies where there is general trust in regulatory agencies. That applies, relatively speaking, in the United States.

According to the 2013 survey by the International Food Information Council Foundation, an industry-supported group, 78 percent in the United States are very or somewhat confident about the safety of the food supply while 64 percent believe government agencies (including the FDA and USDA) are somewhat or very trustworthy to provide accurate food safety information.[58]

Finally, traditional economic logic dictates that a firm's reputation is critical to its success and so is jealously guarded. That, in turn, acts as a brake on dubious, risky activities. And reputation is considered to be especially critical for banks/finance firms, where trust and integrity are viewed as essential. Yet in a recent book titled *The Death of Corporate Reputation,*[59] Jonathan Macey argues that recent changes have greatly diminished the risk-curtailing role of reputation: the economic model no longer applies (Example 5.3).

EXAMPLE 5.3: THE DEATH OF CORPORATE REPUTATION

In his book, Macey describes the economic theory of reputation as follows: firms invest in reputation so that customers will do business with them. Reputations though are difficult and expensive to build but easy to destroy. Hence no rational corporation will act to impugn its reputation, as that will inevitably reduce long-term profits. As trust is particularly important in finance, the reputational model is believed to be particularly relevant in that sector. His thesis with attention to the finance sector is that regulation has undermined the role of reputation, creating a larger problem.

According to Macey there are ten principal causes of the decline of the role of reputation, seven of which are due to changing societal mores, industry structure, and technological change:

1. "People are no longer embarrassed to be sued the way they used to be. It is just a cost of doing business" (p. 23). Moreover, some suits are motivated by the political ambitions of prosecutors like Rudolph Giuliani and Eliot Spitzer, which further undermines the role legal action has had in affecting personal and corporate reputations (pp. 116–17).
2. Individual reputations are distinct from those of the firms they work for, in part because of changes in information technology. This means individuals can readily move from firm to firm and so are not solely dependent on the reputation of their employer (pp. 98–91).
3. Even if convicted, individuals frequently retain much of their ill-gotten spoils and their status in their own cliques (pp. 89–90). Cheating does not affect personal reputations.
4. The change from private partnership to public ownership or the removal of personal liability through the transfer to a limited liability partnership (LLP) structure means losses are borne largely by shareholders and other asset holders while employees benefit from enormous bonuses during flush periods (p. 173). The firm's reputation is capitalized into its value, which is now the property of the shareholders and no longer a direct concern for employees.
5. Accounting firms and other "reputational intermediaries" at one time transferred reputational validity to the firms they audited; to be "fired" by an accounting firm was a blow to a firm's reputation. Then the number of major accounting

firms declined, so there was less choice, and competition is essential to the functioning of the reputational model. And then when accountancy became more competitive for profits, firing a client, particularly a large client who also purchased management consulting services, hurt the auditor more than the firm (pp. 134–38).

6. In a more limited way, the establishment of accounting standards by the SEC and the law undermined the authority of the major stock exchanges which used to provide and verify those standards were followed. As a result and in combination with technological changes like electronic trading, stock exchanges lost the reputational role extension to the firms listed there. They became commodities where listing had no reputational signaling value (pp. 202–03, 207).
7. The success of the SEC is measured by the number of legal cases brought and won, and by the size of the settlements. These metrics though do not reflect its effectiveness.

Regarding the remaining three principal causes of the decline of the importance of reputation, Macey points directly to bad judgment and more sinisterly to malfeasance by the SEC:

8. The SEC is most needed, and receives the greatest increases in its budget, during times of crisis. Hence it has the incentive to emphasize, and even perpetuate, crisis (p. 270).
9. By mandating certain assets achieve a minimum credit rating, a position quickly adopted and expanded by the finance sector, the SEC made credit-rating agencies essential to the system. Subsequently, "quality quickly became irrelevant . . . Those rating agencies that rated quickly and predictably and generously and were the friendliest and easiest to work with were the most in demand" (pp. 170–72).
10. "[T]he SEC purposely pursues a strategy of keeping its rules vague and in flux." In that way the SEC "increas[es] the demand for compliance personnel, creating new job opportunities for SEC alumni . . ." (p. 241). For a similar reason of creating lucrative job opportunities in the legal and finance sectors, the SEC pursues complex fraud cases rather than simple ones (like the Bernie Madoff pyramid scheme), which are more relevant for protecting small investors (p. 221). The SEC further protects powerful incumbents as sources of employment (p. 232).

Based on these observations, Macey concludes with several sharp criticisms of the SEC:

- "The SEC is failing in its mission to protect capital markets, but succeeding in its mission of imposing heavy regulatory burden on those companies whose misfortune it is to be publicly listed on a U.S. trading venue" (p. 270).
- "[T]he SEC has no clearly defined clientele. In other words the SEC has no idea whom it should help" (p. 270).

Certainly this volume presents some important concepts, in part regarding how change, including technological change, has altered the roles of financial institutions and hence the institutions themselves. Reputation clearly is no longer a controlling force in the finance sector as it has been replaced to some significant degree by regulation. They are to a large degree substitutes. But whereas Macey's thesis implies the reputational model served the country well, modern regulation as exemplified by the SEC "undermines rather than strengthens the way reputation functions in the capital markets" (p. 217). Most pointed of his critiques are that (a) ambitious politicians have brought financial cases to enhance their stature, in the process damaging if not outright convicting innocent individuals; and (b) the SEC to a large degree operates to enhance career opportunities for its alumni and not for public benefit.

These are strong charges indeed, and they further undermine the reputational position the SEC requires to respond effectively to the problems evident in our financial system. It is therefore relevant to examine some of the evidence used to substantiate these strong charges.

As regards the "ambitious politician" charges, two are highlighted: former New York City Mayor Rudolph Giuliani in his pursuit of Michael Milken (Drexel Burnham Lambert), and former New York Governor Eliot Spitzer, although more attention is given to Spitzer's attacks on the SEC than any particular cases brought (p. 257). With Giuliani and Milken, Macey notes that Milken pleaded guilty to five (and convicted of six) technical charges of the ninety-eight-point indictment following a "show trial" which "collapsed." What is more, Milken acted only to "avoid the indictment of his brother" (p. 116). Other cited evidence of innocence includes judgments of Gilder, a financial columnist, an editorial in *Business Week*, and the judgment of an editor at the *Wall Street Journal* (pp. 112–13). Perhaps those sources are more knowledgeable than the court, and Milken perhaps did indeed act to protect his brother (although no supportive evidence is presented). Perhaps as well the business community was blind to the faults of one of its stars.

The *Wall Street Journal* editors similarly lashed out again in 2013 against the proposed $13 billion settlement with JPMorgan Chase over the misleading sale of mortgage-backed securities, saying the Justice Department "confiscat[ed]" the funds "for no other reason than because they can and because they want to appease their left-wing populist allies." These actions were portrayed as poor treatment of a firm which did "the country a favor" by taking over two troubled firms, Bear Stearns and Washington Mutual.[60]

Well, give us a break. JPMorgan Chase was given Bear Stearns and Washington Mutual at very favorable prices and full well knew the potential liabilities involved.[61] JPMorgan Chase paid only $1.5 billion for Bear Stearns despite its market capitalization of $11 billion, and is said to have "come out ahead" on the Bear Stearns and Washington Mutual deals even after the proposed fines were paid.[62] The *Wall Street Journal* simply is not a balanced observer of business behavior, meaning that a supportive editorial carries no positive reputational value for Macey's argument.

Macey himself moved well beyond the role of an impartial academic observer when he quoted himself considering Milken's treatment as "worse" than a charge of communism by Joe McCarthy's committee in the 1950s (pp. 112–13). According to Macey, Milken's treatment was "an attack on such fundamental American values as entrepreneurship, individual responsibility, and, ultimately, capitalism itself" (p. 112). That is an extraordinary accusation, for McCarthy attacked democracy itself, certainly a fundamental American value. Macey is no neutral observer on this issue.

Macey continues with a complex rebuttal of a SEC inside-trading case. But he then tips his hand again by chiding the SEC for espousing a "socialist philosophy that valuable information belongs to the people—regardless of how it was obtained" (p. 247). Whatever the values of his argument may have been, they are diminished with name-calling, using words like "socialism" and "McCarthyism." Many of the points raised are valuable but his ideological stance against regulation in general and the SEC in particular should make the reader cautious.

c. Corporate Involvement in Policy Making

This subsection on corporate involvement in policy making could be quite lengthy, for corporations are hardly passive acceptors of regulatory changes, nor should they be. But the intent here is not to discuss the methods used in detail but rather to highlight some significant examples.

Lobbying

According to quarterly lobbying disclosure reports filed with the Secretary of the Senate's Office of Public Records, lobbyists in 2012 self-reported spending $3.3 billion on lobbying activities. The pharmaceutical and health sector alone in 2012 spent $250 million on lobbying.[63]

Of course, entities other than firms and their representatives in the form of trade associations also lobby. Indeed, the top two lobbying organizations in 2012 were associations: the U.S. Chamber of Commerce and the National Association of Realtors. The largest firm was General Electric (GE) at $21 million.[64]

Political Contributions

Prior to 2010, the Federal Election Commission banned direct corporate contributions to political campaigns. Firms and other groups then operated through Political Action Committees (PACs). The top three contributors in 2010–2011 were Honeywell, the National Beer Wholesalers Association, and the International Brotherhood of Electrical Workers. PACs are political committees organized for the purpose of raising and spending money to elect and defeat candidates.

Then in January 2010 the Supreme Court, in a 5–4 decision in *Citizens United vs. Federal Election Commission,* overturned the Federal Election Commission and extended full "free speech" rights to corporations. Free speech in this instance means political speech, which means funding candidates and running advertisements on behalf of candidates, although technically not in direct collaboration with the candidates.

Corporations are not required to disclose such contributions, although some do so voluntarily; the degree of transparency varies by sector (Figure 5.4). Accurate data are difficult to come by, but estimates place the amount from outside groups for the 2010 midterm election cycle at $294 million, up 400 percent from the prior cycle in 2006. Sources for only about half the funds were disclosed.[65] However, it was not until the "big bucks" 2012 presidential campaign that corporate donations rapidly accelerated (Table 5.1).

Some publicly held firms received notable push-back for corporate donations to political parties and candidates, or at least for doing so publicly. Scotts Miracle-Gro, a home-garden fertilizer company with a strong brand franchise, in June 2012 donated $200,000 to Restore Our Future, a super PAC that supported Republican presidential candidate Mitt Romney. James Hagedorn, chairman and CEO, explained his decision in a letter:

Figure 5.4 **Sector Transparency Regarding Political Contributions, 2011**
Baruch Index: Moderate 41–60, Weak 21–40

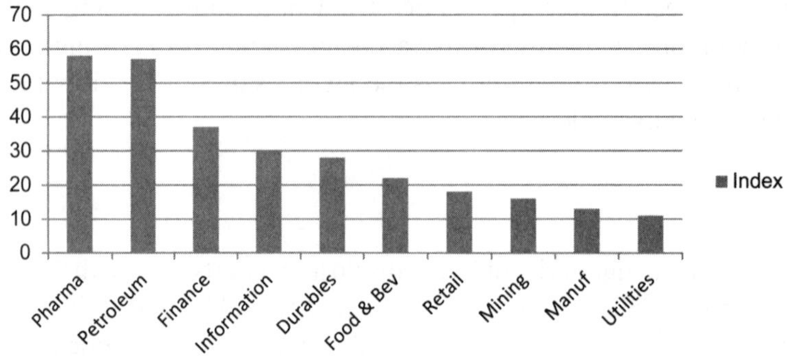

Source: Baruch Index of Corporate Political Disclosure, "2011 Results."

Table 5.1

Top Ten Corporate Political Contributors through Mid-2012

Firm	Donation ($ million)	Republicans %	Democrats %
Las Vegas Sands Corp.	52.4	100	0
Adelson Drug Clinic	42.0	100	0
Contran Corp.	31.4	82	18
Perry Homes	23.7	99	1
Newsweb Corp.	14.2	0	100
Hugo Ent.	12.9	97	3
Renaissance Tech	10.0	40	60
Goldman Sachs	7.9	75	25
Euclidian Capital	6.6	5	95
Bain Capital	5.6	71	29

Source: Open Secrets.org, "Top Overall Donors." www. opensecrets.org/overview/topcontribs.php.

> Business leaders have to make decisions based on what they believe is best for their shareholders and associates. We have a history of supporting candidates and causes we believe will help strengthen our business. The decision to contribute to Restore Our Future was no different, and I felt the contribution should be made in the light of day."[66]

There is no indication of any significant consequences to the firm as a result of the donation.

That was not the case with Target, which in 2010 donated $150,000 to MN (Minnesota) Forward in support of the election of Republican Tom Emmer as Minnesota governor. Emmer has been charged by critics as being opposed to same-sex marriage and gay rights. While other firms have also contributed to MN Forward, Target has been particularly criticized given its declared stance of being in support of diversity. The backlash led CEO Gregg Steinhafel to write a letter to his employees explaining that the purpose of the $150,000 donation to MN Forward was to support economic growth and job creation, but admitting that the contribution affected many employees in unanticipated ways, for which he was "deeply sorry."[67] In addition to financial costs, activists called for a boycott of Target, and megastar Lady Gaga decided against an exclusive Target special album edition due to the firm's continued political activity.[68]

The *Citizens United* decision, which purportedly supports free speech, provides stockholders no specific recourse against a firm using corporate funds—read stockholders' money—for political purposes beyond selling the ownership stake or attempting to place a referendum on the ballot for the shareholders' meeting. In the case of Scotts Miracle-Gro, where the family of CEO James Hagedorn has a 30 percent controlling interest, that is not going to happen.

In a 2012 decision in *Knox vs. SEIU,* the Supreme Court not only specified that labor unions could not compel nonmember workers to contribute to support political speech repugnant to them but that the unions must positively affirm workers who are willing to contribute. A mere opt-out by nonmembers is not permitted under the decision.

Education

Firms and their representatives commit considerable sums to inform individuals of their positions on issues of current importance. An example is the contentious drilling for natural gas known as hydraulic fracturing—called fracking—which involves injecting into a well a water-sand-chemical solution to fracture rock formations and release any trapped deposits of oil or natural gas. The industry contends the practice is completely safe, while the opposition sees multiple problems, especially the pollution of drinking water (the film *Gasland* at www.gaslandthemovie.com explores the problems of fracking).

Corporate information campaigns are also used for public relations purposes and indirectly to avert new regulations. For example, BP spent considerable sums presenting its position following the Deepwater Horizon well leak in 2010 (Figure 5.5).

The soft-drink industry was also active in opposing suggested anti-obesity "sugar" taxes. The beverage industry and a coalition called New Yorkers Against Unfair Taxes say the so-called sugar tax proposed for New York State could cost the state approximately 6,000 jobs[69] (see also Section 5.1g of this chapter).

Returning to Ralph Nader and his book challenging the auto industry and General Motors (GM) in particular (see Chapter 2, Section 2.1b), in March 1966, GM President James Roche was forced to appear before a Senate subcommittee and to apologize to Nader for the company's campaign of harassment and intimidation. Nader later successfully sued GM for excessive invasion of privacy. It was the money from this case that allowed him to lobby for consumer rights leading eventually to his presidential campaigns in 1996 and 2000 on the Green Party line.

Figure 5.5 **In Situ Burn Operations as Part of the Cleanup from the Deepwater Horizon Oil Spill**

Source: National Oceanic and Atmospheric Administration, United States Department of Commerce.

Participation with Regulatory Activities

As knowledgable practitioners, industry representatives are prominent members of many regulatory and related committees. One example is the *Codex Alimentarius* (Latin for "Food Book"). The Codex Alimentarius Commission was created in 1963 by the Food and Agricultural Organization (FAO) and the World Health Organization (WHO) to develop food standards, guidelines, and related texts such as codes of practice under the Joint FAO/WHO Food Standards Program. The Codex standards though are recommendations only with no regulatory authority.

For the electronic media to function, there must be agreement on protocols and standards. Many of the responsible groups are nonprofit organizations like the Internet Society (ISOC), a nonprofit organization founded in 1992 to provide leadership in Internet-related standards, education, and policy. Membership includes corporations, governments, and foundations, as well as interested organizations.[70]

Conversely, firms may choose not to participate with governments in a regulatory process in the hopes of hampering it. The advantages and disadvantages of this choice is the subject of a case study (see Chapter 6, Section 6.4).

5.3 Conclusions

There are typically multiple approaches to a similar outcome, and that applies to regulations as well. Many alternate approaches exist, and indeed Congress mandates that regulations be applied as the last alternative.

The alternatives presented here (others likely exist) fall into four basic categories:

1. Alternate approaches which augment formal regulations (some self-regulation)
2. Voluntary regulations (grades and standards, independent assessments, competitive effects)
3. True substitutes (litigation, taxation, franchise bidding, rating agencies)
4. Self-regulation undertaken to avoid potentially more restrictive formal regulations.

The final alternative listed describes more of a motivation than an outcome, but it does seem to apply, for example, to the American Beverage Association's adoption of the School Beverage Guidelines. There is of course great benefit in having an industry police itself, but it should be recognized that the threat of formal regulation is likely the critical motivating factor. Also critical is that some group evaluates the steps actually taken to confirm they serve the identified public need and are not merely meant to placate the public, as was the case for thirty years in the self-regulation of advertising by the tobacco industry.[71]

Codes of conduct and the like can be highly beneficial when they are actually followed. More complex are insurance and litigation as de facto regulatory levers. They can be effective because responsibility is diffuse and therefore enforcement is more likely. Conversely they can be a heavy-handed instrument, providing a negative financial incentive. Consider all the references to costly and "unnecessary" medical tests undertaken allegedly to protect a physician in the case of a lawsuit. The bottom line though is that these alternatives are critical and ongoing components of the regulatory mix and must be accommodated.

Most firms, for their part (excluding pharmaceutical companies and similar sectors for which regulatory compliance is central to the business), have only recently established their own ethics and compliance offices. The trend is likely to expand, but the authority of those offices remains limited. Where corporations have and continue to act is in influencing the regulatory process through lobbying and sometimes through direct contact with the public through advertising.

These actions are clearly their right. The recent Supreme Court *Citizens United* decision, however, has and will continue to expand the funding for involvement in the election process, which will further encumber the political decision-making process in a period of general paralysis. For publicly owned firms there are few avenues by which shareholders can effectively protest the use of their monies in supporting political positions, whatever those positions may be.

5.4 STUDY QUESTIONS

1. A number of alternatives to regulation (some of which could also serve as complements)—nine in total—are summarized as follows:

   - Litigation
   - Insurance costs
   - Nonmandatory government grade and standards information
   - Private grade standards
   - Independent assessments
   - Competitive effects
   - Taxing socially undesirable products
   - Rating agencies
   - Franchise bidding

   Considering the preceding list, please group those that function similarly and identify how they change behavior—for example, by providing information for consumers. If you believe some items on the list do not fit into a category, please explain why.
2. Some professions use a self-licensing authority to establish high licensing barriers, restricting the supply and raising wages for those who are certified. Can you identify some professions where that approach may be in use?
3. The federal government offers (typically subsidized) flood insurance, which critics charge allows building in inappropriate locals. How would you describe that program in the context of alternatives to regulation?
4. Until the prohibition on rejecting medical coverage for "pre-existing conditions" was prohibited by the Affordable Care Act (Obamacare), many individuals were unable to change jobs for fear of losing critical coverage. Please describe that conundrum in the context of regulatory approaches.
5. As in the case of Goldman Sachs, J.P. Morgan Chase's reputation has been taking some hits recently, including the $900 million settlement over the "London Whale" trading debacle, part of a $13 billion fine for misleading purchasers on the riskiness of mortgage-backed securities,[72] and, in Europe, part of a $2.3 billion fine for rigging benchmark interest rates.[73] What are the reasons for that negative publicity, and how is the firm responding? Are there any explanations for the different approaches of these two major investment banks?
6. Are the recent JPMorgan Chase and Goldman Sachs experiences supportive of or counter to Macey's thesis of the decline of the role of corporate reputation?
7. Identify two examples in which a concern about corporate reputation no longer constrained a firm's actions.
8. One of the dimensions of the Supreme Court's *Citizens United* decision was that corporations have free speech rights under the Constitution akin to individuals' rights. Please trace the Court's argument on this issue, including the distinctions between private and corporate speech. (Note: Answering this question will require reviewing the case, which is available at www.law.cornell.edu/supct/html/08–205.ZS.html. This is not an easy task.).

9. Develop a justification for why the government should be involved in grading a particular product, say chicken eggs, rather than leaving that task to a private firm or for the marketplace to grade on its own.
10. Trace how movie ratings systems have evolved over time in response both to changing social moral standards and explicit regulation.
11. A good reputation has economic value. How can that value be depicted in an economic graph?
12. How might better product information affect the demand curve for a product?

NOTES

1. Wikipedia, "Tobacco Master Settlement Agreement." Available at http://en.wikipedia.org/wiki/Tobacco_Master_Settlement_Agreement#Restrictions_on_youth_targeting. Last visited 9/30/11.

2. Sherman Act, Section 7. Similar language is included in the Clayton Act, Section 4.

3. Emily Walker, "Most Doctors Will Face Malpractice Suit, AMA Says." ABC News, August 5, 2010. Available at http://abcnews.go.com/Health/HealthCare/malpractice-lawsuits-doctors-common-ama/story?id=11332146. Last visited 9/30/11.

4. "Why All the Pharmaceutical Lawsuits?" *Policy and Medicine,* February 2010. Available at www.policymed.com/2010/02/why-all-the-pharmaceutical-lawsuits-.html. Last visited 9/30/11.

5. For more information, see the UL Web site, www.ul.com.

6. For more information on the Energy Star system, see www.energystar.gov/index.cfm?c=about.ab_index. Last visited 0/2/11.

7. For more information on LEED, see www.usgbc.org/DisplayPage.aspx?CMSPageID=1988. Last visited 10/2/11.

8. Cornell University, Cornell Sustainable Campus, "Green Development." Available at www.sustainablecampus.cornell.edu/climate/building.cfm. Last visited10/2/11.

9. Earth Island Institute, "Dolphin Safe Tuna: Consumers." Available at www.earthisland.org/dolphinSafeTuna/consumer/. Last visited 10/2/11.

10. Campaign for Tobacco Free Kids, "Raising Cigarette Taxes Reduces Smoking, Especially Among Kids." Available at www.tobaccofreekids.org/research/factsheets/pdf/0146.pdf. Last visited 10/4/11. (See also references therein.)

11. Anemona Hartocollis, "New York Health Official Calls for Tax on Drinks with Sugar." *New York Times,* April 8, 2009.

12. KidsHealth, "Overweight and Obesity.' Available at http://kidshealth.org/parent/general/body/overweight_obesity.html. Last visited 10/4/11.

13. Emedicinehealth, "Obesity in Children." Available at www.emedicinehealth.com/obesity_in_children/article_em.htm. Last visited 10/4/11.

14. S&P, "Browse Ratings by Practice." Available at www.standardandpoors.com/ratings/en/us/. Last visited 10/2/11.

15. David S. Hilzenrath, "SEC Report Questions Credit Ratings Agencies' Practices." *Washington Post*, September 30, 2011.

16. AMA, "Accreditation and Collaboration." Available at www.ama-assn.org/ama/pub/physician-resources/clinical-practice-improvement/clinical-quality/accreditation-collaboration.page. Last visited 10/13/12.

17. AICPA, "AICPA Ethics Codification Project." Available at www.aicpa.org/interestareas/professionalethics/community/pages/aicpa-ethics-codification-project.aspx. Last visited 8/13/12.

18. FINRA, "About the Financial Industry Regulatory Authority." Available at www.finra.org/AboutFINRA/. Last visited 10/13/12.

19. American Beverage Association, "Alliance School Beverage Guidelines: Final Progress Report."

March 8, 2010. Available at www.ameribev.org/files/240_School%20Beverage%20Guidelines%20 Final%20Progress%20Report.pdf. Guidelines available at www.ameribev.org/nutrition—science/school-beverage-guidelines/. Both last visited 8/14/2012.

20. L.L. Sharma, S.P. Terent, and K.D. Brownell, "The Food Industry and Self-Regulation: Standards to Promote Success and to Avoid Public Health Failures." *Framing Health Matters/American Journal of Public Health* 100 (February 2010): 240–46.

21. Beer Institute, "Beer Institute Advertising and Marketing Code." Available at www.beerinstitute.org/assets/uploads/BI-AdCode-5-2011.pdf. Last visited 7/9/14. The Wine Institute and Distilled Spirits Council have similar advertising guidelines.

22. Federal Trade Commission, "Self-Regulation in the Alcohol Industry: Report of the Federal Trade Commission." June 2008. Available at www.ftc.gov/os/2008/06/080626alcoholreport.pdf. Last visited 8/14/12.

23. Federal Trade Commission, "FTC Releases Fourth Major Study on Alcohol Advertising and Industry Efforts to Reduce Marketing to Underage Audiences," March 20, 2014. Available at www.ftc.gov/news-events/press-releases/2014/03/ftc-releases-fourth-major-study-alcohol-advertising-industry. Last visited 5/27/14.

24. Available at www.ussc.gov/guidelines-manual/2013-ussc-guidelines-manual.

25. PricewaterhouseCoopers and Compliance Week, "Broader perspectives; Higher performance. State of Compliance, 2012 Study." June 2012. Available at www.pwc.com/en_us/us/risk-management/assets/2012-compliance-study.pdf. Last visited 6/23/14.

26. Corporate Compliance Plan, "*Corporate Governance and Regulatory Compliance Programs, Plans and Issues*." Available at www.corporatecomplianceplan.com/. Last visited 10/3/11.

27. See www.corporatecompliance.org. Last visited 10/3/11.

28. See Exhibit 1: Merck Leadership and Organizational Structure. Available at www.merck.com/newsroom/vioxx/pdf/002_exhibit_1_merck_leadership_and_organizational_structure.pdf. Last visited 10/3/11.

29. Detailed listing available at www.cbsnews.com/8301–31727_162–20001981–10391695.html. Last visited 9/6/12.

30. Goldman Sachs, "Business Principles and Standards Committee Report," Executive Summary, January 2011. Available at www.goldmansachs.com/who-we-are/business-standards/committee-report/business-standards-committee-report-pdf.pdf. Last visited 9/6/12.

31. Dina ElBoghdady, "Jury Finds Goldman Executive Liable for Misleading Investors." *Washington Post,* August 1, 2013.

32. Quoted in SEC, "SEC Charges Goldman Sachs With Fraud in Structuring and Marketing of CDO Tied to Subprime Mortgages." April 16, 2010. Available at www.sec.gov/news/press/2010/2010–59.htm. Last visited 9/6/12.

33. Peter J. Henning, "The Litigation That Haunts Goldman Sachs." DealBook, June 25, 2012. Available at http://dealbook.nytimes.com/2012/06/25/the-litigation-that-haunts-goldman-sachs/. Last visited 9/6/12.

34. Quoted in ibid.

35. "A Risk Too Far." *The Economist,* January 11, 2011. Available at www.economist.com/node/17969917. Last visited 9/6/12.

36. Quoted in *Daily Mail*, "Goldman Sachs 'Misled Clients, Manipulated Markets and Profited Off Clients' Losses' Says Scathing Senate Report." April 14, 2011.

37. William D. Cohan, "Wise Up on Goldman: Bloomberg Businessweek Opening Remarks." *BloombergBusinessweek*, March 15, 2012. Available at www.businessweek.com/news/2012–03–14/wise-up-on-goldman-sachs-bloomberg-businessweek-opening-remarks. Last visited 9/7/12.

38. Greg Smith, "Why I Am Leaving Goldman Sachs." *New York Times* Opinion Pages, March 14, 2012.

39. Don Jeffrey, "Morgan Stanley, Goldman Sachs Sued Over Facebook IPO." *Bloomberg,* May 23, 2012.

40. G. Morgenson, "Trying to Pierce a Wall Street Fog." *New York Times,* July 21, 2013.

41. David Kocieniewski, "A Shuffle of Aluminum, but to Banks, Pure Gold." *New York Times,* July 20/21, 2013.

42. Matt Egan, "J.P. Morgan Inks $410M Deal to Settle Electricity Manipulation Probe." *Fox Business,* July 30, 2013. Available at http://www.foxbusiness.com/industries/2013/07/30/jp-morgan-inks-410m-to-settle-electricity-manipulation-probe/#ixzz2adTwp4bB. Last visited 7/31/13.

43. Smith, "Why I Am Leaving Goldman Sachs."

44. Full list available at www.goldmansachs.com/s/2011annual/business-principles/. Last visited 9/7/12.

45. Goldman Sachs, "Business Principles and Standards Committee Report."

46. Ibid.

47. Cohan, "Wise Up on Goldman: BloombergBusinessweek Opening Remarks."

48. John Carney, "The Banality of Goldman's Business Standards" CNBC, January 12, 2011. Available at www.cnbc.com/id/41040099/The_Banality_of_Goldman_s_Business_Standards. Last visited 9/7/12.

49. Simon Johnson, "What Goldman Sachs Failed to Acknowledge." *Economix,* January 13, 2011.

50. See 2011 Annual Report pp. 24–25. Available at www.goldmansachs.com/investor-relations/financials/current/annual-reports/2011-annual-report-files/GS_AR11_Corporate_Engagement.pdf. Last visited 9/10/12. Miriam Kreinin Souccar, "Goldman Sachs Slashes Charitable Giving." *Crain's New York Business,* January 20, 2012.

51. Susanne Craig, "Goldman Sachs, Buying Redemption." *New York Times*, October 26, 2013.

52. "Goldman Sachs: Reform School for Bankers." *The Economist,* October 5, 2013. Available at www.economist.com/news/finance-and-economics/21587212-worlds-leading-investment-bank-puts-itself-under-spotlight-reform-school. Last visited 10/14/13.

53. Rachel Burstein, "Paid Protection—Why Monsanto and Other Industry Giants Love EPA Regulations." *Mother Jones,* January/February 1997. Available at www.mindfully.org/GE/Monsanto-Paid-Protection-EPA.htm. Last visited 10/3/11.

54. Jennifer Ferrara, "Revolving Doors: Monsanto and the Regulators." *The Ecologist,* September/October 1998. Available at http://www.psrast.org/ecologmons.htm. Last visited 12/2/11.

55. Brian Shaffer, "Firm-Level Responses to Government Regulation: Rheoretical and Research Approaches." *Journal of Management* 21, 3 (Fall 1995): 495–514.

56. Quoted in D. Charles, *Lords of the Harvest.* Cambridge, MA: Perseus Publishing, 2001, p. 134.

57. T. Sing, "Details: *Mutual Pharmaceutical Co. vs. Bartlett.*" SCOTUSBlog, June 24, 2013. Available at www.scotusblog.com/?p=165662. Last visited 6/17/13.

58. International Food Information Council Foundation, "2013 Food & Health Survey." Available at www.foodinsight.org/LinkClick.aspx?fileticket=rH%2bcRQoWh2s%3d&tabid=65. Last visited 6/20/13.

59. J.R. Macey, *The Death of Corporate Reputation.* Upper Saddle River, NJ: Pearson Education, 2013.

60. "The Morgan Shakedown." *The Wall Street Journal,* October 20, 2013.

61. Katrina vanden Heuvel, "JPMorgan Settlement is Justice, Not a Shakedown." *Washington Post,* October 29, 2013.

62. Danielle Douglas and Steven Mufson, "JPMorgan Chase CEO Jamie Dimon's Complicated Relationship with Washington." *Washington Post*, November 1, 2013.

63. Elizabeth Rosenthal, "The Soaring Cost of a Simple Breath." *New York Times,* October 12, 2013.

64. OpenSecrets.org, Center for Responsive Politics. "Lobbying." Available at www.opensecrets.org/lobby/methodology.php. Last visited 6/20/13.

65. Public Citizen, "12 Months After." January 2011, p. 9. Available at www.citizen.org/documents/Citizens-United-20110113.pdf. Last visited 10/3/11.

66. Quoted in Stephen Koff, "Scotts Miracle-Gro hopes to seed Mitt Romney's election." *The Plain Dealer,* August 10, 2012.

67. Quoted in Tom Scheck, "Target apologizes for donation to MN Forward." Minnesota Public Radio, August 5, 2010. Available at http://minnesota.publicradio.org/display/web/2010/08/05/target-apology-donation/. Last visited 9/6/12.

68. "Target Pressured to Refrain from Political Donations." *HuffPost Politics,* August 7, 2011. Available at www.huffingtonpost.com/2011/06/07/target-refrain-from-political-donations_n_872830.html. Last visited 9/6/12.

69. News Channel 9, "Local Coke bottling plant to protest 'Sugar Tax' proposal." February 5, 2010. Available at www.9wsyr.com/news/local/story/Local-Coke-bottling-plant-to-protest-Sugar-Tax/KVk1cr8ysEWOorer8b37_g.cspx. Last visited 10/4/11.

70. Internet Society. Available at www.isoc.org/isoc/. Last visited 10/3/11.

71. J.W. Richards, J.B. Tye, and P.M. Fischer, "The Tobacco Industry's Code of Advertising in the United States: Myth and Reality." *Tobacco Control* 5, 4 (December 1996): 295–31. Available at www.ncbi.nlm.nih.gov/pmc/articles/PMC1759528/. Last visited 10/28/13.

72. The agreement however contains few new revelations. Available at www.justice.gov/iso/opa/resources/69520131119191246941958.pdf. Last visited 12/9/13.

73. Danielle Douglas, "JPMorgan Chase, Citigroup First U.S. Banks to be Fined in Rate-Rigging Scandal." *Washington Post*, December 4, 2013. Danielle Douglas, "JPMorgan's Settlement: A Win for Communities Hard Hit by Housing Crisis." *Washington Post,* November 19, 2013.

▪ PART II ▪

MANAGING WITH AND UNDER REGULATION

While Part I presents the whys and wherefores of regulation, Part II addresses how to manage and even prosper in a regulated environment.

6 Consumer Products and Food Safety Regulation

CHAPTER OBJECTIVES

Chapter objectives include providing examples of problems with past unregulated products that led to the adoption of many regulations. The core objective of the chapter though is initiating a consideration of business strategy for working with current regulations, as well as likely future ones, based on ten case studies in different product markets.

There are no easy answers for any of these cases, nor indeed for most regulatory compliance issues. It will become clear that there are different corporate interpretations of regulations and strategies for compliance. This means a true strategy must incorporate expected responses of competitors, and reactions to their actions. To that end, the method of game theory is introduced as a systematic means of considering actions and expected responses by competitors. To make the cases here more complex, several are presented as probable/possible future regulations, meaning corporate strategy must be made based on incomplete information.

Key agencies and acts involved in the cases include: NHTSA (National Highway Traffic Safety Administration); CFPB (Consumer Financial Protection Bureau); LEED (Leadership in Energy and Environmental Design—a voluntary group, not an agency); FDA (Food and Drug Administration); National Labeling and Education Act (1990); USDA (U.S. Department of Agriculture)

Key Terms: *Game theory; Intellectual property rights; rBST (recombinant bovine somatotropin); GRAS (generally recognized as safe)*

Consumer products, including food and pharmaceuticals, were one of the early areas of domestic federal regulation. The reason for this is easy to appreciate as these products touch everyone and can have severe implications. Yet presently there are seemingly more and more news reports of salmonella and other bacterial contamination of feed products causing widespread illness and occasionally even death. For example during the 2011 summer, Cargill recalled 36 million pounds of ground turkey products which had been contaminated with salmonella. At least seventy-six people had become ill and one man died.[1] That case, though, was a result of accidental contamination. In 2008 a Chinese company recalled 700 tons of infant formula after determining it contained melamine, an industrial chemical. The contaminated product was linked to the death of one baby and kidney problems in at least fifty more. And this followed a similar deliberate contamination case which caused the deaths of thirteen infants. None of these products were believed to have been imported into the United States, but in 2007 melamine-contaminated pet food imported from China sickened thousands of U.S. pets and killed an unknown number.

At a more whimsical, or at least fictional, level, there is the conversation in *Huck Finn* after the Duke and the King have been run off by an angry mob. To the question "What got you into trouble?" the Duke replies, "Well, I'd been selling an article to take the tarter off the teeth—and it does take it off, too, and generly the enamel along with it . . ." Like most "patent medicines," the Duke's would not have been patented. "Patent" means from its Latin route "to lay open," as in to inspect, not something the purveyors of those "medicines" wanted at all (Figure 6.1)!

It is important to note that "domestic federal regulation" actually followed state efforts and those focused on export trade (see this chapter, Section 6.3). This was in large part because the Supreme Court interpretation of the Commerce Clause of the Constitution did not until 1824 give the Congress authority to regulate interstate commerce, while the regulation of foreign commerce had been the preserve of the Congress (see Chapter 3, Section 3.7a).

Product safety though is only one aspect, albeit the dominant one, of product regulation. The other is product standards and quality designations. Examples include standards for what can be labeled as "mayonnaise" (as distinct from "salad dressing") and "ice cream" (see Chapter 3, Section 3.3a). There are also food quality standards like "Grade A" and "Prime" (see Chapter 5, Section 5.1c). These standards serve a different regulatory purpose than protection from physical harm. This could be termed *protection from economic harm* or, using more the language of economics, as addressing information asymmetry. Recall that markets cannot function efficiently when buyers in particular are inadequately informed. When an information-based market failure exists, regulation-mandated information can remedy the inefficiency, so the theory goes. In short, consumers are made better off by enhancing their purchase decisions (see Chapter 2, Section 2.2). The lead case in this chapter deals with a particular type of product information, that describing key attributes of tires (see this chapter, Section 6.4).

The need for information is especially critical when it is not possible to evaluate the essential attributes of a product even by using or consuming it. Taste or other sensory evaluations for example cannot be used to determine if a food was produced organically. Economists call these *credence* goods, meaning one must believe the description, as distinct from *experiential* goods, which can be assessed by the buyer.

We proceed in this chapter by first giving an overview of the kinds of consumer product problems which have been regulated (this chapter, Section 6.1), proceeding to the support and controversy of this form of regulation (this chapter, Section 6.2); and following with a synopsis of the major applicable legislation (this chapter, Section 6.3). The fourth section (this chapter, Section 6.4) then presents the case regarding tire standards and raises the question "When is it in the interest of a firm to cooperate with regulators when setting product quality standards?" Next we proceed to nine additional and distinct cases.

Figure 6.1 **Patent Medicines**

Source: Wikimedia Commons. Original author "Deepestbluesea."

Case 6.2 (this chapter, Section 6.5) addresses an update of the tire quality case, focusing on efficiency. Case 6.3 (this chapter, Section 6.6) deals with another current issue and the question to cooperate or not, this time with the Consumer Financial Protection Bureau regarding its management structure, while Case 6.4 (this chapter, Section 6.7) focuses on one of the controversial regulations proposed by the Consumer Financial Protection Bureau to tighten up on the "servicing" or oversight of mortgage payment collections. Case 6.5 (this chapter, Section 6.8) introduces the concept of voluntary compliance, in this instance with building energy efficiency standards. Case 6.6 (this chapter, Section 6.9) extends the voluntary compliance issue by adding the dimension of making a building "bird-safe."

The next three cases relate to food-labeling issues, first regarding the posting of calories at fast-food restaurants (Case 6.7; this chapter, Section 6.10), the costs and uses of nutrition and organic labels (Case 6.8; this chapter, Section 6.11), and finally the labeling of genetically modified foods, dairy foods in particular (Case 6.9; this chapter, Section 6.12). And finally Case 6.10 (this chapter, Section 6.13) adds an international dimension involving intellectual property rights.

6.1 NOTABLE EXAMPLES OF STANDARDS AND SAFETY ISSUES

Chapter 2 emphasizes the importance of tragic events as a springboard for regulations. For consumer products it is not difficult to identify multiple examples of products for which alleged safety lapses have evolved into regulations. According to Consumers Union, annually 34,500 people die and 34 million suffer injuries from consumer products under federal safety jurisdiction.[2] A sampling of dramatic problems with product safety is presented here. Several of these cases are self-evident to many, while others raise more difficult cost/benefit questions. But all are regulations which must be accommodated by the targeted businesses.

a. Baby Cribs

There have been over fifty recalls of baby cribs with drop-side detachments since 2005, which involved more than 7 million drop-side cribs. These recalled cribs have been implicated in at least thirty-two infant and toddler deaths.[3] A voluntary ban on selling drop-side cribs in the United States beginning on June 1, 2010, was made mandatory on June 28, 2011.

At the same time, the Consumer Product Safety Commission has revised standards for full-sized cribs. Past standards require slats to be a maximum of 2⅜ inches apart.[4] The 2011 standards require the wood be stronger and the hardware include anti-loosening devices.[5]

b. Elixir Sulfanilamide

Sulfanilamide was one of the first effective drugs to treat streptococcal infections in the pre-penicillin era but was limited in usefulness by being available only as powder and tablets. The entire pharmaceutical industry was searching for a suitable solvent to convert it to liquid form. Then in 1937, Harold Cole Watkins, head chemist for the small but reputable pharmaceutical firm S. E. Massengill Co., found that it dissolved in diethylene glycol. What was not noted was that glycol—best known as an antifreeze—is a deadly poison, all the more sinister as it has a pleasing, sweet raspberry taste. Before all but 6 gallons of the 240 gallons produced and distributed could be located and seized, over 100 people, many children being treated for a sore throat, had been poisoned. Making the tragedy worse, the deaths from kidney failure were characterized by intense and unrelenting pain. As the mother of one victim described the incident to President Roosevelt, "[W]e can [still] see her little body tossing to and fro and hear that little voice screaming in pain and it seems as though it would drive me insane."[6]

This incident has ongoing national significance for several reasons. One is the alacrity with which the poisonous product was collected in that pre-instant-communication era. Efforts included sending out over 1,000 telegrams followed by dispatching all 239 FDA inspectors and chemists to check the Massengill shipping record and following up with visits to salesmen, druggists, and patients. Notably, the product could not have been seized under the prevailing 1906 Food and Drug Act except that it was mislabeled as an "elixir" (Figure 6.2). Since, technically, an elixir uses an alcohol solvent, it fell under FDA control, whereas if it had been labeled a "solution," the FDA would not have had any authority.[7]

More notably, the law in 1937 did not require safety, toxicity, testing. The fervor created led to the passage of the 1938 Food, Drug, and Cosmetic Act, which gave the FDA the authority to require safety testing for new medicines. The industry as well recognized the need for a government role in protecting the drug supply. "The only way in which the industry can properly protect itself against another accident of the same type is for [an] outside agency, such as the government, to have proper control over manufacturers and their products."[8]

Figure 6.2 **Elixir Sulfanilamide, Implicated in Over 100 Poisonings in 1937, Led to FDA Control Over the Safety of Pharmaceutical Products**

Source: Wikimedia Commons. Author unknown. Circa 1937–1938.

But the deaths from glycol did not end with the seizure of the Massengill product. Harold Cole Watkins, the chemist who was responsible for its creation, committed suicide, but S. E. Massengill, the company president, disclaimed any responsibility. "I do not feel that there was any responsibility on our part." Nor has the lure for the unscrupulous of substituting the cheap, tasty glycol diminished over time. "Toxic syrup has figured in at least eight mass poisonings around the world in the past two decades. Researchers estimate that thousands have died. In many cases, the precise origin of the poison has never been determined. But records and interviews show that in three of the last four cases it was made in China, a major source of counterfeit drugs."[9]

c. Thalidomide

Thalidomide as a cure for morning sickness was sold in a number of countries across the world from 1957 until 1961. It was then withdrawn from the market after being found to be a cause of birth defects in what has been called "one of the biggest medical tragedies of modern times" (Figure 6.3). It is not known exactly how many worldwide victims of the drug there have been, although estimates range from 10,000 to 20,000. At the time of cessation of sales, thalidomide had not been approved in the United States for reliev-

Figure 6.3 **Baby Born in 1962 with an Extra Appendage Connected to the Foot and a Malformation of the Right Arm Caused by the Pregnant Mother Taking the Drug Thalidomide**

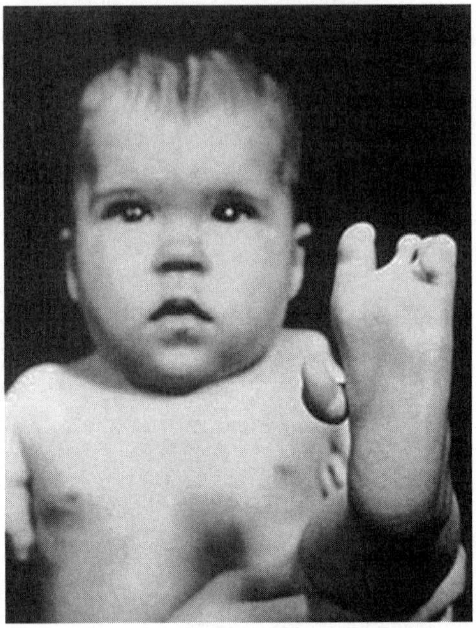

Source: Tony Long, "Oct. 1, 1957: Thalidomide Cures Morning Sickness, But . . ." *Wired*, October 1, 2008. Original photo source National Cancer Institute.

ing morning sickness, so cases of deformed babies were limited to those who used or acquired the product overseas.

The Kefauver-Harris Amendment of 1962, passed in the wake of the thalidomide imbroglio, requires drug manufacturers to demonstrate the effectiveness of their products as well as their safety. Technically, though, the amendment would not have affected the FDA review process as thalidomide is effective for its intended role in suppressing morning sickness; it is the side effects that were so problematic. The thalidomide regulatory experience is nevertheless invoked when there are suggestions the FDA speed up the drug review process. Recently thalidomide has been approved for other uses in the United States for certain cancers, side effects of AIDS, and leprosy, but only under carefully controlled conditions. The name has been changed, though—to Thalomid®.

d. Compounding Pharmacies

It would be a mistake to assume that deadly and debilitating problems with pharmaceuticals are solely issues of the past, often the deep past, and have all been resolved. Very recently—fall 2012 to be specific—thirty-nine people died and 620 stricken with meningitis as a result of the contamination of a spinally injected treatment for back pain. Infections in the spine are nearly impossible to treat and in this case the injections were contaminated with fungal meningitis.

Figure 6.4 **All Early Pharmacies Were Compounding Pharmacies**

Interior of A. E. Lathrop's Drug Store—Simsbury, Conn.

Source: Wikimedia Commons. Original author unknown photographer. Issued by George E. Wright, Hartford, Connecticut.

Each of the thirty-nine avoidable deaths is a personal and family tragedy, but the regulatory issue is with the suspected supplier of the treatment, the New England Compounding Center. Compounding pharmacies go back to the early days of the industry when chemists mixed up drugs as needed in the pre-pill era (see Figure 6.4). Today, however, compounding pharmacies make specialized products in batches too small to interest the majors, or simply at lower cost. The problem is they exist in regulatory ambiguity between the FDA and (less comprehensive) state pharmacy regulation. Compounding pharmacies are not supposed to ship out of state (New England Compounding Center is located in Massachusetts), but they do; the 17,676 vials containing the potentially contaminated steroid were shipped to twenty-three states, with 14,000 patients treated in nineteen states. Faced with heavy lawsuits, the New England Compounding Center subsequently declared bankruptcy;[10] all fifty of the tested vials from the New England Compounding Center were found to be contaminated with mold or fungus.[11]

Nor was this New England's first problem—it had received warning letters from the FDA. And other compounding pharmacies have been implicated in the past as well—in

2002 (one death), 2005 (three deaths), 2007 (two deaths), and 2011 (nine deaths). There is a voluntary accreditation board, the Pharmacy Compounding Accreditation Board, but only some 162 of about 3,000 eligible have sought accreditation to date.[12] The industry nonetheless uses the existence of the voluntary process as a justification for continued non-FDA regulation.[13]

A preliminary House report confirmed that the FDA has more limited authority over compounding pharmacies than with drug manufacturers. Warning letters sent by the FDA are "Guidance documents [which] do not establish legally enforceable rights or responsibilities and do not legally bind the public or the FDA," according to the report.[14] In September 2013 the responsible congressional panels developed a bill, the Drug Quality and Security Act, to rectify the problems. The act grants the FDA greater authority to regulate compounding pharmacies which ship across state lines, as well as establishing a national set of standards to track drugs through the distribution chain. Recall that locating products in the pipeline has been a problem with defective products for more than a century. H.R. 3204 was passed November 21, 2013.

e. Ford Pinto's Exploding Gas Tank

In the late 1960s, Ford Motor Company set out to produce a subcompact automobile, the Pinto, that would compete with the Japanese subcompacts then becoming increasingly popular in the United States. Ford engineers knew that the Pinto's gas tank design location between the differential and the bumper was susceptible to explosions from rear-end collisions due to some exposed bolts. Explosions had previously occurred with a related European model. An alternative to moving the Pinto's tank would have been to install a part protecting the tank from rupturing on impact with the exposed bolts, but costing $6.65 per car, or an estimated $20 million annually.

At the time there were no federal regulations applicable to the placement of gas tanks, nor to impact safety regarding tank explosions. Lawsuits stemming from the burning deaths of multiple victims nonetheless cost Ford millions, and Ford was eventually forced to recall the Pintos—technically a "voluntary" recall as there were no standards or federal authority to compel a recall in order to install the $6.65 part.[15] The publicity surrounding the recall informed drivers about the degree to which crash-worthiness could be designed into cars.[16] (Crash test video "1971 Chevrolet Impala vs. 1972 Ford Pinto Full-Rear Impact [Legendary Crash Test!]" can be seen on YouTube at www.youtube .com/watch?v=lgOxWPGsJNY.)

In a case of déjà vu, Chrysler in 2013 was involved with a related recall of millions of earlier Jeep models associated with fires following rear-end collisions. The National Highway Traffic Saftey Administration (NHTSA) initially called for a recall of 2.7 million Jeeps. Chrysler agreed, but only after two weeks of resistance and then after the number to be recalled was reduced to 1.56 million cars from the 1993–2007 model years. Nor did Chrysler have to declare any were defective. This is expected to help the company defend itself in lawsuits concerning those vehicles. Some of the excluded models will be available for a "customer service action," which will receive similar treatment but technically do not constitute a recall and so are subject to different requirements.[17]

General Motors (GM) was not so successful when in early 2014 a long-standing failure in an ignition switch came to light. The switch could turn from "on" to "accessory" while the vehicle was in motion, disabling power brakes, airbags, and power steering, leading to at least thirteen deaths. Evidence emerged that GM engineers were aware of the problem as far back as 2001 and at one point provided a replacement part, but using the same part number as the original faulty product. The regulatory process eventually led to the recall of 2.6 million cars, and a $ 35 million fine by the NHTSA for not reacting quickly enough to its requests for answers. Some have accused GM of a cover-up while others have been very critical of the NHTSA for being so slow to identify the problem.[18]

f. Tylenol Tampering Scare

On September 29, 1982, twelve-year-old Mary Kellerman of Elk Grove Village, Illinois, woke up at dawn and went to her parents' bedroom. She felt ill and complained of having a sore throat and a runny nose. To ease her discomfort, her parents gave her one Extra-Strength Tylenol capsule. At 7 A.M. they found Mary on the bathroom floor. She was immediately taken to the hospital where she was later pronounced dead. Doctors initially suspected that Mary died from a stroke, but evidence later pointed to a more sinister diagnosis.

Johnson and Johnson experienced a major crisis when it was discovered that numerous bottles of its Extra-Strength Tylenol capsules had been laced with cyanide. Within three days beginning September 29, 1982, seven people took cyanide-laced Tylenol in Chicago and four subsequently died. Following a $100 million product recall, Tylenol products were reintroduced with triple-seal tamper-resistant packaging. It became the first company to comply with the Food and Drug Administration's new mandate of tamper-resistant packaging. Furthermore, Tylenol promoted the use of caplets, oval-shaped pills, which are more resistant to tampering.[19]

This was the first major product tampering case, and remains unsolved. But there is a legacy: "Every time you open a bottle or package (of medicine, food or drink) that has tamper evidence features, a band around the lid or an interior seal, it is because of the Tylenol case," said Pan Demetrakakes, executive editor of *Food & Drug Packaging* magazine.[20]

g. Seismic Building Codes

The San Francisco fire of 1906, which claimed some 3,000 lives and destroyed 80 percent of the city, began with an earthquake (Figure 6.5). Seismic building codes, designed to protect the safety of occupants, have been the most obvious way to minimize such horrendous losses going forward. Structures built according to code should resist minor earthquakes undamaged, resist moderate earthquakes without significant structural dam-

Figure 6.5 **Burning of San Francisco Following the 1906 Earthquake**

Source: Wikimedia Commons. Original source National Archives.

age, and resist major earthquakes without collapse. Codes have only recently begun to address content damage.

In the western United States, codes had begun to make substantial improvements in construction as early as the mid-1970s, but became widely used in the eastern states only in the early or mid-1990s.[21]

h. Substandard Housing

In the early nineteenth century, housing conditions for the poor were abysmal. People often lived in "back-to-backs," which were houses of two or three rooms, one on top of the other, and literally back-to-back. The back of one house joined onto the back of another with windows only on one side. The bottom room was used as a living room cum kitchen. The upstairs rooms were used as bedrooms. The lowliest homes were one-room cellars, which were damp and poorly ventilated. The poorest people slept on piles of straw because they could not afford beds.

In the 1840s, local councils passed bylaws banning cellar dwellings. They also banned any new back-to-backs. The existing ones were gradually demolished and replaced over the following decades.[22]

Substandard and overcrowded housing is not only an issue for the past or for the poor. In Ithaca, New York, home of Cornell University, there has been an ongoing issue between student residents of Collegetown, local permanent residents, and City of Ithaca officials. The city limits occupancy of a nongrandfathered dwelling unit to three unrelated individuals but acknowledges it lacks the staff to enforce the regulations as well as housing quality on a timely basis.

i. All-Terrain Vehicles (ATVs)

ATVs of either the three- or four-wheeled type are popular for off-road use and are often used by teenagers. But due to the rugged terrain they operate in, motorcycle-like lack of protection for drivers and riders (most are intended for driver use only), and often spirited performance, they are the cause of frequent accidents. Estimates are of 781 deaths and nearly 132,000 injuries in 2009. Reporting these figures is one of the responsibilities of the Consumer Products Safety Commission (CPSC).[23] About 170 of those deaths are among children under sixteen, leading to calls for use bans for that age group.[24] Legislation including registration and mandatory helmet use is left to the states.[25]

6.2 SUPPORT AND CONTROVERSY

a. Support for Product Regulation

A recent telephone survey by Consumers Union (publishers of *Consumer Reports*) found strong and general support for CPSC's role in protecting the public from unsafe consumer products. Specific findings include:[26]

- Ninety-five percent of those surveyed agree that the federal government should require testing by manufacturers of children's products like jewelry, pacifiers, and toys to ensure they do not contain any harmful substances.
- Ninety-four percent agree that the federal government should require testing by manufacturers of products like baby carriers or slings, cribs, and strollers to ensure their safety.
- Eighty-seven percent were interested in the opportunity to investigate if another consumer experienced a safety hazard with a consumer product. (Example: The NHTSA at SaferCar.gov has a hotline for reporting or searching auto-safety issues).
- Eighty-two percent were interested in the ability to access a database maintained by the government where they can report and search safety problems with consumer products.
- Ninety-one percent agree that the federal government should set safety standards for all children's products.

The CPSC claims its actions and rules "contributed significantly to the 30 percent decline in the rate of deaths and injuries associated with consumer products over the past 30 years."[27] That was accomplished by a very small department (by Washington standards) of only 500 employees and a budget of $121 million in 2011.[28]

b. Controversy Regarding Product Regulation

The broad and general hostility to regulations shown by Republican legislators in particular, but not exclusively, is evident from the ongoing opposition to the Patient Protection and Affordable Care Act (fifty-four votes and counting to repeal have been introduced in the House) as well as the filibustering of a number of nominees for agency heads. The powerful U.S. Chamber of Commerce recently passed the $1 billion mark in spending on lobbying to influence legislation. Particular targets have been financial and health-care regulation.[29]

Several trade associations are frequently critical of the regulatory process. One example is the National Association of Manufacturers. In a 2012 letter to Representative Darrell Issa (R-CA), the association's president and CEO cited a recent member survey in which 62 percent of the respondents cited "an unfavorable business climate caused by regulations and taxes [as] the top challenge facing business." Many of the specific concerns are environment and labor related, but a CPSC rule making to establish a safety standard for table saws is a consumer product regulation specifically identified.[30]

A number of think tanks, such as the conservative Hoover Institution, particularly target regulations. A 2013 opinion piece identifies an estimated $1.8 trillion annual cost of regulation, "equivalent to an invisible 65 percent surcharge on your federal taxes, or nearly 12 percent of GDP. Especially invidious is the fact that the costs of regulation for small businesses (those with fewer than twenty employees) are 36 percent higher per employee than they are for bigger firms."[31] And then there are extremely wealthy individuals who use their private means to advance antiregulation causes. A leading example is the billionaire brothers David and Charles Koch. According to Common Cause, a liberal organization, "they favor dramatically lower personal and corporate income taxes, less government oversight of industry—particularly when it involves environmental regulations that impact their businesses—and minimal public assistance for the needy."[32]

Regulations are complex and the base for multiple different perspectives, especially when the costs and benefits are unevenly distributed. While brief, this subsection will discuss some of the diverse players who affect the regulatory debate.

6.3 Overview of Major Federal Legislation/Responsible Agencies

Table 6.1 provides a partial list intended only to give an indication of the development and extension of regulations. Among the exclusions are amendments to previously existing acts, and state legislation. A full listing of acts would be very lengthy indeed!

Table 6.1

Overview of Major Federal Regulatory Acts Related to Product Information and Safety

Title	Agency	Year	Authority
Drug Importation Act	Customs Service	1848	Inspect imported drugs
Meat Inspection Act	USDA	1891	Inspect live cattle for export
Tea Importation Act	Sec. Treasury	1897	Customs inspection
Biologics Control Act		1902	Licensing of biologics establishments, inspection of vaccine manufacturers, premarket approval
Pure Food & Drug Act	FDA	1906	Specified drugs labeled with contents and dosage; created FDA (1930)
Federal Meat Inspection Act	FSIS	1906	Prevent sale of adulterated/misbranded meat, sanitary slaughter and procession
Federal Trade Commission Act	FTC	1914	Prevent unfair competition, deceptive acts; created FTC
Federal Food, Drug, and Cosmetic Act	FDA	1938	Authorize FDA to oversee the safety of food, drugs, and cosmetics
Poultry Products Inspection Act	FSIS	1957	Inspection of poultry
Humane Slaughter Act	FSIS	1958	Protect livestock during slaughter
Food Additives Amend. Act	FDA	1958	Exempts GRAS foods; additives must be approved
National Traffic & Motor Vehicle Safety Act	DOT	1966	Safety standards for motor vehicles; save lives
Consumer Products Safety Act	CPSC	1972	Protect public from unreasonable risks of injury or death from thousands of consumer products; created CPSC
Energy Policy Conservation Act	DOT	1975	Establishes car manufacturers' mileage standards
Anti-Tampering Regulations	FDA	1982	Most over-the-counter drugs to be packaged in tamper-resistant packages
Orphan Drug Act	FDA	1983	Promote research on rare diseases
Nutrition Labeling and Education Act	FDA	1990	Use FDA-approved health claims on food labels; food labels include nutrition info (calories, fat)
Mammography Quality Standards Act	FDA	1992	Mammography facilities certified and inspected
Dietary Supplement Health & Education Act	FDA	1994	Vitamins, herbs, and minerals exempt from food additive provisions
Food and Drug Modernization Act	FDA	1997	Fast-track approval for certain new drugs
Consumer Prod. Safety Improvement Act	CPSC	2008	Strengthened Consumer Products Safety Act
Credit CARD Act	Fed. Res.	2009	Consumer protection for credit card users
Consumer Financial Protection Act	Fed. Res.	2010	Part of the Dodd-Frank Act; provide financial information to consumers
Food Safety Modernization Act	FDA	2011	Expand prevention; enhance FDA recall authority

Abbreviations:

CPSC	Consumer Product Safety Commission
DOT	Department of Transportation, National Highway Traffic Safety Administration
Fed. Res.	Federal Reserve
FDA	Food and Drug Administration
FTC	Federal Trade Commission
FSIS	Food Safety and Inspection Service of U.S. Dept. Agriculture

Source: Compiled by W. Lesser.

6.4 ■ CASE 6.1: COOPERATE OR NOT WITH GOVERNMENT TIRE-GRADING SYSTEMS

a. Background

This case deals with the role of the industry and Goodyear, then the sales leader, in the development of tire quality grade standards in the 1980s.

Replacing one's automobile tires is indeed a major consumer decision, one that was made 296 million times in 2011 in the United States.[33] There are approximately seventeen major tire brands available as well as private labels from retailers like Walmart. Within brands there are multiple lines—Goodyear presently offers forty-nine distinct ones, and that is for passenger cars alone! Tires differ by level of traction (snow, ice, rain, dry), wear resistance, intended use (summer, snow, all-season), and speed rating (N, H, Z). One large online retailer offers seventy-eight distinct choices for my present car.

Which to select? This is not only a value-for-money issue but a safety one as well. Tire tread all looks pretty much the same, but there are major differences in traction, particularly on snow. Oh, for the days when you simply knew a tire had good traction because it said so right on the tire—"Non-Skid" (Figure 6.6)! And then a tire must be designed to carry the expected load. John Steinbeck, Nobel Prize–winning author of *The Grapes of Wrath,* had problems with too weak tires during the journeys he reported in *Travels with Charlie.* How though to choose? Polls show 27 percent of replacement-tire buyers simply choose the same ones that came with the car, which may or may not be a good decision.[34]

By 2011, according to *Modern Tire Dealer's* new "Retail Tire Customer Survey," 52.5 percent of retail customers who come into an independent tire dealership do not specify a brand preference. Another 25.7 percent specify a tire brand, but are convinced by the tire dealer to make a different choice.[35]

The Department of Transportation (DOT), acting under a mandate of the National Traffic and Motor Vehicle Safety Act of 1966, developed the three-part Uniform Tire Quality Grading Standards (UTQGS) to be included on each tire sold:

- Temperature resistance: A, B, or C—denotes resistance to the generation of heat
- Tread wear: two- or three-digit number—denotes relative wear resistance
- Traction: AA, A, B, or C—denotes ability to stop on wet pavement under controlled conditions

Testing is done by, or on behalf of, the manufacturer, but the DOT has the authority to inspect the test data.

The temperature standard reflects the top-speed rating of a tire as heat buildup increases with speed, as follows:

A: Over 115 mph
B: Between 100 and 115 mph
C: Between 85 and 100 mph

The tread-wear rating is based on a 7,200-mile road test and extrapolated by the manufacturer based on the expected life of the tire. A two- or three-digit number is used

Figure 6.6 **The Non-Skid Tread Was A Major Improvement Over the Treadless Tires of the First Cars**

Source: W. Lesser.

to represent a percentage of a standard value when a tire is tested in accordance with specified procedures. In theory, this means that a tire with a 200 grade will wear twice as long as a tire with a 100 grade, but the practical implications are not nearly so precise. According to one Web site:

> The problem with UTQG Treadwear Grades is that they are open to some interpretation on the part of the tire manufacturer because they are assigned after the tire has only experienced a little treadwear as it runs the 7,200 miles. This means that the tire manufacturers need to extrapolate their raw wear data when they are assigning Treadwear Grades, and that their grades can to some extent reflect how conservative or optimistic their marketing department is. Typically, comparing the Treadwear Grades of tire lines within a single brand is somewhat helpful, while attempting to compare the grades between different brands is not as helpful.[36]

The same site concludes, "Unfortunately for all of the money spent to test, brand, and label the tires sold in the United States, the Uniform Tire Quality Grading Standards have not fully met their original goal of clearly informing consumers about the capabilities of their tires. Maybe it's because tires are so complex and their uses can be so varied, that the grades don't always reflect their actual performance in real world use."[37] According to About.com, "Each tire manufacturer has its own philosophy about UTQG ratings, especially when it comes to the treadwear rating. Some view the rating as a huge marketing tool, while others tend to think of it as an implied warranty."[38]

A survey conducted by DOT in the early 1990s found more than 50 percent of potential consumers surveyed rated information about all three tire quality grade standards as important in making their tire-purchasing decisions. However, among recent purchasers less than 50 percent said the information helped with their actual purchase decision.[39]

An analytical approach for scrutinizing the competitive effects of strategic choices is called *game theory*. An introduction is provided in Example 6.1.

EXAMPLE 6.1: STRATEGIC ASSESSMENT—A GAME THEORY PRIMER

The topics in this subsection, and indeed most of the case studies presented later in this volume, are issues of strategy. That is, given the options available, which course of action is the best, generally meaning the most profitable? For example, is a public relations campaign likely to return at least the cost of its investment, or might it serve only to antagonize a significant portion of the target audience? Greatly complicating a strategic decision is the typical situation in which a competitor or competitors can be expected to respond to any decision made. Your firm may determine acting alone that a 10 percent price increase will significantly enhance profits. However if the competition raises prices by only 5 percent the anticipated higher profits could indeed result in lower ones due to sales losses. How can a firm systematically weigh the options and make the best strategic choice? And of course any approach which is useful for corporate planners can also be useful for analyzing case studies.

The analytical approach described here goes by the name of *game theory* and is applicable to decisions where the possible outcomes can be characterized in numeric terms. Those terms as we shall see can be "hard" numbers like sales or more relativistic numbers like relative preferences. While applications are particularly prevalent in economics and business, game theory is useful across a wide range of issues, including such subjects as evolutionary biology, gambling, investing, and diplomacy—any situation involving interdependent decisions. Here, applications are limited to business and economics. Game theory can also become very complex so only the most basic uses are covered here. Interested readers are directed to the well-reviewed *Game Theory 101: The Complete Textbook* by William Spaniel (2011) or one of the several free online MOOCs.

Game participants are known as players, of which there may be two to *n* (lots). We here shall limit ourselves to two-player games. Games may be *sequential*, a series of back-and-forth, alternating decisions between competitors, or *simultaneous*, where the players act concurrently. We begin with sequential games.

Sequential Games: In a sequential game, as the name clearly states, the players take turns. The simple cases considered here can be solved using a game tree, which is best described through an example. Say there are two airlines in a market, A (for Agony Airlines, the affectionate term used for Allegany Airlines, a precursor of U.S. Airways), and B (for Belly-Up Airlines). They are in competition for market share. At the beginning of the game both share the market about equally, and B ventures a 10 percent price increase. B's expectation is that A will adopt the increase as well, and in the end shares will remain about equal but revenues will have increased (ignoring for this example any effect of prices on overall demand). A, however, has the option of following the increase or not at the start, and B in the second-round decision may continue or abandon the price increase. That means there are a total of six possible decisions in two rounds, with the expected market share outcomes shown in the game tree as follows:

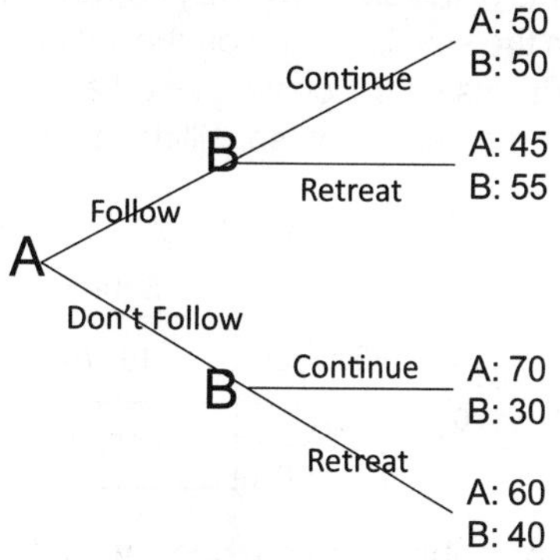

The strategic issue is which choice A should make at the onset—to follow B's increase or not. The solution is to use backward induction, or more simply, look ahead and reason backward. This means we begin the process at the end, always assuming that B will take the optimal rational choice, in this example the highest available market share given the projections shown on the tree. The best option open for B is a 55 percent share, which A rationally assumes it will choose. A now knows that B, after initiating the price increase, will optimally retract it once A has revealed its choice, whether that choice is to follow or not. Knowing this, B now chooses between a payoff of 45 percent market share if it initially follows the price increase, or 60 percent if it does not. Naturally, A chooses the latter, meaning its optimal initial strategic choice is not to follow the price increase. In real life, it was at one time common for an airline to test a price increase, which the other majors may or may not have followed. If the latter, then the initiator usually abandoned the attempt.

When working through these solutions it is important not to get caught up in the "game" terminology and assume the objective is winning, in the sense of achieving an absolutely better result than the opponent. The object rather is to make the optimal strategic choices given the available options. Again referring to the example above, A is the absolute winner if the starting point was indeed near a 50/50 market share balance. However if the starting point was 65/35 for A/B respectively, then A would have lost absolutely but still have made the optimal pricing choice.

Simultaneous Games: For a sequential game to apply, it must be possible for one firm to respond to the decision of the others. That is not always possible, for example, if there is no communication among the players with no second chances. An example would be sealed bids where a player either wins or loses, or the famous example of game theory, the Prisoners' Dilemma. That scenario is as follows: Two parolees are brought in for separate questioning. The police believe they are guilty of a recent robbery but lack the evidence for a conviction. Thus they offer the plea deal that if one rats on the other by confessing, he will get only two years; the other will receive fifteen. However if both confess, they both get ten years in the slammer. Of course, if neither confesses, they both walk. What is a rational crook to do?

The situation is laid out in a game table or payoff matrix as shown below. As suspects we use two of the Beagle Boys from the Mickey Mouse cartoons. The BBs were distinguishable by their prison numbers, which they wear like necklaces: 176–167 and 617–176 (the numbers are variants of the digits 167). By convention, in the playoff matrix the numbers for the player listed on the side is placed on the left (for clarity this is bold in this example; the other number is in italics for the player placed at the top). In this example the numbers are symmetrical, but that need not be so. Filling in the numbers gives the following matrix:

		176–167	
		Squeal	Hang Tough
617–176	Squeal	**10**, *10*	**2**, *15*
	Hang Tough	**15**, *2*	**0**, *0*

To solve, note that while both suspects would benefit if assured the other would not confess, neither can be certain of that outcome (a consequence of being unable to communicate). Hence, each is best off squealing, which will result in a maximum ten-year sentence, with some possibility of serving only two years if the other is not as logical or is excessively trustworthy. The choice of confessing is a dominant strategy as it is not possible for one of the suspects to enhance his situation irrespective of the action of the other. That is, once 617–176 has decided his best option is to squeal, then his eventual sentence will be either ten or two years, depending on 176–167's action. This is a better outcome than if he holds out, which would result in a sentence of zero or fifteen years, again depending on how 176–167 responds to the plea deal.

Since this game is symmetrical, both suspects have the same dominant strategy. Conversely, both have (the same) dominated strategies, which would be hanging tough and not confessing. That choice is dominated because it is optimal only if it is also the choice of the other (not to confess). Indeed, another approach in this case is to strike off the dominated strategies, which leads to the same outcome. In general, dominated strategies should never be selected, while dominant ones should always be used. When both players have selected an individually optimal strategy such that neither can enhance his or her position acting alone, that is known as a Nash equilibrium. A game can have one, multiple, or no Nash equilibria.

Games for which there are no equilibria solutions are more complex to solve as the players can continue to iterate: A makes a move followed by B, which elicits a response by A, and so forth. Solutions involve developing response functions for each player—how A expects B to respond to each of A's possible actions, for example. A's response function for B is then calculated, and where the two cross is the equilibrium outcome.

For a slightly more complicated case, that is, one with nonsymmetrical outcomes, we can use the data from the airline price-leadership example from the sequential game above. This is shown in the following matrix:

		Agony Airline Continue	*Agony Airline* Retreat
Belly-Up Airline	Continue	**50,** *50*	**30,** *70*
	Retreat	**55,** *45*	**40,** *60*

The question is, what decision should Agony Airlines optimally make? Following the example, Agony does indeed have a dominant strategy, which is to retreat (not follow) the price increase. That choice gives a market share of 60 or 70 percent depending on which choice Belly-Up takes, easily dominating the 45 or 50 percent shares if the "Continue" option is followed. Similarly, Belly-Up also has a dominant strategy: retreat as well, with payoffs of 55 or 45 percent. This is, of course, the Nash equilibrium. Now Agony can figure out that Belly-Up will choose retreat as its dominant strategy (and vice versa) and so can predict its ending-market share will be 60 percent. Too bad for Belly-Up!

Application to Case Analysis: Putting a case analysis into a game theory context can be a useful way to seek the optimal resolution. Some cases will provide the playoff results that can be plugged directly into the tree or matrix. In the many cases though when the numbers are not provided, they can be developed by considering the options available to each player. Absolute values are not required; rankings on a 0–10 scale can suffice. Consider, for example, the "cooperate-or-not" cases (e.g., this chapter, Sections 6.4 and 6.5), where one player is the large tire companies and the other the smaller firms. The values entered then reflect the different strategic choices based on the varied underlying characteristics. Often, the thought process itself of establishing the values is of value.

b. Case Questions

Students should prepare to answer the following questions, based on the Harvard Business School case:

Goodyear and the Threat of Government Tire Grading #707-494

1. Should Goodyear back in the 1980s have been concerned about the introduction of a tire-grading system?
2. Would you at that time have recommended that Goodyear continue to fight against the introduction of a tire-grading system, or should it cooperate with the government in the development of such a system?
3. Are there alternative sources of tire-quality information reasonably available to consumers that negate the need for the grading system?
4. Has there been a discernable effect on the tire industry over the past twenty years following the introduction of the grading system?

6.5 ■ CASE 6.2: PROPOSED SYSTEM FOR TIRE FUEL-EFFICIENCY REGULATION

a. Background

Many consumers unknowingly purchase less-efficient tires when replacing original equipment tires. Carmakers install low rolling resistance tires on new vehicles because they have to meet federal automobile fuel economy (CAFE) standards (see Chapter 3, Section 3.2). Tires affect vehicle fuel economy mainly through reduced rolling resistance (RR), with average impacts of 4 percent for urban driving and 7 percent for highway use; the more freely a tire rolls, the less energy it expends, resulting in better gas mileage. Overall, a 10 percent reduction in rolling resistance reduces fuel use by 1 to 2 percent.[40] But tire manufacturers are not required to offer efficient tires on the secondary market. A limited number of replacement tires seem as efficient as the tires that come with new cars, but they are frequently not labeled or marketed as such, making them difficult for consumers to identify. This will change when new information requirements for tire efficiency are implemented. The new system will augment, and supersede, the existing tire-grading system. At present, though, some large online retailers like TireRack do identify energy-efficient tires (marked as LRR for "low rolling resistance"), but only for very few in their extensive inventory, and identifying them takes a concerted effort.[41]

California was the first state to address this issue by adopting in 2003 a requirement for manufacturers to label the efficiency of tires sold in California beginning in 2008. Energy savings were projected to be $50–150 over the life of a tire.[42] The system, delayed because details remain to be worked out, equates "energy efficiency" with rolling resistance because it can be measured. Other states are considering adopting similar legislation.

This rule making would respond to requirements of the Energy Independence & Security Act of 2007 to establish a national tire-fuel efficiency consumer information program for replacement tires designed for use on motor vehicles. On March 30, 2010, the National Highway Traffic Safety Administration (NHTSA) published a final rule (modified 12/21/13) specifying the test procedures to be used to rate the performance of replacement passenger car tires for this new program. This rule making would address how this information would be made available to consumers. The proposal will be released in 2014 for adoption in 2016.

The rule, as well as its associated tire consumer education program, will require tire makers to rank their products for fuel efficiency, safety, and durability "based on test procedures specified." There are many details still needing to be worked out, however. "When this program is fully established, this information will be provided to consumers at the point of sale and online," according to NHTSA agency officials. NHTSA says, though, it is not specifying the content or requirements of the consumer education portion of the program at this time.[43]

A 2006 study of the rolling resistance of tires found the difference in rolling-resistance values among tires often exceeds 20 percent. This suggests the technical feasibility and practicality of lowering rolling resistance while maintaining generally accepted levels of traction. If the average rolling resistance exhibited by replacement tires in the passenger vehicle fleet were to be reduced by 10 percent, motorists would save $24 to $48 per year in fuel expenses with gas at $4/gallon, or roughly $2.40 to $4.80 for every 1 percent reduction in average rolling resistance. Note, however, a drop in tire pressure from 32 to 24 psi—a significant degree of underinflation that would not be apparent by visual inspection—increases a tire's rolling resistance by *more* than 10 percent.

Data on new replacement tires do not show any clear pattern of price differences among tires that vary in rolling resistance but that are comparable in many other respects such as traction, size, and speed rating. This result suggests that consumers buying existing tires with lower rolling resistance will not necessarily pay more for these tires or incur higher tire expenditures overall, as long as average tire wear life is not shortened.[44]

The issue is not one solely for the United States, as a related new European Union (EU) regulation for tire labeling went into effect on November 1, 2012. The regulation requires grading a tire's fuel efficiency, wet grip, and noise, and became mandatory for all car and van tires manufactured after July 1, 2012, for use in EU countries.[45]

Members of the Rubber Manufacturers Association, the national trade association for tire manufacturers, support providing consumer information on the contribution of tires to vehicle fuel efficiency. The information should be provided at the point of sale and be meaningful and easy to understand. The proposal is for a five-point standard based on rolling resistance with manufacturers to self-certify the results.[46]

Manufacturers see wide implications resulting from the rule. The vice president of sales and marketing for Yokohama Tire Corp. estimates testing will cost manufacturers between $50 million and $60 million in the first year. But effects will be far deeper. There are trade-offs between low rolling resistance and other performance characteristics, such as grip. So manufacturers are going to have "to push the envelope on tire performance" in order to reduce those trade-offs.[47]

Other manufacturers are more supportive. "Michelin further supports setting maximum rolling resistance standards for all passenger tires sold in the United States to guarantee minimum levels of tire fuel-efficiency performance and spur further progress in tire performance." "Tires account for up to 20 percent of fuel consumption for passenger vehicles. Allowing consumers to understand this fact and compare fuel economy performance among tire brands at the point of purchase is an important step in improving the overall fuel efficiency of vehicles, reducing fuel costs to consumers and lessening the impact of road transportation on the environment."[48]

The NHTSA for its part calculates the start-up costs for the tire industry, including initial testing, to be $34.8 million with variable costs of $2–6 per tire (average $3) (2008 dollars). Total costs depend on the number of low rolling resistance tires produced.[49]

Note though that multiple external factors affect rolling resistance and its effect on fuel efficiency. Among the more significant are the smoothness of the road (the smoother, the lower the resistance) and the size of the vehicle itself—lighter, more streamlined vehicles are impacted far more than are heaver, less "slippery" cars and SUVs.

However, according to the Rubber Manufacturers Association, just 5 percent of tire buyers chose fuel efficiency as the most important aspect when choosing a tire, while 31 percent put it in the top three decision factors. Top choices were "tire life" and "traction" at 58 percent.[50] A 2010 tire buyer survey by *Consumer Reports* found only 2 percent of buyers claimed that fuel economy was a factor in tire selection decisions. And they expected an 8 mpg improvement, when less than 2 mpg (about 3 percent) is common.[51] Comparison tests, however, have found that LRR tires can be up to 8 percent more fuel efficient than standard ones.[52]

b. Case Questions

Students should prepare the following questions, noting this is not the typical case because the issues under consideration will not be resolved until sometime in the future.

1. Should the tire manufacturers as a group support or resist the development of U.S. consumer information on relative tire efficiency?
2. If the answer to question one is no, then should a single manufacturer participate with DOT in the development of the information?
3. Should the information be included on tires or made available at purchase locations?
4. How do the sweeping changes in the industry structure affect answers to the preceding questions?

6.6 ■ CASE 6.3: CONSUMER FINANCIAL PROTECTION BUREAU STRUCTURE

a. Background

The Consumer Financial Protection Bureau (CFPB) was created in 2010 by the Dodd-Frank Wall Street Reform Act. (For additional discussion of this act, see Chapter 9, Section 9.4c). The act set up a new bureau, temporarily reporting to the Treasury Department, to protect consumers' financial security by regulating credit cards, debit cards, consumer loans, payday loans, credit reporting agencies, debt collection, stored-value cards, and financial advisory services. The bureau is to be an independent unit located within and funded by the Federal Reserve. It is not an entirely new bureau, since it will pick up consumer protection responsibilities from several entities that already exist, such as the Federal Trade Commission. Once the transition is complete, the office will be able to regulate a wide variety of consumer financial services, from online banking to high-interest payday loans.

Specifically, the CFPB mandates that loan disputes be allowed to go to court, not just arbitration. It wrote user-safety rules for all consumer financial products. Enforcement is through levying fines. Other regulations protect consumers in home real-estate transactions, including title, escrow, and financing businesses affiliated with realtors and homebuilders. It oversees equal credit opportunity and fair housing, and set standards for all mortgage offerings. Although the CFPB does not ban risky mortgage products, like interest-only loans, it requires proof that borrowers understand the risks. It also requires banks to verify income, credit history, and job status of mortgage seekers.[53]

The bureau will eventually hold sway over the following financial services:

- Deposits
- Credit extensions and loan services
- Property leases and purchases
- Real estate settlements
- Check cashing, collection, and guaranty services
- Online banking
- Financial advisory services
- Credit reports and other consumer financial reports
- Debt collection

To assist with these efforts the bureau is creating an Office of Financial Literacy and an Office of Financial Protection for Older Americans. Both are designed to help average Americans achieve a measure of financial independence through education. According to HowStuffWorks, "Right away, consumers should notice one thing: Their contracts will become easier to understand. The new law requires banks and other financial entities to do away with the kind of hidden fees and disclosures that they used to bury within the fine print. Congress's goal was to make consumers more aware of the impact of any purchases or financial decisions they make, which would ultimately make them more informed and spur competition."[54]

While the bureau has no independent legislative authority, it would be within the scope of its responsibilities to manage the consumer information components of the Credit CARD Act of 2009. Effective February 22, 2010, for new loans, the act's provisions include, in summary form:[55]

1. No interest rate increases for the first twelve months of your credit card.
2. No interest rate increases on pre-existing balances.
3. Rate increases require advanced notice of forty-five days, including penalty rate increases.
4. No more double billing cycle finance charges.
5. Limited fees for subprime credit cards.
6. Billing statements must be sent twenty-one days before payment due date.
7. Payments received by 5:00 P.M. on the due date are on time.
8. Payments received the next business day after a weekend or holiday are on time.
9. Payments above the minimum are applied to highest interest rate balances.
10. Billing statements must detail the cost of making the minimum payment, listing the number of months it will take to pay off a balance with minimum payments along with the total interest paid.

The bureau's provisions have been contested from the start, with Republicans generally opposed and Democrats supportive. Indeed, due to Republican opposition, President

Obama did not even seek Senate approval for his preferred director, and the nomination of Richard Cordray, submitted in mid-July 2011, was not acted upon (i.e., was filibustered) by the Senate through the remainder of 2011. At the start of 2012 President Obama used a recess appointment to place Cordray as director until the end of the next session of the Senate.[56] It was not until the Majority Leader in July 2013 threatened the "nuclear option" (reducing the vote requirement from 60 to 51 to end a filibuster) that Cordray's nomination was allowed to come to the floor for a vote. He was subsequently confirmed, 66 to 34.

The Heritage Foundation, a conservative think tank, describes the bureau as follows: "Creation of the Consumer Financial Protection Bureau (CFPB) ranks among the most contentious provisions of the vast Dodd-Frank financial regulation statute. Largely unaccountable to Congress and imbued with sweeping powers, the agency is the epitome of regulatory excess." Much of this criticism is focused on the structure with a single director appointed for a five-year term. The budget process is also an issue: "Because the bureau is ensconced within the Federal Reserve, its budget is not subject to congressional control. Instead, CFPB funding is set by law at a fixed percentage of the Fed's 2009 operating budget."[57]

Expanding on this theme, Senator Shelby (R-AL), chairman of the Senate Committee on Banking, Housing and Urban Affairs, wrote in an opinion piece in the *Wall Street Journal* stating, "In its current form, the bureau is headed by a single director. Over a five-year term, the director will have unfettered authority over thousands of American businesses, not just banks. While the bureau receives hundreds of millions of dollars of public money annually, the elected representatives of the American people have no say in how it spends this money. Moreover, other regulators have no meaningful ability to prevent bureau mandates that may threaten the financial health of banks."[58] This position led to Republican legislation described as follows:

> Republicans have proposed three commonsense reforms [in HR 1121; reintroduced as HR 2446] that we believe will enhance consumer protection while ensuring accountability to the American people:
>
> First, we would establish a board of directors to oversee the bureau. This would allow for the consideration of multiple viewpoints in decision-making and would reduce the potential for the politicization of regulations. This is the very same structure proposed by the president and former House Financial Services Committee Chairman Barney Frank at the outset of the financial-reform debate.
>
> Second, we would subject the bureau to the congressional appropriations process to ensure that it doesn't engage in wasteful or unnecessary spending. This also gives Congress the ability to ensure that the bureau is acting in accordance with our legislative intent.
>
> Finally, we would allow bank regulators (such as the FDIC, the Federal Reserve, and the Office of the Comptroller of the Currency) to prevent the bureau from endangering the safety and soundness of financial institutions.

The proposed House bill would establish a five-member commission composed of the Vice Chairman for Supervision of the Federal Reserve System and four additional members appointed by the president, with the advice and consent of the Senate,[59] for staggered five-year terms. No more than three commissioners could represent a single political party, and a commission chairman would be appointed by the president. A similar structure exists at the Federal Trade Commission, the Federal Deposit Insurance Corporation, and the Securities and Exchange Commission. Then on July 16, 2013, Senator Portman (R-OH) introduced a bill that would create an independent Inspector General for the CFPB. The bill (S. 1310), part of the agreement bringing Cordray's name up for a confirmation vote, would require the CFPB to have an independent Inspector General confirmed by the Senate.[60]

The Heritage Foundation though seeks further reform, while acknowledging that a five-person commission could lead to delays and wrangling: "A bipartisan commission may seem less autocratic than a single director vested with bureau control. Arguably, group decision making could slow the regulatory gears, as could partisan bickering. But the rulemaking process is not the fundamental problem with the CFPB, and tinkering with organizational structure will not reduce the harm of regulatory overkill to consumers and the economy. The real problem is the bureau's lack of accountability and the virtually unconstrained power bestowed upon it under the Dodd-Frank statute."[61]

When pressed on that point during congressional testimony, Professor (now Senator) Warren, who assisted with the establishment of the bureau, reminded lawmakers that rules can be nullified by the newly created Financial Stability Oversight Council (FSOC) if the council determines that such rules may affect the safety and soundness of a particular financial institution, which is not true for any other agency.[62]

The banking industry overall is not so negative on the bureau. "How can you be against simplified disclosures? asks Scott Talbott, chief lobbyist for the Financial Services Roundtable. "I mean, it benefits the consumer, it benefits the industry, it benefits the entire transaction. It's all good, and the industry supports what the CFPB is doing."

In fact, so far, Talbott says the industry has been pleased with the direction the bureau is heading. "We may not always agree with them," he says. "Where we don't, we feel so far we have been able to have good dialogue with them. But at the same time, we haven't really hit the road yet. We're about to turn the keys and start it up today. And it will be out on the road for a test drive."[63]

When considering the credit card industry in particular, it is important to recognize how concentrated it is. By 2004, the top ten cards saw their market share leap to an estimated 89.5 percent, with Visa and MasterCard together holding about 70 percent of the credit card market. Meanwhile, although credit cards bear the logo of Visa, MasterCard, or one of the other networks, they are actually issued by banks. The leading U.S. bank credit-card issuers are Bank of America, JPMorgan Chase, Citigroup, Capital One, and HSBC Bank, as shown in Table 6.2.[64]

Another way to measure market share is by number of cards issued, as shown in Table 6.3.

Table 6.2

Top 15 Issuers of General Purpose Credit Cards for First Six Months of 2009
(based on outstanding balances)[65]

Rank	Issuer	Outstanding Balances (in billions)	Market Share	Cumulative Market Share
1	Chase	$165.87	19%	19%
2	Bank of America	$145.10	16%	35%
3	Citi	$102.54	12%	47%
4	American Express	$78.16	9%	55%
5	Capital One	$55.46	6%	62%
6	Discover	$48.90	6%	68%
7	Wells Fargo	$30.89	3%	71%
8	HSBC	$24.80	3%	73%
9	U.S. Bank	$20.17	2%	76%
10	USAA	$12.96	1%	77%
11	Barclays	$10.67	1%	78%
12	Target	$7.78	1%	79%
13	GE Money	$7.17	1%	80%
14	PNC Bank	$5.08	1%	81%
15	First National	$4.32	0.5%	81.5%
	Total Credit Card Debt:	$887.10		

Source: Nilson Report, Federal Reserve. August 2009. www.cardhub.com/edu/market-share-by-credit-card-issuer/.

Table 6.3

Credit Card Market Share Based on Number of Cards in Circulation, 2010

Visa	MasterCard	American Express	Discover
302 million	203 million	48.9 million	54.4 million
49.6%	33.4%	8.0%	8.9%

Source: Card Hub. "Market Share by Credit Card Network." www.cardhub.com/edu/market-share-by-credit-card-network/.

b. Case Questions

Students should prepare the following questions, noting again this is not the typical case, because the issues under consideration will not be resolved until sometime in the future.

1. What are the benefits and costs to the credit-card industry as well as to individual issuers of having a single director of the Consumer Financial Protection Bureau versus the proposed five-person board?
2. Should one of the issuing banks oppose HR 2446, and if so which one(s) might you suggest, and why?
3. What is the role of the industrial trade association, the Financial Services Roundtable, in these processes?

6.7 ■ CASE 6.4: Consumer Financial Protection Bureau Mortgage Service Regulations

a. Background

It is no secret that subprime mortgages were the cause, or at least the tipping point, of the financial near-collapse of 2008. There is plenty of blame to spread around, with borrowers taking on more debt than they could sustain and in some cases allegedly falsifying employment and income information. Brokers for their part frequently did not seek documentation, while investment banks secularized loans into tranches which ratings firms subsequently graded at risk levels well short of true risks (see Chapter 9, Section 9.4). Those issues though did not end the problems with, among other things, banks subsequently attempting to foreclose on mortgagees without clear documentation of ownership,[65] while federal programs to find alternatives to foreclosure met with limited success.[66] One dimension of the would-be foreclosure problem was the so-called robo-signing scandal in which banks did not apply due diligence when reviewing documents leading up to a foreclosure. That problem culminated in a $25 billion settlement with the five largest U.S. mortgage servicers. Certainly there have been multiple complaints from homeowners about the nonresponsiveness of banks:[67] 43 percent ofcalls to the CFPB's complaint hotline related to mortgage issues. And of those, 54 percent involved borrowers who had problems with loan modifications, debt collection, or foreclosure.[68] In January 2013, a $10 billion settlement with the banks was proposed, which translates into a very small compensation for the potentially millions of affected homeowners.[69]

Into this complex mix, on August 10, 2012, the CFPB injected a planned rule to enhance the information available to mortgage holders while holding brokers responsible to respond to customers' inquiries. The rules are focused on mortgage servicers who are responsible for collecting payments for the mortgage owners, usually on a contract basis, and are based on service requirements in the Dodd-Frank bill (see Chapter 9, Section 9.4c). The CFPB is implementing those requirements, as well as exercising additional rule making authority under the Dodd-Frank Act. Comments on the rules were open until October 9, 2012, with some final changes made in January 2013; they were implemented in July 2013 and are described at www.consumerfinance.gov/regulatory-implementation/.

Under the proposed rules, the following nine services are mandated:[70]

1. **Clear monthly mortgage statements:** Provide regular reports, including regular statements that would include a breakdown of payments by principal, interest, fees, and escrow; the amount of and due date of the next payment; recent transaction activity; and warnings about fees.
2. **Warning before interest rate adjusts:** Provide earlier disclosures, including information about alternatives and counseling resources when new rates are unaffordable.
3. **Options for avoiding costly "force-placed" insurance (insurance mandated by the mortgage owner if the borrower cancels—typically more costly than homeowner-held insurance):** Give advance notice and pricing information before charging consumers for this insurance; terminate the insurance within

fifteen days if there is evidence the borrower has the necessary insurance; refund the force-placed insurance premiums.

4. **Early information and options for avoiding foreclosure:** Make good faith efforts to contact delinquent borrowers and inform them of options for avoiding foreclosure.
5. **Payments promptly credited:** Credit consumer's account the day a payment is received.
6. **Maintain accurate and accessible documents and information:** Establish reasonable policies and procedures to provide accurate and current information to borrowers.
7. **Errors corrected quickly:** If a borrower suspects an error has been made, servicer is required to acknowledge receipt of notification, conduct a reasonable investigation, and provide timely information about the resolution to the consumer.
8. **Direct and ongoing access to servicer personnel to assist delinquent borrowers:** Required to provide delinquent borrowers with direct, easy, ongoing access to employees.
9. **Evaluate borrowers for options to avoid foreclosure:** Promptly review applications for available foreclosure options; prohibition for proceeding until application review complete.

Since this regulation had been proposed, in-house mortgage servicing operations in large banks are being spun off to independent firms which work on a contract basis for mortgage owners. At the same time, smaller (community) bankers are seeking an exemption from these mandates, which they see as particularly burdensome for smaller operations.[71] According to KPMG, "Today's mortgage servicing and default management industry is under tremendous pressure to enhance its business practices. Companies are being directed by supervisors and investors to contain costs, improve service levels, capture new markets, and increase profitability—all while addressing a growing range of regulatory requirements."[72]

b. Case Questions

1. What are the final rules adopted by the CFPB, and how do they differ from the draft version described above?
2. What is the structure of the mortgage service industry (depending on data availability, firm numbers, market shares, independent firms versus departments of mortgage providers), and has it changed since the CFPB expressed an intent to regulate the service, say since January 2012?
3. Wells Fargo is one of the largest mortgage servicers. Considering the regulations described in question 1 above, should it hold steady, increase, or decrease its in-house mortgage servicing activities? Why?

6.8 ■ CASE 6.5: VOLUNTARY COMPLIANCE

a. Background

Buildings, particularly when they are corporate or institutional, are not typically thought of as consumer goods. But they are consumer goods—long-lived ones at that, with an ongoing effect on energy use. Buildings overall in the United States are responsible for some 30 percent of all energy use.

Two major standards have been established for building energy efficiency, the EPA Energy Star system, and Leadership in Energy and Environmental Design (LEED), with its Silver, Gold, and Platinum designations (see Chapter 5, Section 5.1e for discussions of each).

This case in large part pivots on the benefits, both hard and soft, to a corporation of having a certified sustainable building. Little information is available documenting those benefits, but a 2011 study by the Cornell School of Hotel Administration did examine the benefits to hotels in Spain of being certified sustainable. The applicable standards used were set by the International Organization for Standardization (ISO) and are known as ISO 14001. Adherance to these standards is strictly voluntary and widely followed in Europe. ISO operates somewhat differently from its U.S. counterparts in that it is not an environmental management system with absolute environmental performance requirements but rather serves as a framework to assist organizations in developing their own environmental management systems. First established in 1996, the current system dates to 2004. It operates by helping organizations identify, and systematically reduce, harmful effects on the environment. Software and consultancies are available to assist firms in establishing their own management systems, and in arranging third-party certification and registration of compliance.[73]

The 2008 Cornell study examined 2,116 hotels, of which 108 had ISO 14001 certification. Results indicated that the certified properties had higher net sales than those lacking the certification. The improved economic performance is attributed to a combination of "reducing costs, improving quality, or improving reputation."[74] The ISO's system of establishing a management approach to sustainability rather than specifying particular activities and undertakings allows for a broad range of benefits, such as those described above. Further study will be required to determine how the benefits are actually achieved, as well as to examine in more detail differences among the hotels other than location.

This case is focused on a publicly held U.S. corporation, which was a pioneer in seeking LEED certification for a new headquarters building.

b. Case Questions

Students should prepare the following questions, based on the Harvard Business School cases.

- Genzyme Center (A) #610-008
- Genzyme Center (B) #610-009
- Genzyme Center (C) #610-010 (suggested but not critical)

1. If you were a Genzyme shareholder, how would you judge the firm's interest in green buildings?
2. Should the firm have made the additional investment to achieve LEED Platinum? Why, or why not?
3. Genzyme had a number of choices for additional features for its goal of LEED Platinum. What decision criteria should guide the decision of which to select? Based on those criteria, which would you choose?
4. Considering the motivations for green buildings, how would you design an evaluation plan to assess the benefits of the Genzyme Center's green building features?
5. How might Genzyme's pioneering effort have affected the building conservation decisions of other corporations?

6.9 ▪ CASE 6.6: BIRD-SAFE BUILDINGS AND LEED CERTIFICATION

a. Background

The collision of birds into buildings is estimated to cause up to one billion deaths each year. Birds cannot see transparent or reflective glass and plastic, and so perceive these surfaces as pathways to, or in the case of reflections, desirable habitats in themselves, particularly if trees and shrubs are being reflected. Because the dead birds are typically hidden from view by the vegetation around structures, the carnage is not readily apparent. Mortality estimates are based on one per building, annually, but indications are that commercial buildings with their large windows cause up to five times this rate of fatalities. Strikes are most common nearer to the ground.

Mortality can occur from flights as short as 3 feet and so both local and migratory species are vulnerable. Indeed, the best predictor of vulnerability is bird density in the immediate vicinity of a window, meaning access to natural and artificially supplied foods, habitats providing cover, and roosting and nesting opportunities. Principal solutions include:

- Physical barriers completely covering a pane
- Lighting turned off or blinds drawn after dark
- Patterns covering the surface and visible from the exterior
- UV reflecting and absorbing patterns visible to birds but invisible to the human eye[75]

Detailed approaches are described at www.abcbirds.org/newsandreports/Bird-FriendlyBuildingDesign.pdf.

An ordinance adopted by San Francisco in September 2011 requires that new buildings in parts of the city use "bird-safe" standards that reduce the risk of winged creatures hitting panes of glass. Some architects are concerned about cost and translucency, but supporters anticipate no major cost factor.[76] Other cities have and are considering similar requirements.

Toronto is both a top contender for the title as the deadliest city for migrating birds as well as for taking the issue most seriously. Toronto's lethalness is due to both location and design factors. It sits on Lake Ontario in the path of several migratory routes, the first obstructions for birds moving to wintering grounds from the vast northern wilderness. At the same time, Toronto has multiple glass towers and parks. The reflective glass on the buildings, which reduces heating and cooling costs, also fools birds into believing the reflection of trees is a resting spot to which they fly with mortal disregard. As of January 31, 2010, all new high-rises must conform to bird mortality-proofing standards as part of the Tier 1 Green Standards.[77] What though of existing structures? The owners of two of the most lethal are being sued under laws initially meant to protect migratory birds from hunting and industrial hazards.[78]

The LEED Pilot Credit Library, which is intended to encourage the testing of new and revised credit language, alternative paths, and new and innovative green building technologies, has adopted a Bird Collision Deterrence Pilot Credit. The LEED credit system is described in Case 6.5 preceeding. The credit, applicable to new construction as well as existing buildings, requires a selection among options for plans for façade design or modification, interior lighting, exterior lighting, and postconstruction monitoring plans.

b. Case Questions

Identify a major building such as a classroom building and calculate whether it would qualify for LEED credits by achieving a Bird Collision Threat Rating of 15 or less. Use the following (somewhat simplified) formula which is based on two "Façade Zones": Zone 1 is the first three floors (where most strikes occur) and Zone 2 the remaining floors.

For each Façade Zone the Threat Factor (TF) is computed using (from www.usgbc.org/Docs/Archive/General/Docs10402.pdf):

FAÇADE ZONE 1 THREAT FACTOR = ((Material Type 1 TF x Material Type 1 Area) + (Material Type 2 TF x Material Type 2 Area) + (etc.))/Total Façade Zone Area

Material Type 1, for example, might be windows and Type 2 bricks. Threat Factor ratings are available at www.usgbc.org/ShowFile.aspx?DocumentID=10397.

With these numbers, the Total Building Bird Collision Threat Rating is calculated using:

TOTAL BUILDING BIRD COLLISION THREAT RATING = ((Façade Zone 1 Threat Factor x 2) + (Façade Zone 2 Threat Factor))/3, which is to say the first three floors are weighted twice as heavily as the remainder due to their importance for collisions.

Additional considerations apply to control of lighting, both interior and exterior, as follows:

INTERIOR LIGHTING:

Option 1: Turned off when unoccupied (excluding safety mandates), or at a minimum from midnight to 6 A.M. OR

Option 2: Automatically shut off when a space is unoccupied for more than thirty minutes.

EXTERIOR LIGHTING:
Option 1: Shield so that shines less than 90 degrees from straight down
Option 2: Complies with LEED exterior lighting standards for new construction

As an example, consider Warren Hall on the Cornell University campus, which was renovated in 2012–2014. Since its completion in 1933, Warren Hall has housed the undergraduate business program at Cornell University, renamed as the Dyson School for Applied Economics and Management in 2010. The building has a total of 128,355 square feet, including a rusticated stone façade on the first floor, above which the second through fourth floors are brick.

Approximate building dimensions are as follows:

- Width: 390 feet
- Depth: 50 feet
- Total height: 60 feet
- Auditorium: 2,000 square feet total

With window surfaces of:

- 1st floor, 4 feet by 6 feet, 87 windows
- 2nd floor, 4.5 feet by 7.8 feet, 90 windows
- 3rd floor, 4.5 feet by 6.5 feet, 89 windows
- 4th floor, 3.4 feet by 4.7 feet, 70 windows
- Auditorium, 5 feet by 13.3 feet, 10 windows

And finally, distance from woods at closest point is 38 feet. Interior lights automatically shut off after twenty minutes of no motion in a room, while the exterior lighting meets the LEED standards.

1. What is the computed Total Building Bird Collision Threat Rating for the building you are evaluating?
2. If the building falls above the cutoff Total Building Bird Collision Threat Rating of 15, what steps might be taken to lower the value? Are there other factors that make it more or less prone to bird strikes?
3. Why might a university or other business/institution/agency be interested to qualify for platinum LEED credits for a building project?

6.10 ▪ CASE 6.7: CALORIE LABELING

a. Background

Not so long ago, being thin was a sign of poverty and ill health while being stout was associated with health and prosperity. President William Howard Taft (1909–1913) weighed over 300 pounds at a time when weight was fashionable. Times change though; just con-

Figure 6.7 **U.S. Obese Population, Percent by State**

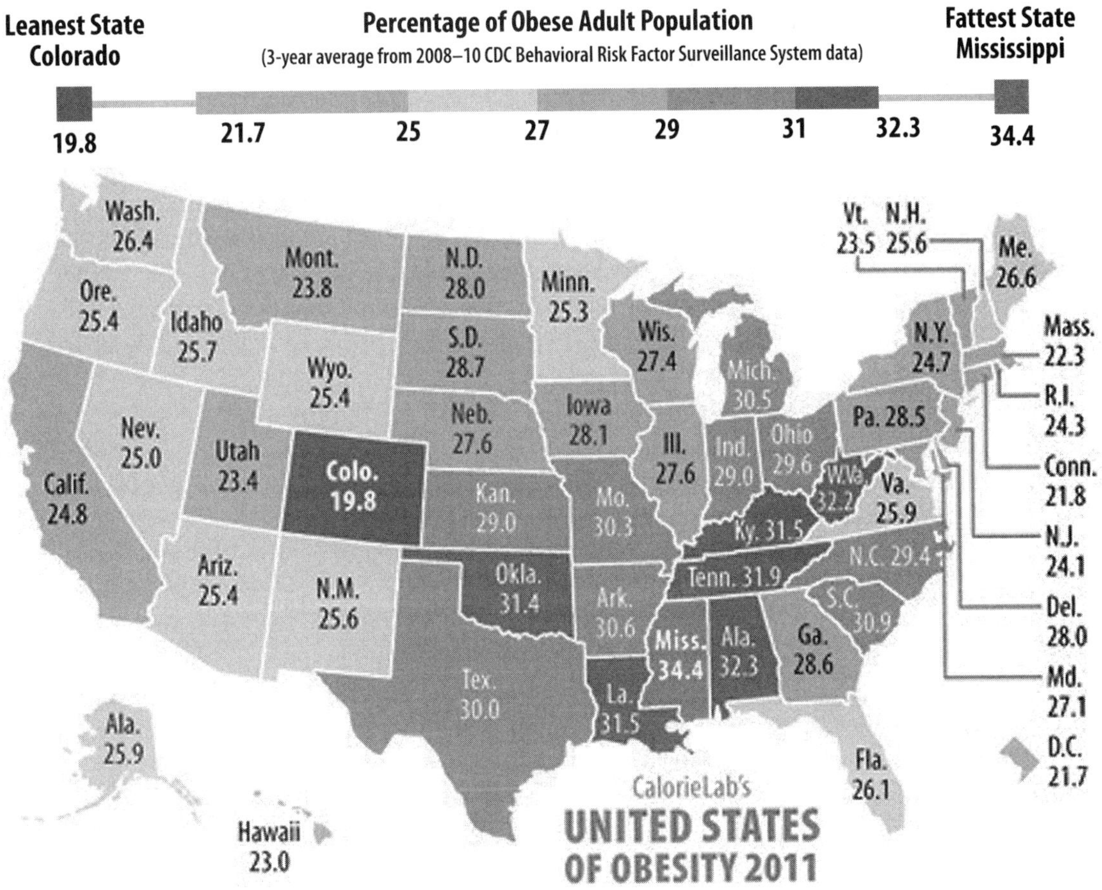

Source: Calorie Lab. "Mississippi is the Fattest State for 6th Straight Year, Colorado Still Leanest, Rhode Island Getting Fatter, Alaska Slimmer." June 30, 2011.

sider the comments made about New Jersey governor Chris Christie's weight. No longer is excess weight considered attractive; it is also recognized as being unhealthy, leading to heart and circulatory problems as well as diabetes, among other issues. That, though, has not stopped many worldwide from being overweight in an era of cheap calories. In the United States, some 30 percent of the adult population is classified as obese (Figure 6.7), a doubling since 1980, with the number of obese children tripling over the same period. The obesity epidemic has been described as a public health crisis, responsible for one-quarter of health care spending.[79]

None of this discussion of excess food intake though should lead to overlooking the fact that 15 percent of U.S. households were "food insecure," at least at times during 2011. Of those, 5.7 percent experienced very low food security—meaning food was unavailable or unavailable in a timely fashion because the household lacked money and other resources for food.[80] Unfortunately, food insecurity and obesity are not mutually exclusive, given the understandable temptation to overeat when food is available and future sources uncertain.

The causes of obesity are varied and complex, but inexpensive, high-calorie foods including soft drinks are clearly implicated. Steps to limit the problem have included restricting access; many school cafeterias now ban vending machines while former Mayor Michael Bloomberg of New York City working with the Board of Health recently banned sweetened drinks in containers larger than 16 ounces at restaurants, street carts, and movie theaters, scheduled to take effect in March 2013.[81] But compulsory steps like these are unpopular and possibly ineffective—anyone can of course always buy *two* smaller soft-drink containers or take advantage of the "free refills" offered by some chains.

And then there are legal hurdles; implementation has been postponed by courts ruling the ban to be unconstitutional while appeals continue.[82] Judge Tingling of the State Supreme Court in Manhattan ruled the ban was "arbitrary and capricious" because of perceived inequalities. The rules applied only to certain sugared drinks (those with a high milk content were exempted) and certain outlets (restaurants but not convenience stores).[83] Subsequently, in June, Mayor Bloomberg appealed the decision to the appeals court where it was also rejected. There is though another approach to reducing caloric intake—that of information through labeling.

Since 1966, manufacturers have been required by the FDA to provide quantity and content information on containers, with food manufacturers subject to additional labeling requirements in 1990 and 1993 (Example 6.2; see also Figure 3.3). However, in an era when half the food budget is spent on away-from-home consumption, constituting about one-third of total caloric intake,[84] a large portion of the consuming public is not reached with those labels, at least for some meals.

The Patient Protection and Affordable Care Act of 2010, Section 4205, requires restaurants with twenty or more locations under the same name to list calorie information on restaurant menus and menu boards for similar menu items. Other nutrient information—total calories, fat, saturated fat, cholesterol, sodium, total carbohydrates, sugars, fiber, and total protein—must be made available in writing on request. Vending machine operators with twenty or more machines must also disclose calorie content for certain items. Smaller operations may voluntarily register to be covered under the regulations.[86]

Although these posting requirements became effective at the time of the Affordable Care Act signing, the FDA used its regulatory discretion to delay implementation until rules could be vetted and published. To that end, in 2010 the FDA solicited comments and other information related to the development of a final rule[87] and draft rules in April 2011.[88] The final regulations are due to be released in 2014. That said, the fast-food industry, a major focus of these regulations and a group frequently the target of criticisms for selling high-fat and high-calorie foods, has been taking initial implementation steps on its own. The complexity of the rule's implementation involves which venders are to be included, and which not. Bowling alleys, for example, are excluded as food sales are not their principal function, but what of supermarkets and convenience stores which sell a myriad of food items?[89]

Example 6.2: Major Food Labeling Regulations

Act	Year	Information/Coverage
Fair Labeling and Packaging Act	1966	Labeling of ingredients, contents, quantity, maker; affecting all consumer products. Veracity of information enforced by FTC.
Amended	1992	Include metric measures; all consumer products
Nutrition Labeling and Education Act	1990	Detailed nutrition information; packaged food products standardizes terms *light* and *low fat*
Organic Foods Production Act	1990	Establishes agricultural products sold and labeled "organic" (USDA)
Amended	1993	Restaurants to comply with health claims terms and definitions
Dietary Supplement Health and Education Act	1994	Manufacturers required to ensure safety prior to marketing; prior approval not required; covers food supplements and ingredients
FDA Modernization	1997	Multiple technical review and information changes, affecting pharmaceuticals, medical devices, food and supplements[85]
Trans-Fat Regulations	2003	List trans-fat ingredients, affecting packaged food and some supplements
Food Allergen Labeling and Consumer Protection Act	2004	Regarding "plain English" labeling—for example, albumin (eggs), not albumen (but need not identify as "allergen"); identify allergenic processing aids; affecting packaged foods

Source: Compiled by W. Lesser.

State restaurant associations initially resisted mandated calorie postings on First Amendment grounds. However, after court losses in numerous states—a New York court determined the regulation is "reasonably related to the government's interest in providing consumers with accurate nutritional information"—the National Restaurant Association has supported a national rule over a hodgepodge of state and local requirements.[90]

The major fast-food firms list nutrition information on their Web sites, but while helpful, this is well removed from point-of-purchase decisions when hunger and temptation can easily obscure memory. Access exclusively through the Internet also disproportionally disadvantages lower-income groups who can be particularly attracted to the low cost of fast food. What is needed is point-of-sale information of the kind to be implemented at an uncertain date by the FDA. Into this regulatory ambiguity McDonald's surprisingly announced on September 12, 2012, that it would voluntarily be listing calories and other nutritional information at its 14,000 locations nationwide beginning the following week.[91]

While McDonald's is not the only fast-food outlet to post nutritional information voluntarily, it is by far the largest and best known and so took a substantial risk with that step. The risk however was not unbounded, for New York City (2008) and Philadelphia (2010) had previously required calories be posted so that the firms have some basis for predicting consumer response. Initial indications are that the effects on purchases—at least the direct effects—are not significant. It should be noted that New York City banned the use of trans fats in restaurants in 2006; the same occurred in Philadelphia in 2007, and similar bans are under consideration or have been adopted in other states and counties.[92]

One study surveyed fast-food consumers in restaurants before and after calorie posting became mandatory in New York City in 2008. Two groups were considered—teenagers and adults buying for small children. Among teenagers, calories purchased (average 725) did not change pre- and post-labeling. For that group, taste, not nutrition, was the compelling factor, followed by cost. The adult customer group frequently indicated the calorie information affected their choices, but a review of receipts for actual purchases indicated no changes. That is not to say these groups were particularly knowledgeable about nutrition: respondents typically underestimated both the number of calories they were consuming (by up to 466) and the number of daily calories needed by adults (1,500 versus the average of 2,000). The study though has limitations; it was small, was conducted only one month following the posting, providing little opportunity for consumers to adjust, and was conducted only in low-income neighborhoods, making it more difficult to project to the entire population. Also, like all of these studies, only current shoppers were included, leaving out any who may have stopped buying fast food altogether.[93]

Another New York City–based study conducted in 2010 found the postings reduced food calories purchased by a small amount, but had no effect on beverage sales. The average calorie purchase reduction was 6 percent. However, for larger food purchases (above 250 calories), calories per transaction declined by 26 percent. This study analyzed cash register receipts and so represents both a larger sample size and longer time frame. Interestingly, Starbucks' New York City revenues were unaffected by the postings, and when a store was near a competitor which did not post calories, sales actually increased.[94]

The foregoing, though, are just the first-round effects. Over time consumers may become more calorie-sensitive, changing from, say, a large to a small order of fries, while the restaurants themselves may introduce new, more nutritious offerings, which is already happening in the form of more salads on fast-food menus. Food choices do indeed change, if slowly. One study documented modest improvements in the nutrient content of offerings at sit-down and quick-serve restaurants in Seattle within eighteen months after a mandatory calorie posting law went into effect (compared to six months pre-law). However, fast food offerings were still considered to be "excessive" in terms of fat and sodium.[95] Indeed, although McDonald's directs one-sixth of its advertising to its salad offerings, they account for only 2–3 percent of sales.[96] Of course, given enough salad dressing, salads are not particularly low-calorie choices. This though is speculative and mid- to long-term, the immediate effects of calorie postings once mandated is likely to be limited: "[C]onsumers don't see fast food as a place to eat healthy."

b. Case Questions

Imagine you are the CEO of KFC (it belongs to Yum! Brands) and you are at a board meeting discussing the corporate response to McDonald's recent decision to post nutritional information in all its U.S. restaurants.

1. What is the market position of KFC, sales, share, and so forth?
2. What is the demographic profile of KFC customers?

3. Should KFC follow McDonald's lead and post calorie information now or wait until it is mandated by the FDA? Please consider what competitors might do, and what other changes might be adopted in operations or menu offerings at the same time.
4. KFC has had a number of controversies over time. How might that situation affect its decision on the calorie-posting decision?

6.11 ▪ CASE 6.8: CORNELL CRISPS

a. Background

For this case imagine that you are Cornell University seniors planning a post-graduation business producing "Cornell Crisps," a baked potato chip using organic potatoes and organic oils. Based on a class project to create five-year business plan, assisted by support from Entrepreneurship@Cornell, you project fifth-year sales of $1.8 million (100,000 cases of 24 bags) with 5 percent real (after inflation) annual sales growth. Gross profits are projected at 20 percent due to the higher cost of organic ingredients, with a net of 10 percent. After five years you plan either to sell out or expand the geographic area for your product.

The target market is twenty-somethings with and without college degrees. Cornell Crisps are being positioned to accompany a typical hamburger dinner with or without beer, or as a TV snack. Package sizes are to be small—around $1.00 retail ($.75 wholesale). Outlets will include supermarkets and convenience-type stores in the upstate New York region. Your marketing plan specifies that you anticipate your customers will pick your organic product to "offset" the less-than-ideal other aspects of their diets. You recognize that you need to comply with USDA organic ingredient specifications in order to list "100% Organic" (Example 6.2; 7 CFR Sec. 205) on the label, but that the high fat and salt content disqualifies you from labeling it "healthy" under the National Labeling and Education Act (NLEA) regulations.

What is undecided at the time is whether to comply with NLEA at all, as your small size does allow an exemption. Products initially marketed after May 8, 1994, are exempt, providing the firm has fewer than 100 FTEs (fulltime employee equivalents) and less than 100,000 units are projected for marketing in the first twelve months.[97] Alternative sales-based exemptions are listed in Table 6.4.

You are aware of research which indicated that the act will place a particular burden on small food firms due to their limited in-house expertise and minimal economies of scale.[98] Other studies have evaluated the use of the nutrition label information by consumers.[99] One finding is that the labels are predominantly used for food labeled or believed to be "healthy." However, because pre-NLEA there was less information available on "unhealthy" foods, the act has proportionally increased the amount of nutrition information labeling on unhealthy foods. But consumers are not uniform in their ability or willingness to comprehend or believe printed nutritional information, a situation exacerbated by the frequent, and frequently contradictory, "health alerts" in the media. The

Table 6.4

Small business food labeling exemptions

Sales in Food	Total Sales (Food & Nonfood)	Status
$50,000 or less	$500,000 or less	Exempt
$50,000 or less	$500,001 or more	Exempt
$50,001 or more	$500,000 or less	Exempt
$50,001 or more	$500,001 or more	Not Exempt

Source: FDA, "Inspections, Compliance, Enforcement, and Criminal Investigations." www.fda.gov/ICECI/Inspections/InspectionGuides/ucm074948.htm.

overall consequence is that nutrition labeling may become a more significant competitive component for "unhealthy food" marketing than in the past, at least for information users and seekers.

Based on several student marketing studies you project that listing the nutritional aspects of your chips (beyond the organic designation) will affect sales from –3 to + 5 percent, depending on the proportion of information users and nonusers in your customer mix. The median value of the several estimates is a positive 2 percent. What is more determinant is the cost of labeling. Upfront costs are projected at $50,000 with annual costs of $5,000. You are so tired from present value (NPV) calculations in all your class exercises you forbid their use in your project planning.

Another option you have is to use a nonorganic trans fat in your processing, which your technical advisers assure you will still allow you to list the product as "Made with Organic Potatoes" under USDA organic regulations. The substitution will save you 6 percent on your costs. You will need to identify on the package that trans fats are used, but you interpret the marketing reports to indicate your consumers will focus on the healthy aspect of the organic potatoes rather than the more problematic trans fats. Because the trans-fat label is straightforward it will cost only $10,000 upfront with no additional costs. Under this positive interpretation projected sales will be only modestly affected. However, not all your marketing advisors are in agreement, citing 2011 survey results from the International Food Information Council that 60 percent of Americans are concerned about some kinds of fats in their diet, and 59 percent are specifically trying to limit the consumption of trans fats.[100]

b. Case Questions

1. Should you voluntarily adopt NLEA labeling or not when selling a 100 percent organic product? What other factors beyond the cost analysis might you consider?
2. Would the trans fat formulation be a viable business choice? What additional factors should be considered?
3. After five years of running Cornell Crisps, what are some potential business options that you might have? How would these options affect your current decisions in questions 1 and 2 above?

6.12 ▪ CASE 6.9: LABELING RBST-FREE DAIRY PRODUCTS

a. Background

BST stands for bovine somatotropin, sometimes called bovine growth hormone or BGH, which is naturally occurring in small concentrations in cows, including in their milk. The "r" in rBST (sometimes rbST) refers to "recombinant" or man-made, in this case using genetically engineered bacteria. Injecting BST into cows has long been known to enhance milk production, but it was not until the major agribusiness firm Monsanto's improvements of the rBST technology in the early 1990s that the practice became viable on a commercial basis.

Experimental trials indicated the product, sold under the trade name Posilac (subsequently sold to Eli Lilly/Elanco), could increase production per cow by up to 40 percent. In commercial operations, however, the reasonably achievable level is closer to 20 percent, more or less.[101] Nothing comes from nothing, and this applies to the increased production from rBST use as well. Cows need to be fed additional amounts to support the increased output so the efficiency comes from the fewer number of cows required for a given level of production. That is, the 20 percent of the ration required to support the cow is spread across an increased output. Farmers can make money using rBST,[102] but the feeding and other management requirements are high and have led numerous dairy farmers to discontinue its use. Present estimates of use are in the 30 percent range of *herds* being treated with rBST—no sales data are provided.[103] The percentage of treated *cows* may be higher than 30 percent as larger farms adopt rBST at a higher rate than smaller ones.

Two levels of approval were required for use of rBST on animals and the sale of milk from the treated cows. The USDA is responsible for animal health. Due to the larger amount of milk produced, treated cows are more susceptible to mastitis, an infection of the udder. Mastitis in turn leads to higher somatic cell counts in the milk, and to increased antibiotic use for treatment. However it should be noted that genetically high-producing cows do not inherently have greater mastitis problems. The infection issue is not about milk production levels but rather more one of management, general cleanliness, and care. So there are no inherent animal health problems with the use of rBST, although there is a somewhat lower pregnancy rate with treated cows. This led to the USDA's approval for use.[104] That though does not mean there is no controversy and dissent regarding animal health.[105]

The USDA standard for milk limits the somatic cell count and prohibits the sale of milk tainted with antibiotics. Approval for the sale of the milk from treated cows however falls to the FDA and was granted in 1993, concluding it was "safe and effective for dairy cows, that milk from rbST-treated cows is safe for human consumption, and that production and use of the product do not have significant impact on the environment."[106] That said, concerns are still expressed about human health effects, including that growth hormones speed puberty and connections with some forms of cancer. Indeed, the Sixth U.S. Court of Appeals concluded that the milk from treated and untreated cows is in fact different.[107] Just how that determination was made is not clear as most experts note there is no detectable difference between the two milks—BST is naturally present and BST and rBST are chemically identical—plus 90 percent is destroyed during pasteurization while the remainder is digested like any protein.[108] Moreover, bovine hormones are specific to bovines with no effect on humans. Nonetheless opinions are strongly held, which brings us to the subject of this case, labeling.

First, some background on U.S. labeling policy towards genetically modified products dating to the 1980s: U.S. policy makers established the basic regulatory approach early on in the biotech era, which can be dated to the 1972–1973 development of the Cohen-Boyer method for DNA engineering. Policy makers interpreted that process as but a different approach to adding and removing genes; conventional cross-breeding for example does much the same thing but using a different approach. Hence, the decision was made in the United States (unlike most countries) to regulate the *product and not the process.* That choice led directly to two ancillary policy decisions: existing agencies could be used, and no new biotech-specific regulations were required. And while the principal food safety focus was on toxicity, allergenicity, and whole food value, as a scientific approach that of "essential equivalents" is used. Establishing essential equivalence at its most basic level involves two steps, the first of which is how conventionally produced foods (say a new tomato variety) are evaluated.

The United States and most systems use the GRAS approach—conventional foods are "generally recognized as safe." Since humankind has been eating tomatoes for a long time with no particular problems, new conventionally bred varieties are generally assumed to be safe as well. From there it is but a small step—considering the product not process approach—to say genetically modified foods which are similar to conventional ones are safe as well. That is not to say there is no safety review, but the expectation is of safety. An example is milk from rBST-treated cows. Since milk from untreated cows is safe, and rBST undetectable, then the "new" milk is anticipated to be safe as well.

It should be noted that the pasteurization of milk was widely resisted when introduced in the 1880–1920 period. Pasteurization kills bacteria, greatly reducing the transmission of diseases like tuberculosis, as well as extending the shelf life of the product. But it was considered by many unnatural and reduced the nutritiousness of milk, while changing the taste to a slightly "cooked" flavor. That opposition delayed the adoption of the procedure for decades, likely at the cost of many lives.[109] Within the current decade, there has been a growing movement to use "raw" (unpasteurized) milk despite the health risks. At the same time in 2002 the FDA, in response to a number of mid-1990s *E. coli* outbreaks, began to require that larger cider and juice producers pasteurize their products, although small operations selling directly to consumers are exempt. That latter group must, however, label their products using the following wording: "This product has not been pasteurized and, therefore, may contain harmful bacteria that can cause serious illness in children, the elderly and persons with weakened immune systems."[110]

From the GRAS and product-not-process train of logic it is but a small step to rule that genetically modified products need not be labeled as such. What indeed would a label say, and what information would that convey to consumers? "Contains genetically modified organisms," or "may contain genetically modified organisms." A label should provide a warning about a health threat—"SURGEON GENERAL'S WARNING: Smoking Causes Lung Cancer, Heart Disease, Emphysema, And May Complicate Pregnancy"—or supply nutrition information which can help in avoiding allergens or less-healthy substances like saturated fats (see Example 6.2). How then are consumers to use the information? One concern is that the mere presence of a label will connote a threat and diminish sales. Indeed, that very thing happened with a tomato paste product sold in Sainsbury supermarkets in the United Kingdom. The product was introduced in 1996 and sold 750,000 cans over three years. It was labeled as containing genetically modified ingredients and sold side by side with the traditional product, but at a lower price. The price was 29 p/170 g versus 29 p/142 g for the traditional product. But when the genetically modified (GM) food controversy took hold of Europe in 1999 the product lost favor and was withdrawn.

This though is the scientific perspective; consumers see the issue differently. Asked, 90 percent will say that GM foods should be labeled, often citing the right to know (Right-2Know march photos at www.right2knowmarch.org/).[111] Unaided, however, only 3 percent will identify GM content as something they would like to see on food labels.[112]

While producers are not required to label GM food products, including milk from rBST-treated cows, non-GM food producers may voluntarily label theirs as being GM-free. Indeed, a federal appeals court struck down a ban in Ohio prohibiting the labeling of rBST-free milk as such. In any case, it is now permissible to label rBST-free milk, provided the label contain a disclaimer indicating that the GM (or rBST) product presents no known health risks (Figure 6.8). Recently, the USDA has allowed labeling as BST-free meat and eggs from animals not fed GM feed.[113]

Figure 6.8 **FDA States: No Significant Difference in Milk from Cows Treated with Artificial Growth Hormones**

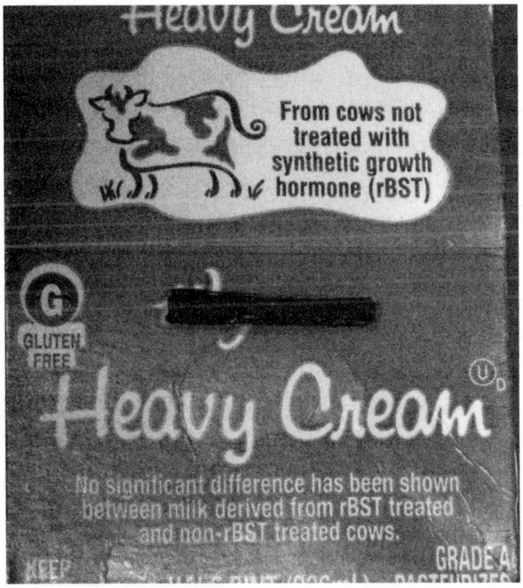

Source: W. Lesser.

In November 2012 Californians voted on Resolution 37 which "Requires labeling of food sold to consumers made from plants or animals with genetic material changed in specified ways," as well as prohibiting "marketing such food, or other processed food, as 'natural.' " Exempted are labeled organic products, meat from animals fed or injected with GM feeds or drugs, foods for immediate consumption such as in restaurants, and small quantities of GM content, until July 2019. The definition of "small" is 0.5 percent, less than other national laws with maximum tolerance levels between 0.9 and 5 percent. It is essentially impossible to provide 100 percent GM-free foods; the contamination potential is too prevelent in the field and supply chains. The animal content exemption means that milk with rBST need not be labeled as such, although some soy milks must be. Labels when required must state "Genetically Engineered" or "May Be Partially Produced with Genetic Engineering."[114]

Pre-vote polls indicated that the "Yes, label" vote was leading by 3:1 despite being outspent 5:1.[115] But in the end the proposition lost by 6 percentage points. Then in 2013 a similar ballot initative in Washington State went down with a similar margin.[116] According to Washington State government sources, the regulations would have cost $3.4 million through 2019.[117]

At that point the mandatory labeling initative shifted to the Northeast with first Connecticut and Maine adopting labeling legislation—but with implementation delayed until contiguous states with 20 million in population had adopted similar laws—and then 2014 in Vermont with an implementation date of 2016. Other Northeastern states are currently considering similar legislation, which is to say with similar exclusions to the California proposition but with a 0.9 percent tolerance for GM ingredients.

While none of these laws would have lead to the mandatory labeling of rBST-containing milk in California, that labeling decision is being made on a business level by milk processors and retailers large and small. It was not unanticipated, given the firm's corporate philosophy and positioning, that Ben & Jerry's label its ice cream as rBST-free. More surprising was the 2008 decision by Walmart to make its private label Great Value milk non-rBST.[118] Other supermarket chains and dairies have made similar pledges. In Walmart's case, the decision was based on concerns expressed by its consumers. Those concerns appear to be only partly human-health related and partly associated with the "industrial farming" techniques associated with its use.[119] Indeed, Walmart's position is decidely not anti-GMO, nor pro-labeling, for it recently announced plans to sell unlabeled *Bt* sweet corn.[120] Rather the decision is consumer oriented. The demand for rBST-free milk has been increasing rapidly, more so than for organic milk.

One informal study in 2010 found that the price for rBST-free milk was 65 percent higher than for conventional milk and close to the price of organic.[121] By mid-2012, the differential had dropped to about 40 percent, with the average price for a half gallon of rBST-free milk $3.57, compared to the reported retail price for a half gallon of regular milk ($2.21),[122] and then in 2014 back to 2010 levels with half gallons of the rBST-free product at $3.87 while regular milk was priced at $2.46.[123] However, milk prices vary across stores and locations, so it is difficult to be precise about these particular values. At the farm level, the average 2013 March price difference (the last of the price series) between conventional and rBST-free milk was about $.023 per pound, or 19 cents per gallon (2 percent milk weighs 8.4 lbs/gallon).[124]

b. Case Questions

The management of Kraft Foods Group *for the purposes of this hypothetical case* of course was aware of the California Proposition 37 vote. Also for the purposes of this case and despite the rejection of the measure, imagine polling indicates similar legislation will and indeed has been adopted and within a decade will extend across the country, either as law or as manufacturer practice. Management is also aware that milk produced using rBST need not be so labeled under the California law, but that many consumers are now seeking out rBST-free milk.

Of course, milk labeling is not a direct concern to Kraft since fresh milk is not one of their many products. Kraft is, however, very involved in the cheese business with about 50 percent of the 4.3 billion pound-a-year American-type cheese (primarily cheddar) business.[125] Indeed, cheese can be considered the signature Kraft product, although its market share has been slipping slightly in recent years due to lower price competition from store-brand cheeses.

Kraft is considering whether using only rBST-free milk and labeled cheese packages will give it a market advantage even though presently only a very few companies like Ben & Jerry's label processed dairy products as rBST-free. The raw material cost bump will be considerable even at a nineteen-cents-per-gallon cost differential, as ten pounds of milk are required to make one pound of cheese. And then there will be the monitoring costs of the dairy farms since Kraft certainly does not want to be caught selling a product with a misrepresented label. But there is an additional consideration.

Presently some 80–90 percent of American-type cheeses are produced using genetically modified rennin (chymosin) in place of the natural product from calves' stomachs.[126] There is insufficient calves' rennin available for all the cheese currently produced, although plant-based substitutes exist as well. Cheeses are not presently labeled as containing GM rennin, and indeed few consumers appear even to be aware of its existence. The EU required labeling for products containing GM rennin beginning in 2013. The average city price of cheddar in June 2013 was $5.50 per pound, according to the Bureau of Labor Statistics, which collects these prices nationally for computing the Consumer Price Index.[127]

This brings us to the following three questions:

1. How much would the additional cost to Kraft be of using rBST-free milk in the production of its American-type cheese products, and how large a premium would it require over prevailing chedder prices to cover the additional expense?
2. What additional considerations might Kraft wish to apply when considering whether or not to label its American-type cheeses as rBST-free? And what about GM chymosin—how should management approach that issue?
3. Considering your answers to questions1 and 2 above, how would you recommend

Kraft label its cheeses: as rBST-free, GM chymosin-free, both, or neither?

4. In October 2012, Kraft spun off its snack foods and international operations to Mondelez International. Does that recent change affect your recommendation?

6.13 ■ CASE 6.10: INTELLECTUAL PROPERTY AND INTERNATIONAL COSMETIC MARKETING

a. Background

In an introductory public lecture on intellectual property (IP), the speaker began with a prop, a liter Coke bottle. That bottle, he posited, represented the scope of intellectual property protection and its use by companies:

- The Coke *formula* is protected as a trade secret (said to be held in a vault in the Atlanta headquarters with several keys in the possession of as many top officials, who must coordinate in order to open it)
- The *bottle shape* (the familiar "hourglass" design) is patented
- The traditional Coke *color* is trademarked
- The Coke *name* and *script* in its several forms, along with marketing slogans, are trademarked

This introduction emphasized two aspects of the strategic use of IP by firms. Companies strive for a strong "fence" of protection around their products and marketing approaches. Individually a single form may have a limited effect, but jointly they are highly effective in preventing direct or misleading copying. This issue is particularly important for a product like Coke where, quite frankly, the product per se is not really distinct but nonetheless commands a substantial price premium and channel access. How many of us have participated in or read about blind taste tests where participants are unable to distinguish between Coke and Pepsi?

For technical products lacking marketing-generated distinctions the protection reality can be quite different. Process or product-by-process patents for example provide limited protection because (a) small changes in the process can bypass the patent protection, and (b) process patent holders generally can prevent the importation of products that infringe the patent but it is difficult to prove that the process used was indeed the one protected in the importing country. And then there is the issue of differences in interpretation across countries so that what is patentable in the United States may not be in France (and the EU member states in general) and visa versa. Furthermore, there is the reality that protection must be secured independently in each country where it is needed. The composite is a costly and complex entity to manage and monitor; IP protection that is not enforced is worthless because there is no disincentive for competitors to violate it. All said, a well-executed IP strategy is invaluable in most sectors. Just how to construct such a strategy is the subject of the case study below.

For background information on intellectual property rights systems, readers are directed to Chapter 3, Section 3.6.

b. Case Questions

Students should prepare the following questions, based on the Harvard Business School case (the IP aspects of the case are being emphasized):

Radiant Cosmetics: What's in a Pout? #310-003

1. Should Radiant protect the "pout" formula with a patent or as a trade secret? Among the categories of patents (product, product-by-process, process, and so forth—see Chapter 3, Section 3.6b), how would this formula be categorized, and what does that mean for the degree of protection granted? What are the advantages/disadvantages of patents versus trade secrets? How do the considerations differ between the United States and France?
2. In what ways are the product-positioning (luxury versus mass market) and IP issues interrelated?
3. IP in its several forms is intended to prevent unauthorized copying. Which aspects of the "Four Carat Pout" product are critical to its commercial success and how effectively can each be protected in the United States and France? Your answer needs to recognize the differences between the luxury and mass-market product.
4. In your judgment should the differences in IP law and practice in the United States and France change Radiant's marketing strategies between the two countries? Please explain your reasoning, emphasizing the kinds of copying risks involved.

6.14 CONCLUSIONS

At one level the justification for regulating consumer products is easy to identify—over time there have been numerous examples of tragedies, of outrages, of exploitation that unsurprisingly led to regulation intended to prevent reoccurrences. Many of those incidents happened in the past, some the deep past, but they are ongoing—consider the compounding pharmacy tragedy of 2012. Yet while regulations are typically (but not universally) supported in particular instances and conceptually, resistance, both individual and political, arises to the aggregate of regulations. And a plethora of regulations we do have, as is evident from the list of just the major product regulations presented in Table 6.1. Most of those regulations are directed towards overcoming the incomplete information market failure. Be assured, there will continue to be tensions between individual regulatory decisions and the aggregate effects.

The bulk of the chapter though is focused on a range of case studies pertaining to consumer product categories, ten in all. These ten can be placed into three categories, as follows:

1.	Labeling and other information provision:	4 (numbers 4, 7–9)
2.	Cooperation and voluntary compliance:	5 (numbers 1, 2, 3, 5, 6)
3.	Intellectual property:	1 (number 10)

The grouping of food-product labeling with CFPB financial information (numbers 4, 7–9) might seem strained, but both provide information with which consumers can make better informed choices, whether they be having a meal or considering an investment. Both respond to information limitations in the marketplace—a market failure. The operational notion here is the degree to which consumers actually use the information provided. Food nutrition labels are used, but not regularly by consumers, but frequency need not be necessary to have the desired effect. I personally love coconut custard pie, but one look years ago at the calorie count put it deep in the "occasional treat" category for me. Routine viewings of the label were not needed! In any case, food companies are presently tightly bound on what they must and what they can say on labels. The details of the labeling stipulations (font size, location, and so forth) may seem excessive, but then any flexibility can be exploited to the detriment of consumers and compliant firms alike. Now financial information seems headed the same way, which is likely a good thing, for consumers anyway.

Issues of regulatory compliance have more strategic involvement. The "correct" answers depend very much on the specific details of a case, as can be seen when contrasting cases 1 and 2. Typically lead firms benefit from the status quo, while followers gain from some kind of equilibrium-disrupting action. Industry leaders need to consider the position of the followers in judging the optimal strategic decision, cooperate or not. Game theory (see Example 6.1) provides a systematic way to do that and is an appropriate approach in evaluating such strategic choices.

The LEED-related cases emphasize the point that regulation is not always necessary to achieve a goal, in this case environmental compatibility. Sometimes it is done voluntarily, whether based on moral commitments, prestige, or simply a different cost/benefit calculus.

These categories have overlaps as well. The tire fuel-efficiency case (# 2) partly applies to how and where information is supplied. Indeed, the posting of calories by fast-food firms (#7) also involves where it is done—on the Web or at the restaurant. The distinction is significant for consumers, producers, and retailers. Operationally, it seems the closer to the purchase decision the information is provided the more likely it is to be used.

Placing the final case in a distinct category is regrettable as it implies that intellectual property issues are separate from other strategic choices made by firms; but they are not. Intellectual property protection in its many forms is absolutely critical in many sectors and must be integrated into other strategic decisions. The question "Is a foreign market attractive?" often devolves into "Can our IP be protected there?" GM, for example, withdrew its technology licenses from Saab, forcing the company into bankruptcy based on fears the Chinese buyers would usurp the technology.[128] For Radiant Cosmetics, the subject of Case 6.10, the decision of where and how to enter markets is heavily IP-dependent. The product, according to the case, is a good one. Success then depends on the combination of marketing and IP strategies, along with competitors' responses. Notably, the product is no longer listed on the Radiant Web site.

This said, the following broad conclusions, at minimum, can be drawn from the chapter cases:

- Firms within a sector can and do take different positions on regulatory compliance, in part because of differential circumstances
- Regulations can generate new business opportunities, especially as regards the labeling of products and consumers' use of those labels
- Corporate support or lack thereof for developing regulations can have major effects on how the regulatory process evolves
- IP options are key strategic regulatory decisions in many product markets and should not be viewed as something apart, abstract, esoteric

6.15 STUDY QUESTIONS

1. For each of the ten cases presented here, please identify the regulatory act or acts on which they are based.
2. For each of the ten cases, please identify if there was a market failure(s) which it was intended, even partially, to address.
3. At the beginning of the chapter a distinction is drawn between "experiential" and "credence" goods. Into which category does each of the products discussed in this chapter fit? How does that distinction affect the regulatory response?
4. J.Q. Wilson (see Chapter 2, Section 2.2e) refers to "entrepreneurial regulators" who use one justification for a regulation to expand its scope. Are there any examples in this chapter of the work of such a regulator?
5. Can you identify any other recent tragedies that have contributed to the promulgation of a new regulation?
6. Pick a consumer product (e.g., baby cribs, smokeless tobacco, etc.) and lay out the regulatory process controlling it.
7. While not strictly a regulatory matter, Johnson & Johnson has won considerable praise for its management of the Tylenol tampering case back in the 1980s. Can you identify a situation in which a firm mismanaged a product safety issue like tampering? How might the situation have been better managed?
8. The LEED building standards are described as combining process and performance approaches to regulation. Can you describe why this is so?
9. The Cornell Crisp case (Case 6.8) raises the prospect of using cheaper (but less healthy) trans fats while not revealing that fact under the small-firm labeling exemption. At the same time, the firm could label its product as made from

"organic potatoes." From regulatory and marketing perspectives what would your evaluation of this approach be?

10. The two initial cases in this chapter (Cases 6.1 and 6.2) both relate to regulations applied to tires. Please describe the similarities and differences between the two cases and what in your judgment are the critical dimensions that led to differences in the recommended corporate responses.
11. Firms clearly take different approaches on the development of regulations. Some but not all of these differences are based on distinct business situations, like relative costs and market positions. Are there though other factors which at least partially explain the different corporate responses?
12. Set up a game theory matrix for evaluating the IP issues facing Radiant Cosmetics in France in Case 6.10.
13. Can you find any information about what happened to Radiant's Four Carat Pout product? Were any of the problems encountered by the company IP-related?

NOTES

1. Shaya Tayefe Mohajer, "Cargill Recall: Turkey Recalled after Salmonella Poisoning." *Christian Science Monitor,* August 3, 2011.
2. Consumers Union, Letter to Senators Opposing SA-199. March 16, 2011. Available at www.consumerfed.org/pdfs/Oppose-SA-199-Defunding-CPSC.pdf. Last visited 7/24/13.
3. Vincent Iannelli, "Crib Recall—Latest Crib Recall List." About.com, October 5, 2011. Available at http://pediatrics.about.com/od/babyproducts/a/510_crib_recall.htm. Last visited 10/14/11.
4. Consumer Products Safety Commission, Office of Compliance, "Requirements for Full Sized Baby Cribs." 16 C.F.R. 1508. Available at www.cpsc.gov/businfo/regsumcrib.pdf. Last visited 10/12/11.
5. Consumer Products Safety Commission, "A Safer Generation of Cribs: New Federal Requirements." Available at www.cpsc.gov/nsn/cribrules.pdf. Last visited 10/12/11.
6. Carol Ballentine, "Taste of Raspberries, Taste of Death: The 1937 Elixir Sulfanilamide Incident." *FDA Consumer Magazine*, June 1981. Available at www.fda.gov/AboutFDA/WhatWeDo/History/ProductRegulation/SulfanilamideDisaster/default.htm. Last visited 7/10/14.
7. Barbara Martin, "Elixir Sulfanilamide Tragedy: Calls for Improved Legislation." *Pathophilia,* March 13, 2009. Available at http://bmartinmd.com/2009/03/elixir-sulfanilamide-legislation.html.
8. Editors, "The Deadly 'Elixir.' " *Drug and Cosmetic Industry* 41 (1937): 611, 614, 615, 619.
9. Walt Bogdanich and Jake Hooker, "From China to Panama, a Trail of Poisoned Medicine." *New York Times,* May 6, 2007.
10. Zachary T. Sampson, "New England Compounding Center, Blamed for Meningitis Outbreak, Files for Bankruptcy." *Boston Globe,* December 21, 2012.
11. Lena H. Sun, "Report Faults States' Oversight of Specialty Pharmacies." *Washington Post,* October 28, 2012.
12. Denise Grady, Sabrina Tavernise, and Andrew Pollack, "In a Drug Linked to a Deadly Meningitis Outbreak, a Question of Oversight." *New York Times,* October 4, 2012.
13. Sarah Kliff and Lena H. Sun, "Critics Charge That Drug-Compounding Pharmacies Require Government Oversight." *Washington Post,* October 18, 2012.
14. David Morgan, "U.S. Regulator Needs New Authority over Compounding Pharmacies: Report." *Chicago Tribune*, October 28, 2012.
15. Charles B. Fleddermann, "The Ford Pinto Exploding Gas Tank." In *Engineering Ethics,* 2nd ed. Upper Saddle River, NJ: Prentice Hall, 2004, pp. 72–73.

16. Matthew T. Lee, "The Ford Pinto Case and the Development of Auto Safety Regulations, 1893–1978." *Business and Economic History* 27, 2 (1998): 390–401.

17. James R. Healey, "Chrysler Wins Cut from Feds, Recalls 1.56 Million Jeeps." *USA Today,* June 19, 2013 (updated June 20).

18. Angelo Young, "GM Ignition Switch Recall: Valukas Report Expected Out This Week, Could Answer Key Questions About What GM Knew and When About Fatal Design Flaw." *International Business Times,* June 2, 2014.

19. "The Tylenol Crisis, 1982." Available at http://iml.jou.ufl.edu/projects/fall02/susi/tylenol.htm. Last visited 10/16/11.

20. Quoted in Don Babwin, "Tylenol Tampering Case Remains Unsolved, in 25 Years." *USA Today,* September 29, 2007.

21. "The ABCs of Seismic Building Codes." Available at http://mceer.buffalo.edu/publications/Tricenter/04-sp02/1–03abcs.pdf. Last visited 10/16/11.

22. "The Industrial Revolution." Available at www.localhistories.org/industrial.html. Last visited 10/16/11.

23. Consumer Product Safety Commission, "ATV-Related Deaths and Injuries for All Ages." Available at www.atvsafety.gov/stats.html. Last visited 2/12/12.

24. Brian Dakss, "Kids' ATV Death Rate Up, Study Says." CBS News, February 11, 2009. Available at www.cbsnews.com/stories/2007/07/31/earlyshow/living/parenting/main3116736.shtml. Last visited 2/12/12.

25. Consumer Product Safety Commission, "ATV State Legislative Resource Bank." Available at www.atvsafety.gov/legislation/legislation.html. Last visited 2/12/12.

26. Quoted in Committee on Energy and Commerce, "Waxman and Butterfield: New Poll Shows 'Very Strong' Support for Federal Consumer Product Safety Efforts." Available at http://democrats.energycommerce.house.gov/index.php?q=news/waxman-and-butterfield-new-poll-shows-very-strong-support-for-federal-consumer-product-safety-e. Last visited 2/12/12.

27. CPSC Overview. Available at www.cpsc.gov/about/about.html. Last visited 2/13/12.

28. Timothy Noah, "Who's Afraid of the CPSC?" *Slate,* March 8, 2011. Available at www.slate.com/articles/business/the_customer/2011/03/whos_afraid_of_the_cpsc.html. See also CPSC "2011 Performance and Accountability Report" November 2011. Available at www.cpsc.gov/cpscpub/pubs/reports/2011par.pdf. Both last visited 2/13/12.

29. Kent Hoover, "What Does $1 Billion Buy in Washington? For U.S. Chamber, Not as Much as They'd Like." *Washington Journal,* July 13, 2013.

30. Jay Timmons, President and CEO, National Association of Manufacturers, letter to Representative Issa dated June 4, 2012. Available at www.nam.org/~/media/82F55BECFC744B5C81A718CFD31C0FD9/NAMIssaJordanRegulation6_4_12.pdf. Last visited 8/1/13.

31. Niall Ferguson, "The Regulated States of America." June 18, 2013. Available at www.hoover.org/news/daily-report/149941. Last visited 8/1/13.

32. Common Cause, "About the Koch Brothers." Undated. Available at www.commoncause.org/site/pp.asp?c=dkLNK1MQIwG&b=6460127. Last visited 8/1/13.

33. Tire Manufacturers Association, "2011 Tire Shipments to Grow Nearly 4 Percent." Available at www.rma.org/newsroom/release.cfm?ID=312. Last visited 10/18/11. Includes all tire sizes, replacements as well as original equipment sales.

34. Rubber Manufacturers Association, "RMA's comments on NHTSA proposed Tire Fuel Efficiency Regulation," August 21, 2009. Available at www.rma.org/rma_resources/government_affairs/federal_issues/RMA%20COMMENTS%20TO%20NHTSA-2008–0121%2008–21–09.pdf. Last visited 10/21/11.

35. "Which OE brand is highest in customer loyalty? Hint: It begins with an 'M.' " *Modern Tire Dealer,* May 3, 2011. Available at www.moderntiredealer.com/News/Story/2011/05/Which-OE-brand-is-highest-in-customer-loyalty-Hint-It-begins-with-an-M.aspx. Last visited 10/19/11.

36. TireRack.com, "Uniform Tire Quality Grade (UTQG) Standards." Available at www.tirerack.com/tires/tiretech/techpage.jsp?techid=48. Last visited 10/18/11.

37. Ibid.

38. Vincent Ciulla, "Uniform Tire Quality Grading (UTQG)." Available at http://autorepair.about.com/cs/generalinfo/a/aa120603a.htm. Last visited 12/2/11.

39. Sandra Weiss, "An Evaluation of the Uniform Tire Quality Grading Standards and Other Tire Labeling Requirements." NHTSA Report Number DOT HS 807 805, January 1992. Available at www.nhtsa.gov/cars/rules/regrev/evaluate/807805.html. Last visited 10/19/11.

40. TireRack.com, "Tire Rolling Resistance, Part 2: Defining Rolling Resistance" Available at www.tirerack.com/tires/tiretech/techpage.jsp?techid=175. Last visited 10/17/12.

41. See, for example, Hunter Leffel, "Bridgestone Ecopia Low Rolling Resistance Tires." September 17, 2010. Available at http://blog.tirerack.com/blog/hunters-ramblings/bridgestone-ecopia-low-rolling-resistance-tires www.tirerack.com. Last visited 10/17/12.

42. Natural Resources Defense Council, "California Adopts World's First Fuel-Efficient Tires Law." October 2, 2003. Available at www.nrdc.org/media/pressreleases/031002.asp. Last visited 10/18/11.

43. "NHTSA sets final rule for fuel efficiency testing." *Modern Tire Dealer,* March 26, 2010. Available at www.moderntiredealer.com/news/story/2010/03/NHTSA-sets-final-rule-for-fuel-efficiency-testing.aspx. Last visited 10/19/11.

44. Board on Energy and Environmental Systems, Tires and Passenger Vehicle Fuel Economy: Informing Consumers, Improving Performance—Special Report 286. *National Academy Press,* 2006, Chapter 6. Available at www.nap.edu/openbook.php?record_id=11620&page=131. Last visited 10/18/11.

45. Greg Smith, "Low rolling resistance, high expectations: The world was watching at the Reifen Trade Fair." *Modern Tire Dealer,* July 26, 2010. Available at www.moderntiredealer.com/Article/Story/2010/07/Low-rolling-resistance-high-expectations/Page/2.aspx. Last visited 10/19/11.

46. Rubber Manufacturers Association, "RMA's comments on NHTSA proposed Tire Fuel Efficiency Regulation."

47. Bob Ulrich, "Tire labeling law will have wide-ranging effect, says King." *Modern Tire Dealer,* January 23, 2010. Available at www.moderntiredealer.com/blog/B-O-B/story/2010/01/Tire-labeling-law-will-have-wide-ranging-effect-says-King.aspx. Last visited 10/19/11.

48. "Michelin supports tire fuel efficiency ratings." *Modern Tire Dealer,* August 26, 2009. Available at www.moderntiredealer.com/news/story/2009/08/Michelin-supports-NHTSA-tire-fuel-efficiency-ratings.aspx. Last visited 10/18/11.

49. NHTSA, "Replacement Tire Consumer Information Program: Final Regulatory Impact Analysis." March 2010. Available at www.nhtsa.gov/staticfiles/rulemaking/pdf/Rolling_Resistance_FRIA.pdf. Last visited 6/4/14.

50. Rubber Manufacturers Association, "RMA's comments on NHTSA proposed Tire Fuel Efficiency Regulation," Appendix 5 (2005 data).

51. Eric Loveday, "*Consumer Reports:* Low-Rolling Resistance Tires Fail to Meet Buyers' Expectations." *Autobloggreen,* November 20, 2010. Available at http://green.autoblog.com/2010/11/20/consumer-reports-low-rolling-resistance-tires-fail-to-meet-buye/. Last visited 9/17/12.

52. hybridCARS, "Choosing Low Rolling Resistance Tires." November 3, 2009. Available at www.hybridcars.com/decision-process/choosing-low-rolling-resistance-tires-26214.html. Last visited 9/17/12.

53. Kimberly Amadeo, "Consumer Financial Protection Bureau" About.com. Available at http://useconomy.about.com/od/candidatesandtheeconomy/g/Consumer_Financial_Protection_Agency.htm. Last visited 10/19/11.

54. Chanel Lee, "What's the Bureau of Consumer Financial Protection?" HowStuffWorks. Available at http://money.howstuffworks.com/bureau-of-consumer-financial-protection1.htm. Last visited 10/20/11.

55. LaToya Irby, "10 Key Changes of the New Credit Card Rules Highlights of the Credit CARD Act of 2009." About.com. Available at http://credit.about.com/od/consumercreditlaws/tp/new-credit-card-rules.htm. Last visited 10/20/11.

56. Specifically, recess appointments expire at the end of the Senate's next session, or when the recess appointee is formally confirmed by the Senate, or when another nomination is submitted and confirmed. In Cordray's case, he in any case can serve until the end of 2013.

57. Diane Katz, "Reforming Consumer Financial Protection Bureau Necessary to Protect Consumers." Heritage Foundation, April 7, 2011. Available at www.heritage.org/research/reports/2011/04/reforming-consumer-financial-protection-bureau-necessary-to-protect-consumers. Last visited 10/20/11.

58. Richard Shelby, "The Danger of an Unaccountable 'Consumer-Protection' Czar." *Wall Street Journal,* July 21, 2011.

59. Govtrack.us, "H.R. 1121: Responsible Consumer Financial Protection Regulations Act of 2011." Available at www.govtrack.us/congress/bill.xpd?bill=h112–1121&tab=summary. Last visited 10/20/11.

60. Consumer Bankers Association, "CFPB Resource Center." July 19, 2013. Available at www.cbanet.org/Advocacy/CFPB%20Resource%20Center/Resource_landing.aspx. Last visited 7/15/13.

61. Katz, "Reforming Consumer Financial Protection Bureau Necessary to Protect Consumers."

62. Elizabeth Warren, "Testimony of Elizabeth Warren Before the Subcommittee on TARP, Financial Services, and Bailouts of Public and Private Programs." May 24, 2011. Available at www.consumerfinance.gov/newsroom/testimony-of-elizabeth-warren-before-the-subcommittee-on-tarp-financial-services-and-bailouts-of-public-and-private-programs. Last visited 6/23/14.

63. Tamara Keith, "New Consumer Protection Agency Faces Opposition." NPR, July 21, 2011. Available at www.npr.org/2011/07/21/138550502/new-consumer-protection-agency-faces-opposition. Last visited 10/21/11.

64. Jeremy Simon, "For credit card issuers, there's plenty of room at the top." CreditCards.com. Available at www.creditcards.com/credit-card-news/us-bank-credit-card-issuers-acquisitions-1264.php#ixzz1bP0o9sId. Last visited 10/21/11.

65. See, for example, Brady Dennis and Ariana Eunjung Cha, "In Foreclosure Controversy, Problems Run Deeper Than Flawed Paperwork." *Washington Post,* October 7, 2010.

66. FreddieMac, "Home Affordable Modification Program." Available at www.freddiemac.com/singlefamily/service/mha_modification.html. Last visited 9/17/12.

67. See, for example, Peter S. Goodman, "Foreclosure Settlement Fails to Force Mortgage Companies to Improve." *HuffPost Business,* August 7, 2012.

68. David Dayen, "CFPB Gets Plurality of Complaints about Mortgages." *FDL,* July 30, 2012. Available at http://news.firedoglake.com/2012/07/30/cfpb-gets-plurality-of-complaints-about-mortgages/. Last visited 9/17/12.

69. Gretchen Morgenson, "Surprise, Surprise: The Banks Win." *New York Times,* January 5, 2013. Also see Paul Kiel, "The Great American Foreclosure Story: The Struggle for Justice and a Place to Call Home." ProPublica, April 10, 2012, Available at www.propublica.org/article/the-great-american-foreclosure-story-the-struggle-for-justice-and-a-place-t/single. Last visited 6/2/14.

70. CFPB, "Consumer Financial Protection Bureau Proposes Rules to Protect Mortgage Borrowers." August 10, 2012. Available at www.consumerfinance.gov/pressreleases/consumer-financial-protection-bureau-proposes-rules-to-protect-mortgage-borrowers/. Full rules available at http://files.consumerfinance.gov/f/201208_cfpb_tila_proposed_rules.pdf and http://files.consumerfinance.gov/f/201208_cfpb_respa_proposed_rules.pdf. Last visited 9/17/12.

71. Carter Dougherty, "Smaller U.S. Banks Seeking Exemption from CFPB Mortgage Rules." *Bloomberg Businessweek,* August 2, 2012. Available at www.businessweek.com/news/2012–08–02/smaller-u-dot-s-dot-banks-seeking-exemption-from-cfpb-mortgage-rules. Last visited 9/25/12.

72. KPMG, "Mortgage Servicing Operations." Available at www.kpmg.com/US/en/IssuesAndInsights/ArticlesPublications/Documents/mortgage-servicing-operations-brochure.pdf. Last visited 9/25/12.

73. See, for example, BSi, "ISO Environment." Available at www.bsigroup.com/en/Assessment-and-certification-services/management-systems/Standards-and-Schemes/ISO-14001/. Last visited 3/7/12.

74. María-del-Val Segarra-Oña, Ángel Peiró-Signes, and Rohit Verma, "Environmental Management Certification and Performance in the Hospitality Industry: A Comparative Analysis of ISO14001 Hotels in Spain." *Cornell Hospitality Report* 11, 22 (December 2011): Exhibit 3 and p. 10.

75. Daniel Klem, Jr., "Avian Mortality at Windows: The Second Largest Human Source of Bird Mortality on Earth." In T.D. Rich, C. Arizmendi, D. Demarest, and C. Thompson, *Proceedings of the Fourth International Partners in Flight Conference: Tundra to Tropics.* February 13–16, 2008 (pp. 244–51). McAllen, TX.

76. William M. Welch, "San Francisco OKs 'Bird-Safe' Building Standard." *USA Today,* September 11, 2011.

77. Available at www.toronto.ca/planning/environment/greendevelopment.htm. Last visited 11/5/12.

78. Ian Austen, "Casualties of Toronto's Urban Skies." *New York Times,* October 28, 2012, pp. 6 and 12.

79. Trust for America's Health, "Obesity." Available at www.healthyamericans.org/obesity/. Last visited 9/25/12.

80. Alisha Coleman-Jensen, Mark Nord, Margaret Andrews, and Steven Carlson, "Household Food Security in the United States in 2011." USDA, ERS, Economic Research Report No. (ERR-141), September 2012. Available at www.ers.usda.gov/publications/err-economic-research-report/err141.aspx. Last visited 9/26/12.

81. Michael M. Grynbaum, "Health Panel Approves Restriction on Sale of Large Sugary Drinks." *New York Times,* September 13, 2012.

82. David B. Caruso, "Appeals judges say NYC's ban on big, sugary drinks at restaurants is unconstitutional." Associated Press, July 30, 2013. Available at www.startribune.com/lifestyle/health/217602801.html. Last visited 7/31/13.

83. Michael M. Grynbaum, "Judge Blocks New York City's Limits on Big Sugary Drinks." *New York Times,* March 11, 2013.

84. FDA News Release, "FDA proposes draft menu and vending machine labeling requirements, invites public to comment on proposals." April 1, 2011. Available at www.fda.gov/NewsEvents/Newsroom/PressAnnouncements/ucm249471.htm. Last visited 9/25/12.

85. See FDA, "Food and Drug Administration Modernization Act of 1997." Available at www.fda.gov/RegulatoryInformation/Legislation/FederalFoodDrugandCosmeticActFDCAct/SignificantAmendmentstotheFDCAct/FDAMA/FullTextofFDAMAlaw/default.htm. Last visited 9/27/12.

86. FDA, "New Menu and Vending Machines Labeling Requirements." Available at www.fda.gov/food/labelingnutrition/ucm217762.htm. Last visited 9/25/12.

87. FDA, " Disclosure of Nutrient Content Information for Standard Menu Items Offered for Sale at Chain Restaurants or Similar Retail Food Establishments and for Articles of Food Sold From Vending Machines." *Federal Register* 75, 129 (July 7, 2010): 39026–39028.

88. FDA News Release, "FDA proposes draft menu and vending machine labeling requirements, invites public to comment on proposals." April 1, 2011.

89. "Restaurant calorie counts may have to wait: FDA." *Associated Press*, March 12, 2013. Available at www.wjla.com/articles/2013/03/restaurant-calorie-counts-may-have-to-wait-fda-86125.html. Last visited 7/31/13.

90. James Barron, "Restaurants Must Post Calories, Judge Affirms." *New York Times,* April 17, 2008.

91. Stephanie Strom, "McDonald's Menu to Post Calorie Data." *New York Times,* September 12, 2012.

92. *News Medical,* "Trans Fat Regulation." Available at www.news-medical.net/health/Trans-Fat-Regulation.aspx. Last visited 6/23/14.

93. Meredith Melnick, "Calorie Counts on Menus: Apparently, Nobody Cares." *Time,* February 16, 2011. Available at http://healthland.time.com/2011/02/16/calorie-counts-on-menus-apparently-nobody-cares/. Last visited 9/26/12. Full study available at http://content.healthaffairs.org/content/28/6/w1110.full.pdf+html. Last visited 7/9/13.

94. Bryan Bollinger, Phillip Leslie, and Alan Sorenson, "Caloric Posting in Chain Restaurants." NBER Working Paper No. 15648, January 2010. Available at www.nber.org/papers/w15648. Last visited 9/26/12.

95. B. Bruemmer, J. Krieger, B.E. Saelens, and N. Chan, "Energy, Saturated Fat, and Sodium Were Lower in Entrées at Chain Restaurants at 18 Months Compared with 6 Months Following the Implementation of Mandatory Menu Labeling Regulation in King County, Washington." *Journal of the Academy of Nutrition and Dietetics* 112, 8 (August 2012): 1169–76.

96. Stephanie Clifford, "Why Healthy Eaters Fall for Fries." *New York Times,* June 30, 2013, Sunday Review p. 5.

97. 21 CFR 101.9(i).

98. See, for example, C. Moorman, R. Du, and C.F. Mela, "The Effect of Standardized Information on Firm Survival and Marketing Strategies." *Marketing Science,* 24 (2005): 263–74.

99. See for example C. Moorman, "The Quasi Experiment to Assess the Consumer and Informational Determinants of Nutrition Information Processing Activities: The Case of the Nutrition Labeling and Education Act." *Journal of Public Policy & Marketing,* 15 (1996): 28–44.

100. International Food Information Council, "2011 Food and Health Survey: Consumer Attitudes toward Food Safety, Nutrition & Health." Available at www.foodinsight.org/Content/3840/2011%20IFIC%20FDTN%20Food%20and%20Health%20Survey.pdf. Last visited 9/27/12.

101. Josh Flint, "Retailers Still Demand rBST-Free Milk." *Wisconsin Agriculturalist,* August 2011. Available at http://magissues.farmprogress.com/WSA/WA08Aug11/wsa037.pdf. Last visited 9/27/12.

102. Jeffrey Gillespie, Richard Nehring, Charlie Hallahan, Carmen Sandretto, and Loren Tauer. "Adoption of Recombinant Bovine Somatotropin and Farm Profitability: Does Farm Size Matter?" *AgBioForum* 13 (2010): 251–62.

103. Chemista, "Posilac (rBST or bovine somatotropin) Eli Lilly/Elanco product information." May 5, 2010. Available at http://renchemista.wordpress.com/2010/05/05/posilac-rbst-or-bovine-somatotropin-eli-lillyelanco-product-information/. Last visited 9/27/12.

104. Full list of animal health impacts available at "POSILAC (rBGH) Insert." Available at www.psr.org/assets/pdfs/posilac-insert.doc. Last visited 9/27/12.

105. See, for example, Michael Hansen, Jean M. Halloran, Edward Groth III, and Lisa Y. Lefferts, "Potential Public Health Impacts of the Use of Recombinant Bovine Somatotropin in Dairy Production." September 1997. Available at www.consumersunion.org/pub/core_food_safety/002272.html. Last visited 9/27/12.

106. Quoted in Carolyn Scott-Thomas, "Court Overturns Ohio Ban on rbST-Free Milk Labeling." Foodnavigator-usa, October 4, 2010. Available at www.foodnavigator-usa.com/Regulation/Court-overturns-Ohio-ban-on-rbST-free-milk-labeling. Last visited 9/27/12.

107. Quoted in ibid.

108. Cate Vojdik, "Got Milk? Got Hormones? Got a Problem with That?" CNN, April 9, 2008. Available at http://ac360.blogs.cnn.com/2008/04/09/got-milk-got-hormones-got-a-problem-with-that/. Last visited 9/27/12.

109. Joseph H. Hotchkiss, "Lambasting Pasteur: Lessons from Pasteurization." Undated. Available at http://nabc-cals-ssl.hosting.cornell.edu/pubs/nabc_13/HOTCHKISS.pdf. Last visited 10/1/12.

110. Jenan Jones Benson, "To Pasteurize or Not?" Growing North Features, undated. Available at www.growingmagazine.com/print-2373.aspx. Last visited 10/1/12.

111. Ronnie Cummins, "Prop 37: The Moment of Truth for GMO Labeling." NaturalNews.com, September 24, 2012. Available at www.naturalnews.com/037300_Proposition_37_GMO_labeling_food.html. Last visited 10/8/12.

112. International Food Information Council, "Consumer Perceptions of Food Technology and Sustainability." Available at www.foodinsight.org/Content/5438/FINAL-%20HP%20Webcast%20Slides_5-10-12.pdf. Last visited 10/8/12.

113. Ethan A. Huff, "First Ever Non-GMO Meat and Egg Product Label Hits the Market."

NaturalNews. com, July 11, 2013. Available at www.naturalnews.com/041148_GMO_labeling_USDA_genetically_modified_foods.html. Last visited 7/31/13.

114. Text of the act available at www.noprop37.com/uploads/1343936210-NoonProp37ReadProp.37.pdf. Last visited 10/5/12.

115. Donation data available at www.kcet.org/news/ballotbrief/elections2012/propositions/prop-37-funding-genetically-engineered-food.html. Last visited 10/5/12.

116. DLA Piper, et al., "Defeat on Washington I-522 GMO Labeling." Association of Corporate Council, November 20, 2013. Available at www.lexology.com/library/detail.aspx?g=3228d1c5-fce8–4a05–8289-a076ed4f8e59. Last visited 11/22/13.

117. Niraj Chokshi, "Washington State Voters Are About to Weigh in on a Multi-Million Dollar Food Fight." *Washington Post,* October 29, 2013.

118. Josh Flint, "Retailers Still Demand rBST-Free Milk." *Wisconsin Agriculturalist,* August 2011. Available at http://magissues.farmprogress.com/WSA/WA08Aug11/wsa037.pdf. Last visited 10/5/12.

119. Dan Shapley, "Wal-Mart Brand Milk Will Be rBST-Free." *Daily Green,* March 21, 2008. Available at www.thedailygreen.com/environmental-news/latest/milk-hormones-rbst-47032108. Last visited 10/5/12.

120. Ethan A. Huff, "Monsanto's Bt GMO Corn to Be Sold at Wal-Mart with No Indication It Is Genetically Modified." NaturalNews.com, February 21, 2012. Available at www.naturalnews.com/035029_GM_corn_Walmart_Monsanto.html. Last visited 10/5/12.

121. Terry D. Etherton, "The 'Smoke and Mirrors' of rbST-Free Milk Pricing Keeps Rolling On . . . and On." *PennState Animal Science Blog*, October 7, 2010. Available at http://blogs.das.psu.edu/tetherton/2010/10/07/the-smoke-and-mirrors-of-rbst-free-milk-pricing-keeps-rolling-on-and-on/. Last visited 10/5/12.

122. American Farm Bureau Federation,"Retail Prices for Meats, Dairy and Eggs Decline Slightly." *The Voice of Agriculture,* July 16, 2012. Available at www.fb.org/index.php?action=newsroom.news&year=2012&file=nr0716.html. Last visited 10/5/12.

123. American Farm Bureau Federation, "Bacon Prices Up, Eggs Too." *The Voice of Agriculture*, April 3, 2014. Available at www.fb.org/index.php?action=newsroom.news&year=2014&file=nr0403.html. Last visited 6/3/14.

124. Approximate in the sense that the cooperative price that includes the rBST—non-rBST price differential is used as the differential. Prices available at www.ams.usda.gov/AMSv1.0/getfile?dDocName=STELPRDC5060352. Last visited 7/31/13.

125. Volume data at USDA, National Agricultural Statistics Service, "Dairy Products Production by Product and Month—United States: 2011." April 2012. Available at www.usda.gov/nass/PUBS/TODAYRPT/daryan12.txt. Last visited 10/8/12.

126. *GMO Compass,* "Chymosin." Available at www.gmo-ompass.org/eng/database/enzymes/83.chymosin.html. Last visited 10/8/12.

127. Bureau Labor Statistics, "Average Prices." Available at www.bls.gov/ro3/apmw.htm. Last visited 7/31/13.

128. "GM halts sale of Saab to Chinese firms." *The Local: Sweden's News in English,* November 8, 2011. Available at www.thelocal.se/37218/20111107/. Last visited 9/25/13.

7 Environment: Clean Air Act

Chapter Objectives

This chapter addresses the major area of environmental regulations. This topic is so broad that we have limited the scope of this chapter to the Environmental Protection Agency (EPA), and to the Clean Air Act in particular. This is not a significant narrowing of the topic because the Clean Air Act is generally considered to be the major piece of domestic regulatory legislation, and to account for the major part of the estimated costs and benefits of regulation. The objective of this chapter is to impart an understanding of how the Clean Air Act functions, with particular attention to the electricity generation sector. Electricity generation, particularly when using coal, is the single largest source of air pollution, notably sulfur dioxide, carbon dioxide, and mercury.

The act, it is now very clear, was initially way overambitious and poorly constructed, leading to amendments over time. This is a good case example of the effects the structure of a regulatory act has on its implementation, impacts, general support, and compliance by business. The involvement of the courts is also an important component to trace.

The initial focus of reducing sulfur dioxide (acid rain) is widely considered to have been successful, in part because the EPA implemented a *cap-and-trade system* with tradable permits. Our first case applies to a major financial decision by the managers of a power plant on how to comply with the sulfur dioxide restrictions at a time of uncertainty over the price of traded permits. More complex is the matter of carbon dioxide emissions, considered by most scientists to be a man-made contributor to climate change. Efforts to restrict carbon emissions nationally are ongoing. Initial legislative efforts failed, bringing to an end a voluntary carbon trading system, and administrative-based mandates are just getting under way with some specific limitations to begin in 2015. Understanding corporate incentives for voluntary participation provides insights into how the corporate world is beginning to prepare for carbon emission restrictions in an as-yet unpredictable future.

Due to the technical issues involved there are numerous terms included in the chapter discussion.

Key Terms: *New Source Review; Prevention of Significant Deterioration; SO_2, CO_2, NO, NO_x, CH_4; Kyoto Protocol; Provisions for the Prevention of Significant Deterioration; Best available control technologies; Maximum achievable control technology; Cap and trade*

Potential environmental issues are to say the least manifest, including the quality of air (smog, particulates, climate change), water (lakes, rivers, oceans, ground and drinking water), land and soil (erosion, contamination), species (extinction, invasive plants and animals), and so forth. The number of issues is far too broad to be addressed herein. Instead we focus on an important but limited subset—air pollution—and on acid rain and climate change in particular. These and other air-related issues are addressed in the Clean Air Act of 1963, with major amendments in 1970, 1977, and 1990; an overview is presented in this chapter, Section 7.1. Environmental regulations are primarily intended to overcome the market failure of nonpriced inputs and outputs, pollution in particular.

The two cases in this chapter pertain to acid rain and climate change in Sections 7.4 and 7.6, respectively. Since regulations on these two areas are administered by the Environmental Protection Agency (EPA), it should be noted that the agency itself was created on December 2, 1970, by executive order of President Richard Nixon to "permit coordinated and effective government action on behalf of the environment." Fifteen different environmental programs from three departments involving nearly 6,000 employees were combined and placed under the jurisdiction of the newly created EPA. The EPA was designed to serve as an "umbrella agency," actually an office representing environmental interests first and in contrast to departments with particular industry foci, through which most federal environmental laws, regulations, and policies would be administered.

7.1 Overview of the Clean Air Act Experience

Congress can, and has, established broad regulatory laws which effectively give wide discretion to the administering agency over exactly what and when to regulate. A recent example is the establishment of the Consumer Financial Protection Bureau (see Chapter 6, Section 6.6). The formation of the EPA in 1970 represented a regulatory experiment, forming an encompassing agency with a specific charge and deadlines. It is useful therefore to consider what the experience has been and the lessons learned for effective regulatory legislation. Here attention is on the Clean Air Act of 1970 as a focused background for the treatment of air pollution legislation, but much the same thing could be said about the experiences under the 1972 federal Water Pollution Control Act.[1]

The formation of the EPA in 1970 was a massive undertaking with nearly 6,000 employees assembled from three departments and fifteen programs. That same year was the celebration of the first Earth Day, a reflection of the environmental consciousness which sprang up along with many other causes in the 1960s. The idea for Earth Day was that of founder Gaylord Nelson, then a U.S. Senator from Wisconsin, after witnessing the ravages of the massive 1969 oil spill in Santa Barbara, California. Inspired by the student antiwar movement, he realized that if he could infuse that energy with an emerging public consciousness about air and water pollution, it would force environmental protection onto the national political agenda.[2]

Also relevant is that the EPA's founding followed (by a year) the development of the "capture theory" of regulation, which states that over time regulators will begin to represent the interests of the regulated rather than the public (see Chapter 2, Section 2.2e). It was believed at the time that general regulatory laws granting agencies considerable discretion contributed to "capture." Combining this belief with environmental activism established the basis for a narrowly targeted environmental law known as the Clean Air Act of 1970. Moreover, and reflecting the same concern, a single administrator was placed in charge, rather than the more common practice of a board of commissioners. The act established the following tasks for the agency to meet its mandate for achieving "healthy air" by 1975 (in addition to the mandate to eliminate the discharge of pollutants into waterways by 1985):

- Within thirty days of passage propose national ambient air quality standards for protection of public health and welfare (primary and secondary standards, respectively)
- Within one year of the setting of the standards, approve state implementation plans specifying specific emission limitations or types of polluters
- Set emission levels for new and modified statutory sources of pollution (i.e., power plants), for pollutants considered toxic, and for motor vehicles to achieve a 90 percent reduction in emissions within five years

There additionally was a major research agenda, corresponding to 30 percent of the EPA's budget. The research mandate was a significant one because the need for technologies to reduce emissions was not addressed in many sectors. Indeed, the EPA staff did not have even a clear understanding of current industry practices, while industry had little incentive to assist EPA's efforts. The EPA staff could identify efficient component practices at individual operations, but none that combined all for a "best available technology" package. Nonetheless the cobbled-together standard was proposed in order to meet the strict task deadline, and in line with the agency mandate, which did not consider cost. Further complicating the process was the Arab oil embargo of 1973–1974, which led to a quadrupling of oil prices and subsequently to rationing (and long gas lines) for consumers, as well as a reduction in the national speed limit to 55 mph to conserve fuel. Also problematic was the new auto emission technologies which tended to reduce gas mileage. Power plants were placed in a different kind of bind as they were required to meet the new effluent standards but were prohibited from converting from coal to cleaner energy sources such as oil and gas.

The Nixon administration understandably did wish to impose some cost considerations for the standards and so the EPA was informed that regulations required the approval of the Office of Management and Budget (OMB). The initial concept was for an intra-EPA office of economists to evaluate the benefits and costs of the regulations so as to maintain agency control. However it soon became apparent that there were far too many to be considered for the staff economists to manage and the effort was abandoned.

A final group to weigh in on the process was the courts. Industry had every incentive to sue the EPA and cause delays as that halted the regulatory process. Other groups sued as well, one over a proposal to allow a two-year extension for communities to develop plans for transportation controls. Transportation controls, primarily in the form of limits to driving, came into play as the only means of achieving the required 90 percent auto-emission reductions in five years in heavily polluted areas like Los Angeles. Not surprisingly, residents were shocked that such a dramatic step was being considered. The courts though denied the time extension, granting states only a few months to develop plans. They also denied a request by the auto industry for any extension over the five-year timetable set in the Clean Air Act, a standard considered by many to be infeasible. The courts also ruled that the EPA was controlled by the 1970 National Environmental Policy Act. The upshot was a requirement to prepare environmental impact statements for over 50,000 emission permits, further delaying the process.

As a consequence of these and other factors, on the day that all effluent guidelines were to have been established, in fact not a single one had been promulgated. In 1977, the acts were amended to modify or in cases eliminate the original deadlines. The revisions favored the industry perspective, just as the original had favored the environmentalists' viewpoint.

So what are the lessons learned? On the positive side, by 1977, new auto emissions had been reduced by two-thirds—not 90 percent but very substantially nonetheless. Over 90 percent of water polluters were utilizing best-practicable technology. The strict standards and time lines were instrumental in these achievements. At the same time the process resulted in higher costs than required. And because so many of the initial goals were granted extensions, many in the public lost faith in the effectiveness of the EPA and similar agencies. EPA management contributed to some of the problems. In its efforts to maintain independence from the administration, it cultivated public over political support, which meant that when public support declined due to delays, little support remained. But most of the lessons learned are for the legislators in Congress.

Laws must have flexible goals, which requires that significant study be invested in such factors as available technologies prior to the adoption of regulations. Flexibility is also required for agencies to accommodate unexpected events and industry needs. Laws also cannot get too far ahead of societal norms as a high level of support and acceptance is required for any law to function. The 1970 act was too extreme for many industries and citizens. And finally, if the courts impose unrealistic standards, then the legislature must be prepared to adjust the law in a timely manner. Regrettably, given the polarization of the current Congress, none of this seems likely to happen soon.

7.2 CLEAN AIR ACT

The Clean Air Act is considered by the EPA to be the most significant piece of environmental legislation in terms of its benefits. It is also by far the most costly, contributing an estimated 46–53 percent of costs and 62–84 percent of benefits of quantified environmental legislation, respectively. The costs and benefits of the Clean Air Act as estimated by the EPA are reviewed in Chapter 4, Section 4.2c and Example 4.5. Generally, the Clean Air Act is recognized to be highly ambitious, and hence was and remains controversial. On several occasions, goals were scaled back to those considered to be more realistic.

The focus here is on the federal components only, although the 1990 amendments to the Clean Air Act rely heavily on states to enforce the regulations, in exchange for funding. State enforcement responsibility is however not mandatory, and not all states are involved. Example 7.1 lays out the major aspects of the original act and its significant amendments. Example 7.2 identifies several aspects of clean air legislation where California regulations preceded federal actions, and in some cases were subsequently folded into federal regulations.

EXAMPLE 7.1: THE CLEAN AIR ACT OF 1963, AND MAJOR AMENDMENTS[3]

Clean Air Act of 1963

> An act to improve, strengthen, and accelerate programs for the prevention and abatement of air pollution.

This first piece of legislation bearing the name "Clean Air" sought to promote public health and welfare. It granted $95 million over a three-year period to state and local governments and air-pollution control agencies to conduct research and create control programs. This act also recognized the dangers of motor vehicle exhaust and encouraged the development of emissions standards from these sources as well as from stationary sources. Interstate air pollution from the use of high-sulfur coal and oil also needed to be reduced and so this act encouraged the use of technology which removed sulfur as needed. To continue action in this area, the Clean Air Act promoted ongoing research, investigations, surveys, and experiments.

Amendments of 1965: Motor Vehicle Air Pollution Control Act

These amendments focused on establishing standards for automobile emissions. They also recognized the serious problem of transboundary air pollution and promoted research on its damaging effects on health and welfare in Canada and Mexico.

Amendments of 1966

These amendments in brief expanded local air pollution control programs.

Amendments of 1967: Air Quality Act

These revolutionary amendments divided parts of the nation into Air Quality Control Regions as a means of monitoring ambient air quality. The government also established a single national emissions standards for stationary sources. These standards established a fixed timetable for state implementation plans, and recommended control technologies to achieve the identified goals. Again, appropriations were granted to continue research in the area of air pollution control.

Amendments of 1969

These amendments extended authorization for research on low emissions fuels and automobiles.

Amendments of 1970

> An Act to amend the Clean Air Act to provide for a more effective program to improve the quality of the Nation's air.

The amendments in 1970 comprised a rewritten version of the original Clean Air Act.

Section 109: National Ambient Air Quality Standards are standards that apply for outdoor air throughout the country. Primary standards are designed to protect human health, with an adequate margin of safety, including sensitive populations such as children, the elderly, and individuals suffering from respiratory diseases.

Section 110: State Implementation Plan is a federal state plan for complying with the Clean Air Act. The plan consists of narrative, rules, technical documentation, and agreements that an individual state will use to clean up polluted areas.

Section 111: New Source Performance Standards dictate the level of pollution that a new stationary source may produce. These sources include landfills, air emissions from wastewater treatment plants, boilers, petroleum refineries, and the like.

Section 112: National Emissions Standards for Hazardous Air Pollutants are set for air pollutants not otherwise covered that may cause an increase in fatalities or in serious, irreversible, or incapacitating illness. The standards for a particular source category require the maximum degree of emission reduction the EPA determines to be achievable, known as the Maximum Achievable Control Technology.

Section 202: Allows emission standards to be set for the emission of any air pollutant from any class or classes of new motor vehicles or new motor vehicle engines.

As a result of these and subsequent standards, emissions from a new car purchased today, according to the EPA, are well over 90 percent cleaner than a new vehicle purchased in 1970. SUVs and pickup trucks were added beginning in 2004. This is significant because motor vehicles are responsible for nearly one half of smog-forming volatile organic compounds, more than half of the nitrogen oxide emissions, and about half of the toxic air pollutant emissions in the United States. Motor vehicles, including nonroad vehicles, account for 75 percent of carbon monoxide emissions nationwide.[4]

Section 211: Fuels and fuel additives must be registered.

Section 231: Allows the Administrator to propose emission standards applicable to any air pollutant from aircraft engines.

Funds of $30 million went toward research on the growing problem of noise pollution in larger cities. Also, as a new principle, this Clean Air Act allowed citizens the right to take legal action against anyone or any organization, including the government, in violation of the emissions standards.

1977 Amendments

The 1977 amendments primarily concerned provisions for the "Prevention of Significant Deterioration" of air quality. Major stationary sources of air pollution and certain modifications to those sources are required by the act to obtain a permit before commencing construction. This permit-issuing process is known as *New Source Review.* The New Source Review program applies to sources that are located in areas that meet National Ambient Air Quality Standards ("attainment areas"), sources in areas that do not meet the standards (nonattainment areas), and areas that are unclassifiable. Permits for sources in attainment or unclassifiable areas are referred to as *Prevention of Significant Deterioration* of air-quality permits, while permits for sources located in nonattainment areas are referred to as *nonattainment area permits*. Nonattainment areas for 2013 are shown in Figure 7.1.

The New Source Review essentially mandated all new coal-fired power plants install scrubbers, although old coal plants were grandfathered and exempted. Instead, the amendment to the Clean Air Act required that, before any expansions, older industrial facilities submit an EPA assessment to see if they were required to install modern pollution control technologies.[5]

Section 161: Plan requirements—implementation plans are to contain emission limitations.

Section 172: Nonattainment plan provisions—calls for the classification of areas and availability and feasibility of the pollution control measures that are believed necessary to provide for attainment of such standard in such area.

Figure 7.1 **Air Quality Nonattainment Counties, 2013**

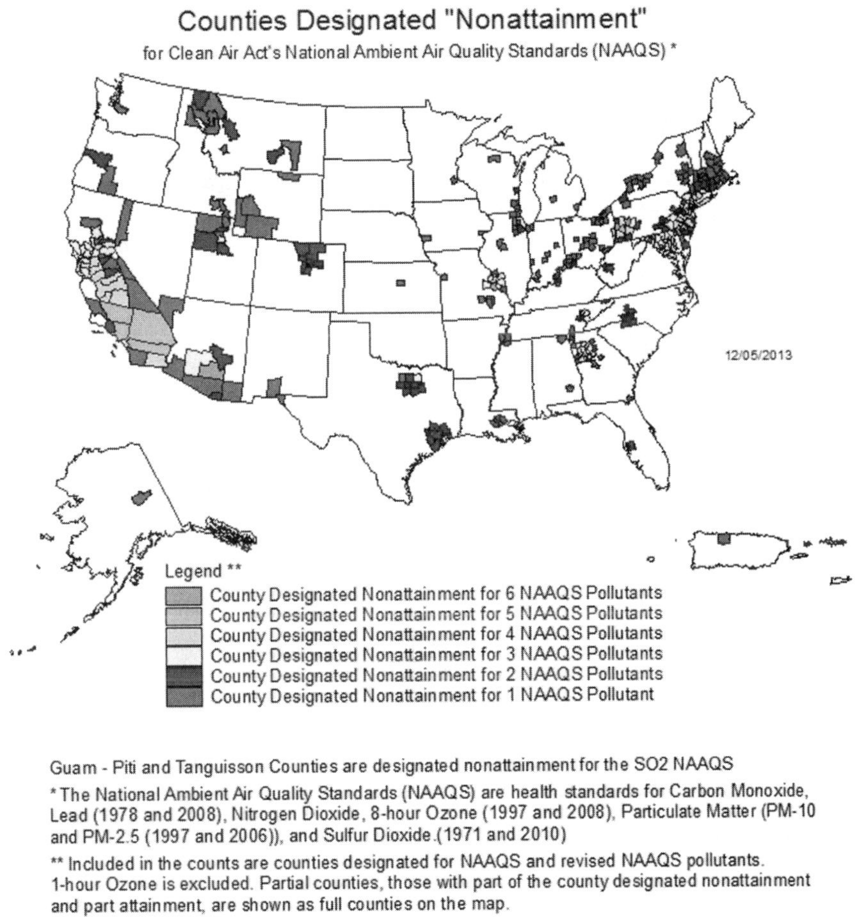

Source: United States Environmental Protection Agency. "Green Book." December 5, 2013.

1990 Amendments

> An Act to amend the Clean Air Act to provide for attainment and maintenance of health protective national ambient air quality standards, and for other purposes.

Congress drastically amended the Clean Air Act again to attempt to solve problems of the past as well as to deal with new issues. As in the past, the federal government designated states as being responsible for nonattainment areas, but it allowed them to establish compliance deadlines for each source considering the severity of its pollution. It also expanded automobile emissions standards and set a definite timetable for adherance to tighten control in this area. Through this legislation, the government encouraged the use of low-sulfur fuels as well as alternative fuels as a means of reducing sulfur dioxide in the atmosphere, which is a main component of acid precipitation, and one of the new issues to be dealt with. Also, it mandated the installment of the "Best Available Control Technology" to reduce the amount of air toxics. The government further called for a reduction in chlorofluorocarbon (CFC) use as a way of preventing ozone depletion, a recent issue needing attention.

Title 1: Provisions for Attainment and Maintenance of National Ambient Air Quality Standards: Title 1 clarifies how areas are designated and redesignated as "attainment." It also allows the EPA to define the boundaries of "nonattainment" areas: geographical areas whose air quality does not meet federal air-quality standards designed to protect public health.

The new law also establishes provisions defining when and how the federal government can impose sanctions on areas of the country that have not met certain conditions.

For the pollutant ozone, the new law establishes nonattainment-area classifications ranked according to the severity of an area's air pollution problem. These classifications are "marginal," "moderate," "serious," "severe," and "extreme." The EPA assigns each nonattainment area one of these categories, triggering varying requirements the area must comply with in order to meet the ozone standard. The new law also establishes similar programs for areas that do not meet the federal health standards for the pollutants carbon monoxide and particulate matter.

Title II: Provisions Relating to Mobile Sources: The Clean Air Act of 1990 establishes tighter pollution standards for emissions from automobiles and trucks.

Title III: Air Toxics: The new law includes a list of 189 toxic air pollutants for which emissions must be reduced. The EPA then must issue "Maximum Achievable Control Technology" standards for each listed source.

Title IV: Acid Deposition Control: The new Clean Air Act will result in a permanent 10-million-ton reduction in sulfur dioxide (SO_2) emissions from 1980 levels. To achieve this, the EPA allocates allowances in two phases permitting utilities to emit one ton of sulfur dioxide per allowance. The new law also allows utilities to trade allowances within their systems and to buy or sell allowances to and from other affected sources.

Title V: Permits: The new law introduces an operating permits program. The permit program will ensure that all of a source's obligations with respect to its pollutants will be contained in one permit document, and that the source will file periodic reports identifying the extent to which it has complied with those obligations.

Title VI: Stratospheric Ozone and Global Climate Protection: The new law builds on the market-based structure and requirements currently contained in the EPA's regulations to phase out the production of substances that deplete the ozone layer. The law requires a complete phase-out of CFCs and halons with interim reductions and some related changes to the existing Montreal Protocol. The law also requires the EPA to publish a list of safe and unsafe substitutes for Class I and II chemicals and to ban the use of unsafe substitutes.

Title VII: Provisions Relating to Enforcement: While the 1990 Title III amendments required that the EPA must specify limits and control technologies for a lengthy list of toxic pollutants, it did not act for fossil fuel–powered power plants and other industrial steam-producing operations for a decade, indeed until several lawsuits and court decisions compelled it to.[6] Then on December 21, 2011, the EPA announced standards to limit mercury, acid gases, and other toxic pollution from power plants.

The EPA is setting emission standards for existing sources in the category that are at least as stringent as the emission reductions achieved by the average of the top 12 percent best-controlled sources.[7] Along with mercury, regulated toxins include arsenic, chromium, selenium, cyanide and nickel, among others, along with several acid gases. The rule is expected to hasten the retirement of roughly one-tenth of the nation's coal-fired power plants, mostly the oldest and dirtiest, which will have the ancillary effect of reducing greenhouse-gas emissions.[8]

According to the EPA, reducing toxic power plant emissions will prevent as many as 11,000 premature deaths and 4,700 heart attacks each year. The final standards would also avert more than 5,700 emergency room visits and hospital admissions and 540,000 fewer days of work missed due to illness. The EPA estimates the value of these health benefits alone will total between $37 billion and $90 billion each year compared to costs of $11 billion, returning $3–$9 in health benefits for every dollar spent to reduce pollution.[9]

These benefits are based primarily on reductions in particulate matter, not mercury poisoning. This is because although mercury is known to be a strong toxin, particularly to young children, the benefits of reductions are difficult to calculate (Figure 7.2).

Source: Compiled by W. Lesser.

Figure 7.2 **The Mad Hatter's Tea Party from *Alice's Adventures in Wonderland.* At the time of its writing, hatters often suffered "madness" caused by mercury poisoning from the felt they handled.**

Source: Wikimedia Commons. Original author John Tenniel.

EXAMPLE 7.2: CALIFORNIA LEADS IN REDUCING AUTO POLLUTION

California is the only state vested with the authority to develop its own emission regulations. Other states have a choice either to implement the federal emission standards, or else to adopt California requirements.[10] California's Low Emission Vehicle (LEV) program defines automotive emission standards that are stricter than the U.S. national "Tier" regulations.

Here are two examples from California, which—due to its particularly heavy auto traffic and geography, especially in Los Angeles—has been notably stringent in this area.

1. The PCV (positive crankcase ventilation) system: This process draws crankcase fumes heavy in unburned hydrocarbons into the engine so they are burned rather than released directly into the atmosphere. Positive crankcase ventilation was first installed on a widespread basis by law on all new 1961 model-year cars first sold in California. The following year, it was required in New York. By 1964, most new cars sold in the United States were so equipped.
2. Exhaust (tailpipe) emission standards: Initially established by the State of California for 1966 model-year cars sold in that state, followed by the United States as a whole for model year 1968.

7.3 REGULATING ACID RAIN

As case 7.1 relates to acid rain, more detail on its effects and regulatory approaches to alleviate it are provided here.

a. Effects and Sources

The basic human health, environmental, and structural problems caused by sulfur dioxide (SO_2)/acid rain are presented in Chapter 4, Section 4.2c, and the reader is kindly referred there. Nitrogen oxides (NO_x) are the other principal pollutants that cause acid precipitation, and so emissions of NO_x are regulated as well. For simplicity attention here is focused solely on SO_2.

When discussing SO_2 emissions, we are largely referring to those from coal-burning electric power plants (Figure 7.3). Coal power in the United States accounts for about 40 percent of the country's electricity production, down from 50 percent as recently as 2003 due to low natural gas prices.[11] Utilities buy more than 90 percent of the coal mined in the United States. Those plants are predominately located in the Midwest (Figure 7.4).

Figure 7.3 **U.S. Electricity Generation by Energy Source, 2005–2014**
(thousand megawatt hours per day)

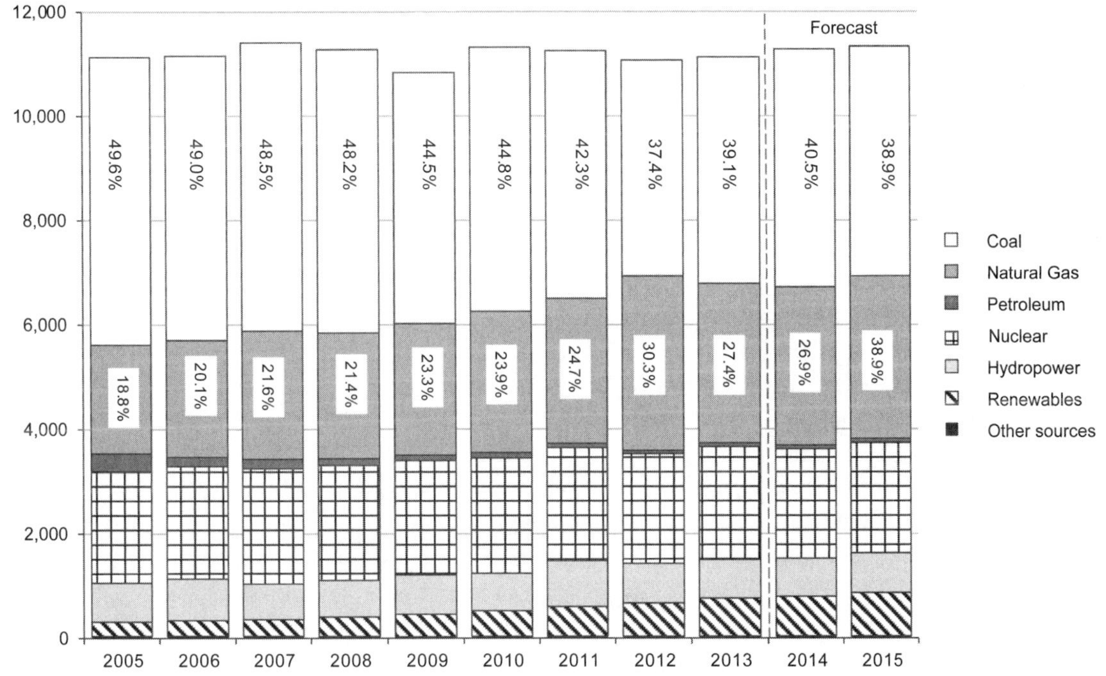

Source: U.S. Energy Information Administration, "Short Term Energy Outlook," November 2013.
Note: Labels show percentage share of total generation provided by coal and natural gas.

Figure 7.4 **Carbon Dioxide Emissions by Power Plants by Size and Location, 2013**

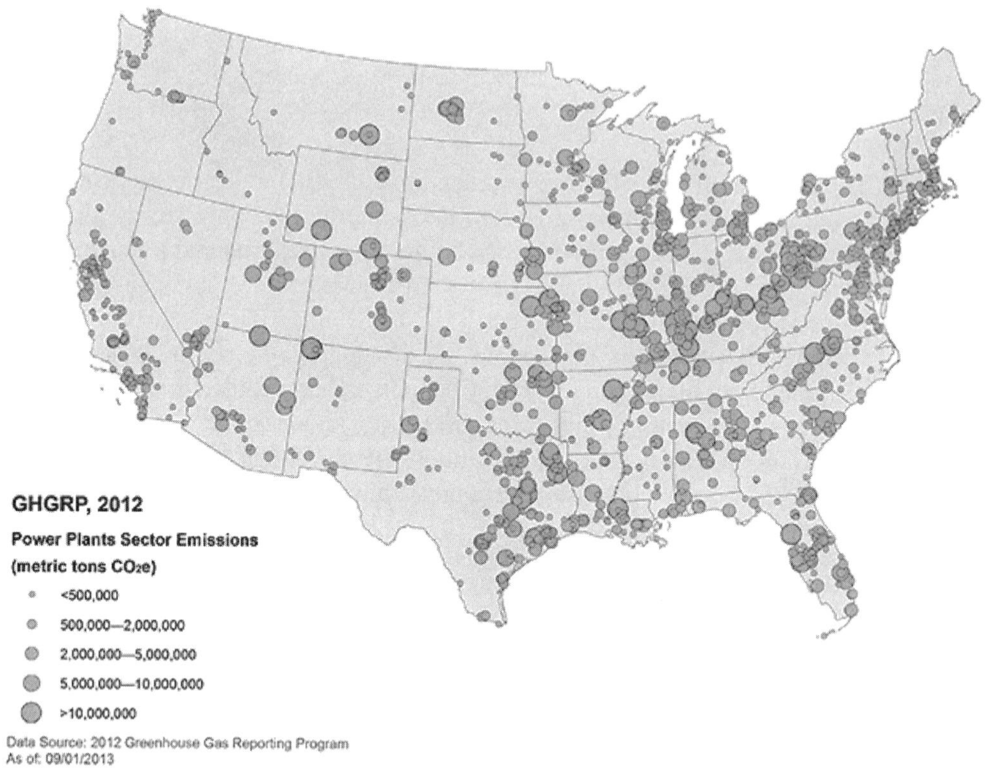

Source: U.S. EPA Greenhouse Gas Reporting System. September 1, 2013.

Among power plants, the 100 largest coal-fired operations are the dominant contributors to emissions. In 2012 this group of large plants produced 33 percent of the CO_2, 25 percent of the SO_2, and 27 percent of the NOx effluents among all coal-powered plants.[12]

b. Acid Rain Legislation[13]

As part of the Clean Air Act 1970 amendments, air-quality standards were established under Section 109 for major pollutants (see Example 7.1). The 1977 amendments, as noted above, essentially required scrubbers for all new plants while existing ones were grandfathered. Major changes occurred with the 1990 amendments in the form of the Acid Rain Program (Title IV).

The Acid Rain Program is a so-called cap-and-trade program whereby the limit of SO_2 emissions from (mostly) coal-burning power plants is set, with planned reductions over time. The program set a final 2010 SO_2 cap at 8.95 million tons, a level of about one-half of the emissions from the power sector in 1980. By way of comparison, the average emission rates in the United States from coal-fired generation are 2,249 lbs./MWh of carbon dioxide, 13 lbs./MWh of sulfur dioxide, and 6 lbs./MWh of nitrogen oxides.

To achieve this goal, the EPA allocated in two phases allowances permitting utilities to emit one ton of sulfur dioxide per permit. The first phase, effective January 1, 1995, requires 110 power plants to reduce their emissions to a level equivalent to the product of an emissions rate of 2.5 lbs. of SO_2/mmBtu x an average of their 1985–1987 fuel use. It affected 263 units at 110 mostly coal-burning electric utility plants located in twenty-one eastern and midwestern states. An additional 182 units joined Phase I of the program as substitution or compensating units, bringing the total of Phase I–affected units to 445. Emissions data indicate that 1995 SO_2 emissions at these units nationwide were reduced by almost 40 percent below their required level.

Phase II beginning in the year 2000, tightened the annual emissions limits imposed on these large, higher-emitting plants and also set restrictions on smaller, cleaner plants fired by coal, oil, and gas, encompassing over 2,000 units in all. The program affects existing utility units serving generators with an output capacity of greater than 25 megawatts and all new utility units.

Then on March 10, 2005, the EPA issued the Clean Air Interstate Rule (CAIR). This rule provides states with a solution to the problem of power plant pollution that drifts from one state to another. CAIR covers twenty-eight eastern states and the District of Columbia. The rule uses a cap-and-trade system to reduce the target pollutants—SO_2 and NO_x—by 70 percent. States must achieve the required emission reductions using one of two compliance options: (1) meet the state's emission budget by requiring power plants to participate in an EPA-administered interstate cap-and-trade system that caps emissions in two stages, or (2) meet an individual state emissions budget through measures of the state's choosing.[14]

c. Permit Trading[15]

To achieve the program goals more efficiently than under a "command-and-control" system, the EPA allocated affected utility units allowances based on their historic fuel consumption and a specific emissions rate. Each allowance permits a unit to emit 1 ton of SO_2 during or after a specified year. For each ton of SO_2 emitted in a given year, one allowance is retired. During Phase II of the program (now in effect), the act set a permanent ceiling (or cap) of 8.95 million allowances for total annual allowance allocations to utilities. Affected plants must by the end of a year (a 60-day grace period is allowed) have sufficient permits (whether granted, purchased, or held over from a prior period) to cover all SO_2 emissions. Permit shortfalls are penalized at a rate of $2,000 (adjusted for inflation) per excess ton of SO_2 (or NO_x) emissions. In addition, violating utilities must offset the excess SO_2 emissions with allowances in an amount equivalent to the excess.

At the onset of the program in 1995, spot SO_2 permits were priced at $150 a ton, with projected prices in the $250–500 range for Phase I (1995–1999) and $500–1,000 for Phase II (2000 onward). Actual prices typically were notably lower, in the $100–200 range and less than $200 for Phases I and II, respectively, where it has remained except for a brief period around the phase-in for CAIR in 2005 (when prices briefly spiked to $1,600).[16]

The EPA assists with the provision of permits in two ways. First, the EPA held a direct sale offering allowances at a fixed price of $1,500 (adjusted for inflation). The idea of this market was to send a price signal and price cap, as well as furnish utilities with an additional avenue for purchasing needed allowances. However, the plan was deemed unnecessary and discontinued in 1997.

Second, once a year the EPA auctions a certain number of SO_2 allowances at the end of March. Utilities, environmental groups, allowance brokers, and anyone else interested in purchasing allowances can participate. Other than the annual auction, permits are available directly from power companies or through brokers. Table 7.1 lists auction prices for 2012 for permits first used that year. Falling electric demand attributable in part to conservation or alternative sources, and in part to the ongoing recession, are contributors to these low permit prices.

Table 7.1

EPA spot SO_2 auction results for use in 2012

Allowances	# Bids	# Bidders	Bid Price
Bid For: 400,415 Sold: 125,000	Successful: 28 Unsuccessful: 11	Successful: 11 Unsuccessful: 2	Highest: $10.00 Clearing:* $0.56
	Total: 39	Total: 13	Lowest: $.01 Weighted Av: $0.67

*The clearing price is the lowest price at which a successful bid was made.

Source: EPA, "Allowance Markets Assessment: A Closer Look at the Two Biggest Price Changes with Federal SO_2 and NO_X Allowance Markets." White Paper, April 23, 2009, p. 2 and Figure 1. http://www.epa.gov/airmarkets/resource/docs/marketassessmnt.pdf.

The approach of giving away permits based on historical power production means that effects on electricity costs at least initially are minimal. An alternative approach is to auction *all* permits, which raises the cost of power generation, but provides greater incentives for conservation. Indeed if a plant receives sufficient permits gratis, there is little economic incentive for emissions reductions (beyond what the generated surplus permits might be worth, which as Table 7.1 shows is not much). A gratis permit program effectively places great emphasis on estimating the needed number of permits, something not required when all are auctioned.

A class simulation for mercury emissions (element symbol: Hg) demonstrating (hopefully) that a cap-and-trade system can achieve the same abatement levels at a lower cost than command and control is described in Example 7.3. The simulation involves three rounds (the third is optional): command and control, permit trading with fixed permit prices, and permit trading with negotiated permit prices. The Excel spreadsheet is included in the chapter appendix.

EXAMPLE 7.3: PERMIT TRADING SIMULATION

Cap and trade allows the trading of pollution permits among electricity-generating firms so that the ones which can most economically reduce emission levels may sell permits to higher cost polluters. The objective is a similar or greater reduction in pollutants at a lower cost for the plants and for electricity consumers. Typically cap-and-trade systems allocate annual permits at no cost but reduce the number allocated year by year. That approach simultaneously provides an incentive to reduce emissions while allowing time for plants to adjust.

As a class exercise, try a simplified Excel-based simulation for mercury pollution which will allow a more tangible familiarity with the issues involved in permit trading. Groups need to be assigned a plant number (1–6) and asked to work through three rounds:

1. Command and control
2. Cap and trade with fixed permit prices
3. Cap and trade with permit prices to be negotiated among plant "operators" (time permitting)

On the Excel simulation (see appendix to this chapter), the Background Data describe the plant age (see Age: older plants are more expensive to upgrade), the kind of coal burned in 2005 (see Coal), pounds of mercury emitted per megawatt (Mw) electricity produced (Hg emissions), and the generation cost per Mw.

Under simulation A, firms have three years to comply with the lower permitted emission level of 90 lbs./Mw (see Allow #). All plants have the same limit. Options for meeting the lower emission levels include (a) changing the kind of coal used and (b) upgrading the plant, which costs annually for fixed and variable costs at $15/lb. Hg x age of plant. The mercury content of the different kinds of coal is listed with the conversion cost per Mw and Hg reduction: lignite (Lig)—highest mercury and cheapest—bituminous (Bit)—most commonly used and next in Hg level and cost—and anthracite (Ant)—the lowest Hg level but most expensive to burn. Costs from Background Data should be entered for your assigned plant. The task is then to determine the least-cost combination of Upgrades and Coal to meet the allowance (Allow #). The spreadsheet will compute your profit or loss (P(L)) as well as the total compliance costs. Note that there is no financial incentive to reduce below the mandated emission level.

For plant one the entries would begin with background data:

Plant #	Age	Coal	Hg emis	Costs $Mw
1	70	Ant	113	925

The next table shows the spreadsheet for the initial four years.

Year	Allow #	Costs	Upgrade	Coal	Elec$Mw	Ann P(L)
2005	142				1,000	1,000
2006	142				1,000	1,000
2007	142				1,000	1,000
2008	90				1,000	1,000

(continued)

For the initial three years (2005–2007) the mercury emissions of 113 pounds per Mw are less than the allowance (142 lbs.) so no adjustments are needed. Costs then are (as given above) $925/Mg, leaving a net profit of $75/Mw ($1,000 – 925). Indeed for those years the plant could increase its profits by switching to bituminous coal at a savings of $200/Mw. Note that would increase emissions by 25 lbs./Mw (from Appendix data) but the plant is operating 29 lbs. below the allowance (142 – 113).

Beginning with 2008, however, the operators must reduce emissions per Mw by 23 lbs. (113 current – 90 allowed). Three reduction options are allowed, as described above. Selecting the upgrade option would cost $15/lb. x 70 (age of plant) x 23 lbs. = $!?x&/Mw—not viable. The second option is using a lower-mercury-containing type of coal. But for Plant # 1 that is not a viable choice either, as it already is using anthracite, the lowest Hg-emitting type of coal. Hence, Plant #1 would cease operation under the EPA command and control plan.

Simulation B is similar to A except that you now have the additional option to buy or sell pollution permits at $20/lb. Hg. In the class exercise the interest is in comparing the total costs and emission levels of A and B to see if cap and trade is indeed a more efficient form of compliance (while allowing enough profit for the plants to continue in service).

Under this plan Plant #1 could increase profits for the first five years (2005–2009) by selling permits at the set price of $20/lb.; the sixth year (2010) would be a wash as the allowance of 113 lbs. is equal to the output. (However, could the plant earn even more by using cheaper coal at the cost of fewer permits to sell?) Beginning in 2011 the plant is in trouble again as none of the compliance options allow a profitable operation.

Time permitting, Simulation C is like B except that the price of permits must be negotiated among the plants. One group for example can announce the availability of permits for sale and either auction publicly or negotiate privately. Demand (and thus prices) will be low in the initial years when few plants need to buy permits, but will rise over time. However, prices are likely to remain cheaper than the set $20/lb. because at that price many plants will cease production as it becomes unprofitable, reducing demand for permits.

7.4 ■ CASE 7.1: ACID RAIN

a. Case Questions

Students should prepare the following questions, based on the following Harvard Business School cases:

Acid Rain: The Southern Company (A) #792-060
Acid Rain: The Southern Company (B) #793-040

The following case provides additional useful background on acid rain and business, but is not mandatory:
Acid Rain: Burlington Northern, Inc. (A) #792-018

1. What is the impact of the EPA's Acid Rain Program on the Bowen plant?

2. What options does the Southern Co. have in complying with the program?
3. What is the least-cost compliance option (in NPV terms) when considering the two "high sulfur'" options—that is, with and without a scrubber? Note: computations (pre-tax) must be included with the case.
4. What are the uncertainties that might advise against the least-cost solution?
5. Which is your recommended choice for the Bowen plant?
6. In the nearly twenty years since the case was written, the price of SO_2 permits has declined to a low level. What factors do you believe led to that decline, and might any of them have been foreseen back in the early 1990s?
7. Is there any evidence that the tradable permits option was beneficial to industry, to the public? Please note that the Southern Co., in addition to complying with the Clean Air Act, was operating in a "rate of return" regulated environment. That regulatory system is described in Chapter 3, Section 3.4.

7.5 GREENHOUSE GASES AND CLIMATE CHANGE

The issues of climate change and greenhouse gases are much in the news, domestically and internationally. Thus far there is no legislation in the United States affecting business to any notable extent, but that will end for the coal-fired electrical power sector beginning mid-2015 if proposed EPA regulations go through. This subsection looks ahead to consider what actions, if any, businesses in the power generation and broader sectors might take now on a voluntary basis to position themselves both from a public relations perspective and to manage better regulations that may be applied at some future date. Thus the case in this chapter, Section 7.6, has connections both with the voluntary compliance case described in Chapter 6, Section 6.8, as well as the permit trading case in this chapter, Section 7.4. That is because the most likely regulations would involve a cap-and-permit trading system as at least one option.

The case is presented in this chapter, Section 7.6. First, though, it is relevant to review at least briefly the international and domestic issues surrounding climate change. This is done not to affect readers' personal opinions in any way, but rather to indicate the great uncertainty affecting business in this important regard.

a. Climate Change and Greenhouse Gases

At this point, there is little debate but what the earth's atmosphere is warming, although the rate of that warming is documented only incompletely. Major recent studies with conclusions include:

- UN Intergovernmental Panel on Climate Change: A .64°C rise from 1961 to 1990; sea-level rises and snow-pack declines commensurate with that rise (Figure 7.5).
- EPA: Since 1901, temperatures across the lower forty-eight states have risen by 1.3°F per century, with the rise more rapid since the late 1970s, 0.35–0.51°F per decade.[17]

- Berkeley Earth Surface Temperature Project: Assessed 1.6 billion measurements from more than 39,000 temperature stations around the world and found typically between a 1–2°C rise.

The Berkeley project results warrant particular attention as the lead author is a noted skeptic of past studies. "When we began our study, we felt that skeptics had raised legitimate issues, and we didn't know what we'd find. Our results turned out to be close to those published by prior groups. We think that means that those groups had truly been very careful in their work, despite their inability to convince some skeptics of that."[18]

Figure 7.5 **Changes in Temperature, Sea Level, and Northern Hemisphere Snow Cover**

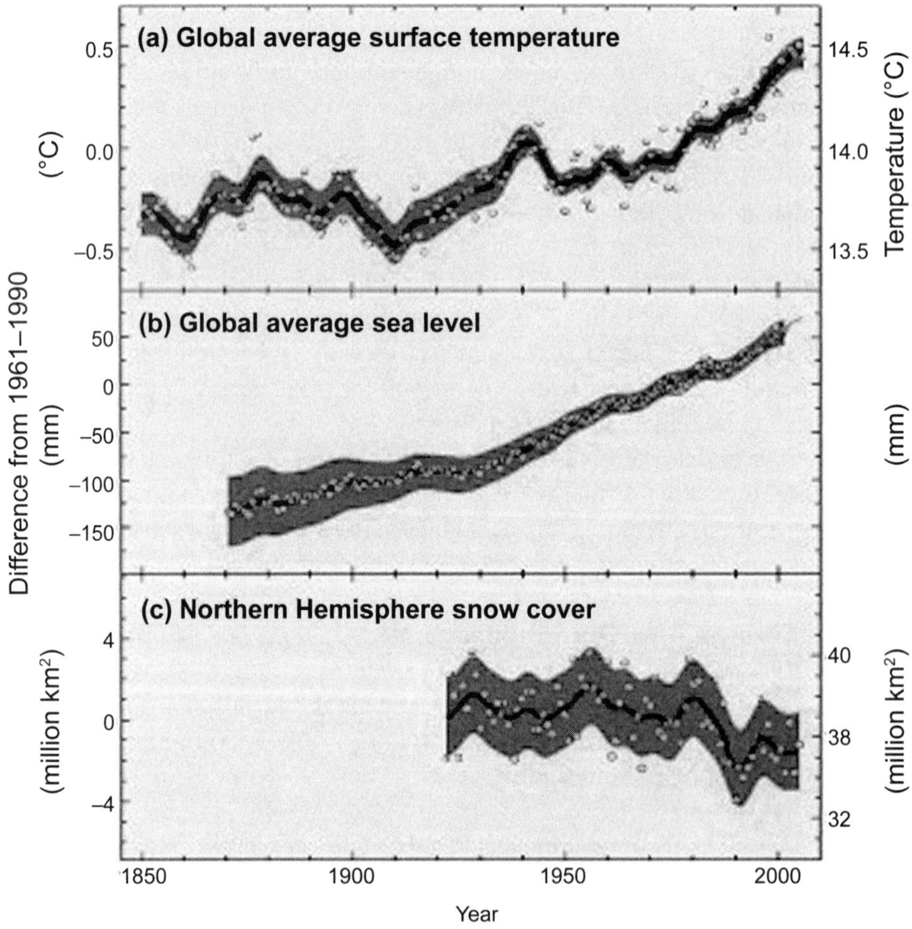

Source: Intergovernmental Panel on Climate Change 2007: Synthesis Report.

The effects of the temperature rise are well reported—changing weather patterns, drought, melting polar ice caps which reached their smallest area on record in September 2012, rising sea water, and the like— and are ever increasing. In addition to humans, many plant and animal species are also being affected, including the polar bear, as receding sea ice reduces access to seals, a prime food source (Figure 7.6).[19]

Figure 7.6 **Reduced Sea Ice Due to Climate Change Hampers Polar Bears' Access to Seals**

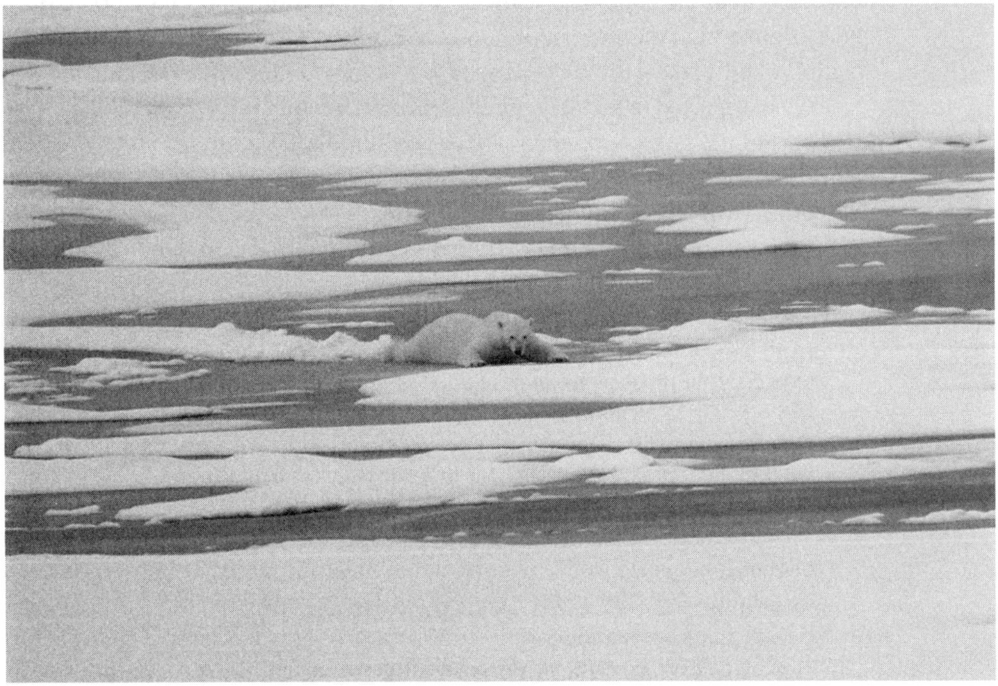

Source: Public Domain Images Online: Archive for the "US Coast Guard" Category. Original source Patrick Kelley, U.S. Coast Guard.

The causes of this warming are somewhat more difficult to establish and achieve consensus over. Nonetheless there is overwhelming agreement among scientists that human-generated carbon dioxide and related emissions are the principal causal factor. Among the major recent studies:

- America's Climate Choices: "Climate change is occurring, is very likely caused primarily by the emission of greenhouse gases from human activities. . . ."[20]
- EPA: "From 1990 to 2008 the radiative forcing of all the greenhouse gases in the Earth's atmosphere increased by about 26 percent (the United States contributed more than half of that amount). The rise in carbon dioxide concentrations accounts for approximately 80 percent of that increase.[21]

- UN Intergovernmental Panel on Climate Change: "Carbon dioxide (CO_2) is the most important anthropogenic [greenhouse gas]. Its annual emissions grew by about 80 percent between 1970 and 2004."[22]

Of course on the issue of global warming, like all complex issues, there will never be complete agreement. The scientific consensus over CO_2 and related gases being the overriding causal factor of climate change is nonetheless very broad. A 2010 study which reviewed 1,372 climate change scientists and their publications found that 97–98 percent concurred with the conclusions of the UN Intergovernmental Panel on Climate Change, and moreover that the experience and credibility of the 2 to 3 percent doubters are "substantially below that of the convinced researchers."[23]

A recent reported in the *Bulletin of the American Meteorological Society* provides some estimates of the degree to which twelve extreme weather events worldwide in 2012 can be attributed to human-caused sources, namely greenhouse gases. The study concludes that natural weather and climate weather fluctuations played a key role, but that in some instances there was evidence that human-caused climate change was a contributing factor. Examples include the following:

> High temperatures, such as those experienced in the United States in 2012 are now likely to occur four times as frequently due to human-induced climate change.
>
> Ongoing natural and human-induced forcing of sea level ensures that [Hurricane] Sandy–level inundation events will occur more frequently in the future. . . .
>
> The extremely low Arctic sea ice extent in summer 2012 resulted primarily from the melting of younger, thin ice from a warmed atmosphere and ocean. This event cannot be explained by natural variability alone.[24]

In close succession to the American Meteorological Society report, the UN Intergovernmental Panel on Climate Change issued its Fifth Assessment Report, which identifies human activity as the highly likely cause of global warming. "It is extremely likely that human influence has been the dominant cause of the observed warming since the mid-20th century." The report also identified a "carbon budget," specifying the maximum amount of carbon dioxide accumulation from industrial activities and forest clearing for the earth to stay below a 3.6°F average temperature increase. The limit is specified as one trillion metric tons of carbon burned, of which one-half trillion has been consumed since the beginning of the Industrial Revolution. At current use levels the one trillionth ton is expected to be consumed around 2014.[25]

The year 2014 has proven to be a bumper year for studies connecting climate change to human activity, namely the release of greenhouse gases. Three major reports from leading scientific bodies, all reaching the same basic conclusion, were released. First, the Intergovernmental Panel on Climate Change in its Fifth Assessment Report goes beyond documenting the existence of climate change to pointing the finger directly at human activity. "Human influence on the climate system is clear."[26] The majority of the report then documents the vulnerabilities of the human and natural world, and mitigation strategies. Second, the Royal Society (U.K.) and the National Academy of Science (U.S.) in a joint report begin with the following statement," It is now more certain than ever, based on many lines of evidence, that humans are changing Earth's climate. The atmosphere and oceans have warmed, accompanied by sea-level rise, a strong decline in Arctic sea ice, and other climate-related changes."[27]

Finally, and closer to the U.S.-focus of this book, the United States Climate Action Report 2014 begins by emphasizing, "The most significant long-term environmental challenge facing the United States and the world is climate change that results from anthropogenic emissions of GHGs [greenhouse gasses]. The scientific consensus, as reflected in the most recent Assessment Reports of the Intergovernmental Panel on Climate Change [] is that anthropogenic emissions of GHGs are causing changes in the climate that include rising average national and global temperatures, warming oceans, rising average sea levels, more extreme heat waves and storms, extinctions of species, and loss of biodiversity[28]

Thus whatever a reader's personal opinion may be, and those of business leaders, there is nonetheless compelling and expanding evidence that carbon dioxide is a leading contributor to climate change, that climate change is indeed real and largely man-induced, is having significant global impacts, and that there is and will continue to be considerable pressure to limit those emissions and their impacts. That is, a prudent business leader would conclude some regulatory action in the United States is highly likely, even beyond the electricity power sector. What remains unclear is the form and date.

b. Political Responses

International Agreements

The Kyoto Protocol treaty related to the United Nations Framework Convention on Climate Change is aimed at limiting global warming through the "stabilization of greenhouse gas concentrations in the atmosphere at a level that would prevent dangerous anthropogenic interference with the climate system." The protocol was adopted in 1997 and came into force in 2005 with 191 states having both signed and ratified; key provisions expired in December 2012. The United States is the only signatory not to have ratified to date; Canada, Japan, and Russia, along with a few other nations, effectively withdrew in 2012. Thirty-seven countries (the Annex 1 countries) have committed themselves to reduce their collective greenhouse gas emissions by 5.2 percent from the 1990 level.

Note that the commitments on reducing greenhouse emissions made under the Kyoto Protocol are not legally binding. An attempt at such a binding agreement, the Copenhagen Accord, was drafted in 2009. It recognizes that climate change is one of the greatest challenges of the present day and that actions should be taken to keep any temperature increases to below 2°C, but commitments to the accord remain voluntary and nonbinding. The Doha Climate Change Conference, held in 2012, extended the agreement until 2020;

at which time a major new unified agreement (one negotiating group for both developed and developing economies) to be negotiated by 2015 will be implemented.

Domestic Action

As a new candidate for president, Barack Obama pledged to classify carbon dioxide as a dangerous pollutant that can be regulated, opening the way for new rules on greenhouse gas emissions. The initial step in the regulatory process was for the EPA to formally declare carbon dioxide and five other heat-trapping gases to be pollutants that endanger public health and welfare, which would allow their regulation under the Clean Air Act. That was done in April 2009.[29] The EPA in 2007 had been under a Supreme Court order in *Massachusetts vs. EPA* to make that determination to move forward with any proposed regulations of carbon dioxide. The regulatory authority of the EPA was reaffirmed unanimously (with one judge recusing) by the Supreme Court in 2011 in *American Electric Power Co. vs. Connecticut.*

A tussle nonetheless arose over regulation through a Congressional bill, or via the EPA's regulatory authority. In May 2010, Senators John Kerry (D-MA) and Joseph Lieberman (D-CT) submitted the American Power Act, which would establish a carbon cap that aims to reduce U.S. greenhouse-gas emissions to 17 percent below 2005 levels by 2020, and ultimately 80 percent below those levels by midcentury. It would also devote billions of dollars in aid to transportation, including public transit, and expand funding for carbon sequestration and clean-energy research and development.[30] The House had passed an even stronger cap-and-trade act the prior year, the American Clean Energy and Security Act, known as the Waxman-Markey bill.

The bill would accomplish its goals by requiring the largest sources of pollution—those that produce more than 25,000 tons of carbon dioxide equivalent annually—to comply with emissions reduction targets. This means the program focuses on but 7,500 factories and power plants. Republicans, slamming the bill as a "national energy tax" and jobs killer, argued that costs would be passed on to consumers in the form of higher electricity bills and fuel costs that would lead manufacturers to take their factories overseas; the bill was abandoned by the Democrats the following month.[31] The bill also did not receive enthusiastic support from many environmental groups, in part because of the allowance for offshore drilling, as well as permitting the continual use of "dirty" coal.

Meanwhile, the EPA was proceeding on a separate track. In 2007 the EPA decided not to set carbon dioxide standards for boilers, but reconsidered the following year when faced with lawsuits from several environmental groups, as well as states and local governments.[32] Following up in 2011, the EPA undertook initial steps to establish carbon dioxide emission permitting requirements for the largest CO_2 emitters. Major requirements include:[33]

- January 2011: Facilities already required to obtain Clean Air Permits must include greenhouse gas emission requirements in the permit requests if newly constructed or modified to increase greenhouse gas emissions by 75,000 tons per year of carbon dioxide equivalent

- July 2011: All new facilities emitting over 100,000 tons of carbon dioxide equivalent or modified ones increasing emissions by 75,000 tons are required to obtain permits addressing greenhouse emissions
- July 2011: All sources emitting over 100,000 tons of carbon dioxide equivalent require operating permits
- 2016: Earliest date that emitters of 50,000 tons of carbon dioxide equivalent will be required to obtain permits for emitting greenhouse gases
- In addition: EPA will on request delegate authority for issuing greenhouse gas permits to states

The proposed rule for oil refineries will be released later. Together, fossil-fueled power plants and oil refineries produce almost 40 percent of greenhouse gas emissions in the United States, according to the EPA.

Regulations applied to mobile sources—cars and trucks—have been more straightforward. On July 29, 2011, EPA and the National Highway Traffic Safety Administration announced plans to propose stringent federal greenhouse gas and fuel economy standards for model year (MY) 2017–2025 passenger cars and light-duty trucks. The standards under consideration are projected to reduce greenhouse gases by approximately two billion metric tons and save four billion barrels of oil over the lifetime of MY 2017–2025 vehicles.[34]

2012 Election

The meanderings of the legislative process regarding carbon emissions is sufficient to cause great uncertainty within the business community about when, and even if, any limitations will be applied, including some form of cap-and-trade system. President Obama's position is clear, based on his past proposed legislation and prior campaign promises, but in the second term of his administration, the ability to pass legislation in the face of likely ongoing Republication opposition is very much in doubt. Actual and would-be Republican presidential candidates were uniformly hostile to the proposals.

Once re-elected, President Obama pledged to reduce the nation's production of greenhouse gases by 2020 to 17 percent below those of 2005. By 2013 progress was being made with a 7 percent cumulative reduction, but more was needed, especially as some of the reductions are attributable to the ongoing recession. Recognizing the limited likelihood of getting significant legislation through the deadlocked Congress, on June 25, 2013, noting that twelve of the warmest years in recorded history occurred in the last fifteen years, the president established a series of steps that could be taken by executive order. The major of these included:

- Ordering the EPA to issue rules by September 20 for the reduction of greenhouse gases by new power plants, and rules for existing ones a year later
- Tightening energy efficiency standards for federal buildings: a 15 percent reduction has been achieved since President Obama took office

- Directing the Interior Department to encourage renewable energy production on public lands. The federal government for its part has established a goal to consume 20 percent of its energy from renewable sources within seven years
- Attempting to have mortgage lenders recognize energy efficiency in home sales

Also in June 2013, the president issued a Climate Action Plan, with the initial step listed as "Cutting Carbon Pollution from Power Plants." A new standard for reduction of carbon pollution by new power plants was proposed in April that year (and was revised in September).[35] The proposed regulations are to go into effect in a year and call for CO_2 emission limits per megawatt-hour of:

- 1,100 lbs. for coal-fired plants (current average 1,760 lbs.)
- 850 for gas-fired plants (current average 800–850 lbs.)
- Proposals for existing plants are planned for June 2014

However, the proposed rule is almost certainly headed for court challenges on the grounds that the requisite technology has not been "adequately demonstrated" in practice.[36] As *The Economist* warns, President Obama will be out of office before that process is completed.[37] The timeframe, though, did not deter President Obama from issuing another executive order related to his Climate Action Plan. On June 2, 2014 a proposed EPA regulation was released for public comment,[38] to be implemented by June 2015, while the president is still in office. The proposed rule is intended to reduce carbon pollution from power plants 30 percent from 2005 levels by 2030. The regulation particularly targets the largest 600 coal-fired power plants, potentially leading to the closure of hundreds. Operationally, the rule takes a flexible approach allowing states choices in the most cost-effective means of implementation.[39]

The rule is anticipated to have a major pushback from business and political groups with lawsuits threatened. Coal industry representatives are already referring to this act as part of the president's 'War on Coal."[40] At the political level, Senate Minority Leader Mitch McConnell referred to the proposal as "a dagger in the heart of the American middle class."[41] Ironically for the regulatory process, the flexibility proposed under the rule may make it more legally vulnerable. However, in late June 2014 the Supreme Court did validate the authority of the EPA to limit carbon emissions from major sources, any source which had a prior restriction on at least one other pollutant. At the international level, though, the proposal has been better accepted as placing the United States in a stronger moral position to pressure China and India in particular to reduce their greenhouse gas emissions, although questions remain if it is sufficient to achieve that goal.[42]

c. State Requirements

The purpose in reporting these positions is to highlight the uncertainty under which business operates at present, and power producers in particular. While there seems little imminent likelihood of a broad-based national greenhouse control legislation in the United States, that could change at some future date and industry will need time to prepare. At the same time, the European Union cap-and-trade system launched in 2005, was significantly tightened in 2013. Permits are increasingly being traded rather than allocated (i.e., granted free) with 40 percent of permits being auctioned beginning in 2013.[43] In July that year permits for 900 metric tons of carbon were withheld from the market in a bid to raise permit prices, considered necessary to encourage emissions reductions.[44] Tightening by EU regulators continued into 2014 when the auction of new permits was delayed, having the effect of reducing permit supply by more than 50 percent. The result was permits gained more than 40 percent in price during the first two months of the year.[45] These are issues for multinational companies to be concerned with. And then there are state requirements, particularly California's.

California is again a leading force in the nation in limiting carbon emissions. A cap-and-trade system is the basis of the Global Warming Solutions Act of 2006 (AB 32). AB 32 requires the California Air Resources Board (CARB) to develop regulations and market mechanisms to reduce California's greenhouse gas emissions to 1990 levels by 2020, representing a 25 percent reduction statewide, with mandatory caps beginning in 2012 for significant emissions sources. California as it happens is the twelfth-largest emitter of carbon worldwide.

In 2010 a cap-and-trade program was adopted to place an upper limit on statewide greenhouse gas emissions beginning in 2012, with a limit placed that year that will be reduced by 2 percent each year through 2015 and 3 percent each year from 2015 to 2020. The rules apply to a list of sectors, including mining, oil, and gas extraction, transportation and refining, electric generation (including when done for institutions), fruit and vegetable processing operations, breweries, wineries, paper mills, glass manufacturing, cement producers, and steel mills.[46] Free credits will be distributed to businesses to account for about 90 percent of overall emissions in their sector, but businesses must buy allowances, or credits, to account for additional emissions.[47] Offset/sequestration procedures—that is, identifying reduction options such as planting trees or burning methane, or removing carbon from emissions for example by injecting it underground—are also in place.[48]

The Air Resources Board, the administrative body, will hold quarterly permit auctions beginning August 15, 2012.[49] The CARB also allows offset credits for specified greenhouse gas emission reductions or sequestered carbon that meet regulatory criteria and may be used by an entity to meet up to 8 percent of its obligation under the cap-and-trade program.[50] The third auction held in May 2013 sold all 14.5 million available allowances for a total sales amount of $203.3 million. With a reserve price of $10.78, the median price was $13.49 (maximum $50.01 and minimum $10.71).[51] The auction went ahead despite a lawsuit by the Chamber of Commerce charging the sale was an illegal tax or fee; a hearing before the Superior Court was held May 31, 2012.[52] In a November 2013 decision Judge Frawley ruled against the Chamber and a similar case by the Pacific Legal Foundation determining that the permit costs were more akin to regulatory fees than a tax. Under California law, initiating a tax requires a two-thirds vote of the state legislature.[53]

Taking a different approach is a consortium of ten Northeastern states which have used a Memorandum of Understanding committing the governors to introduce regulatory legislation establishing a cap-and-trade system for power plants called the Regional Greenhouse

Gas Initiative (RGGI).[54] Under the system, beginning in January 2009, the affected plants are required to purchase sufficient permits, each of which applies to one ton of CO_2, to cover their total emissions. The participating states are the six New England states and New Jersey, New York, Delaware, and Maryland, with the eastern Canadian provinces and several additional states holding observer status. New Jersey, however, withdrew in 2012 and several other states have considered the move, but to date none have acted. The permits are auctioned quarterly with the revenues flowing to each state.

From 2009–2014, the RGGI cap stabilizes power sector CO_2 emissions at 188 million short tons of CO_2 per year. Beginning in 2015, the cap will decrease by 2.5 percent per year, for a total reduction of 10 percent by 2018.[55] At the same time, the funds generated from permit sales support alternative energy projects and similar ventures. The consortium rejected the more common approach of distributing all or most permits without charge because "Selling the allowances ensures that their proceeds will benefit the public by funding projects to conserve energy, reduce CO_2 emissions and develop clean technologies."[56] A study of the economic effects of the system projected permits would sell for about $2 per ton in 2009, and increase wholesale electricity prices by about 1.6 percent (78 cents per month for a typical residential customer) in 2015 and 2.4 percent ($1.13 per month for a typical residential customer) in 2021.[57]

New Jersey officials justified their decision to withdraw because the December auction brought prices of only $1.89 per ton, the minimum price allowed, and then only 63 percent of the available permits sold. The low permit price, explained as the consequence of cutbacks by consumers during the Great Recession, was seen as too low to have any real effect on emission decisions by plant operators. By June 2013 the clearing price had risen to $3.21 per ton, and bids were twice the available supply.[58] Claimed benefits include CO_2 emission reductions, enhancements in efficiency and alternative energy production, as well as bill relief for low-income consumers.[59]

d. Greenhouse Gases and Electrical Generation

Just as fossil fuel–burning generators of electricity received special regulations under acid rain regulations due to their large contributory role (see Chapter 3, Section 3.3a, and this chapter, Section 7.3a), they are vulnerable as well as major contributors of greenhouse gases. Consider President Obama's recent executive orders (see this chapter, Section 7.5b). Indeed, power generation is the single largest contributor—about 25 percent (Figure 7.7). A more recent report however puts that number closer to 38 percent of CO_2 emissions in the United States in 2012.[60] The report also indicates that CO_2 emissions from power plants rose 30 percent since 1990. However, CO_2 emissions have declined by 2.1 percent from 2007 levels due to several reasons including the economic recession and increased use of natural gas, renewable energy, and energy efficiency.

The major greenhouse gas in volume and effect is of course CO_2, but methane and nitrous oxide (NO) also contribute. NO is a major greenhouse gas; considered over a 100-year period, it has 298 times more impact per unit weight (climate change potential) than carbon dioxide. Methane (CH_4) for its part is a principal component of natural gas. It is

Figure 7.7 **Global Anthropogenic Greenhouse Gas Emissions**

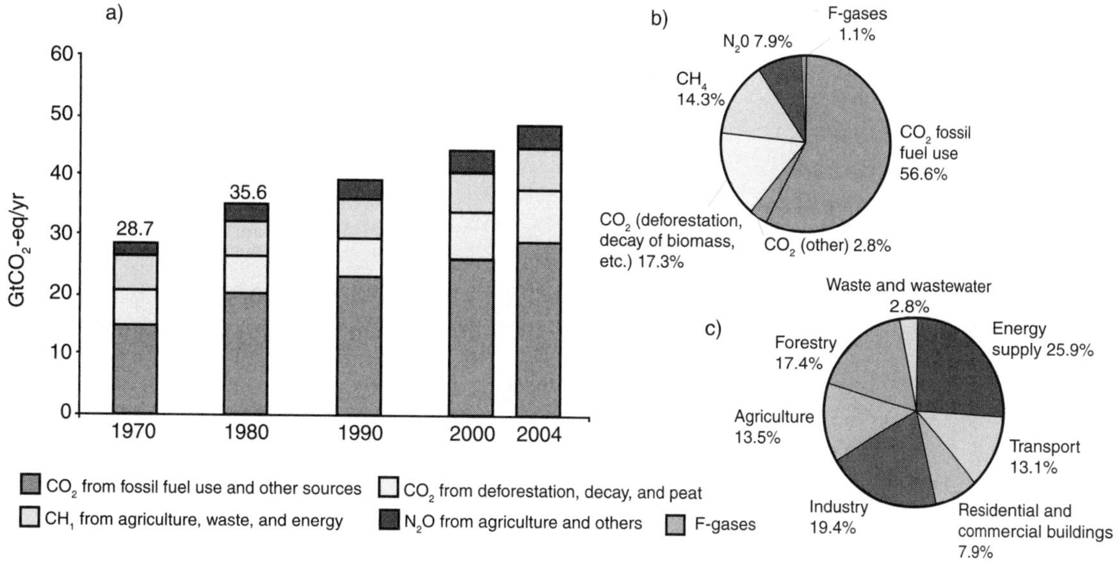

Source: Intergovernmental Panel for Climate Change, "Climate Change 2007: Synthesis Report."

also formed and released to the atmosphere by biological processes occurring in anaerobic environments—read ungulate's stomachs (cows principally). Methane is about twenty-one times more powerful at warming the atmosphere than carbon dioxide by weight.

Because methane is a much more potent greenhouse gas than carbon dioxide, a simple method of mitigation is simply to burn methane and emit CO_2 rather than CH_4. Despite this, methane has been building up rapidly in the atmosphere (Figure 7.8). Methane constitutes about 14 percent of emissions versus nearly 60 percent for carbon dioxide.

In an attempt to quantify the costs of air pollution, including greenhouse gas emissions, the Congress commissioned a report from the National Research Council. *Hidden Costs of Energy: Unpriced Consequences of Energy Production and Use* examines those "hidden costs" in an effort to inform energy-related policy decisions. The damages that the committee was able to quantify were an estimated $120 billion in the United States in 2005, a number that reflects damages from air pollution associated with electricity generation relying on fossil fuels, motor vehicle transportation, and heat generation.[61]

e. Voluntary Actions—Chicago Climate Exchange

Several voluntary climate exchanges have been in operation in the United States, but have ceased trading. The Chicago Climate Exchange (CCX) was North America's largest and longest running greenhouse gas emission reduction program. From 2003 through 2010 CCX operated as a comprehensive cap-and-trade program with an offsets component, but ceased trading permits in 2010.[62] For its part, the Chicago Climate Futures Exchange

Figure 7.8 **Methane Accumulations in the Atmosphere Over Time**

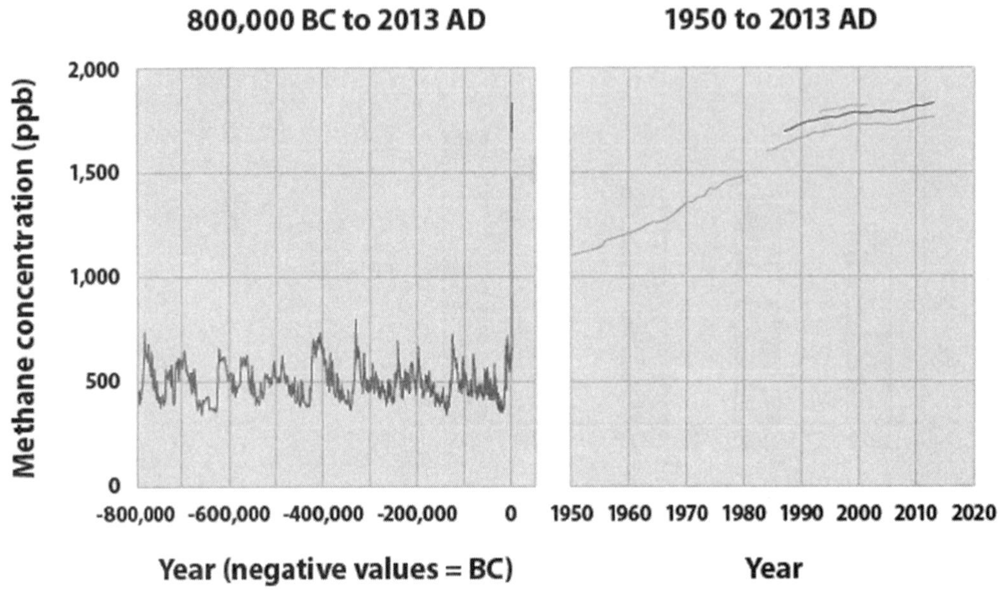

Source: EPA "Climate Change Indicators in the United States." www.epa.gov/climatechange/science/indicators/ghg/ghg-concentrations.html.

traded CO_2 and other permits since 2004, but ceased trading following the first quarter of 2012. Only twenty contracts were traded in mid-2011. U.S. contracts were for 1,000 metric tons of CO_2 equivalent. Quoted prices for December 2011 were \$.50, and \$2.86 for December 2013.[63]

The CCX was a voluntary market whose 450 members pledged to purchase a specified number of permits. The underlying reason for the collapse of these markets was failure of a national cap-and-trade program to get Congressional approval. The purpose of voluntary participation in these markets was after all to gain experience with allowances and trading. However, according to a *New York Times* assessment, there were other more specific factors involved in the collapse of the permit market as well. Basically, demand for permits was relatively fixed while the supply of offset permits (from say converting methane to carbon dioxide) was "seemingly endless." As a result, emission permit prices sometimes fell to as low as \$.05. The European exchange suffers from a related fate, but for a different reason. There, too many permits were issued so there was no market,[64] but that situation is being rectified (see this chapter, Section 7.5c).

Despite this outcome, some members of the CCX were nonetheless pleased with the experience. According to Jennifer Orgolini, sustainability director at New Belgium Brewing, a small craft beer-maker based in Fort Collins, Colorado, the chance to join the nation's only carbon trading platform back in 2003 was an opportunity her environmentally conscious firm couldn't pass up. "We're glad to have had the experience."[65]

7.6 ■ CASE 7.2: VOLUNTARY CARBON PERMIT TRADING

a. Background[66]

New Belgium Brewing Company opened in 1991. By 2011, it produced over 712,800 barrels of its various labels making it the third-largest craft brewery and seventh-largest overall brewery in the United States. Their mission statement is "to operate a profitable company which is socially, ethically and environmentally responsible, that produces high quality beer true to Belgian brewing styles" (see Example 7.4).

EXAMPLE 7.4: NEW BELGIUM BREWING COMPANY'S ENVIRONMENTAL STEWARDSHIP COMMITMENT[67]

"Alternatively Empowered" means making business decisions based on minimizing environmental impact, encouraging the growth of our employee owners, and being a socially responsible contributor to our community. It's rewarding, challenging, and educational. It's what makes us New Belgium.

We believe, to be environmental stewards, we need to:

1. Lovingly care for the planet that sustains us.
2. Honor natural resources by closing the loops between waste and input.
3. Minimize the environmental impact of shipping our beer.
4. Reduce our dependence on coal-fired electricity.
5. Protect our precious Rocky Mountain water resources.
6. Focus our efforts on conservation and efficiency.
7. Support innovative technology.
8. Model joyful environmentalism through our commitment to relationships, continuous improvement, and the camaraderie and cheer of beer.

In 2008, New Belgium Brewing Company was named the best place to work in America by *Outside* magazine. That designation is particularly notable because New Belgium Brewing Company is employee owned. The company emphasizes "open-book" management. "The way it works here is that each employee knows precisely what it costs to make a barrel of beer, and how much their department contributes to that cost. Since they have a vested interest in the profits, they often meet to set performance targets to bring those costs down."

New Belgium Brewery has made it a goal to be entirely wind-powered. This proposal was made at a staff meeting of owners and owner-employees: what did they think of the idea of meeting the facility's entire electrical needs with wind power? The company would have to pay a premium for the power, and that expense would come out of the company's profits, possibly affecting employee/owner wages. Rather than directly using wind-generated power, the brewery elected to pay an increased rate for wind-derived electrical energy. There was stone silence in the group as they thought about it, but the silence did not last long. Within a minute or so the employee/owners had decided as a group to become the world's largest single user of wind power.

The beer is apparently pretty good as well, according to online reviews.[68]

b. Case Questions

Students are requested to prepare the following questions.

1. What were the benefits to the New Belgium Brewing Company of participating in the CCX?
2. If you were a New Belgium Brewing Company employee, would you have supported that participation? Why or why not?
3. Now imagine New Belgium Brewing Company were based in California and not Colorado. How might your answers to questions 1 and 2 change?
4. Now suppose you are a stockholder in an electric utility in California and management was holding a referendum at the stockholders' meeting on whether or not to trade carbon permits, when possible. Would you support or not? Why?

7.7 CONCLUSIONS

The EPA is the 800-pound gorilla in the regulatory room. It is responsible for the majority of the computed regulatory benefits as well as costs, particularly through enforcing the Clean Air Act. It also has an unusual structure with a single director rather than five commissioners, and it is not mandated to document that regulatory benefits exceed costs (although it is accountable to other laws).

Regarding the Clean Air Act, there were many missteps in implementation—delays, unattainable goals, political posturing—caused by Congress, the courts, and the EPA itself. That said, major (literally visible) benefits have been documented, although the cost effectiveness can be (and is) debated. Acid rain reduction has been a success, mercury reduction is just under way, and reduction in auto emissions is another success.

The process, though, has been a messy one, and the regulations complex. That is one of the messages from this chapter—complex regulations are just that, complex and unclear for individuals and certainly for the regulated. The underlying issue is that pollution is traditionally not priced—a market failure. Using regulations to replace the market will always be an imperfect process, but is the main option available in the instance of market failure.

To some degree business itself contributed to the uncertainty by not cooperating with the EPA (for instance, by lobbying against regulations and by creating delays with lawsuits). Delay was indeed achieved, but at the expense of some higher long-term costs. One cost is ongoing uncertainty, another the rise of state and regional regulations to operate where the EPA was unable. California led the way with auto emission standards and is again doing so with carbon permitting, although the Northeast states also have their own operating program. For business, a complex of local regulations is often more onerous than strict national ones. That is why the auto industry voluntarily agreed to new, stricter mileage standards.

The pending big issue, the biggest to date, is climate change and greenhouse gases. How this issue is approached has huge consequences for business and individuals. Industry understandably has resisted any mandates through lobbying, which has caused delays in the establishment of effective regulation and such ancillary matters as the collapse of voluntary permit trading markets. Increasingly, however, there is evidence that climate change is real and we are both a major cause and the victims of its consequences. The Obama administration, having failed to institute a successful approach legislatively, is now acting administratively. The implementation process for achieving needed change will be a long one, but if past experiences are any guide, the EPA will prevail in the long term. Certainly the requisite technologies are far from fully established, but that too was the case in the past. With hindsight, the results are likely to prove beneficial. Business should be taking the time to prepare and support workable legislation, and not be satisfied merely with opposition and delay.

The two cases presented in this chapter are quite different. The first case is largely a matter of financial planning; finding the least cost option. The planning, though, is done in a clouded environment—the projected cost of future permits is a determining factor in the analysis. And who knew at the time? More relevant for the future is just how might a firm know? The New Belgium Brewing Company, subject of the second case, attempted to know by participating in a voluntary carbon permit trading exchange. Was it helpful? Is it a relevant example for other corporations as an employee-owned and socially conscious firm?

7.8 STUDY QUESTIONS

1. What are some of the unique aspects of how the EPA was formed and the concepts underlying the Clean Air Act of 1970? Does the subsequent experience support or contradict the approaches used?
2. What were the associated problems with establishing cost/benefit mandates for the act?
3. How did the courts fit into the complex of managing the requirements of the Clean Air Act?
4. One of the impediments to the EPA's timely fulfillment of the Congressional mandates of the Clean Air Act of 1970 was gaining cooperation from the electrical generation industry. The EPA was required among other things to specify a "Best Available Control Technology," which meant working with industry to understand how pollution-control technologies actually function. The industry for its part had every incentive not to cooperate to delay implementation. In this the generation sector generally succeeded while the auto industry did not—at no insignificant cost in the form of rushed engineering designs and damaged

customer relations (early efforts performed poorly and were not reliable). Please compare and contrast these experiences with the EPA under the Clean Air Act with the other cooperation/resistance cases we considered—for example, tire grading and the Consumer Financial Protection Bureau and the credit card industry. In what ways are they similar or different from the industry incentive perspective?

5. We are told by observers of the process of formulating the Clean Air Act of 1970 that the specific targets and dates were set in the law as a way of minimizing the prospect of regulatory capture. The capture theory, however, is based on the limited perception of economists about the creators and implementers of regulation. The perceptions of political scientists like J.Q. Wilson are more nuanced (Chapter 2, Section 2.2e). If the Congress had been more conversant with the political science description of the regulatory process, do you believe the Clean Air Act might have come out differently? Why or why not?
6. For the two cases presented, please identify if there was a market failure that each regulation is intended, even partially, to address.
7. What conditions are required for a regulatory system to function effectively?
8. How do the concepts of "attainment" and "nonattainment" areas function?
9. What factors explain the State of California's leadership role in controlling air pollution?
10. Some individuals oppose the very concept of permit trading systems as "licenses to pollute." How would you counter that position?
11. How might you assess RGGI's success or lack of it?
12. If you were the manager of a large coal-fired power plant (a) what future regulatory issues should you be considering, and (b) selecting two from the list, what current steps would be appropriate?
13. Please summarize the economic arguments for permit trading systems. What are the arguments against it?
14. What are the parallels, if any, between voluntary participation in the tire grading and LEED cases, and that of the New Belgium Brewing Company?
15. Explaining their opposition to carbon dioxide emission restrictions, many Republicans described them as raising costs which will be passed on to consumers. Are they correct? Please explain. (Hint: Recall that regulation costs can be modeled as tax increases.)

APPENDIX: TRADING SIMULATION SPREADSHEET FOR EXAMPLE 7.3

Notes for spreadsheet formulas:

[1] $1,000—cost-upgrade-coal
[2] Row sums for cost, upgrade, and coal
[3] Column sums for cost, upgrade, and coal
[4] As for #1 above but add in permit costs (revenue)

EPA	Regulations	MERCRY Imposed	(Hg) SIMULATION 2005	
Background Plant#	Data Age	Coal	Hg emis	Costs $Mw
1	70	Ant	113	925
2	55	Bit	108	900
3	2	Bit	94	950
4	35	Lig	140	850
5	40	Bit	92	850
6	20	Bit	104	900

A. Command and Control

2005	3 Year	Phase to	90lbs./Mw	
Options				
1. Upgrade	Age x $15	Fixed/lb.	Mercury	
2. Switch	Coal			
Lignite to	Bit	$200/Mw	25-lbs./Hg	Reduction
Lignite to	Ant	$300/Mw	35-lbs./Hg	Reduction
Bit to	Ant	$100/Mw	10-lbs./Hg	Reduction

Year	Allow #	Costs	Upgrade	Coal	Elec$/Mww	Ann P(L)
2005	142				1000	1000[1]
2006	142				1000	1000
2007	142				1000	1000
2008	90				1000	1000
2009	90				1000	1000
2010	90				1000	1000
2011	90				1000	1000
2012	90				1000	1000
2013	90				1000	1000
Total[2]	966	0	0	0		
Total Compliance Costs[3]				0		

B. Cap and Trade

Year	Allow #	Costs	Permits Upgrade	$20/lb. Trading	Coal	Elec/$Mw
2005	142					1000
2006	136					1000
2007	132					1000
2008	129					1000
2009	121					1000
2010	113					1000
2011	96					1000
2012	58					1000
2013	44					1000
Total:	971	0	0	0	0	
Total Compliance Costs:					0	

C. As with B, but negotiate permit price with other plant

Year	Allow #	Costs	Upgrade	Trading	Coal	Elec/$Mw	Ann P(L)
2005	142					1000	1000[4]
2006	136					1000	1000
2007	132					1000	1000
2008	129					1000	1000
2009	121					1000	1000
2010	113					1000	1000
2011	96					1000	1000
2012	58					1000	1000
2013	44					1000	1000
Total:	971	0	0	0	0		
Total Compliance Costs:					0		

NOTES

1. This material draws heavily on Alfred Marcus, "Environmental Protection Agency." *The Politics of Regulation,* ed. J.Q. Wilson, chapter 8. New York: Basic Books, 1980.

2. Earth Day Network, "Earth Day: The History of a Movement." Available at www.earthday.org/earth-day-history-movement/. Last visited 8/9/12.

3. Drawn in part from "A look at U.S. air pollution laws and their amendments: Clean Air Acts of 1955, 1963, 1970, 1990." Available at www.ametsoc.org/sloan/cleanair/cleanairlegisl.html. See also EPA, "Clean Air Act." Available at www.epa.gov/air/caa/. Last visited 10/23/11.

4. EPA, "Cars, Trucks, Buses, and 'Nonroad' Equipment." Available at www.epa.gov/air/caa/peg/carstrucks.html. Last visited 10/23/11.

5. *Sourcewatch,* "Scrubbers." Available at www.sourcewatch.org/index.php?title=Scrubbers. Last visited 10/25/11.

6. Port of Entry, "US: Lawsuits filed challenging EPA approach at curbing power plant toxic air emissions." May 18, 2005. Available at www.medioambienteonline.com/web/guest/green_economy_news/article/-/article/iY0h/14137/-1/2866/us:-lawsuits-filed-challenging-epa-approach-at-curbing-power-plant-toxic-air-emissions. Last visited 12/23/11.

7. Standards available at EPA, "National Emission Standards for Hazardous Air Pollutants." 6560–50-P. Available at www.epa.gov/mats/pdfs/20111216MATSfinal.pdf. Summarized in EPA "Basic Information." Available at http://epa.gov/mats/basic.html. "Fact Sheet." Available at http://epa.gov/mats/pdfs/20111221MATSsummaryfs.pdf. All last visited 1/2/12.

8. Brad Plumer, "How to Tally Up the Benefits from EPA's Mercury Rule." *Washington Post,* December 22, 2011.

9. EPA, "Healthier Americans." Available at www.epa.gov/mats/health.html. Last visited 1/2/12.

10. DieselNet, "Emission Standards: United States." Available at www.dieselnet.com/standards/us/. Last visited 10/24/11.

11. "FACTBOX-U.S. coal-fired power plants scheduled to shut." Reuters, August 5, 2013. Available at http://in.reuters.com/article/2013/08/05/utilities-firstenergy-coal-idINL1N0G60S820130805. Last visited 8/7/13.

12. EPA, "Emission Tracking Highlights," 2012 data. Available at www.epa.gov/airmarkets/quarterlytracking.html. Last visited 8/14/13.

13. EPA, "Acid Rain Program." Available at www.epa.gov/airmarkets/progsregs/arp/basic.html#phases. Last visited 10/25/11.

14. EPA, "Clean Air Interstate Rule (CAIR)." Available at www.epa.gov/cair/. Last visited 3/11/12.

15. EPA. "Acid Rain Program."

16. EPA, "Allowance Markets Assessment: A Closer Look at the Two Biggest Price Changes with Federal SO_2 and NO_X Allowance Markets." White Paper, April 23, 2009, p. 2 and Figure 1. Available at www.epa.gov/airmarkets/resource/docs/marketassessmnt.pdf. Last visited 3/11/12.

17. EPA, *Climate Change Indicators in the United States,* April 2010, p. 22. Available at http://epa.gov/climatechange/indicators/pdfs/ClimateIndicators_full.pdf. Last visited 10/27/11.

18. Richard A. Mueller, "The Case against Global-Warming Skepticism: There Were Good Reasons for Doubt, until Now." *Wall Street Journal,* October 21, 2011.

19. "Protecting Polar Bears Must Include Mitigating Global Warming, Group Argues." *Science-Daily,* May 21, 2008. Available at www.sciencedaily.com/releases/2008/05/080521100419.htm. Last visited 10/27/11.

20. National Academies, "America's Climate Choices: Final Report." Available at http://americas-climatechoices.org/ACC_Final_Report_Brief04.pdf. Last visited 10/27/11.

21. EPA, *Climate Change,* p. 4.

22. IPCC Fourth Assessment Report: Climate Change 2007: 2. Causes of Change. Available at www.ipcc.ch/publications_and_data/ar4/syr/en/spms2.html. Last visited 10/27/11.

23. William A.R. Anderegg et al., "Expert Credibility in Climate Change." *Proceedings of the National Academy of Science,* Early Edition, April 9, 2010. Available at www.pnas.org/content/early/2010/06/04/1003187107.full.pdf. Last visited 10/27/11.

24. Synopsis in NOAA, "New analyses find evidence of human-caused climate change in half of the 12 extreme weather and climate events analyzed from 2012." September 5, 2013. Available at www.noaanews.noaa.gov/stories2013/20130905-extremeweatherandclimateevents.html. The underlying study is T.C. Pearson et al. (eds.), "Explaining Extreme Events of 2012 from a Climate Perspective." *Bulletin of the American Metrological Society* Special Supplement, 94, 9 (September 2013). Available at www.ametsoc.org/2012extremeeventsclimate.pdf. Both last visited 9/26/13.

25. Justin Gillis, "UN Climate Panel Endorses Ceiling on Global Emissions." *New York Times,* September 27, 2013.

26. IPCC, Summary for Policymakers. In *Climate Change 2014: Impacts, Adaptation, and Vulnerability. Part A: Global and Sectoral Aspects. Contribution of Working Group II to the Fifth Assessment Report of the Intergovernmental Panel on Climate Change,* p.12. Available at http://ipcc-wg2.gov/AR5/images/uploads/WG2AR5_SPM_FINAL.pdf. Last visited 6/4/14.

27. Royal Society and the National Academy of Science, "Climate Change: Evidence and Causes." Foreword. February 27, 2014. Available at http://dels.nas.edu/resources/static-assets/exec-office-other/climate-change-full.pdf. Last visited 6/4/14.

28. U.S. Department of State, "United States Climate Action Report 2014," p. 6. Available at http://www.state.gov/documents/organization/219038.pdf. Last visited 6/4/14.

29. Decision available at EPA, "Endangerment and Cause or Contribute Findings for Greenhouse Gases under Section 202(a) of the Clean Air Act." Available at http://epa.gov/climatechange/endangerment.html. Last visited 10/28/11.

30. Details at www.time.com/time/magazine/article/0,9171,1989130,00.html#ixzz1c3yvOnz9. Last visited 10/28/11.

31. Matthew Daly, "Climate Bill: Senate Democrats Abandon Comprehensive Energy Bill." *Huffington Post,* July 22, 2010.

32. EPA, "Settlement Agreement to Address Greenhouse Gas Emissions from Electric Generation Facilities and Refineries." Available at www.epa.gov/airquality/pdfs/settlementfactsheet.pdf. Last visited 10/28/11.

33. EPA, "Fact Sheet: Clean Air Act Permitting for Greenhouse Gas Emissions—Final Rules." Available at www.epa.gov/NSR/ghgdocs/20101223factsheet.pdf. Last visited 12/5/11.

34. EPA, "Regulatory Initiatives." Available at www.epa.gov/climatechange/initiatives/index.html. Last visited 10/28/11.

35. Executive Office of the President, "The President's Climate Action Plan." June 2013. Available at www.whitehouse.gov/sites/default/files/image/president27sclimateactionplan.pdf. Last visited 9/26/13.

36. Lenny Bernstein and Juliet Eilperin, "EPA Moves to Limit Emissions of Future Coal- and Gas-Fired Power Plants." *Washington Post,* September 19, 2013.

37. "Climate Change: While Congress Sleeps." *The Economist*, June 29, 2013. Available at www.economist.com/news/united-states/21580186-barack-obama-offers-stopgap-measures-slow-global-warming-while-congress-sleeps Transcript available through Bloomberg News at www.bloomberg.com/news/print/2013–06–25/-we-need-to-act-transcript-of-obama-s-climate-change-speech.html. Both last visited 8/7/13.

38. EPA, "Clean Power Plan Proposed Rule. June 2, 2014." Available at http://www2.epa.gov/carbon-pollution-standards/clean-power-plan-proposed-rule. Last visited 6/4/14.

39. Coral Davenport, "Obama to Take Action to Slash Coal Pollution." *New York Times,* June 1, 2014. Available at http://www.nytimes.com/2014/06/02/us/politics/epa-to-seek-30-percent-cut-in-carbon-emissions.html. Last visited 6/4/14.

40. Melissa Clyne, "Obama Environmental Plan Part of a 'War on Coal,' Executive Says." *Newsmax*, June 2, 2014. Available at http://www.newsmax.com/US/Obama-EPA-coal-greenhouse-gases/2014/06/02/id/574538/. Last visited 6/4/14.

41. Quoted in Steven Mufson, "Will the New EPA Rules for Coal Plants Inspire Other Countries?" *Washington Post,* June 4, 2014.

42. Ibid.

43. European Commission, Climate Action, "The EU Emissions Trading System (EU ETS)." Available at http://ec.europa.eu/clima/policies/ets/index_en.htm. Last visited 7/14/14.

44. Damian Carrington, "Emissions Trading Reforms Raise Price of Pollution Permits." *The Guardian*, July 3, 2013.

45. *Bloomberg New Energy Finance,* "Auction Cuts to Breathe New Life into EU Carbon Market." March 3, 2014. Available at http://about.bnef.com/press-releases/auction-cuts-to-breath-new-life-into-eu-carbon-markets/. Last visited 6/5/14.

46. California Air Resources Board, "Preliminary List of Entities Covered by the Cap and Trade Program." Updated 10/27/11. Available at www.arb.ca.gov/cc/capandtrade/covered_entities_list.pdf. Last visitied 3/12/12.

47. Act details at CA.Gov, "Assembly Bill 32: Global Warming Solutions Act." Available at www.arb.ca.gov/cc/ab32/ab32.htm. Last visited 11/1/11.

48. Regional Greenhouse Gas Initiative, "CO2 Offsets." Available at www.rggi.org/market/offsets. Last visited 8/7/13.

49. California Air Resources Board, "Major Activities for the Cap-and-Trade Mandatory Reporting Program in 2012." Available at www.arb.ca.gov/cc/capandtrade/2012activities.pdf. Last visited 3/12/12.

50. California Air Resources Board, "Compliance Offset Program." Available at www.arb.ca.gov/cc/capandtrade/offsets/offsets.htm. Last visited 3/12/12.

51. "California Air Resources Board Quarterly Auction 3, May 2013—Summary Results Report." Available at www.arb.ca.gov/cc/capandtrade/auction/may-2013/results.pdf. Last visited 8/7/13.

52. Karen Gullo and Lynn Doan, "California's First Carbon Auction Challenged in Lawsuit." Bloomberg.com, November 14, 2012.

53. William Sloan, Peter Hsiao, Michael Steel, and Jennifer Jeffers, "California's Cap-and-Trade Auction Is Not a Tax: Court Decides 'Close Question.'" Morrison/Foerster, November 15, 2013. Available at http://media.mofo.com/files/Uploads/Images/131115-Cap-and-Trade-Not-a-Tax.pdf. Last visited 6/5/14.

54. For example, New York's Budget Trading Program and its share of the total regional cap was established through a new rule (6 NYCRR Part 242) while revisions to an existing rule (6 NYCRR Part 200, General Provisions Part 242) establish the cap-and-trade provisions.

55. Regional Greenhouse Gas Initiative, "The RGGI CO2 Cap." Available at http://rggi.org/design/overview/cap. Last visited 12/14/11.

56. New York Department of Environmental Conservation, "The Economic Effects of RGGI." Available at www.dec.ny.gov/energy/39282.html. Last visited 12/14/11.

57. Ibid.

58. RGGI, Inc., "Market Monitor Report for Auction 20." June 7, 2013. Available at www.rggi.org/docs/Auctions/20/Auction_20_Market_Monitor_Report.pdf. Last visited 8/7/13.

59. RGGI, Inc., "RGGI Benefits." Available at www.rggi.org/rggi_benefits. Last visited 8/7/13.

60. EPA, "Overview of Greenhouse Gases." Available at www.epa.gov/climatechange/ghgemissions/gases/co2.html. Last visited 6/23/14.

61. National Research Council, *Hidden Costs of Energy: Unpriced Consequences of Energy Production and Use.* October 2009. Available at www.nap.edu/catalog.php?record_id=12794. Last visited 10/31/11.

62. Chicago Climate Exchange. Available at www.theice.com/ccx.jhtml. Last visited 10/31/11.

63. Chicago Climate Futures Exchange. Available at www.ccfe.com/. Last visited 10/31/11.

64. Nathanial Gronewold, "Chicago Climate Exchange Closes Nation's First Cap-and-Trade System but Keeps Eye to the Future." *New York Times,* January 3, 2011.

65. Quoted in ibid.

66. David Wann, "Brewing a Sustainable Industry." Terrain.org, no. 9, Spring/Summer 2001. Available at www.terrain.org/articles/9/wann.htm. Also New Belgium Brewing. Available at www.newbelgium.com/home.aspx. Last visited 11/1/11.

67. New Belgium Brewing Co., "Alternatively Empowered." Available at www.newbelgium.com/culture/alternatively_empowered.aspx. Last visited 3/8/12.

68. Reviews available at www.yelp.com/biz/new-belgium-brewing-company-fort-collins. Last visited 11/1/11.

8 The Regulation, and Deregulation, of the Communications Sector with Emphasis on Cable

Chapter Objectives

The concept of a rate-of-return regulatory approach to natural monopolies is described in Chapter 3 with a focus on the electricity sector. Well, much of the communication sector is also a natural monopoly, but with the added twist that the airwaves are public property. The objective of this chapter then is the gaining of an understanding of how the U.S. approach to regulating the sector has evolved with changing societal values and technology, with differential effects on business.

The regulatory trail is convoluted for sure and so for a fuller understanding it is useful to trace the progression of regulatory approaches, including the following stages:

- Origins of the regulatory concept (especially common carriers)
- Protection of free speech and oversight of obscenity laws
- Equal access, equal time, fairness doctrine, must-carry rules
- Mergers, divestiture, and rate control
- Role of intellectual property rights in international marketing

Cases consider firm options and opportunities under deregulation, as well as the potential of forming municipally owned cable systems. Much of the growth of the sector is based on mergers and acquisitions. One case provides an opportunity to apply the Merger Guidelines described in Chapter 3, Section 3.5, to judge the likelihood the merger will be approved, and consider alternatives to growth by merger. Those considerations are particularly relevant in light of the communications mega-mergers which landed on the Federal Communications Commission's desk shortly before this book went to press. The applicable international case study highlights the importance of intellectual property rights in protecting music and movies and other such ventures, and the need to become familiar with the rights in each market country.

Key Terms and Agencies: *ICC; FCC; NAICS; Interconnectivity; Local-into-local; Common carrier; "Must carry"; "Overbuilder"; "à la carte"; Net neutrality*

To paraphrase Will Rogers, the great American humorist and philosopher, when the government settled Indians on reservations they were promised the land until the grass no longer grew and the water didn't flow. So the government gave them land where the grass didn't grow and the water didn't flow. In many ways the regulation of the airwaves, and subsequently cable, over time has been similar: promise a lot but deliver little. With the Native Americans, though, it was clear who was benefiting and who was losing. With communication regulation and deregulation the gainers and losers over time are not always so clear, as we shall see.

The management of the airwaves is a classic example of the need for regulation, as we saw in Chapter 2, Section 2.1a, regarding the additional delays in sending assistance to the sinking *Titanic* caused by the unregulated use of the airwaves. That led to the first of many regulatory laws, the Radio Act of 1913. With the airwaves there are as well equity issues for they belong to all but can be used by only a few. Indeed special controls are needed to space properly transmission frequencies as overlapping transmissions render the signals worthless for everyone. So how does a government equitably allocate a finite resource like broadcast frequencies? Should allocation be on a financial basis only? Or should the government seek some degree of "variety" and "balance"? Then when cable television began a presence in the 1950s there followed the classic issue of managing a natural monopoly for in most markets it is not economically viable to have multiple service providers when relying on landline technologies (Figure 8.1). Satellite broadcasting, emerging in North America in the 1970s, promised

Figure 8.1 **Early Cable: Laying the First Transatlantic Telegraph Cable, 1850s**

Source: Wikimedia Commons. Original source W.H. Russell.

to provide competition to hardwired cable systems, but for a variety of reasons has not been very effective in that role.

So regulation and deregulation are complex tasks and one government has subjected to multiple approaches. The outcome has been some highly profitable cable and entertainment companies—four firms have a 57-percent share of the cable market (see this chapter, Section 8.2)—with shifting business opportunities and management issues each time the law has changed. We explore these issues first in this chapter, Section 8.1, with an overview of major regulations beginning in 1910. Section 8.2 of this chapter then reviews reports on the effects of the several laws on the sector, as well as on service, variety, and, particularly, price. Sections 8.3–8.7 of this chapter present five cases related to different aspects of regulation and deregulation. The fourth of these is another in our series of ongoing cases—this one pivoting from the (hypothetical) proposed merger between Comcast and NBC Universal. The consideration and regulations of mergers involves a different set of economic issues, regulations, and agencies than we have seen heretofore. The final case applies to the effect of intellectual property rights on the expansion into international markets—in this case into a mega-developing country, India.

8.1 MAJOR REGULATORY ACTS FOR RADIO AND TELEVISION, INCLUDING CABLE

Table 8.1 lists the major regulatory acts applied to the communications sector, followed by a description of their principal components. While the focus of this chapter is not on telephone regulation, telephones are part of the communication mix and regulations of the airwaves need to be considered in that context as does the mixed legacy of telephone regulation (Example 8.1). Besides, technological changes in recent decades have blurred the distinctions among the previously separate sectors of telephone, radio, and TV. A fuller understanding of telecommunications regulation also requires some background in general regulatory policy, such as transportation, as much of the regulatory concepts and methods for telecommunications are extensions of those for transport, initially railroads, then trucking. So the relevant transportation-related laws are identified in brief. Following the table is more detailed information on the key legislation.

a. Radio Act of 1927[6]

At one level, the Radio Act is predominately technical. Previously, the sector was self-regulated regarding the frequencies (and power levels) used for transmission, but that approach quickly became unworkable as radio grew in the 1920s. The act allowed the Federal Radio Commission (FRC) (which it established, superseding the Department of Commerce) to assign frequencies as part of the licensing process. The concern was that the undisciplined and unregulated voice of the public (there were at the time 15,000-plus

Table 8.1

Major Regulatory Acts for Radio and Television, Including Cable

Title	Date	Agency	Mandates
Interstate Commerce Act	1887	ICC	Regulate railroad industry Established ICC
Hepburn Act	1906	ICC	Authority to set maximum railroad rates
Mann–Elkins Act	1910	ICC	Extended authority to regulate telecommunications Designated telephone, telegraph, and wireless as common carriers (authorized transporters)
Radio Act	1913	Dept. Commerce	Transmitters and operators licensed
Radio Act	1927	FRC	Regulated frequencies Created FRC (Federal Radio Commission) "Equal time" access for politicians
Communications Act	1934	FCC	Created FCC to parallel ICC
Communications Satellite Act	1962	COMSAT	Create COMSAT Allows communication industry to share satellite use
1st Cable TV Report & Order	1965	FCC	
2nd Cable TV Report & Order	1966	FCC	Require cable carry local broadcast Limit duplicative imported programs
Telecommunications Act	1966	FCC	Deregulated access to sector Incorporated cable service Allows cross-ownership
Cable TV Report & Order	1972	FCC	Eased content restrictions Continued local programming requirement
Cable Communications Policy Act	1984	FCC	Removed rate regulation Standardize franchise renewal Legalized scrambling Limit local franchise fee to 5 percent
Children's Television Act	1990	FCC	Increase quantity educational and informational TV for children Regulate commercials time Consider childrens' programming when licensing
Cable Consumer Protection & Communication Act	1992	FCC	Mandate lower cable rates Cable companies must compensate content providers
Telecommunications Act	1996	FCC	Emphasis on telephone industry Allows media cross ownership Access to be given by incumbents Spectrum allotments to internet
Satellite Home Viewers Improvement Act	1999	FCC	Permits "local-into-local" Allows distant or national programs

Abbreviations:

COMSAT	Communications Satellite Corporation
ICC	Interstate Commerce Commission
FCC	Federal Communications Commission
FRC	Federal Radio Commission

Source: Compiled by W. Lesser.

EXAMPLE 8.1: THE RISE AND FALL, AND RISE, OF AT&T, OR THE HISTORY OF U.S. VOICE COMMUNICATION AND ITS REGULATION[1]

Early History: Rarely does a single firm, albeit in many different forms, capture the entire U.S. history of a vital sector along with the evolution of regulatory approaches and concepts as they interacted with technological change. AT&T, formerly American Telephone and Telegraph, is one such firm, tracing its roots back to the very invention of the telephone in 1875. Its inventor, Alexander Graham Bell, arranged with two major financial supporters, Gardiner Hubbard and Thomas Sanders, to form the Bell Telephone Company in 1877. Commercialization of the invention was rapid; within three years exchanges had been established in most major cities and towns. Next, in 1882, a controlling interest in the Western Electric Co. was acquired from Western Union (the telegraph company) to manufacture its equipment.

The name AT&T appeared first in 1885 with the creation of AT&T Long Lines, which was to become a nationwide long-distance system. Late in 1899, AT&T took over American Bell (as it was then named). This was the first regulatory-induced structural change for the firm. The Massachusetts corporate laws under which American Bell operated restricted growth by limiting market capitalization at $10 million. New York State, where AT&T was headquartered, was more accommodating of size and so the assets were transferred there. The system became known as the Bell System, later rechristened in the vernacular as "Ma Bell."

A second regulation-based change occurred in 1894 when Bell's last key patent expired (see Chapter 3, Section 3.6, for a discussion of patents). That led within a decade to the entrance of over 6,000 independent phone companies. Access was enhanced and with competition prices were reduced, but there was a key problem: lack of connectivity. Current mobile phone users experience some of this with "roaming" problems and the need to access different devices for connectivity in Europe and elsewhere in the world.

On to a Regulated Monopoly: Under a corporate policy of "One Policy, One System, Universal Service," AT&T began acquiring local telephone companies which would facilitate connectivity. It would also facilitate monopoly pricing by AT&T, which led to the government filing an antitrust suit (see Chapter 3, Section 3.5, for an overview of antitrust law). The case was resolved through an agreement, the Kingsbury Commitment of 1913 (really a form of consent decree). In exchange for dropping the case, AT&T agreed to stop acquiring independent phone companies except when authorized by the Interstate Commerce Commission (ICC). AT&T was also required to divest Western Union and to allow the independents to connect with its long-distance lines. However, there was no requirement to interconnect local service, nor with independent long-distance carriers. As a result AT&T continued to dominate, and the lax approval requirements of the ICC (99 percent of acquisition requests were approved) meant AT&T controlled the U.S. telephone industry.

When the Federal Communications Commission (FCC) was created in 1934, it was given regulatory authority over telephone rates. Previously, some states and municipalities regulated rates, often with the effect of urban users subsidizing those in rural areas, while limiting competition through restrictions on duplication of service areas. A regulated monopoly had come into existence, whether by intent or a slippery slope based on lax enforcement of regulatory levers.

The control over the system exercised by AT&T was quite extraordinary by contemporary standards. Phones and lines were rented, not owned (think cable boxes). At the time one never imagined owning the home phone, and even moving it involved a call to a service technician even though phones need only simple two-wire connections. The controlled rental market was a highly profitable one for AT&T. It was not until 1956 in *Hush-A-Phone Corporation vs. United States* that non–AT&T devices were permitted to be added to the AT&T licensed/rented equipment. Specifically, Hush-A-Phone was a device covering the mouthpiece to allow greater privacy. Recall that at the time phones were immobile. The regulatory issue regarded § 203(a) of the Communications Act of 1934 related to "tariffs" (rates). These tariffs forbade attachment to the telephone of any device "not furnished by the telephone company." The FCC, which was petitioned by Hush-A-Phone, agreed that its use does not impair telephone service. Nevertheless the FCC ruled that its use was "deleterious to the telephone system and injures the service rendered by it."

The question for the court to which the regulatory decision was appealed was whether the FCC had sufficient authority to control subscribers' legitimate use of their telephones. AT&T argued that the same privacy effect could be achieved without an external device by cupping a hand around the mouthpiece, but that was found to cause distortion. The court determined that restricting the use of a useful external device is "neither just nor reasonable. The interveners' tariffs, under the commission's decision, are an unwarranted interference with the telephone subscriber's right reasonably to use his telephone in ways that are privately beneficial without being publicly detrimental."[2]

Then in 1968 the FCC permitted the Carterfone to be connected to the AT&T network. The Carterfone is an acoustic cradle which permitted, for example, a CB caller to connect with a landline. (Functionally, it is similar to the cradle for the earliest telephone Internet dial-up connections.) That ruling (13 F.C.C. 2d 420) opened the way for connecting other devices like fax machines, while marking the beginning of the end of the lease-only option for AT&T.

Legal Action: The Justice Department instituted two antitrust actions against AT&T, the first in 1949, which was not resolved until the 1956 consent decree. The department sought to separate the Bell System's manufacturing (Western Electric) from its operating (AT&T) and research (Bell Labs, whose technological advancements greatly strengthened the firm's position). The outcome was:[3]

- AT&T not permitted to enter computer and information services business
- Western Electric maintained as a separate subsidiary
- AT&T Long Distance established as a long-distance telecommunications company
- Bell Companies separated from AT&T
- Bell Labs separated as a telecommunication research company

Second, and with greater consequence, was *United States vs. AT&T*, begun in 1974 and settled 1982. By that time in history technological change had eased the entry cost into long-distance voice transmission, leading the FCC to consider only local service to be a natural monopoly. This view is similar to the separation of electricity production from distribution—see Chapter 3, Section 3.4. The consent decree which settled the case included:[4]

- AT&T ("Ma Bell") would divest the local parts of the Bell operating telephone companies
- The twenty-two Bell Operating Companies became seven Regional Bell Operating Companies (known as "Baby Bells")
- AT&T would keep its manufacturing facilities and its long-distance network
- The Baby Bells would not be allowed to manufacture nor would they be allowed to enter the long-distance business within their territories
- AT&T would not be allowed entry to the local-exchange business nor to acquire the stock or assets of any Baby Bell

AT&T was permitted at that point to enter into the computer business, partly overturning the 1956 consent decree. The firm additionally retained its long-distance services through its AT&T Communications division (previously AT&T Long Lines), but at much reduced profitability due to competition from specialized carriers like Sprint and MCI.

On to Deregulation: In 1996 the Congress passed the Telecommunications Act of that year to spur competition by allowing any firm in the communications sector to compete against any firm in any other sector (see this chapter, Section 8.1f). Thus freed of a major constraint, AT&T plunged into the cable business, simultaneously spinning off its tech operations as Lucent Technologies. Through a series of cable acquisitions, AT&T became the largest domestic provider. The acquisitions though were costly and with falling long-distance revenues they became unsustainable. Bits and pieces were spun off to Comcast and Cingular, until in 2005 Southwestern Bell, one of the "Baby Bells" created in 1982, acquired AT&T, its former parent. The merged company was named AT&T Inc. to distinguish it from the preceding AT&T Corporation.

The new AT&T acquired BellSouth the subsequent year along with a number of additional wireless and spectrum up to the present. At present, AT&T Inc. has reassembled most of the Baby Bells from the earlier AT&T Corp. period. That is, AT&T Inc. owns:[5]

- Bell South
- Southwestern Bell (which had acquired AT&T Corp.)
- Pacific Telesis Group (combining Pacific, and California and Nevada Bell)
- Ameritech Corp. (combining five Baby Bells in the upper Midwest)
- Southern New England Telecommunications

Lessons Learned: AT&T in its several configurations has gone nearly full circle in terms of structure for landline and long-distance service from essential monopoly a century ago to the same currently. Of course there has been considerable technological change, meaning there are presently multiple alternatives to landline service so the price effect today is not at all the same as in the earlier period. One nevertheless can reasonably ask, to what ultimate end was all the regulation, particularly the divestiture of the Baby

Bells in 1982? Here are some lessons that may be derived from this experience in utility regulation:

- Technological advances can fundamentally change the competitive dynamics of an industry. This means regulations must be flexible to accommodate those changes. Flexibility may be introduced within a regulatory system (very difficult given the uncertainty of predicting change) or by amending the regulations as change occurs.
- Divestiture is a drastic process. The newly formed firms may not function well in the new environment and hence be ineffective competition.
- Congress is not good at directing change through regulatory adjustments, especially those changes which attempt to incentivize competition.
- Many of the problems with the regulation of AT&T are attributable to lax enforcement, particularly by the ICC and the FCC, rather than to faulty regulatory policies per se.
- The regulated system, despite the evident limitations, did for decades provide an excellent telephone system with adoption in the 90 percent–plus range along with ongoing technological change.

amateur stations) interfered with corporate goals of delivering programming and advertising on a dependable schedule to a mass audience.

The FRC, managed by a group of five commissioners, was free to control radio to serve whatever interests it deemed were within the scope of "public interest, convenience, and necessity," as the act's purpose is described, as long as the commission did not deny "free speech" to broadcasters. However, Congress did not really mean to allow complete free speech by including the clause, "No person within the jurisdiction of the United States shall utter any obscene, indecent, or profane language by means of radio communication." In practice, the commissioners, with their authority to grant and deny licenses, had some control over program content.

That radio had wide ramifications for political messages, and hence political power, was evident from an early date. This was also an era of broad concern over monopolies (see Chapter 3, Section 3.5) in broadcasting taking the form of radio networks, notably NBC but soon to be joined by CBS. Nonetheless the act makes but one reference to networks, granting the commissioners "authority to make special regulations applicable to stations engaged in chain broadcasting." No rules regulating advertising were authorized. Significantly though, a forerunner of the "equal-time rule" was stated in Section 18, which ordered stations to give equal opportunities for political candidates.

These considerations initially applied only to AM stations as FM was not patented until 1933 with the first experimental broadcast license issued in 1937. In 1928 the commission issued the first license for television.

b. Communications Act of 1934[7]

The stated purposes of the Communication Act are:

> regulating interstate and foreign commerce in communication by wire and radio so as to make available, so far as possible, to all the people of the United States a rapid, efficient, nationwide, and worldwide wire and radio communication service with adequate facilities at reasonable charges, for the purpose of the national defense, and for the purpose of securing a more effective execution of this policy by centralizing authority theretofore granted by law to several agencies and by granting additional authority with respect to interstate and foreign commerce in wire and radio communication, there is hereby created a commission to be known as the "Federal Communications Commission," which shall be constituted as hereinafter provided, and which shall execute and enforce the provisions of this Act.

The act is based on the Commerce Clause of the U.S. Constitution (Article I, Section 8, Clause 3), regulating commerce "among the several states" (see Chapter 3, Section 3.7a). In 1914, the Supreme Court ruling in *Houston, East and West Texas Railway Co. vs. United States* set limits on railroad price discrimination that were effectively restricting interstate commerce. The underlying concern then was that discriminatory intra- and interstate rates would damage other states. Under the 1934 Communications Act, communications technology, both wired and wireless, was deemed to be an interstate good with the regulatory goal to be similar to that by which the ICC regulates the railways and interstate commerce. Unlike the ICC, however, the FCC was not granted authority to regulate prices, but it has used auctions as a means of determining who would be awarded licenses.

The act is composed of eight "Titles," of which numbers III and VI are most relevant here. Title VI, added via the Cable Communications Policy Act of 1984 (see below), describes provisions related to cable regulation and is an example of how as new communications technologies have been created (such as broadcast, cable, and satellite television), new provisions governing these communications have been added to the act.

Title III applies to broadcast station requirements. Among the significant components are:

- Section 326 prevents the commission from exercising censorship over broadcast stations.
- Section 315, the Equal-Time Rule, requires broadcasters to afford equal opportunity to candidates seeking political office. A 1999 amendment by the FCC ruled that "a broadcast station should not be allowed to refuse a request for political advertising time solely on the ground that the station does not sell or program such lengths of time."

- A connection with U.S. code bars individuals from uttering obscene or indecent language over a broadcast station.

The Supreme Court held in *National Broadcasting Co. Inc. et al. vs. United States et al.* (1943) that the FCC had the right to issue regulations pertaining to associations between broadcasting networks and their affiliated stations. The FCC until 1958 interpreted that Supreme Court decisions to mean that potential economic injury to an existing licensee was not grounds for refusing to license a competitor.

c. Telecommunications Act of 1966

The FCC was granted authority to preempt state or local legal requirements that acted as a barrier to entry by new firms.

Since the earliest days, the FRC and then the FCC insisted that because of "scarcity" a licensee must operate a broadcast station in the public trust rather than promote only one point of view. The constitutionality of the Fairness Doctrine and Section 315 was upheld by the courts in *Red Lion Broadcasting vs. FCC* (1969). That case established broadcasters as full First Amendment speakers whose editorial speech could not be regulated absent good reason. However, because they were granted government licenses on a scarce radio spectrum, they could be regulated by the FCC to preserve openness in covering news.

Broadcasters complained that the doctrine produced a "chilling effect" on speech and cited the possibility of fighting protracted legal battles in Fairness Doctrine challenges. The courts reaffirmed the notion that licensees were not obligated to sell or give time to specific opposing groups to meet Fairness Doctrine requirements as long as the licensee met its public trustee obligations. In 1987, the FCC repealed the Fairness Doctrine and in 2000 the courts ordered the FCC to rescind the personal attack and political editorializing rules as well.

d. Cable Communications Policy Act of 1984[8]

The Supreme Court had affirmed the FCC's jurisdiction over cable in *United States vs. Southwestern Cable Co.* (1968), noting regulation was needed for the commission to execute its responsibilities. The 1984 act established policies in the areas of ownership, channel usage, franchise provisions and renewals, subscriber rates and privacy, obscenity and lockboxes, unauthorized reception of services, equal employment opportunity, and pole attachments.

The new law also defined jurisdictional boundaries among federal, state, and local authorities for regulating cable television systems. That is, many local governments were being criticized for trying to obtain lucrative contracts and perks from their local cable operators. As a result, the pressure to deregulate in order to provide more competition gained substantial momentum leading in 1984 to Congress passing legislation to deregulate cable TV rates and limit local government control. Its major provisions created a standard procedure for renewing franchises that assured operators of relatively certain renewal and it deregulated rates so that operators could charge what they wanted for different service tiers as long as there was "effective competition" to the service. This was defined as the presence of three or more over-the-air signals, a very easy standard that over 90 percent of all cable markets could meet.[9]

e. Cable Consumer Protection and Communication Act of 1992

The 1992 Cable Act codified, and the commission has adopted, a regulatory plan allowing local and/or state authorities to select a cable franchisee and to regulate in any areas that the commission did not preempt. Local franchising authorities have adopted laws and regulations in areas such as subscriber service requirements, public access requirements, and franchise renewal standards.

Under the 1992 Cable Act, local franchising authorities have specific responsibility for regulating the rates for basic cable service and equipment. The FCC itself required cable operators to cut rates by an average of 7 percent; all subscribers were to have been benefited, but that was not the case. Finally, it required that the FCC generate a plan (called must-carry/retransmission consent) by which broadcasters would receive compensation for their programming.

f. Telecommunications Act of 1996[10]

The stated purpose of the act is: "to provide for a pro-competitive, de-regulatory national policy framework designed to accelerate rapidly private sector deployment of advanced telecommunications and information technologies and services to all Americans by opening up all telecommunications markets to competition." Essentially, Congress attempted to create a regulatory framework for the transition from primarily monopoly provision to competitive provision of telecommunications services by allowing any communications business to compete in any market against any other. In essence, telecommunications were deregulated with the intention of enhancing competition through the removal of regulatory barriers to entry (Figure 8.2). Emphasis was on the restructuring of the telephone industry, but it also affected the cable industry. Regulation of telephones has a lengthy and convoluted history that does not reflect well on either the industry or regulators.

The act attempts to enhance competition by establishing distinct regulations for each technology platform. That is, it creates separate regulatory regimes for carriers providing voice telephone service, a second for providers of cable television, and a third for information services.

Key provisions include:

- Oblige incumbent carriers and new entrants to interconnect their networks with one another, imposing additional requirements on the incumbents because they might

Figure 8.2 **Satellite Dishes Were Intended under the Telecommunications Act of 1996 to Provide Competition for Cable**

Source: All-Free-download.com. Original source Alex Borland.

desire to restrict competitive entry by denying such interconnection or by setting terms, conditions, and rates that could undermine the ability of the new entrants to compete.

- Compel local telephone companies to share their lines with competitors at regulated rates if "the failure to provide access to such network elements would impair the ability of the telecommunications carrier seeking access to provide the services that it seeks to offer."
- Base intercarrier compensation rates among competing local exchange carriers on the "additional costs of terminating such calls." Intercarrier compensation rates apply when a call initiates and terminates in the jurisdiction of different companies; traditionally the company of the call initiator pays the recipient caller's supplier and recovers the cost through general service charges.
- Create competition in both local and long-distance telephone markets through a process by which the regional Bell operating companies would be allowed to offer

long-distance service once they made a showing that their local markets had been opened up to competition.

- Regulate obscene programming on cable television.
- Allow for the scrambling of satellite channels for nonsubscribers, and the scrambling of sexually explicit adult-video service programming, including a requirement for the manufacture of televisions to facilitate program-blocking V-chip technology.
- Allow greater latitude for mergers, since cable companies can now enter the telecommunications business, and vice versa.
- Ease multiple outlet restrictions in individual markets. The act permits a single entity to own up to eight individual properties in a market of forty-five or more, and five individual properties in a market of fourteen or fewer stations. Previously, operators were allowed to own no more than twenty-four stations nationally, and just two AM and two FM stations per market.
- Deregulate cable rates. Deregulation is not absolute, but cable operators are allowed to raise rates to account for inflation and/or the expense of providing new channels and programming. The intent of the act rather is to encourage the competitive marketplace to work toward lower prices.

g. Satellite Home Viewers Improvement Act of 1999[11]

One of the key elements of the act is the allowance, for the first time, for satellite carriers to transmit local television broadcast signals into local markets, also known as *local-into-local*. Local-into-local means that if a satellite customer lives in an area where the satellite company has decided to provide the service, the customer can receive local TV channels. Should, however, the company decide not to provide local broadcast stations in an area, a consumer may still be able to receive local broadcast stations by using an antenna or basic cable service. Subscribers who cannot receive such an over-the-air signal of Grade B intensity using a conventional, stationary rooftop antenna are eligible to receive these distant signals from "local" stations via the dish service.

h. Free Speech Issues[12]

The early decision to treat radio, and then TV, as "common carriers" set the basis for restrictions on their activities, and notably mandates for carrying local programs, and not duplicating local programs when available with imported ones. There was as well a component of regulatory protection of local broadcasters vis-à-vis cable networks. By the early 1970s, however, the cable industry began to liken itself more to newspapers as "electronic publishers" and to claim the First Amendment free speech rights of print journalism. In *HBO vs. FCC* (1977), and reiterated in *United States vs. Midwest Video Corp.* (1979), the courts ruled the FCC "must-carry" mandates and the like placed unacceptable obligations on cable operators. Rather, cable operators should be free to package and offer content at their own discretion.

8.2 STUDIES OF EFFECTS OF TELECOMMUNICATION REGULATION AND DEREGULATION

The regulatory history of cable is indeed a complex and convoluted one. There are several reasons for that. One is the initial base of regulation on the Communications Act of 1934, which clearly did not and could not anticipate the emergence of cable service. A second factor is the varied structure of the cable sector itself. Some participants are mere carriers, others buy content while still others produce content as well as buying it, and so forth. Few sectors are as complex. And then there is the fact that the sector is highly visible to consumers; we see electric bills monthly but so long as service is available think little of it in the interim. But cable comes into the home continuously and so is frequently on the minds of users.

Another complicating dimension is the free speech issues involved. TV has enormous influence on what people think, so some kind of "balance" in the material presented would seem to be in the public's interest, and indeed that was mandated for decades. In fact, cable television service is available to 95 percent of all television households in the United States, and about two-thirds of all television households subscribe to it. But such efforts are in the end hopeless to accomplish, and it seems as well, not legal. Yet when regulatory changes in terms of required content or "balance" are amended, the effects on the sector are enormous.

Deregulation has directly contributed to the number of channels available to subscribers. Most of those systems offer at least thirty channels; 57 percent have between thirty and fifty-three channels and 13 percent have fifty-four or more channels.[13] Contributing to this channel growth was the emergence of Home Box Office nationally in 1975 with the "Thrilla in Manila" the title bout between Muhammad Ali and Joe Frazier (and first national broadcast by HBO), and CNN in 1980. This content, unavailable on network TV, gave viewers additional reasons to subscribe to cable. This expansion in cable viewership has occasioned a substantial drop in the broadcast network viewing from 1983 to 1994 when weekly broadcast audience shares dropped from sixty-nine to fifty-two, while basic cable networks' shares rose from nine to twenty-six during the same period.[14]

To see other examples of the influence of regulation on the operation of the cable industry, one need only look at the period following the Cable Communications Policy Act of 1984. With rate deregulation and franchise renewal assured, the cable industry's value soared. Cable rates jumped tremendously, according to Government Accounting Office surveys, by an average of 25 to 30 percent from 1986 to 1988 alone, vastly greater than the inflation rate.[15] Indeed, rates have risen virtually steadily from 1983 through at least 1999; the Consumer Price Index (CPI) for cable TV has increased by 6.1 percent per year on average from 1983 to 1999, while the CPI-U (the CPI for all urban consumers) grew 3.2 percent per year (see Figure 8.3). The only perturbation was around 1992 when the Cable Consumer Protection and Communication Act restored rate regulation, only to lift it again several years later.

Figure 8.3 **National Cable Rates 1983–1999**

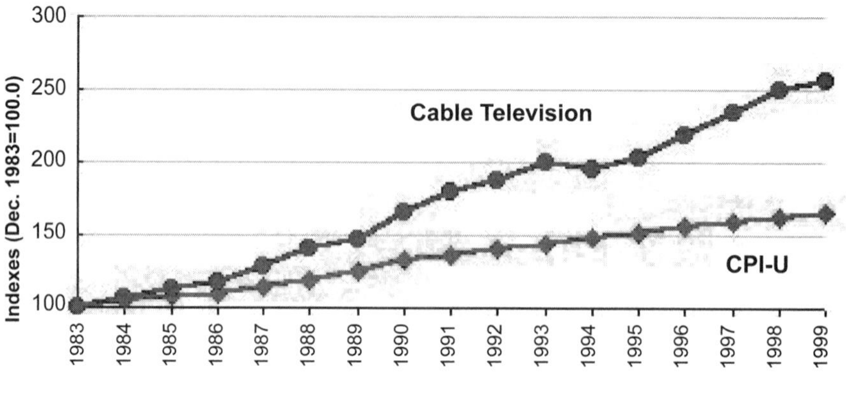

Source: Bureau Labor Statistics, "Cable TV Providers Plug in to Higher Prices."

Under the 1992 act, the FCC is required to collect and report cable rates annually. Using those data, the rate of continuing subscription price increases is evident (see Figure 8.4). Clearly the rate rise on a per-channel basis is far lower, but questions have been raised about the value of many of these channels as under the bundling approach to cable offerings there is no control over the selection of channels such as HBO below the "super premium" tier.

Typically, cable companies have justified the higher rates by a combination of (a) more channels offered and (b) higher license fees for content providers. Recall that under the Telecommunications Act of 1996 cable operators are allowed to raise rates to account for inflation and/or the expense of providing new channels and programming (see this chapter, Section 8.1f). The General Accounting Office (GAO) found that license fees for predominately sports-related programming rose 59 percent from 1999–2002 versus an average of 26 percent for the nonsports networks.[16] By 2013 it was estimated that access to ESPN alone added nearly $5 monthly to the typical cable bill.[17] U.S. PIRG, a public advocacy group, looked into those explanations and, using FCC data, concluded that rates were rising even on a per-channel basis.[18] As regards program costs, New York PIRG finds that 40 percent of the content providers are wholly or partially owned by the major cable companies, so they are paying themselves. Moreover, the greater advertisement and service revenues more than compensate for the program costs without the need for major rate increases.[19]

The issue of sharply rising subscription rates has not been lost on viewers. According to a 2011 survey of 54,000 subscribers by *Consumer Reports,* the two major satellite TV service providers were ranked as below average for "value" but above average for channel selection. However, the leading cable subscribers, accounting for 87 percent of subscribers, rated cable TV value as much below average ("worse") while channel selection received mostly average ratings, with one above average and one below.[20]

Figure 8.4 **Cable Subscription Rates and the CPI, 1995–2009**

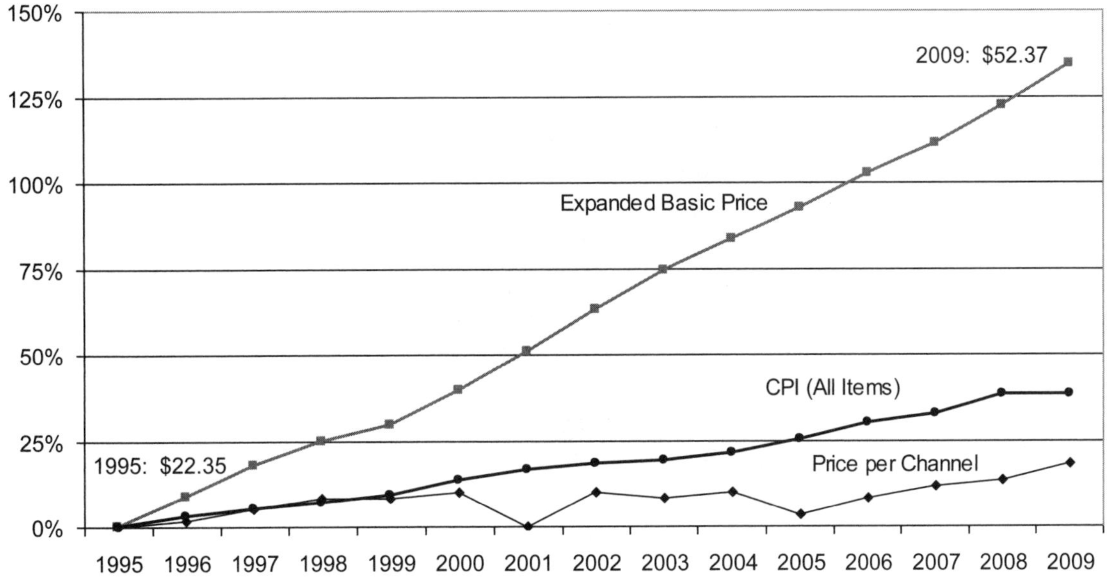

Source: FCC, "Report on Cable Industry Prices." DA 11–284, February 14, 2011. Chart 1.

Expectations of heightened competition fostered by deregulation under the 1996 act and subsequently have, however, not materialized, as is evidenced overall by rapidly rising cable fees. Two sources of competition in particular were anticipated to constrain price increases, the emergence of a second cable operator in a market, and satellite broadcasts. In 2003 the GAO conducted a survey and empirical study of the effects of these and other factors on cable rates. The results indicated a second operator (known as an "overbuilder"), when present, held down rates by 15 percent. As regards satellite providers, the study found a 10 percent higher penetration rate by satellite subscribers led to a 15 percent reduction in cable rates, as well as enhancing service by cable companies.[21] Regarding overbuilder competition, though, the Consumers Union found only around 10 percent of markets have options for cable access,[22] while the FCC put the level of "effectively competitive markets" at 6 percent, with only 2 percent having real competition from alternative wired providers.[23]

The limitation of satellite competition has been its slowly rising penetration rate, now about 32 percent nationally in 2010 (Figure 8.5) but subscriber growth rates have subsequently slowed substantially, from 6 percent annually to a weak 1 percent.[24] And about half of those subscribers live in rural areas lacking wired cable access so that the level of direct competition is even lower. In urban areas, only south-facing dwellings can receive satellite broadcasts, further limiting the potential for effective competition. U.S. PIRG further found many subscribers have both cable and satellite to gain access to particular

Figure 8.5 **Sources of TV Signals, 2010**

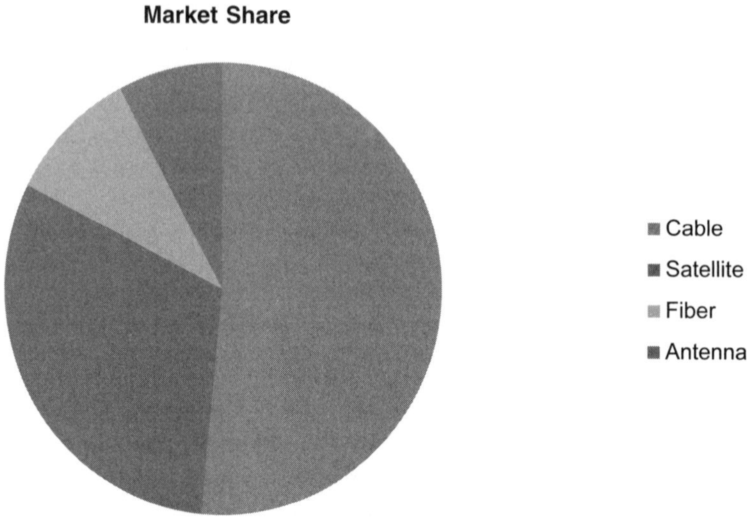

Source: W. Lesser. Data from Free by 50, "What Percent of Homes Have Cable, Satellite, Fiber or Antenna Only?" Original source Consumer Electronics Association.

programs like certain sport events. And then there is the overlapping ownership of cable services and content providers. This means cable companies can, and according to U.S. PIRG do, refuse access for satellite providers to key programs, including sport events, or charge particularly high prices for that access.[25]

The American Cable Association in responding to the GAO study countered that too much of the study's attention was focused on the larger cable operators, while the smaller ones (the bulk of the association's membership) faced direct competition from satellite providers as well as higher programming costs. As a result, the association does not believe that greater competition is a solution to rising cable rates.[26] The National Cable and Telecommunications Association for its part raised questions about the interpretation of the results of competition from overbuilders, noting they are present in only forty-five of the 10,000 franchise communities. Hence, in the opinion of the association, it is inappropriate for the GAO effectively to extrapolate the statistical findings from a few markets to the nation. The basis for the rate analysis was also challenged. The GAO examined rates per channel provided, while the association contends that the base should be per viewing hour, which rate has fallen, according to one study.[27] Other contributing factors were found to be the rising concentration of cable ownership—the share of the cable market controlled by the largest firms—as well as the combined ownership of cable service and programming.

Presently, the FCC uses auctions as:

> one of the primary means of choosing among two or more mutually exclusive applications for an initial license for most commercial services, including wireless, television and radio.

> In a spectrum auction, parties apply to become qualified bidders for one or more spectrum licenses and take part in an online auction for those licenses. By using auctions, the FCC seeks to award licenses to those who value them most and who will have an incentive to use them most effectively. Prior to Congress granting the FCC auction authority in 1993, the Commission relied upon comparative hearings and lotteries to select a licensee from mutually exclusive applicants.[28]

According to a 1997 Congressional Budget Office study, "Auctions have distributed licenses rapidly, efficiently, and at a low cost compared with the alternatives of assigning licenses by comparative hearings or lotteries."[29] Academic studies have supported the finding that the auctions are being operated efficiently.[30]

Currently, the FCC is proposing, or at least considering, recovering 40 percent of the broadcast TV spectrum (120 MHz of 300 MHz) to be made available for allocation to smartphones, iPads, and other broadband mobile uses. A bill (S.911/HR 2482) was introduced in the 112th Congress, but subsequently died, would among other provisions have permitted the FCC to auction TV spectrum that broadcasters voluntarily give up in exchange for a share of the auction proceeds.[31] The National Association of Broadcasters warned that the program would lead to the loss of multiple free TV stations channels 31–51; firms choosing to retain those stations must reallocate them to lower-numbered stations. The association projected 40 percent or more of stations will go off the air, 100 in Detroit alone with several upstate New York cities hit hard as well.[32]

8.3 ■ CASE 8.1: CABLE TV REGULATION

Students should prepare the following questions, based on the Harvard Business School case:

Note on Cable Television Regulation #391-022

1. To what extent has regulation of the cable television industry at the local level been consistent with the public interest—being sure to identify what you and the several regulatory acts define as "public interest"? Why has federal regulation of the cable TV sector been so variable over time?
2. What were the primary determinants of profitability in the cable TV industry after the passage of the Cable Communications Act of 1984? How well did Continental Cablevision perform over the period 1984–1991? Why?
3. What have been the implications of the Telecommunications Act of 1996? How might you have expected a large operator like Continental Cablevision to have responded at the time of passage?

8.4 ■ CASE 8.2: RADIO DEREGULATION

Students should prepare the following questions, based on the Harvard Business School case:

Clear Channel Communications, Inc. #707-523

1. Why is Clear Channel Communications' radio business so financially successful?
2. In 2000, Air Virginia announced it was selling WUMX-FM in Charlottesville. Clear Channel intended to bid, in part because it expected Erie Communications, its main Charlottesville competitor, was planning to bid. Noting that the industry rule of thumb is to bid 42 percent of sales, what would you advise Clear Channel to bid for WUMX-FM?
3. Do you believe Clear Channel has the appropriate corporate scope? Would you recommend selling any of its divisions?

8.5 ■ CASE 8.3: MUNICIPAL CABLE COMPETITION

One of the ways for a municipality to contend with high cable prices and limited competition is to start a publicly owned system of its own. This case deals with one such effort. Some may consider a publicly run cable system an oddity, and numerically it certainly is. But it should not be forgotten that in most communities water and sewer systems are public utilities, some of which for larger cities are major businesses indeed.

a. Chattanooga's Municipal Electric, Internet, Telephone, and TV System

The subject area of this case study, Paragould, Arkansas, is certainly not the only locally owned and operated communication system. Chattanooga, Tennessee, has had a municipal system since 1935 which currently serves nearly 170,000 homes and businesses with electricity, Internet, telephone, and TV cable service. That places it eighth in size of municipally operated electric utility services in 2000 (the Long Island Power Authority is largest).[33] What the Chattanooga system, EPB, is receiving attention for presently though is its enhanced fiber-optic service. In particular, EPB is now offering one gigabit-per-second service to all its customers. By comparison, when Google wires Kansas City for its equally fast service, only a quarter of the residential districts ("fiber-hoods") will have access.[34]

The EPB system cost about $220 million, about half of which was supported from stimulus funds and the remainder through bonds. As of early 2012, the system had 35,000 Fiber to the Premises customers, 9,000 more than its initial goal of 26,000 customers by the third year in operation. It is also ahead of its third-year financial projections, reporting $57.3 million in revenue. That means the service provider could be out of debt by 2020 instead of its original target of 2027. Only a handful of those customers though are opting for the gigabit-per-second service, which costs $350 a month.[35]

Impacts are being felt by the two private Internet and cable TV suppliers in the city, Comcast and AT&T. Comcast has roughly 100,000 TV customers in the area with EPB second at 35,000 and AT&T a distant third with fewer than 1,000. Comcast's strength remains programming, but with the rise of streaming that relevance is declining. Eight of the nine largest subscription-TV providers in the United States lost 195,700 subscribers in the April-to-June 2011 quarter, or about 0.2 percent. Where competition is greater the loss is correspondingly greater. Comcast's revenues fell by 8.4 percent for the first half of 2011 as customers signed up for EPB's new fiber-optic service.[36] In 2012, Standard and Poor's upgraded EPB's bond rating to AA+.[37] That was the first quarterly loss for the group, which serves about 70 percent of households. The loss amounts to only 0.2 percent of their 83.2 million video subscribers, the Associated Press reported.

A third municipality presently offering cable and Internet services is San Bruno, California.[38] Presently about half the states have laws restricting municipal broadband services.[39]

b. Paragould, Arkansas, City Cable Case

Students should prepare the following questions, based on the Harvard Business School case:

Paragould City Cable #794-030

1. Who are the winners and losers from the public/private competition in Paragould's cable TV market?
2. Is cable TV in Paragould a natural monopoly? Does the government of the City of Paragould have options other than direct municipal competition to improve the cable system there?
3. How well do you believe City Cable has performed through August 1993? What is its breakeven number of subscribers at prevailing rates? Alternatively, what is the breakeven rate with the current number of subscribers?
4. What changes, if any, would you recommend with City Cable's current strategy? What changes would you recommend for Paragould Cablevision?

8.6 ▪ CASE 8.4: THE COMCAST/AT&T/NBC CABLE TV MERGERS

a. Comcast Mergers[40]

In 2002, Comcast acquired the assets of AT&T Broadband, AT&T's spun-off cable TV service, for $44.5 billion (Figure 8.6). The merged company had at the time 21.4 million cable subscribers, up from 8.5 million. That number of subscribers makes it the market leader in the United States in a market valued at $60 billion, or $80 billion when direct-broadcast satellite company revenues are added. Prior to the merger Comcast was number two in the segment, but subsequently had twice the number of subscribers as Time Warner, which was relegated to the number two spot. Comcast is also a leader in related market segments like digital video and broadband, but to make it more tractable those markets are not considered as part of this case.

Subsequently in 2004 Comcast made an unsuccessful bid for The Walt Disney Company in an attempt to acquire ESPN to expand its sports offerings. Then in December 2009 Comcast entered a joint venture with NBC Universal under which Comcast would own 51 percent of the company; NBC Universal (GE) will retain ownership of the residual

Figure 8.6 **A Comcast Logo**

COMCAST

Source: Wikimedia Commons, June 1, 2006. Comcast_Logo.svg.png.

49 percent. The venture was approved by the FCC and the Department of Justice in January 2011 with several conditions. Under the conditions, Comcast committed to expanding local news coverage, expand programs for Spanish-speaking viewers, and offer Internet access to schools and libraries. It also agreed not to manage Hulu, a provider of streaming videos. Nor is Comcast permitted to discriminate in terms of access and price between its own subscribers and other subscribers.[41] The merger gives Comcast ownership over the majority of the NBC network's channels, including CNBC and Bravo, as well as the Universal Pictures movie studio. "After a thorough review, we have adopted strong and fair merger conditions to ensure this transaction serves the public interest," FCC Chairman Julius Genachowski said in a statement. In 2013 Comcast acquired the remaining 49 percent ownership share in NBC Universal.

Comcast, as reported in its 2012 Annual Review, had a FY 2012 revenue growth of 12 percent to $62.6 billion, inclusive of revenues from the NBC Universal joint venture. It has a 2012 video cable subscription base of market share of 22 million[42] despite losing 60,000 subscribers during the first quarter of 2013 alone. The reduced customer base was offset by a rate increase to 72 percent of its subscribers.[43] The firm then saw its future based on a high-quality technology platform, increased services provided to subscribers, and added programming such as that provided by NBC Universal. New threats to Comcast's lucrative cable business are nonetheless appearing (Example 8.2).

EXAMPLE 8.2: NEW THREATS TO THE CABLE BUSINESS

Cable service remains a highly profitable business; Comcast earned a 14 percent return on equity for the year ending mid-2013. All, though, is not well as the industry looks ahead to multiple challenges and new forms of competition. Most directly there is satellite TV, but placement limitations (multiple apartment complexes, for example) and the fact that satellite providers must negotiate for content from the same sources as the cable operators (indeed, cable companies own some of the content providers) inherently limit competition from that source.

Second is the new streaming options, some from pay services like Netflix and Hulu, some from online content. Noncable sourcing seems to account for most of the loss in cable subscribers in recent years—down 400,000 subscribers for 2012.[44] That streaming activity is likely to grow, especially as Viacom has made an agreement with Sony to make its popular content and channels available as paid Internet TV services. Channels such as Comedy Central and Nickelodeon may soon be available on devices such as the Sony Playstation 3 and PS4.[45]

A major new threat is arising on the back of a Time Warner imbroglio over fees paid to CBS. On August 2, 2013, Time Warner Cable, the second-largest domestic cable operator, suspended carrying CBS in eight markets (including Dallas and Los Angeles) over a rate dispute.[46] That contentious matter has elevated the discussion over the cable providers' practice of bundling stations into tiers, meaning customers receive—and pay for—many stations they never watch.[47] And those stations can be costly—$10 a month directly to the cable bill for three sports stations alone (ESPN, Fox Sports West, Fox Sports Prime Time).[48] As an alternative, there have been calls for allowing users to select and pay for only the channels of their choice, known as "à la carte."

Senator John McCain (with Senator Richard Blumenthal as cosponsor) introduced the Television Consumer Freedom Act of 2013 (S.912), which would have the following provisions:[49]

- Allows multichannel video programming distributors (MVPDs) (including cable operators, multichannel multipoint distribution services, direct broadcast satellite services, or television receive-only satellite program distributors), except with respect to the minimum contents of programming required for basic tier service, to provide subscribers with any channel of video programming on an à la carte basis.
- Defines *à la carte* as offering video programming for wholesale or retail purchase on an individual, per-channel basis rather than as part of a package or tier of video programming.
- Amends the Communications Act of 1934 to modify the types of programming constituting the minimum contents of basic tier service.
- Conditions the availability of the statutory copyright license to an MVPD on the MVPD offering local commercial television stations, and any other channels of video programming under common control with such stations, for purchase by subscribers on an à la carte basis. An MVPD is a service provider like cable and satellite TV that delivers video programming services, usually for a subscription fee.

Unsurprisingly, the Multicultural Motion Picture Association and other affected sectors oppose the bill. The association in a statement noted, "The marketplace is vibrant, providing audiences more choices in high quality television programming than ever before. And, with rapidly changing technologies and business models, there are more ways than ever for consumers to enjoy their favorite content and to discover new programming. Government intervention now would likely short-circuit this innovation, providing consumers fewer options at higher prices."[50]

In that regard, only 20 percent of current ESPN subscribers are projected to continue it if priced separately. That reduction in subscribers would raise the cost to the residual pool to $30 monthly, assuming the revenue level remained unchanged.[51] More likely, revenue would fall, bringing down the payments to televised sports teams. From the perspective of viewers though, "If the industry isn't willing to give consumers real choice, perhaps it's time for the government to step in."[52] It however went nowhere in the Senate.

Figure 8.7 **Cable Losing Market Share to Satellite and Telephone Market Shares, December 2010 and June 2012**

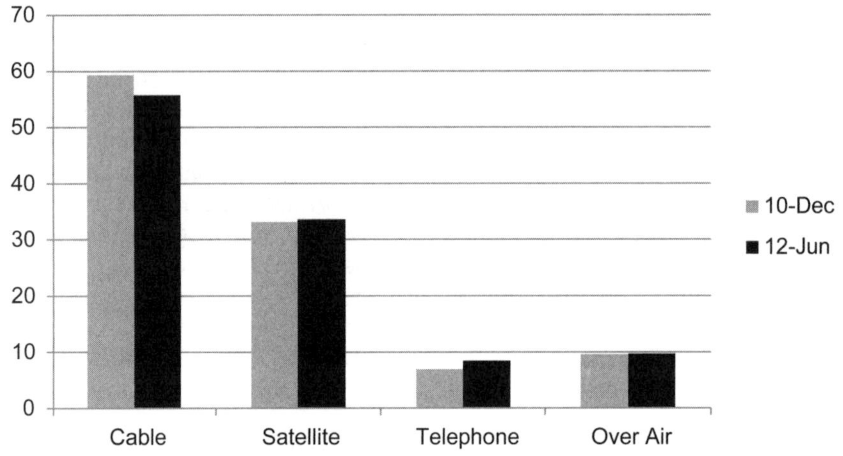

Source: W. Lesser. Data source FCC, "FCC Adopts 15th Report."

As one looks further ahead for Comcast, two aspects are evident. First, the company has grown since its founding as American Cable Systems in 1963 largely through mergers.[53] However as the government signaled through its opposition to the proposed AT&T merger with T-Mobile (see antitrust law review in Chapter 3, Section 3.5, for more on merger regulation) future merger approvals may prove far more difficult, particularly under Democratic presidents. At the same time technology changes (undoubtedly hastened by the ongoing steep price increases for cable service) are allowing video streaming, which along with rises in the use of satellite receivers is credited with reducing the number of cable subscribers, and Comcast's consumers in particular (Figure 8.7).

This uneasy, one might say unsustainable, situation with cable companies' eroding market share to Internet streaming sources began to take a new course in 2014. First up was a court rejection of a 1010 FCC rule covering "net neutrality."[54] Net neutrality is the approach that all Internet service providers (ISPs)—read Comcast, Verizon—should treat all traffic equally. The FCC rule supporting net neutrality was struck down on January 14, 2014, by the U.S. Court of Appeals, largely on a technicality. The commission has the legislative authority to regulate utilities like the telephone system, according to the court. But it has classified the Internet as an "information service," placing it outside the scope of FCC regulatory authority.[55]

The commission passed on the option to appeal the court ruling, choosing instead to revise the regulation. The May 15, 2014 revision allows ISPs to charge content companies—read Netflix and Google—for faster access to homes, with the proviso that those firms which do not pay for the enhanced service not be unfairly allocated to slower service. The plan, though, is short on details on just how the commission would measure and detect unfairness making consumer advocates suspicious but what the control mechanism will be inoperable. Concerns for consumers are threefold: first that ISP fees will be passed along to consumers, second that the system disadvantages start-ups with fewer resources to pay the fees compared to established firms, and most significantly than the large ISPs will become de facto gatekeepers of political speech and other online content.[56] The revision is open for comment until mid-September with the expectation of having a revision adopted by the end of 2014.

That is the regulatory situation. The industry has acted even more quickly. In February Netflix and Comcast reached an agreement under which Netflix is to pay Comcast for faster, more reliable access to Comcast's subscribers. The terms of the arrangement have not been made public but a knowledgeable observer places it at several million dollars annually.[57] A similar arrangement was established with Verizon within a few months, with the prediction of many more to follow.[58]

The big news though is a series of sector mega-mergers proposed in early 2014. First up was Comcast's offer to acquire Time Warner in an all-stock deal valued at $45.2 billion. If approved by shareholders and regulators, the combined firm would give Comcast a one-third share of the TV cable system and almost 40 percent of high-speed Internet access.[59] At present the two firms rank first and second in cable subscribers and one and three in broadband services. Not to be outdone, AT&T (second in broadband services) offered to buy DirectTV, the largest satellite-TV service provider, for $48.5 billion in cash and stock.[60] And finally, there is an ongoing expectation that Sprint will make an offer for T-Mobile.[61]

The involved firms are arguing that the combined firms will achieve real savings which can be used to improve consumer service, such as by expanding high-speed Internet access, particularly in rural areas.[62] But the real prizes seem to be accessing content—DirectTV, for example, would provide AT&T with access to National Football League Sunday games—while providing greater bargaining power with third-party content providers.[63] For regulators they must consider the effects on users of not just marginal changes but rather a complete restructuring of the communications sector. For example, are consumers better off with four notable mobile telephone providers or with a more forceful third firm if the Sprint–T-Mobile merger is approved (assuming of course it is proposed, as is widely expected)? The decisions being made now will affect the communications sector for decades and influence not just entertainment but basic information and business functions which increasingly flow through the Internet.

As regulators ponder these significant issues they should reflect on how past deregulation, the Telecommunications Act of 1996 in particular (see subsections 8.1f and 8.2 this chapter), led not to more competition, but less with higher prices. Service too has remained poor at those steeper prices. Time Warner Cable's Internet service recently was ranked 236th out of 236 companies or brands in the American Customer Satisfaction Index[64] while Internet speeds are far below levels in other countries. The average speed in the United States is 6.5 megabits per second, placing it just ahead of the Philippines. Japan by contrast has an average speed of 21.3 megabits per second.[65] In one aspect though the deals excel; the golden parachute proposal for the Time Warner CEO is valued at $80 million, subject to shareholder approval.

Americans are often led to believe they have the best of everything, but in the communications sector there is overwhelming evidence that just is not true. Much remains to be improved, and at lower costs. Greater consolidation has had the opposite effect on the sector in the past, with little justification that the currently proposed round, if approved, will lead to better outcomes for the public.

This case then focuses on growth strategies for Comcast operating as it does within regulatory limitations and technological change. However, considering the regulatory dimension requires some background into antitrust law and economics, which is presented in Chapter 3, Section 3.5.

b. Concentration in the Cable Industry

As described in Chapter 3, Section 3.5e, ownership concentration is often measured based on data from the Department of Commerce's Economic Census. That census classifies industries according to the two- to seven-digit North American Industry Classification System (NAICS), with the seven-digit industries the most detailed ones. For the cable system, three six-digit industries apply:

515210 Cable and Other Subscription Programming

This industry comprises establishments primarily engaged in operating studios and facilities for the broadcasting of programs on a subscription or fee basis. The broadcast programming is typically narrowcast in nature (e.g., limited format, such as news, sports, education, or youth-oriented). These establishments produce programming in their own facilities or acquire programming from external sources. The programming material is usually delivered to a third party, such as cable systems or direct-to-home satellite systems, for transmission to viewers.

517110 Wired Telecommunications Carriers

These establishments are primarily engaged in operating and/or providing access to transmission facilities and infrastructure that they own and/or lease for the transmission of voice, data, text, sound, and video using wired telecommunications networks. Transmission facilities may be based on a single technology or a combination of technologies. Establishments in this industry use the wired telecommunications network facilities that they operate to provide a variety of services, such as wired telephony services, including voice-over-Internet protocol (VoIP) services; wired (cable) audio and video programming distribution; and wired broadband Internet services. By exception, establishments providing satellite television distribution services using facilities and infrastructure that they operate are included in this industry.

Incorporating three seven-digit industries:

- **5171101 Wired telecommunications carriers:** Establishments engaged in (1) operating and maintaining switching and transmission facilities to provide point-to-point communications via landlines, microwave, or a combination of landlines and satellite linkups; or (2) furnishing telegraph and other nonvocal communications using their own facilities.

- **5171102 Cable and other program distribution:** Establishments primarily engaged as third-party distribution systems for broadcast programming. These establishments deliver visual, aural, or textual programming received from cable networks, local television stations, or radio networks to consumers via cable or direct-to-home satellite systems on a subscription or fee basis. These establishments do not generally originate programming material.
- **5171103 Internet service providers (broadband):** Establishments known as Internet service providers (ISPs) using broadband (cable, DSL) primarily engaged in providing clients access to the Internet and related services such as Web hosting, Web page designing, and hardware or software consulting related to Internet connectivity. These establishments may provide local, regional, or national coverage for clients or provide backbone services (except telecommunications carriers) for other ISPs.

517210 Wireless Telecommunications Carriers (Except Satellite)

This industry comprises establishments engaged in operating and maintaining switching and transmission facilities to provide communications via the airwaves. Establishments in this industry have spectrum licenses and provide services using that spectrum, such as cellular phone services, paging services, wireless Internet access, and wireless video services.

Data from the 2007 Economic Census provide the concentration values (rounded to the nearest tenth) for the cable industry in Table 8.2.

Additional details of cable merger entities are included in the FCC's review report,[66] which is required under the "public interest, convenience, and necessity" mandate of the commission. Regrettably, large sections, including equations and tables, have been redacted making it far more difficult to understand the review process and the data upon which it was based.

Table 8.2 **Concentration in the Cable Industry**

NAICS #	Sales $	CR4	CR8	CR20
517110	290.8b	57	73	86
5171101	186.0	76	83	89
5171102	100.4	68	88	95
5171103	4.3	34	49	67
515210	44.9b	62	79	94

Source: Compiled from Census Bureau Economic Census American Fact Finder.

c. Case Questions

Students are requested to prepare the following questions, noting that this case is a hypothetical in a rapidly evolving sector:

1. If Comcast were to propose an additional horizontal or vertical merger with a major player—say one of the top ten firms—do you believe the merger would be approved? Why or why not?

   Hints: The HHI (see Chapter 3, Section 3.5e) must be calculated from market share data; it is possible for the purposes of this case to use either sales or subscriber numbers in its calculation. Data on the "tail" of very small firm market shares are difficult to find and for this case may be ignored in the HHI calculation. That is to say, if fifty firms have a combined market share of thirty, then they individually add little to the computed HHI. Possible sources of data include the following Web site, and there are likely others:

   www.businessweek.com/ap/2012–03/D9TR15RO0.htm.

2. Will the ongoing decline in cable subscribers (even if revenues are holding up) likely have any effect on the Department of Justice's decision to allow or oppose the merger?
3. If additional mergers were to be denied to Comcast, what other growth strategies might it pursue?
4. What evolving services/products present a treat to Comcast's existing business operations? Are regulations implicated in establishing or thwarting those threats?

8.7 ■ CASE 8.5: HOLLYWOOD IN INDIA: PROTECTING INTELLECTUAL PROPERTY

Hollywood often draws heavily on nostalgia for creating its wares. But producers themselves may soon be nostalgic for the past when domestic box office receipts dominated earnings. That situation, though, has not applied for many years; in 2011 international sales contributed 69 percent of total revenues of $32.6 billion.[67] At the same time, competition from other sources of filmmaking has been advancing. Principal among these is "Bollywood," the name given to the Mumbai-based Indian film industry which produces twice as many movies annually as does Hollywood, about 1,000 in all. Bollywood receipts in 2011 were $3 billion, and rising by 10 percent annually.[68] Imitation may be flattery, but flattery is not profitable, so it was a matter of time before Hollywood film studios attempted to collaborate with their Indian counterparts.

This case applies to one such collaborative effort. How, though, does that involve regulation? Because movies are expensive forms of intellectual property (IP), property which can be and is easily appropriated. Just consider the many unauthorized music and movie copies available on the Web in the United States. And Indian IP is somewhat different in construct than similar systems in the United States, and very different in enforcement. Thus for U.S. studios making money in Indian film requires a careful management of IP in India. This case applies to one pioneering attempt by U.S. Fox Star Studios. Before proceeding though it is necessary to identify some of the ways U.S. and Indian IP regimes differ; more specific details are included in the case. U.S. IP systems are explored in Chapter 3, Section 3.6.

a. IP Issues in India

India has IP systems including patents, copyright, trademarks, and trade secret protection generally in line with the rest of the world. The reason is not coincidence or even necessarily perceived need but rather the outcome of the TRIPS harmonization agreements (see Chapter 3, Section 3.6f). There are nonetheless key regards in which Indian laws and practices differ from those in the United States, even if much of the world is more closely aligned with Indian law than that of the United States. For firms familiar with U.S. practice the differences can nonetheless be significant, critical. And then there are the India-only differences. We begin this brief overview by first looking at the differences in the law and then consider practice.

Patents (Patents Act of 1970, as Amended)

In line with TRIPS, India does not allow patents for plant varieties (e.g., seeds), but rather has a specialized system (known as a *sui generis* or special purpose system) commonly referred to as Plant Variety Protection (PVP) (The Protection of Plant Varieties and Farmers' Rights Act, 2001). Patents are allowed for microorganisms, as is required by TRIPS. As regards patenting genes, the guiding principles are to date a limited case law making generalizations difficult. The Indian Patent Office though has since 2002 granted patents for modified genes—the patentability of human genes is as yet untried—but isolated genes are not patentable by statute.[69]

Pharmaceutical patents have long been a conundrum in India due seemingly to a commitment not to outprice medicines for the poor as well as India's stature as the largest producer and exporter of generic drugs, an industry benefiting from not having patent protection. Until recently India allowed only product-by-process patents for pharmaceuticals and then for only seven years, which is to say not much protection at all. Following TRIPS, standard twenty-year product patents must be, and are being, allowed. However, the courts nonetheless take a determined stand on pharma patents. Recently, the international IP community has been jolted by the revocation of leading medicines in India based on lack of innovation. In 2012, India revoked patents granted to Pfizer Inc.'s cancer drug Sutent, Roche Holding AG's hepatitis C drug Pegasys, and Merck and Co.'s asthma treatment aerosol suspension formulation. Then in April 2013 India's Supreme Court rejected a patent for Novartis AG's cancer drug Glivec, calling it an amended version of a known molecule called imatinib.[70] While every national patent office has the right to interpret the innovativeness requirement (nonobviousness/inventive step) for national patents, the fact that India's, at least for pharma, are more stringent than those in major developed countries has caused consternation in the sector.

Another area where India takes a far stronger position than in the United States is in the granting of compulsory licenses. (In the United States, however, the courts frequently overturn patents for various reasons.) Compulsory licenses apply when the government overrides the right of the patent holder to exclude others by offering licenses or even revoking patents based on the lack of use (see Chapter 3, Section 3.6b). While the United States lacks general language for compulsory licenses, India in line with TRIPS permits them based on unfilled need and use. It should be noted that these same conditions are specifically allowed under TRIPS and are included in many national laws. Equitable royalty payments to the patent owner are required. Indian law further allows the rejection of patentability based on *morality* and *ordre public* (public order). While these terms are pliant and have not been fully scrutinized by the Indian courts, it is worth noting that the recent Supreme Court rejection of the Novartis drug Glivic (see immediately above) was based in part on public order. The high price of the medicine was judged to "seriously prejudice" the health of the poor.[71]

Copyright (Copyright Act of 1957, as Amended)

Indian copyright law has been amended every three years post-1957 with significant changes made in 2012 in the Copyright Amendment Bill of that year.[72]

Indian copyrights last for the life of the author plus sixty years except for films and sound recordings, which last sixty years, covering:

- Original literary, dramatic, musical, and artistic works
- Cinematographic films
- Sound recordings
- Computer programs

The 2012 amendments primarily extend the protection of artistic works, films, and recordings to the "storing" in any medium, including electronic. However, the act also extends the so-called "first sale" exclusion from literary, dramatic, and artistic works to films and sound recordings. The exclusion means that once the work has been sold, the new owner has a broad right to use it, as in movie rentals, but not extending to reproduction. Performers are now granted the right to receive royalties if a work is subject to commercial use.

Trademark (Trade Marks Act of 1999, as Amended)

In India a trademark can be acquired either through registration or "first use" anywhere in the world. Use may be anticipatory up to five years, although use must be within India. Often an advertisement or other limited act is sufficient to establish use. Well-known brands can prevent a similar mark (along of course with a fraudulently identical one) being used on an unrelated product on the basis of preventing dilution or tarnishing.[73]

Trademarks are granted for ten-year periods, and must be renewed. A mark must have at least one of the following characteristics:

- The name of a company, individual, or firm represented in a particular or special manner
- The signature of the applicant for registration
- One or more invented words
- One or more words having no direct reference to the character or quality of the goods excluding the exceptions listed below
- Any other distinctive trademark
- A trademark which has acquired distinctiveness by use over a prolonged period of time

Trade Secrets

India lacks formal legislation governing the protection of trade secrets, the misappropriation of confidential information. Rather, confidential information and trade secrets are protected through contracts such as employment (nondisclosure and confidentiality) or technology transfer (licensing) agreements. Such clauses, however, place no restrictions on anyone not a direct party who somehow acquired the confidential information. Moreover, Indian courts have been reluctant to enforce restrictive covenants and nondisclosure agreements, considering them unenforceable under the Indian Contract Act of 1872. Thus, the only remedy is through civil law.[74]

Enforcement

IP is personal property, meaning it is the responsibility of the owner to seek rectification. These are not criminal cases for which the state acts. And seeking justice brings one before the court system, which in India is not a happy position to be in. Presently there is a backlog of some 32 million cases of all kinds, 26 percent of which have been pending for more than five years, some for thirty years or more. Part of the problem is a shortage of judges; 25 percent of seats are vacant leaving only 10.5 judges per million population compared to 107 in the United States and 159 in China. This is in part attributable to a system which allows frequent delays as a legal tactic. Concerned the decision will go against you? Simply delay final judgment.[75]

And then there is, there always is, the issue of corruption, which is endemic in India. One group, Transparency International, a nongovernmental organization, attempts to measure and rank the degree of corruption in different nations. For India in 2012, 54 percent of the population reported having paid a bribe; countries range from 1 to 84 percent of citizens paying bribes. On a 1 (low) to 5 scale of perceptions of corruption in the judiciary, India ranks 3.3 (range is 1.7–4.6).[76] So India is far from the worst nation, but the chances of corruption influencing the outcome of a court case are very present, and worrying.

Further complicating IP cases is technical complexity. Courts must determine how similar two products must be to constitute infringement. Often these are highly technical issues. Further compounding the decision is the requirement that the judgment must reflect the state of the art at the time of creation, not the present. For fast-moving science fields, tasks which must be performed by experienced PhDs can be reduced to the level of high-school experiments in merely a decade. Often courts lack the technical sophistication to address such matters in a satisfactory manner leading to major errors and bad law.

b. Case Questions

Students should prepare the following questions, based on the Harvard Business School cases:

Hollywood in India: Protecting Intellectual Property (A) # 711-017

Hollywood in India: Protecting Intellectual Property (B) # 711-018

1. How can a movie studio prevent plagiarism in India?
2. What strategies should Fox Star adopt to combat potential piracy of *My Name Is Khan*? For your answer please estimate the costs and benefits of each approach you identify.
3. Do the copyright modifications of 2012 that occurred after the case was written change any of the strategies identified for question 2 above?
4. If you were a Fox Star executive given the opportunity to change one component of one of the Indian IP laws, what would you choose, and why?

8.8 CONCLUSIONS

Regulating a critical, complex, and technologically dynamic industry like communications is a difficult and, frankly, tedious task. The underlying issue for cable is the large economies-of-scale market failure, to which rate-of-return regulation is typically applied. The crowding-out aspect of uncontrolled use of the airwaves is an example of the overuse of a public resource, the Tragedy of the Commons. In these cases, though, the regulatory process is additionally burdened by technological change, the public ownership of the air waves, and the public safety and education aspects of communication, as well as changing social mores. This is not an easy undertaking for either the regulators, or the regulated.

Limitations in the regulatory approaches applied are easy to identify and critique: Why was AT&T broken up only to be allowed to reassemble? Why did efforts to invigorate competition through deregulation fail so badly? Regulatory successes though should not be overlooked: The United States has had excellent and innovative telephone and cable systems. The most evident failing has been in maintaining low prices. Divestiture through antitrust is an effective if very blunt instrument with the ultimate outcome dependent on subsequent regulatory actions.

A proposal for à la carte sales of cable channels is a reasonable option to achieve lower user costs. The industry is disinclined, so there is a clear role for a regulatory mandate, even if that option seems unlikely. Rather, "reform" will likely come through technological change as users move away from cable, an effective but perhaps not the quickest nor most efficient route.

Regulating the media involves more than economics, and changes in attitudes greatly complicate the process. The public is now much more accepting of graphic acts and language on TV so long as efforts are made to shield younger viewers. These looser attitudes were not always the case, and the regulatory system has had to adjust. Perhaps more significant is changes to mandating "balanced" reporting and prohibiting political attack ads. True, the past regulatory justification based on "scarcity" of the airways has been supplanted by technological advances, and it is difficult given the current public mind-set to imagine banning almost anything from the airwaves. But the consequences of deregulation have been far greater political polarization and a less informed public, which is threatening the very effectiveness of democratic governance. Perhaps there is a continuing role for regulation divorced from a single focus on efficiency?

Returning to the commercial sphere, internationalization and rapid technological progress are necessitating more international activities by U.S.-based firms. That need brings them into direct contact with other nations' IP systems. IP law is national but harmonization is essential. Strides were made in the 1990s but more is needed.

The first three cases emphasize the natural monopoly dimension of communications, be it by air or wire. This makes it difficult to develop a competitive sector, but as the Paragould, Arkansas, case demonstrates, entry is possible if the initial focus is on service and not necessarily profit maximization. Or did Paragould simply receive unfair subsidies? The fourth case highlights the fact that it is far easier to prevent a highly concentrated sector through limiting mergers than it is to deal with a concentrated sector once it exists. The merger issue is very much before the FCC and other governmental agencies as Comcast and Time Warner, AT&T and DirectTV, and (widely expected but not presented as this book goes to press) Sprint–T-Mobile. Decisions being made now, including the future of net neutrality, will influence the communications sector for decades.

And the international case, the fifth, points to the role of IP rights as critical regulatory acts enabling internationalization of business, but with the limitation that the laws are national and so complex to manage and oft inadequate from the perspective of the international investor.

8.9 STUDY QUESTIONS

1. While the Comcast "merger" case above (this chapter, Section 8.6) is hypothetical, the DOJ during summer 2013 did indicate an intent to block a proposed merger between U.S. Airways and American Airlines, which would have created the largest U.S. national carrier. (The merger was subsequently approved with some modest limitations.) What were the issues involved, or alternatively on what analysis did the DOJ make its decision to oppose the merger? Some observers complained that

it was not fair to block U.S. Airways/American when it had recently allowed large mergers between Delta and Northwest (2009) and United and Continental (2010). Do you agree with that position, and why? Were there any new or additional issues involved in the recent proposal which did not apply previously?

2. If Viacom is sued under the antitrust laws for requiring bundled channel sales to cable companies, what law(s) would it likely be charged under?
3. Indian IP law is clearly "weaker" than that in the United States and other developed countries in numerous regards, which presumably should limit the inventive/creative industries there in some way(s). Can you identify an example in any sector where that limitation is evident?
4. Trace the Fairness Doctrine including the effects that technological change has had on this policy.
5. Identify the key court decisions in the communications sector and their lasting effects.
6. Describe the regulations controlling access to and payment for local programming. What have the effects of these regulations been on firms and viewers?
7. While competition is desirable, "too much" competition can be problematic as well. Please identify examples of excessive competition in the communications sector and how regulation was designed to rectify these problems.
8. Two major antitrust actions were the breakups of Standard Oil and AT&T. What were the parallels leading up to those actions and the long-term consequences of the forced divestitures?
9. What regulations and public benefits can be cited as justification for the reclaiming of underused TV bandwidth to be allocated to smartphones and the like?
10. Develop an argument against the à la carte channel offerings on cable.
11. Discuss the merits of using the NAICS measures of concentration in the cable sector versus using the HHI based on cable providers' revenues or subscriber numbers.
12. For each of the five cases presented here please identify the regulatory act or acts on which they are based.
13. For each of the five cases please identify if there was a market failure which the regulation is intended, even partially, to address.
14. Discuss the appropriateness of using as a base for tracking cable bills over time either (a) the average bill, (b) price per channel offered, or (c) price per viewing hour.
15. Suppose the tide was turned, as the saying goes, and an Indian film studio sought to invest in a U.S.-based movie. What kinds of IP issue might it expect to encounter, such as streaming and the like?
16. If cable has many of the attributes of a natural monopoly, why has it been treated so differently from utilities regarding regulatory requirements?
17. How do the FCC decisions on the proposed Comcast-Time Warner, AT&T-DirectTV, and (expected) Sprint–T-Mobile fit with past regulatory decisions? What do those decisions say about the FCC's vision of the future of the communications sector?

NOTES

1. Wikipedia, "History of AT&T." Available at http://en.wikipedia.org/wiki/History_of_AT%26T. Winlab Rutgers, "LL1.doc The History of AT&T)." Available at www.winlab.rutgers.edu. Both last visited 8/30/13.

2. *Hush-A-Phone Corporation vs. United States*, 238 F.2d 266 (1956). Available at http://scholar.google.com/scholar_case?case=3157605393289179824&q=Hush-A-Phone+v.+United+States&hl=en&as_sdt=2,33&as_vis=1. Last visited 8/28/13.

3. Legal History of Telecommunication. Available at www.technologyforall.com/TechForAll/legalHistory.html. Last visited 8/28/13.

4. Ibid.

5. Corporate History, "AT&T Inc." Available at http://transition.fcc.gov/wcb/armis/carrier_filing_history/COSA_History/attr.htm. Last visited 8/30/13.

6. Mark Goodman, "The Radio Act of 1927 as a Product of Progressivism." Vol. 2, No. 2. Available at www.scripps.ohiou.edu/mediahistory/mhmjour2–2.htm. Last visited 11/3/11.

7. Fritz Messere, "Analysis of the Federal Communications Commission." In *Encyclopedia of Television.* Available at www.oswego.edu/~messere/FCC1.html. Last visited 11/3/11.

8. FCC, "Fact Sheet, Cable Television." Available at http://transition.fcc.gov/mb/facts/csgen.html. Last visited 11/4/11.

9. Museum of Broadcast Communications, "United States: Cable Television." Available at www.museum.tv/eotvsection.php?entrycode=unitedstatesc. Last visited 11/4/11.

10. FCC, "Telecommunications Act of 1996." Available at http://transition.fcc.gov/telecom.html. Russell H. Mouritsen, "Telecommunications Act of 1996: Relationships to Functional Theory." Available at https://43f7cb640225fbfc67686e0928f1de5be0b26d7e.googledrive.com/host/0BwYZA6eD9SMqN0k5QV9YMkhGZ00/Perspectives/Perspectives2002/Mouritsen.htm. Both last visited 7/14/14.

11. FCC, "The FCC's Satellite Home Viewer Improvement Act Page." Available at http://transition.fcc.gov/mb/shva/. Last visited 11/4/11.

12. Museum of Broadcast Communications, "United States: Cable Television."

13. 1995 *Television and Cable Factbook,* quoted in ibid.

14. A. C. Nielsen data of 1995, quoted in Museum of Broadcast Communications, "United States: Cable Television."

15. Quoted in ibid.

16. General Accounting Office (GAO), "Issues Related to Competition and Subscriber Rates in the Cable Television Industry." GAO-04–8, October 2003, p. 22. Available at www.gao.gov/new.items/d048.pdf. Last visited 11/6/11.

17. Matt Solinsky, "A la carte ESPN could cost consumers $30 per month." My Dessert.com, July 16, 2013. Available at http://voices.mydesert.com/2013/07/16/a-la-carte-espn-could-cost-consumers-30-per-month/. Last visited 8/21/13.

18. U.S. Public Interest Research Group (PIRG), "The Failure of Cable Deregulation: A Blueprint for Creating a Competitive, Pro-Consumer Cable Television Marketplace." August 2003. Available at http://cdn.publicinterestnetwork.org/assets/qZPECxJiK5daxX6nCmUS8g/failureofcabledereg.pdf. Last visited 11/4/11.

19. Ibid.

20. *Consumer Reports,* "Cut Your Telecom Bill." June 2012, p. 21. Cable share data from Cable Metrics—Nat. Cable & Communications Association. Available at www.ncta.com/Statistics.aspx. Last visited 5/8/12.

21. GAO, "Issues Related to Competition and Subscriber Rates in the Cable Television Industry," Table 3; Cable Prices Equation.

22. Gene Kimmelman, "Testimony on Cable Television and the Dangers of Deregulation." Consumers Union, May 6, 2003. Available at www.consumersunion.org/pdf/0506-cable.pdf. Last visited 11/4/11.

23. FCC results quoted in U.S. PIRG, "The Failure of Cable Deregulation," pp. 29–30.

24. "Bundles and Bulk: AT&T Buys DirectTV." *The Economist*, May 24, 2014, pp. 58 & 60.

25. U.S. PIRG, "The Failure of Cable Deregulation."

26. Reported in GAO, "Issues Related to Competition and Subscriber Rates in the Cable Television Industry," p. 80.

27. Reported in ibid., p. 84.

28. FCC, "Auctions." Available at www.fcc.gov/topic/auctions. Last visited 12/21/11.

29. Congressional Budget Office, "Where Do We Go from Here? The FCC Auctions and the Future of Radio Spectrum Management." April 1997. Available at www.cbo.gov/doc.cfm?index=9&type=0&sequence=1. Last visited 12/22/11.

30. Peter Cramton, "The Efficiency of the FCC Spectrum Auctions." *Journal of Law and Economics,* 41 (1998): 727–736.

31. Govtrack.us, "S.911, SPECTRUM Act." Available at https://www.govtrack.us/congress/bills/112/s911. Last visited 6/6/14.

32. National Association of Broadcasters, "The Potential Impact of the FCC's National Broadcast Plan on Broadcasters and Viewers." July 2011. Available at www.nab.org/documents/newsRoom/pdfs/072511_spectrum_presentation.pdf. Last visited 12/22/11.

33. Table C4. "Twenty Largest U.S. Publicly Owned Electric Utilities Ranked by Purchase Power Expenses for All Respondents, 2000." Available at www.eia.gov/cneaf/electricity/public/tc4p01p1.html. Last visited 8/24/12.

34. "Municipal Broadband: The Need for Speed." *The Economist,* August 11, 2012. Available at www.economist.com/node/21560288. Last visited 8/24/12.

35. Sean Buckley, "Chattanooga's EPB Fiber defies tough telecom odds." FierceTelecom, February 24, 2012. Available at www.fiercetelecom.com/story/chattanoogas-epb-fiber-defies-tough-telecom-odds/2012–02–24. Last visited 8/24/12.

36. Ellis Smith, "EPB, AT&T, and Comcast Compete for Chattanooga Customers." *Timesfreepress,* December 5, 2011.

37. EPB, "Standard & Poors Upgrades EPB's Bond Rating to AA+." October, 20, 2012. Available at www.epb.net/news/news-archive/standard-poors-upgrades-epbs-bond-rating-to-aa/. Last visited 10/2/13.

38. San Bruno Municipal Cable TV. Available at www.sanbrunocable.com/. Last visited 6/5/14.

39. John Murawski, "Cable TV fights municipal broadband." NewsObserver.com, June 22, 2010. Available at www.newsobserver.com/2010/06/22/545221/cable-tv-fights-municipal-broadband.html. Last visited 6/5/14.

40. Erin Joyce, "Comcast, AT&T Broadband Close Merger." *InternetNews.com,* November 18, 2001. Jeffrey F. Rayport, "Cable TV vs. Cable Broadband." *Businessweek,* June 3, 2009. Kristen Hamill, "U.S. Approves Comcast-NBC Merger." CNN, January 18, 2011. Available at http://money.cnn.com/2011/01/18/technology/fcc_comcast_nbc/index.htm. Last visited 11/8/11.

41. Details at FCC, Memorandum Option and Order, FCC 11–4, revised January 20, 2011. Available at http://transition.fcc.gov/FCC-11-4.pdf. Last visited 11/10/11.

42. Kirsten Acuna, "The Death of TV: Comcast Lost Nearly 400,000 Cable Subscribers in Last Year." *Business Insider,* August 1, 2012.

43. Amy Chozick, "Higher Cable Bills Help Comcast Increase Profit by 17 Percent." *New York Times,* May 1, 2013.

44. Acuna, "The Death of TV."

45. Franklin McMahon, "CBS/Time Warner Fight Helps Slowly Unravel Cable TV." Broadcast Engineering Blog, August 19, 2013. Available at http://broadcastengineering.com/blog/cbs-time-warner-fight-helps-slowly-unravel-cable-tv. Last visited 8/22/13.

46. Roger Yu, "CBS, Time Warner Cable Lift Blackout for Mayor Debates." *USA Today,* August 22, 2013.

47. Jonathan Berr, "The Time Has Come for a la Carte Pricing" *Investor Place,* August 21, 2013.

48. Matt Solinsky, "A la cart ESPN could cost consumers $30 per month." *Sports Blog,* July 16, 2013. Available at http://voices.mydesert.com/2013/07/16/a-la-carte-espn-could-cost-consumers-30-per-month/. Last visited 8/22/13.

49. Summary: S.912—113th Congress (2013–2014). Available at http://beta.congress.gov/bill/113th/senate-bill/912. Last visited 8/22/13.

50. Quoted in Alex Ben Block, "Broadcasters, MPAA Line Up against Proposed a la Carte Bill." *Hollywood Reporter,* August 2, 2013. Available at www.hollywoodreporter.com/print/598054. Last visited 8/22/13.

51. Solinsky, "A la Cart ESPN Could Cost Consumers $30 per Month."

52. Berr, "The Time Has Come for a la Carte Pricing."

53. History available at Wikipedia, "Comcast." Available at http://en.wikipedia.org/wiki/Comcast. Last visited 11/8/11.

54. FCC 10-102, December 23, 2010. Available at https://apps.fcc.gov/edocs_public/attachmatch/FCC-10-201A1_Rcd.pdf. Last visited 6/6/14.

55. Cecelia Kang, "Court Strikes Down FCC 'Net Neutrality' Rule." *Washington Post,* January 15, 2014. Available at www.washingtonpost.com/business/technology/court-creates-new-game-for-web-access-in-america/2014/01/14/539c9a2a-7d3e-11e3-95c6-0a7aa80874bc_print.html. Last visited 6/6/14.

56. Cecelia Kang, "FCC Chair Tries to Salvage Net Neutrality Plan, Promises To Be Strong Cop in Revised Rules." *Washington Post,* May 11, 2014. Available at www.washingtonpost.com/blogs/the-switch/wp/2014/05/11/fcc-chair-tries-to-salvage-net-neutrality-plan-promises-to-be-strong-cop-in-revised-rules//?print=1. Last visited 6/6/14.

57. Edward Wyatt and Noam Cohenfeb, "Comcast and Netflix Reach Deal on Service." *New York Times,* February 23, 2014. Available at www.nytimes.com/2014/02/24/business/media/comcast-and-netflix-reach-a-streaming-agreement.html?_r=0. Last visited 6/6/14.

58. Kwame Opam, "After Comcast, Netflix signs a traffic deal with Verizon." *Verge,* April 28, 2014. Available at www.theverge.com/2014/4/28/5662580/netflix-signs-traffic-deal-with-verizon. Last visited 6/6/14.

59. Wyatt and Cohenfeb, "Comcast and Netflix Reach Deal on Service."

60. "Bundles and Bulk: AT&T Buys DirectTV." *The Economist*, May 24, 2014, pp. 58 & 60.

61. Michael J. de la Merced, "The Biggest Champion of a Sprint–T-Mobile Deal: SoftBank's Chief." *New York Times,* June 5, 2014. Available at http://dealbook.nytimes.com/2014/06/05/the-biggest-champion-of-a-sprint-t-mobile-deal-softbanks-chief/. Last visited 6/6/14.

62. "Bundles and Bulk: AT&T Buys DirectTV." *The Economist.*

63. Ibid.

64. Bob Ferandez, "Time Warner Cable Shareholders' Meeting: Lacking in Comcast Drama." *The Inquirer,* June 6, 2014. Available at /www.philly.com/philly/business/20140606_Time_Warner_Cable_shareholders__meeting__Lacking_in_Comcast_drama.html. Last visited 6/6/14.

65. de la Merced, "The Biggest Champion of a Sprint–T-Mobile Deal: SoftBank's Chief."

66. FCC, Memorandum Option and Order.

67. Pamela McClintock, "Global Box Office Hit $32.6 Billion in 2011, Fueled by Exploding International Growth." *Hollywood Reporter,* March 22, 2012. Available at www.hollywoodreporter.com/print/303324. Last visited 9/3/13.

68. Palash Ghosh, "Bollywood at 100: How Big Is India's Mammoth Film Industry?" *International Business Times,* May 3, 2013. Available at www.ibtimes.com/bollywood-100-how-big-indias-mammoth-film-industry-1236299. Last visited 9/3/13.

69. Bhavishyavani Ravi, "Gene Patents in India: Gauging Policy by an Analysis of the Grants Made by the Indian Patent Office." *Journal of Intellectual Property Rights* 18 (July 2013): 323–329. Available at http://nopr.niscair.res.in/bitstream/123456789/20283/1/JIPR%2018%284%29%20323–329.pdf. Last visited 9/4/13. See also IIPTA, "15 New Guidelines for Examining Biotech Patent Applications." Available at www.iipta.com/ipr/blog/15-new-guidelines-examining-biotech-patent-applications-1055. Last visited 9/4/13.

70. "Update 2–India revokes GSK cancer drug patent in latest Big Pharma blow." Reuters, August 2, 2013. Available at www.reuters.com/article/2013/08/02/india-gsk-idUSL4N0G318920130802. Last visited 9/4/13.

71. "Public Health and IP in India: Novartis Loses Gleevec Patent Appeal at the Supreme Court." *Time,* April 3, 2013. Available at http://ipkitten.blogspot.com/2013/04/public-health-and-ip-in-india-novartis.html. Last visited 9/4/13.

72. Abhai Pandey, "Inside Views: Development in Indian IP Law: The Copyright (Amendment) Act of 2012." Intellectual Property Watch. Available at www.ip-watch.org/2013/01/22/development-in-indian-ip-law-the-copyright-amendment-act-2012/print/. Last visited 9/4/13.

73. Shwetasree Majumder et al., "Indian Trademark Law: A Comparison with EU and U.S. Laws." *INTABulletin* 65, 7 (April 1, 2010). Available at www.inta.org/INTABulletin/Pages/IndianTrademarkLawAComparisonwithEUandUSLaws.aspx#. Last visited 9/4/13.

74. For more detail see, for example, A.S. Dalal, "Law Relating to Trade Secrets in India." *IUP Law Review* 2, 4 (October 2012): 5–27. Available at SSRN: http://ssrn.com/abstract=2185310. Last visited 9/4/13.

75. Sunrita Sen, "Backlog Stalls Justice in India." *IOLnews,* January 21, 2013. Available at http://www.iol.co.za/news/world/backlog-stalls-justice-in-india-1.1455345#.Uiecg3-yBrA. Last visited 9/4/13.

76. Transparency International, "Global Corruption Barometer 2013." Available at http://issuu.com/transparencyinternational/docs/2013_globalcorruptionbarometer_en/1?e=2496456/3903358. Last visited 9/4/13.

9 The Hodgepodge of Financial Regulation and Deregulation

Chapter Objectives

The management of money and assets is a complex matter whether at the national or personal level. We as a nation were ambivalent about the role and even existence of a national bank until the Panic of 1907 made its continued absence untenable, leading to the passage of the Federal Reserve Act of 1913. The next round of banking regulation followed the Great Depression.

As these examples indicate, regulation followed financial traumas, while deregulation crept in when lessons learned were unlearned. The objective of this chapter is an understanding of the forms and effects of financial regulation following the ongoing Great Recession. Two examples of those vast and evolving regulations are examined: the 2010 Dodd-Frank Act and its effect on smaller banks and the JOBS (Jumpstart Our Business Startups) Act of 2012. The passage of the Dodd-Frank Act was followed rapidly by a partial relaxation in requirements in order to enhance funding options for start-ups. Relief for small businesses came in the JOBS Act, which is discussed as it applied to the 2012 Facebook initial public offering (IPO; see Section 9.6f of this chapter).

That said, it is not possible to understand the motivations or the public or private consequences of Dodd-Frank and the JOBS Act without some appreciation of past actions (and inactions), as follows:

Regulation:

Glass-Steagall Act (1933): Due to speculation by banks using depositors' funds, this act separated commercial from investment banking, disallowed insurance underwriting, and created the *Federal Deposit Insurance Corporation* (FDIC) to insure deposits.

Securities Exchange Act (1934): Created the Securities and Exchange Commission (SEC), which mandates financial disclosures for shareholders while prohibiting certain fraudulent activities (such as insider trading).

Deregulation and Consequences:

Garn-St. Germain Depository Institutions Act (1982): Relaxed requirements for Savings & Loans (S&L), a class of banks, giving more latitude in mortgage lending and in raising funds in riskier ways. The consequence was the S&L collapse of the 1980s, which cost taxpayers $124 billion.

Gramm-Leach-Bliley Act (1999): Revoked parts of Glass-Steagall, allowing the mixing of investment and commercial banking activities.

Regulation:

Sarbanes-Oxley Act (2002): A response to the collapse of Enron and then WorldCom, six months later, debacles caused by fraudulent financial reporting. This act requires accurate statements, including off-balance sheet liabilities, mandates internal control mechanisms, and imposes criminal penalties.

Dodd-Frank Act (2012): Adopted in the wake of the subprime mortgage crisis and the $700 billion federal bailout—the Troubled Asset Relief Program (TARP)—Dodd-Frank is having widespread effects (such as regulating the hedge fund industry), even while many detailed regulations remain pending. Particularly controversial components are the Volcker Rule prohibiting banks from proprietary trading, and the "too big to fail" stipulation, limiting responses to liquidation. Turf uncertainty between the SEC and the Commodity Futures Trading Commission (CFTC), which regulates futures and options, has led to complications concerning regulation of swap markets. Incorporated in Dodd-Frank is Basel III, an international agreement raising bank equity requirements.

Key Terms and Agencies: *Commodity Futures Trading Commission (CFTC); Federal Deposit Insurance Corporation (FDIC); Fannie Mae; Freddie Mac; Federal Reserve Act of 1913; Glass-Steagall Act; Sarbanes-Oxley Act; Dodd-Frank Act; JOBS Act; Volcker Rule; Basel III; Great Depression; Futures; Option; Swap; Emerging growth companies; Crowdfunding; Stress test; Initial Public Offering (IPO); Subprime mortgage crisis; "Too big to fail"; Troubled Asset Relief Program (TARP); Blue sky laws*

Any undergraduate can commiserate with, if not fully appreciate, the complexities of banking for college students in past years. In this case the student was me and the place Seattle, Washington.

Come 2:30 P.M. every Friday I would suddenly recall that the banks closed for the weekend at 3 P.M. (a practice known then as "bankers hours") and as there were no automatic teller machines (ATMs) in those days and local merchants were as suspicious as now of accepting checks from students, while credit cards were not for the likes of college students, missing closing time meant a lean weekend indeed. So I chased up there—I cannot recall the name of the bank but it was a Washington State bank for in those days there were no multistate banks—and withdrew my weekly stipend in $2 bills (Figure 9.1). The bills had nothing to do with banking per se, just something a little different with which to entertain myself.

This little anecdote is intended to highlight the changes in personal banking over the years: state banks are disappearing, bank branches work largely through ATMs, and many transactions bypass cash altogether in favor of plastic. Some of these changes are attributable to technological and managerial innovations, but as we shall see, no

Figure 9.1 **Legal Tender**

Source: Public Domain Clip Art. Original source Department of Treasury.

small aspect is the consequence of regulatory adjustments. Other less visible changes are under way as well in higher levels of finance. Stock and futures exchanges, for example, are shifting—some already have—from floor trading to electronic transactions (Figure 9.2).

All the news, though, is not happy for there have been two major financial meltdowns—the Great Depression (1929–1940 or so) and the Great Recession (December 2007 to June 2009)—not that one would have noticed by 2014 that the recession is over.

This chapter discusses the rises and falls of the U.S. financial system and the regulatory responses. Section 9.1 focuses on crises and responses up until the 1930s, Section 9.2 describes regulations adopted during the Great Depression and its aftermath, while Section 9.3 examines the period 1940–2007. Section 9.4 examines in more detail the causes of the Great Recession and its regulatory aftermath, which remains very much a work in progress.

As always in this volume, attention is principally focused on regulations and their consequences and opportunities for business. The treatment of causes is included only to help understand the motivation for the regulations, and enhance an appreciation of whether the invoked regulations will indeed address the underlying issues. For the Great Recession, though, the causes remain only imperfectly understood, which further complicates the business/regulatory environment. Finally, in Section 9.5 we proceed to a case regarding Tompkins Financial, and Section 9.6 discusses a case regarding the Facebook IPO and the JOBS Act.

Just because the causes of the Great Recession are incompletely understood by the experts does not mean there are not lots of strongly held opinions. The Occupy Wall Street movement as it spread worldwide represented one pole. The message was not concise, focused, but it greatly enhanced attention to the widening distribution of income in the

Figure 9.2 **Floor Trading of Equities, Going, Going . . . Passé**

Source: Wikimedia Commons. Original source Ryan Lawler.

United States, as well as anger over the bailouts of banks during the threatened collapse of the banking system in 2007–2008 (Figure 9.3).

From a very different perspective, a number of contenders for the Republican 2012 presidential nomination saw regulation as the problem and its lifting as a solution. Republican presidential candidate Mitt Romney during the 2012 campaign pledged to repeal Dodd-Frank and replace it with a "streamlined framework" of financial regulation that would be simpler and less burdensome for banks.[1]

9.1 Bringing Order to a Fragmented System: Banking Regulation to the 1930s

a. The First and Second Bank of the United States[2]

The apparent confusion in banking and financial regulation at present has a long history, dating back indeed to the Founding Fathers. Secretary of the Treasury Alexander Hamilton saw the need for a central bank, while others such as Thomas Jefferson—whose vision was one of independent farmers, yeomen—saw a danger in such a powerful central institution. The role of a national bank was to manage the government's money and credit. In that instance, in 1791, Hamilton prevailed, although questions of the constitutionality of

Figure 9.3 **Example of Occupy Wall Street's Focus on Income Inequality and Bank Bailouts**

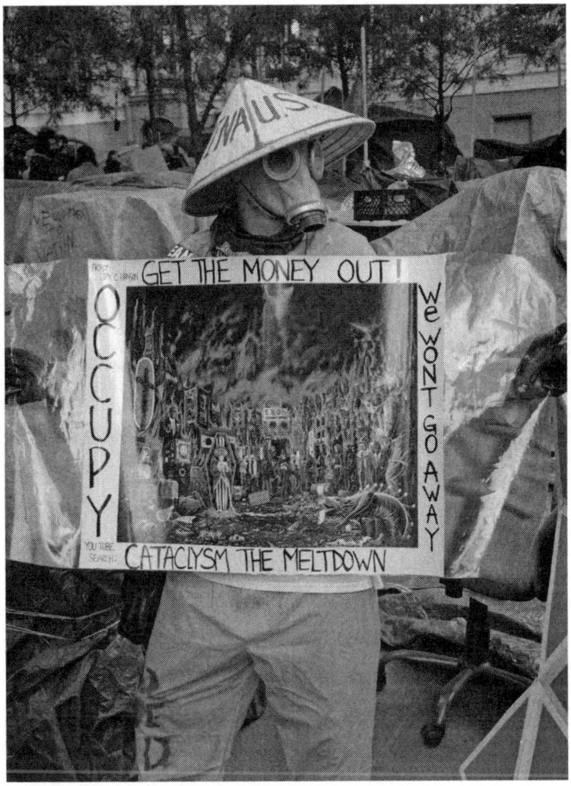

Source: Wikimedia Commons. Original author JoeInQueens.

a federal bank—no such institution is authorized in the Constitution—have persisted to this day even though the issue was decided positively and unanimously by the Supreme Court in *McCulloch vs. Maryland* (1819).[3]

This First Bank, managed by twenty-five directors, five public and twenty private, soon became a national bank, and indeed the largest corporation in the United States at the time. The bank, however, was chartered for only twenty years, and when the charter expired in 1811 the bill to recharter it failed. In that round, the Jeffersonian Republicans prevailed. Chaos ensued, in part because the government lacked a central system for managing banking and credit, including marketing its securities. To complicate matters, the nation was again at war with Great Britain, the War of 1812.

The Second Bank of the United States was chartered in 1816, again for twenty years. It functioned much like the First Bank but was much larger. Its size enhanced concerns about its possible role as a threat to democracy during that populist era. When vetoing a rechartering bill, President Andrew Jackson evoked the dangers of "such a concentration of power in the hands of a few men irresponsible to the people." The Second Bank then disappeared when its charter expired in 1836.

Figure 9.4 **Dubious Legal Tender: State Chartered Banks Issued Their Own Banknotes in the Absence of a National Bank**

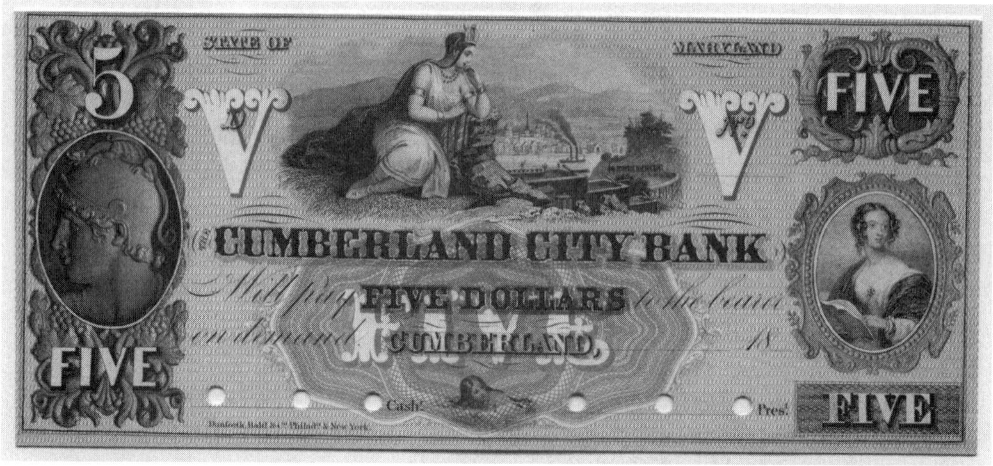

Source: Wikimedia Commons. Cumberland City Bank of Cumberland, Maryland, 1800s.

Into this gap stepped state chartered banks, which even issued their own banknotes, of varying value (Figure 9.4). By 1920, there were almost 30,000 banks in the United States, more than the rest of the world put together.[4] Some argue that the fees for state chartered banks became a major source of state revenue, to the point where states, protecting their own economic interest, vehemently opposed a national bank. Some states also allowed state chartered banks to sell insurance (the insurance sector remains predominately state-regulated), and so there was another sector opposed to seeing a national banking system established.[5] A state-centric view of banking, as we will see, carried over through the 1970s.

Other limitations of the decentralized, state-based banking system were the great variations in the money supply, which carried over into prices. Moreover the bank reserve levels that supported the issued currencies as well as loans were erratic and all too often inadequate.

b. National Banking Act of 1863

For all the anguish caused by the Civil War, it did have the effect of speeding the U.S. economy, beginning in the North, in the transformation from a rural agricultural base to an urban industrial one. The new economic system, and indeed the war itself, could not have advanced without a more focused banking system. That change took the form of the National Banking Act of 1863, with the following major components:

- Created nationally chartered banks
- Established stringent capital requirements for those banks
- Mandated reserves for both banknotes and deposits
- Effectively provided for (through the mechanism of taxing state banknotes out of existence) the issuance of banknotes only by those banks

This act, though, did not extinguish state-chartered banks. They were able to endure as a result of the expansion of demand deposits—also known as checking accounts—that provided a new source of funds at a time the use of checks was growing rapidly.

These are the achievements of the National Banking Act. It, though, did not establish the centralization of reserves. Rather, reserves were held by individual banks with some classes of banks required to place reserves with higher echelon banks. Three tiers of banks were created: rural banks, forty-seven reserve city banks, and three central reserve banks. Since the reserve requirements were inflexible and to be held in either government securities or cash, the money and credit supply depended on the changing value of the government securities.

That system placed a burden on rural banks when cash requirements rose during harvest season and then drew on their reserves at the reserve banks, which put the latter's reserve holdings under pressure. The problems only became more acute as rapid industrialization raised the needs for credit. With limitations in credit, depressions became more frequent, occurring in 1873 and 1893, after the country had endured ones in 1807 and 1837. Not good.

But it was the financial panic of 1907 that finally led to a recognition that banking regulation was not all it should be. The 1907 crisis resulted from a failed speculation that led to the collapse of two New York brokerage firms and in turn to runs on banks in New York City and other American cities in October and early November 1907 (Figure 9.5). The root cause, though, was on the other coast—the 1906 San Francisco fire drew gold out of the world's major money centers creating a liquidity crunch that caused a recession starting in June 1907.[6] Something finally would be done about unstable banking practices, but it would take some years.

c. Creation of the Federal Reserve

Initial responses to the Panic of 1907 were limited and largely ineffectual. The Aldrich-Vreeland Act (1908) allowed national banks to issue notes on a wider range of securities than previously permitted. In addition to federal government bonds, the act allowed banks to use the bonds of states, cities, and counties, along with commercial paper. The effect of that liberalization of policy was to put more money into circulation.[7]

The Aldrich-Vreeland Act also created the National Monetary Commission, which met into 1913. The commission, though, failed in its efforts as the result of an impasse among the Populist, Progressive, and Conservative members. The Conservatives supported what was known as a "money trust," which was anathema to the other political groups. The next, and as it turned out far more relevant, event for stabilizing financial systems was the election of Woodrow Wilson as president in 1912.

Although not personally knowledgeable about banking, Wilson was committed to banking reform, but of a variant which did not involve a central bank. As advisers he enlisted Carter Glass and H. Parker Willis, who drafted a proposal for Wilson which evolved into the Federal Reserve Act, signed into law on December 23, 1913. Once Wilson had the best he could get, he did not hesitate.

Figure 9.5 **The Financial Panic of 1907, or There Is Nothing New about Marching on Wall Street**

Source: Wikimedia Commons. Original source soerfm.

Of course the process was anything but easy politically, because Wilson needed to balance the expectations of the Populists and Progressives who opposed bankers controlling the banking system against bankers who, for their part, opposed government regulation dominated by political appointees. The Conservatives recognized the Federal Reserve Act as a sharp break with prevailing laissez-faire economic policy. But in the end the bankers did not prevail.

The original Federal Reserve Act contains thirty sections, the most relevant of which are:

- Sections 2 and 3: That the Federal Reserve establish a minimum of eight and maximum of twelve districts, each with a branch bank
- Section 4: National banks located within each district must apply for membership in the Federal Reserve system
- Section 5: A member bank must own capital stock in the system in proportion to its assets
- Sections 8 and 9: A qualified state chartered bank may on request be converted into a national chartered bank, and state chartered banks may apply for membership in the Reserve
- Section 10: The Federal Reserve Board is to have seven members appointed by the president and confirmed by the Senate

- Section 11: Federal Reserve is to oversee and manage financial affairs of the member Federal Reserve and other banks
- Section 13: Member banks are eligible for discount loans
- Section 15: Federal Reserve banks are empowered to act as fiscal agents for the government
- Section 19: Member banks must maintain a specified amount of non-interest-bearing reserves for deposits
- Section 24: Allows the use of farmland to secure loans

Eventually—following another political fight—twelve regional banks were established: Boston, New York, Philadelphia, Cleveland, Richmond, Atlanta, Chicago, St. Louis, Minneapolis, Kansas City, Dallas, and San Francisco. Because reserve requirements are proportional to the size of the deposits and not the geographical area, the banks differed in magnitude.

One concern did not materialize—that many of the federally chartered banks would choose to go out of business rather than subject themselves to the new regulations. In practice and within months 99 percent of eligible banks requested a Federal Reserve charter. From that point on the system stumbled along reasonably effectively until the next huge challenge—the Great Depression.

9.2 FINANCIAL REGULATION DURING THE GREAT DEPRESSION

a. Bank Regulation

It is not the intent here to attempt a summary of the underlying causes of the Great Depression. It can, though, be mentioned that Americans were increasingly buying on credit, and so by 1929 considerable debt had accumulated, reducing demand. Another sector of the U.S. economy experiencing difficulty was agriculture, which then accounted for 25–30 percent of the U.S. population. Farmers had been overproducing since the end of World War I (1914–1918). The glut of farm products had driven farm prices so low that farmers could barely sustain themselves much less buy consumer goods. Here, though, we focus principally on how the financial system functioned, or did not function, and how regulations were adjusted to overcome the apparent shortcomings.

But if the causes of the Great Depression are not clear, the beginning can be pinpointed as Black Thursday, October 24, 1929, when the equities markets lost a total of $9 billion. (In reality, the market gyrated for a time, but Black Thursday provides a convenient start point.) The major symptoms of the Great Depression were high unemployment, reaching an official 25 percent in 1933, although that figure likely underestimates the true number of people who needed a job. Demand fell by over 20 percent while investment in the face of weak (at best) demand tanked—from $92 billion in 1929 to $10 in 1932. Due to the lack of demand the country experienced considerable disinflation, 11 percent in 1932 alone, so that real interest rates reached nearly 16 percent. That rate of course was devastating for borrowers who had borrowed cheap dollars but had to repay with dear ones.[8]

The stock market crash and even the high Smoot-Hawley Tariffs enacted in 1930 to spur internal demand were in themselves probably not sufficient to cause such a rapid descent into depression. However, beginning in October 1930 a series of small Midwestern banks failed and a full-scale nationwide banking panic began. This panic was the first of three banking crises that would culminate with the "banking holiday" of March 1933, when the entire U.S. banking system was closed by presidential directive.

The Emergency Banking Act of 1933, passed by Congress on March 9, 1933, four days after President Roosevelt declared the nationwide bank holiday, combined with the Federal Reserve's commitment to supply unlimited amounts of currency to reopened banks, created de facto 100 percent deposit insurance. Within two weeks, nearly half the funds which had been withdrawn were redeposited.

From a banking regulatory perspective, much of the liquidity problem was the Federal Reserve Act's requirement that when banks came to the discount window to borrow funds, they were required to present as collateral viable business interests, which they did not have, after the crash of 1929. The Great Depression was an exacerbated form of the classic banking panics of the late 1800s. But because the U.S. economy had become more complex and dependent on the smooth functioning of capital markets, the damage caused by the bank runs of the early 1930s was much greater than previously.[9]

Among the first laws passed under the Roosevelt administration was the Banking Act of 1933, also known as the Glass-Steagall Act. In the perception of the public, banks were not only using their assets to invest, but were also buying new stock issues for resale to the public, taking risks with depositors' money. Banking objectives became blurred. Unsound loans were issued to companies in which the bank had invested, and clients would be encouraged to invest in the stocks of those same companies.

Under the Glass-Steagall Act, banks were given a year to decide whether they would specialize in commercial or in investment banking. Only 10 percent of commercial banks' total income could stem from securities; however, an exception allowed commercial banks to underwrite government-issued bonds.[10]

The Glass-Steagall Act contained several other provisions including prohibiting banks from paying interest on short-term deposits (known as "Regulation Q"), and prohibiting banks from engaging in many other forms of nonbank activities such as underwriting insurance. In other words the Glass-Steagall Act established a fire wall around commercial banking. That wall was dismantled as part of the banking deregulation movement in 1999, and became a contributing factor to the financial meltdown of 2007–2008.

This act also provided the first nationally guaranteed system of insuring bank deposits by creating the Federal Deposit Insurance Corporation (FDIC). Deposit insurance ended forever the problem of bank runs and banking panics. The system is self-funded through payments from member banks. Currently, deposits are guaranteed up to $250,000 per account.

The Banking Act of 1935 renewed and extended many of the 1933 provisions to banks outside the Federal Reserve System—that is, the state-chartered banks. However, this act is of particular note because it finally clarified that the Federal Reserve Board was *the* supreme institution and renamed it the Board of Governors. The act also made other changes to the management structure of the Federal Reserve System.

b. Equities Regulation

We have already seen how the government increasingly controlled business activities in a range of dimensions. These included food and product safety regulations (Chapter 6), communications (Chapter 8), environment (Chapter 7), and antitrust (Chapter 3, Section 3.5). Our focus now is on the other dimension of business regulation: equities and derivative markets. Accounting standards are also incorporated, for that is the basis on which the worth of a business is judged.

Prior to the Great Depression, equity markets were regulated at the state level under what is known as *blue sky laws*—the origin of that term is not entirely clear. States continue to maintain those laws, now generally patterned after federal law,[11] but with notable differences among them, including exempt transactions.[12] Black Thursday raised questions about the effectiveness of that hodgepodge of regulations. But it was not until 1932—March 2 to be exact—that the Senate passed Senate Resolution 84 authorizing the Committee on Banking and Currency to investigate "practices with respect to the buying and selling and the borrowing and lending" of stocks and securities. Not much happened until early 1933 when Ferdinand Pecora was appointed chief council and the scope of the inquiry was expanded.

The formal title of the inquiry was the Subcommittee on Senate Resolutions 84 and 234, but it is better known as the Pecora Committee. Pecora obtained the records of the nation's largest financial institutions, uncovering accounts like the investment of National City Bank in Cuban sugar interests. In the early 1920s, the National City Bank had made several loans to Cuban sugar interests, but by 1927 the loans were in default. The bank issued $50 million in stocks and, without the knowledge of investors, transferred this money to the National City Company to purchase controlling interest in the Cuban sugar industry.[13]

Of course, buying into a losing proposition was a bad investment for the bank's stockholders, but they were unaware of this action because of the lax financial disclosure requirements of the time. The resulting Pecora Committee report led not only to the Banking Act of 1933, but also to equities regulation, including the establishment of the Securities and Exchange Commission.

Actually, there were five major securities-related pieces of legislation passed in close succession:[14]

1. **Securities Act of 1933:** Often referred to as the "truth in securities" law, it has two basic objectives:
    - Require that investors receive financial and other significant information concerning securities being offered for public sale
    - Prohibit deceit, misrepresentations, and other fraud in the sale of securities

This act functions by mandating the registration of securities through the provision of essential financial facts about the business.

2. **Securities Exchange Act of 1934:** Created the Securities and Exchange Commission (SEC).
3. **Trust Indenture Act of 1939:** Applies to debt securities such as bonds, debentures, and notes offered for public sale. The agreement between the issuer of bonds and the bondholder, known as the trust indenture, must conform to the standards of this act.
4. **Investment Company Act of 1940:** Regulates companies, including mutual funds, engaged primarily in investing, reinvesting, and trading in securities. The act requires these companies to disclose their financial condition and investment policies and minimize conflicts of interest. It was amended by the National Securities Markets Improvement Act of 1996 in an attempt to make management more efficient, such as by specifying "covered securities" as defined by the act are exempt from state registration and review.
5. **Investment Advisers Act of 1940:** Regulates investment advisers by requiring entities compensated for advising about security investments must register with the SEC and conform to regulations designed to protect investors. A 1996 amendment generally restricted registration to advisers who have at least $25 million of assets under management.

Of these several acts, the creation of the SEC has the most far-reaching effects with broad authority over all aspects of the securities industry. This includes the power to register, regulate, and oversee brokerage firms, transfer agents, and clearing agencies as well as the nation's securities industry self-regulatory organizations, which include the various stock exchanges, such as the New York Stock Exchange and the American Stock Exchange. Among the significant stipulations are:

- Govern the disclosure in materials used to solicit shareholders' votes in annual or special meetings
- Require disclosure of important information by anyone seeking to acquire more than 5 percent of a company's securities
- Broadly prohibit fraudulent activities of any kind

These provisions are the basis for many types of disciplinary actions, including actions against fraudulent insider trading.

Insider trading charges (and convictions, with jail terms) have been applied to a number of celebrity investors, including Martha Stewart and Rajat Gupta (Figure 9.6).[15] The SEC reports more insider trading cases over the past three years than for any prior three-year period in the agency's history, fifty-eight in FY2012 but down to forty-four in FY2013 but with a record $ 3.4 billion in sanctions.[16]

Figure 9.6 **Mug shot of Rajat Gupta, the fity-sixth person charged with insider trading by federal prosecutors in New York during 2010–2011. Fifty-one have been convicted or pleaded guilty.* Authority is granted by the Securities Exchange Act of 1934.**

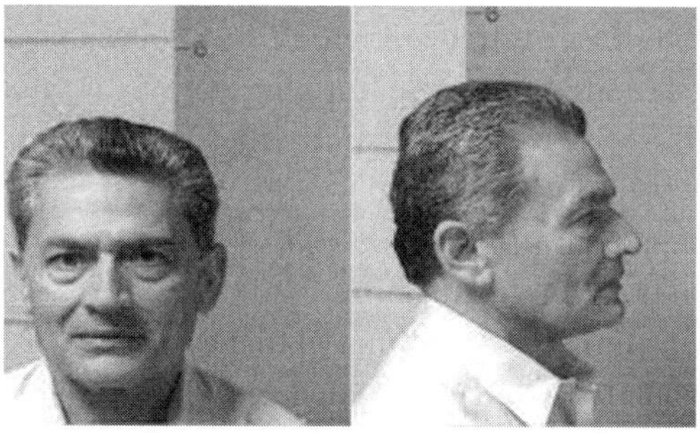

Source: The Smoking Gun. Original source U.S. Marshals Service.
*Michael Rothfeld, Susan Pulliam, and S. Mitra Kalita, "Gupta Case Targets Insider Culture." *Wall Street Journal,* October 27, 2011.

9.3 REGULATION AND DEREGULATION, 1940–2007

a. Banking Regulation and Deregulation

Jumping ahead by some decades and passing over the regulations imposed during World War II, the Employment Act of 1946 directed the Federal Reserve System to implement policies designed to balance the two goals of full employment and low inflation. Achieving these goals has been the guiding principle of the system ever since. However, as a result of spiraling government spending during wartime, an impasse developed over the responsibilities of the Federal Reserve as a buyer of last resort for Treasury debt. Rising debt implied an expansionist, inflationary monetary policy which conflicted with the Fed's inflation mandate.

Under the terms of the Treasury Accord of 1951, the Federal Reserve System was relieved of the responsibility of keeping interest rates low when required to purchase Treasuries.[17] In the context of the twenty-first century, it should be noted that the absence of the authority of the European Central Bank to buy Euro member states' debt is one of the confounding issues in the resolution of that debt crisis.

In 1956, in an effort to prevent financial conglomerates from amassing too much power, a new act focused on banks involved in the insurance sector. Congress agreed that bearing the high risks of underwriting insurance is not good banking practice. Thus, as an extension of the Glass-Steagall Act, the Bank Holding Company Act further separated financial activities by creating a wall between insurance and banking. Even though banks could, and can still, sell insurance and insurance products, underwriting insurance was forbidden.

More generally, the Bank Holding Company Act authorizes the Federal Reserve to oversee bank holding companies, which are the dominant ownership structure of

U.S. banks. Under the act, a bank holding company may engage directly in—or establish or acquire subsidiaries that engage in—nonbanking activities determined by the Federal Reserve Board to be closely related to banking (e.g., mortgage banking, consumer and commercial finance and loan servicing, leasing, collection agency, asset management, trust company, real estate appraisal, financial and investment advisory activities, management consulting, employee benefits consulting, career counseling services, and certain insurance-related activities). A bank holding company can also make investments in companies not engaged in activities closely related to banking, but these investments cannot exceed 5 percent of the target company's outstanding voting stock.

In the 1980s, the Federal Reserve issued a policy statement (Appendix C to Regulation Y) recognizing the importance of community banking in the financial system and providing certain advantages to facilitate ownership and transfer of small banks by bank holding companies.

Until this point, we have used the term "bank" to refer to many types of financial institutions. In addition to a (chartered) bank, the term can apply to a trust company, a savings bank, savings and loan institution, credit union, thrift, or a thrift and loan. While these institutions may appear quite similar, they actually have different rights, powers, and obligations. They may even have different tax obligations. For example, savings and loan associations must invest more of their assets in home mortgages than traditional banks. Trust companies manage and administer trust funds of individuals and pension plans but may not take deposits into checking or savings accounts. Credit unions enjoy certain tax advantages, and so forth.[18]

We stray beyond the focus of this book to go into great detail on the activities and regulatory oversight of these alternative forms of banks. But two key pieces of legislation which enhanced their scope of activities are worth noting: the Depository Institutions Deregulation and Monetary Control Act of 1980[19] and the Garn-St. Germain Depository Institutions Act of 1982.[20] These lifted restrictions on checking and money market accounts, deregulated savings and loan associations, and allowed banks to provide adjustable-rate mortgage loans.

Coincidentally, the Garn-St. Germain Depository Institutions Act is implicated in the S&Ls, debacle of the later 1980s. Recall that the principle activity of savings and loans (S&Ls) is to fund mortgages using monies from savings accounts. Problems arose in the 1980s when money market accounts were paying higher interest than the S&Ls, siphoning away deposits. Under the Garn-St. Germain Depository Institutions Act, S&Ls were permitted to raise interest rates on deposits and to make commercial and consumer loans. The act also removed restrictions on the proportion of the purchase price which could be paid by a mortgage. In a further effort to raise capital, banks invested in speculative real estate and commercial loans, along with some illegal activities.

Then that bubble burst. By 1983, 35 percent of the country's S&Ls were unprofitable, and 9 percent were technically bankrupt. Since the deposits were insured by the FDIC, those bankruptcies drained monies from the fund, and a taxpayer-funded infusion of $50 billion was required to close the failing banks. Costs accumulated at the state level as well—half of the failed S&Ls were in Texas. Overall, between 1986–1995, over 1,000 banks with total assets of over $500 billion failed. By 1999, the S&L crisis cost $153 billion, with taxpayers footing the bill for $124 billion and the S&L industry paying the rest.[21]

What ensued—no big surprise—was an era of reregulation with the passage of:

- **Competitive Equality Banking Act of 1987:** To regulate nonbank banks,[22] impose a moratorium on certain securities and insurance activities by banks, recapitalize the Federal Savings and Loan Insurance Corporation, allow emergency interstate bank acquisitions, streamline credit union operations, regulate consumer check holds, and for other purposes[23]
- **Financial Institutions Reform, Recovery and Enforcement Act of 1989:** To reform, recapitalize, and consolidate the federal deposit insurance system, to enhance the regulatory and enforcement powers of federal financial institutions regulatory agencies, and for other purposes[24]
- **FDIC Improvement Act of 1991:** To require the least-cost resolution of insured depository institutions, to improve supervision and examinations, to provide additional resources to the Bank Insurance Fund, and for other purposes[25]

Meanwhile, states had been slowly adopting intra- and interstate bank branching deregulation. In 1994 the Riegle-Neal Interstate Banking and Branching Efficiency Act repealed the 1927 McFadden Act, allowed banks to open limited service bank branches across state lines by merging with other banks, effectively phasing out all barriers to interstate banking and branching by 1997.[26] Importantly, the courts had ruled that ATM machines did not constitute bank branches.

Then, to the delight of many in the banking industry, in November 1999 Congress repealed much of the Glass-Steagall Act with the establishment of the Gramm-Leach-Bliley Act, which eliminated the earlier act's restrictions against affiliations between commercial and investment banks. The act functioned by allowing a bank holding company to declare itself a financial holding company and thereby engage in financial activities, including securities underwriting and dealing, insurance agency and underwriting activities, and merchant banking activities. For a bank holding company to be eligible to declare itself a financial holding company, all of the bank holding company's depository institution subsidiaries must be well-capitalized and well-managed and have satisfactory or better ratings.[27]

Finally, in 2006, the president signed the Federal Deposit Insurance Reform Act of 2005 into law. The Reform Act merged the Bank Insurance Fund and the Saving Association Insurance Fund into a new fund called the Deposit Insurance Fund.[28] These are the member-supported funds which cover depositors' losses in the case of the bankruptcy of a member bank. Foreclosures are not uncommon: the FDIC listed some fifty-two bank failures in 2012. [29]

b. Securities Regulation

On July 30, 2002, President Bush signed into law the Sarbanes-Oxley Act of 2002, which he characterized as "the most far-reaching reforms of American business practices since the time of Franklin Delano Roosevelt." The act mandated a number of reforms to enhance corporate responsibility, enhance financial disclosures, and combat corporate and accounting fraud, and created the Public Company Accounting Oversight Board, to oversee the activities of the auditing profession.

This was the biggest change in securities regulation since the 1930s and came about as no accident. According to PBS's *Nightly Business Report*,[30]

> The roots of Sarbanes-Oxley can be traced to the collapse of Enron, which caused some $70 billion in investment losses and shook investor confidence to the core. As news reports focused on employees who lost their jobs and life savings, it soon became clear Enron was no ordinary business collapse, but the result of a massive conspiracy by insiders to inflate the company's earnings.
>
> People started to wonder how this could happen, even though the company's accountants and a supposedly independent auditor, Arthur Andersen, had signed off on the company's books. Soon stock prices overall were plummeting as investors began to question the accuracy of corporate earnings reports. When another massive accounting fraud was exposed at WorldCom just six months later, investors demanded reform of the corporate accounting system and Capitol Hill got the message.

The act is arranged into eleven titles, the most important sections considered to be the following:[31]

- **Title III, Section 302:** Pertains to "Corporate Responsibility for Financial Reports" and among other requirements specifies that signing officers have reviewed the report and the report does not contain any materially untrue statements or material omission or be considered misleading.
- **Title III, Section 304:** Corporate officials are required to return compensation based on bogus financial statements even if they personally were not involved in the deception.
- **Title IV, Section 401** (Enhanced Financial Disclosures): Pertains to "Disclosures in Periodic Reports," which requires reports be accurate and presented in a manner that does not contain incorrect statements or omit material information. These financial statements shall also include all material off-balance sheet liabilities, obligations, or transactions.
- **Also under Title IV, Section 404:** Pertains to "Management Assessment of Internal Controls." Firms are required to publish information in their annual reports concerning the scope and adequacy of the internal control structure and procedures for financial reporting. This statement shall also assess the effectiveness of such internal controls and procedures. The registered accounting firm shall, in the same report, attest to and report on the effectiveness of the internal control structure and procedures for financial reporting.
- **Further under Title IV, Section 409:** Pertains to "Real Time Issuer Disclosures." Issuers are required to disclose to the public, on an urgent basis, information on material changes in their financial condition or operations.
- Sections 802 and 902 specify civil and criminal penalties.

The act applies narrowly to publicly traded companies. Yet some not-for-profits have either voluntarily chosen to comply, or state laws have been enacted to compel nonprofits to comply in some regards.[32]

The law has not been without its critics. According to the same PBS *Nightly Business Report*,

> At first, Wall Street seemed to like the new law. . . . But as public companies began implementing the law, some began to wonder whether Congress had acted too hastily. While the SEC originally estimated it would cost the average company $91,000 a year to comply with the law, by some estimates that cost has turned out to be over $4 million.[33]

In other instances, enforcement has been minimal. A 2011 study of Section 304 enforcement reported in the *New York Times* that the SEC required refunds by only thirty-one executives in twenty companies, with only $12.2 million recovered to date. SEC initiative is essential because under the act neither companies nor shareholders are permitted to bring lawsuits.[34]

Understandably, most executives wondered why they should be subjected to the same compliance burdens as those who had been negligent or dishonest. Smaller companies in particular complained about the monopolization of executives' time and costs running into the millions of dollars. The most burdensome element proved to be Section 404, which places the responsibility on management to maintain a sound internal-control structure for financial reporting and to assess its effectiveness.

A 2009 SEC study of compliance costs placed the Section 404–related costs at a median $1 million.[35] However, small companies (those with a "public float" of less than $75 million) do not have to comply with Section 404(b), which constitutes about a third of the 404 costs. Section 404(b) requires a publicly held company's auditor to attest to, and report on, management's assessment of its internal controls. Section 404 costs vary by company size, which might be expected, as follows:[36]

- Small (< $75 million) $.5 million
- Medium ($75–$700 million) $.7 million
- Large (> $700 million) $2.0 million

Compliance has also involved changes in accounting standards. The U.S. Chamber of Commerce has expressed concerns that the ensuing compliance costs are making U.S. business uncompetitive internationally.[37] Firms, however, have noted benefits from improved internal control. United Technologies Corp. (UTC) used the new control systems to standardize checks on bookkeeping in its disparate businesses around the world. "We had a fair degree of latitude in how people document things. We've tightened that up," says Jay Haberland, UTC's vice-president for business controls, reports *Businessweek*.[38]

c. Derivatives Regulation

A financial derivative can be thought of as an instrument related to but removed from the underlying transaction. A derivative is to a transaction what the purchase of an engagement ring is to the engagement: the two are distinct but obviously related and roughly parallel in time.

Financial derivatives are quite prevalent, and not only recently with hedge funds. Widespread use extends back to the Civil War when there was a large demand for food to feed the troops, but disruptions made filling that demand chancy. In any case, the Chicago Board of Trade (CBOT) was established in 1848 and is the world's oldest futures and options (F&O) exchange, trading initially in agricultural F&O. Subsequently the number and form of products traded has expanded outside agricultural products to metals (copper, gold), energy (crude oil and gas), exchange rates, stock indexes, and interest rates. Indeed, the new products have long eclipsed the agricultural staples in terms of trading volume (Figure 9.7). There is now even a contract for weather futures (farmers, ski resorts, cruise lines, and so forth are very dependent on weather conditions for the success of their businesses) and also, more recently, a futures contract based on motion picture box-office receipts.

A futures (always used in the plural) contract is a fixed commitment to buy or sell a specified product at a particular future date at the then-prevailing price. An option is the opportunity but not the requirement to buy or sell a specified product at a particular future date and price.

Consider, for example, a corn farmer who, based on good price forecasts, takes out a loan for fertilizer in June and is obviously concerned if the price of corn drops by September when the crop is harvested. He or she uses a futures contract in June to "lock in"

Figure 9.7 **Change in Futures Contract Trading Over Time**

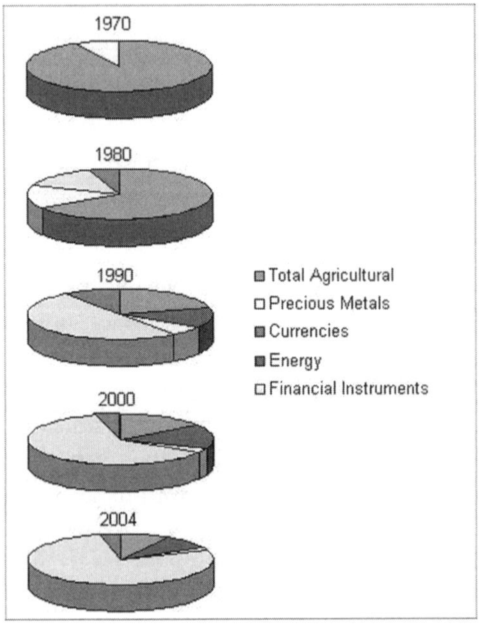

Source: Wikipedia Commons. Original source Tony Wikrent.

the September price. Conversely, an ethanol producer who uses corn as the feedstock is concerned about future price rises. He or she can also use the futures market to gain protection against a price rise. The systems really do work, but as with any financial system there are many details which require oversight.

The concept of established F&O markets is to specify closely the product and terms so that price is the only variable, resulting in reduced transaction costs. The markets, which are highly leveraged (5–10 percent margin typically required), also attract speculators. Speculation often gets a bad name, but it does provide liquidity to the F&O markets, which is another of their attractions.

The government has been regulating established futures markets since the 1920s,[39] but the big regulatory step occurred in 1974 with the establishment of the Commodity Futures Trading Commission (CFTC) under the Commodity Futures Trading Commission Act. The act creates the CFTC, an independent agency granted exclusive jurisdiction over futures trading in all commodities.[40] The act is to be renewed every four years or so. In 1982 the Futures Trading Act clarified commission jurisdiction in a number of areas including importantly codifying the Shad-Johnson Accord, which gave the CFTC jurisdiction over broad-based stock index futures and banned single-stock and narrow-based stock index futures. Due to a change of regulations, trading limits were removed effective August 2003.[41]

Underlying all of these particulars were careful controls over the financial resources needed to make good on the contract commitments being made. In short, F&O markets are highly transparent, with data on prices and outstanding contracts public knowledge.

In the 1990s the Futures Trading Practices Act of 1992, among other things, granted the commission the authority to exempt over-the-counter (OTC) derivatives and other transactions from CFTC regulation. Soon thereafter, certain swap agreements and hybrid instruments were exempted from regulation under the Commodity Exchange Act.[42]

The next major regulatory change was the Commodity Futures Modernization Act of 2000. It was an attempt to solve a dispute between the SEC and the CFTC over what constituted a "commodity." A single stock futures contract had features of both a commodity, which is governed by the CFTC, and a stock, which is governed by the SEC. Both agencies wanted jurisdiction over transactions of this type of financial instrument. The Commodity Futures Modernization Act allowed single stock futures to be sold again (following an eighteen-year ban) in U.S. markets, but did not specify which exchange would be allowed to trade them. The ultimate resolution was to trade primarily on the OneChicago Exchange, a joint venture among F&O exchanges.[43]

Throughout these regulatory processes no clear jurisdiction by either the SEC or CFTC over the trading of swaps was established. A swap is the mutually beneficial exchange of financial instruments. Traditionally, they involved exchanging one security for another for the purpose of changing the maturity (bonds), the quality of issues (stocks or bonds), or investment objectives. Another form of swap from a group known as "plain vanilla" involves the exchange of a fixed for a variable interest rate commitment. Swaps however grew more complex in the first decade of the 2000s—the most infamous of which is the credit default swap—while remaining largely unregulated, a situation that came back to bite all of us, as described below.

In 2004, the SEC voted unanimously to permit the largest broker-dealers (those with capital of more than $5 billion) to apply for exemptions from the established "haircut" method of calculating reserve requirements. Upon receiving SEC approval, those firms were permitted to use mathematical models to compute the so-called "haircuts" on their securities based on international standards used by commercial banks. By contrast, the rule requires smaller firms to value their securities at market prices and to apply to those values a haircut (i.e., a discount) based on each security's risk characteristics. The haircut values of securities are used to compute the liquidation value of a broker-dealer's assets to determine whether the broker-dealer holds enough liquid assets to pay all its nonsubordinated liabilities and to still retain a "cushion" of required liquid assets.

Finally, in the lead-up to the financial near collapse of 2007–2008, the Credit Rating Agency Reform Act of 2006 was adopted. It is intended to open up the credit rating industry to more competition and abolish the SEC's authority to designate credit-rating agencies as "nationally recognized rating agencies." Instead, a credit-rating company with three years of experience that meets certain standards would be allowed to register with the SEC as a "statistical ratings organization." The act also grants the SEC new authority to inspect credit-rating agencies, although the commission would have no say over their rating methodologies.[44] Credit-rating agencies rate securities—bonds primarily—for the likelihood of default on an AAA, AAa, or similar system. Some regulations and many private systems require a minimum credit score for bonds to be investment grade (i.e., not junk bonds) and therefore qualified for certain kinds of investments such as pension funds. The authority, and responsibilities, of the SEC were enhanced under Title IX, section 939A of the Dodd-Frank Act (see section 9.4c this chapter).

In May 2011, the SEC's five commissioners voted unanimously to propose new, tougher regulations for credit-rating agencies. The proposed rules would implement certain provisions of the Dodd-Frank Wall Street Reform and Consumer Protection Act and enhance the SEC's existing rules governing credit ratings that are registered as Nationally Recognized Statistical Rating Organizations. Under the SEC's proposals, these organizations would be required to:[45]

- Report on internal controls
- Protect against conflicts of interest
- Establish professional standards for credit analysts
- Publicly provide—along with the publication of the credit rating—disclosure about the credit rating and the methodology used to determine it
- Enhance their public disclosures about the performance of their credit ratings
- Require disclosure concerning third-party due diligence reports for asset-backed securities

The regulations have (mid-2014) yet to be implemented, which is both a surprise and frustration to many observers.[46] Much SEC activity to date has been focused on removing credit rating references from several financial laws.

9.4 THE GREAT RECESSION AND ITS REGULATORY AFTERMATH

a. What Happened?

Describing what happened is easier than deciphering just why it happened. The stunning series of events culminated a weekend of frantic around-the-clock negotiations in September 2007 as Wall Street bankers met at the request of Bush administration officials to try to avoid a downward spiral in the markets stemming from a crisis of confidence. The following fateful occurrences date to that week.

Bear Stearns, once the country's fifth-largest investment bank, faltered and subsequently agreed to be sold for just $2 (subsequently raised to $10) a share to JPMorgan Chase (with a $30 billion infusion from the Federal Reserve), down 93 percent from its closing price the preceding Friday. Bear Stearns failed because its investors no longer believed it could repay its loans despite the firm's having $18 billion of cash on hand. Bear Stearns was one of the biggest underwriters of complex investments linked to mortgages, which led to two of its hedge funds, heavily invested in subprime mortgages, to fold in July 2007, leading to over $3 billion in losses.

Even worse, investors concluded the investment bank no longer could stand behind the complex agreements it had with other financial institutions. Bear Stearns had a web of intertwined agreements with other banks, investment houses, and corporations, which explains the Fed's cash infusion to purchase securities not easily marketable. But their's was a confidence business and with major losses Bear Stearn's investors became increasingly reluctant to do business with the company. Thereafter its downward spiral was rapid. "As far as Wall Street securities houses go, Bear Stearns wasn't too big to fail," said a leading Wall Street economist at the time. "It was too interconnected to fail."[47]

Then the problems spread. On Sunday, September 6, Merrill Lynch agreed to sell itself to the Bank of America for roughly $50 billion to avert a deepening financial crisis. At the same time, another prominent securities firm, Lehman Brothers, filed for bankruptcy protection and subsequently collapsed after failing to find a buyer. Bank of America eventually ended talks with Lehman after the government refused to take responsibility for losses on some of Lehman's most troubled real estate assets, something it did when JPMorgan Chase bought Bear Stearns.

Yet another crisis loomed as the insurance giant American International Group (AIG) appeared to teeter. Staggered by losses stemming from the credit crisis, AIG sought a $40 billion guarantee from the Federal Reserve, without which the company had only days to survive.[48]

The $40 billion proved to be a grand underestimate as the U.S. government that fateful September seized control of AIG, one of the world's biggest insurers, in an $85 billion deal that indicated that, unlike Lehman, AIG was determined to be truly too big to fail. The Fed would lend up to $85 billion in a two-year loan to AIG, and the U.S. government effectively received a 79.9 percent equity stake in the insurer. The loan is secured by AIG's assets, including its profitable insurance businesses.[49] Taxpayer aid to AIG ultimately mounted to $182 billion.

Much of the rescue money went to meet the company's obligations to its Wall Street trading partners on credit default swaps. Goldman Sachs Group was given $12.9 billion in AIG money; Bank of America, $5.2 billion; Merrill Lynch, $6.8 billion; and Citigroup, $2.3 billion.[50] The AIG investment is posed to do well for the Treasury. In September 2012 the fourth and largest tranche of AIG stock was placed on the market and, if sold at the then-current price of $32.50 a share, above the $28.72 needed for the government to break even, would earn the Treasury $12.4 billion.[51]

This was not the first time regulators were confronted with the imminent failure of a large fund which threatened the stability of the global financial system. The key incident involved Long-Term Capital Management, formed in 1993 by highly respected Wall Street financial figures.

The trading strategy of that large hedge fund was to make trades taking advantage of arbitrage between securities that are incorrectly priced relative to each other. Due to the small spread in arbitrage opportunities, the fund had required leverage to make money using massive amounts of borrowed funds. At its height in 1998, the fund had $5 billion in assets, controlled over $100 billion, and had positions whose total worth was over $1 trillion.

Due to its highly leveraged nature and a default of government bonds in Russia which led to a flight to quality bonds, the fund sustained massive losses and was in danger of defaulting on its loans. The fund held huge positions in the market, totaling roughly 5 percent of the total global fixed-income market. Had it gone into default, it could have triggered a global financial crisis, caused by the massive write-offs its creditors would have had to make. In September 1998, the fund, which continued to post losses, was bailed out with the help of the Federal Reserve and its creditors and taken over.[52] This near collapse was a clear indication that the new financial tools and models were anything but foolproof.

b. Why Did It Happen?[53]

Imagine this scenario: To promote its export-led industrialization policy, the Chinese leadership in the 1990s kept export prices low, in part by undervaluing its currency, the yuan, as well as by subsidizing state corporations through cheap credit and other means.[54] This helped to keep U.S. inflation levels low.

At the same time, the Chinese government was willing to accept low returns on its investment in U.S. bonds in exchange for "recycling" its trade surplus back to the United States. That kept interest rates on U.S. debt low so that the Federal Reserve could follow a low-interest rate policy. Low-interest rates in turn made housing more affordable for many, and a housing boom ensued (Figure 9.8).

Of course, with cheap, easily obtained credit, demand increased pushing housing prices to economically unsustainable levels. In response, banks and other lenders created new types of mortgages, making loans affordable to people who normally would not qualify for a conventional thirty-year mortgage. Some of these mortgagees—the system is still attempting to determine the extent—were made to buyers who did not have the income

Figure 9.8 **Inflation-Adjusted House Prices, 1970–2012**

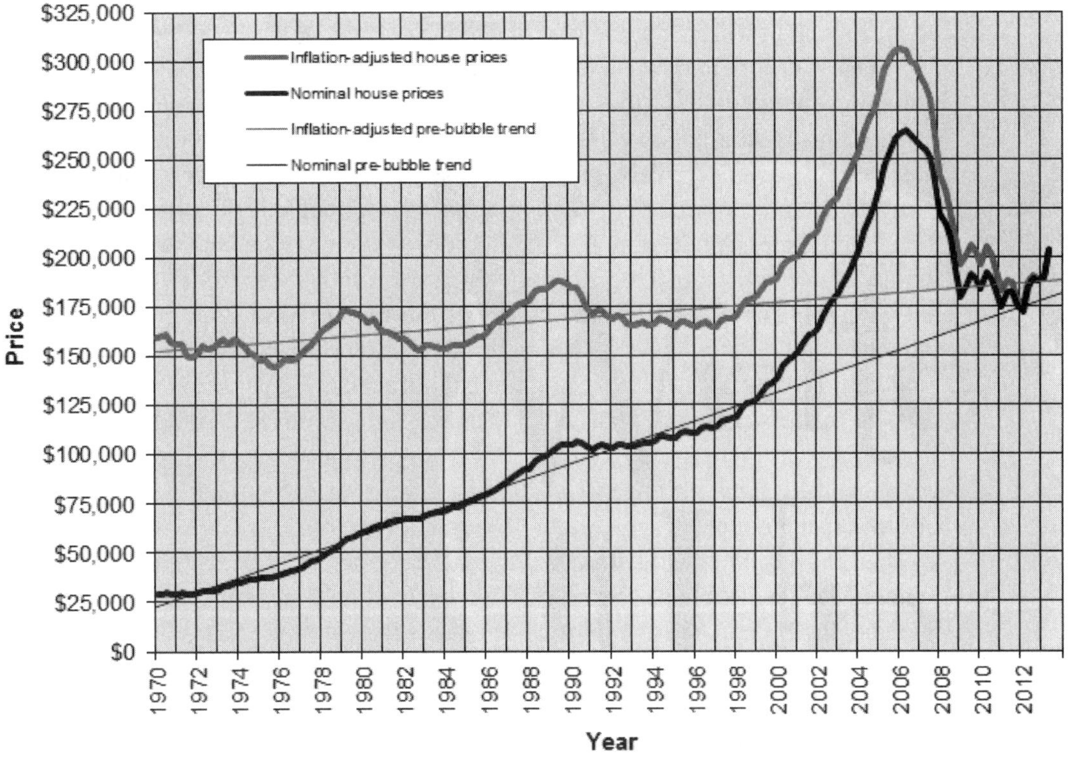

Source: "JP's Real Estate Charts," Jparsons.net.

to sustain them. Indeed there are many stories of loans to individuals who had neither jobs nor assets. In other instances, low introductory rates were used or interest-only loans offered, which for many just pushed payment problems off into the future. These are subprime mortgagees—subprime is defined as below some specified credit rating.

From a mortgage broker's point of view, these so-called subprime mortgages sustained the market, allowing banks and brokers to collect fees for closing the deals but face no risk once they sold the loans to Wall Street. Wall Street for its part was eager to buy subprime loans, mix them with other types of debt, package them into complex securities (called tranches) and sell them to other investors. As long as housing prices continued to soar, everything seemed fine. Borrowers in shaky loans could refinance their loans or sell their homes for big gains. Investors in the new securities Wall Street created received rich interest payments at a time when other fixed-income securities carried low rates.

And then there were Fannie Mae and Freddie Mac, which were so instrumental to the mortgage debacle. Indeed, a 2012 presidential nominee hopeful laid much of the near financial collapse to pressure by the Congress on these two government-sponsored entities to lend to individuals with poorer and poorer credit risks.[55] Fannie Mae (officially the Federal National Mortgage Association) was founded during the Great Depression as a government-sponsored enterprise, though it has been a publicly traded company since

1968. Fannie Mae purchases mortgage-backed securities on the secondary market and pools them for sale to investors on the open market as a means of expanding mortgage credit to make owning a home more affordable. Freddie Mac (the Federal Home Loan Mortgage Corporation) was created in 1970 to extend the role of Fannie Mae while providing competition. It, too, is a government-sponsored enterprise, which means that when so many mortgages went bad in the first decade of the 2000s, the government (i.e., tax payers) covered the substantial losses. Fannie Mae and Freddie Mac together own or guarantee around $5 trillion in mortgages, about half of the total outstanding in the United States. A failure of that magnitude would have shaken the housing market in unimaginable ways.[56] In a recent book, Morgenson and Rosner see the blame as internal, not external. They identify three pillars of the Fannie Mae strategy, including undue influence on Congress, and, partly with the assistance of a compliant Congress, marginalizing regulators with the result that capital requirements were dangerously low. In part, the authors charge this was done to enrich the Fannie Mae/Freddie Mac executives whose pay was increasingly tied to profits. James Johnson, Fannie Mae's head for nine years, walked away with nearly $100 million; taxpayers were left with a bill hundreds of times that amount.[57]

Then in December 2011, Daniel Mudd, the former chief executive officer (CEO) of Fannie Mae, and Richard Syron, ex-CEO of Freddie Mac, were sued by the SEC for understating by hundreds of billions of dollars the subprime loans held by the firms.[58] The lawsuit caused Daniel Mudd to take a leave of absence as CEO of Fortress Investment Group.[59]

Once the housing market began to fall, though, borrowers started to default on mortgages. As defaults piled up, the complex securities Wall Street had created from those mortgages began to shed value. More and more lenders grew wary of making loans, especially if the collateral was mortgage-backed securities. The resultant credit squeeze helped push the economy into a recession, the effects of which are still with us. As regards housing, in late 2011 nearly 30 percent of homes are worth less than the purchase price, and half of mortgage holders were underwater—that is, owing more than their properties were worth.[60] Yet 2013 brought a strong recovery with real prices up by 18.4 percent over the prior sixteen months. This has raised the prospect of (yet) another housing bubble, although the boom mentality does not appear to be dominating the market at present.[61] By 2014, though, the housing market was again down except for a few major cities like New York and San Francisco. A major explanation for the protracted sector recovery seems to be a dearth of new household formulation as younger people have chosen (or been compelled by a weak job market) to live longer with their parents.[62]

As regards the role of regulation, some commentators have identified the 2004 SEC rule change (see this chapter, Section 9.3c) as an important cause of the crisis on the basis it permitted certain large investment banks to increase dramatically their leverage. Financial reports filed by those companies show an increase in their leverage ratios from 2004 through 2007 (and into 2008).

Another group considered complicit is the rating agencies. These agencies rate the riskiness of financial products, including bonds and mortgages for use by investors. In some cases, investment rules prohibit advisers for pension funds from investing in risky securities such as subprime mortgages. Where corporate and government bonds are concerned, this rating system has proved reliable and enables investors to diversify their portfolios. Markets for structured products could not have developed without the quality assurance provided by rating agencies about inherently complex financial products. However, the ratings for structured credit have turned out to be much less robust predictors of future developments than were the ratings for traditional securities.[63]

Others, less generously, see complicity or at minimum laxness in these agencies, which gave their highest security ratings to mortgage tranches which turned out to contain many subprime notes. In any case there is a clear case of conflict of interest because the credit rating agencies are paid by the broker firms, which benefit most by a high rating. According to knowledgeable observers, once investor groups were restricted by regulations to investments in certain rating categories (i.e., investment grade), the conflict of interest expanded. "[R]atings agencies began to sell not only information but also valuable property rights associated with compliance with regulation."[64] The Financial Economists Roundtable has called for three reforms in the ratings system:[65]

- Increase the transparency of modeling practices while holding management accountable for negligent ratings errors
- Not include ratings organizations ratings in security and banking regulations
- State an express margin of error in the ratings for all tranches of securitized instruments

c. Regulatory Response

The governmental response to the evolving financial crisis of September 2008 was in fact one of the last acts of the Bush administration which on October 3, 2008, adopted the Emergency Economic Stabilization Act. The act, which established the Troubled Asset Relief Program (TARP), gave the U.S. Treasury authority to purchase up to $700 billion of illiquid mortgage-backed securities and, at the discretion of the secretary of the treasury, other illiquid assets from financial institutions in an attempt to create liquidity and free up the money markets. When the purchases were made in a market with no established prices (a common situation for these dubious securities) or in the absence of an auction, the government was in exchange to receive a "meaningful equity or debt position" in the selling firms, although the government would not exercise any voting rights. For participating firms there are also some restrictions on executive compensation.[66]

The initial post-crisis response was the passage of the Fraud Enforcement and Recovery Act of 2009 to enhance, strengthen, and rebuild the government's ability to investigate and prosecute the increasing instances of mortgage and corporate fraud.[67] Then, much more significantly, on July 21, 2010, President Obama signed the Dodd-Frank Wall Street Reform and Consumer Protection Act (known as the Dodd-Frank Act) into law: "A bill to promote the financial stability of the United States by improving accountability and transparency in the financial system, to end 'too big to fail,' to protect the American taxpayer by ending bailouts, to protect consumers from abusive financial services practices, and for other purposes."

In addition to the headline regulatory changes covering capital investment by banks and insurance companies, the act introduces new regulation of hedge funds, alters the definition of accredited investors, requires reporting by all public companies on CEO to median employee pay ratios and other compensation data, enforces equitable access to credit for consumers, and provides incentives to promote banking among low- and medium-income residents.

The legislation is complex, with sixteen titles, summarized on the relevant points as follows:[68]

- Title I, Financial Stability: Creates the Financial Stability Oversight Council that will regulate particular nonbank financial firms in ways that are possibly stricter than banks. Also ensures that large banks and bank holding companies will remain subject to heightened prudential requirements.
- Title II, Orderly Liquidation Authority: Allows the FDIC to seize control of a financial company (excluding insurance companies under state regulation) whose imminent collapse is determined to be a threat to the entire U.S. economy. Also addressed is companies considered to be "too big to fail." If judged to be failing, the only permitted outcome is liquidation (see Example 9.1).
- Title III, Transfer Powers and FDIC Amendments: Changes the fee structure for the FDIC as well as raising the coverage limit to $250,000 per institution. Eliminates and redistributes the responsibilities (but not the roles) of the Office of Thrift Supervision.
- Title IV, Regulation of Advisers to Hedge Funds and Other Institutions: Changes the registration and reporting requirements of hedge fund managers and other investment advisers.
- Title V, Insurance: Creates the Federal Insurance Office with authority over all lines of insurance (excluding health).
- Title VI, Improvements to Regulation over Depository Institutions: Allows heightened authority, including the "Volcker Rule," which prohibits any "banking entity" from engaging in proprietary trading or sponsoring or investing in a hedge fund (but with a few limited exceptions).
- Title VII, Derivatives Legislation: Gives authority to the CFTC and SEC to regulate swaps, with some to be traded on exchanges and others publicly reported. Specifically, (a) providing for the registration and comprehensive regulation of swap dealers and major swap participants; (b) imposing clearing and trade execution requirements on standardized derivative products; (c) creating robust recordkeeping and real-time reporting regimes; and (d) enhancing the commission's rulemaking and enforcement.

  New CFTC rules went into effect October 2, 2013, mandating that trading be conducted on an approved swap execution facility, which is to say one permitting multiple bids and offers while allowing the observation of bids and offers by other

EXAMPLE 9.1: ORDERLY LIQUIDATION OF LEHMAN BROTHERS HOLDINGS UNDER THE DODD-FRANK ACT

The Dodd-Frank in Title II grants the FDIC authority to take control of a teetering, too-big-to-fail financial institution. As a demonstration/exercise, the FDIC released a report describing how it would have managed the Lehman Brothers collapse. The Lehman bankruptcy almost exactly four years prior (September 15, 2008) is what catapulted a mortgage-backed security strain into a near collapse of the international banking system. Hence it is important to understand how, at least in the minds of the FDIC, the bankruptcy could have been managed to a more secure resolution for the U.S./world economy as well as for Lehman's creditors.

At the time of its insolvency, the FDIC had the authority to intervene only with failing U.S.-chartered banks while Lehman Holdings consisted of thousands of companies, many of which were not banks. The government could have rescued all or none of those entities, and chose none. As it was (and is—the liquidation of Lehman Brothers assets has been restarted following its emergence from bankruptcy and is expected to continue until 2017 or so), creditors are receiving only about 20 cents on the dollar, although some classes are returned more.[71]

Based on their scenario, the FDIC computes unsecured creditors would have received 90 percent of their investments following these steps now authorized under Dodd-Frank:

- Advance resolution planning: Collect and analyze information for resolution planning prefailure
- Domestic and international preplanning: Help FDIC and other domestic regulators better understand Lehman's business and how it could be resolved
- Source of liquidity: FDIC provides liquidity to fund Lehman's critical operations for stability and preserving valuable assets and operations pending a sale
- Speed of execution: Complete transfer prior to Lehman's failure, assisted by Dodd-Frank mandate contractors continue to perform until the restructuring is completed
- Flexible transactions: Provide flexibility to bid on troubled assets

According to the FDIC, "These [Dodd-Frank] powers would enable the FDIC to act to preserve the financial stability of the United States and to maximize value for creditors by preserving franchise value and by rapidly moving proceeds into creditors' hands." All at no cost to taxpayers.[72]

Davidson, though, raised some questions about the practicality of this happy FDIC scenario. Large financial institutions are required to identify their important subsidiaries, but it is within their discretion to determine which indeed are "important." And the FDIC assumes global regulators will be fully cooperative in the liquidation process, even as it eliminates all shareholder value for domestic and international investors alike.[73] An actual liquidation of a financial institution in the $600-plus asset category would likely be far messier.

market participants. Required transactions are delineated in the Commodity Exchange Act Section 2(h)(8) (added by the Dodd-Frank Act). The initial step required the registering of the approved execution facilities. The deadline for the beginning of trading is expected in early 2014.[69]

- Title IX, Investor Protection: Multifaceted, including changes to executive compensation with mandatory nonbinding shareholder votes (Subtitles E and G). In a different dimension, imposes more stringent internal control requirements and creates new rules dictating credit-rating procedures and processes. Furthermore, requires credit-rating agencies to file disclosures analyzing the accuracy of prior credit ratings (Subtitle C).
- Title X: Bureau of Consumer Financial Protection: Established as an independent bureau within the Federal Reserve (see Chapter 6, Section 6.6a).
- Title XIV: Mortgage Reform and Anti-Predatory Lending Act: Increases the regulation of mortgage loan origination and servicing practices with increased disclosure requirements.

The Dodd-Frank Act has been severely criticized for being horrendously complex, and hence costly. *The Economist* quotes the costs to individual hedge funds of completing just two forms (for Sections 404 and 406) at $100,000–$150,000 initially, dropping to about $40,000 annually. But for that publication, the real concern is that the "apparatus will smother financial institutions in so much red tape that innovation is stifled and America's economy suffers."[70]

d. International Dimension: Basel III

The regulation of banking within the confines of a single country, though, is not sufficient or effective today. One reason is international competition among banks: If one country has a higher reserve requirement than another, its banks effectively have higher costs and are uncompetitive in the internationalized banking system. Uncontrolled, countries one after another are pulled to reduce requirements, potentially leading to an equilibrium well short of adequate.

A second reason was highlighted by the Eurozone debt crisis. Questions about the ability of governments in Ireland, Greece, and Portugal, and possibly other larger economy nations, to repay their loans weakened banks in their respective countries, which hold considerable amounts of that paper, which in turn weakens other banks that have invested in the first-line banks, and so on. The collapse of any in the chain due to inadequate reserve holdings threatens all their creditor banks in turn.

To address these issues the Basel Committee on Banking Supervision was established in 1975 by the governors of the central banks with its Committee's Secretariat (the administrative body) located at the Bank for International Settlements in Basel, Switzerland. Presently there are twenty-seven member central banks.[74] The most recent Basel Accord, Basel III, was adopted in December 2010 (revised June 2011) with its major provisions going into effect in 2013. Basel III requires banks to hold 4.5 percent of common equity (up from 2 percent in Basel II) and 6 percent of Tier I capital (generally common stock and retained earnings) (up from 4 percent in Basel II). There is also a new leverage ratio requirement (minimum 3 percent).[75] The U.S. Federal Reserve announced in December 2011 that it would implement substantially all of the Basel III rules applied to banks and all other institutions with more than US $50 billion in assets.[76]

Then in 2013 the Fed proposed a rule which would place U.S. reserve requirements at a higher level than under Basel III. The proposed rule at its most stringent for banks with more than $250 billion is assets establishes a "liquidity coverage ration" which specifies a sufficient amount of liquid assets be held for a bank to withstand a thirty-day run on the bank. The intention is to prevent a repeat of 2008 when large banks in particular had to seek liquidity infusions from the Fed to avoid collapse.[77] Comments have been received and the rule, strongly opposed by banking interests, is presently under review.[78]

The added reserve requirements are having effects on large bank profitability, but are particularly noticeable for smaller ones, especially the 5 percent of loans issued through mortgage-backed securities which must be held by the bank. Further costs relate to compliance with Dodd-Frank, said to be proportionally heaviest for small banks with less than $500 million in assets. Another profit-reducing factor is the squeeze between short- and long-term interest rates, a traditional source of profits for community banks. As a consequence banks are looking for scale economies through mergers.[79] Fifty-one bank mergers were announced in the first quarter of 2012, up from thirty-nine in the first quarter of 2011.[80]

e. What Next?

As the TARP program expired, it had dispersed $600 billion of the authorized $700 billion. Moreover, a number of the loans were repaid or are in the process of being repaid and therefore the eventual cost to taxpayers is set at about $20 billion by the White House Office of Management and Budget (the Treasury Department is projecting a small profit).[81] And the program may even make a profit.[82] However, the most costly component is the receivership of Fannie Mae and Freddie Mac.

While the Standard & Poor's/Experian credit default index continues to decline below 1.3, at the height of the housing collapse it stood at 5.5,[83] meaning homes were going into default—reverting to government ownership when the mortgage was held by Fannie Mae or Freddie Mac. As a result, the Congressional Budget Office estimated the government's receivership cost to be $291 billion in 2009 and an additional $99 billion over 2010–2019. The Office of Management and Budget approaches the accounting slightly differently by considering only direct cash infusions. Its estimates are $95.6 and $65 billion respectively.[84] By either measure, these are large numbers indeed.

Whatever the final financial tally is, the impact on public opinion is clear—Americans hate the bailouts. The Occupy Wall Streeters, claiming to represent the 99 percent of less-well-off Americans, saw the process as a benefit to wealthy bankers at the expense of ordinary taxpayers. Indeed, one common perspective is that U.S. citizens have paid twice, once for the bailout and again through the unemployment and stock market turmoil caused by the fallout from the toxic mortgage securities. In addition, it is evident that there has been no cost to bankers or Wall Street: No one has gone to jail, and bonuses continue to be paid, $16 billion–worth for Goldman Sachs employees alone in 2009 (an average of $430,000 each) and $15.3 billion in 2010 (but declining thereafter due to reduced profits).[85] For 2013 the bonus pool was down 3 percent from 2012 to $12.61 billion as investment bank profits are squeezed by regulatory limits on some past lucrative businesses activities.[86] At the other end of the political spectrum is the Tea Party, which is equally aghast, but on a different free-market basis:

> If Congress had the best long-term interests of the American public in mind, it would have allowed the free market to recover from the loose credit problem government created, resulting in tighter credit, reduced consumer debt, greater savings, and more investment in industry that actually produces exportable goods that increase U.S. wealth and reduce our debilitating trade deficit. But, motivated by its own short-term interest, Congress did the opposite: it rewarded real-estate risk-takers, penalized conservative investors, paid off political supporters, and encouraged greater consumer spending of borrowed money.[87]

In some instances both groups seem to confuse TARP with the subsequent stimulus package intended to jump-start the economy, but that does not reduce the anger.

One of the debatable issues is if some financial institutions are "too big to fail" in the sense that their collapse will create widespread financial havoc, due to their size and interconnectedness with other financial institutions. The right sees the support of these firms as a harmful interference with the workings of the private sector while the left sees another example of those who are already powerful being rewarded for excessive risk taking.

The Dodd-Frank bill is supposed to address that issue by prescribing that the only solution for a faltering "too-big-to-fail" firm is liquidation (see this chapter, Section 9.4c). Yet evidence to date is that the problem is worse, not better, with the largest banks having more assets than ever. "The structural problems are worse," said Simon Johnson, a professor at the MIT Sloan School of Management and a former chief economist at the International Monetary Fund. "Their size, incentives—none of that has changed."[88]

The situation is unlikely to improve in the future, if one is persuaded by the results of a recent simulation by *The Economist*. The simulation involved a fictional but teetering $1 trillion bank holding company and involved some very experienced former officials. A private takeover was excluded because banks are now better able to unravel their relationships, eliminating the need for such a takeover, while bankruptcy was judged too risky for the financial system. Those exclusions threw the situation into the realm of the Dodd-Frank bill, which prohibits bailouts of large banks (see this chapter, Section 9.4c). A "forced" takeover by another large bank would create a yet larger one, and violate the Dodd-Frank cap of a 10 percent market share.

Another option was recapitalization under which unsecured creditors would have their obligations converted into shares. The process, though, was considered to take too long to resolve the immediate problem. Nonetheless that was the option of choice, as problematic as it was.

It seems Dodd-Frank creates some problems en route to resolving others.[89] The Fed has been attempting to avoid, or at least anticipate, any failure problems through the use of a "stress test" (Example 9.2).

EXAMPLE 9.2: "STRESS TEST" FOR TOO-BIG-TO-FAIL INSTITUTIONS

With the Comprehensive Capital Analysis and Review, commonly known as the "stress test," the Federal Reserve evaluates the capital planning processes and capital adequacy of the largest bank holding companies with the intent of determining whether firms would have sufficient capital in times of severe economic and financial stress to continue to lend to households and businesses. The test posits an intentionally severe scenario—a peak unemployment rate of 13 percent, a 50 percent drop in equity prices, and a 21 percent decline in housing prices. These conditions are as intended more stringent than for the first round of tests in 2009.

Nineteen bank holding companies were required to participate in the 2011 and 2012 tests over a hypothetical nine-quarter test period. Total losses at the nineteen participating holding companies in 2012 were estimated at $534 billion. The aggregate Tier 1 common capital ratio, which compares high-quality capital to risk-weighted assets, fell from 10.1 percent to 6.3 percent. Despite these projected losses, fifteen of the nineteen bank holding companies were estimated to maintain capital ratios above all four of the regulatory minimum levels; four banks failed to do so in the context of the test: Citigroup (the third-largest U.S. bank), SunTrust, Ally Financial, and MetLife. In large part this result is the consequence of significant increases in capital levels from 2011–2012, a weighted average increase to 10.4 percent from 5.4 percent, made possible by a substantially lower capital distributions in response to the Federal Reserve's move to ensure the firms reduced or eliminated dividends to maintain safety and soundness.

Many of the banks which "passed" the test were permitted to reduce their capital, either through dividends or stock buybacks.[90] That decision by the Fed has been criticized as increasing the likelihood of a future public bailout. Among other factors, the tests assume a mild recession in the European Union, which is anything but clear at this time, as well as ignoring the effect of interest rates.[91] Other commentators fault the use of a very few point estimates, stressing the importance of computing how banks fare as economy parameters such as employment rates deteriorate. "Because point estimates are so prone to errors from faulty model assumptions, measuring the distance between them to detect how quickly losses pile up as the economic shock gets larger becomes a vastly more reliable measure of risk."[92]

For their part, banks have been critical of the fact that they are not notified of the conditions of the test, greatly complicating management.[93] However, prior information would permit the firms to adjust their reporting to the standards, to "game" the system.

For the foreseeable future, the Fed's stress tests are likely to continue and become more stringent. Indeed for 2014 stress conditions included an unemployment rate reaching 11.25 percent, home prices declining nearly 25 percent, and the U.S. gross domestic product decreasing 4.75 percent. Five of the thirty largest banks (assets over $ 50 billion) failed, the most prominent being Citigroup. As a result the Fed did not approve its capital plan and it has been prevented from a share buyback plan and an increase in the dividend.[94]

Nor have the accounting firms necessarily been filling their mandated role under Dodd-Frank of protecting investors, as best as the public can glean. The big accounting firm Deloitte & Touche has taken the word of companies that it audited instead of properly performing its watchdog function, according to a recent report. Though Deloitte was alerted to the problems in spring 2008, a year later it had failed to fix them, according to the oversight board. "The firm's apparent failure to appropriately challenge management's representations occurred in numerous areas," the report by an industry oversight board said. Details, though, are lacking as the law restricts what can be publicly disclosed, assuring that certain findings would come to light only after a long delay, if ever.[95]

One area where the application of Dodd-Frank has advanced has been with the oversight of swap trading, and in particular the implementation of the Title VII requirement that the CFTC oversee swap execution facilities. The CFTC recently proposed a rule requiring any firm applying for designation as a swap execution facility be required to post swap prices that are widely accessible. Direct one-to-one transactions over the phone, heretofore the dominant market mechanism, would no longer be allowed.

However, the Swap Execution Facilities Clarification Act (HR2586) was approved by a House committee on November 15, 2011; this act would have, among other mandates, barred the mandated posting of swap prices and repealed the Dodd-Frank prohibition of the government bailout of swap dealers, but it was not adopted.[96] A second bill, the Swap Jurisdiction Certainty Act (HR1256), "would prevent the CFTC and the SEC from regulating derivative trades by overseas subsidiaries of American companies—even if the regulators determined those trades threatened the stability of the American economy or were being conducted purely to avoid regulation in America."[97] The bill passed the House in June 2013 and remains under committee review in the Senate. Critics express a concern that any swap trading reforms under Dodd-Frank could, if the act is adopted, be bypassed by U.S.-based firms simply by transferring trading overseas.[98]

In 2011 a UBS trader in London engaged in unauthorized trades which cost the bank $2.3 billion in losses at a time it was still recovering from a near collapse during the 2008 financial crisis.[99] UBS is a Swiss bank; the trades were made from the London office, while it also has a major position in the United States. This emphasizes how losses in one part of the world can affect bank stability worldwide.

Implementation of the Dodd-Frank Act has been proceeding slowly with just 40 percent of the 400 provisions cast into final regulatory language as of fall 2013, but banks still face the compliance deadline of July 21, 2014, increasing uncertainty.[100] One rule which has received particular scrutiny and pushback is the Volcker Rule (Section 619), which limits banks taking excessive risks by speculating with their own funds (called proprietary trading). Exemptions are allowed to banks for market-making—buying and selling assets on behalf of others—as well as hedging activities. The final rule was adopted December 10, 2013 (effective date April 1, 2014) with full compliance required by July 21, 2015, soon extended two years to July 21, 2017. That is, banks were allowed two additional years to unwind their collateralized loan obligations (CLOs). CLOs are a form of bank loans favored in leveraged buyouts which can be removed from a bank's balance sheet by selling (securitization), possibly to another bank.[101] The new rules limit banks' investments in hedge funds and other risk activities like private equity funds, which has an indirect effect on CLOs. Other prohibitions of the rule include:

- Engaging in short-term proprietary trading of securities, derivatives, commodity futures and options on these instruments for their own account
- Owning, sponsoring, or having certain relationships with hedge funds or private equity funds, referred to as "covered funds"

To be sure there are asset class exemptions to these sweeping prohibitions. These include U.S. Treasuries and municipal securities.[102]

Others have pointed out that a series of other exemptions, asset classes as well as administrative, significantly limit the effect of the Volcker Rule on controlling risk taking by banks, and large banks in particular. These exemptions as but one example allow banks to own physical commodities while banning trading in commodity derivatives. The "ownership" of physical commodities is sometimes used for a temporary purchase of the inventories of oil companies to enhance the firms' balance sheets, prior to "selling" them back. Those commodity transfers have been linked to the manipulation of commodity prices. And banks may engage in derivatives trading if they operate a clearinghouse, an institution which verifies the buyers and sellers of recently completed trades along with other administrative functions. However, clearinghouses also act as the opposite party for all clearinghouse members—buyers for member sellers and sellers for member buyers.[103] For that reason clearinghouses can take on significant risk and so while the Dodd-Frank Act requires the use of clearinghouses it does not create them, leading to the existence of many club-like, underfunded clearinghouses which themselves can become too big to fail.[104] The rule is estimated to cost $ 4.3 billion for the forty-seven largest banks alone, not including agency costs and those of smaller banks. Most of that cost will result from unwinding CLO and other positions at a loss, although there are something like $500 million in annual compliance costs projected.[105]

Delays in completing the language irritated both President Obama and Treasury Secretary Lew Delays were attributable to four principal causes:[106]

- Threat of court challenge: The SEC lost a case regarding "proxy access" (a process by which shareholders can remove directors) brought by the U.S. Chamber of Commerce and the Business Roundtable on the grounds of an insufficient cost/benefit analysis. In 2012 the CFTC lost the first round of a court challenge over a rule placing position limits on futures and options contracts. That decision is presently under appeal but at minimum the implementation of any rule is being delayed. The pressure is therefore on to complete the analysis by the end of the year, despite the fact that there are few hard numbers, especially as regards benefits. Yet whatever is the outcome, the banking industry is promising a legal challenge.
- Massive lobbying leading to the passage of "technical loopholes" in the regulations: Lobbying contributed to the flat funding of the CFTC in 2012 despite the great increase in its responsibilities under Dodd-Frank, to the passage of HR3283 (see above), which prohibits the CFTC and the SEC from regulating derivative trades

by overseas subsidiaries,[107] and dropping the minimum 20 percent down-payment requirement for mortgages to none at all.[108]

- Infighting and differences in approaches and responsibilities among the five responsible regulatory authorities: the Federal Reserve, FDIC, Office of the Comptroller of the Currency, CFTC, and the SEC.
- Difficulty of defining "proprietary trading" and "market making"—often when placing trades for clients, banks must also lay down complex hedges involving the buying and selling of multiple instruments. Under those conditions it is complex to determine just what market activity is on the account of the bank and what is undertaken for clients.[109] Proprietary trading can be highly profitable for banks but does leave them open to large trading losses, as in the "London whale" debacle (see immediately below).

There is an open debate over whether the Volcker Rule, as adopted, would have prevented substantial trading losses by JPMorgan Chase during summer 2012. Initially estimated to cost the bank $2 billion, the estimate rose as high as $9 billion, but could settle in the $6–7 billion range. The trades, established by a trader known as the "London whale" (Bruno Iksil, who was never charged, while two alleged co-conspirators are under U.S. indictment), established a bullish bet on an index of investment-grade corporate debt, subsequently combined with a bearish wager on high-yield securities.[110]

The losses came at a particularly bad time for bankers as the Volcker Rule details were then under discussion, with JP Morgan Chase's CEO, Jamie Dimon, being noted as both a skilled risk manager and outspoken critic of the Volcker Rule. The trades were subsequently the subject of Senate Banking Committee hearings. The firm agreed in a settlement to pay $920 million in penalties and admitted violating securities laws in 2012 as top managers withheld information from the board.[111] Complicating matters, Dimon was a member of the board of directors of the New York Federal Reserve at the time of the illegal trades. There were calls at the time for him to step down, but he completed his second term in December 2012 and has not continued (which is common following a second term).

While media opinion is important, it is also valuable to consider the positions of knowledgeable participants. We turn here to a statement made by Paul Volcker, former chairman of the Federal Reserve, regarding the Dodd-Frank bill and the status of the financial reform in general:[112]

> I think it is fair to say that in passing the Dodd-Frank legislation, the United States has taken an important step in the needed direction.
>
> But there are real, behavioral consequences of the rescue effort that was made. The expectation that taxpayers will help absorb potential losses can only reassure creditors that risks will be minimized and help induce risk-taking on the assumption that losses will be repaid out of public funds—with the potential gains all private.

He leaves little doubt, though, that to his mind much remains to be done:

> It should be clear that among the causes of the recent financial crisis was an unjustified faith in rational expectations, market efficiencies, and the techniques of modern finance. That faith was stoked in part by the huge financial rewards that enabled the extremes of

borrowing, the economic imbalances, and the pretenses and assurances of the credit-rating agencies to persist so long. A relaxed approach by regulators and legislators reflected the new financial zeitgeist.

All the seeming mathematical precision that was brought to investment, all the complicated new products, including the explosion of derivatives, that were intended to diffuse and minimize risk, did not work as had been claimed.

Those were fundamentally matters of public policy—the result of decisions on taxing, spending, and exchange rates; they were not a reflection of the characteristics of the financial market. But neither can we ignore the fact that financial practices helped sustain such imbalances. In the end, the build-up in leverage, the failure of credit discipline, and the opaqueness of new kinds of securities and derivatives such as credit default swaps helped facilitate, to a truly dangerous extent, accommodation to the underlying imbalances and to the eventual bubbles.

All these developments derive in some part from the complexity implicit in the growth of the so-called shadow banking system—the nondepository banks, hedge funds, insurers, money market funds, and other largely unregulated entities that grew enormously in size after 2000—a system that by June 2008 was roughly the size of the traditional banking system. In the end, the consequence was to intensify the financial crisis and to severely wound the real-world economy.

There is the larger conceptual and unsettled question of the extent to which such standards should be applied to the "shadow" banking system I have referred to.

Several observations and recommendations for reform were made by Volcker, some more sweeping than others, including:

- Role of money market funds which are unregulated including with no reserve requirements are subject to runs during perilous times
- Proprietary trading needs stronger limits
- Derivatives require strong, simple, and standardized clearinghouses
- The interest rates on mortgage-backed securities have been held down due to a perception (correct as it turned out) they had a government guarantee, which led directly to overleverage and heightened risk

As we see now, most of Volcker's policy recommendations have been incorporated into the rule carrying his name. Whether they and other components of the Dodd-Frank Act are sufficient to avoid future financial collapses remains to be seen. Certainly overregulation of finance, as some warn of, is a potential risk, but underregulation has proven to be hugely costly to taxpayers as well.

9.5 ▪ CASE 9.1: TOMPKINS FINANCIAL

a. Background on Tompkins Financial[113]

Tompkins Financial has $5 billion in assets and is traded on the NYSE Amex under the symbol "TMP." Headquartered in Ithaca, New York, Tompkins Financial traces its roots to 1836 through Tompkins Trust Company.

It operates approximately thirty-five banking offices in New York. The banks provide individual retirement, money market, checking, and savings accounts, as well as certificates of deposit. In addition, the banks originate real estate, business, home equity, and consumer loans. Subsidiary Tompkins Insurance Agencies mainly offers property and casualty insurance in western New York. Major divisions include:

- **Tompkins Trust Company**: Community bankers serving Ithaca and central New York since 1836
- **The Bank of Castile**: Community bankers serving western New York since 1869
- **Mahopac National Bank**: Community bankers serving the Hudson Valley in New York since 1927
- **VIST Bank**: Headquartered in Wyomissing, Pennsylvania, providing banking, insurance, investment, and mortgage services throughout southeastern Pennsylvania with roots back to 1909
- **Tompkins Financial Advisors**: Wealth and risk managers since 1891 serving western, central, and downstate New York
- **Tompkins Insurance Agencies**: Insurance and risk managers since 1875 serving western and central New York

Like most banks, Tompkins Financial was hard hit by the financial crisis of the late 2000s but has been performing stably since (Figure 9.9). It can be considered to be ably and conservatively managed with a focus on the upstate New York market. The firm received the Bauer Financial four-star (excellent) rating for financial stability in 2013.[114]

b. Case

Students are asked to prepare the following case questions.

Tompkins Financial is clearly a well, if somewhat conservatively, run regional bank. It was clearly affected by the recent financial crisis, as were all listed stocks, but has held its stock value well in uncertain times. It, like all businesses under recent regulations, has additional reporting responsibilities and has some restrictions over its activities, but to a large degree its small size exempts it from the most onerous of these regulations. At the same time the changing banking/finance environment presumably creates new opportunities.

This case then considers:

1. How has regulatory reform since 2000 likely affected Tompkins Financial, directly as well as indirectly?
2. What opportunities does Tompkins Financial have under the new regulatory environment, and which would you suggest it act on? Options include switching its charter from commercial to investment banking (a long shot), looking for takeover opportunities to enhance its market share in New York, or establishing a regional presence by seeking acquisitions in neighboring states. Alternatively,

Figure 9.9 **Tompkins Financial Stock Prices 2009–2013, Third Quarter**

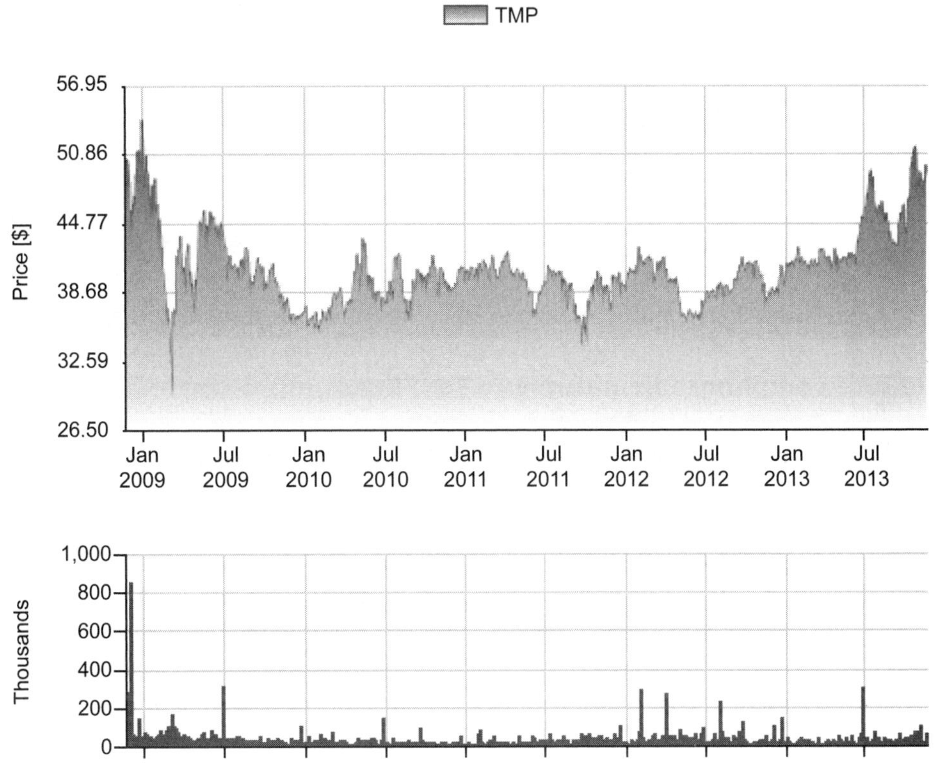

Source: Tompkins Trust Co.

Tompkins Financial may look to be acquired by a larger bank or perhaps seek a leveraged purchase by a hedge fund which is looking for a steady-performing asset. Are any of these options appealing, or are there other alternatives?

9.6 THE JOBS ACT

With unemployment languishing in the 7 percent range five years after the beginning of the current recession, and with unemployment having been a major dimension of the 2012 presidential campaign, it is not surprising that the government has been seeking ways to boost employment. With "start-up" firms credited with the majority of new job creation,[115] it is also not surprising that sector is a focus of interest. From there it is but a small step to connect start-ups with capital formulation, and from there to the use of IPOs as capital generators for new, growing firms.

IPO refers to the initial offering of stock to the public by a privately held company. IPOs provide an opportunity for early investors such as venture capitalists as well as for the founders to cash out on a successful firm while providing the newly public company with additional capital for financing growth.

Policy makers have not been unattentive to the fact that IPO numbers have been and remain low since the start of the current recession. Subsequent years showed some uptick from the depth of the recession—thirty-one in 2008, sixty-three in 2009, 154 in 2011 and down again, to 128 in 2012 and then rebounding in 2013 to 222—but still below the prerecession numbers.[116] Of course, IPO numbers are affected by the strength of the stock market overall.

There are of course many reasons why firms choose, or not, the IPO route, and the recession has to be a big component. But the regulations controlling the reporting of financial figures and solicitations of pre-IPO share sales are also factors, and ones the JOBS Act is intended to ease. The act, signed into law in April 2012, contains a number of provisions which can be placed in the following four categories.

a. Reduce Compliance Requirements for "Emerging Growth Companies"

This provision creates a new category of "Emerging Growth Companies" (EGCs), companies with annual gross revenues of less than $1 billion, that have been public reporting companies for less than five years, and that have a capitalization held by nonaffiliates under $700 million. This applies to companies completing their IPO after December 8, 2011. Firms qualifying as EGCs will have many public, and potentially burdensome, reporting requirements eased:[117]

- Include only two years of audited financial statements in the initial registration documents
- Exempt from the enhanced compensation disclosure and analysis requirements under Dodd-Frank, and not required to comply with shareholder voting requirements on named executive officer compensation ("say on pay")
- Not be required to supply an auditor attestation of their financial reporting controls in their annual reports on Form 10-K
- Generally exempt from any audit firm rotation or supplemental auditor disclosure requirements
- Not required to comply with new U.S. Generally Accepted Accounting Principles (GAAP) accounting standards
- File registration statements with the SEC in draft form and on a confidential basis; delay public availability of their registration materials until twenty-one days prior to publicizing IPO

The $1 billion in revenues cap set under the act would qualify 94 percent or all IPOs over the past thirty years to qualify for the relaxed rules.[118]

b. Relax Analyst Communication Rules

- Investment bank analysts, even if an underwriter, are permitted to publish research reports on EGCs while IPO registrations are pending

- Exempt underwriters' analysts from the conflict-of-interest rules by permitting communication with EGC management and investment bankers
- Issuer will be able to communicate with and canvass interest from qualified institutional buyers (QIBs) and institutional accredited investors, prior to or during registration
- Prohibition from imposing restrictions on publishing EGC-related research or public appearances during the post-IPO "quiet" and "lock-up" periods

c. Liberalized Private Placement Rules: General Solicitation and Advertisement of Private Offerings

- Modifies Rule 506 of Regulation D by requiring the SEC to adopt rules permitting companies to engage in public solicitation of "accredited investors" in a private offering
- Amends the private offering exemptions under the Securities Act to permit certain general solicitation and advertisement of ostensibly private offerings
- Public advertising and solicitation are permitted

d. Enhance Flexibility to Sell Securities, Including "Crowdfunding"

- Expand the maximum offering under Regulation A offerings from $5 million to $50 million, allowing issuers to solicit investor interest prior to filing an offering statement with the SEC, and allow public solicitation of investment interest
- Raises the shareholder ceiling prior to filing with the SEC from 500 to a new maximum of 2,000 holders of record of which no more than 500 may be nonaccredited investors
- Allow small issuers to use online tools to raise capital in small amounts from a broad investor base, while instituting investor safeguards, primarily in the form of enhanced disclosure requirements (referred to as the "CROWDFUND Act"). This part of the act relies on the emergence of crowdfunding portals, which have their own requirements/stipulations

The limitations of crowdfunding are significant and include under a proposed rule of October 23, 2013:[119]

- **Offering Limit:** Not to exceed $1 million in any twelve-month period
- **Individual Investor Limit in Any Twelve-Month Period:** For investors with annual income or net worth of less than $100,000, greater of $2,000 or 5 percent of the investor's annual income or net worth; for other investors, 10 percent of the investor's annual income or net worth, to a maximum of $100,000
- **Public Disclosure Requirements:** Financial information with scope keyed to the size of the offering, the business and business plan, and intended use of proceeds from the offering, target offering amount, the pricing of the securities or a description

of the pricing method, and disclosure about the issuer's management and current ownership

The crowdfunding rule is under review with a decision expected by the end of 2014. This is in addition to tax reduction provisions to be implemented over the next several years for qualified small businesses.[120]

e. SEC Regulatory Proposals for Accrediting Investors

The SEC was given 270 days following enactment to complete all the implementing regulations, but many rules under Regulation D lagged. Those which have been adopted allow for general solicitation of sales to the public went into effect on September 23, 2013 (see this chapter, Section 9.6b).[121] And Rule 501: An investor is an accredited investor if "he or she has individual net worth—or joint net worth with a spouse—that exceeds $1 million at the time of the purchase, excluding the value of the primary residence of such person. Or, if he or she has income exceeding $200,000 in each of the two most recent years or joint income with a spouse exceeding $300,000 for those years and a reasonable expectation of the same income level in the current year." This rule went into effect in September 2013.[122] Additionally, under Rule 144A investors can be accredited if the "issuer reasonably believes that they meet one of the categories at the time of the sale of the securities."[123] The issuer is charged with verifying that investors are indeed accredited.

f. The Effects of the Facebook IPO on the JOBS Act

Although the JOBS Act was one of the few pieces of legislation to receive strong bipartisan support in 2012, observers have expressed concern about protecting investors. There are actually two concerns—the provision of adequate information for investors to make informed decisions, and drawing in unsophisticated investors. One perspective (that of a self-identified cheat) is available at Reuters.com in a video titled "JOBS Act Is Fraud Made Easy: Sam Antar (2:41)": www.reuters.com/video/2012/04/13/jobs-act-is-fraud-made-easy-sam-antar?videoId=233309052&videoChannel=5.

Ironically, at the time the JOBS rules were being discussed the Facebook IPO debacle gave credence to the critics' concerns. Facebook stock at $65.36 is at the time of writing (summer 2014) finally trading well above its opening price on May 18, 2012, of $42.05 (Figure 9.10). The IPO price was $38, valuing the company at $100 million.

Now of course stock prices go up and down, but with the Facebook IPO that is only part of the story. The pre-IPO price had risen steadily (Figure 9.11), particularly as anticipation and hype accelerated in the IPO date grew closer, which placed great pressure on the underwriters, led by Morgan Stanley and with JPMorgan Chase and Goldman Sachs, to set the IPO price high to justify the valuation. "The bankers needed to drum up enough interest that they could set the IPO price at least as high as it was on [the pre-IPO market]. Anything short of that would have been viewed as a flop."[124] The IPO raised a

Figure 9.10 **Facebook Post-IPO Price Chart: Quarterly Closing Prices**

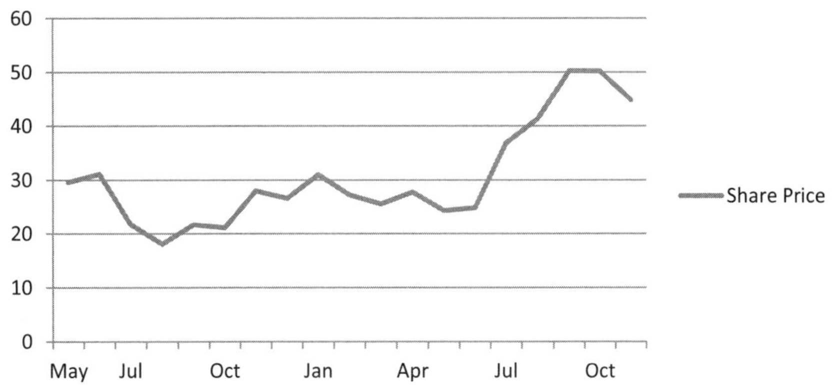

Source: W. Lesser. Date source Yahoo Finance.

Figure 9.11 **Facebook Pre-IPO Price Chart: April 2009–April 2012**

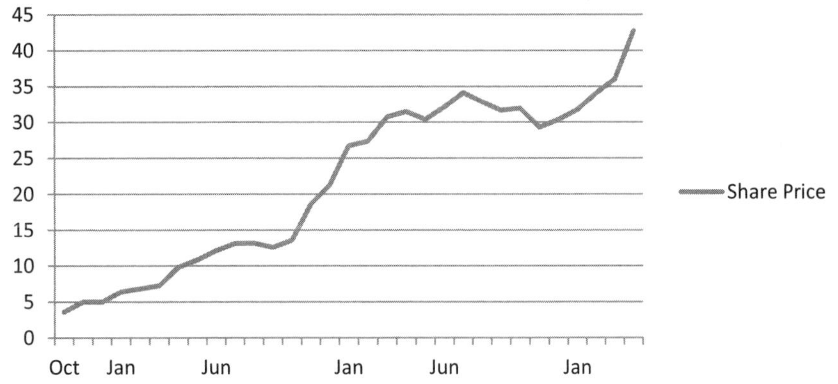

Source: W. Lesser. Data from Secondmarket.

record $16 billion for Facebook, which led to the unresolved question if the firm pressured Morgan Stanley to set the stratospheric valuation.

The Facebook IPO valuation was in sharp contrast to the pricing of other IPO offerings, according to an ongoing lawsuit by eToys against Goldman Sachs, the underwriter. According to eToys executives, Goldman intentionally set the stock offer price low so as to provide a guaranteed profit to its corporate clients, which immediately flipped them. What was in this arrangement for Goldman? A kickback of 30–50 percent of the profits as "commissions," according to the suit. An IPO with a big first-day price jump traditionally is seen as a success, but of course what it really means is that others are taking the profits that rightly belonged to the firm.[125]

The subsequent sharp Facebook price declines led to some forty shareholder law suits (the underwriters are attempting to have these consolidated into a single suit) claiming they were provided with inadequate earnings information. What happened was a bit murky—and unusual. On May 9, shortly before the scheduled IPO, Facebook filed with the SEC an amended S-1 filing acknowledging the growth of users on the platform was "outpacing" the number of ads reaching its 901-plus million users. That is, recent user growth was from mobile devices (cell phones), which have proven to be a less successful platform for ads, the source of revenues. What the Facebook filing said was:

> Based upon our experience in the second quarter of 2012 to date, the trend we saw in the first quarter of [Daily Active Users] increasing more rapidly than the increase in number of ads delivered has continued. We believe this trend is driven in part by increased usage of Facebook on mobile devices where we have only recently begun showing an immaterial number of sponsored stories in News Feed, and in part due to certain pages having fewer ads per page as a result of product decisions.

The underwriters soon thereafter reduced their 2012 revenue forecast to $4.85 billion from more than $5 billion earlier. Such a reduction by underwriters so close to the stock launch date is considered highly unusual.[126] What happened next remains unclear. It does seem that Morgan Stanley told its top clients about the new revenue forecasts; the information was passed on verbally as published revenue forecasts or other analysis by an underwriter are illegal until forty days following the IPO. This is known as the "second quiet period" under SEC rules (pre–JOBS Act). The "first" quiet period has three subperiods:

- The "prefiling period," which begins with the decision to publicly offer securities and continues until the filing of an SEC registration statement
- The "waiting period" or "quiet period" which begins with the filing of a registration statement and continues until the SEC declares that registration statement effective
- The "posteffective period," which begins once the registration statement is declared effective

Pre–JOBS Act, oral and written offers were generally prohibited during the prefiling period, while during the quiet period there were no explicit restrictions on oral offers,[127] which are apparently what Morgan Stanley solicited during its "road show" presentations to major clients.[128] So Morgan Stanley did not necessarily act illegally, according to these reports. Still, there is a serious ethical question about informing one group of investors and not the other. Institutional clients did act, often selling rather than buying shares during the IPO, profiting in the act and passing along losses to small investors.

Nor were these the only problems associated with the IPO. Nasdaq technical glitches caused a thirty-minute delay in trading on opening day. There were reports of trouble with canceling orders and at times trading on the platform. These problems were the basis for Facebook's lawsuit against Nasdaq, which is blamed in the suit for the IPO debacle.[129]

It is, though, the information issues which concern us here in regard to the JOBS Act. Small investors did not participate directly in the IPO; direct purchases were allocated to large institutional clients.[130] As a result of the future earning prediction cut, combined with an increase in the size and price of the deal (25 percent more shares were allocated by Facebook just days prior to the IPO) and the number of shares sold by insiders, some institutional investors recognized pending problems and unloaded shares, placing further downward pressure on the stock price. Individual investors, meanwhile, were oblivious. According to analyst Henry Blodget:

> In the wake of these revelations, Facebook's lead underwriter, Morgan Stanley, said that it had followed the rules. And it may have. If Morgan Stanley followed the rules, however, the rules themselves are grossly unfair. Because they allowed big institutional investors to learn just before the IPO that Facebook's business had deteriorated, while smaller investors were left thinking everything was just fine.[131]

The unequal treatment of small investors in the Facebook IPO has clear ramifications for the forms and timing of financial information required under the JOBS Act. A related information factor is the "quiet period" (see above), originally intended to enhance the equality of informational access by limiting all interested parties to the prospectus. Of course, it has always been difficult to prevent the spread of information, and that applies doubly today with the proliferation of communication media. The JOBS Act significantly reduces quiet period requirements for emerging growth companies (see above), which is at the heart of the debate over the act. Make that two questions: "One is whether all investors should have equal access to information. The other is whether allowing looser corporate tongues is good, leading to better pricing, or bad, leading to hype."[132]

The debut of the relaxation of the advertising role in September 2013 under the JOBS Act brought another media giant into the media spotlight. This time it was Twitter which announced it had filed with the SEC an S-1 form declaring an intent to hold an IPO. Twitter, which does not release sales figures, is unofficially estimated to have revenues of $600 million, rising to $950 million over a year, placing it near the top of the generous JOBS Act cap.[133]

The seventy million shares offered quickly rose 73 percent from the offer price of $26 ($45.10 opening) to $44.90 by the end of the initial trading day on November 7, 2013. Shares reached a high of almost $50 before falling back to $44 a week later. The $50 price values the company at $25 billion, essentially twice the estimated worth of $12.8 billion as reported in the IPO filing. With only negative net revenues Twitter cannot be valued in traditional ways, but an alternative approach comparing capitalization to annual sales lead to a calculated value of $18.50, midpoint in the pre-IPO planned offer price range of $17–20.[134]

Twitter management is being criticized both for setting too low a price, leaving $1 billion on the table, as well as allowing and encouraging the enormous hype, leading[135] to little upside potential for investors.[136] "But at anything above $18 each, its shares will be a poor long-term investment."[137] Many observers feel that Twitter is the kind of large, established firm which does not need the options allowed under the JOBS Act.

For small investors the Twitter IPO experience was echoed in about half the IPOs for 2013–2014. That is, after a year that half of IPO shares are still trading at prices below the opening levels. Twitter itself is trading seven months following the IPO at $10 off the opening price. Of course, not all investors have lost money; institutional investors which paid the $26 offering price were well rewarded.[138]

9.7 ■ CASE 9.2: WOULD THE JOBS ACT HAVE ENHANCED OR DENIGRATED THE EXPERIENCE WITH A FACEBOOK-LIKE IPO?

As has been described, there were and are significant issues with the Facebook IPO, major among them the questions of information distribution and equity. The offering however did raise a record amount of funds for the firm for financing future growth. At the same time the JOBS Act is being implemented, which has at its core a reduction in information reporting requirements in an attempt to expedite the IPO process. Of course, the Facebook IPO was too early and too large (revenues exceeding $1 billion) to fall under the JOBS Act rules, but other similar offerings will follow.

Case questions

Students should prepare the following questions:

1. What have been the costs, financial and reputational, to Facebook and its underwriters of their faulty IPO?
2. Who actually suffered the losses from the initial IPO?
3. Imagine you are advising a $25 million annual revenue private firm interested in raising at least $50 million through a stock offering. The firm, tentatively valued at $500 million, is in the volatile social media sector and so is widely known. Would you recommend using pre-IPO placements to accredited investors, crowdfunding from small investors, and/or a public IPO? How would you recommend the prospectus and "forward looking" projection be managed, including the "road show" pitches to institutional investors and possible public advertising? Please provide details as needed on your "client's" business and/or interpretation of JOBS Act rules if relevant to your answer.
4. As events unfold, how has the experience of the Twitter IPO differed from that of Facebook due to measures allowed by the JOBS Act?

9.8 CONCLUSIONS

If nothing else, the material in this chapter emphasizes that financial regulation is both detailed and complex, possibly to a fault. Perhaps that is why few among the public pay much attention to it despite its importance. But even at a peripheral level several factors become apparent:

- The government cannot function without a central bank, and its role increases rather than declines over time.

- Similarly, the financial sector cannot function without regulation. The sector follows a pattern of no/limited regulation followed by catastrophe, then forgetfulness and deregulation, another catastrophe, and reregulation.
- At the level of specific regulations there is a tendency to be overstrict when responding to a new problem and to relax on details with time and experience. That seems to be happening with financial regulation. This point though is distinct from that of broad deregulation led from the legislative level.

While the details can be confusing, a key concept of financial regulations current and past is simple: enhance transparency. That is, financial regulation in the main is a response to incomplete information leading to market failure. Transparency was initiated in reaction to an opaque financial world in the 1930s, enhanced with Sarbanes-Oxley, and continued in parts of Dodd-Frank such as "say-on-pay" (under which shareholders are informed of the top executives' full compensation with comps).

We know from economic theory and from experience that complete information is essential for markets to function efficiently. Bankers also know that, which is why they so strongly oppose the standardization of swap markets, a lucrative opportunity for insiders. The movement to public trading platforms is just getting under way with a trading target of 2014. Conversely, insider trading in its many forms is the misappropriation of information, which also is counter to efficient market operation.

On a broader scale, we believe we have learned some truths under Sarbanes-Oxley. One is that the requirement that chief executive officers and chief financial officers sign off on the accuracy of their financial statements has made them aware that the correctness of the reports is their responsibility and not that of the auditors and others. Second, and related, since these top officials now take direct responsibility they are seeing that appropriate control mechanisms are in place, including safeguards so that no one in a firm can bypass the systems.[139] These points may seem narrow considering the scope of Sarbanes-Oxley, but they are fundamental to preventing future Enrons and their ilk.

Other simple, apparent truths are the need (a) for adequate reserve requirements and (b) for individuals to be protected from losses caused by bank failure. The latter issue is well resolved with the creation of the FDIC, but the form and adequacy of reserves remains a perplexing issue. We do now know, thanks to an expensive lesson, that the regulated should not establish their own requirements, no matter how sophisticated that approach may seem. We are beginning to question the different classes of reserves à la Basel III, both for the same reasons. Unexpected events, concurrences of events, can change risk profiles, rendering the projections/distinctions worthless.

With the several opportunities for regulation over the past eighty years, one would think the country would get it right, but that is far from the case. Indeed there are those who argue that on balance regulation exacerbates the problems, whether by undermining the need for reputation (which is a partial substitute for regulation), by increasing moral hazard (in this case the belief that the public will cover the costs of misadventures as was done in 2007–2008), or simply by raising compliance costs so high as to stultify the necessary work of the sector. Many recent hires into commercial and investment banking find a large portion of their time is spent in regulatory compliance. Yet if regulations have been suboptimal (to put it nicely) there is much blame to share—by agencies, by politicians, by the courts, and by the sector itself which lobbies hard against regulations.

An example could be the JOBS Act, which rolls back important investor protections of full information disclosure while the needs and benefits are less clear. Certainly there is no need to set the limits so high that virtually all IPOs are encompassed. Twitter by most reasonable standards is no start-up firm yet it is using the JOBS Act cloak potentially to double its initial share offering.

Going ahead, a more assertive SEC (Professor Macey aside; see Chapter 5, Example 5.3) is a good thing, overdue. Yet the incomplete state of the Dodd-Frank regulations means significant parts of financial infrastructure remain potentially at risk from the same forces that caused the last problems. We may lack the smarts to identify and prevent future issues, but past ones? No excuse. Particularly problematic are strategies for enhancing the quality of credit-rating agency evaluations (although charging buyers and not sellers of those ratings would be a good start) and resolving the "too big to fail" issue. The top banks are indeed too big to fail. Perhaps one strategy would be to encourage the growth through merger of the second-tier banks (which is already happening due to monetary penalties regarding size imposed on smaller banks—note Tompkins Trust). More, though, is required.

The two cases point out the differential effects of regulations—in this case based on the size of the firms. Tompkins Trust had little to do with the impetus for Dodd-Frank but still faces a cost penalty for compliance. The Facebook IPO debacle pointed out why the financial reporting requirements the JOBS Act reverses were instituted in the first place.

9.9 STUDY QUESTIONS

1. Draw the parallels in early political debates over a central bank and federal control over the money supply with the issues and political position following the 2007–2008 financial near collapse.
2. What is a "bank panic" and why does it no longer happen in the United States?
3. Detail the role of bank reserve requirements, credit, and recession up to the Great Depression. What subsequent regulations limited that destructive pattern?
4. What are the connections among security reporting requirements and banking regulations? What are the principal acts involved?
5. What is the regulatory basis for insider trading cases?
6. The Federal Reserve is required to balance the goals of full employment with low inflation. In the 2010s inflation has been low but unemployment remains high by historical standards. What is the Federal Reserve doing now to fulfill its full employment policy obligation?
7. In what ways does Tompkins Financial qualify as a bank holding company under Federal Reserve policy?
8. In what ways did the Garn-St. Germain Depository Institutions Act deregulation of S&Ls in the 1980s presage the mortgage problems of the 2000s?

9. A series of reregulation acts followed the S&L crisis of the 1980s. How successful was that regulation in resolving the underlying problems for that group of banks?
10. In the finance area few would dispute that the really significant regulations include the SEC, Glass-Steagall, Sarbanes-Oxley, Gramm-Leach-Bliley, and of course Dodd-Frank. Would you add any other acts to this heavyweight list? Please explain.
11. Why has the regulation of swap trading been such a complex matter for regulators and regulatory law?
12. What are the roles of the credit-rating agencies and how did they contribute to the Great Recession? How are credit-rating agencies regulated?
13. Large brokers and investment banks were allowed to use their own mathematical models to calculate their risk exposure, from which their reserve requirements were derived. What went wrong with that approach?
14. How do the Dodd-Frank and Basel III reserve requirements differ? Are the differences significant?
15. What are the key obstacles to completing the regulations under Dodd-Frank?
16. Why is the Volcker Rule proving to be so difficult to implement?
17. Is the U.S. economy under ongoing threat due to the incomplete regulation of the finance sector? Justify your position. If so, what are the ongoing gaps in regulations?
18. What are the economic principles underlying the JOBS Act?
19. Economists among others are concerned about what they call "moral hazard," the incentive to take large risks on the belief that others will cover the losses. What are moral hazard issues evident in this chapter? How are they mitigated or enhanced by regulation?
20. In what ways have financial regulations enhanced the "moral hazard" problem in the finance sector?

NOTES

1. Claes Bell, "Obama versus Romney on Financial Reform." *Fox*Business, October 10, 2012. Available at www.foxbusiness.com/personal-finance/2012/10/10/obama-versus-romney-on-financial-reform//. Last visited 10/3/13.

2. Roger T. Johnson, *Historical Beginnings . . . The Federal Reserve.* Federal Reserve Bank of Boston, 2010. Available at www.bos.frb.org/about/pubs/begin.pdf. Last visited 11/14/11.

3. The Court held that Congress had the power to incorporate the bank and that Maryland could not tax instruments of the national government employed in the execution of constitutional powers. Writing for the Court, Chief Justice Marshall noted that Congress possessed unenumerated powers not explicitly outlined in the Constitution.

4. John Steele Gordon, "A Short Banking History of the United States." *Wall Street Journal*, October 10, 2008.

5. Randall S. Kroszner, "The Motivations behind Banking Reform." Available at www.cato.org/pubs/regulation/regv24n2/kroszner.pdf. Last visited 11/14/11.

6. Abigail Tucker, "The Financial Panic of 1907: Running from History." *Smithsonian.com,* October 10, 2008. Available at www.smithsonianmag.com/history-archaeology/1907_Panic.html. Last visited 11/15/11.

7. "Aldrich-Vreeland Act: Responding to the Panic of 1907." *United States History*. Available at www.u-s-history.com/pages/h953.html. Last visited 11/15/11.

8. Data from San Jose State University, Department of Economics, "Economic History of the United States." Available at www.sjsu.edu/faculty/watkins/useconhist.htm#DEPRESSIONS. Last visited 11/15/11.

9. Answers.com, "Federal Reserve Act." Available at www.answers.com/topic/federal-reserve-act. Last visited 11/15/11.

10. Investopedia, "What Was the Glass-Steagall Act?" July 16, 2003. Available at www.investopedia.com/articles/03/071603.asp#axzz1doczCUWu. Last visited 11/15/11.

11. The Uniform Securities Act of 1956 is a model statute designed to assist each state in the drafting of its securities laws.

12. Richard I. Alvarez and Mark J. Astarita, "Introduction to the Blue Sky Laws." SECLaw.com. Available at www.seclaw.com/bluesky.htm. Last visited 11/16/11.

13. U.S. Senate, "Subcommittee on Senate Resolutions 84 and 234." Available at www.senate.gov/artandhistory/history/common/investigations/Pecora.htm. Last visited 11/16/11.

14. SEC, "The Laws that Govern the Securities Industry." Available at www.sec.gov/about/laws.shtml. Last visited 11/17/11.

15. SEC, "SEC Files Insider Trading Charges against Rajat Gupta." October 26, 2011. Available at www.sec.gov/news/press/2011/2011-223.htm. Last visited 11/17/11.

16. SEC, "Year-by-Year SEC Enforcement Statistics." Available at www.sec.gov/news/newsroom/images/enfstats.pdf. See also "SEC Announces Enforcement Results for FY 2013." Available at www.sec.gov/News/PressRelease/Detail/PressRelease/1370540503617#.U5XpwhBMKky. Last visited 6/9/14.

17. Answers.com.

18. "Banks, Savings & Loans, Credit Unions."*Encyclopedia of Everyday Law.* Available at www.enotes.com/everyday-law-encyclopedia/banks-savings-and-loans-credit-unions. Last visited 11/16/11.

19. Federal Reserve Bank of Boston, "Depository Institutions Deregulation and Monetary Control Act of 1980." Available at www.bos.frb.org/about/pubs/deposito.pdf. Last visited 11/16/11.

20. G. Garcia et al., Federal Reserve Bank of Chicago, "Garn-St. Germain Depository Institutions Act of 1982." Available at www.chicagofed.org/digital_assets/publications/economic_perspectives/1983/ep_mar_apr1983_part1_garcia.pdf. Last visited 11/16/11.

21. Kimberly Amadeo, "Savings and Loan Crisis." About.com. Available at http://useconomy.about.com/od/grossdomesticproduct/p/89_Bank_Crisis.htm. FDIC, *History of the Eighties—Lessons for the Future,* "Banking Legislation and Regulation." Volume I: An Examination of the Banking Crises of the 1980s and Early 1990s, 1997, Chapter 2. Available at www.fdic.gov/bank/historical/history/87_136.pdf. Both last visited 11/16/11.

22. Defined in section 2(c) of the Bank Holding Company Act of 1956.

23. FDIC, "Competitive Equality Banking Act of 1987." Available at www.fdic.gov/regulations/laws/rules/6500-3240.html. Last visited 11/16/11.

24. FDIC, "Financial Institutions Reform, Recovery, and Enforcement Act of 1989." Available at www.fdic.gov/regulations/laws/rules/8000-3100.html. Last visited 11/16/11.

25. FDIC, "FDIC Improvement Act of 1991." Available at www.fdic.gov/regulations/laws/rules/8000-2400.html. Last visited 11/16/11.

26. Kroszner, "The Motivations Behind Banking Reform."

27. Partnership for Progress, "Bank Holding Companies and Financial Holding Companies." Available at www.fedpartnership.gov/bank-life-cycle/grow-shareholder-value/bank-holding-companies.cfm. Last visited 11/16/11.

28. FDIC, "Deposit Insurance Fund." Available at www.fdic.gov/deposit/insurance/index.html. Last visited 11/16/11.

29. FDIC, "Failed Bank List." Available at www.fdic.gov/bank/individual/failed/banklist.html. Last visited 10/7/13.

30. PBS *Nightly Business Report*. "Sarbanes-Oxley: The Original Objective." April 6, 2007. Available at www.pbs.org/nbr/site/onair/transcripts/070406a/. Last visited 11/17/11.

31. "Sarbanes-Oxley Act 2002." Available soxlaw.com, Sarbanes-Oxley Act. Last visited 11/17/11.

32. BroadSource and Independent Sector, "The Sarbanes-Oxley Act and Implications for Nonprofit Organizations." Available at www.boardsource.org/dl.asp?document_id=558. Last visited 11/17/11.

33. PBS *Nightly Business Report*. "Sarbanes-Oxley: The Original Objective."

34. Gretchen Morgenson, "Clawbacks without Claws." *New York Times*, September 11, 2011.

35. SEC, Office Economic Analysis, "Study of the Sarbanes-Oxley Act of 2002, Section 404, Internal Control over Financial Reporting Requirements." September 2009, Table 8. Available at www.sec.gov/news/studies/2009/sox-404_study.pdf. Last visited 11/17/11.

36. Ibid., Table 9.

37. Chamber of Commerce of the United States, February 26, 2007. Available at www.uschamber.com/sites/default/files/comments/070226_chavern_sox.pdf. Last visited 11/17/11.

38. "Death, Taxes, and Sarbanes-Oxley?" *Businessweek*, January 17, 2005.

39. The initial Futures Trading Act of 1921 was declared unconstitutional due to the imposition of a prohibitive tax of 20 cents per bushel on all options trades and on grain futures trades that are not executed on a designated contract market. Its replacement, the Grain Futures Act of 1922, passed the constitutionality test by banning off-contract-market futures trading rather than taxing it. The Grain Futures Administration was formed as an agency of the U.S. Department of Agriculture to administer the Grain Futures Act. CFTC, "U.S. Futures Trading and Regulation before the Creation of the CFTC." Available at www.cftc.gov/About/HistoryoftheCFTC/history_precftc. Last visited 11/18/11.

40. CFTC, "CFTC History in the 1970s." Available at www.cftc.gov/About/HistoryoftheCFTC/history_1970s. Last visited 11/18/11.

41. CFTC, "CFTC History in the 1980s." Available at www.cftc.gov/About/HistoryoftheCFTC/history_1980s. Last visited 11/18/11.

42. CFTC, "CFTC History in the 1990s." Available at www.cftc.gov/About/HistoryoftheCFTC/history_1990s. Last visited 11/18/11.

43. *wiseGEEK*, "What Is the Commodity Futures Modernization Act of 2000?" Available at http://p.wisegeek.com/what-is-the-commodity-futures-modernization-act.htm. Last visited 11/17/11.

44. Marie Leone, "Credit Rating Agency Reform Act of 2006." CFO.com, October 2, 2006. Available at www.cfo.com/article.cfm/7991492. Last visited 11/18/11.

45. Richard B. Margolies, "The SEC Proposes Tougher Regulations for Credit Rating Agencies." Abbey Spanier, Rodd, and Abrams, June 1, 2011. Available at http://blog.abbeyspanier.com/2011/06/01/the-sec-proposes-tougher-regulations-for-credit-rating-agencies/. Last visited 11/19/11.

46. Gretchen Morgenstern, "The Stone Unturned: Credit Ratings." *New York Times,* March 22, 2014. Available at www.nytimes.com/2014/03/23/business/the-stone-unturned-credit-ratings.html?_r=0. Last visited 6/9/14.

47. John Waggoner and David J. Lynch, "Red Flags in Bear Stearns's Collapse." *USA Today,* March 19, 2008. Roddy Boyd, "The Last Days of Bear Stearns." *CNN Money,* March 31, 2008. Available at http://money.cnn.com/2008/03/28/magazines/fortune/boyd_bear.fortune/. Both last visited 11/19/11.

48. Andrew Ross Sorkin, "Lehman Files for Bankruptcy; Merrill Is Sold." *New York Times,* September 14, 2008.

49. Matthew Karnitschnig et al., "U.S. to Take Over AIG in $85 Billion Bailout; Central Banks Inject Cash as Credit Dries Up." *Wall Street Journal,* September 16, 2008.

50. CBS News, "Panel: $182B AIG Bailout May Not Be Recouped." June 10, 2010. Available at www.cbsnews.com/stories/2010/06/10/politics/main6568652.shtml. Last visited 11/19/11.

51. "AIG bailout earns U.S. treasury $12.4 billion profit after selling shares." Reuters, September 10, 2012. Available at www.huffingtonpost.com/2012/09/10/aig-bailout-treasury-shares_n_1872551.html?utm_hp_ref=business. Last visited 9/11/12.

52. Investopedia, "Long-Term Capital Management." Available at www.investopedia.com/terms/l/longtermcapital.asp#axzz1e4nZkQfZ. Last visited 11/19/11.

53. For a full account, see Financial Crisis Inquiry Commission Report, January 2011. Available at www.gpo.gov/fdsys/pkg/GPO-FCIC/pdf/GPO-FCIC.pdf. Last visited 11/27/11.

54. See Roselyn Hseuh, *China's Regulatory State*. Ithaca, NY: Cornell University Press, 2011.

55. Kirsten West Savali, "Mitt Romney in Profitable Threesome with Freddie Mac and Fannie Mae." *YourBlackWorld*, September 20, 2011.

56. HubPages, "The Government Bailout of Fannie Mae and Freddie Mac Explained."Available at http://ohtwosmitha.hubpages.com/hub/The-government-officially-bails-out-Fannie-Mae-and-Freddie-Mac. Last visited 11/19/11.

57. Gretchen Morgenson and Joshua Rosner, *Reckless Endangerment: How Outsized Ambition, Greed, and Corruption Led to Economic Armageddon*. New York: Times Books, 2011.

58. David Glovin and Joshua Gallu, "Freddie Mac, Fannie Mae Ex-CEOs Sued for Understating Loans." *Bloomberg*, December 16, 2011.

59. Cristina Alesci and Devin Banerjee, "Fortress CEO Mudd Takes Leave Amid SEC's Fannie Mae Lawsuit." *Bloomberg*, December 21, 2011.

60. Diana Olick, "Half of U.S. Mortgages Are Effectively Underwater." CNBC, November 8, 2011. Available at www.cnbc.com/id/45209336/Half_of_US_Mortgages_Are_Effectively_Underwater. Last visited 11/19/11.

61. Robert J. Shiller, "Housing Market Is Heating Up, if Not Yet Bubbling." *New York Times,* September 28, 2013.

62. Neil Irwin, "Why the Housing Market Is Still Stalling the Economy." *New York Times*, April 24, 2014.

63. ADB Institute, "The Role Played by Credit Rating Agencies in the Financial Crisis." Available at www.adbi.org/working-paper/2010/01/26/3446.credit.rating.agencies.european.banking/the.role.played.by.credit.rating.agencies.in.the.financial.crisis/. Last visited 11/19/11.

64. Frank Partnoy, quoted in Financial Economists Roundtable, "Statement on Reforming the Role of the Statistical Ratings Organizations in the Securitization Process." December 1, 2008. Available at http://fic.wharton.upenn.edu/fic/policy%20page/FER12%201%2008rev.pdf. Last visited 9/11/12.

65. Ibid.

66. Simpson Thacher Client Memorandum, "Emergency Economic Stabilization Act of 2008." October 3, 2008. Available at www.stblaw.com/content/publications/pub754.pdf. Last visited 11/20/11. Act details at *Washington Post,* "Breakdown of the Final Bailout Bill." September 28, 2008.

67. Democratic Policy Committee, "The Fraud Enforcement and Recovery Act of 2009." Available at http://dpc.senate.gov/dpcdoc.cfm?doc_name=lb-111-1-58. Last visited 11/18/11.

68. Cadwalader, "Summary of the Dodd-Frank Wall Street Reform and Consumer Protection Act." August 12, 2010. Available at www.cadwalader.com/assets/client_friend/072010_DF1.pdf. Last visited 11/18/11.

69. Synopsis available at CFTC, "Final Rulemaking Regarding Core Principals and Other Requirements for Swap Execution Facilities." Available at www.cftc.gov/ucm/groups/public/@newsroom/documents/file/sef_factsheet_final.pdf. Last visited 10/14/13.

70. "Too Big Not to Fail." *The Economist*, February 18, 2012. Available at www.economist.com/node/21547784. Last visited 9/11/12.

71. Adam Davidson, "Dead Bank Walking." *New York Times Magazine*, September 16, 2012, pp. 16, 18, 20.

72. FDIC, "The Orderly Liquidation of Lehman Brothers Holdings under the Dodd-Frank Act." April 18, 2011. Available at www.fdic.gov/regulations/reform/lehman.html. Full report available at www.fdic.gov/bank/analytical/quarterly/2011_vol5_2/lehman.pdf. Both last visited 9/17/12.

73. Davidson, "Dead Bank Walking."

74. Membership list at Bank for International Settlements, "Fact Sheet—Basel Committee on Banking Supervision." Available at www.bis.org/about/factbcbs.htm. Last visited 1/10/12.

75. Details at Basel Committee on Banking Supervision. Available at www.bis.org/publ/bcbs189.pdf and www.bis.org/publ/bcbs188.pdf; synopsis at www.bis.org/press/p100912.pdf. All last visited 1/10/12.

76. Governor Daniel K. Tarullo, Federal Reserve System, "Capital and Liquidity Standards." Statement before the Committee on Financial Services, U.S. House of Representatives, Washington, D.C., June 16, 2011. Available at www.federalreserve.gov/newsevents/testimony/tarullo20110616a.htm. Last visited 1/10/12.

77. Shahien Nasiripour, "Federal Reserve Toughens Requirements for Biggest Banks." *Huffington Post*, October 25, 2013. Available at www.huffingtonpost.com/2013/10/24/federal-reserve-liquidity_n_4158388.html. Last visited 6/9/14.

78. Board of Governors of the Federal Reserve, "Press Release." October 24, 2014. Available at www.federalreserve.gov/newsevents/press/bcreg/20131024a.htm. Last visited 6/9/14.

79. Danielle Douglas, "Consolidation of Small Banks on the Rise." *Washington Post,* August 27, 2012.

80. Marcy Gordon, "As U.S. economy steadies, bank closings become rarer." *Public Opinion.* Available at www.publicopiniononline.com/news/ci_21012580/us-economy-steadies-bank-closings-become-rarer. Last visited 10/7/13.

81. Mark Gongloff, "Banks Stockpile Cash for Government Default They Say Won't Happen." *Huffington Post,* October 4, 2013. Available at www.huffingtonpost.com/2013/10/04/banks-cash-default_n_4044294.html. Last visited 10/7/13.

82. At the time of writing the board of AIG, one of the principal recipients of government support under TARP, is considering whether to join a multibillion-dollar lawsuit claiming the compensation given to AIG was inadequate. See Ben Berkowitz, "AIG board meets on possible lawsuit vs. government as public rages." Reuters, January 9, 2013. Available at www.reuters.com/article/2013/01/09/us-aig-lawsuit-government-idUSBRE9080S720130109. Last visited 1/9/13.

83. S&P Dow Jones Index, "S&P/Experian Consumer Credit Default Composite Index."Available at http://us.spindices.com/indices/specialty/sp-experian-consumer-credit-default-composite-index. Last visited 6/9/14.

84. Congressional Budget Office, "CBO's Budgetary Treatment of Fannie Mae and Freddie Mac." January 2010. Available at www.cbo.gov/ftpdocs/108xx/doc10878/01-13-FannieFreddie.pdf. Last visited 11/20/11.

85. Jill Treanor, "Goldman Sachs Bankers to Receive $15.3bn in Pay and Bonuses." *The Guardian*, January 19, 2011.

86. Lianna Brinded, "Goldman Sachs Pay and Bonuses Hit $12.61bn in 2013." *International Business Times*, January 16, 2014. Available at www.ibtimes.co.uk/goldman-sachs-pay-bonuses-hit-12-61bn-2013-1432575. Last visited 6/9/14.

87. NJTEAPARTY.com, "T.A.R.P. and Bailouts." Available at http://njteaparty.com/index.php?option=com_content&view=category&id=3&layout=blog&Itemid=11. Last visited 11/21/11.

88. Quoted in Shahien Nasiripour, "A Year after Dodd-Frank, Too Big to Fail Remains Bigger Problem than Ever." *Huffington Post,* November 21, 2011. Available at www.huffingtonpost.com/2011/07/20/-dodd-frank-too-big-to-fail_n_903969.html. Last visited 11/21/11.

89. "Fright Simulator." *The Economist*, November 12–18, 2011, p. 86.

90. J. B. Silver-Greenberg, "Questions as Banks Increase Dividends." *New York Times,* March 14, 2012.

91. Simon Johnson, "Federal Reserve Stress Tests Make Us All Muppets." *Bloomberg,* March 18, 2012.

92. Matthew Boesler, "NASSIM TALEB: The Fed Is Looking at the Banking System All Wrong." *Business Insider,* August 31, 2012.

93. Craig Torres, Dakin Campbell, and Dawn Kopecki, "Fed Said to Criticize Banks on Risk Models in Stress Test." *Bloomberg*, May 1, 2012.

94. "Stress Tests Round 2: Citi Fails Fed's Most Important Exam, 25 Banks Pass." *Forbes,* March 26, 2014. Available at www.forbes.com/sites/halahtouryalai/2014/03/26/stress-tests-round-2-citi-fails-feds-most-important-exam-25-banks-pass/. Last visited 6/9/14.

95. David S. Hilzenrath, "Oversight Board Faults Deloitte Audits." *Washington Post,* October 17, 2011.

96. H.R. 2586, 2779, and 1838. Reported and commented on in Gretchen Morgenson, "Slipping Backwards on Swaps." *New York Times,* January 27, 2011, pp. 1 and 5.

97. George Zornick, "House Posed to Gut Derivatives Reform." *The Nation*, April 4, 2012. Available at www.thenation.com/blog/167219/house-poised-gut-derivative-reforms. Last visited 9/11/12.

98. Erika Eichelberger, "House Passes Bill that Could Lead to Another Financial Crash—But Reformers Claim Victory."*Mother Jones,* June 13, 2013. Available at www.motherjones.com/mojo/2013/06/swap-jurisdiction-certainty-act-house-cross-border. Last visited 6/10/14.

99. Estelle Shirbon, "Fraud trial jury for former UBS trader selected." Reuters, September 10, 2012. Available at www.reuters.com/article/2012/09/10/us-ubs-trial-idUSBRE8890BO20120910. Last visited 9/11/12.

100. Scott Patterson and Deborah Solomon, "Volcker Rule to Curb Bank Trading Proves Hard to Write." *Wall Street Journal,* September 10, 2013.

101. Douwe Miedema, "Fed gives banks more time on Volcker Rule detail." Reuters, April 7, 2014. Available at www.reuters.com/article/2014/04/07/us-fed-volcker-idUSBREA361R820140407. Last visited 6/10/14.

102. SIMFA, "Volcker Rule Resource Center." Available at www.sifma.org/issues/regulatory-reform/volcker-rule/overview/. Last visited 6/10/14.

103. See Investopedia, "Clearing House." Available at www.investopedia.com/terms/c/clearinghouse.asp. Last visited 6/10/14.

104. Lee Sheppard, "The Loopholes in the Volcker Rule." *Forbes,* January 8, 2014. Available at www.forbes.com/sites/leesheppard/2014/01/08/the-loopholes-in-the-volcker-rule/. Last visited 6/10/14.

105. Jesse Hamilton, "Volcker Rule Will Cost Banks Up to $4.3 Billion, OCC Says."*Bloomberg,* March 21, 2014. Available at www.bloomberg.com/news/2014-03-20/volcker-rule-will-cost-banks-up-to-4-3-billion-occ-says.html. Last visited 6/10/14.

106. "Volcker Rule Costs Tallied as U.S. Regulators Press Deadline." *Financial Planning*, October 2, 2013. Available at www.financial-planning.com/news/volcker-rule-costs-tallied-regulators-press-deadline-2686810-1.html?zkPrintable=true. Last visited 10/3/13.

107. Matt Taibbi, "How Wall Street Killed Financial Reform." *Rolling Stone,* May 10, 2012. Available at www.rollingstone.com/politics/news/how-wall-street-killed-financial-reform-20120510. Last visited 10/3/13.

108. Editorial Board, "A Dodd-Frank Capitulation on Mortgage Down Payments." *Washington Post,* September 5, 2013.

109. Patterson and Solomon, "Volcker Rule to Curb Bank Trading Proves Hard to Write."

110. Jessica Silver-Greenberg and Susanne Craig, "JPMorgan Trading Loss May Reach $9 Billion." *New York Times*, June 28, 2012.

111. Dawn Kopecki, "JPMorgan Pays $920 Million to Settle London Whale Probes." *Bloomberg,* September 20, 2013.

112. Paul Volcker, "Financial Reform: Unfinished Business." *New York Review of Books*, November 24, 2011.

113. Tompkins Financial. Available at www.tompkinsfinancial.com/about-us/corporate-profile/ Last visited 6/10/14.

114. Bauer Financial Rating. Available at www.bauerfinancial.com/btc_ratings.asp. Last visited 10/7/13.

115. Tim Kane, "The Importance of Startups in Job Creation and Job Destruction." Kauffman Foundation, July 2010. Available at www.kauffman.org/uploadedFiles/firm_formation_importance_of_startups.pdf. Last visited 10/8/13.

116. Matt Krantz, "IPO Market Showing Signs of Life as 2011 Looks Promising." *USA Today,* January 26, 2011. "Signs of Life in IPO Market? 2011 Global Review and 2012 Outlook." *Seeking*

Alpha, December 22, 2011. Available at http://seekingalpha.com/article/315593-signs-of-life-in-ipo-market-2011-global-review-and-2012-outlook. Last visited 9/13/12. Matt Krantz, "IPOs Have Good, but Not Great, 2012." *USA Today,* January 1, 2013. Renaissance Capital IPO Intelligence, "2013 Annual Review." Available at www.renaissancecapital.com/ipohome/review/2013usreviewpublic.pdf. Last visited 6/10/14.

117. Adapted from M. Margolis, "Jobs Act Summary: The Reed Smith Bulletin." *Onemediaplace,* April 6, 2012. Available at www.onemedplace.com/blog/archives/10520. Last visited 9/13/12.

118. Jeff Sommer, "With a Tweet, Twitter Starts a Debate." *New York Times,* September 21, 2013.

119. SEC, "SEC Issues Proposal on Crowdfunding." October 23, 2013. Available at www.sec.gov/News/PressRelease/Detail/PressRelease/1370540017677#.U5c21hBMKkw. Last visited 6/10/14.

120. IRS, "Small Business Jobs Act of 2010 Tax Provisions." Available at www.irs.gov/Businesses/Small-Businesses-&-Self-Employed/Small-Business-Jobs-Act-of-2010-Tax-Provisions. Last visited 9/13/12.

121. Rule available at www.sec.gov/rules/final/2013/33-9415.pdf. Last visited 10/8/13.

122. SEC, "Fact Sheet: Eliminating the Prohibition on General Solicitation and General Advertising in Certain Offerings." Available at www.sec.gov/news/press/2013/2013-124-item1.htm. Last visited 6/10/14.

123. SEC, "SEC Proposes Rules to Implement JOBS Act Provision about General Solicitation and Advertising in Securities Offerings." August 29, 2012. Available at www.sec.gov/news/press/2012/2012-170.htm. Last visited 9/13/12.

124. Paul Sloan, "Here's the Chart that Explains Facebook's IPO Mess." *CNET News,* May 30, 2012.

125. Joe Nocera, "Rigging the I.P.O. game." *New York Times*, March 10, 2013.

126. Alistair Barr, "Insight: Morgan Stanley cut Facebook estimates just before IPO." Reuters, May 22, 2012. Available at www.reuters.com/article/2012/05/22/us-facebook-forecasts-idUSBRE84L06920120522. Last visited 9/14/12.

127. Vanessa Schoenthaler, "The JOBS Act in a Nutshell—Part II: Research Reports and Communications Related to Emerging Growth Companies."*100 F Street,* April 19, 2012. Available at http://100fstreet.com/index.php/2012/04/the-jobs-act-in-a-nutshell-part-ii-research-reports-and-communications-related-to-emerging-growth-companies/. Last visited 9/14/12.

128. Lauren Indvik, "What Went Wrong with Facebook's IPO?" *Mashable Business,* May 22, 2012. Available at http://mashable.com/2012/05/22/facebook-ipo-whats-wrong/. Last visited 9/14/12.

129. Joann Pan, "Facebook Blames Nasdaq Errors for Its Weak Market Debut."*Mashable Business,* June 16, 2012. Available at http://mashable.com/2012/06/16/facebook-ipo-lawsuits/. Last visited 9/14/12.

130. Michael Hiltzik, "Investment Frenzies Almost Never End Prettily for the Participants." *Los Angeles Times,* May 16, 2012.

131. Henry Blodget, "Facebook IPO Fiasco: Here's How Small Investors Got Rolled Over." *Daily Ticker,* May 24, 2012. Available at http://finance.yahoo.com/blogs/daily-ticker/facebook-ipo-fiasco-small-investors-got-rolled-over-114216627.html. Last visited 9/14/12.

132. "Initial Public Offerings: Suspiciously Quiet." *The Economist*, September 1, 2012. Available at www.economist.com/node/21561911. Last visited 9/14/12.

133. Sommer, "With a Tweet, Twitter Starts a Debate."

134. "Twitter's IPO: Going Cheep?" *The Economist*, November 2, 2013. Available at www.economist.com/news/business/21588940-microblogging-firms-shares-may-not-be-bargain-investors-are-hoping-going-cheep. Last visited 11/14/13.

135. Matt Egan, "Report: Twitter Willing to Double IPO Size to $2 Billion." *Fox Business,* October 7, 2013. Available at www.foxbusiness.com/technology/2013/10/07/report-twitter-willing-to-double-ipo-size-to-2-billion/. Last visited 10/8/13.

136. Olivia Oran and Gerry Shih, "Twitter shares soar in frenzied NYSE debut." Reuters, November 7, 2013. Available at www.reuters.com/article/2013/11/07/us-twitter-ipo-idUSBRE99N1AE20131107. Last visited 11/14/13.

137. "Twitter's IPO: Going Cheep?"

138. Matt Krantz, "Insiders Outpace Masses on IPOs." *USA Today,* May 12, 2014.

139. I would like to recognize and thank my colleague Jack Little for bringing these points to my attention.

Index

Note: Italicized locators indicate figures.

B

C

D